(Continued on back endsheets)

German Writers and Works of the High Middle Ages: 1170–1280

Dictionary of Literary Biography® • Volume One Hundred Thirty-Eight

German Writers and Works of the High Middle Ages: 1170–1280

Edited by
James Hardin
University of South Carolina
and
Will Hasty
University of Florida

A Bruccoli Clark Layman Book
Gale Research Inc.
Detroit, Washington, D.C., London

Printed in the United States of America

Published simultaneously in the United Kingdom
by Gale Research International Limited
(An affiliated company of Gale Research Inc.)

The paper used in this publication meets the minimum requirements
of American National Standard for Information Sciences–Permanence
Paper for Printed Library Materials, ANSI Z39.48-1984. ∞™

Library of Congress Catalog Card Number 94–075221
ISBN 0–8103–5397–0

I(T)P

The trademark ITP is used under license.

10 9 8 7 6 5 4 3 2 1

Contents

Plan of the Series

. . . Almost the most prodigious asset of a country, and perhaps its most precious possession, is its native literary product — when that product is fine and noble and enduring.

Mark Twain*

The advisory board, the editors, and the publisher of the *Dictionary of Literary Biography* are joined in endorsing Mark Twain's declaration. The literature of a nation provides an inexhaustible resource of permanent worth. We intend to make literature and its creators better understood and more accessible to students and the reading public, while satisfying the standards of teachers and scholars.

To meet these requirements, *literary biography* has been construed in terms of the author's achievement. The most important thing about a writer is his writing. Accordingly, the entries in *DLB* are career biographies, tracing the development of the author's canon and the evolution of his reputation.

The purpose of *DLB* is not only to provide reliable information in a convenient format but also to place the figures in the larger perspective of literary history and to offer appraisals of their accomplishments by qualified scholars.

The publication plan for *DLB* resulted from two years of preparation. The project was proposed to Bruccoli Clark by Frederick C. Ruffner, president of the Gale Research Company, in November 1975. After specimen entries were prepared and typeset, an advisory board was formed to refine the entry format and develop the series rationale. In meetings held during 1976, the publisher, series editors, and advisory board approved the scheme for a comprehensive biographical dictionary of persons who contributed to North American literature. Editorial work on the first volume began in January 1977, and it was published in 1978. In order to make *DLB* more than a reference tool and to compile volumes that individually have claim to status as literary history, it was decided to organize volumes by topic, period, or genre. Each of these freestanding volumes provides a biographical-bibliographical guide and overview for a particular area of literature. We are convinced that this organization — as opposed to a single alphabet method — constitutes a valuable innovation in the presentation of reference material. The volume plan necessarily requires many decisions for the placement and treatment of authors who might properly be included in two or three volumes. In some instances a major figure will be included in separate volumes, but with different entries emphasizing the aspect of his career appropriate to each volume. Ernest Hemingway, for example, is represented in *American Writers in Paris, 1920–1939* by an entry focusing on his expatriate apprenticeship; he is also in *American Novelists, 1910–1945* with an entry surveying his entire career. Each volume includes a cumulative index of the subject authors and articles. Comprehensive indexes to the entire series are planned.

With volume ten in 1982 it was decided to enlarge the scope of *DLB*. By the end of 1986 twenty-one volumes treating British literature had been published, and volumes for Commonwealth and Modern European literature were in progress. The series has been further augmented by the *DLB Yearbooks* (since 1981) which update published entries and add new entries to keep the *DLB* current with contemporary activity. There have also been *DLB Documentary Series* volumes which provide biographical and critical source materials for figures whose work is judged to have particular interest for students. One of these companion volumes is entirely devoted to Tennessee Williams.

We define literature as the *intellectual commerce of a nation:* not merely as belles lettres but as that ample and complex process by which ideas are generated, shaped, and transmitted. *DLB* entries are not limited to "creative writers" but extend to other figures who in their time and in their way influenced the mind of a people. Thus the series encompasses historians, journalists, publishers, and screenwriters. By this means readers of *DLB* may be aided to perceive literature not as cult scripture in the keeping of intellectual high priests but firmly positioned at the center of a nation's life.

*From an unpublished section of Mark Twain's autobiography, copyright by the Mark Twain Company

DLB includes the major writers appropriate to each volume and those standing in the ranks immediately behind them. Scholarly and critical counsel has been sought in deciding which minor figures to include and how full their entries should be. Wherever possible, useful references are made to figures who do not warrant separate entries.

Each *DLB* volume has a volume editor responsible for planning the volume, selecting the figures for inclusion, and assigning the entries. Volume editors are also responsible for preparing, where appropriate, appendices surveying the major periodicals and literary and intellectual movements for their volumes, as well as lists of further readings. Work on the series as a whole is coordinated at the Bruccoli Clark Layman editorial center in Columbia, South Carolina, where the editorial staff is responsible for accuracy of the published volumes.

One feature that distinguishes *DLB* is the illustration policy – its concern with the iconography of literature. Just as an author is influenced by his surroundings, so is the reader's understanding of the author enhanced by a knowledge of his environment. Therefore *DLB* volumes include not only drawings, paintings, and photographs of authors, often depicting them at various stages in their careers, but also illustrations of their families and places where they lived. Title pages are regularly reproduced in facsimile along with dust jackets for modern authors. The dust jackets are a special feature of *DLB* because they often document better than anything else the way in which an author's work was perceived in its own time. Specimens of the writers' manuscripts are included when feasible.

Samuel Johnson rightly decreed that "The chief glory of every people arises from its authors." The purpose of the *Dictionary of Literary Biography* is to compile literary history in the surest way available to us – by accurate and comprehensive treatment of the lives and work of those who contributed to it.

The *DLB* Advisory Board

Introduction

The word *biography* was first widely used at the end of the seventeenth century, when John Dryden defined it as "the history of particular men's lives." While the Middle Ages did not possess such an understanding of biography, works of a biographical kind were produced during that period. Runic inscriptions and Germanic songs celebrated the lives of heroes and legendary figures, chroniclers documented the great events in the lives of emperors and kings, and hagiographical literature commemorated the virtues of pious men and women. But the flaws of heroes, emperors, and the pious tended to be overlooked, and such portrayals were largely shaped by considerations other than historical accuracy. References to the lives of authors in their own works are scarce, seemingly accidental, and difficult to interpret; and unambiguous references to the lives of authors outside their works are rare. Generally, only the broadest of outlines can be conjectured about the authors' lives on the basis of their literary works. From a modern perspective, medieval literature seems anonymous in character: instead of reflecting the lives and personalities of the authors who produced it, it reaffirms the interests and values of the communities to which they belonged. Wherever one looks for the particular in medieval literature, one is confronted by the typical.

Another difficulty is what might be called the open-endedness of medieval literature. Works often survive only in fragments; others are preserved not in their original forms but in copies, often made centuries later. Editors of a medieval work that does not survive in its original form have attempted, in the tradition of nineteenth-century philology, to arrive at a hypothetical reconstruction of the original, or archetype, based on a critical assessment and comparison of the available manuscripts, which often contain revisions and errors, and on educated guesses.

The relationship of the extant manuscripts to the reconstructed original and to one another is frequently represented as a *Stammbaum* (genealogical tree). Recently this strategy has been called into question by editors who consider the search for an "original" a characteristically modern enterprise that does not do justice to the life of medieval literature. The attempt to arrive at an original strives for a kind of closure that belies the inherent open-endedness of a medieval work, its ability to adapt itself over the years to different priorities and tastes. This new philological approach has resulted in an editing strategy in which variations among manuscripts are seen as corresponding to different possible uses of a given work, and not necessarily as errors that have to be "corrected" to reconstruct the original. Another aspect of the open-endedness of medieval literature is its performative nature. The works of courtly authors were in all likelihood dramatically recited to their audiences, and it has been suggested that the *Nibelungenlied* (Song of the Nibelungs, circa 1200) was sung. Thus, many medieval works were originally linked to the skill with which an author (and, perhaps, later emulators of him) acted also as a performer, adapting the presentation of his (or another's) works to the expectations and demands of his audiences in concrete situations, and in many instances engaging in polemics with rival authors. Similarly, the popularity of the minnesingers, the German troubadours, was based not only on the lyrics that have survived but also on the effect of the accompanying music and of the voices that sang it. Medieval drama, perhaps the most overtly performance-based literature, was a communal product, an outgrowth of church liturgy that evolved over several centuries. The works as they exist today are like snapshots of dynamic events, irrecoverable in their totality, that typically involved the authors as performers in immediate contact with their audiences.

The attempt to extrapolate information about the authors from their works is fraught with interpretive difficulties, since there is often little or no historical information to indicate whether a self-reference in literature is biographical or fictional. Even if it is doubtful that it would have occurred to medieval authors that anyone would be interested in their particular lives, however, it would be a mistake to dismiss as anachronistic the endeavor to find out about them. Still firmly anchored in literary traditions and in the values of the communities to which they belonged, the authors of the high medieval period were becoming increasingly aware of what they as individuals brought to literary activity. Nowhere is this awareness more pronounced than in authors such as Wolfram von Eschenbach and Walther von der Vogelweide, who stressed the distinctive characteristics of their works with a pride that seems almost provocatively individualistic within a cultural context still largely characterized by anonymous traditions and communal forms of identity. Tradition was employed in a different manner but to the same effect by Mechthild von Magdeburg, who achieved something resembling self-expression in the medium of mystical literature. Although the works of these authors are still a long way from literary biography in the modern sense, significant steps in that direction were being taken during this time.

The first efflorescence (*Blütezeit*) of literature in the German vernacular occurred between 1170 and 1280, a period that also saw the rising political influence of the Holy Roman Empire of the German nation, which had been founded in 800 with the coronation of Charlemagne. The beginning of this artistic flowering was marked by the composition of some of the great masterpieces of German literature, most of which were written within a few decades of the year 1200. These great works shaped literary history throughout the thirteenth century, with later courtly authors looking back to them as models for emulation, and they continued to have an appeal beyond the Middle Ages in their cogent expression of universal concerns of human existence such as love, honor, and humanity's relationship to God. By the middle of the thirteenth century the historical and cultural forces that accompanied this first efflorescence of German literature had begun to weaken. While courtly traditions continued to thrive into the fourteenth century and beyond, the careers of courtly authors who could regard themselves as immediately linked to the great writers and works from around 1200 coincided approximately with the so-called Interregnum, which began in 1256 and lasted until the selection by the electoral princes (*Kurfürsten*) of Rudolf of Hapsburg as emperor in 1273.

The complex historical and cultural forces accompanying this efflorescence of German literature included the political and cultural ambitions of the Hohenstaufen emperors, the most significant of whom was Friedrich I, known as "Barbarossa" for his red beard. Friedrich's greatest achievement was to revive the traditional claim of emperors to preeminence over all of Western Christianity, and he centralized political and cultural power to a greater extent than any emperor since the Saxon Emperor Otto I in the early tenth century. By birth and by disposition Friedrich was in an excellent position to

assert himself against the two major rivals to imperial power. The first of these rivals were the powerful German princes, who desired a monarch strong enough to defend the empire against external dangers but not so strong as to infringe on the authority they wielded within their own territories – an authority that they increasingly regarded as a hereditary prerogative rather than as a feudal right conferred by the emperor. The other rival was the papacy, which in the wake of the Cluniac reform – a religious movement beginning in 910 that strove for a spiritual separation of the church from worldly matters – had begun to argue that it, and not the emperor, was the leader of Western Christianity. Although the popes' argument was based on a posited ascendancy of the spiritual over the secular realm, the two spheres were not yet clearly differentiated, and the more ambitious popes clearly envisioned their leadership as both spiritual and worldly.

Friedrich was in a good position to deal with the German princes by virtue of his blood relationships to the two most powerful German families, the Staufer and the Welfs. These relationships made him an acceptable compromise among bitter rivals and enabled him to garner the support and resources he needed to rule with authority and to conduct his military campaigns. Friedrich's authority was, for the most part, unquestioned by the German princes, even if he was frequently unable to bend them to his will. He was in a position late in his reign to ban the most powerful German prince, the Welf Heinrich der Löwe (Henry the Lion), Duke of Saxony, for not supporting the Italian campaign of 1174. At the September diet of 1157 Friedrich's authority among European monarchs was underscored in a striking manner when the English ambassadors presented the emperor a letter asserting the absolute allegiance of King Henry II: "We place our kingdom and everything subject to our rule anywhere at your disposal and entrust it to your power so that all things shall be arranged at your nod and that the will of your command [*imperium*] shall be done in everything." While Henry's true intentions are debatable, this letter was subsequently employed by imperial propagandists as support for Friedrich's claim to universal leadership. It is the role of such a leader that he played in his final endeavor, the Third Crusade, during which he died in 1190 en route to the Holy Land.

Friedrich was less successful in his dealings with the popes. The contest between *imperium* and *sacerdotium* – which, in the persons of Heinrich IV and Pope Gregory VII, had reached an initial high-point in 1077 at Canossa, when the emperor was freed from the ban of absolution after standing barefoot in the snow for three days – was revived when Friedrich initially refused during his coronation in 1155 in Rome to act as Pope Adrian IV's squire by holding his bridle and stirrup. This symbolic denial of the papacy's implicit claim to preeminence over the empire marked the beginning of a protracted conflict between the emperor and the popes, who based their claims on Roman and canon law, respectively. This ideological conflict issued inevitably into military conflict when Friedrich attempted to impose imperial control over the rich and powerful cities of northern Italy. In alliance with the popes, these cities successfully resisted Friedrich and compelled him to accept only nominal sovereignty and to recognize their right to self-government in the Peace of Constance in 1183. The conflict between empire and papacy was unresolved on the death of Barbarossa and was to be taken up again in the thirteenth century by his grandson, Friedrich II, and Pope Innocent III.

Despite the failure of his Italian policy, Friedrich Barbarossa managed to harness, at least temporarily, the conflicting forces of his age, thus creating in Germany (that is, the German-speaking part of the empire) a situation favorable to the efflorescence of German literature. It was during the reign of Friedrich, who styled himself as both emperor over all Christendom and as a knight who was first among equals, that imperial power first allied itself with the ideals of chivalry, thus providing a political and social foundation for the great literary achievements composed at courts throughout Germany during the late twelfth and early thirteenth centuries. Prominent in this literary activity were the *ministeriales,* a class of unfree servants at larger courts who rose gradually in importance, in some instances – for example, the minnesinger Friedrich von Hausen – occupying high administrative posts, and eventually solidified a position in the lower tiers of the nobility. Basing themselves on classical, foreign (especially French and Provençal), and indigenous literary traditions, German authors produced a corpus of works dealing with love, honor, and adventure that was, despite its great diversity of forms, demonstrative of a cultural unity grounded in the values of courtly knighthood. Exemplary of the connection between the ideals embodied by Friedrich I and the rise of courtly literature in Germany is the great Whitsuntide Festival of 1184 at Mainz, at which the emperor's two eldest sons were knighted. Tens of thousands from all of Europe gathered

for this event, at which jousts were fought and crowds were entertained with tales of knightly exploits and courtly love.

The major themes of the court literature of the Staufer period are *minne* (love) and *âventiure* (adventure). Besides presenting an ethos of courtly knighthood that was fostered by imperial politics, these themes were linked to fundamental changes in the emotional life of the Middle Ages. The love lyrics of *Minnesang* seem to indicate a different attitude in the relationship between the sexes. In its idealized portrayal of the lady as the embodiment of worldly perfection and an object of worship and service, these lyrics portray a relationship in which it is not acceptable for the man to achieve the fulfillment of his sexual desire by the employment of force. According to the historian Norbert Elias in his *The Civilizing Process,* volume 2 (New York: Urizen, 1978), *Minnesang* can be viewed in terms of an internalization and sublimation of aggressive impulses within the social context of large courts. At these courts women, particularly the wives of powerful lords, held positions of great cultural importance. Generally more literate than men, whose business was not learning but fighting, such women could function, following the model of Eleanor of Aquitaine, as patrons and as inspirations for the minnesingers' lyrical portrayal of their beloved ladies. If *Minnesang* indicates a less violent form of sexual interaction outside the literary context, such progress was probably quite limited and confined to the larger courts. Elsewhere the kinds of violent behavior that characterized relationships between men and women in the earlier Middle Ages continued.

Adventure, which in the Arthurian romances involved armed conflict against a series of knightly opponents, also suggests a curbing of aggression. The tournament, which provided, however imperfectly, a controlled space in which armed conflict became sport, figures prominently in the romances. Even combat situations that are far less controlled than the tournament demonstrate an unprecedented degree of restraint (*mâze*). Wolfram's Parzival, for example, receives this following advice from his mentor, Gurnemanz, with respect to warfare: "an swem ir strîtes sicherheit / bezalt, er enhabe iu solhiu leit / getan diu herzen kumber wesen, / die nemet und lâzet in genesen" (when someone offers you his surrender – unless he has done you harm that is grievous to your heart – you should accept it and allow him to live, 171,27–30). It is unlikely that the warriors in the days of Charlemagne and the Saxon emperors would have concluded hostilities with such ethical pondering. As is the case with the less violent relationship to women suggested in *Minnesang*, it is difficult to assess how far this curbing of aggression in knightly adventure reached beyond the literary works. Even in the Arthurian romances there are knightly fatalities in abundance, and the curbing of aggression, while visible as a tendency, does not take the form of a coherent and consistent program.

The medium for the first great flowering of German literary culture was Middle High German, a language of great subtlety and expressiveness that flourished from around 1100 to 1400. Middle High German was distinguished from Old High German by a flattening of the full-sounding middle and end syllables (from *o* and *u* to *e*) and by a partial diphthongization of *î, û,* and *iu* to *ei, au,* and *eu* and the monophthongization of *ie, uo,* and *üe* to *î, û,* and *ü.* Despite regional variations, a standard version of this language was sought by authors throughout Germany, another significant indication of the cultural unity achieved during this time. Middle High German has roughly the same relationship to modern German (technically, New High German) as does Middle English to modern English. It can be learned in a relatively short time by speakers of German.

The ethos of knighthood that arose during Barbarossa's lifetime had a power and fascination that allowed it to survive after his death; but the power he achieved for the imperial cause was of short duration, for it was based on personal qualities rather than on stable institutions providing for a lasting centralization of political authority. Friedrich himself contributed to the collapse of political order after his death by making political and territorial concessions to the German princes to gain their support for his endeavors in Italy. It is likely that Friedrich controlled the disintegrative, centrifugal forces in the short term only by strengthening them for the future; at any rate, these forces became unmanageable not long after his death. Friedrich was succeeded as emperor by his son Heinrich VI, who wielded a power equal to or greater than that of his father. Heinrich's fostering of the connection of imperial power to chivalric values seems to be demonstrated by three *Minnelieder* (love songs) transmitted under his name, although his authorship remains a matter for debate. When Heinrich died in the seventh year of his reign, leaving as his heir his four-year-old son Friedrich II, imperial power quickly crumbled. The rivalries and conflicts of the German princes reemerged, some of them choosing Heinrich's brother Philip of Swabia as emperor, while others chose Otto of Brunswick,

the son of Heinrich der Löwe. This period of political and social turbulence in Germany was fully exploited by Pope Innocent III, who was able to assert himself as arbiter in the dispute. Implicitly claiming the prerogative not only to place the imperial crown on head of the German king but to choose the king as well, Innocent III brought papal power in temporal matters to heights it would never again achieve.

Imperial power was revived by Barbarossa's grandson, Friedrich II, who grew up in cosmopolitan Sicily, where Western and Arab civilizations mingled. Friedrich II, who has been called the first modern ruler, pursued the goal of imperial supremacy against the papacy in a Machiavellian fashion, for the most part unconcerned with excommunication, the epithet *Antichrist,* and other such papal weapons that would have troubled emperors and their subjects in the past. The reign of Friedrich II has been viewed as one of the channels through which elements of Eastern learning and statecraft were introduced to the empire. Friedrich himself was the author of a book on falconry that reveals a close observation of nature rare for the Middle Ages, and the learned men who surrounded him translated texts by the Arab philosophers Avicenna and Averroës and studied algebra. Although a patron of court literature in Germany – he gave the aged Walther von der Vogelweide his long-desired piece of land – Friedrich II's importance for cultural developments north of the Alps was not equal to that of his grandfather Barbarossa. Friedrich II spent less than eight years of his thirty-eight-year reign in Germany. His absence, combined with concessions to princes to gain their support for his Italian wars, further contributed to the princes' independence from imperial overlordship. Thus, there was an increasing discrepancy between the ideals embodied by the emperor and the actual disintegration of imperial power in Germany. The imperial power that had, in the days of Barbarossa, given impetus to the literary expression of chivalric ideals became increasingly hollow, and, as the chaos of the Interregnum indicates, it did not long survive Friedrich II's death. By this time court literature exercised its own power and attraction, independently of the social and political context in which it arose. Nevertheless, one can observe in the court literature of the thirteenth century a frequent expression of resigned longing for *temporis acti,* past times when the values of knighthood seemed to be something more than a mere literary exercise or an aristocratic diversion.

The literature of the Staufer period is part of a broader cultural synthesis of conflicting historical forces that has been called the twelfth-century Renaissance. Besides the literary activity in vernacular languages throughout Europe, this synthesis included Scholasticism and Gothic architecture, each of which manifested a fruitful and novel tension between the individual and the universal. Scholasticism incorporated both poles in its juxtaposition of philosophy and theology. Experiencing a revival in figures such as Peter Abelard, philosophical inquiry was energized during the twelfth and thirteenth centuries by newly discovered Aristotelian works and their Arabic commentaries. The increasing importance of philosophy was linked both to the content of these works, such as the emphasis on the development of natural wisdom and the implicit message that scientific inquiry could be pursued for its own sake, and to the attempt to reconcile such contents with church dogma, which was grounded in a Christianized Platonism that located meaning in a transcendental realm of universals beyond the transitory world of individual phenomena. The increasing tension between the philosophical emphasis on human reason and the theological emphasis on grace and revelation was resolved in the thirteenth century by Saint Thomas Aquinas, who arrived at a powerful synthesis of Aristotelianism and Christian dogma that posited the inherence of universal qualities within the individual objects of human perception. Aquinas's synthesis of the individual and the universal achieved a reconciliation of philosophy and theology that permitted human reason to be viewed as an independent power, capable within its own limitations of arriving at truth.

Intellectual currents of the twelfth-century Renaissance took material form in the Gothic cathedrals, which began first in France and then throughout Europe to replace the older Romanesque churches. The spiritual priorities of the age are exemplified by the immense amount of material and human resources that went into the cathedrals, the construction of which typically lasted for decades: the cathedral of Chartres was begun around 1194, and its roof was completed in 1220; the cathedral of Cologne, begun in the thirteenth century, was not completed until the late nineteenth century. Although originally imported from France, the spiritual intensity and dramatic perspectives of the Gothic style, particularly in painting and wood carving, was destined to become particularly German, retaining its hold in Germany after much of Europe had returned during the Renaissance to the more symmetrical and worldly forms of classical an-

tiquity. The motivation behind the construction of Gothic cathedrals in the High Middle Ages was economic as well as spiritual: although representing a significant investment of resources, a Gothic church, constructed around the relics of some holy figure, helped to establish the reputation of a city and to fill its coffers with the coins of visiting pilgrims. The spirituality expressed by the Gothic churches is akin to the synthesis of the individual and the universal as formulated by Thomas Aquinas: Gothic architecture seemed to wield the individual elements of construction in such a way that the universal within them could manifest itself. These elements included innovations such as the pointed arch, perhaps the most recognizable feature of Gothic, and flying buttresses, which displaced the weight of the roof to the outside of the building so that the upper nave no longer had to support the entire weight of the roof and could become, in some instances, rows of high windows. These and other innovations achieved an impression of verticality and weightlessness, suggestive of a state of spiritual transcendence. Perhaps most significant in Gothic architecture was the interaction of these elements with light, which was understood in Neoplatonic mysticism as an emanation of the divine. Gothic architecture thus created a space that seemed to capture the moment at which the individual merged with the universal.

Both Scholasticism and Gothic architecture testify to the increasing importance of cities as cultural centers. It is in the cities that one finds the newest religious orders, the Dominicans and the Franciscans, whose urban evangelism rejected the traditional monastic ideal of isolation from the world even as their ideal of poverty criticized, in a traditional monastic way, the worldliness and ostentatious wealth of the church. It was in the cities that economic forces were at work that eventually undermined the medieval Christian conviction that it was sinful to lend money at interest or to accumulate wealth so as to live significantly better than one's neighbors. In general, cities provided a greater amount of latitude for individual thought and action – a well-known saying in the Middle Ages was "Stadtluft macht frei" (city air makes one free). Cities were typically connected with markets, and their value as a source of income was recognized by the princes, who provided them with special rights and protection in return for a share of their wealth. It was in the cities, ultimately, that the twelfth-century Renaissance came to an end, as the forces constituting it – philosophical, spiritual, social, political, and economic – increasingly developed according to their own internal logic.

This volume treats significant authors who were active between 1170 and 1280 – the High Middle Ages – and anonymous works that were composed during the same period. Since little is known about even those authors who can be identified, the entries on writers concentrate, by necessity, on their works. Each entry discussses critical reception of the author or work, and the attempt has been made to treat major works in such a way that the reader will have a sense of their atmosphere, language, and significance. Within entries on writers, their works are discussed in chronological order, as well as this order can be determined, rather than thematically.

Entries on writers are headed with the full name by which the author is generally known, and birth and death dates, as well as they can be determined, are given. In entries on anonymous works the approximate date of the work's composition is given. In entries on writers, under the rubric Major Works, the author's works are listed in chronological order with their approximate dates of composition. Titles of works are listed as they generally appear in standard editions. Groups of works with no clear title are referred to in English (for example, *Songs*). For each work a brief description of its transmission – the number, age, quality, location of significant manuscripts – is given. The goal of this description is to provide the reader with a sense of the medieval "life" of a given work without becoming involved in disputes about the merits of different manuscripts. For each work, standard editions of the original Middle High German text are given, followed by lists of modern German editions and English translations, if available. The text of the entry assesses the writer's or work's place in the literary history of the period, and, in the case of entries on writers, includes any available information on the writer's life. Whenever possible, the author's works are discussed chronologically. Line numbers following quotations from medieval works correspond to the standard editions; citations of *Minnesang* lyrics follow the numbering system of Karl Lachmann in *Des Minnesangs Frühling,* which

was first published in 1857. All non-English words and quotations are translated into English. The editors have attempted to keep everything comprehensible to a reader unfamiliar with the German language, history, and culture. The References section lists a selection of books and articles on the writer or work that is the subject of the entry.

– *Will Hasty, with the collaboration of James Hardin*

ACKNOWLEDGMENTS

This book was produced by Bruccoli Clark Layman, Inc. Karen L. Rood is senior editor for the *Dictionary of Literary Biography* series. Philip B. Dematteis was the in-house editor.

Production coordinator is George F. Dodge. Photography editors are Edward Scott, Timothy C. Lundy, and Robert S. McConnell. Layout and graphics supervisor is Penney L. Haughton. Copyediting supervisor is Bill Adams. Typesetting supervisor is Kathleen M. Flanagan. Julie E. Frick is editorial associate. The production staff includes Phyllis Avant, Joseph Matthew Bruccoli, Ann M. Cheschi, Patricia Coate, Denise Edwards, Sarah A. Estes, Joyce Fowler, Laurel Gladden, Jolyon M. Helterman, Rebecca Mayo, Kathy Lawler Merlette, Sean Moriarty, Pamela D. Norton, Patricia F. Salisbury, Maxine K. Smalls, William L. Thomas, Jr., and Wilma Weant.

Walter W. Ross and Deborah M. Chasteen did library research. They were assisted by the following librarians at the Thomas Cooper Library of the University of South Carolina: Linda Holderfield and the interlibrary-loan staff; reference librarians Gwen Baxter, Daniel Boice, Faye Chadwell, Cathy Eckman, Gary Geer, Qun "Gerry" Jiao, Jean Rhyne, Carol Tobin, Carolyn Tyler, Virginia Weathers, Elizabeth Whiznant, and Connie Widney; circulation-department head Thomas Marcil; and acquisitions-searching supervisor David Haggard.

Professor Hasty would like to express his appreciation to Yale University for its support during his work on this project.

German Writers and Works of the High Middle Ages: 1170–1280

Dictionary of Literary Biography

Konrad Fleck

(flourished circa 1220)

Danielle Egan
University of Southern California

MAJOR WORK: *Flore und Blanscheflur* (circa 1220)

Manuscript: The Middle High German *Flore und Blanscheflur* is extant in two manuscripts from the fifteenth century: ms. H (Heidelberg, no. 362) and ms. B (Berlin ms. germ. fol. 18). Ms. B contains many errors, corrections, and additions by the scribe, and its final ninety verses are lost. There are also two fragments from the thirteenth century: ms. P (Prague UB, cod. XVII) and ms. F (Frauenfeld, cod. III Bg.).

Standard edition: *Flore und Blanscheflur: Eine Erzählung von Konrad Fleck,* edited by Emil Sommer (Quedlinburg & Leipzig: Basse, 1846).

Konrad Fleck humbly withheld his name from his major work, *Flore und Blanscheflur* (circa 1220). Only through Rudolf von Ems's *Alexander* (circa 1230–1254) is it known that "der Vlec der guote Kuonrat" (the good Konrad Fleck) is the poet of the romance *Flore und Blanscheflur.* Rudolf also provides an approximate date for Fleck's existence by placing him between Freidank and der Stricker; based on Fleck's style, which shows Hartmann von Aue's influence, it is assumed that Fleck must have worked around 1220. Rudolf's attribution of a nonextant *Clies* to Fleck has not been proven. Scholars today seem to agree that although Fleck might have begun such an attempt, Ulrich von Türheim probably finished the work. Fleck's dwelling place is also open to speculation. Based on his dialect it is assumed that he must have been of Alemannic origin, possibly from Basel or Swabia.

Flore und Blanscheflur is an adaption of a highly popular story from an Old French source. Fleck's claimed source, "Ruopreht von Orbent," remains obscure. The prologue to *Flore und Blanscheflur,* however, is not based on the French source and is the poet's

contribution. In it the author emphatically praises the courtly virtues of "tugent" (chastity) and "minne" (love) and stresses the importance of "staete" (constancy) in this world. These are high ideals, but Fleck's didactic prologue reverberates with optimism: through learning and listening to wise men and poets humankind can achieve such perfection. Flore and Blanscheflur personify *tugent, minne,* and *staete* in the absolute. Achieving this they are able to transcend social and religious barriers. Their love represents the *hohe minne* (platonic love that reflects God's love). The *Valsche minne* (false love) is generally practiced by heathens who do not espouse courtly virtues and is, of course, set against *hohe minne.*

After Fleck's prologue *Flore und Blanscheflur* follows its French source and introduces the frame within which the story will be told. During an idyllic summer day a lady of the court tells the story of Flore and Blanscheflur to entertain her entourage. The lady situates the narrative in an indefinite past that is characteristic of romance, a past in which Christians and heathens are at war. King Fenix of Spain attacks Christian pilgrims on their way to Santiago de Compostella. A pregnant lady sees her father die, but she is saved because of her astounding beauty. Fenix takes her to Spain to serve as a companion to his pregnant wife. At Fenix's court there is no tension between the heathens and the Christian lady: the latter continues to practice her faith. When both women give birth on the same day, Easter Sunday, the heathen Flore and the Christian Blanscheflur grow up together in complete harmony and childlike innocence, and Flore insists on having Blanscheflur educated with him. Flore and Blanscheflur learn at an early age, however, that love is always in close proximity to sorrow: their devotion to each other displeases the king and queen,

Illustration accompanying Konrad Fleck's Flore und Blanscheflur *in the Heidelberg manuscript H (cpg. 362, f.94v). Flore, accompanied by his servants, rides in search of Blanscheflur, who is being held in captivity by the ruler of Babylon.*

who send Flore away to Montore. This decision to separate the lovers is based on the social inequality between the king's son and a servant's daughter; another reason, however, based on religious differences, is given later in the tale by an innkeeper: "ich waen si ist getoufet, und ist er ein heiden: / dar umbe waren sie gescheiden" (I think she is baptized, and he a heathen: / that is why they were separated). In Flore's words, they were separated because of "nit und haz" (jealousy and hate). Flore is frequently described in Christian moral terms. Although Flore seems unable to distinguish between a heathen and a Christian god, he acts and speaks as a Christian.

While Flore is away, Blanscheflur is sold to rich merchants from Babylon for a beautiful and precious cup that is described at length. On Flore's return the queen tells him Blanscheflur has died and shows him a lavish grave, richly decorated with magnificent statues of animals that stun Flore by their lifelike appearance. Fleck's penchant for minute and descriptive details — he added some five thousand lines to the three-thousand-line French source — are fully displayed here as well as

later in the tale in the descriptions of Blanscheflur's tower and Flore's horse. The gravestone tells the story of Flore and Blanscheflur's love, and the inscription is so wondrously executed that the dialogue, eternally chiseled into rock, comes to life:

> Floren bilde sprach alsus:
> "kuesset mich, frouwe sueze
> da im uebel geschehen mueze,
> der uns dirre minne nîde;
> wan ich niemer doch vermîde
> ich ensi iu rehte holt."

> (Flore's picture spoke thus:
> "kiss me, sweet lady
> because evil things will happen
> to the one that is envious of this love;
> I just cannot avoid
> being true to you always.")

Blanscheflur's response is

> "ist das war, so bin ich rîch;
> wan ich iuch in mînem sinne

vor al der werlde minne;
also helfe mir nu got,
daz ist mîn ernest âne spot."

("If that is true, then I am rich;
because I love you in my own mind
before the whole world;
as God is my witness,
I mean it truly.")

Seeing Flore's utter despair at the graveside and narrowly preventing him from committing suicide, the queen tells him the truth. This revelation starts Flore's travels in search of Blanscheflur. But, unlike the heroes of Arthurian romances, Flore is not looking for adventure. He does not need to prove himself to gain honor because he has already proven himself in his absolute devotion to Blanscheflur. He always was and always will be a "helt" (hero), even if the poet calls him a "kind" (child) through most of the tale. Only when Flore leaves the emir's court will he become a man.

Flore has only an approximate idea of where he might find Blanscheflur, but he is helped along the way by people who recognize him as a relative of hers. (Blanscheflur, conveniently, has traveled the same route.) More than once the text refers to Flore's resemblance to Blanscheflur. It is partly an outward resemblance based on their display of splendor, but it also manifests their firm belief in their constancy in *tugent* and *minne*. It is these factors that make Flore and Blanscheflur resemble each other and seem almost interchangeable to outsiders.

The innkeeper Darius is especially helpful: through him Flore learns that Blanscheflur is being held in a well-guarded tower by an emir who desires her as his wife. The emir has had many wives; he keeps each one for a year before putting her to the stake. Darius also teaches Flore how to deal with the ferocious doorkeeper of the tower, and by following the innkeeper's instructions Flore turns the doorkeeper into his trusted vassal. Flore reminds the doorkeeper of the virtues of "staete" and "triuwe" (loyalty), and the doorkeeper fabricates a plot by which Flore can gain access to Blanscheflur's chambers: Flore is to wear red clothes and hide in a bucket of roses that will be delivered to the ladies in the tower. But Flore is brought into the chamber of Blanscheflur's confidante, Claris. Claris, however, does not reveal to the guards Flore's presence in the roses. Blanscheflur's subsequent speech on *minne* demonstrates once more her unwavering devotion to Flore. The couple are reunited, but they must now face the angry emir. The emir wants to put them to the stake, but Flore's and Blanscheflur's pleas to die in the place of the other demonstrate their love and triggers deep pity in the audience. The emir finally agrees to setting them free, and he heaps Flore with treasures. A double wedding takes place in which the emir marries Claris and Flore marries Blanscheflur.

Learning that his father has died, Flore returns to Spain. At Flore's court everyone converts to Christianity because "der heilige Krist . . . warer minne meister ist" (the holy Christ is the true master of love). Flore and Blanscheflur live happily ever after, dying together on their one hundredth birthday; their daughter Berthe becomes the mother of Charlemagne, which places the narrative into a pseudohistorical context.

References:

Johanna Belkin, "Das Mechanische Menschenbild in der Floredichtung Konrad Flecks," *Zeitschrift für deutsches Altertum und deutsche Literatur*, 100, no. 4 (1971): 325–346;

Alfred Ebenauer, "Das Dilemma mit der Wahrheit," in *Geschichtsbewußtsein in der deutschen Literatur des Mittelalters*, edited by Christoph Gerhardt, Nigel F. Palmer, and Burghart Wachinger (Tübingen: Niemeyer, 1985), pp. 52–71;

Klaus Bernhard Hupfeld, "Aufbau und Erzähltechnik in Konrad Flecks *Floire und Blanscheflur*," Ph.D. dissertation, University of Hamburg, 1967;

T. R. Jackson, "Religion and Love in *Flore und Blanscheflur*," *Studia Germanica Gandensia*, 9 (1967): 157–196;

Hans-Adolf Klein, *Erzählabsicht im Heldenepos und im höfischen Epos: Studien zum Ethos im* Nibelungenlied *und in Konrad Flecks* Flore und Blanscheflur (Göppingen: Kümmerle, 1978);

Eva Klingenberg, "Helt Flore," *Zeitschrift für deutsches Altertum und deutsche Literatur*, 92 (1963): 275–276;

Roland Lane, "A Critical Review of the Major Studies of the Relationship between the Old French *Floire et Blancheflor* and Its Germanic Adaptations," *Nottingham Medieval Studies*, 30 (1986): 1–19;

Karen Pratt, "The Rhetoric of Adaptation: The Middle Dutch and Middle High German Versions of *Floire et Blanscefloir*," in *Courtly Literature: Culture and Context*, edited by Keith Busby and Erik Kooper (Amsterdam: Benjamins, 1990), pp. 483–497;

R. Sprenger, *Zu Konrad Flecks* Floire und Blanscheflur (Northeim: Rohrs, 1887).

Freidank

(circa 1170 – circa 1233)

Albrecht Classen
University of Arizona

MAJOR WORK: *Bescheidenheit* (circa 1215–1230)

Manuscripts: Of the many medieval manuscripts containing all or parts of this work the most important are ms. A (Heidelberg, Universitätsbibliothek, cpg 349 and 360; late 1200s), ms. B (Gotha, Landesbibliothek, Ch. B 53), ms. C (Salzburg, Universitätsbibliothek, M I 137), ms. D (Bremen, Staatsbibliothek, Ms. b 42b), ms. D* (Frankfurt am Main, Stadt- und Universitätsbibliothek, ms. germ. Quart. 32), ms. E (Wolfenbüttel, Herzog-August-Bibliothek, cod. 2. 4 Aug. 2), ms. G (Berlin: Staatsbibliothek Preußischer Kulturbesitz, ms. germ. fol. 1428), ms. H (Munich, Bayerische Staatsbibliothek, cgm 444), ms. J (Munich, Universitätsbibliothek, 2 cod. ms. 731), ms. K (Vienna, Österreichische Nationalbibliothek, cod. 2705), ms. L (Dresden, Landesbibliothek M 209), ms. M (Wolfenbüttel, Herzog-August-Bibliothek, cod. 417 Helmst.), ms. O (Gotha, Landesbibliothek, cod. Ch. A 823), ms. P (Donaueschingen, Fürstlich Fürstenbergsische Hofbibliothek, Hs. 104), ms. T (Fulda, Landesbibliothek, Aa 46), ms. U (Tübingen, Universitätsbibliothek, Mc 113), ms. V (Nuremberg, Germanisches Nationalmuseum, 2 L 1915 [Hs. 1611]), ms. W (Cologne, Stadtarchiv, G. B. Kasten A Nr. 51.52), ms. X (Dresden, Landesbibliothek, M 67), ms. Y (Munich, Bayerische Staatsbibliothek, clm 4660), and ms. Z (Innsbrück, Universitätsbibliothek, Hs. 669).

First publication: *Proverbia Fridanci* (Leipzig, circa 1493).

Editions: *Der Freidanck,* edited by Sebastian Brant (Strasbourg: Johannes Grüninger, 1508); *Vridankes Bescheidenheit,* edited by Wilhelm Grimm (Göttingen: Dieterich, 1834); *Freidank's Bescheidenheit: Spruchsammlung aus dem 13. Jahrhundert; neudeutsch,* translated and edited by Adolf Bacmeister (Stuttgart: Neff, 1860); *Freidanks Bescheidenheit: Ein Laienbrevier. Neudeutsch,* edited by Karl Simrock (Stuttgart: Cotta, 1867); *Fridangi discretio: Freidanks Bescheidenheit lateinisch und deutsch aus der Stettiner Handschrift,* edited by Hugo Lemcke (Stettin: Stettiner Gymnasium, 1868); *Bescheidenheit,* edited by Heinrich Ernst Bezzenberger (Halle: Waisenhaus, 1872); *Freidank: Mit kritisch-exegetischen Anmerkungen,* edited by Franz Sandvoss (Berlin: Berntraeger, 1877); *Freidanks Bescheidenheit: Aus dem Mittelhochdeutschen übersetzt,* translated and edited by Karl Pannier (Leipzig: Reclam, 1878).

Edition in Modern German: *Freidank's Bescheidenheit Auswahl, Mittelhochdeutsch-Neuhochdeutsch,* edited and translated by Wolfgang Spiewok (Leipzig: Reclam, 1985).

Although hardly anything is known of Freidank's life, his work exerted a profound impact far into the sixteenth century. The poet achieved a rank unparalleled by most of his lay contemporaries and found recognition even among the clergy. After his texts were translated into Latin, sometime before 1384–1385, they became reading material for the schools and important sources for sermons aimed at the general populace. A selection of his poems appeared in print in Leipzig around 1493 under the title *Proverbia Fridanci;* revised versions of the Middle High German texts were published by Sebastian Brant in 1508 and by an anonymous Protestant writer in 1538. The last edition seems to have appeared in Frankfurt in 1567. Many of his verses were quotable pieces of "wisdom literature" throughout the Middle Ages. In *Alexander* (circa 1230) Rudolf von Ems praises Freidank as the "sinnerîche Vrîgedanc" (insightful Freidank), and in *Willehalm von Orlens* (1240) Rudolph labels him "maister Freidank" (master Freidank). Oswald von Wolkenstein (1376/1377–1445) adapted

Opening of Freidank's series of didactic poems, commonly called
Bescheidenheit, *in manuscript O (Gotha, Landesbibliothek,*
ch. A 823, f 43r)

some of Freidank's verses for his canto "Wer hie umb diser welde lust" (He who for worldly pleasure kills). Freidank's name was soon transformed into a genre term for didactic poetry. A sixteenth-century manuscript from Basel or Colmar says that "Frydancus vagus fecit rithmos Theutonicos gratiosos" (The goliard Freidank created graceful German verse).

The *Annales Caesariensis,* the historical annals of the Cistercian convent Kaisheim, north of Donauwörth, reports that a Freidank died in 1233. The poet's own statements indicate that he participated in the Fifth Crusade under Emperor Friedrich II in 1228–1229 and spent some time in Akko in Palestine. Other sources emphasize that he was a "magister" or "meister," suggesting academic learning on his part. In some of his verses Freidank

speaks of a visit to Rome. Otherwise, there is scant information about his life. His social background cannot be determined with certainty, although he stresses the value of inner nobility over external trappings: "sost nieman edel âne tugend" (nobody possesses nobility without virtue), or "Swer tugende hât, derst wol geborn: / ân tugent ist edele gar verlorn" (he who has virtue is well born: / those born without virtue have lost their nobility).

The 181 *Sprüche* (didactic poems in rhymed, four-beat couplets) that constitute Freidank's *Bescheidenheit* (Wisdom, circa 1215–1230) are original in their pragmatic outlook and concise formulations. Overall, however, they contain ideas that can be traced back to the Bible, Aesop's fables, the *Physiologus,* Latin proverbs, and perhaps Provençal texts. Freidank also uses popular sayings in the vernacu-

Lines from Bescheidenheit *in Heidelberg manuscript A (Heidelberg, Universitätsbibliothek, cpg. 349, Sp. lc)*

lar and molds them into the literary form of the epigram. He reflects on his own oeuvre:

> Mîne sprüche sint niht beladen
> mit lügen sünde schande schaden.
> in disen vier worten stât
> aller werlde missetât:
> swer ân diu vieriu sprichet baz
> dann ich, daz lâz ich âne haz.

> (My poems are not filled
> with lies, sin, shamefulness, damage.
> In these four words are contained
> all wrongdoings of this world:
> he who can speak better without these four
> than I, will be accepted by me without anger.)

The beginning and the end of *Bescheidenheit*, with their religious verses reminiscent of biblical narratives and liturgical models, provide a tradiional framework within which the poet feels free to deal with the spectrum of human existence. It appears that Freidank composed his texts as immediate reflections on his personal experiences; no internal order can be detected. Beginning in the fourteenth century, however, various scribes seem to have attempted to sort the poems according to theme. The title *Bescheidenheit* implies a thorough understanding of this world, of God's wishes, and of humanity's shortcomings. Those who serve God, Freidank says at the outset, have found the basic direction toward wisdom. There follows an extensive discussion of humanity's relationship with God and of the human condition in this life. Freidank asks what the foundation of earth and heaven might be but accepts his ignorance and refers to God, the Creator, for further explanations.

Freidank's early verses reflect the generally accepted theology of his time, but he individualizes it by expressing his personal puzzlement over the intricacies of the divinely created cosmos. Freidank admits that for him the mystery of the Holy Trinity remains inexplicable. Similarly, he confesses that the devil and the nature of death are enigmas; nevertheless, he is deeply afraid of both.

Turning to worldly concerns, Freidank examines the God-given feudal society that is divided into peasantry, nobility, and clergy. The devil, however, created usury: "daz slindet liute unde lant" (it devours people and countries). The poet condemns arrogance, greediness, and envy. It is not worth giving oneself up to earthly existence, since its honey always turns to gall. Freidank admonishes against wealth, but he stresses that anybody who increases his or her wisdom and honor must face new worries. He laments that the world is filled with dishonest profits, improper love, and disloyalty and that people are not even ashamed of their wrongdoings. The devil primarily attacks those who enjoy a good life, making them restless and anxious to improve their worldly existence. The greatest dangers for the human soul are the world, the devil's trickery, and one's own heart. Freidank recognizes that he, too, is bound by his human existence, which exposes him to the lure of his senses and opens avenues toward sinfulness:

> Ich kan mit allen sinnen
> mir selbe niht entrinnen;
> ich entrünne gerne, wiste ich war:
> nû bin ich mensche, swar ich var.
>
> (With all my senses
> I cannot escape from myself;
> I would like to escape,
> if I knew where to:
> alas, I am human, wherever I go.)

Although here Freidank is following the model of Isidor of Seville's *Sentenciae,* the verses reveal his inner struggle with the human condition.

Almost every facet of human life finds mention in Freidank's work, be it gambling, old age, virtue, envy, self-praise, unreasonable toll barriers, or unfair taxation. He discusses violence, rhetoric, marriage, behavior that takes one to hell or heaven, the difference between wise and foolish people, ways to gain honor and wisdom, the ideals of chivalry, the vice of drunkenness, and the value of friendship. He condemns prostitution and analyzes at length the nature of love. The litany of misogynist complaints about women in Freidank's work

appears to be included for the benefit of his male audience.

At times the poet reduces his discussions to proverbs: "Der hunger ist der beste koch" (hunger is the best cook); "swaz mit varwe ist überzogen, / dâ wirt ein kint lîhte an betrogen" (things colorfully painted easily deceive children); and "Swer sich flîzet guoter site, / dem volget dicke saelde mite" (he who strives for good habits, will often find good fortune). Freidank's teachings do not represent new insights but summarize a vast body of didactic literature from antiquity through the Middle Ages. His literary genius rests in his ability to give a new twist to the expression of well-known truths:

> Nieman ist sô vollekomen,
> daz er dem wandel sî benomen;
> ân wandel niemen mac gesîn,
> deist an al der werlde schîn.
>
> (Nobody is so perfect
> that he is not subject to change;
> nobody is exempt from change,
> which is apparent all over the world.)

Although his didacticism might appear dry and lacking in originality, he often presents significant introspective comments in which he explores the dialectics of human existence:

> Ichn weiz von nieman alsô vil
> als von mir selben; doch ichz hil.
> Swer in sîn selbes herze siht,
> der sprichet nieman arges niht.
>
> (I do not know of anyone as much
> as of myself, but I conceal this.
> He who looks into his own heart,
> does not speak badly about others.)

When Freidank says: "Swer berlîn schüttet für diu swîn, / diu mugen niht lange reine sîn" (when you throw pearls before pigs, / they will not stay clean for long), he might be sarcastically anticipating what could happen to his own poetry. Freidank teaches his listeners to withhold their own knowledge rather than cause conflict. At the same time, he insists on freedom of thought. He emphasizes that he will accept as truth only what he has verified with his own eyes. He views astrology, above all, as highly untrustworthy. He rejects book learning that is not tested by reality. For him it is better to rely on oneself than to trust even one's best friend, although he feels pity for people who have no friends.

As is to be expected from a didactic poet, Freidank expresses a strong belief in Christianity.

He demonstrates his love of God as much as his fear of death. The poet prays for his soul and begs God to have mercy on him and on humanity in general. Freidank admits that all his wisdom does not make it easier to watch the approach of death: "die wîle ich iemer mac geleben, / so wil ich wider den tôt streben" (as long as I live, / I will fight against death). Those who are successful in their earthly lives will eventually die, so it is better to be filled with the pure spirit of poor people than to be as rich as the emperor. *Bescheidenheit* concludes with a prayer to God to safeguard the poet's soul in the name of the Holy Trinity.

Freidank puts into verse the basic value system and ideals of his time, emphasizing morality and ethics and submitting himself to God. He recognizes fate as a dominant force in life but erects solid barriers against it through his moralizing and pragmatic teachings.

References:

Günther Eifler, *Die ethischen Anschauungen in Freidanks "Bescheidenheit"* (Tübingen: Niemeyer, 1969);

Jutta Goheen, "Societas humana in Freidanks 'Bescheidenheit,' " *Euphorion,* 77 (1983): 95–111;

Wilhelm Grimm, *Über Freidank* (Berlin: Druckerei der Königlichen Akademie der Wissenschaften, 1850);

Nikolaus Henkel, *Deutsche Übersetzungen lateinischer Schultexte* (Munich: Artemis, 1988);

Christoph Huber, *Wort sint der dinge zeichen: Untersuchungen zum Sprachdenken der mittelhochdeutschen Spruchdichter bis Frauenlob* (Munich: Artemis, 1977);

Berndt Jäger, *"Durch reimen gute lere geben": Untersuchungen zu Überlieferung und Rezeption Freidanks im Spätmittelalter* (Göppingen: Kümmerle, 1978);

Joseph Klapper, *Die Sprichwörter der Freidankpredigten: Proverbia Fridanci. Ein Beitrag zur Geschichte des ostmitteldeutschen Sprichworts und seiner lateinischen Quellen* (Breslau: Marcus, 1927);

Albert Leitzmann, "Studien zu Freidanks Bescheidenheit," in *Sitzungsberichte der Deutschen Akademie der Wissenschaften zu Berlin, Philosophisch-historische Klasse 1948, Nr. 2* (Berlin: Deutsche Akademie der Wissenschaften, 1950): 3–30;

Friedrich Neumann, "Freidank," in *Die deutsche Literatur des Mittelalters: Verfasserlexikon,* volume 2, revised edition, edited by Kurt Ruh and others (Berlin & New York: De Gruyter, 1980), cols. 897–903;

Neumann, "Freidanks Leben und Schaffenszeit," *Zeitschrift für deutsches Altertum und Literaturgeschichte,* 89 (1958–1959): 213–241;

Neumann, "Meister Freidank," *Wirkendes Wort,* 1 (1950–1951): 321–331;

Christoph Petzsch, "Freidank-Überlieferung im cgm 811," *Zeitschrift für deutsches Altertum und Literaturgeschichte,* 98, no. 2 (1969): 116–125;

Leslie Seiffert, *Wortfeldtheorie und Strukturalismus: Studien zum Sprachgebrauch Freidanks,* Studien zur Poetik und Geschichte der Literatur, no. 4 (Stuttgart & Berlin: Kohlhammer, 1968);

Samuel Singer, *Sprichwörter des Mittelalters,* volume 2 (Bern: Lang, 1946), pp. 153–187; volume 3 (Bern: Lang, 1947), pp. 7–119;

Wolfgang Spiewok, *Freidanks Bescheidenheit: Auswahl mittelhochdeutsch-neuhochdeutsch* (Leipzig: Reclam, 1991);

O. von Zingerle, "Die Heimat des Dichters Freidank," *Zeitschrift für deutsche Philologie,* 52 (1927): 93–110.

Friedrich von Hausen

(circa 1171 – 6 May 1190)

Albrecht Classen
University of Arizona

MAJOR WORKS: *Seventeen Minnesongs* (except for the crusade songs, which were composed circa 1170–1180, the chronology is unknown)

Manuscripts: Thirty-six stanzas are in the Weingartner (or Stuttgarter) Liederhandschrift (Stuttgart, Württembergische Landesbibliothek, Sigla B, cod. HB XIII poetae germ. 1), written around 1306 in Constance, fols. 10–18; fifty-three stanzas are in the Große Heidelberger (or Manessische) Liederhandschrift (Heidelberg, Universitätsbibliothek, Sigla C, cod. pal. germ. 848), copied at the beginning of the fourteenth century in Zurich for the Manesse family, fols. 117^r–119^r; five stanzas are in the Weimarer Liederhandschrift (Weimar, Zentralbibliothek der Deutschen Klassik, Sigla F, cod. quart 564), a fifteenth-century manuscript; and one stanza is in the Berner Handschrift (Bern, Staatsbibliothek, Sigla p, Hs. 260), from the second half of the fifteenth century.

First publication: In *Sammlung von Minnesingern aus dem schwäbischen Zeitpuncte, CXL Dichter enthaltend: Durch Ruedger Manessen, weiland des Rathes der uralten Zyrich, aus der Handschrift der königlich-französischen Bibliothek herausgegeben,* edited by Johann Jakob Bodmer and Johann Jakob Breitinger, 2 volumes (Zurich: Orell, 1758–1759).

Standard edition: In *Des Minnesangs Frühling: I. Texte,* edited by Hugo Moser and Helmut Tervooren (Stuttgart: Hirzel, 1988), pp. 73–96.

Edition in modern German: *Friedrich von Hausen: Lieder. Mittelhochdeutsch/Neuhochdeutsch. Text, Übersetzung und Kommentar,* edited by Günther Schweikle (Stuttgart: Reclam, 1984).

Editions in English: Translated by Frank C. Nicholson, in *Old German Love Songs* (London: Unwin, 1907); translated by Jethro Bithell, in *The Minnesingers,* volume 1 (New York: Longmans, 1909); translated by M. F. Richey, in *Medieval German Lyrics* (Edinburgh: Oliver & Boyd, 1958); translated by Hubert Creekmore, in *Lyrics of the Middle Ages* (New York: Grove, 1959); translated by J. W. Thomas, in *Medieval German Lyric Verse,* University of North Carolina Studies in the Germanic Languages and Literatures, no. 60 (Chapel Hill: University of North Carolina Press, 1968).

Friedrich von Hausen was a respected member of the court of Emperor Friedrich I (Barbarossa) and a well-known love poet among the German minnesingers. He is considered the leader of a circle of composers from the Rhine area, near the Staufer courts in southwest Germany, that also included Emperor Heinrich VI, Bernger von Horheim, Bligger von Steinach, Ulrich von Gutenburg, and Count Otto von Botenlauben. These poets came either from the class of *ministeriales* (aristocrats who had risen since the eleventh century from servants to nobles) or from the traditional aristocracy. None was a professional poet, dependent on a patron's munificence; they composed their songs to entertain and to discuss courtly love.

Friedrich is acclaimed for having established the ideal of *hohe minne* (courtly love) in Germany through his poetic compositions and for being a source of inspiration for the other minnesingers dedicated to this ideal. Heinrich von dem Türlin in his *Diû Crône* (circa 1220), Reinmar von Brennenberg in the mid thirteenth century, and Der von Gliers in the second half of the thirteenth century praise him as an important poet.

Friedrich von Hausen is known through documents from 1171 to 1190 in which he is referred to as Fridericus de Husen or Husa. He was the son of a "homo liber Waltherus de Husen" (free man Walther of Hausen), whose testimony is recorded in more than twenty documents from 1140 to 1173. The father owned property in Oppenheim, Bingen,

*"Portrait" of Friedrich von Hausen, pointing at battling sea monsters, in
the Große Heidelberger Liederhandschrift (Heidelberg,
Universitätsbibliothek, cpg. 848, f.116v)*

Bensheim, and Worms. Several times he donated gifts to monasteries near Heidelberg and Bingen. His son Friedrich is mentioned for the first time in documents by Archbishop Christian of Mainz (1171) and Bishop Konrad of Worms (1173). Despite the unusual wealth of biographical information on Friedrich, his castle cannot be located more precisely than in the area between Bingen and Mannheim. In 1175 he is still mentioned as Walther's son, but in 1186, in an Italian document issued by King Heinrich VI, he is named without any reference to his father. Friedrich's legal and political activities are recorded in manuscripts until 1188. The only other report, in a note, is that he died through a fall from his horse while on the Third Crusade near Philomelium (today Aksehir, Turkey) on 6 May 1190.

Friedrich von Hausen appears to have been a close associate of Emperor Friedrich I and his fam-

ily. He traveled to Italy in 1175 accompanying Archbishop Christian of Mainz, the emperor's political and military ally, and in 1187 with Heinrich VI, the emperor's son. In 1184 he participated at the magnificent Whitsun Festival at Mainz on the occasion of the knighting of Friedrich I's sons, Friedrich of Swabia and Heinrich. Forty thousand guests are said to have attended, among them not only the whole gamut of European nobility and royalty but also musicians, artists, and other entertainers. The presence of the French poets Guiot de Provins and Conon de Béthune would prove to be of particular significance for Friedrich von Hausen. Other intellectual contacts probably took place during his visits to Italy.

In 1187 he was present at the meeting of Friedrich I and King Philipp II August of France at Meuzon on the Maas. In 1188 he was the head of an imperial embassy to Count Balduin von Hennegau, leading the latter to Worms to receive the earldom of Namur as a fief. It can be assumed from such indications that the poet enjoyed a considerable reputation in political power circles. His poetry further enhanced his social standing.

The only known "portrait" of Friedrich von Hausen is a stylized representation of the narrator of his crusade song "Mîn herze und mîn lîp diu wellent scheiden" (My heart and my body want to go separate ways) in the Codex Manesse or Große Heidelberger Liederhandschrift. It shows him standing on a ship, pointing with his right hand down into the water, where two monsters are battling each other, and holding his left hand in the air. He is wearing a long red coat with a hood and a white fur cap. The illuminator obviously did not know what the Hausen coat of arms looked like and left it out of the picture.

Friedrich is recognized for having introduced the ideal of *hohe minne,* a concept of esoteric love in which the physical and spiritual distance between the lover and his mistress seems insurmountable. Unavoidable suffering is the result, and the poet uses his love songs to express his emotions. The lover has to submit to the commands of the lady, who orders him to refine his manners and code of honor. Despite his willingness to fulfill every requirement, the male narrator of the love poems does not achieve his end and is left in despair. Sometimes in *Wechsel* poems with separate female and male voices, the woman is distraught over the social pressure to refrain from physical contact with her lover; she longs for love and erotic passion, which she does not find in her marriage. In the anonymous narrative poem *Morîz von Craûn* (circa 1180–1190 or 1210–1220) the lady dismisses her lover and renounces *minne* altogether; her wooer had outdone himself in his service for her but had fallen asleep while waiting for his reward. Her rejection is severely criticized because it represents a violation of one of the major principles of courtly culture. Friedrich, on the other hand, has the lady in one of his songs express her deep sorrow that she cannot reward her lover because society prevents it. She does not want to lose his friendship, yet she does not see an alternative: "daz ist mir leit und muoz doch sîn" (it gives me pain, yet it has to be).

Friedrich's narrator is filled both with burning longing for his lady and also with anger over her refusal. In "Ich muoz von schulden sîn unvrô" (I must be unhappy because of my own fault) he relates that the lady compared him with Aeneas but flatly refused to become his Dido (a clear indication of Friedrich's classical learning and probable familiar-

ity with Heinrich von Veldeke's *Eneit* [circa 1170–1185], in which Dido, queen of Carthage, kills herself after her lover Eneas leaves her). Nevertheless, he consoles himself that his heart will be the only place for his lady to retreat, since no other woman will find space enough in there. But then, surprisingly, he declares himself to be through with his mistress and will never have any further contact with her. This is a playful mode of expression, however, since he declares in the following poem, "An der genâden al mîn vröide stât" (All my joy is bound to the noble lady), that his beloved is the only source of his happiness and joy and that nobody, not even the jealous court detractors, will keep him from pursuing her. Nevertheless, she causes him profound pain because his amorous desires for her are not fulfilled. As a consequence, the narrator recognizes that joy cannot be sustained without pain – an insight that would become one of the essential concepts of medieval love poetry and courtly romances. By doubting the suitor's reliability, the lady forces him constantly to strive for self-improvement to increase his attractiveness in her eyes. The narrator is at least able to receive some degree of happiness by seeing her from a distance. Friedrich here outlines the most important concept of courtly love: that it refrains from physical contact and is content with gazing on the beloved object. The narrator goes on to say that he does not hear other people's greetings because he is thinking exclusively about his mistress ("und swer mich gruozte, daz ich sîn niht vernan"). Love makes people lose their reason, wherefore God remains the only solution for the desolate lover. He laments that the lady is under constant "huote" (guard) by the courtiers, but he also praises this situation: through *huote* his *hohe minne* will achieve refinement and esoteric fulfillment. Friedrich's concept of love is not desire for physical union but the never-ending quest for the lady's love.

Friedrich's most important statement comes in his crusade song "Mîn herze und mîn lîp diu wellent scheiden," where he describes the tension between religious and erotic ideals. The dilemma forces him to make a choice, as painful as it may be, against his mistress and in favor of God. It is worthier to fight the heathens in Palestine than to dedicate his love to his lady; she has turned a deaf ear to his pleas and now gets the reward she deserves: "swie vil ich sî gevlêhte oder gebaete, / sô tuot si rehte, als sis niht verstê" (how often I pleaded with her or begged her, / she acted as if she did not understand anything). In "Si waenent dem tôde entrunnen sîn" (They are convinced they have escaped death)

Friedrich explains that those who die for God are on their way to heaven.

Like many medieval poets, Friedrich believed in the veracity of dreams, and in his song "In mînem troume ich sach" (In my dream I saw) the narrator confesses to having dreamed of his ideal mistress. But when he woke up, both the dream image and his hope were taken away. In "Dô ich vón der guoten schiet" (When I left the good woman) the narrator insists that the river Rhine would be transformed into the river Po before he would consent to abandon his love for his lady; after all, she is worthy to be kissed by the emperor and has received from God the power to do good. Moreover, from his early childhood the narrator has dedicated his service to this lady without ever turning to falsehood and disloyalty. This faithfulness represents, in courtly terms, his never-ending *triuwe* (loyalty) and *staete* (constancy). The lover says that he has always loved his mistress not only by looking at her with his eyes but also by taking her into his heart.

The concept of *hohe minne* is especially evident when the narrator emphasizes his servitude, irrespective of how his mistress has treated him. His songs tell her of his deep love for her. At the same time he complains bitterly about her cold treatment, particularly when she does not return his greetings. The narrator questions himself and his courtly audience as to the meaning of courtly love: "Waz mac daz sîn, daz diu welt heizet minne" (What might it be, which the world calls love), thereby introducing a powerful reflective element into courtly love poetry. In all likelihood, however, Friedrich's question is merely rhetorical. *Minne* continues to vex him: "dâ von mir ist geschehen alsô vil herzesêre" (I received much heartfelt pain from it). Personifying *minne,* he proclaims that he wishes to take revenge against her because she has stolen all his heart's happiness. If it were possible, he would gouge her eyes out; if love were dead, he would feel relieved and free from her oppression.

Friedrich's poems were noticeably influenced by French troubadour and trouvère poetry, whose melodies he borrowed. The four-beat verse and the Romance decasyllabic line dominate the new poetry of *hohe minne,* but Friedrich also uses two- , five- , and six-beat verses. In contrast to those of the earlier poets, his songs excel by their hypotactic sentence structure, which allows him to formulate complex ideas about courtly love. Moreover, Friedrich was the first to use enjambment, giving his verses fluidity. It has been possible to identify some of Friedrich's models. His "Sî darf mich des zîhen niet" (She must not blame me for it) follows a song by Folquet de Marseille; "Mir ist das herze wunt" (My heart is hurt) copies an anonymous troubadour song; "Ich denke underwîlen" (I am thinking at times) uses a melody by Guiot. Friedrich's "Diu süezen wort habent mir getân" (The sweet words have affected me) was perhaps based on poems by Gaucelm Faidit or Chrétien de Troyes; "Gelebt ich noch die lieben zeit" (If I still experience that sweet moment) may have been modeled on a work by Blondel de Nesle; "Ich lobe got der sîner güete" (I praise God for his mercy) might be patterned after a song by Gace Brulé.

References:

Ursula Aarburg and Hennig Brinkmann, "Sinn und Klang in Hausens Lied 'Ich lobe got der siner güete,' " *Wirkendes Wort,* 9 (1959): 139–147;

Oskar Baumgarten, "Die Chronologie der Gedichte Friedrichs von Hausen," *Zeitschrift für deutsches Altertum und deutsche Literatur,* 26 (1882): 105–145;

Arnold Becker, "Zu Friedrich von Hausen," *Germania,* 28 (1883): 272–296;

Hugo Bekker, *Friedrich von Hausen: Inquiries into His Poetry,* University of North Carolina Studies in the Germanic Languages and Literatures, no. 87 (Chapel Hill: University of North Carolina Press, 1977);

Helmut de Boor, "Zu Hausens Kreuzzugslied 47, 9," *Beiträge zur Geschichte der deutschen Sprache und Literatur,* 87 (1965): 390–393;

Hennig Brinkmann, *Friedrich von Hausen* (Bad Oenhausen: Lutzeyer, 1948);

Doo-Hwan Choi, "Die Bedeutung Friedrichs von Hausen in der mittelalterlichen deutschen Literatur," *Zeitschrift für deutsche Sprache und Literatur* (Korea), 17 (1982): 83–94;

Karl-Huber Fischer, *Zwischen Minne und Gott: Die geistesgeschichtlichen Voraussetzungen des deutschen Minnesangs mit besonderer Berücksichtigung der Frömmigkeitsgeschichte* (Frankfurt am Main, Bern & New York: Lang, 1985);

Arne Holtdorf, "Friedrich von Hausen und das Trierer Schisma von 1183–1189: Zu MF 47, 9ff. und zur Biographie des rheinischen Minnesängers," *Rheinische Vierteljahresblätter,* 40 (1976): 72–102;

Günther Jungbluth, "Neue Forschungen zur mittelhochdeutschen Lyrik," *Euphorion,* 51 (1957): 192–221;

Richard Kienast, *Hausens scheltliet (MF 47, 33) und der "sumer von triere,"* Sitzungsberichte der deutschen Akademie der Wissenschaften zu

Berlin: Klasse für Sprachen, Literatur und Kunst, no. 3 (Berlin: Akademie, 1961);

Richard Lehfeld, "Über Friedrich von Hausen," *Beiträge zur Geschichte der deutschen Sprache und Literatur,* 2 (1876): 345–405;

Friedrich Maurer, "Zu den Liedern Friedrichs von Hausen," *Neuphilologische Mitteilungen,* 53 (1952): 149–170;

Ulrich Mehler, "Friedrich von Hausen: Sî darf mich des zîhen niet: Beobachtungen zur Form von Hau V (= MF 45, 37)," *Euphorion,* 72 (1978): 323–331;

Volker Mertens, "Der 'heiße Sommer' 1187 von Trier: Ein weiterer Erklärungsversuch zu Hausens MF 47, 38," *Zeitschrift für deutsche Philologie,* 95 (1976): 344–356;

D. G. Mowatt, *Friderich von Hûsen: Introduction, Text, Commentary and Glossary,* Anglica Germanica Series, no. 2 (Cambridge: Cambridge University Press, 1971);

Karl von Müllenhoff, "Zu Friedrich von Hausen," *Zeitschrift für deutsches Altertum und deutsche Literatur,* 14 (1867): 133–147;

Ulrich Müller, "Klassische Lyrik des deutschen Hochmittelalters – Entfaltung von Minnesang und politischer Lyrik zu weltliterarischem Rang," in *Geschichte der deutschen Literatur. Mitte des 12. bis Mitte des 13. Jahrhunderts,* edited by Rolf Bräuer and others, Geschichte der deut-schen Literatur von den Anfängen bis zur Gegenwart, no. 2 (Berlin: Volk und Wissen, 1990), pp. 503–644;

Hermann Patzig, "Zu Friedrich von Hausen," *Zeitschrift für deutsches Altertum und deutsche Literatur,* 65 (1928): 142–144;

Hans-Herbert S. Räkel, *Der deutsche Minnesang: Eine Einführung mit Texten und Materialien* (Munich: Beck, 1986), pp. 42–76;

Hans Jürgen Rieckenberg, "Leben und Stand des Minnesängers Friedrich von Hausen," *Archiv für Kulturgeschichte,* 43 (1961): 163–176;

Olive Sayce, *The Medieval German Lyric 1150–1300: The Development of Its Themes and Forms in Their European Context* (Oxford: Clarendon Press, 1982), pp. 114–119;

Franz Rolf Schröder, "Zu Friedrich von Hausen, 42, 1," *Germanisch-Romanische Monatsschrift,* 42 (1961): 330–331;

Günter Schweikle, "Friedrich von Hausen," in *Die deutsche Literatur des Mittelalters: Verfasserlexikon,* volume 2/3, edited by Kurt Ruh and others (Berlin & New York: De Gruyter, 1979), cols. 935–947;

Max Spirgatis, *Die Lieder Friedrichs von Hausen* (Tübingen: Fues, 1876);

Norbert Wagner, "Zum Wohnsitz des Friedrich von Hausen," *Zeitschrift für deutsches Altertum und deutsche Literatur,* 104 (1975): 126–130.

Gottfried von Straßburg

(died before 1230)

Michael S. Batts
University of British Columbia

MAJOR WORK: *Tristan und Isolde* (circa 1210)

Manuscripts: There are eleven complete manuscripts of this work: B (Cologne, Historisches Archiv, no. *88), E (Modena, Biblioteca Estense, MS. Est. 57), F (Florence, Biblioteca Nazionale Centrale, MS. B. R. 226), H (Heidelberg, Universitätsbibliothek, cod. pal. germ. 360), M (Munich, Bayerische Staatsbibliothek, cod. germ. 51), N (Berlin, Staatsbibliothek Preußischer Kulturbesitz, MS. germ. qu. 284), P (Berlin, Staatsbibliothek Preußischer Kulturbesitz, MS. germ. fol. 640), R (Brussels, Bibliothèque Royale de Belgique, M.S. 14967), S (Hamburg, Staats- und Universitätsbibliothek, MS. germ. 12), and W (Vienna, Österreichische Nationalbibliothek, cod. vindob. 2707, 3). Two of these manuscripts date from the thirteenth century (M, H), four from the fourteenth (F, W, B, N), and four from the fifteenth (D, E, R); S is an eighteenth-century copy of a fifteenth-century manuscript. Manuscripts B, H, M, N, R, and S include the continuation by Ulrich von Türheim; E, F, and O include the continuation by Heinrich von Freiberg; P includes a continuation adapted from one by Eilhard von Oberge. There are also fragments of thirteen other manuscripts dating from the thirteenth, fourteenth, and fifteenth centuries.

First publication: "Tristan, ein Rittergedicht aus dem XIII. Jahrhundert," in *Samlung deutscher Gedichte aus dem XII., XIII. und XIV. Jahrhundert,* edited by Christoph Heinrich Müller, volume 2 (Berlin, 1785).

Standard editions: *Tristan: Erster Teil. Text,* edited by Karl Marold (Leipzig: Avenarius, 1906); revised by Werner Schröder (Berlin: De Gruyter, 1969); *Tristan und Isold,* edited by Friedrich Ranke (Berlin: Weidmann, 1930).

Editions in modern German: *Tristan und Isolde,* 2 volumes, translated by Karl Simrock (Leipzig: Brockhaus, 1855); *Tristan,* 2 volumes, edited by Reinhold Bechstein (Leipzig: Brockhaus, 1869–1870); *Tristan und Isolde: Gedicht,* translated by Hermann Kurz (Stuttgart: Cotta, 1844); *Tristan und Isolde: Neu bearbeitet und nach den altfranzösischen Tristanfragmenten des Trouvère Thomas ergänzt,* edited by Wilhelm Hertz (Stuttgart: Kröner, 1877); *Tristan und Isolde: Hofisches Epos. Aus dem Mittelhochdeutschen übersetzt,* 2 volumes, translated by Karl Pannier (Leipzig: Reclam, 1903); *Tristan und Isolt: A Poem,* edited by August Closs (Oxford: Blackwell, 1944); *Tristan und Isold: In Auswahl,* edited by Friedrich Ranke (Berlin: Francke, 1946).

Editions in English: *The Story of Tristan and Iseult,* 2 volumes, translated by Jessie L. Weston (London: Nutt, 1889; New York: New Amsterdam, 1900); *The "Tristan and Isolde" of Gottfried von Strassburg,* edited and translated by Edwin H. Zeydel (Princeton: Princeton University Press, 1948); *Tristan, Translated Entire for the First Time: With the Surviving Fragments of the Tristan of Thomas, Newly Translated,* edited and translated by A. T. Hatto (Harmondsworth, U.K.: Penguin, 1960; Baltimore: Penguin, 1960); *Tristan and Isolde,* edited and revised by Francis G. Gentry (New York: Continuum, 1988).

Gottfried von Straßburg was highly regarded by writers who came after him, and his reputation was never greater than it is today. His work, like that of most writers of the high medieval period, was lost from sight with the advent of the Renaissance and was only rediscovered in the latter part of the eighteenth century. During the first half of the eighteenth century Gottfried's *Tristan und Isolde* (circa 1210; translated as *The Story of Tristan and Iseult,* 1889) was appreciated for its virtuosity, but

Miniature of Gottfried von Straßburg (with diptych on knee) reciting from his Tristan und Isolde *(Heidelberg, Universitätsbibliothek, cpg 360, f.364a)*

the moral codes of the day, coupled with the belief that the actions and statements of literary figures represented the philosophy of the author, led to condemnation of the work on moral grounds. Today *Tristan und Isolde* is recognized not simply as the height of stylistic virtuosity in its genre but as a masterpiece of characterization, a subtle and moving portrayal of the psychological forces that move men and women. Superior to all other poets of the German High Middle Ages as a versifier, Gottfried also outshines them in his knowledge of the human psyche and can be said to constitute one of the twin peaks of this period in German literature – the other being Wolfram von Eschenbach, who takes not individuals but the whole of German society, if not the whole world, as his subject.

As is the case with so many other poets of this time, and despite the evident popularity of his work, there is no documentary evidence about Gottfried's life. One must, therefore, seek biographical data in his literary works and in those of his contemporaries and successors. Gottfried is almost always referred to as *meister* (master); this title has traditionally been taken to mean that he was of bourgeois rather than noble birth, but the term may also imply that he was a learned man, a master of arts. The initial letters of the quatrains with which *Tristan und Isolde* begins are *G, D, I, E, T, E, R, I, C, H, T, and I;* the *G* presumably stands for *Gottfried,* while *T* and *I* are the first letters of *Tristan* and *Isolde.* The remaining letters of the names of the protagonists occur at irregular intervals throughout the remainder of the work, as do also – possibly – some further letters of Gottfried's name. The name *Dieterich* is likely that of a patron.

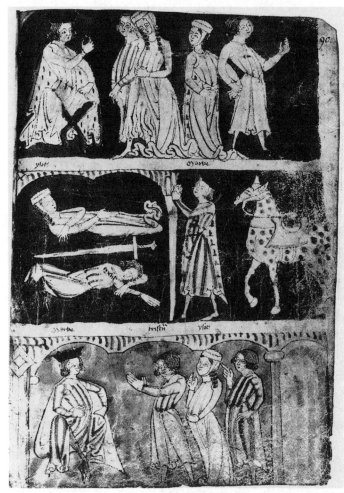

Illustrations of scenes from Gottfried's Tristan und Isolde *in the thirteenth-century manuscript M (Munich, Bayerische Staatsbibliothek, cgm 51, f.902)*

The existence of the incomplete acrostic is evidence that a much longer work was planned than the approximately 19,500 lines that have been preserved. Ulrich von Türheim completed the work from 1230 to 1235; his comment "that death interrupted his living days unfortunately before his time" may mean that Gottfried died at an early age. Rudolf von Ems eulogizes Gottfried in his *Alexander the Great,* a poem written probably around 1230. It is, therefore, clear that Gottfried died before 1230, but there is no evidence as to when he was born.

The only evidence for the date of composition of *Tristan und Isolde* is to be found in the poem itself. When Tristan is knighted by his uncle, King Mark, Gottfried refuses to describe the ceremony; such events traditionally involved great pomp and pageantry, and their depiction was frequently an excuse for poets to display their virtuosity. Instead, Gottfried provides a brief overview of recent liter-

ary history in which he refers to Hartmann von Aue in the present tense and to the minnesinger Reinmar der Alte as having fallen silent (died) and castigates an unnamed poet who is presumed to be Wolfram. Since Reinmar had died by 1210 and Hartmann did not die until after that year, possibly not until about 1220, it can be assumed that Gottfried wrote *Tristan und Isolde* between these dates – certainly earlier rather than later in the decade, since he knew Wolfram's *Parzival* (completed around 1210) well enough to criticize it and since Wolfram responded to Gottfried's criticism in his *Willehalm,* which was commenced around 1212.

There is sufficient evidence in *Tristan und Isolde* to indicate that, whether bourgeois or not, Gottfried was, for his time, well educated. He knew a good deal about the literature of his own country (besides his discussions of Hartmann, Reinmar, and Wolfram, he gives high praise to Bligger von Steinach, of whom today virtually nothing is known); in addition, he had a thorough knowledge of French, for he makes no errors in using his French source and claims to have seen other French versions of the same story. He was familiar with the standard works of classical antiquity and seems to have had some acquaintance with the law. He was well versed in theology, even making use for secular purposes of a form of allegorical interpretation that had previously been applied only in the religious sphere. And while he may have had bourgeois origins, he was fully cognizant of the lifestyle of the nobility, from court ceremony and hunting techniques to political councils. Above all, it is evident that Gottfried studied literature and composition: he rhymes with apparent ease and employs, with great skill and evident enjoyment, all manner of rhetorical and stylistic devices.

The historical origins of the story of Tristan and Isolde are obscure. A Prince Drust (Drostan), son of a Pictish king Talorc (the names Trystan and Tallwch are found in Welsh literary works) lived at the end of the eighth century, and a King Mark is recorded by a ninth-century chronicler as having lived in Cornwall in the sixth century. There is no evidence of a historical Isolde, and the etymology of her name is unknown. How these figures came to be associated with one another and with this story is impossible to tell, but the basic plot is Celtic and originally resembled the story of Potiphar's wife, who tried to seduce Joseph, her husband's head servant. In the evolution of the Tristan and Isolde story Isolde's unsuccessful attempt to seduce Tristan was replaced by a successful one and finally by a love potion that draws them irresistibly to one another. Various stock elements were also added to the story as time passed, such as the fight of the young man against a giant or dragon, the poisoned sword for which only one person has the cure, the life in the forest, and the black and white sails; and the work was extended at one end by the stories of the protagonists' parents (primarily those of Tristan) and at the other by the introduction of a second Isolde. Such elements may have been borrowings from myth, from the literature of classical antiquity, or from oriental sources. By the middle of the twelfth century the story was largely complete; there existed, in addition, short works that recounted episodes from the story, it being assumed that the listener or reader would know the general outline of the story as a whole.

This version of approximately 1150, on which the extant works are assumed to have been based, is commonly referred to as the *estoire* and was written in French. The link between the Celtic peoples and the European continent was provided by Henry II of England, who, as Count Henry of Anjou, had married Eleanor of Aquitaine. From the *estoire* derive, on the one hand, the works of Eilhard von Oberge and Béroul, and, on the other, that of Thomas of Brittany. It is generally assumed that Béroul wrote around 1170 and Eilhard at the same time or ten to twenty years later; the version by Thomas may have been written as early as 1150 or as late as 1190. No complete manuscript of any of these works has been preserved. Gottfried makes a strong point of having selected Thomas's version as the true one, but Gottfried's work ends just after the point at which the surviving text of Thomas's work begins. A comparison of Gottfried's work with its source must therefore be carried out on the basis of a reconstruction of Thomas's, using primarily a Norwegian translation of Thomas's made in 1226 that is somewhat abbreviated, and an even more abbreviated English stanzaic poem of about 1300, *Sir Tristrem*.

It is, however, fairly evident why Gottfried chose Thomas's work rather than that of the Frenchman Béroul or the German Eilhard. In the latter works the effect of the potion wears off after some years; also the flight of the lovers into the forest is occasioned by their being caught in flagrante dilicto and condemned to death. In Eilhard's version they are to be burned at the stake; when Tristan escapes, the king is so furious that he orders Isolde to be given over to a crowd of lepers – a fate worse than death. Such uncourtly behavior is not acceptable to Gottfried, who is concerned not only with the proprieties but also with verisimilitude: he is critical, for example, of Eilhard's story of the golden hair, dropped by a swallow, which prompts the king to send Tristan out to find the owner of the hair so that the king can marry her. In Thomas's version the material is organized much more carefully and consistently, and with due regard for courtly convention. The lovers are banished from court rather than fleeing to escape execution; their sojourn in the forest is an idyll rather than a period of suffering; and the permanence of the effect of the potion makes Tristan's continued love for Isolde while in exile, despite his entanglement with the second Isolde, understandable and meaningful. The whole plot hangs together.

Gottfried's *Tristan und Isolde* is much more than the story of the love of two individuals. Rather, it is an analysis of the quality of love in various forms, of the role of love in society, and of the relationship of love to life and death. Precisely what

Manuscript leaf with the opening lines of Tristan und Isolde *(Heidelberg, Universitätsbibliothek, cpg. 360, f.1r)*

Pages from manuscript M, with text and illustrations for Tristan und Isolde *(Munich, Bayerische Staatsbibliothek, cgm 51, f.75v–76r)*

lesson, if any, Gottfried intended his audience to draw from his work is by no means clear, and interpretation has perhaps been hindered rather than assisted by the involved introduction and frequent authorial interpolations.

The story of Tristan and Isolde in Gottfried's version is preceded by a brief history of Tristan's parents. Rivalin, Lord of Parmenie, after successfully waging war against his neighbor, Morgan, sets off to visit the famed court of King Mark at Tintagel in Cornwall. Here he meets Mark's sister, Blancheflor; they fall in love, but neither at first understands what is happening. Rivalin is a man of action, untutored in the arts, though not entirely without social graces, while Blancheflor has been brought up, to judge by her comments about her brother, largely in seclusion. Blancheflor takes the initiative in their relationship; Gottfried allows his female figures a far more active role than is customary in chivalric literature. They declare their love to each other but keep it secret from the outside world.

Rivalin is severely wounded in a battle against Mark's enemies; Blancheflor gains entry to his sickroom, and their love is consummated while Rivalin is apparently dying. Their blind passion is symbolized by their union in the darkness of the sickroom. The power of love brings her at first "geliche als ob si waere tot" (almost to the point of death), but the same power revives her and enables him to consummate their love and to recover from what had seemed a mortal wound. Their union takes place in concealment, foreshadowing the union of Tristan and Isolde in the cabin of their ship and later in the grotto. The sexual union of Rivalin and Blancheflor also takes place in the shadow of Rivalin's expected death; it results in his recovery, but she now carries the child that will be brought into the world in the shadow of both their deaths. Tristan's life and death are prefigured in and to be understood in relationship to the lives and deaths of Rivalin and Blancheflor. When Rivalin recovers, he is forced to return to Parmenie to protect his property against renewed attacks by Morgan, secretly taking Blancheflor with him. In the fighting Rivalin is killed, and Blancheflor dies giving birth to a son. The son is named Tristan, from the French *triste* (sad), and is brought up as the child of a couple faithful to Rivalin, Rual and Floraete, to protect him from Morgan.

The early life of Tristan is described in great detail and is intended to qualify him for the experience of a much deeper kind of love. Although he acquires the chivalric skills to a high degree, much greater emphasis is placed on his knowledge and appreciation of the arts. He is a skilled linguist, versed in literature, and above all a musician; his understanding of human nature is based both on these arts and on personal experience gained during the travels that are part of his education. In the guise of the minstrel Tantris, Tristan will transmit much of his knowledge and understanding to Isolde; thus, in her case too, there is emphasis on her ability as a musician, and she is clearly a fitting companion for Tristan. When the moment comes, she, like Blancheflor, will take the initiative.

In the flower of his youth Tristan is abducted by a visiting Norwegian merchant but hastily put ashore on the coast of Cornwall when a storm breaks out that seems to be the wrath of God for this crime. Tristan makes his way, unknown and unknowingly, to the court of Mark at Tintagel, where he becomes a great favorite on account of his many accomplishments. Finally Rual, who has searched everywhere for him, arrives at Tintagel and reveals the story of Tristan's parentage. Mark, his uncle, knights Tristan and sends him back to Parmenie, where he kills Morgan and regains the lands of his father.

Tristan leaves the land in Rual's charge and returns to Cornwall, where he finds that the "giant" champion of Ireland, Morold, has arrived to demand the tribute laid on the country by the Irish king when Mark was a child. The alternative to paying the tribute is single combat with Morold, which only Tristan dares to undertake. He kills Morold but receives a poisoned wound, which only Morold's sister, Isolde, queen of Ireland, can cure.

Tristan goes to Ireland disguised as the minstrel Tantris and is so successful as a teacher of the younger Isolde, the daughter of the queen, that the queen cures him. He returns to Cornwall, where he becomes more popular than ever with his uncle, who wants to make him his heir. But the barons insist that Mark take a wife. When Mark agrees, they select the princess Isolde, whose beauty and nobility have been so highly praised by Tristan, as the only possible wife and Tristan as the best person to undertake the embassy.

Arriving in Ireland for the second time, Tristan finds the countryside ravaged by a dragon and hears that the reward for killing the beast is the hand of the princess. He kills the dragon, cuts out its tongue, and conceals it on his person, but he is overcome by the fumes from the tongue and falls unconscious. A steward, enamored of the princess, finds the dead dragon and claims to have killed it. Neither mother nor daughter believes him; they search for and find the real hero, convey him secretly to the palace, and revive him. He promises to appear and confound the steward, but before he can do so Princess Isolde notices that "Tantris's" sword has a piece missing that exactly fits the piece found in Morold's skull when his body was returned to Ireland, and she realizes that the minstrel is Tristan. Unable to take revenge herself and caught in a dilemma because of the steward, she abandons the idea of revenge. The steward is confounded by the evidence of the tongue, and Tristan claims Isolde on behalf of his uncle. Through their marriage the old enmity between the two kingdoms will be ended.

On the voyage back to Cornwall, Tristan and Isolde inadvertently drink a love potion that was put in the safekeeping of Brangane, Isolde's maidservant, and intended for Isolde and Mark. They subsequently consummate their love. The love potion has been interpreted as necessary to justify an otherwise unacceptable adultery; this view was taken in the sixteenth century and related in part to versions in which Mark also partakes of the potion (Gottfried, however, insists that the remainder of the potion was destroyed and not given to Mark) or the efficacy is of limited duration. Alternatively, the potion has been interpreted as symbolic of a love that has already sprung up between the two. The prevailing modern view is that Gottfried does not depict Tristan and Isolde as falling in love before drinking the potion, but that its function is, nevertheless, largely symbolic. The position can, however, be taken that the potion is meant to be taken literally and that no symbolism is intended; belief in such things was, after all, current in Gottfried's day and remained so for a long time to come. Gottfried portrays Tristan and Isolde as being made for one another; but the potion initiates their relationship, and it may, therefore, be taken as symbolic both of the unpredictability of love and of the dangers love may bring: "ezn was niht mit wine / . . . / ez was diu wernde swaere, / die endelose herzenot, / von der si beide lagen tot" (it was no wine / . . . / it was their lasting sorrow, / their never-ending anguish, / from which they both found death).

Isolde takes the initiative in a manner similar to that of Blancheflor, but the physical union with Tristan is delayed. Brangane realizes that their love, if it remains unconsummated, could lead to their deaths, and she therefore allows them their will. After they have admitted their love to Brangane and obtained her consent to their union, it is Tristan who comes to Isolde; he is led by love, which, as the narrator Gottfried puts it, is acting as their physician: sexual union is the medicine prescribed by love as a cure for their sickness. When Brangane later tells them of the potion and suggests that it will bring about their deaths, Tristan claims that if Isolde is to be his death in this manner, he would wish to die eternally. They willingly embrace the risk. Life, love, and death, linked involuntarily in the union of Rivalin and Blancheflor, are consciously accepted as inextricably linked in the future of Tristan and Isolde.

Tristan and Isolde persuade Brangane, who is a virgin, to take Isolde's place on the wedding night, since the wedding must take place as planned. Subsequently Isolde plots to have Brangane killed; but the plot fails, and the two are reconciled. That neither Tristan nor Isolde for a moment considers that Isolde's marriage to Mark should not take place has nothing to do with fears for their personal safety or concern for the political situation, but everything to do with the medieval concept of society. An existence outside society, which any form of elopement – such as that described in similar Celtic tales – would entail, was simply unthinkable. The noble hearts to whom Gottfried dedicates the work in his prologue understand the quality of true love and accept that it brings both pleasure and pain. Both emotions are experienced by the lovers as they meet in secret or are foiled in their attempts to do so.

There follows a series of episodes in which suspicions of infidelity are aroused in the king – primarily by his followers Melot and Marjodo – and then allayed, until the king becomes so confused that he insists on a formal trial: Isolde is to swear an oath of innocence while holding a red-hot iron. The purpose of these episodes, which are closely linked with major themes running throughout the work – darkness and light, blindness and seeing, hunter and quarry – is to contrast the true love of Tristan and Isolde with false kinds of love and to portray the difficulties encountered by true lovers in a society where love has become salable. There is a distinct progression in these episodes, inasmuch as the circle of those involved widens and the dispute is eventually carried into the public arena. The trou-

ble begins with Tristan's "friend," the steward Marjodo, who discovers Tristan's affair with Isolde and tries to betray them to the king – not out of loyalty to the latter, but because he himself is in love with Isolde and is jealous of Tristan. The king is also in love with Isolde, but his love does not go beyond the desire for physical possession: he was unable to distinguish on the wedding night between Brangane and Isolde, and his concern is the safeguarding of his property.

As Isolde approaches the place where the oath is to be taken she asks a pilgrim – Tristan in disguise – to lift her from the boat and carry her ashore. He stumbles and falls down with her, so that she is able to swear an oath never to have lain with any man except her husband and the person in whose arms she just fell. Isolde passes the test (occasioning a sarcastic comment from the author about the way God blows with the wind), but the lovers are now kept apart as much as possible, and the king sees that Isolde loves Tristan better than she loves him. He banishes them, and they retire to a grotto far out in the wilderness. In this grotto, which is described in great detail as the abode of true love, they remain for some time, playing, singing, telling tales of love, and hunting for pleasure but not for food; they need no sustenance besides the presence of the other.

Mark's lack of any deeper feeling for Isolde is not criticized by Gottfried, and Mark gains the reader's sympathy to some extent: first by his desire not to suspect his wife and nephew of wrongdoing, and second by sending them away when he thinks that their love for each other is greater than their love for him and that his situation is, consequently, ignominious. In so doing, he overrides the official and public evidence of the trial by ordeal, an episode that has caused a great deal of discussion over the years. The so-called false oath (the oath is literally true but deceptive) was long considered blasphemous but is now generally accepted as Gottfried's criticism of the manner in which individuals take the name of the Lord in vain in the pursuit of their own ends. Although there are other references to matters religious, Gottfried attacks neither the church nor individual representatives of the church, and he does not set up a "religion of love" as a substitute for Christianity.

Banished from a situation of hardship and suffering into paradise, the lovers remain aware of society beyond the wilderness that surrounds them (they send Curvenal, Tristan's faithful servant, back to keep an eye on things for them). In this idyllic situation they pass the time with all manner of

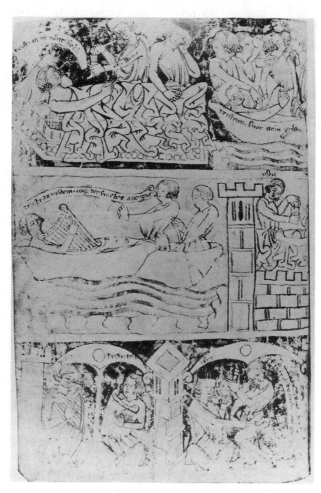

Illustrations of scenes from Tristan und Isolde *(Munich,
Bayerische Staatsbibliothek, cgm 51, f.46v)*

pleasures, especially with music and the telling of
tales of lovers of the past. The grotto is described as
dating from heathen times, but the detailed description and the allegorical interpretation of its shape,
dimensions, and colors (for example, the roundness
and smoothness of the chamber signify the simplicity of love, the breadth of its power, and the height
of its aspiration) are derived from Christian interpretations of the fabric of church buildings, and the
recognition of this derivation in Friedrich Ranke's
Die Allegorie der Minnegrotte in Gottfrieds "Tristan"
(The Allegory of the Love Grotto in Gottfried's
"Tristan," 1925) has been the most important factor
in the modern interpretation of this episode. Other
interpretations range from the religious (the grotto
as a temple in a religion of love) to the Freudian
(the grotto as womb), some of which are summa-
rized in Vlastimil Vrablik's "Die Minnegrotte in
Gottfrieds von Strassburg 'Tristan und Isolde': Ein
Versuch zur Typologie der Liebe" (The Love Grotto

in Gottfried von Straßburg's "Tristan und Isolde":
An Attempt at a Typology of Love, 1989). Vrablik's
comment that Gottfried's concept of love flies in the
face of the *Minnesang* Tradition, however, is mistaken: sexual love is a constant factor in *Minnesang*.
The traditional dawn song, for example, is based on
what is in effect a brief sojourn in a love grotto.

The specific details of the grotto contribute to
an understanding of the nature of true love, but its
most important aspect is its location. Gottfried describes it at first as in Cornwall and attainable only
across a pathless wilderness (which reminds one of
the wilderness through which Hartmann's Gregorius passes on his way to a different epiphany). He
later claims to have reached the grotto himself and
to have known it since his early days, but he also
says he has never been in Cornwall. In other words,
the grotto represents a state of existence rather than
a real place, a state that can only be attained with
commitment and suffering and only for a limited

time. The ultimate experience of love is akin to the mystic's momentary experience of union with God; the connection is, presumably, deliberately made when Gottfried refers to the grotto as a "kluse" (hermit's cell) and to the lovers as "klusenaere" (anchorites).

When Tristan and Isolde fear that they are about to be discovered by the king, they lie down on their bed with a sword between them. The king, who wants Isolde back, interprets this act as evidence of their innocence, and they return to court. Their deception of Mark and his response to it make it evident that he is compelled by the desire for the physical possession of Isolde to blind himself to the truth. Nevertheless, he surrounds Isolde with watchers to prevent her and Tristan from coming together, and she is impelled to circumvent the restrictions imposed upon her.

The lovers become careless, however, and are one day seen by the king sleeping in each others' arms. They awaken as he leaves to fetch witnesses, and by the time the king returns with the witnesses Tristan has fled. Mark cannot, therefore, prove Isolde's guilt, and she remains with him. The scene in which Mark finds Tristan and Isolde sleeping together in broad daylight in the orchard is prefaced by a diatribe in which Gottfried criticizes those who feel it necessary to lay down rules to protect their honor and argues that Eve would never have offered Adam the fruit if God had not expressly forbidden it. By drawing this parallel Gottfried suggests that Isolde, by inviting Tristan to bed in the orchard, is sinning against true love. Their love has been dragged down to Mark's level, to the level of physical desire. Their discovery by Mark means for him the end of all doubt. Although by the time the witnesses arrive Isolde is alone, Mark knows the truth and can no longer deceive himself. For the lovers, separation cannot mean the end of love, for true love such as theirs survives it.

In exile Tristan meets another woman named Isolde – Isolde Whitehands – and is tempted to fall in love with her, persuading himself that "his" Isolde is happy with her husband. It is at this point that Gottfried's poem breaks off. Tristan becomes involved in yet another kind of love when he meets the second Isolde. It is true that he is initially attracted to her by her name, but the manner in which he behaves is reminiscent of *Minnesang*, of love as a social game. In the playful wooing of Isolde Whitehands, Gottfried depicts Tristan's deviation from the true path of love, a path to which he later would return, just as Isolde has returned to it after the brief lapse in the orchard.

There is sufficient evidence that Gottfried was following his source fairly closely and that the poem would, therefore, have continued, as Thomas's version does, with Tristan's unconsummated marriage to Isolde Whitehands, with Tristan's visits in disguise to his first love, and with his receipt of a second poisoned wound. The first Isolde, who has inherited her mother's skills, is sent for, and the messenger is told to hoist a white sail if she is on board, a black sail if she is not. She does come; but out of jealousy Isolde Whitehands tells Tristan that the sail is black, and he dies. When Isolde arrives and finds Tristan dead, she dies over his corpse. They are buried together. The episodes in which Tristan makes brief visits to Isolde would again exemplify the mixture of joy and suffering experienced by true lovers and together with the second poisoned wound would provide a kind of mirror image of the first stages of their love; the end, which was prefigured in the beginning, is their union in death.

No discussion of Gottfried's great work would be complete without some reference to the vast number of works of literature, art, and music that have been based on it. Gottfried took over the work of his predecessors, of course, and to that extent he is only a link, if one of the greatest, in a long and broad European tradition. But it is undoubtedly his work that made the story so popular in Germany that motifs from it were used in the following centuries to decorate domestic objects, carpets, and tapestries. Since the rediscovery of his work in the eighteenth century there has been an uninterrupted succession of translations, reworkings in literary form, and adaptations into other media. In music the best-known example is, of course, Richard Wagner's music drama *Tristan und Isolde* (1859; translated as *Tristan and Isolde,* 1889). Hans Werner Henze's *Tristan: Preludes für Klavier, Tonbänder und Orchester* (Tristan: Preludes for Piano, Tapes, and Orchestra, 1973) was subsequently used as the score of a ballet on the same subject. Thomas Mann's novella "Tristan" (1903; translated, 1925) is fairly well known, as is Georg Kaiser's play *König Hahnrei* (King Cuckold, 1913), a Freudian version of the story. Mann also drafted an outline for a film on Tristan and Isolde that was never produced. There have been film versions of this story, however, among them Veith von Fürstenberg's *Feuer und Schwert* (Fire and Sword).

Bibliography:

Hans-Hugo Steinhoff, *Bibliographie zu Gottfried von Straßburg,* 2 volumes (Berlin: Schmidt, 1971, 1986).

References:

Michael S. Batts, *Gottfried von Strassburg* (New York: Twayne, 1971);

Otfried Ehrismann, "Isolde, der Zauber, die Liebe – der Minnetrank in Gottfrieds *Tristan* zwischen Symbolik und Magie," in *Ergebnisse und Aufgaben der Germanistik am Ende des 20. Jahrhunderts: Festschrift für Ludwig Erich Schmidt zum 80. Geburtsag* (Hildesheim: Olms, 1989), pp. 282–301;

Michael Huby, *Prolegomena zu einer Untersuchung von Gottfrieds "Tristan,"* 2 volumes (Göppingen: Kümmerle, 1984);

William T. H. Jackson, *The Anatomy of Love: The "Tristan" of Gottfried von Strassburg* (New York: Columbia University Press, 1971);

Stephen Jaeger, *Medieval Humanism in Gottfried von Strassburg's "Tristan und Isolde"* (Heidelberg: Winter, 1977);

Alain Kerdehelue, "Feuer und Schwert," in *Tristan et Iseut, mythe européen et mondial,* edited by Danielle Buschinger (Göppingen: Kümmerle, 1987);

Lambertus Okken, *Kommentar zum Tristan-Roman Gottfrieds von Straßburg,* 3 volumes (Amsterdam: Rodopi, 1984–1988);

Friedrich Ranke, *Die Allegorie der Minnegrotte in Gottfrieds "Tristan"* (Berlin: Deutsche Verlagsgesellschaft für Politik und Geschichte, 1925);

Ranke, "Die Überlieferung von Gottfrieds Tristan," *Zeitschrift für deutsches Altertum,* 55 (1917): 157–278, 381–438;

Neil Thomas, *Tristan in the Underworld: A Study of Gottfried von Strassburg's "Tristan" together with the "Tristan" of Thomas* (Lampeter, Wales: Mellen, 1991);

Tomas Tomasek, *Die Utopie im "Tristan" Gotfrids von Straßburg* (Tübingen: Niemeyer, 1985);

Vlastimil Vrablik, "Die Minnegrotte in Gottfrieds von Strassburg 'Tristan und Isolde': Ein Versuch zur Typologie der Liebe," in *Ist zwîvel herzen nâchgebûr: Günther Schweikle zum 60. Geburtstag* (Stuttgart: Helfant, 1989), pp. 181–192;

Franziska Wessel, *Probleme der Metaphorik und die Minnemetaphorik in Gottfrieds von Strassburg "Tristan und Isolde"* (Munich: Fink, 1984);

Alois Wolf, *Gottfried von Strasburg und die Mythe von Tristan und Isolde* (Darmstadt: Wissenschaftliche Buchgesellschaft, 1989).

Hartmann von Aue

(circa 1160 – circa 1205)

Will Hasty
University of Florida

MAJOR WORKS: *Die Klage* or *Das Büchlein* (circa 1180)

Manuscript: This work is preserved only in the Ambraser Heldenbuch (Österreichische Nationalbibliothek, Vienna; cod. Vind. ser. nov. 2663), a large parchment manuscript containing twenty-five works by Hartmann and other authors that was commissioned by Emperor Maximilian I and completed by his secretary, Hans Ried of Bozen, between 1504 and 1516; the title *Das Büchlein* is based on an error by its first editor, Moriz Haupt, who mistakenly associated this poem with another poem in the Ambraser Heldenbuch (*Das zweite Büchlein*).

First publication: In *Die Lieder und Büchlein und Der arme Heinrich,* edited by Moriz Haupt (Leipzig: Weidmann, 1842).

Standard editions: *Die Klage–Das (zweite) Büchlein,* edited by Herta Zutt (Berlin: De Gruyter, 1968); *Das Klagebüchlein Hartmanns von Aue und das zweite Büchlein,* edited by Ludwig Wolff (Munich: Fink, 1972); *Hartmann von Aue: Das Büchlein; nach den Vorarbeiten von Arno Schirokauer zu Ende geführt und herausgegeben,* edited by Petrus W. Tax (Berlin: Schmidt, 1977).

Eighteen Songs (circa 1180)

Manuscripts: Strophes of Hartmann's songs are transmitted in the three major manuscripts containing *Minnesang* which were all assembled around the year 1300; sixty strophes in Die große Heidelberger (or Die Mannessiche) Liederhandschrift (Universitätsbibliothek, Heidelberg; cpg 848), ten strophes in Die kleine Heidelberger Liederhandschrift (Universitätsbibliothek, Heidelberg; cpg 357), and twenty-eight strophes in Die Weingartner Liederhandschrift (Württembergische Landesbibliothek, Stuttgart; cod. HB XIII 1); the number of strophes and their order differ from one manuscript to another; formal characteristics of the strophes indicate eighteen different melodies, or Töne.

First publication: In *Sammlung von Minnesingern aus dem schwaebischen Zeitpuncte, CXL Dichter enthältend: durch Ruedger Manessen, weiland des Rathes der uralten Zyrich, aus der Handschrift der königlich-französischen Bibliothek herausgegeben,* 2 volumes, edited by Johann Jakob Bodmer and Johann Jakob Breitinger (Zurich: Orell, 1758, 1759).

Standard edition: *Des Minnesangs Frühling,* edited by Karl Lachmann and Moriz Haupt (Leipzig: Hirzel, 1857); revised by Hugo Moser and Helmut Tervooren, 2 volumes (Stuttgart: Hirzel, 1987).

Edition in modern German: *Lieder: Mittelhochdeutsch/Neuhochdeutsch,* edited and translated by Ernst von Reusner (Stuttgart: Reclam, 1985).

Editions in English: Translated by Frank C. Nicholson, in *Old German Love Songs* (London: Unwin, 1907); translated by Jethro Bithell, in *The Minnesingers,* volume 1 (New York: Longmans, 1909); translated by M. F. Richey, in *Medieval German Lyrics* (Edinburgh: Oliver & Boyd, 1958); translated by Barbara G. Seagrave and J. W. Thomas, in *The Songs of the Minnesingers* (Urbana: University of Illinois Press, 1966).

Erec (circa 1180)

Manuscripts: The only complete version, which lacks several lines from the beginning of the poem, is preserved along with *Die Klage, Iwein,* and works by other authors in the Ambraser Heldenbuch. There are also fragments of manuscripts in Wolfenbüttel (Herzog August Bibliothek, cod. 19.26.9 Aug.4^0 and in Koblenz (Landeshauptarchiv, Best.701 Nr.759,14) from the thirteenth century, and in Vienna (Nordösterreichisches Landesarchiv, Nr.821) from the fourteenth century.

First publication: *Erec: Eine Erzählung von*

Miniature depicting Hartmann von Aue as a knight, from the Große Heidelberger Liederhandschrift (Heidelberg, Universitätsbibliothek, cpg. 848, f. 184v)

Hartmann von Aue, edited by Moritz Haupt (Leipzig: Weidmann, 1839).

Standard edition: *Hartmann von Aue: Erec,* edited by Albert Leitzmann (Halle: Niemeyer, 1939); revised by Christoph Cormeau and Kurt Gärtner (Tübingen: Niemeyer, 1985).

Edition in modern German: *Erec,* edited and translated by Wolfgang Mohr (Stuttgart: Kümmerle, 1980).

Editions in English: Translated by J. Wesley Thomas as *Erec* (Lincoln: University of Nebraska Press, 1982); translated by R. W. Fischer as "Erec" in *The Narrative Works of Hartmann von Aue* (Göppingen: Kümmerle, 1983); translated by Michael Resler as *Erec* (Philadelphia: University of Pennsylvania Press, 1987).

Gregorius (circa 1187)

Manuscripts: Six manuscripts and five frag-

ments are preserved from the thirteenth to the fifteenth century; the prologue, in which the author introduces himself and his story, is preserved in only two of the manuscripts, designated *J* (Staatsbibliothek Stiftung Preußischer Kulturbesitz, Berlin; Ms. germ. qu. 979) and *K* (Stadtarchiv, Constance; Hs. A I 1), and its relationship to Hartmann is questionable.

First publications: *Gregorius: Eine Erzählung von Hartmann von Aue,* edited by Karl Lachmann (Berlin: Reimer, 1838); in *Spicilegium Vaticanum: Beiträge zur näheren Kenntnis der Vaticanischen Bibliothek für deutsche Poesie des Mittelalters,* edited by Carl Greith (Frauenfeld, 1838), pp. 135–303.

Edition in modern German: *Gregorius der gute Sünder,* edited by Friedrick Neumann, translated by Burkhard Kippenberg (Stuttgart: Reclam, 1976).

Editions in English: Translated by Edwin H. Zeydel and Bayard Q. Morgan as *Gregorius: A Medieval Oedipus Legend* (Chapel Hill: University of North Carolina Press, 1955; New York: AMS Press, 1966); translated by Sheema Z. Buehne as *Gregorius: The Good Sinner* (New York: Ungar, 1966).

Der arme Heinrich (circa 1191)

Manuscripts: This work is preserved in three manuscripts, a fragment, and a dozen verses in a Latin manuscript from the fourteenth century, and in two fragments from the thirteenth century; the manuscripts present two widely divergent versions of the work.

First publication: In *Samlung deutscher Gedichte aus dem XII., XIII. und XIV. Jahrhundert,* edited by Christoph Heinrich Myller, volume 1 (Berlin, 1784).

Standard editions: *Der arme Heinrich von Hartmann von Aue,* edited by Hermann Paul (Halle: Niemeyer, 1882); revised by Gesa Bonath (Tübingen: Niemeyer, 1984); *Der arme Heinrich: Überlieferung und Herstellung,* edited by Erich Gierach (Heidelberg: Winter, 1913).

Edition in modern German: Der arme Heinrich: Mittelhochdeutscher Text und Ubertragung, edited and translated by Helmust de Boor (Frankfurt am Main & Hamburg: Fischer, 1967).

Editions in English: Paraphrased by Dante Gabriel Rossetti as *Henry the Leper,* 2 volumes (Boston: Printed for the Members of the Bibliophile Society, 1905); translated by C. H. Bell as *Peasant Life in Old German Epics: Meier Helmbrecht and Der arme Heinrich* (New York: Columbia University Press, 1931); translated by J. Wesley Thomas as "Poor Heinrich," in *The Best Novellas of Medieval Germany* (Columbia, S.C.: Camden House, 1984).

Iwein (circa 1203)

Manuscripts: Fifteen complete manuscripts and seventeen fragments have been preserved from the thirteenth to the sixteenth century; more than 40 percent of the manuscripts are from the thirteenth century, another 30 percent are from the fourteenth century; this is the best preserved of Hartmann's works.

First publication: In *Samlung deutscher Gedichte aus dem XII., XIII. und XIV. Jahrhundert,* edited by Christoph Heinrich Myller, volume 2 (Berlin, 1784).

Standard editions: *Iwein der riter mit dem lewen getihtet von dem hern Hartmann dienstman ze Ouwe,* edited by G. F. Benecke and Lachmann (Berlin: Reimer, 1827); revised by Ludwig Wolff (Berlin: De Gruyter, 1968).

Edition in modern German: *Iwein: aus dem Mittelhochdeutscher ubertragen,* translated by Max Wehrli (Zurich: Manesse, 1988).

Editions in English: Translated by J. Wesley Thomas as *Iwein* (Lincoln: University of Nebraska Press, 1982); edited and translated by Patrick McConeghy as *Iwein* (New York: Garland, 1984).

Hartmann von Aue stands out as one of the most significant authors of the flourishing of literary activity that occurred in German-speaking lands at the end of the twelfth and the beginning of the thirteenth centuries. Hartmann is a seminal figure: his versions of works by the French author Chrétien de Troyes introduced what is regarded as the classical form of the Arthurian epic to subsequent German authors. During an age when many authors concentrated their efforts on a single epic or lyrical genre, Hartmann is also a rarity in the variety of his literary production. Next to his worldly works dealing with Arthur and the Round Table, *Erec* (circa 1180) and *Iwein* (circa 1203), are two works of a spiritual, if not ascetic, tone: *Gregorius* (circa 1187) and *Der arme Heinrich* (circa 1191) as well as a relatively large group of songs in the *Minnesang* tradition. No other author of this period so distinguished himself both by the variety and by the significance of his literary work. Perhaps the best testimony to the importance of Hartmann comes from another author of the same period, Gottfried von Straßburg, who in his *Tristan und Isolde* (circa 1210) speaks highly of his predecessor while passing review on several of the significant poets of his age:

> ahi, wie der diu mære
> beid uzen unde innen
> mit worten und mit sinnen
> durchverwet und durchzieret!
> wie er mit rede figieret
> der aventiure meine!
>
> (Oh, how he
> colors and adorns the tales
> Both inside and out
> With words and with wit!
> How he grasps with words
> the meaning of the adventure!)

These words are not only a tribute to Hartmann's literary style, which is regarded as a model by later authors; they portray him as a prime example of what an author of his day and age is supposed to be: a combination of craftsman, entertainer, and pedagogue, whose skillful renditions of existing literary traditions convey their true meaning.

Despite Hartmann's literary importance, almost nothing is known about his life; there is no historical documentation of his existence. This situation is the rule rather than the exception even for the major authors of court literature. It is possible to say some things about Hartmann's life based on a few passages in literary works, but doing so involves interpretive problems. When Hartmann sings about his participation in a Crusade, for example, should one understand this as an autobiographical statement, or is he merely availing himself of the purely literary possibilities afforded by the Crusade song, a subgenre within the *minne* (love) lyrics? In other words, is it possible to separate the biographical Hartmann from the Hartmann who is stylized according to the demands of different literary traditions? Despite such problems and many differences of opinion among scholars with regard to the details, there exists a consensus concerning the rough outline of Hartmann's life.

The beginning point for establishing when Hartmann lived and worked is a passage from Wolfram von Eschenbach's *Parzival* (circa 1200–1210). To illustrate the consequences of a rowdy knightly tournament he has portrayed, Wolfram makes an extremely rare allusion to a historical event: "Erffurter wîngarte giht / von treten noch der selben nôt: / maneg orses fuoz die slâge bôt" (The vineyards at Erfurt still show the effects of trampling from the foot of many a horse). Thanks to this offhand comparison between Wolfram's fictional knightly tournament and an actual conflict at Erfurt in 1203 between two rivals for the crown of the empire, Philipp von Schwaben and Otto IV, it is possible to determine that Wolfram's work was composed around 1205. In an earlier section of the work a reference is made to *Iwein,* which for stylistic reasons is presumed to be Hartmann's last work. Hence, all of Hartmann's works were likely written before the year 1205. It is impossible to say whether Hartmann lived beyond this year or whether he produced other works after *Iwein* which have been lost. Establishing the approximate year of his birth and the beginning of Hartmann's literary activity is much more difficult. *Erec,* which is presumed to be among Hartmann's first works, contains a reference to a place called Connelant, or Ikonium, with which diplomatic contacts were made by the emperor Friedrich I ("Barbarossa") by 1179 or 1180 in preparation for the third Crusade, from 1189 to 1192. The approximate date of Chrétien's first Arthurian

work, *Erec et Enide,* is 1165, but it is improbable that Hartmann would have been able to get a manuscript and produce his own work until many years later. For lack of a better clue, the connection to Ikonium suggests that Hartmann's first works were written around 1180. Assuming that he was twenty years old at the time, his date of birth would be around 1160. Consequently, Hartmann's literary activity must have occurred for the most part during the last two decades of the twelfth century. The chronology of his works during this period is tenuous; it is based on the criterion of literary style as well as on certain assumptions about Hartmann's philosophy or psychology that ultimately remain conjectual.

The language of Hartmann's works indicates an Alemannic origin, meaning that he probably came from a region that today encompasses parts of Baden-Württemberg and Bavaria in Germany, the Thurgau and Zürichgau in Switzerland, and the French Alsace. Hartmann's Alemannic origin is supported by a later medieval author, Heinrich von dem Türlîn, who designates this region when he says that Hartmann was "von der Swâbe lande" (from the land of Swabians). In *Der arme Heinrich* Hartmann refers to himself as a *dienstman* ; this designation means that he belonged to the unfree class of *ministeriales,* a social class consisting of functionaries, administrators, and servants who performed duties of various kinds at the larger courts. In the prologues of *Iwein* and *Der arme Heinrich,* Hartmann calls himself a *rîter* (knight) who can read and write, indicating that the combination of knighthood and literacy is not self-evident. During this age an education could only be obtained in a cloister or a cathedral school. Hence, sometime during his youth, perhaps before entering the service of his feudal lord(s) and literary patron(s), Hartmann may have received teaching in the liberal arts; if so, he would have known Latin. On the basis of a passage in *Die Klage* (circa 1180) that mentions a *Krûtzouber von Kärlingen* (magical root from France), some scholars have posited that Hartmann may have spent some time in France. Although a stay in France cannot be confirmed, Hartmann's intimate knowledge of works by Chrétien makes it fairly certain that he was familiar with the French language.

Two manuscripts of *Minnesang* containing illustrations of singers, Die große Heidelberger and Die Weingartner, depict Hartmann with a coat of arms consisting of white eagles' heads on a blue or black background. The same coat of arms is documented for the Wespersbühler family in Thurgau as of 1238. Unfortunately, this family reveals no connec-

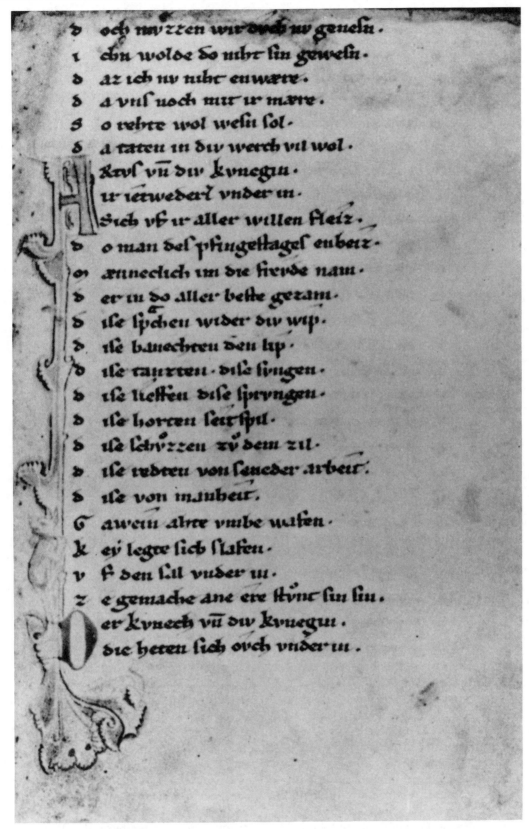

Lines 53–78 of Hartmann's Iwein *(Gießen, Universitätsbibliothek, MS. no. 97, Handschrift B)*

tion to the name Aue. An association has also been made to the coat of arms of the Zähringer, a powerful noble family in the Swabian region of Germany that can be connected to families named Aue. Another clue about Hartmann may be contained in *Der arme Heinrich,* whose protagonist is named Heinrich von Aue. Scholars have considered this similarity of names too striking to be merely coincidental and have theorized that this literary figure may have been one of Hartmann's ancestors. Heinrich, who at the work's beginning is a rich and powerful noble, marries the daughter of a peasant at the end of the work. In the Middle Ages marriage tended to be a matter of political alliance rather than personal preference. A good marriage could bolster the fortunes of a family for generations, while a bad one could result in a loss of economic and political power. Some scholars perceive the rough outlines of Hartmann's own family history in the events described in *Der arme Heinrich:* the Aues may have been free nobles who fell into feudal servitude (that is, into the *ministeriales*) as the result of a bad marriage. Such a conclusion involves, of course, the questionable assumptions that the Heinrich depicted in this work really existed, that he was related to Hartmann, and that his actions had a direct influence on Hartmann's existence, none of which can be proved.

Another assumption can be made on the preconditions of literary activity in general. Manuscripts of source works, such as the works of Chrétien, had to be obtained; the high cost of parchment and the financial support of scribes and authors had to be paid. The activity of an author such as Hartmann could only be supported by a lord and patron with connections at high levels of the nobility and a great deal of financial wherewithal. In the region in question there would appear to be only three families that would have been in a position to employ an author such as Hartmann: the Staufer, the Welfs, and the Zähringer. Links to any or all of these families are possible. Nevertheless, associations between the Zähringer and the patrons of Chrétien, the source of Hartmann's Arthurian works, provide good reason for viewing this family as Hartmann's patrons. The similarity of the coat of arms carried by Hartmann in the illustrations to that of the Zähringer gives further support to this link. The name Aue is found in association with that of the Zähringer in three places, any one of which might have been the locus of Hartmann's literary activity: Obernau, Owen/Teck, and Au bei Freiburg. The last place is especially interesting because there are records of a Heinricus de Owen or

Owon as of 1112, and it is possible that this family fell into the status of servitude characteristic of the *ministeriales*.

Almost everything that is known about Hartmann is based on literary works. Each of these works belongs to a specific literary tradition that shapes and limits what Hartmann says about himself. While it is certainly possible to define Hartmann in a literary rather than biographical way in terms of the contributions he makes to these literary traditions, it is difficult to relate the lives and personal experiences of medieval authors to their literary works in the same way one might relate Johann Wolfgang von Goethe to *Die Leiden des jungen Werthers* (The Sorrows of Young Werther, 1774) or Thomas Mann to *Buddenbrooks* (1901). Literature is not, in the Middle Ages, the vehicle of self-expression or catharsis for the author that it was to become later. Hence, in turning to the works of Hartmann one turns primarily to these literary traditions and Hartmann's versions of them. At the same time, one must remain open to the possibility that Hartmann may reveal something about himself despite the dictates of the literary traditions within which he worked.

Die Klage is considered Hartmann's first work. Like all of Hartmann's narrative poems, it is composed in rhymed couplets, except for the final part (from line 1645), when a crossing-rhyme pattern is employed. The source of the poem is unknown, but it shows similarities to the traditions of the French *complaintes d'amour* and *saluts.* The poem takes the form of an allegorical disputation between personifications of the *herz* (heart) and the *lîp* (body) of a certain unnamed *jungelinc* (youth), and it consists of four parts. In the first (lines 1–484) the body reproachfully addresses the heart for forcing it to seek the love of a lady who repudiated it. As a result the body has suffered unending torment and has lost its desire to continue living. In the second part (lines 485–972) the heart responds that the body shares responsibility for falling in love, since it was through the eyes of the body that the image of the beloved reached the heart. This notion of love as the result of an image that passes through the eyes to the heart is standard in medieval love literature and is found, for example, in André le Chapelain's treatise *De amore.* The heart also chastises the body for not pursuing the lady's love with greater diligence and provides a bit of advice: "swer ahte hât ûf minne / der darf wol schœner sinne" (whoever values love / must refine himself). This advice on the part of the heart allows this work to be placed in the tradition of courtly love because of its conception of love as an ennobling force. During the third section of the poem (lines 973–1644), which is a dialogue between the heart and the body, the advice of the heart to the body culminates in the *krûtzouber von Kärlingen,* which is a formula for achieving the love of God and of fellow man. The *krûtzouber* consists of *milte* (generosity), *zuht* (appropriate behavior), *diemut* (modesty), *triuwe* (loyalty), *staete* (constancy), *kiuscheit* (purity), and *gewislîchiu manheit* (dependable manhood) mixed in a heart without hatred. The elements of this recipe are qualities that describe the ideal courtly lover and are found everywhere in the literature of this period. The body promises to avail itself of the *krûtzouber* and is sent back to the beloved lady to renew the suit in the fourth and final section of the work (lines 1645–1914). By this time it is abundantly clear that the outcome of the suit is not as important as the manner in which it is pursued.

This disputation is a highly conventional literary form, and it would be an error to see in this debate between the body and the heart a reflection of the psychology of Hartmann. What is at stake is the value of love, which is portrayed not as a personal or subjective emotion, as a modern reader might expect, but as a principle that leads to the self-perfection of the lover not only in the eyes of his beloved but also in the eyes of God and his fellow man. The heart/body dialogue would seem to be a secularized version of soul/body dialogues encountered in many religious treatises. The position has been taken that this work reveals close ties to early Scholasticism, which would support the thesis that Hartmann attended a cathedral or cloister school in his youth.

Erec was probably completed within a few years of *Die Klage.* Hartmann names Chrétien as his source; but he takes many liberties with his stated source, leaving open the possibility that he may have consulted other versions of this tale, such as the ones contained in the Welsh *Gereint* and *Enid* and the Norse *Erexsaga.* In all likelihood Hartmann's differences from Chrétien have more to do with his own literary conception than with other versions of the Erec tale. With his *Erec,* Hartmann introduces into German literature the "classical" bipartite structure of Chrétien's Arthurian works.

The beginning of Hartmann's *Erec* is missing, but in all liklihood it would not have been much different from that of Chrétien. Hartmann would have introduced himself in the prologue and begun his tale by describing the court of King Arthur. The court resolves at the beginning of the work to embark on a hunt for a white stag. The hunter who brings down the stag will enjoy the honor of be-

stowing a kiss upon the most beautiful lady at court. For reasons that are not explained, the young knight Erec, the son of King Lac, is not with the other knights on the hunt but rather accompanies the queen and a lady attendant. It is at this point that the preserved verses of Hartmann's work take up the tale. The three come across an unknown knight, his lady, and a dwarf. The queen's attendant, sent to discover who the strangers are, receives a whipping at the hands of the dwarf, and Erec receives the same rough treatment when he attempts to find out their identity. Because he is without armor and weapons Erec is unable to react and must content himself with following the strangers in the hope that he will have an opportunity to overcome this insult to his honor.

The strangers lead Erec to a castle called Tulmein. The castle and surrounding town are full of people, and Erec, who has no money with him, is forced to accept the hospitality of a destitute count named Koralus, who possesses little more than his humble abode, a suit of armor, and a pretty young daughter named Enite. From Koralus, Erec discovers the identity of the unknown knight he has followed as well as the reason for the multitude of people at Tulmein: there is to be a beauty contest on the following day. The lady of the unknown knight has won the contest for the last two years, and if she wins again this year, she will receive a sparrow hawk to symbolize her ultimate victory and the conclusion of the contest. This lady's success has been based not so much on her beauty as on the strength of her knight, Iders, who has intimidated the competition. The old count provides Erec with armor and weapons, in exchange for which Erec promises to marry the beautiful Enite. On the appointed day, when Ider's lady moves to take possession of the falcon, Erec protests her claim and insists that Enite is the more beautiful. The sought-after battle between Iders and Erec ensues, and the victory of the latter overcomes the insult to Erec's honor. Iders's dwarf is given a sound beating, and Iders is sent back to the court of Arthur to announce what has transpired. The importance of Arthur's court as the source of courtly values such as honor is underscored by the practice, visible here and in other Arthurian works of this period, of sending defeated knightly opponents back to that court. There they spread the fame of the knights who have defeated them, ask for forgiveness, and are generally taken into the fold of the king's court. In the meantime, it was Arthur who succeeded in bringing down the white stag. Because of concern about Erec, he has not yet bestowed the distinguishing kiss. When the victorious Erec returns to court with Enite, the two narrative strands are tied neatly together: Enite receives the kiss due the most beautiful lady. A knightly tournament, in which Erec further distinguishes himself, follows Erec and Enite's wedding. The first segment of the work nears its end when Erec returns to his homeland with his bride.

Erec's knightly fame and courtly honor, at their apogee on his return to the family castle, are short-lived. Erec is so enamored of his wife that he spends the entire day in bed with her and neglects the activities that make him a lord to be respected and a knight to be honored. Eros disrupts the socially responsible attitude that previously characterized Erec's actions:

> Êrec wente sînen lîp
> grôzes gemaches durch sîn wîp.
> die minnete er sô sêre
> daz er aller êre
> durch si einen verphlac,
> unz daz er sich sô gar verlac
> daz niemen dehein ahte ûf in gehaben mahte. (2966–2973)

> (Erec turned to a life of ease
> because of his wife,
> whom he loved with such passion
> that, to be with her,
> he gave up all striving for honor
> and became indolent
> to the point where no one could respect him.)

The second segment of the work is instigated by the shame Erec's lying around in bed with his wife brings upon him. It is not the distracted Erec but Enite who discovers the disrepute into which her husband has fallen. While in bed one sunny day she sighs and utters words of regret at a moment when she assumes Erec to be asleep. Erec overhears his wife and, after forcing her to reveal the source of her unhappiness and the cause of his shame, abruptly resolves to depart with Enite from the castle and seek adventures. At the outset of their mutual adventure, Erec commands Enite to ride ahead of him. By so doing, Enite will be in a position to perceive dangers before Erec. But she is also commanded by her husband to hold her tongue, on pain of death, no matter what she may see.

The second segment is divided into two parts that mirror each other structurally. In the first part Erec and Enite confront a group of robber knights, a count who attempts to take Enite away from Erec, and a knightly opponent named Guivreiz le petiz. In the second part Erec encounters two rampaging giants, a count named Oringles who wishes to wed Enite against her will, and Guivreiz le petiz for a

second time. The two parts of the second segment are divided by a short stay at the court of Arthur, to which Erec is unwittingly led by his knightly friend Gawein. The latter two adventures are the most significant. At Oringles's castle Enite suffers physical abuse at the hands of the count because she will not stop grieving for her husband. Erec, whom all believe to be dead after his battle with the giants, hears the cries of his wife, arises from his deathlike stupor, and falls with sword in hand upon the surprised Oringles and his men, killing the importunate count and escaping with Enite into the forest. This episode underscores Enite's loyalty to Erec in an exemplary way, and it is also suggested that Erec's former identity has been shed and that a new and wiser Erec has arisen to replace the old. Above all, the relationship between Erec and Enite seems to have gained a depth that it did not possess before, and it is not coincidental that Erec chooses this moment to reconcile with his wife.

The second battle with the dwarf-king Guivreiz seems by its outcome to suggest that Erec's single-minded pursuit of adventures and knightly activity has been as unbalanced as the erotic activity that resulted in his *verligen*. The two knights meet in the forest; neither recognizes the other. Erec insists on battle, although he is still weak from his wounds and has nothing to gain from the fight. After losing the contest and discovering the identity of his opponent, who swore allegiance and friendship to him after their first battle, Erec seems to question the value of knighthood pursued for its own sake when he says of himself: "swelh man tœrlîche tuot, / wirts im gelônet, daz ist guot" (If a man behaves foolishly, it is fitting that he receive a fool's reward). Nevertheless, despite this apparent insight, Erec does not put an end here to his knightly pursuit of honor.

The adventures of the second segment, however interesting and colorful in themselves, have two basic functions. One of these is to demonstrate the *triuwe* of Enite to her husband. Despite her fear of punishment, she breaks Erec's command to silence and warns her husband every time she perceives imminent danger to him. She also spurns the advances of the two counts, who promise to deliver her from her tribulations. Enite's loyalty to her husband, despite his harsh treatment of her, transcends even life itself in one memorable instance. After Erec has apparently died in his battle with the giants, Enite chastises God for taking a husband away from his wife when the two, according to God's own law, are of one flesh. Enite sets about to commit suicide to rejoin her husband, but God mercifully sends the count Oringles to stop her before she can carry out her intention. The only puzzling thing about the demonstration of Enite's loyalty, which is clearly a concern of the work, is why such a demonstration should be necessary. It is difficult to locate any grave lapse on her part that would justify such a grueling test. It is probable that the remnants of a literary tradition dealing with the test of a wife who is presumed to be unfaithful may have found their way into Hartmann's work.

More significant than the proven loyalty of Enite is the test that Erec has passed. Hartmann's increased emphasis on Erec's rehabilitation is the most important difference between this work and that of Chrétien. Most scholars believe that the honor and fame so quickly achieved by Erec in the first segment of the work were hollow and incomplete. The socially destructive eruption of erotic *minne* that ensued was not an indictment of love per se but served to demonstrate that his social standing had not yet been placed on a solid foundation. There is a broad critical consensus that the second segment of adventures, although involving an extreme devotion to knightly activity that is itself faulty, provides him with a depth he did not possess before – a depth that carries over into his social standing and his marriage. This depth is exemplified in the final adventure of the work, "Joie de la curt" (Joy of the Court), which receives special emphasis because it occurs after the end of the second structural segment. In it Erec meets the formidable knight Mabonagrin, who has sworn to his wife to live in total isolation with her until he has suffered defeat at the hands of another knight. The garden in which he lives with his beloved is surrounded with stakes on which are impaled the heads of his defeated opponents. The isolation of Mabonagrin and his wife from courtly society seems to allude to the earlier erotic lapse of Erec and Enite, which also isolated them from the court. Erec's victory over Mabonagrin achieves what has been present at this castle in name only: the joy of the court. Mabonagrin is able to return to court society and place his formidable knightly talents at its disposal. It would appear that the lesson learned by Erec, which is transferred to Mabonagrin in somewhat abbreviated fashion, has something to do with recognizing one's responsibilities to society. " 'Bî den liuten ist sô guot' " (It is so good to be with other people), says Erec to Mabonagrin after their battle, apparently divulging an insight that has caused him and his wife a good deal of pain during the course of their joint adventure.

Concurrently with the writing of these early narrative works it is likely that Hartmann was also composing songs. Sixty strophes composed for eighteen separate melodies have been preserved in the three major manuscripts of *Minnesang*. Important in this context are several songs that have been understood as a demonstration of a psychological or philosophical transformation on the part of the poet, if not of biographical events. This presumed transformation is based, in turn, on a hypothetical chronology of Hartmann's songs. Peter Wapnewski, for example, speaks of a "seelische Entwicklung" (spiritual development) and distinguishes four chronological phases in Hartmann's lyrical poetry. In the first phase Hartmann more or less directly emulates the conventions of the Provençal and German lyrical traditions that preceded him. This attitude shows the same uncritical acceptance of the conventions of courtly love that are visible in *Die Klage*. The second phase is characterized by a loss of the feeling of joy stemming from love's ennobling power that elsewhere in the *minne* tradition accompanies the pain of unrewarded service. In this phase falls a song that shatters for a brief and rare moment the conventionality of the lyrical language of *Minnesang*. In this song Hartmann laments the death of his overlord: "mich hât beswæret mînes herren tôt" (the death of my liege has saddened me). This line almost certainly refers to a real event in the life of Hartmann and allows a rare glimpse of individual sentiment in the otherwise opaque and conventional language of the courtly love lyric. It is possible that such a moving event in Hartmann's life may have gradually led him to regard *Minnesang* and the values conveyed in it as vain and frivolous. The third phase of Hartmann's lyrical development involves what Wapnewski calls a rejection of *minne* based on practical reason. This rejection of a love that holds no promise whatsoever of fulfillment, which anticipates the songs of *niedere minne* (low love) by Walther von der Vogelweide, is exemplified by the so-called *Unmutslied* (song of discontent), in which the singer Hartmann arrives at a highly unusual conclusion after being rejected by a highborn lady: "ich mac baz vertrîben / die zît mit armen wîben" (I can spend my time better with low-born women). *Unmut* is certainly not exceptional in the German love lyrics of this time, but Hartmann is the first to suggest that the challenges posed by *minne* in its classical or "high" form (characterized by unrequited love) are simply not worth the trouble and that ladies of a lower social status offer the possibility of a satisfying love that is mutual rather than hopelessly one-sided. In Hartmann's Crusade songs Wapnewski perceives a final rejection of *minne* and of the worldly values propagated by the love and service of highborn ladies in favor of the love of God. Wapnewski views the Crusade songs as the last in Hartmann's lyrical oeuvre, positing that there is no way back to the worldly lyric once this spiritualized form of *minne* has been adopted. At this point Hartmann may have participated in a Crusade. Two of them come into question, the Third Crusade (1189 to 1192) and the Fourth Crusade (1197 to 1198). The determination hinges on a passage that seems to indicate that the great Muslim leader Saladin is still alive (218, 19ff.). The meaning of this passage is disputed, however, and either Crusade appears to be possible. Despite the plausibility of many of the points made by Wapnewski with regard to this proposed spiritual development on the part of Hartmann, it is important to recognize that this development posits a chronology of the songs that cannot be proved.

The spiritual development posited for Hartmann is based not only on his lyrics but also on *Gregorius,* which is presumed to be his next narrative work. The oldest preserved version of the Gregorius story is the French *Vie du Pape Gregoire.* Whether one of the six preserved versions of this work served as Hartmann's source or whether he based his work on a lost manuscript is a matter of debate. The Gregorius story, which reveals broad similarities to the story of Oedipus, is one of many tales in the Middle Ages that revolve around the theme of incest. It is not known upon whom the story is based: the protagonist cannot be identified with any of the historical popes named Gregorius.

It is somewhat convenient to think that *Gregorius* was written at about the same time Hartmann wrote his Crusade songs. In the same way that the singer's higher love of God is construed by some as a rejection of the courtly love of ladies that characterized his earlier lyrical work, the religious theme of *Gregorius* is seen as a turn away from the worldly themes of Hartmann's early narrative works. Such a turn is suggested in a direct way in the prologue of the work:

> Mîn herze hât betwungen
> dicke mîne zungen
> daz si des vil gesprochen hât
> daz nâch der werlde lône stât:
> daz rieten im diu tumben jâr. (1–5)

> (My heart has often
> induced my tongue

> to speak of many matters
> that attract the rewards of this world:
> in this it was persuaded by youthful inexperience.)

These lines have been taken both as an overt reference to Hartmann's earlier works – that is, as a sort of biographical statement – and as a literary trope that belongs to all works with a religious theme. However its relationship to Hartmann's other works is viewed, there is little doubt that this work presents a clear departure from the themes present in the Arthurian works and in *Die Klage.* The story is supposed to exemplify the power of God's grace in an exceptional case of human sinfulness. A brother and sister share a relationship of special fondness after the death of their parents, the rulers of the land of Aquitaine. Due to the power of *minne* (here portrayed most negatively), the devil's evil designs, and his own inexperience, the brother begins to desire his sister sexually; their relationship culminates in incest. To atone for this deed, the brother eventually embarks on a Crusade and dies of lovesickness for his sister along the way. The sister, now princess of Aquitaine, gives birth secretly to a son, whom she places in a boat and leaves at the mercy of God and the waves. Into the boat she places twenty marks of gold and an ivory tablet on which the baby's noble status and sinful origin are written. She also imparts a message to her son: he should devote his life to atonement for the sins of his mother and father. Because she has devoted her life to God, the princess rejects the suit of a powerful neighbor who seeks her hand in marriage. The neighbor responds by attacking Aquitaine and taking nearly all her lands and castles. Still the princess rejects marriage, and she holds out in her capital city in the only castle that has not been taken by the invader.

The baby is found after three days by fishermen of an island cloister. The abbot gives the child his own name, Gregorius, and places him in the care of a fisher family. After he has grown to manhood, Gregorius's foster mother reveals to him in a moment of anger that he is a foundling, and from the abbot he discovers the full truth about himself. Although shattered by the story of his sinful origin, Gregorius is encouraged by the news of his noble heritage to adopt a profession to which he has long felt a deep inner affinity. Against the advice of the abbot, who admonishes him to follow the wish of his mother that he spend his life atoning for his parents' sins, Gregorius becomes a knight and sets out into the world, taking with him the ivory tablet to remind him of his sinful origin. In a series of events that closely resemble episodes in Hartmann's Arthurian works, Gregorius helps to free a city ruled by a lady from the siege of an undesirable suitor. As a reward Gregorius receives the hand of the lady. A crucial difference makes the distance of this work from the Arthurian ones quite clear: the lady is the princess of Aquitaine; unbeknownst to Gregorius, the lady he has won is his own mother. The adoption of the profession of knighthood has preceded, if not caused, a relapse into the sinfulness to which Gregorius owes his existence. The tablet on which Gregorius's story is written is eventually discovered by the mother, and thus the two become aware of this recurrence of incest. They resolve to devote their lives to atonement. Gregorius's atonement takes a most unconventional and extreme form: he has a fisherman chain him to a rock in the sea, where he miraculously lives for seventeen years on nothing but water. After this long atonement he is sought by two legates from Rome, who have been told by God in a vision that Gregorius is to succeed the recently deceased pope. A miracle aids them in their attempt to find Gregorius and provides another proof of his beatitude: while the legates are dining with the fisherman who chained Gregorius to the rock, the key to the chains, which the fisherman had thrown into the waves some seventeen years earlier, is found in the stomach of a fish. A final miracle occurs three days before Gregorius enters Rome to take up the holy scepter, when all the bells of the city begin to chime (Thomas Mann's *Der Erwählte* [translated as *The Holy Sinner,* 1951], which is based on this work, begins with the miraculous chiming of Rome's bells). The new pope is visited by a woman who carries such a horrible sin that only the pontiff himself could grant her absolution. Mother and son recognize each other a final time, not in sinfulness but in the grace of God.

From the lowest depths of sinfulness, Gregorius is raised by God's grace to the position of God's highest earthly servant. Nobody disputes that the power of grace is a central theme, but there is a good deal of scholarly debate concerning the kind of religiosity that manifests itself in this work. In the prologue Hartmann makes use of concepts (for example, *buoze* [atonement], *bîhte* [confession], *zwîvel* [doubt]) that have their place in official church doctrine. The story itself, however, seems to be characterized by a religiosity that more closely corresponds to the values and customs of the lay nobility than to the practices of the church. The most striking example of this religiosity is the "sinfulness" of Gregorius: according to church doctrine, a necessary prerequisite of sin is the *voluntas* (will) of the

sinner; since Gregorius never knowingly committed incest, his sinfulness would appear to be questionable from a theological standpoint. Despite the vocabulary used by Hartmann in the prologue, it would seem that the stigma attached to incest is more social than religious in nature. According to medieval law, the son of an incestuous relationship was a social nonperson, incapable of owning or inheriting property. Related to this point, and important for assessing Hartmann's presumed religious development, is the status of worldly values in general. Does the work present a categorical condemnation of worldly values such as *minne* and *êre* (honor)? Or does it invoke a realm of spiritual experience which only qualifies the validity of worldly values? Although even less is known about Hartmann's audience than about the author, it is unlikely that this work was written for monks or priests. If it was written for lay nobility, as is generally assumed, then it seems improbable that he wished categorically to reject worldly values, even if his primary goal was to get his listeners to think about the welfare of their souls.

A spiritual concern is also visible in what is presumed to be Hartmann's penultimate work, *Der arme Heinrich*. It is not known if the author had a particular source for this work (its relationship to two Latin exempla from the fourteenth and fifteenth centuries – *Heinricus pauper* and *Albertus pauper* – is unclear), but it is clear that he availed himself of two literary traditions that involve the medieval belief that leprosy can be cured by the blood of a human sacrifice. One tradition, the so-called Sylvester legend, is linked to the Roman emperor Constantine, who, after contracting leprosy, forgoes the sacrifice of young boys to achieve a cure. Subsequently he is healed in the sacrament of baptism administered by Pope Sylvester. The other tradition focuses on the individual who has to make the sacrifice. Konrad von Würzburg's *Engelhard* (circa 1260?), for example, presents a situation in which the protagonist must sacrifice his children to achieve the cure of a friend. While it is possible that Hartmann's source had already combined these two traditions, there is no good reason to assume that the combination was not Hartmann's own achievement. Although the preservation of *Der arme Heinrich* does not indicate that it was popular in the Middle Ages, it is perhaps the best known of Hartmann's works among modern readers. One of the more noteworthy of these was Goethe, who found it "ein an und für sich betrachtet höchst schätzenswerthes Gedicht" (all things considered a most estimable poem), which nevertheless caused him "physisch-ästhetischen Schmerz" (physical-aesthetic pain).

In contrast to *Gregorius,* the short prologue of this work does not prepare its audience for the religious theme that is to come. After alluding to his literacy and naming himself, Hartmann sets about to relate "ein rede die er geschriben vant" (a written story that he has found). The only indication that the work is of a religious nature is Hartmann's request that his audience reward him by praying for his soul. The story proper begins with an introduction of Heinrich von Aue, who is in every respect exemplary of the values of the lay nobility. He is by birth equal to princes and possesses great wealth. These qualities that come automatically with high birth are complemented by more-individual accomplishments. Heinrich possesses *êre, tugent* (chastity), *stæte, zuht,* and *milte.* Described in the most glowing terms, Heinrich's ideal existence comes to an abrupt end that shows that it is seemingly rotten to the core: he is stricken by leprosy, a disease that attacks in a most visible way the things this world holds dearest. In the Middle Ages lepers were considered unclean in both a physical and a spiritual sense. It was also thought that the disease was a form of divine punishment that not only attacked the flesh of lepers but also their souls; this belief resulted in the exclusion of lepers from society.

Heinrich, who is not immediately willing to accept the new "identity" that leprosy involves, responds with denial and attempts in consultations with several doctors to find a cure for his ailment. Not until he discovers that he can only be cured by the sacrifice of a young maiden who is willing to give her life freely for him does he accept the apparent impossibility of a cure and the social ramifications of his illness. He empties his treasury in alms to the poor and to the church, leaves behind his life among noble peers, and moves in with a free peasant family that lives in his territory. His friendship with the eight-year-old daughter of the peasant couple deepens to the point of containing an erotic element. Heinrich gives her little gifts that one would ordinarily associate with *Minne* at court: a ring, a sash, a mirror. He calls her, curiously, his *gemahel* (bride). After three years the girl learns from Heinrich what is necessary to achieve his cure, and she resolves to make the ultimate sacrifice for him. She reveals her resolution to her parents and, against their objections, defends it with great rhetorical skill. The parents, believing that God is speaking through her, finally acquiesce to her wish. Heinrich departs with the girl to Salerno, where her sacrifice is to be performed. The doctor who is to perform the procedure first verifies that the girl is acting of her own free will. In an attempt to dissuade her, he explains that the procedure involves cutting the still-beating heart out of her body. Finding her resolute, the doctor takes her into a room, where she is bound naked to a large table. Struck by the great beauty of her body, the doctor takes pity on the girl and begins to sharpen the knife so that the ordeal will at least be over quickly. Outside the door Heinrich, hearing the sound of the blade against the stone, suddenly realizes that he will never see the girl again. He finds a hole in the wall and looks into the other room. The beauty of the girl's body, perhaps increased by her proximity to death and by the selflessness of her sacrifice, causes a transformation within Heinrich, which is described by Hartmann as "eine niuwe güete" (a new sense of charity). At this moment Heinrich decides to accept the illness as God's will and to reject the sacrifice of the girl.

The girl's ranting and raving fail to reverse Heinrich's decision not to allow the sacrifice. The position has been taken that the girl's fanatical desire to die and her belief that she is predestined for a life of glory in heaven indicate a degree of self-aggrandizement that is equivalent to that revealed by Heinrich's former desire to cling to his earthly existence. Although the story is clearly oriented toward Heinrich, the girl's importance as a protagonist is underscored by the fact that she, too, has a lesson to learn. This lesson is not stated directly but seems to follow from the program of the work: the goal is neither to become wrapped up in this world nor to escape from it but to find the proper manner of living in it. The two begin their return home, and while they are en route, God's mercy manifests itself: he has tested Heinrich and the girl as he once tested Job and has found them worthy of his grace. Heinrich is cured of his disease and rejuvenated. The girl, who was in a condition near death after being deprived of her heavenly crown, is also restored to health. As miraculous as the cure itself is Heinrich's immediate resumption of his former life, now with even more wealth and honor than before. There is, however, one crucial difference in Heinrich's attitude – one that sheds light on all the events of this work:

> er wart rîcher vil dan ê
> des guotes und der êren.
> daz begunde er allez kêren
> stæteclîchen hin ze gote
> und warte sînem gebote
> baz dan er ê tæte.
> des ist sîn êre stæte. (1430–1436)

Thirteenth-century frescoes on the walls of Castle Rodenegg, in the southern Tirol, depicting scenes from Iwein: *the wild man; the duel between Iwein and Ascalon; Iwein proposing marriage to Ascalon's widow, Laudine*

(He became much wealthier than before
in possessions and in prestige.
All this he proceeded to devote
faithfully to God
and observed his command
better than he did before.
Thus his honor is now secure.)

Like the empty glory of Erec before his fall into erotic excess, Heinrich's life before leprosy was only externally correct. It lacked the substance that comes only from a proper relationship to the Source of All Things.

Restored to power, Heinrich rewards the peasant family by giving them the piece of land on which they live. Finally, at the urging of his advisers to marry, he takes the peasant girl as his bride. One need not fall back on the thesis that Heinrich may have been a real ancestor of Hartmann, and that this unfavorable marriage may have been a part of the author's own family history, to understand the marriage in its literary context. The utopian, fairy-tale ending of this work, in which everything is contingent on the proper personal attitude, occurs independently of realistic concerns involving social class.

There is some difference of opinion with regard to the status of worldly/courtly values in this work. Wapnewski is of the opinion that Hartmann's critique of these values in this work is "unerbitt-licher" (more relentless) than in *Gregorius:* "anders als im Erec, im Iwein und im Gregorius versagt hier nicht einer in der höfischen Welt, sondern in ihm versagt die höfische Welt!" (as opposed to *Erec, Iwein,* and *Gregorius,* this work is not about a hero who fails in the courtly world but about the courtly world failing in the hero!). Nevertheless, in light of the generally positive depiction of worldly values, one tends to agree with Christoph Cormeau and Wilhelm Störmer, who view the spirituality postulated by Hartmann not as antithetical but rather as a necessary complement to worldly values.

Probably around 1200 Hartmann composed *Iwein,* a work that shows the author at the height of his artistic ability. Indeed, it is this work's merits that have led many scholars to view it as Hartmann's final and most significant achievement. Nowhere is his simple elegance of style and aesthetic conception more evident than in *Iwein.* Its medieval popularity is demonstrated by the many manuscripts of the work and by the many representations of episodes from this work in tapestries and frescoes. It seems more than appropriate to regard *Iwein* as what Helmut de Boor and Richard Newald call "das klassische Werk der hochhöfischen, stau-

fischen Zeit" *(the* classical work of the courtly period of the Hohenstauffen dynasty). With *Iwein* Hartmann returns to the literary world of King Arthur and the knights of the Round Table and to the source of his first Arthurian work, Chrétien, whom he follows much more closely than in *Erec.* At the beginning of the Iwein tradition stands a historical Owen, son of King Uriens, who lived in the sixth century; but it is unlikely that Iwein shares much with this historical figure beyond his name. As is the case with *Erec,* the Iwein story is present in many versions during this period. Besides the works of Chrétien and Hartmann, there is the story of Owen and Lunet in the Welsh "Mabinogion," a Norse *Ivens Saga,* and a Middle English poem, *Ywain and Gawein.* The latter two works, along with that of Hartmann, are all dependent on the version of Chrétien.

Iwein shares with *Erec* the bipartite structure that is definitive of the classical Arthurian works following in the tradition of Chrétien. In the first segment Iwein achieves honor and fame as he wins a wife and land. An ensuing crisis demonstrates that this initial glory is insubstantial and initiates the second segment of adventures, in which a solid foundation for Iwein's achievements is established. In contrast to Erec, however, whose insufficiency was manifested by a socially irresponsible sexual excess, it is difficult to define where Iwein's fault lies. Despite the acclaim that *Iwein* has enjoyed, it has proved to be an extremely difficult work to interpret. A reason for this difficulty may be that the Iwein story incorporates many magical elements from Celtic mythology. Such elements are inherent to all of the stories within the *matière de Bretagne* (matter of Britain; that is, Arthurian legends), but the Iwein tradition seems to be especially replete with them. The land of the fountain, for example, is similar to an enchanted, fairy-tale landscape; the queen of the land, Laudine, may originally be related to a race of water nymphs; the drawbridge across which Iwein pursues his opponent shows similarities to a mythical bridge into the realm of the dead; and the year given by Laudine to Iwein for knightly adventures may correspond to conditions issued by fairies to people returning to a former life. These and other mythical elements, which are discussed by Wapnewski, operate according to rules that are not always in accord with the values and priorities of Arthurian knighthood, which are more social and ethical in nature. The killing of the watchman of the fountain, for example, may be a necessary step in a fairy tale, but it involves moral issues in the world of Arthur.

The tale begins at the court of Arthur, during a festival in celebration of Whitsuntide. Knights and ladies are amusing themselves in a typically ideal Arthurian scenario. The harmony is almost predictably deceptive. While the king is napping, the queen comes upon a group of knights that includes Iwein, his cousin Kalogreant, and Sir Kay, the marshal of the court. The last is a stock character in the Arthurian tradition, whose abrasiveness and disgraceful manners contribute to the motivations of the heroes in their adventures. After some verbal sparring mainly involving the queen and Kay, Kalogreant begins to tell of an adventure that he undertook ten years earlier.

His adventure began at the castle of a most courtly host, where he was generously wined and dined. On the following day Kalogreant left these comfortable surroundings and came upon a clearing where a wild man, who looked more like an animal than a human, held scores of wild beasts at his beck and call. The wild man turned out to be congenial, despite his appearance, but he did not know what knightly *aventiure* (adventure) was, so Kalogreant defined it for him: two armed men fight, and the winner becomes more honorable than he was before. Some scholars have considered this crude definition to be an implicit criticism by Hartmann of the motivations that guide Kalogreant here and that will guide Iwein later. It is also possible that the exchange concerning the meaning of adventure serves to illustrate that Kalogreant's path has taken him into a magical realm where the rules and customs are different from those to which the Arthurian knight is accustomed.

Despite his ignorance about the meaning of adventure, the wild man was able to direct Kalogreant to the land of the fountain and to instruct him how to achieve his goal of combat. Kalogreant followed these instructions on his arrival at the fountain by pouring water onto a stone, thus triggering a magical sequence of events. A terrible storm was unleashed, which Kalogreant barely survived. Following the storm, the original harmony and beauty of the place was immediately restored. The watchman of the land, Ascalon, then appeared, accused Kalogreant of causing the storm, and challenged him to combat. Kalogreant was summarily unhorsed by his opponent, who, according to the rules of knightly combat, led away his steed. Horseless and with a bruised ego, Kalogreant made his way back to the court of Arthur and has remained quiet about his disgrace until this moment.

The story undermines the harmony of the festive situation. Iwein immediately declares his intention to avenge the disgrace of his cousin, an intention that draws the derision of Kay. When Arthur discovers the shame inflicted upon a member of his court, he resolves to travel two weeks later to the fountain with his entire retinue. Because Iwein fears that the renowned Gawein will be given first permission to undertake the adventure, he secretly departs from the court and follows the same path taken by Kalogreant. This time, after receiving a stunning blow from Iwein, Ascalon flees. Concerned that he will have no proof that he has won the contest, Iwein pursues his opponent over the drawbridge of the castle. As he leans forward to deal a mortal blow to his fleeing opponent, a trapdoor falls down behind him, splitting his horse in two but leaving Iwein unscathed. Another door falls in front of Iwein and behind the dying Ascalon, leaving the victor confined in the castle of his enemies.

Iwein gains the assistance of a servant named Lunete, who protects him from the castle's angry inhabitants by giving him a ring that makes him invisible. She eventually achieves a reconciliation between Iwein and the lady of the castle, Laudine, with whom Iwein has fallen in love at first sight. Concerned about the defense of her land and honor and aware of the planned invasion by Arthur, Laudine agrees, after some resistance, to marry the killer of her husband. Medieval and modern sensibilities have been disturbed by this marriage of mutual convenience, but Hartmann himself does not criticize it. It seems more likely that this marriage is determined by fairy-tale elements in the Iwein tradition than that a criticism of Laudine or Iwein is intended. As lord of the land Iwein responds to the invading Arthur. Narrative logic dictates that none other than Kay is granted permission to try the adventure by pouring water on the stone. Iwein duly avenges himself on Kay, reveals his identity, and basks in the fame and honor his adventure has won for him in the eyes of Arthur's court.

The first segment of Iwein's adventures ends with an episode which structurally parallels the episode in which Erec's erotic excess occurred. On the advice of his friend Gawein, the paragon of Arthurian knighthood, who warns about the dangers of inactivity and even brings up the example of Erec, Iwein resolves to depart from his newly won wife and land to seek more adventures. From Laudine he receives permission to be absent for one year. She states that she will wait no longer for him, however, since her honor and the defense of their land are at stake. As a token of these words she gives him a ring. Caught up in knightly activity in the company of Gawein, Iwein forgets about his promise to return until several months after the deadline. While at the court of Arthur, enjoying the increased honor his adventures have won for him, Iwein suddenly realizes that he has not returned to his wife on time. The resulting regret makes him dumb to the world. Iwein's fall from the high position he has reached begins with the arrival of Lunete, who takes back his lady's ring and formally rejects Iwein on the basis of his lack of *triuwe*. The sudden, apparently irrevocable loss of wife, land, and honor are too much for Iwein: he becomes insane, strips off his clothing, runs into the forest, and lives as a wild beast.

The cause of Iwein's fall is a matter of debate. Some scholars say that the killing of Ascalon violated the spirit of knighthood, which is supposed to be selfless service on behalf of others and not merely a vehicle for obtaining honor for oneself. This interpretation is supported by the words "âne zuht" (unscrupulously), which Hartmann uses to describe Iwein's relentless pursuit of the fleeing Ascalon. The argument has also been made, however, that Iwein's motivations during this battle correspond in every way to accepted practices of knighthood. Iwein's failure to return to his wife during the allotted year has also been viewed as the main reason for his fall; but although it would be an error to expect psychological realism in this work, the overstepping of a deadline would seem to be a purely formal offense that could hardly hurl the protagonist into madness. The deadline has even been viewed as an egotistical whim on the part of Laudine.

The second segment of Iwein's adventures provides evidence for both his pursuit of Ascalon and his neglect of Laudine's deadline as the reason for his fall. After he has been cured by the magic salve of the Lady of Narison, Iwein undertakes six adventures: the liberation of the Lady of Narison from the count Aliers, of a lion from a dragon, of some relatives of Gawein from a vicious giant named Harpin, of Lunete from death by fire at the hands of two angry marshals, of three hundred ladies from demeaning labor imposed by two other giants, and of a young lady from the tyranny of an elder sister who attempts to deprive her of her inheritance. The adventures involving Lunete and the younger sister were preceded by promises on the part of Iwein to appear at an appointed hour, and he did so despite conflicting engagements. The logic and order of these adventures are determined both by the principle of knightly service on behalf of others and by the necessity of fulfilling promises. Underlying both these priorities is the principle of *triuwe*, for which the lion that becomes Iwein's companion and helper is a symbol. Whether Iwein's original lack of *triuwe* was exemplified by the knightly pursuit of fame for himself that resulted in the death of Ascalon, by his overstepping of Laudine's deadline, or by both of these actions, the general emphasis of the second segment indicates that it is Iwein's *triuwe* that had to be put to the test. It is noteworthy – and indicative of the elusiveness of a satisfactory interpretation of this work that Iwein achieves a final reconciliation with his wife by leading her to believe that her land is being invaded again. Closure is achieved not by *triuwe*, but by force.

If there is a single principle underlying all of Hartmann's works, despite their diversity, it is the necessity of being pleasing both to God and to one's fellow man. This principle, which is a defining characteristic of court literature, is formulated at the end of Wolfram's *Parzival*:

swes lebn sich sô verendet,
daz got niht wirt gepfendet
der sêle durch des lîbes schulde,
und der doch der werlde hulde
behalten kan mit werdekeit,
daz ist ein nütziu arbeit (827, 19–24).

(A life that ends in such a way
that God is not deprived
of the soul through the guilt of the body,
and that can still obtain the praise of the world
with dignity,
that is a worthy task.)

Besides the elegant clarity of his style, Hartmann's individual mark on German courtly literature may well be the social concern of his works. Even those works addressing religious questions deal with one's obligations to others, with conflicts that can result from such obligations, and with false and legitimate solutions to these conflicts. Although clothed in the garb of medieval knights and popes, the social orientation of Hartmann's works is frequently general enough to address the experience of modern readers.

Bibliographies:

Ingrid Klemt, *Hartmann von Aue: Eine Zusammenstellung der über ihn und sein werk von 1927–1965 erschienenen Literatur* (Cologne: Greven, 1968);

Elfriede Neubuhr, *Bibliographie zu Hartmann von Aue* (Berlin: Schmidt, 1977).

Biographies:

Ludwig Schmidt, *Des Minnesängers Hartmann von Aue. Stand, Heimat und Geschlecht: Eine kritisch-historische Untersuchung* (Tübingen: Fues, 1874);

Hendricus Spaarnay, *Hartmann von Aue: Studien zu einer Biographie,* 2 volumes (Halle: Niemeyer, 1933, 1938).

References:

Hans Blosen, "Noch einmal: Zu Enites Schuld in Hartmanns Erec," *Orbis Litterarum,* 31, no. 2 (1976): 81–109;

Helmut de Boor and Richard Newald, *Geschichte der deutschen Literatur,* volume 2, *Die höfische Literatur: Vorbereitung, Blüte, Ausklang (1170–1250),* fifth edition (Munich: Beck, 1953);

M. A. Bossy, "Medieval Debates of Body and Soul," *Comparative Literature,* 28 (Spring 1976): 144–163;

Saul Nathaniel Brody, *The Disease of the Soul: Leprosy in Medieval Literature* (Ithaca, N.Y.: Cornell University Press, 1974);

Susan Clark, *Hartmann von Aue: Landscapes of Mind* (Houston: Rice University Press, 1989);

Christoph Cormeau, "Hartmann von Aue," in *Die deutsche Literatur des Mittelalters: Verfasserlexikon,* volume 3, edited by Kurt Ruh (Berlin: De Gruyter, 1987);

Cormeau and Wilhelm Störmer, *Hartmann von Aue: Epoche-Werk-Wirkung* (Munich: Beck, 1985);

Thomas Cramer, "Saelde und êre in Hartmanns Iwein," *Euphorion,* 60, no. 1–2 (1966): 30–47;

Otfried Ehrismann, "Höfisches Leben und Individualität – Hartmanns *Erec,*" in *Aspekte der Germanistik,* edited by Walter Tauber (Göppingen: Kümmerle, 1989);

Humbertus Fischer, *Ehre, Hof und Abenteuer in Hartmanns* Iwein: *Vorarbeiten zu einer historischen Poetik des höfischen Epos* (Munich: Fink, 1983);

Wolf Gewehr, *Hartmanns Klage-Büchlein im Lichte der Frühscholastik* (Göppingen: Kümmerle, 1975);

Gewehr, "Der Topos 'Augen des Herzens' – Versuch einer Deutung durch die scholastische Erkenntnistheorie," *Deutsche Vierteljahrsschrift,* 46 (November 1972): 626–649;

D. H. Green, "Hartmann's Ironic Praise of Erec," *Modern Language Review,* 70 (October 1975): 795–807;

Gudrun Haase, *Die germanistische Forschung zum* Erec *Hartmanns von Aue* (Frankfurt am Main: Lang, 1988);

Beate Hennig, *"Maere" und "werc": Zur Funktion von erzählerischem Handeln im "Iwein" Hartmanns von Aue* (Göppingen: Kümmerle, 1981);

Gert Kaiser, *Textauslegung und gesellschaftliche Selbstdeutung: Aspekte einer sozialgeschichtlichen Interpretation von Hartmanns Artusepen* (Frankfurt am Main: Athenäum, 1973);

Marianne Kalinke, "Hartmann's *Gregorius:* A Lesson in the Inscrutability of God's Will," *Journal of English and Germanic Philology,* 74 (October 1975): 485–501;

Irmgard Klemt, *Hartmann von Aue: Eine Zusammenstellung der über ihn und sein Werk von 1929 bis 1965 erschienenen Literatur* (Cologne: Greven, 1968);

Hugo Kuhn, "Erec," in *Dichtung und Welt im Mittelalter* (Stuttgart: Metzler, 1959);

Timothy McFarland and Silvia Ranawake, eds., *Hartmann von Aue: Changing Perspectives* (Göppingen: Kümmerle, 1988);

Volker Mertens, *Laudine: Soziale Problematik im "Iwein" Hartmanns von Aue* (Berlin: Schmidt, 1978);

Kurt Ruh, *Höfische Epik des deutschen Mittelalters,* volume 1 (Berlin: Schmidt, 1967);

Paul Salmon, "The Wild Man in *Iwein* and Medieval Descriptive Technique," *Modern Language Review,* 56 (October 1961): 520–528;

Thomas Perry Thornton, "Love, Uncertainty, and Despair: The Use of *zwîvel* by the *Minnesänger,*" *Journal of English and Germanic Philology,* 60 (April 1961): 213–227;

Frank Tobin, "Fallen Man and Hartmann's *Gregorius,*" *Germanic Review,* 50 (March 1975): 85–98;

Tobin, Gregorius *and* Der arme Heinrich: *Hartmann's Dualistic and Gradualistic Views of Reality* (Frankfurt am Main: Lang, 1973);

Frederic C. Tubach, "Postulates for an Approach to Medieval German Lyric Poetry," *Journal of English and Germanic Philology,* 70 (July 1971): 458–467;

Rudolf Voß, "Handlungsschematismus und anthropologische Konzeption – Zur Ästhetik des klassischen Artusromans am Beispiel des Erec und Iwein Hartmanns von Aue," *Amsterdamer Beiträge zur älteren Germanistik,* 18 (1982): 95–114;

Peter Wapnewski, *Hartmann von Aue,* fourth edition (Stuttgart: Metzler, 1969).

Heinrich von dem Türlîn

(flourished circa 1230)

Ernst S. Dick
University of Kansas

MAJOR WORK: *Diu Crône* (circa 1230)

Manuscripts: The text has been preserved in an unusually small number of manuscripts, of which the only complete one is the not-very-accurate Heidelberg codex of 1479 (Universitätsbibliothek, Cod. Pal. Germ. 374 [P]). Of the six fragments, only V (Vienna, Österreichische Nationalbibliothek, Cod. 2779) from the early fourteenth century contains a major portion of the text (lines 1–12,281). The Linz MS. D (Oberösterreichisches Landesarchiv, Cod. ab 104 2°) is part of V. The Berlin fragment G (Staatsbibliothek Preußischer Kulturbesitz, mfg 923,9) is from the end of the thirteenth century. One fragment is at Kiel (Universitätsbibliothek, Ms. K.B.48[i] fol [K]), another at Cologne (Universitätsbibliothek, Cod. 5 P 62 [Kö]). Ms. g, from Schwäbish-Hall, is now lost.

First publication and standard edition: *Diu Crône von Heinrîch von dem Türlîn zum ersten Male herausgegeben,* edited by Gottlob Heinrich Friedrich Scholl (Stuttgart: Litterarischer Verein, 1852; reprinted, Amsterdam: Rodopi, 1966).

Edition in English: Translated by J. Wesley Thomas as *The Crown: A Tale of Sir Gawein and King Arthur's Court by Heinrich von dem Türlin* (Lincoln: University of Nebraska Press, 1989).

As the author of *Diu Crône* (circa 1230; translated as *The Crown,* 1989), Heinrich von dem Türlîn holds a towering position in the later stages of Arthurian romance in Germany. Written after – and in opposition to – Wolfram von Eschenbach's *Parzival* (circa 1200–1210), *Diu Crône* is one of the most unusual creations in the genre that is often referred to as "postclassical." Building on the huge corpus of French and German works that constitute the "supertext" of Arthurian romance, Heinrich produced a courtly epic that is both highly traditional and daringly innovative. In a gigantic attempt to recast the *matière de Bretagne* (matter of Britain; that is, the Arthurian legends), Heinrich created what his contemporary Rudolf von Ems, following the author's own reference to his work as a "crown," calls in his *Alexander* (circa 1230–circa 1254) "Allr Aventiure Krône" (the Crown of All Adventures, line 3219). With thirty thousand lines (not counting a forty-one-line appendix presumably added by a later hand), *Diu Crône* is the longest Arthurian romance written in Germany during the High Middle Ages. It is also the only German romance entirely devoted to Gawein, the prototype of the Arthurian knight.

What is known about the author is little more than what he reveals about himself in his work. He mentions his name in four places, once in an acrostic. For a long time it was thought that he also revealed his family, his birthplace, and his social status. That the family name von dem Türlîn ("of the Small Gate") is also mentioned in an early-fourteenth-century chronicle by Ottokar of Styria. Since this reference links the name with the Carinthian town of Saint Veit, it was long assumed that it yeilded the missing information about about Heinrich's family, birthplace, and possibly even his social status. Finally even the name Heinrich von dem Türlein, with the title *Herr,* was found in a record believed to be from 1229. Thus Heinrich came to be associated with a well-to-do patrician family of Saint Veit, and since his status as a poet called for an influential patron, the next step was to link him to the court of Duke Bernhard of Sponheim.

A critical reexamination of the evidence by Bernd Kratz in 1976, however, showed these assumptions to be largely unfounded. Neither Heinrich's work nor that of Rudolf, who calls him *meister* (master), indicates that he was a knight. His reference to himself as *"werlt kint"* (worldly, line 10,444) suggests, according to J. Wesley Thomas, that he may have been a clerically trained layman. His language, which is generally regarded as Bavarian, and his knowledge of regional coats of arms have led Lewis Jillings to associate him with the counts of Görz. The language, in any case, points toward the eastern Alps. Some Italian influence may argue for his acquaintance with southern regions such as Friaul or Krain.

An excellent education is suggested by his knowledge of French and Latin and, to some extent, also of Italian. Even more impressive is his unique command of a vast body of German and French literature. He must have been familiar with most of the important German romances, especially the works by Hartmann von Aue, Wolfram, and Wirnt von Grafenberg, and he apparently also knew Heinrich von Veldeke's *Eneit* (circa 1185), Ulrich von Zatzikhoven's *Lanzelet* (circa 1194–1214), and Gottfried von Straßburg's *Tristan und Isolde* (circa 1210). Among the French texts, he knew not only Chrétien de Troyes's Grail romance, *Perceval,* and *Lancelot* but also the continuations of *Perceval.* He must also have known several further works, because he seems to have adapted them in the first part of *Diu Crône:* Paien de Maisières's *La Mule sanz Frain* (for the two-sisters plot) and *Les enfances Gauvain* (for the story of Arthur), Robert Biquet's *Lai du cor* (for the virtue test with the cup), *Le chevalier à l'épée* (for the sword over Amurfina's bed), and the *Livre de Caradoc* (for the beheading game).

To answer the question of Heinrich's patronage, it is necessary to identify a court that had the connections to provide access to this wealth of literature; of particular importance is the existence of dynastic connections with the French courts of the time. Various possibilities have been examined without definitive results, including the courts of Duke Bernhard of Sponheim, Duke Friedrich II in Vienna, and the counts of Görz, but the case made by Fritz Peter Knapp for the powerful house of Andechs-Meran in Bavaria deserves special attention on account of that house's close dynastic ties with Burgundy. At the time Heinrich composed *Diu Crône,* Otto of Andechs-Meran had the title of count palatine of Burgundy. Since his influence also extended to Brixen and to some of the eastern and southern regions that may have played a role in Heinrich's life, this connection

looks especially promising. Heinrich may, thus, have enjoyed the same courtly patronage as did Wirnt, whose *Wigalois* (circa 1210–1215 or circa 1235) may have served as one of his models for portraying Arthurian society, including a strong role for Gawein.

Heinrich's re-creation of the Arthurian utopia turns Arthur's nephew Gawein into a superhero, a protégé of Vrowe Fortûne (Lady Fortune) who appropriates some of the missions of Parzival and Lancelot and finds himself in the role of a ubiquitous redeemer. While he continues to be Arthur's chief knight errant and remains attached to the court, the universe of his adventures is now vastly expanded: it ranges from the otherworldly palace of Lady Fortune to the magic castles of a uniquely romantic mountain world and finally to the realm of the Grail as an otherworld of the living dead.

In the beginning it is not apparent that *Diu Crône* is a romance about Gawein. The narrator's declared intention is to tell a story about King Arthur: "Nu wil iu der tihtære / Von künec Artûs ein mære / Sagen . . ." (Now the poet will tell you a story about King Arthur . . .). More specifically, the story he sets out to tell is about Arthur's youth; but at the end he says "daz alle âventiure / von Gâweines tiure / Sagent" (that all adventures tell of Gawein's distinction).

The predominant thematic strand seems to be the continuous threat to, and concern for the preservation of, Arthur's court. Next in importance in terms of narrative momentum is the role of savior assumed by Gawein, with regard both to the court and to the countless victims of violence outside the court. His redemption of the Grail community is another major theme; but, in contrast to *Parzival,* this community in *Diu Crône* lacks the utopian element of a superior order of humanity. Heinrich's rejection of any model of spirituality appears to reverse Wolfram's value system. The foundation of his world consists in the secular order of his Arthurian society, which derives its spiritual strength chiefly from Lady Fortune – a power associated not with God but with the secular realm. Thus, *Saelde* (Fortune) as a deity becomes a theme in Heinrich's work. *Diu Crône* may be called a romance about *Saelde*; and Gawein, apart from being a *chevalier errant,* a prototypical redeemer, and a Grail quester, also carries out the new function of mediator between Arthur's court and Lady Fortune.

The stability of Arthur's court is open to question from the beginning. When the arrival at the court in Caridol of the typical stranger knight disrupts the sumptuous Christmas festivities, a virtue test – the test of the drinking cup – exposes the court's shaky moral condition. Since its application to the ladies amounts to a chastity test, it gives the knight Keie ample cause for sarcastic comments and provides a great deal of frivolous entertainment at the expense of the victims. Only Arthur himself is able to pass the test. A series of events following in rapid succession accentuates the impression of a state of decline and finally of an acute crisis. First, all but three of Arthur's knights secretly leave the court to take part in a tournament; since they do so on the advice of Gawein, this act does not speak well for the model knight, the court's traditional pillar of strength. When a deserted and clearly frustrated Arthur returns from hunting on a cold winter day, his instinctive move to warm his hands over an open fire invites ridicule from Queen Ginover that implicitly aims at his manhood. She contrasts Arthur with the mysterious stranger, Gasozein, who, dressed only in a white shirt, spends the winter nights in the woods singing love songs.

Gasozein has come to claim the queen on the basis of an earlier engagement. At this point, however, the story shifts to the adventures of Gawein. Two subplots follow. The first involves Gawein's rescue of King Flois from the giant Assiles; but before he can defeat Assiles he is sidetracked by another call for his assistance. This call starts the second subplot, the so-called bridle plot, in which Amurfina attempts to assure herself of Gawein's help in an inheritance dispute with her sister, Sgoidamur. Gawein immediately falls in love with Amurfina. But a love potion intended to strengthen the union with Amurfina causes him to lose his memory; only when he looks at a golden bowl displaying a cycle of illustrations of his own heroic deeds – some of them yet to happen – does he realize who he is. After recovering his memory he resumes his mission against Assiles and concludes it successfully, despite many life-threatening occurrences in the forest. The narration abruptly switches back to Caridol, where Arthur is to fight a joust with Gasozein over Ginover. Gasozein breaks off the fight and suggests leaving the decision to the queen herself; Ginover – after some embarrassing hesitation – rejects Gasozein, and he departs angrily. The queen's own brother, Gotegrin, offended by her recent behavior, kidnaps her and takes her to a secluded spot in the mountains, where he intends to kill her. Gasozein turns up just at the right moment to rescue the queen. In a shockingly explicit scene, however, Ginover's rescue turns into an attempted rape. Gawein, on his way back to the court, turns up by chance and rescues the queen from Gasozein. Back at the court, where the badly wounded antagonists are recovering, Gasozein confesses that his claim was based on lies; surprisingly, he receives Arthur's pardon, and the crisis is resolved. The next festival celebrated is Pentecost, a time associated with Arthur's birth.

At this point the bridle plot is resumed. Now it is Sgoidamur who asks for help against her sister, Amurfina. Arriving on a white mule, she pleads for assistance in regaining her land from Amurfina, who is in possession of the magic bridle that gives the holder the right to the inheritance.

After the rash volunteer Keie fails her, Sgoidamur turns to Gawein, who wins the bridle at the magic castle of Gansguoter, the sisters' uncle. Confronted with a series of tests of courage, he proves himself in all of them – even in the frightful beheading game. Gansguoter, being the second husband of Arthur's mother, Igern, turns out to be closely related to Gawein; he explains to Gawein that the latter has won the all-important bridle from himself and that, consequently, he has been needlessly fighting against himself. Nevertheless, this story can now end. Gawein finds Amurfina in Gansguoter's castle, marries her at Arthur's court, and has Sgoidamur, who had pledged her love to the winner of the bridle, accept Gasozein as a substitute husband.

What emerges from the various strands of action that come together at the end of this first part is a remarkable thematic consistency revolving around the threat to the court's stability. Gawein rescues the queen from Gasozein, wins Amurfina, and serves as a matchmaker for Sgoidamur and Gasozein; by reconciling conflicting forces he increases the court's stability. It is of the greatest importance, therefore, that after winning Amurfina as well as her land he does not embark on a career as a ruler in his own right but brings Amurfina to Arthur's court. He thus remains the indispensable guarantor of the stability of the court. At the same time, he has established himself as the only knight capable of dealing with the forces of the preternatural realm, thus assuming a role of virtually superhuman dimensions.

There is a relatively simple narrative scheme behind the first part of the work. It is framed at the beginning and end by a feast. The initiating force of the action is an outside figure who threatens the court's stability. This threat may take the form of a virtue test, which exposes the discrepancy between ideal and reality, or it may be a direct threat to a central member of the court. Any threat to the court will sooner or later involve Gawein in the role of the court's savior. In its dealings with outside forces, the court depends exclusively on Gawein. The plots and subplots are handled with skill.

The bewildering course of events and the sheer quantity of narrative detail characterizing the work after the major break at line 13,901 can be presented as a relatively coherent structure of two further parts: Gawein's *katabasis* (descent) in the form of his "death" and reappearance as well as his Grail quest.

The first of these two parts (lines 13,902–22,563), following the double wedding of Gawein and Gasozein, again opens with a crisis and ends with a wedding feast in Caridol. When, on the way to a tournament, Gawein loses his way, his archenemy Giramphiel, the sister of Lady Fortune, seizes the opportunity to direct him toward a presumably fatal encounter with a dragon. This plan is delayed by Gawein's accidental visit to the Grail castle and the first of two sequences of fantastic events, and it eventually leads him to the palace of Lady Fortune, where the Wheel of Fortune comes to a complete stop upon his entrance. The result is a temporary reversal of Giramphiel's scheme. From Lady Fortune, Gawein receives a ring for Arthur that implies a guarantee of the court's continuance.

In another adventure Gawein defeats the knight Aamanz, who is called "the other Gawein." When Aamanz refuses to swear fealty to Gawein, two other knights substitute for him. After Gawein's departure they decapitate Aamanz. When his head is brought to Arthur's court, the psychological effect is disastrous. Gawein's existence is clearly indispensable for the stability of the court.

In a third turn of this plot, Gawein engages in combat with the Black Knight, who, as an instrument of God, brings death to an entire land. Gawein, having received from the Land of Maidens the gift of eternal youth, promptly disposes of this death figure and is recognized as the predestined savior. Thus a three-step development designed to eliminate Gawein elevates him to the level of a mythical redeemer.

But before Gawein returns to Arthur, one more plot – this one inherited from Chrétien's and Wolfram's Gawein sequences – remains to be carried through. It corresponds to the events in books 7 through 14 of *Parzival*. The joyful reunion with Arthur's court at the end concludes Gawein's *katabasis*. His descent, marked by two Wunderketten (fantastic sequence); his first visit to the Grail castle; and his reception in the other-worldly realm of Lady Fortune and the Land of Maidens have again restored the threatened balance of the Arthurian world.

The final part, Gawein's Grail quest (lines 22,564–29,908), actually represents another *katabasis*, triggered again by Giramphiel's determination to destroy Arthur's court. It parallels the first part of the work in that it starts with a virtue test and is framed by two feasts at Caridol. The main plot begins with Gawein's departure from the court and ends with his return. Gawein now has three companions: Calocreant, Lanzelet, and Keie. This device of extending Gawein's savior role to a quartet acting in unison heightens the importance attached to this mission, while it does not lessen the personal merit of his success and its significance for the court. At the end the court is once more restored to a state of stability, and joy has returned for good.

As in *Parzival*, the Grail quest is the hero's ultimate task, but its significance no longer lies in the establishment of a utopia. The focus here is on redeeming the living dead, including the old lord of the Grail castle, from a state of suffering that was brought upon them by the wrath of God so that they can die in peace. The Grail maidens, who alive, are redeemed at the same time. For Arthur, however, the significance of Gawein's mission lies in the overcoming of the ultimate crisis of his court. Even the motivation of the quest downplays the traditional importance of Gawein's search for the Grail: instead of a spiritual quest, his Grail mission is the outcome of a chivalrous obligation forced on him by Angaras (the character corresponding to Wolfram's Vergulaht in *Parzival*).

The virtue test at the beginning of this part is a pretext for Giramphiel to rob Gawein of the magic objects that are the indispensable source of strength for his fearful Grail expedition, especially the stone that he won in combat from her husband, Fimbeus. Without his magic objects, Gawein seems to be doomed. The very strategy designed to effect his downfall, however, proves him to be stronger than before: he now passes the virtue test, just as Arthur does. It appears that the source of his strength has shifted from the power of magic to the power of intrinsic human virtue.

Nevertheless, the recovery of the lost objects becomes a primary concern and leads Gawein to seek the help of Gansguoter, the magician, who lives in an almost inaccessible mountain realm. The mountain expedition, in turn, produces a further subplot when the giant Baingranz sees a chance to take revenge for the death of his brother, Assiles. Gawein, however, miraculously escapes the trap, kills the dragon that guards the well containing the life-restoring water, and, together with his companions, overcomes the giant. Strengthened by the supernatural water, Gawein proceeds to Gansguoter's castle and regains the crucial magic objects from Fimbeus.

The highly adventurous journey to the Grail involves further setbacks, among them the capture of Keie and the inability of Gawein's companions to avoid falling asleep at the most critical moments – another test passed only by Gawein. Also, this journey contains one more sequence of the fantastic events that seem to be part of the scenario for journeys in the symbolic domain of death. There is even a reprise of the strategy to fabricate a false report of Gawein's death; it fails due to the intervention of Gansguoter's sister, who becomes the pivotal figure in the last phase of the Grail journey: she not only assumes the role of the hero's guide but also turns out to be the goddess of the Grail castle. Thus ends the hero's story. But since the Grail territory is a realm of the dead, this tale has been a story of descent, lacking the more ambitious component of the traditional Grail story: there is no ascent to an ideal society within the spiritual realm. The final destination remains Arthur's court.

Heinrich attempted to create a form of romance that, despite its indebtedness to the Arthurian corpus, follows no particular structural paradigm of courtly romance. No longer committed to the aesthetics of his predecessors, he redefines the genre by striking a precarious balance between the literary conventions, on the one hand, and an original blend of fairy-tale stereotypes and unprecedented projections of the fantastic, on the other. In redesigning the Arthurian cosmos, he cultivates a form of narrative that is unparalleled in German romance. In some ways it suggests the compositional style of the French continuations of Chrétien's *Perceval,* especially in the portrayal of the Grail adventure.

Diu Crône includes many traditional motifs while following an aesthetic conception of its own. Perhaps its most striking difference from Hartmann's and Wolfram's romances is its lack of interest in the spiritual side of the hero's progress. What Christoph Cormeau calls the "preformed" nature of Gawein's character, which assumes his perfection as given, does not allow for a spiritual crisis and, consequently, for the typical two-step development of heroes such as Hartmann's Erec and Iwein.

In the absence of a spiritual goal, the preservation of Arthur's court becomes an end in itself. Although its Christian foundation is never called into question, the court sometimes appears to be more closely related to Lady Fortune than to God. The emphasis of the work is on the secular, and Gawein assumes the role of a secular savior. For Heinrich, it must have been a challenging project to put a model of society into the center of attention and to use perspectives and techniques that were in line with the secular outlook of the later Middle Ages and that in some instances – the fantastic sequences are a prime example – even anticipate much later forms of fiction.

References:

Christoph Cormeau, *"Wigalois" und "Diu Crône": Zwei Kapitel zur Gattungsgeschichte des nachklassischen Aventiureromans* (Munich: Artemis, 1977);

Ernst S. Dick, "The Hero and the Magician: On the Proliferation of Dark Figures from *Li Contes del Graal* and *Parzival* to *Diu Crône*," in *The Dark Figure in Medieval German and Germanic Literature,* edited by Edward R. Haymes and Stephanie Cain Van D'Elden (Göppingen: Kümmerle, 1986), pp. 128–150;

Dick, "Tradition and Emancipation: The Generic Aspect of Heinrich's *Crône*," in *Genres in Medieval German Literature,* edited by Hubert Heinen and Ingeborg Henderson (Göppingen: Kümmerle, 1986), pp. 74–92;

Alfred Ebenbauer, "Fortuna und Artushof: Bemerkungen zum 'Sinn' der *Krone* Heinrichs von dem Türlin," in *Österreichische Literatur zur Zeit der Babenberger: Vorträge der Lilienfelder Tagung 1976,* edited by Ebenbauer and others (Vienna: Halosar, 1977), pp. 25–49;

Karl Heinz Göller, ed., *Spätmittelalterliche Artusliteratur: Ein Symposion der neusprachlichen Philologien auf der Generalversammlung der Görres-Gesellschaft Bonn, 25.–29. September 1982* (Paderborn: Schöningh, 1984);

Walter Haug, *Literaturtheorie im deutschen Mittelalter: Von den Anfängen bis zum Ende des 13. Jahrhunderts. Eine Einführung* (Darmstadt: Wissenschaftliche Buchgesellschaft, 1985);

Haug, "Paradigmatische Poesie: Der spätere deutsche Artusroman auf dem Weg zu einer 'nachklassischen' Ästhetik," *Deutsche Vierteljahrsschrift für Literaturwissenschaft und Geistesgeschichte,* 54 (June 1980): 204–231;

Lewis Jillings, *Diu Crône of Heinrich von dem Türlein: The Attempted Emancipation of Secular Narrative* (Göppingen: Kümmerle, 1980);

Fritz Peter Knapp, Chevalier errant *und* fin'amor. *Das Ritterideal des 13. Jahrhunderts in Nord-*

frankreich und im deutschsprachigen Südosten: Studien zum Lancelot en prose, *zum* Moriz von Craûn, *zur* Krone *Heinrichs von dem Türlin, zu* Werken des Strickers *und zum* Frauendienst Ulrichs von Lichtenstein (Passau: Universitätsverlag, 1986);

Peter Krämer, ed., *Die mittelalterliche Literatur in Kärnten: Vorträge des Symposions in St. Georgen/Längsee vom 8. bis 13. 9. 1980* (Vienna: Halosar, 1981);

Bernd Kratz, "Die Ambraser *Mantel* — Erzählung und ihr Autor," *Euphorion,* 71, no. 1 (1977): 1–17;

Kratz, "Zur Biographie Heinrichs von dem Türlin," *Amsterdamer Beiträge zur älteren Germanistik,* 11 (1976): 123–167;

Kratz, "Zur Kompositionstechnik Heinrichs von dem Türlin," *Amsterdamer Beiträge zur älteren Germanistik,* 5 (1973): 141–153;

Arno Mentzel-Reuters, *Vröude: Artusbild, Fortuna- und Gralkonzeption in der "Crône" des Heinrich von dem Türlin als Verteidigung des höfischen Lebensideals* (Frankfurt am Main: Lang, 1989);

Werner Schröder, "Zur Literaturverarbeitung durch Heinrich von dem Türlin in seinem Gawein-Roman 'Diu Crône,' " *Zeitschrift für deutsches Altertum,* 121, no. 2 (1992): 131–174;

Rosemary E. Wallbank, "König Artus und Frau Saelde in der 'Crône' Heinrichs von dem Türlin," in *Geistliche und weltliche Epik des Mittelalters in Österreich,* edited by David McLintock and others (Göppingen: Kümmerle, 1987), pp. 129–136;

Franz Josef Worstbrock, "Über den Titel der 'Krone' Heinrichs von dem Türlin," *Zeitschrift für deutsches Altertum,* 95 (May 1966): 182–186;

Christine Zach, *Die Erzählmotive der* Crône *Heinrichs von dem Türlin und ihre altfranzösischen Quellen: Ein kommentiertes Register* (Passau: Rothe, 1990).

Heinrich von Veldeke

(circa 1145 – circa 1190)

J. Wesley Thomas
University of Kentucky

MAJOR WORKS: *Songs* (circa 1165–circa 1190)

Manuscripts: The lyric verse of Heinrich von Veldeke appears with that of many other poet-composers in three manuscripts of the late thirteenth and early fourteenth centuries: the Small Heidelberg Song Manuscript and the Manesse or Large Heidelberg Song Manuscript, both in the Heidelberg University Library (cpg 357 and cpg 848, respectively), and the Weingarten Song Manuscript of the Württemberg State Library in Stuttgart (cod. HB XIII poetae germanici 1).

First publication: In *Die Weingartner Liederhandschrift,* edited by Franz Pfeiffer and F. Feltner (Stuttgart: Bibliothek des Literarischen Vereins in Stuttgart, 1843), pp. 60–71.

Standard editions: "Heinrich von Veldeke: Die Lieder," edited by Theodor Frings and Gabriele Schieb, *Beiträge zur Geschichte der deutschen Sprache und Literatur,* 69 (1947): 1–284; in *Des Minnesangs Frühling,* edited by Karl Lachmann and Moriz Haupt (Leipzig: Hirzel, 1857; revised by Hugo Moser and Helmut Tervooren, 2 volumes, Stuttgart: Hirzel, 1988).

Editions in English: Translated by Frank C. Nicholson, in *Old German Love Songs* (London: Unwin, 1907), pp. 22–25; translated by Jethro Bithell, in *The Minnesingers,* volume 1 (New York: Longmans, 1909), pp. 23–27; translated by Margaret Fitzgerald Richey, in *Medieval German Lyrics* (Edinburgh: Oliver & Boyd, 1958), pp. 43–44; translated by Barbara G. Seagrave and J. W. Thomas, in *The Songs of the Minnesingers* (Urbana: University of Illinois Press, 1966), pp. 51–54.

Servatius, part 1 (circa 1165); part 2 (circa 1175)

Manuscripts: This verse adaptation of the Latin *Vita Sancti Servatii* is extant in a fifteenth-century paper manuscript in the library of the University of Leiden (BPL cod. 1215) and in fragments of a late-twelfth- or early-thirteenth-century manuscript that preserve about 350

Miniature of Heinrich von Veldeke in the Große Heidelberger Liederhandschrift (Universitätsbibliothek Heidelberg, cpg 848, f.30r)

verses. Some of the fragments were lost in an air attack on Munich in 1944; the location of the rest of the fragments is unknown.

First publication: *Sinte Servatius Legende van Heynrijck van Veldeken, naer een handschrift uit het midden der XVde eeuw,* edited by J. H. Bormans (Maastricht, Netherlands: Leiter-Nypels, 1858).

Standard edition: *Die epischen Werke des Henric*

van Veldeken I: Sente Servas, Sanctus Servatius, edited by Theodor Frings and Gabriele Schieb (Halle: Niemeyer, 1956).

Eneit (circa 1185)

Manuscripts: The three most important manuscripts are in the state libraries in Berlin, Munich, and Gotha. That in Berlin (mgf 282) is parchment and was written early in the thirteenth century; the Munich Manuscript (cgm 57) is parchment and dates from the late thirteenth or early fourteenth century; the paper Gotha Manuscript (cod. chart. A 584) of the fifteenth century is in Thuringian, the dialect in which Heinrich is thought by many to have completed his romance.

First publication: "*Die Eneidt:* Ein Helden-Gedicht aus dem 12. Jahrhundert von Heinrich von Veldeke," in *Sammlung deutscher Gedichte aus dem XII., XIII., und XIV. Jahrhundert,* volume 1, edited by Christoph Heinrich Müller (Berlin, 1783), pp. 1–102.

Standard edition: *Eneide,* 3 volumes, edited by Gabriele Schieb, Theodor Frings, Günter Kramer, and Elisabeth Mager (Berlin: Akademie, 1964–1970).

Edition in modern German: *Eneasroman: Mittelhochdeutsch/Neuhochdeutsch. Nach dem Text von Ludwig Ettmüller,* translated by Dieter Kartschoke (Stuttgart: Reclam, 1986).

Edition in English: *Eneit,* translated by J. W. Thomas (New York: Garland, 1985).

The importance of Heinrich von Veldeke for the literature of the German High Middle Ages was well stated some twenty years after his death by Gottfried von Straßburg. In the literary excursus of his *Tristan und Isolde* (circa 1210) Gottfried extols the beauty of Veldeke's expression and declares that the best poets of the time praised him highly, agreeing that it was Veldeke who made the first graft on the tree of German verse that produced the branches and the blossoms from which they took the art of fine composition. Veldeke taught them to value pure rhyme, a fairly regular rhythm, courtly language, and romance sources.

Veldeke is not mentioned in any official record, but biographical references in his works and documents of the years 1195 to 1264 that name persons who apparently were his relatives provide considerable information about him. He belonged to a family of minor nobility that resided at Veldeke, near Hasselt in the present-day Belgian province of Limburg; held a fief from the abbey of Sankt Truiden; and was subject to the counts of Loon.

The author was born around 1145 and received a good education. He knew Latin and French and was familiar with the German literature of his time.

None of Veldeke's melodies has survived. The poet's treatment of his subject matter and the forms he employed are sufficiently varied to suggest that the songs were composed over a long period of time, perhaps throughout his entire career. Almost all of them deal with love: from the standpoint of the happy lover, the unhappy lover, the irritated ladylove, and the wise and objective counselor. The summum bonum is joy. The singer cares little for the nobility of character that is revealed by those heroes of the conventional courtly love song who constantly suffer the pangs of unrequited love. This poetic conceit is treated with amused parody.

Many of the songs begin with an account of the beauties of spring – green meadows, blooming flowers, and singing birds – and it is in such a scene that the illustrators of the Weingarten and Manesse Manuscripts depict the carefree poet. These nature introductions, together with his spritely rhythms, suggest that the songs were composed for outdoor group dances at the court of Count Ludwig of Loon and later at those of Countess Margareta of Cleve and Count Palatine Hermann of Saxony. Although the songs are extant only in High German, the traces of Old Limburg they contain indicate that they originally may have been in the poet's native dialect.

Around 1165 Countess Agnes of Loon and Sacristan Hessel of the Maastricht Cathedral asked the young poet to prepare a Limburg version in rhymed couplets of a church legend, *Vita Sancti Servatii,* to honor Servatius, a fourth-century bishop who became the patron saint of Maastricht. Veldeke's work consists of two narratives, each with an epilogue and in a somewhat different style, which leads one to conclude that the second account was written later in his career.

After a prologue that includes a short sermon, part 1 gives a genealogy of Servatius, according to which his grandfather was a cousin of the Virgin Mary. The future saint is born in Armenia, takes holy orders in Jerusalem, and is sent by an angel to Gaul. When he enters the cathedral at Tongeren as a pilgrim, an angel appears and hands him the staff of a former bishop, whereupon Servatius becomes the latter's successor. He performs miracles of healing, but the people eventually turn against him. Warned by an angel, he leaves for nearby Maastricht.

Not long afterward God reveals to Servatius that Attila will devastate Gaul, including Tongeren, so the bishop journeys to the grave of Saint Peter in

Rome to pray that the city will be saved. There Saint Peter appears to him in a vision to say that the evil citizens of Tongeren will not be spared. The journey home is marked by a brief detainment by the Huns and several miracles. He dies soon after arriving in Maastricht and is buried there.

The second part of *Servatius* covers the period from the fifth century to about the end of the eleventh century. It tells how the saint's remains were exhumed by order of Charlemagne and records the miracles connected with them. At the behest of Emperor Otto I they were transferred to the abbey at Quedlinburg, but certain citizens of Maastricht went there at midnight, stole the shrine containing the saint's bones, and hurried home with it. Later Emperor Heinrich (which Heinrich is not clear) chose Servatius as his patron saint and obtained a chinbone as a relic for a new church in Goslar. Some of the miraculous deeds connected with the saint's remains were punishments inflicted on those who tried to steal from Servatius's church or withhold tribute due it.

If one assumes that the dominant tone in his account of the saint's life reflects the author's own feelings, rather than those of his sponsors, then the work reveals another side of Veldeke: here there is no humor or wit; the astounding miracles are told with a sober piety that accepts them without question, and the prevailing mood is that of *vanitas mundi*. But, however devout the author may have been, one is inclined to believe that his other works provide a better mirror of his disposition. It has also been argued that some of the digressions in the manuscript are not by Veldeke but are later interpolations by a scribe.

Veldeke's *Eneit* (circa 1185) has been called the first courtly romance of German literature. Although he was familiar with Virgil's epic, *The Aeneid,* and seems to have gotten certain information from Ovid's *Metamorphoses,* his chief source was an anonymous French adaptation of the *Aeneid* that was written about 1160 and is known as *Eneas.* Several allusions point also to a familiarity with the *Roman de Thèbes* and the *Roman de Troie* or their Latin sources. German works from which Veldeke drew include the *Annolied* (Song of Anno, circa 1075), the *Rolandslied* (Song of Roland, circa 1170), the *Kaiserchronik* (Chronicle of the Emperors, circa 1135–1150), and possibly Heinrich von Melk's *Von des todes gehugde* (Reminder of Death, 1150–1160) and Eilhart von Oberge's *Tristrant und Isolde* (circa 1170–1190). But the only important German influence was that exerted by the *Straßburg Alexander* (circa 1170). By refining its prosody he created the

poetic medium for storytelling that Gottfried so much admired.

When his *Eneit* was about four-fifths completed the author lent it to the countess of Cleve; it was stolen from her during the celebration of her wedding to Landgrave Ludwig III of Thuringia (probably in 1174) by the landgrave's brother Count Heinrich, who sent it back to his homeland. Angry and discouraged, Veldeke gave up the project. It has been suggested that he went back to the Servatius legend at this time and wrote part 2.

Nine years after the theft of his manuscript and three years after the death of Count Heinrich, Veldeke journeyed to Thuringia to request that his work be returned. The landgrave gave it to him and asked him to stay and finish it; at the urging of Ludwig's brother Count Hermann, whose court at the Wartburg later became a famous cultural center, the poet agreed to do so. A year later, probably in the entourage of either Hermann or Ludwig, Veldeke was present at the magnificent festival that Emperor Friedrich I (Barbarossa) arranged at Mainz in the spring of 1184 for the knighting of his two sons. Although Veldeke apparently lived for several more years, he could not have passed middle age, for Wolfram von Eschenbach in *Parzival* (circa 1210) laments his early death.

Unlike Virgil, who begins his account of Aeneas with the hero on the high seas, Veldeke starts his tale with the burning of Troy. Before the Greek victory the gods had told Duke Aeneas, the mortal son of the goddess Venus, that Troy would be destroyed and that he was to escape across the sea to Italy. Therefore, when he sees the city in flames, he sails away with his friends and vassals, but fierce storms drive his battered fleet to the coast of Libya. The exiles are welcomed by the mighty queen Dido, who soon falls passionately in love with their lord, gives herself to him, and publicly declares herself his bride. Yet he cannot stay long, for the gods wish him to set out again for Italy. The forsaken Dido builds a great fire, thrusts a sword into her heart, and springs into the flames.

One night Aeneas's dead father appears to him in a dream and tells him to go to the sibyl at Cumae, who will lead him into hell; there he will learn what the future will bring. Aeneas goes to her, and she guides him past the horrors below to the Elysian Fields and his father. The latter lets him see everything that is to come and declares that one of his descendants will found Rome, the chief city of Earth. Returning from the underworld, Aeneas sails to the mouth of the Tiber and builds a strong fortress on a mountain above the river.

When the ruler of the land, Latinus, is informed of the arrival of Aeneas, he sends word that the duke should have his daughter Lavinia in marriage and inherit the realm after Latinus's death, adding that this outcome had been foreseen and made known to him by the gods. But at the insistence of his wife the king has already promised daughter and land to Prince Turnus, and the latter gathers a great army from far and near to drive out the Trojans. On learning of this move, Venus sends her son armor that no weapon can pierce and advises him to form an alliance with King Evander, the ruler of a neighboring country and an enemy of Turnus.

After arranging for the defense of the fortress, Aeneas starts up the river with a large escort in two ships. The crews row all night and arrive at Evander's capital the following day. The king gladly promises him aid and quickly gathers a host of ten thousand men, whom he sends back with Aeneas in fifty ships. Evander's son Pallas also returns with the Trojan. In the meantime, Turnus's forces have been repulsed from the fortress with great losses, and two of Aeneas's warriors have been killed after entering the enemy camp at night and slaying at least two hundred men in their sleep. The assault on the fortress is renewed the following day, and many men on both sides die before the attackers are again driven off.

Just as the conflict begins on the third morning, Turnus and his army catch sight of the ships approaching and hurry down to engage Aeneas and his allies on the plain below. In the ensuing conflict the young Pallas, who has been knighted only recently, distinguishes himself by slaying more than a hundred men. Turnus boards one of the ships to look for an archer who wounded him, the wind carries him out to sea, and in his absence a truce is arranged. But after two days the wind blows him back and the fighting breaks out again. The Trojans suffer especially from the wondrous deeds of the warrior queen Camilla, whose spear and sword take the lives of many before she is slain by a javelin thrown by an arrant coward.

With the death of Camilla and the departure of her troops the army of Turnus is so weakened that it retreats to Latinus's capital city, and the Trojans encamp on a hill nearby. Arrangements are made for the dispute to be settled by a duel between Aeneas and Turnus to take place two weeks later; the victor is to be heir to Latinus's kingdom. When Aeneas rides up to the city wall during the interim, he and Lavinia see each other and, struck by the arrows of Venus and Amor, fall in love. In the duel

Aeneas kills Turnus. After giving a detailed account of Aeneas and Lavinia's splendid wedding celebration, the author lists their descendants up to Emperor Augustus and tells of the birth and death of Christ. The work ends with an epilogue that tells about the theft of the manuscript and its completion.

Veldeke's verse romance is, above all, a tale of adventure, with single combats, massed battles, strange places and creatures, colorful festivals, and great loves. What holds the diverse scenes together is not the unfolding of a divine plan, as with Virgil, but two themes: the struggle of the characters for self-fulfillment and the role of fate in their lives. The greatly reduced attention given to the individual gods, compared to the Latin epic, and the absence of a patriotic theme – there is no glorification of Rome as in the *Aeneid* – focus attention on the human actors and their ambitions.

It is difficult for Aeneas to desert his wife and friends in Troy and Dido in Carthage, but the gods had told him that he was to be a king, and he never loses sight of his goal. Dido's ambition is much greater: she pays homage to Juno so that the goddess will make Carthage the capital of Earth. The dramatic growth of the lady's power since coming to Libya justifies such extravagant hopes, and she does not fail for lack of wisdom and ability but because of the overwhelming passion for Aeneas induced by Venus. Dido's fateful attraction for Aeneas turns her vassals against her; when he leaves, her vast plans are ruined, and she is torn by unrequited love. Although her death comes at her own hands rather than by a decree of the gods, her nature, as Veldeke portrays it, would not permit her to live on under these circumstances.

A third person who strives valiantly for self-fulfillment is Pallas. Though only seventeen, he has long wanted to become a knight. His wish is granted, and he accompanies Aeneas in search of honor and glory. The youth proves to be a bold and faultless warrior and performs great deeds of valor before being slain by Turnus, who barely survives his attack. Aeneas and the youth's mother blame the gods for not protecting him, and the father declares that Pallas was given bravery and ability in excess and too soon. But Pallas achieved his goal: his daring and the magnificent tomb that is prepared for him ensure the youth the immortal fame he had sought.

The last of Veldeke's heroic strivers is Turnus. As a boy he had ten times the ability of his peers, and as a young man he had demonstrated that he had all the qualities needed to be a great

Illustrations from the Berlin manuscript for Heinrich von Veldeke's Eneit: *(top left) Aeneas and Dido at the table; (bottom left) Aeneas telling Dido of the fall of Troy; (top right) the queen going to Lavinia; (bottom right) the queen telling Lavinia that she must not love Aeneas (Berlin, Stiftung Preußischer Kulturbesitz, mgf 282, f.22, f.64r)*

king. His renown already is such that he can summon a vast army of great allies from distant lands. Latinus thinks highly of Turnus and had made a promise, supported by a legal contract, to give him Lavinia and the realm. The nobleman could look forward to a distinguished future up to the time when the king disinherited him, saying that this act is the will of the gods. In the weeks that follow, Turnus repeatedly refers to the contract. He struggles on through one defeat after another because he knows that he is in the right and cannot believe that the gods would be unjust or that the forces that control human destiny would not be concerned with human concepts of rectitude. Yet the unfairness of fate becomes clear in the final combat as he stands on the field with his mail torn, half his shield gone, and his sword broken, facing an opponent who wears armor that no weapon can pierce and wields a sword that no armor can withstand. If he had not been destined to die, says the narrator, Turnus would have won. While the gods had decreed that Aeneas was to have the princess and the land, Turnus's defeat is the result of his unquenchable ambition and passion for justice, but his death may simply be the result of bad luck: Aeneas slays his helpless foe because he sees that Turnus is wearing a ring that, on a thoughtless whim, he had taken from the dead Pallas – a ring that Aeneas had given the youth. Three minor episodes tell of other warriors who, like Turnus, go to deaths that are predestined by their own natures.

There is something approaching modern determinism in Veldeke's story, because the fates of his characters depend neither on the will of the gods – who are largely symbolic – nor on the characters' own volition but on their natures and pure chance. It is therefore fitting that, for all the strife and bloodshed, there is no division of the participants into the virtuous and the villainous but only into those with happy and those with tragic destinies. Two elements that contribute to the artistic unity of the *Eneit* are the laments and the foreshadowings. The laments – for Dido, Pallas, Camilla, and Turnus – reinforce the omnipresent theme of inexorable fate and make up a leitmotiv of direct or implied protest against the workings of fate. The foreshadowings, many of which also deal with destiny, anticipate all the significant happenings.

Veldeke's style tends to be descriptive rather than dramatic. He portrays his subjects in detail, usually by means of adjectives rather than by similes or metaphors, and sometimes at greater length than is warranted by their importance to the story. The author seems to have greatly enjoyed himself as he graphically depicted the wonders and horrors of hell and the marvelous architecture of two mausoleums. These descriptive scenes serve as interludes in the main action and, coming directly after the deaths of Dido, Pallas, and Camilla, respectively, tend to clear the atmosphere of gloom.

Although the narrator sometimes refers to himself and occasionally speaks directly to his audience, there is little attempt on the part of the author to present his story through the medium of a specific personality. Nevertheless, one forms a definite impression of the storyteller, primarily through his characteristic sense of humor. There is situation comedy in the trepidation of Aeneas as he is led through hell, in the trials caused the henpecked Latinus by his shrewish wife, and in the latter instructing her unbelievably naive daughter in matters of love. There is also considerable wit in some of the remarks with which enemies address each other. But the most typical humor of the work appears in the narrator's facetious remarks concerning his tale. These comments reveal the same detached and lighthearted attitude that appears in Veldeke's love songs and help to create a more consistent interplay of comedy and tragedy than does the occasional humor of his French source.

Eneit is composed in rhymed couplets of tetrameter (occasionally trimeter) lines, a verse form that was used in most of the narrative poetry of its successors. Since about three fourths of the work was written in or near Veldeke's Limburg homeland it was presumably composed in his native dialect, but he may have translated it into High German while in Thuringia or have supervised a translation. *Eneit* exerted a significant influence on younger writers, providing them with a German model of polished narrative verse, of high adventure with a love story and a leading idea, and of tragedy interspersed with good-natured humor.

References:

Susan L. Clark, "Said and Unsaid, Male and Female; Leaving, Left, and Left Out in Heinrich von Veldeke's *Eneide*," *Proceedings of the PMR Conference: Annual Publication of the International Patristic, Mediaeval and Renaissance Conference 1986,* 11 (1986): 51–70;

Marie-Luise Dittrich, *Die "Eneide" Heinrichs von Veldeke: I. Teil: Quellenkritischer Vergleich mit dem "Roman d'Eneas" und Vergils "Aeneis"* (Wiesbaden: Steiner, 1966);

Jane Emberson, "Favored and Unfavored Characters in Veldeke's *Eneide*," *Parergon*, 30 (August 1981): 29–33;

Theodor Frings and Gabriele Schieb, *Drei Veldekestudien: Das Veldekeproblem, der Eneideepilog, die beiden Stauferpartien*, Abhandlungen der Deutschen Akademie der Wissenschaften zu Berlin, Philosophisch-historische Klasse, 1947, no. 6 (Berlin: Akademie, 1949);

Hans Fromm, "Die Unterwelt des Eneas: Topographie und Seelenvorstellung," in *Philologie als Kulturwissenschaft: Studien zur Literatur und Geschichte des Mittelalters: Festschrift für Karl Stackmann zum 65. Geburtstag*, edited by Ludger Grenzmann (Göttingen: Vandenhoeck & Ruprecht, 1987), pp. 71–89;

Arthur Groos, " 'Amor and his Brother Cupid': The 'Two Loves' in Heinrich von Veldeke's *Eneit*," *Traditio*, 32 (1976): 239–255;

Niklaus Henkel, "Bildtexte: Die Spruchbänder in der Berliner Handschrift von Heinrichs von Veldeke Eneasroman," in *Poesis et pictura: Studien zum Verhältnis von Text und Bild in Handschriften und alten Drucken: Festschrift für Dieter Wuttke zum 60. Geburtstag*, edited by Stephan Füssel and Joachim Knape (Baden-Baden: Koerner, 1989), pp. 1–47;

J. A. Huisman, "Die Funktion der Ortsnamen in Veldekes Servatiuslegende," in *Namen in deutschen literarischen Texten des Mittelalters: Vorträge, Symposion Kiel 9.-12.9. 1987*, edited by

Friedheim Debus and Horst Pütz (Neumünster: Wachholz, 1989), pp. 225–239;

Stephen J. Kaplowitt, "Heinrich von Veldeke's Song Cycle of 'Hohe Minne,' " *Seminar*, 11 (September 1975): 125–140;

Ingrid Kasten, "Herrschaft und Liebe: Zur Rolle und Darstellung des 'Helden' im *Roman d'Eneas* und in Veldekes *Eneasroman*," *Deutsche Vierteljahrsschrift für Literaturwissenschaft und Geistesgeschichte*, 62 (1988): 227–245;

Bernd Kratz, "Die Pferde des Mesapus in Veldekes 'Eneit' und im französischen 'Roman d'Eneas,' " *Zeitschrift für deutsches Altertum und deutsche Literatur*, 117 (Second Quarter 1988): 97–104;

Gabriele Schieb, *Henric van Veldeken: Heinrich von Veldeke* (Stuttgart: Metzler, 1965);

Werner Schröder, *Veldeke-Studien* (Berlin: Schmidt, 1969);

John R. Sinnema, *Hendrik van Veldeke* (New York: Twayne, 1972);

Heinz Thomas, "Matière de Rome – matière de Bretagne: Zu den politischen Implicationen von Veldekes 'Eneide' und Hartmanns 'Erec,' " *Zeitschrift für deutsche Philologie*, special issue, 108 (1989): 65–104;

Ludwig Wolff and Werner Schröder, "Heinrich von Veldeke," in *Die deutsche Literatur des Mittelalters: Verfasserlexikon*, volume 3, edited by Kurt Ruh and others (Berlin & New York: De Gruyter, 1981), cols. 899–918.

Konrad von Würzburg

(circa 1230 – 1287)

Timothy R. Jackson
Trinity College, Dublin

MAJOR WORKS: *Thirty-two Lyric Poems* (circa 1257–1287?)

Manuscripts: The Große Heidelberger (or Manessische) Liederhandschrift (Heidelberg, Universitätsbibliothek, cpg 848), composed between 1310 and 1330, is the only source for Konrad's two leiche (lays) and the great majority of his Minnelieder (love songs) and is the principal source for his Sprüche (didactic poems).

First publication: In *Minnesinger: Deutsche Liederdichter des zwölften, dreizehnten und vierzehnten Jahrhunderts,* 4 volumes, edited by Friedrich Heinrich von der Hagen (Leipzig: Barth, 1838–1856), II: 310–335.

Standard edition: "Leiche, Lieder und Sprüche," in *Kleinere Dichtungen Konrads von Würzburg,* volume 3, edited by Edward Schröder (Berlin: Weidmann, 1926; reprinted, Dublin & Zurich: Weidmann, 1970).

Der Schwanritter (circa 1257–1258)

Manuscript: This work is preserved on the first ten remaining leaves of a manuscript from the second half of the fourteenth century (Frankfurt am Main, Stadt- und Universitätsbibliothek, Ms. germ. 4° 2 [formerly Kloss No. 6]). The first folio is missing.

First publication: "Der Schwann-Ritter von Conrad von Würzburg," in *Altdeutsche Wälder,* volume 3, edited by Jacob and Wilhelm Grimm (Frankfurt am Main: Körner, 1816);

Standard edition: "Der Schwannritter," in *Kleinere Dichtungen Konrads von Würzburg,* volume 2, edited by Edward Schröder (Berlin: Weidmann, 1925; reprinted, Dublin & Zurich: Weidmann, 1974).

Das Turnier von Nantes (1257–1258)

Manuscript: This work is found only in the "Hausbuch" of Michael de Leone (Munich, Universitätsbibliothek, 2° cod. ms. 731).

First publication: "Das Turnier zu Nantes von Konrad von Würzburg," edited by Bernhard Joseph Docen, in Hans Ferdinand Maßmann, *Denkmäler deutscher Sprache und Literatur,* volume 1 (Munich: Michaelis, 1828), pp. 138–148.

Standard edition: "Das Turnier von Nantes," in *Kleinere Dichtungen Konrads von Würzburg,* volume 2, edited by Edward Schröder (1925; reprinted, 1974).

Engelhard (circa 1260?)

Manuscript: No manuscript version of this work exists.

First publication: *Eine schöne Historia von Engelhart auß Burgunt: Hertzog Dietherichen von Brabant, seinem Gesellen und Engeltrud* (Frankfurt am Main: Printed by Kilian Han, 1573); reprinted in *Eine schöne Historia von Engelhart auss Burgund: Der "Engelhard" Konrads von Würzburg in Abbildung des Frankfurter Drucks von 1573. Mit einer bibliographischen Notiz zu Kilian Han,* edited by Hans-Hugo Steinhoff (Göppingen: Kümmerle, 1985).

Standard editions: *Engelhard: Eine Erzählung von Konrad von Würzburg,* edited by Moriz Haupt (Leipzig: Weidmann, 1844; revised edition, edited by Eugen Joseph, Leipzig: Hirzel, 1890); *Engelhard,* edited by Paul Gereke (Halle: Niemeyer, 1912; revised edition, edited by Ingo Reiffenstein, Tübingen: Niemeyer, 1982).

Edition in modern German: *Engelhard,* edited by Ingo Reiffenstein, translated by Klaus Jorg Schmitz (Göppingen: Kümmerle, 1989).

Das Herzmaere (circa 1260?)

Manuscripts: This work is recorded in at least twelve manuscripts, including one in Heidelberg (Universitätsbibliothek, cod. Pal. germ. 341).

First publication: "Das Herzmaere," in

*Miniature of Konrad von Würzburg in the Große Heidelberger
Liederhandschrift (Heidelberg, Universitätsbibliothek,
cpg 848 f.383r)*

*Samlung deutscher Gedichte aus dem XII., XIII. und
XIV. Jahrhundert,* volume 1, edited by
Christoph Heinrich Myller (Berlin, 1784), pp.
208–212.
Standard editions: "Das Herzmaere," in
Kleinere Dichtungen Konrads von Wurzburg, vol-
ume 1, edited by Edward Schröder (Berlin:
Weidmann, 1924; reprinted, Dublin & Zurich:
Weidmann, 1970); "Das Herzmaere," in
*Heinrich von Kempten; Der Welt Lohn; Das
Herzmaere,* edited by Heinz Rölleke (Stuttgart:
Reclam, 1968).
Edition in modern German: *Heinrich von
Kempten; Der Welt Lohn; Das Herzmaere,* edited
by Schröder, translated by Rölleke (Stuttgart:
Reclam, 1968).

Der Welt Lohn (circa 1260?)

Manuscripts: Seven complete and two fragmentary manuscripts of this work, dating from
the thirteenth to the fifteenth centuries, survive.
Of these manuscripts, one in Munich (Staatsbibliothek, cod. germ. 16) was written in 1284 –
that is, during Konrad's lifetime. The work is
also included in the Heidelberg manuscript
(Universitätsbibliothek, cod. Pal. germ. 341).
First publication: In "Erzählungen von dem
Striker und Conrad von Würzburg," edited by
Bernhard Joseph Docen, *Beiträge zur Geschichte
und Literatur vorzüglich aus den Schätzen der
Pfalzbarischen Centralbibliothek zu München,* 6
(1808): 168–175.
Standard editions: "Der Welt Lohn," in

Kleinere Dichtungen Konrads von Würzburg, volume 1, edited by Edward Schröder (1924; reprinted, 1970); "Der Welt Lohn," in *Heinrich von Kempten; Der Welt Lohn; Das Herzmaere,* edited by Heinz Rölleke (1968).

Edition in modern German: *Heinrich von Kempten; Der Welt Lohn; Das Herzmaere,* edited by Schröder, translated by Rölleke (Stuttgart: Reclam, 1968).

Die Klage der Kunst (circa 1260?)

Manuscript: This work, like *Das Turnier von Nantes,* is found only in the "Hausbuch" of Michael de Leone (Munich, Universitätsbibliothek, 2 cod. ms. 731").

First publication: "Konrads von Würzburg Klage der Kunst," edited by Bernhard Joseph Docen, *Museum für altdeutsche Literatur und Kunst,* 1 (1809): 62–72.

Standard edition: "Die Klage der Kunst," in *Kleinere Dichtungen Konrads von Würzburg,* volume 3, edited by Edward Schröder (1926; reprinted, 1970).

Heinrich von Kempten, also known as *Olle mit dem Barte* (between 1261 and 1277)

Manuscripts: This poem is preserved in six complete manuscripts and one fragment, stemming for the most part from the fourteenth and fifteenth centuries.

First publication: *Olle mit dem Barte,* edited by Karl August Hahn (Quedlinburg & Leipzig: Basse, 1838).

Standard editions: "Heinrich von Kempten," in *Kleinere Dichtungen Konrads von Würzburg,* volume 1, edited by Schröder (1924; reprinted, 1970); "Heinrich von Kempten," in *Heinrich von Kempten; Der Welt Lohn; Das Herzmaere,* edited by Heinz Rölleke (1968).

Edition in modern German: *Heinrich von Kempten; Der Welt Lohn; Das Herzmaere,* edited by Edward Schröder, translated by Rölleke (Stuttgart: Reclam, 1968).

Silvester (early 1270s?)

Manuscript: This work is preserved in a thirteenth-century manuscript in Trier (Stadtbibliothek ms. 1990/17).

First publication: *Silvester,* edited by Wilhelm Grimm (Göttingen: Dieterich, 1841).

Standard edition: *Silvester,* volume 1 of *Die Legenden,* edited by Paul Gereke (Halle: Niemeyer, 1925).

Alexius (not later than 1275)

Manuscripts: This work, the most widely preserved of Konrad's saints' legends, is found in four manuscripts; one of them is a prose version

(Berlin, SBPK Ms. germ. quart. 188), a legendary from the Strasbourg monastery of Sankt Nikolaus believed to have been compiled in the 1430s.

First publications: *Sanct Alexius Leben in acht gereimten mittelhochdeutschen Behandlungen: Nebst geschichtlicher Einleitung sowie deutschen, griechischen und lateinischen Anhängen,* edited by Hans Ferdinand Maßmann (Quedlinburg & Leipzig: Basse, 1843); "Der heilige Alexius von Konrad von Würzburg," edited by Moriz Haupt, *Zeitschrift für deutsches Altertum,* 3 (1843): 534–576.

Standard editions: *Alexius,* volume 2 of *Die Legenden,* edited by Paul Gereke (Halle: Niemeyer, 1926); "Eine Prosabearbeitung der Alexiuslegende Konrads von Würzburg," edited by Nigel F. Palmer, *Zeitschrift für deutsches Altertum,* 108 (1979): 158–180.

Pantaleon (circa 1275–1277?)

Manuscript: This work is found in the cod. Vind. 2884, composed circa 1380–1390.

First publication: "Pantaleon von Konrad von Würzburg," edited by Moriz Haupt, *Zeitschrift für deutsches Altertum,* 6 (1848): 193–253.

Standard edition: *Pantaleon,* volume 3 of *Die Legenden,* edited by Paul Gereke (Halle: Niemeyer, 1927; revised edition, edited by Winfried Woesler, Tubingen: Niemeyer, 1974).

Die goldene Schmiede (circa 1275–1287?)

Manuscripts: The work is found in twenty complete manuscripts and fourteen fragments, composed from the late thirteenth century to the end of the fifteenth century.

First publication: "Die Goldene Schmiede von Conrad von Würzburg," edited by Wilhelm Grimm, in *Altdeutsche Wälder,* volume 2, edited by Jacob and Wilhelm Grimm (Frankfurt am Main: Körner, 1815).

Standard editions: *Die goldene Schmiede,* edited by Schröder (Göttingen: Vandenhoeck & Ruprecht, 1926; reprinted, 1969); *Marien Voerspan of Sapeel: Eine mittelniederländische Bearbeitung der "Goldene Schmiede" des Konrad von Würzburg,* edited by Joachim Moschall (Erlangen: Palm & Enke, 1983).

Partonopier und Meliur (completed 1277?)

Manuscripts: This work is found in two parchment manuscripts from the end of the thirteenth century, probably belonging to the same gathering, and a paper manuscript from 1471 (Berlin, SBPK Ms. germ. fol. 1064) with 21,784 lines.

First publication: Excerpts in *Sammlung critischer, poetischer und andrer geistvoller Schriften,* edited by Johann Jakob Bodmer (Zurich: Orell, 1743), pp. 36–46.
Standard editions: In *Konrads von Würzburg Partonopier und Meliur – Turnei von Nantheiz – Sant Nicolaus – Lieder und Sprüche: Aus dem Nachlasse von Franz Pfeiffer und Franz Roth,* edited by Karl Bartsch (Vienna: Braumüller, 1871); *Partonopier und Meliur,* edited by Bartsch (Berlin: De Gruyter, 1970).
Der Trojanerkrieg (left incomplete in 1287)
Manuscripts: This work exists in five complete manuscripts from the fifteenth century, four fragments from the thirteenth century, and five fragments from the fourteenth and fifteenth centuries. In addition, two short sections of the text are included in two fifteenth-century manuscripts.
First publication: "Der Trojanerkrieg," lines 1–25245, in *Samlung deutscher Gedichte aus dem XII., XIII. und XIV. Jahrhundert,* volume 3, edited by Christoph Heinrich Myller (Berlin, 1785).
Standard edition: *Der trojanische Krieg,* edited by Georg Karl Frommann, Johann Franz Roth, and Adelbert von Keller (Stuttgart: Litterarischer Verein, 1858; reprinted, Amsterdam: Rodopi, 1965).

No German poet of the second half of the thirteenth century enjoys a richer manuscript tradition than Konrad von Würzburg. The generic diversity of his poetic output is astonishing, ranging from relatively conventional *Minnesang* (courtly love poetry) to social and moral *Sprüche* (didactic poems), from somewhat plain saints' legends to the virtuosity and rhetorical force of *Die goldene Schmiede* (The Golden Smithies, circa 1275–1287?), and from small-scale *Mären* (stories) to a conception of the Trojan War so grandiose that he was ultimately unable to realize it. Such variety – of the major medieval genres only the Arthurian romance is missing – sets him apart from almost every other author of the German Middle Ages. He is virtually unique in writing both *Sprüche* and romances.

In comparison with information about other authors who lived before the end of the thirteenth century, modern knowledge of Konrad's life and of the circumstances of his literary production is outstanding – yet still fragmentary. It is likely that he was born in Würzburg in the early thirteenth century. Traces of his Franconian origins have been identified in his language. In *Spruch* 32,189 he says:

"wær ich edel" (if I were noble), giving evidence of nonaristocratic birth. His works show him to have been widely read in the literature of classical Rome: in addition to the writings of Ovid, Horace, and Virgil, he was familiar with works by Dares and Statius and with the Alexander tradition. In many of his works, principally the saints' legends, he says that he is translating from a Latin version. He confesses to a lesser acquaintance with French, crediting Heinrich Marschant in the prologue to *Partonopier und Meliur* (completed 1277?) with having translated the unidentified French source for him.

Among Konrad's early works, *Das Turnier von Nantes* (The Tournament of Nantes, 1257–1258) is now thought to have been written for the counts of Kleve on the Lower Rhine, *Der Schwanritter* (The Swan Knight, circa 1257–1258) for the same family or for the counts of Rieneck in East Franconia; these suppositions are the more likely because the latter work brings these two families together (along with the houses of Brabant and Geldern) and celebrates their legendary joint descent from the Swan Knight. *Engelhard* (circa 1260?) has increasingly been seen as also an early work and may belong within this complex, in connection with either Kleve or Brabant. A second center of Konrad's literary activity was Strasbourg. The epilogue to *Heinrich von Kempten* (between 1261 and 1277) names as its instigator the provost of the cathedral, Berthold von Tiersberg, who is recorded in documents between 1261 and 1277, the year of his death, as the holder of that position. The man praised in *Spruch* 32,361–375 may well have been Konrad von Lichtenberg, bishop of Strasbourg from 1273 to 1299, or his brother Ludwig, *Stadtvogt* (municipal magistrate) of Strasbourg from 1253 to 1282. There may be a connection between Strasbourg and the commissioning of *Die goldene Schmiede;* Gottfried, the city's famous son, is mentioned in flattering terms in the text, but other internal evidence and external factors, such as the need to encourage the faithful to make a larger contribution to the cost of building a cathedral dedicated to the subject of the poem, the Virgin Mary, point as easily to Basel or Freiburg.

Whatever the uncertainties of tracing his earlier career – and the themes of some of his *Sprüche* could be taken as indicating a period as a wandering poet – there is no doubt that the more substantial part of Konrad's working life, perhaps the last twenty years, was spent in Basel; given the close personal and institutional connections between the two cities, commissions from Strasbourg might easily have been carried out there. Of the works that can be ascribed to the Basel period, *Silvester* (early

1270s?) is likely to be the earliest. Both the prologue and the epilogue of the work identify Liutold von Roeteln, a member of the Basel nobility, as its patron and refer to him as a canon of the cathedral, a post he held from 1260 until 1274 or 1277. Of the other saints' legends, *Alexius* (not later than 1275), as the epilogue says, was commissioned by "von Basel zwêne bürger" (two lay citizens of Basel), Johannes von Bermeswil and Heinrich Isenlin. The former is mentioned in a document of 1273, but otherwise little is known of him; the latter appears in various documents between 1265 and 1294, one dated 1288 recording that he was a governor of a municipal hospice for the poor and sick. The third legend, *Pantaleon* (circa 1275–1277?) has as its patron Johannes von Arguel, another lay burgher, whose name is found in documents between 1277 and 1311; a young man at the time *Pantaleon* was written, as the epilogue implies, he later also became a governor of a hospice and a man of considerable political importance in the city, seemingly as a defender of the interests of the guilds. In this connection he came into conflict with the man who commissioned the romance *Partonopier und Meliur*, Peter Schaler, a member of an important noble family and leader of the aristocratic Psitticher party in the city (so called after their symbol, the parrot; the other party, the Sterner, had a star as its motif). In addition to Schaler and Marschant, the translator, the prologue also names Arnolt Fuchs as having assisted in the production of this book. The last work to be assigned definitely to the Basel period, *Der Trojanerkrieg* (The Trojan War, left incomplete in 1287), was commissioned by Dieterich an dem Orte (or de Fine), also a member of an important family and a canon of the cathedral. Konrad refers to him as *singer,* that is, cantor, a position which he is recorded as having held from 1281 or 1278. Konrad was promoted by a cross section of the men who formed the political, economic, and ecclesiastical elite of the city of Basel in the later thirteenth century – though none of this patronage prevented him from complaining in *Sprüche* and elsewhere of the reluctance of the nobility to support poetic skill.

A document of 1290 or 1295 records that he had occupied a house in the Spiegelgasse (today the Augustinergasse) in Basel, a location that would indicate close links to the bishop's court. The *Anniversarienbuch* of Basel Cathedral says that he was married to Berchta and had two daughters, Gerina and Agnesa, and that all four were buried there, in the chapel of Maria Magdalena. An entry in the "Hausbuch" of Michael de Leone indicates, however, that he was buried in Freiburg, and a document in the Dominican convent there refers to one Brůder Cůnrat von Wurczburg. The *Annals of Colmar* record the year of his death as 1287, between 8 and 22 October, while the entry in the *Anniversarienbuch* is under 31 August of that year. Whatever the lack of clarity in this information, much more is known about Konrad's life than about the lives of any of his literary contemporaries.

In *Der Schwanritter,* which may originally have consisted of 1,642 lines – the missing folio is assumed to have contained 140 lines – Konrad takes the combination of historical and fairy-tale elements that characterized the Old French *Chevalier au Cygne* and that was also used by Wolfram von Eschenbach in his *Parzival* (circa 1200–1210). The widow of Duke Gottfried of Brabant, conqueror of Jerusalem and grandson of the Chevalier au Cygne, is rescued from the Duke of Saxony's attempt to deprive her of her inheritance by the Swan Knight, who arrives in a boat pulled by a swan and defeats the duke in a trial by combat. The forbidden question that lies at the narrative center of the work is later asked by the duchess's daughter, whom the knight has subsequently married: so that her children may have a name, she asks who he is, whereupon he disappears immediately with his swan. Charlemagne appears in the important, if wholly anachronistic, role of the representative of law and justice. Konrad's work supports the assertion that divine favor rests on the successors of Duke Gottfried of Brabant, and it closes with the claim, buttressed by assertions of God's power to work miracles, that this story linking the Swan Knight with the house of Brabant is deserving of belief.

Although the 1,156-line *Das Turnier von Nantes* does not mention Konrad by name, doubts as to his authorship have only rarely been expressed. Recent research has shown that the function of the work is by no means exhausted in the lengthy heraldic descriptions that claimed the attention of earlier scholars. It comprises a strange mixture of static and dynamic elements: within the framework of the narrative of a tournament, some two-fifths of the work is devoted to the presentation of the participating kings and noblemen, with elaborate descriptions of their coats of arms. At the center of the work stands the figure of King Rîchart von Engellanden (Richard of England), who is characterized as the embodiment of generosity and courage. In the jousting that takes place on the eve of the tournament proper he shows his prowess by unhorsing Gotfrit von Gâne (Caen); in the tournament the next day he leads the German company to victory over that commanded by the king of France, in the course of which he defeats the king of Spain in single combat. The work's support for Rîchart's side, which is suggested by the disproportionately long description of his company, has been seen as having a political intention that indicates an early dating (others have seen *Das Turnier von Nantes* as belonging to the Basel period). The character referred to as the king of England can be identified with Richard of Cornwall, and in the aftermath of his election and coronation as king of Germany in 1257 the work would be aimed at gaining support and recognition from those who opposed him or were undecided in their allegiance; they are invited to create in political reality the unity of purpose shown by Rîchart and his company in the text. The setting in Nantes, with its Arthurian associations, is not accidental.

If the gradually evolving understanding of the chronology of Konrad's oeuvre is correct, the 6,504-line *Engelhard* represents his first larger work. Like some of his shorter stories, such as *Das Herzmaere* (circa 1260?) and *Der Welt Lohn* (The World's Reward, circa 1260?), it is ostensibly an exemplum. In a relatively long prologue – 216 lines, of which the first 88 comprise eleven eight-line stanzas on the model of the prologue to Gottfried's *Tristan und Isolde* (circa 1210) – he extols the value of friendship, which he fears is a virtue little practiced in his day. A brief epilogue, in which he names himself as the author and mentions a Latin source, takes up this theme again, presenting the story as a "bilde . . . ze lûterlicher triuwe" (exemplum . . . inspiring pure loyalty). The intervening narrative provides examples of friendship in action. In addition, the work contains a love interest such as one might find in any romance, while the concluding episode exhibits motifs that recall the tradition of Christian legend. The broad outline of Konrad's story belongs to a widespread European literary tradition: in Latin it is represented by *Amicus et Amelius* (the relationship of which to Konrad's work has still not been clarified), in Old French by *Amis et Amiles,* and in Middle English by *Amis and Amiloun.* But rather than being set in Italy in the time of Pépin and Charlemagne, Konrad's version (for reasons that may relate to the commissioning of the work) is set in Burgundy, Brabant, and Denmark, and he has also changed the names of the principal characters.

Three episodes demonstrate the value of friendship. In the first Engelhard, the son of a noble yet poor family, leaves home in the hope that his qualities of character will enable him to find his fortune at the court of King Fruote of Denmark. On his journey he offers an apple to each of three young men whom he meets. Neither of the first two

reacts in the way that he seeks; the third, Dietrich of Brabant, insists on sharing the fruit with him and thus demonstrates the qualities of a potential friend; this capacity is confirmed symbolically by the fact that he is also identical in appearance to Engelhard. The second test of friendship occurs at Fruote's court, where Engelhard makes his mark and then – in socially inappropriate fashion – falls in love with Engeltrud, the king's daughter. Konrad develops this romantic strand to an extent that some have found disproportionate, but recent research sees it as belonging intrinsically to the theme of fidelity. Discovered by the jealous Ritschier in flagrante delicto with the princess, Engelhard denies all; but he is forced to agree to fight Ritschier in a trial by combat. Dietrich saves him by pretending to be Engelhard and fighting in his stead: the issue thus becomes less one of the establishment of objective truth than of the vindication of *triuwe* (loyalty) between friends in the face of the *untriuwe* represented by the faithless and ill-intentioned Ritschier. (The moral issues involved here are reminiscent of the deceitful stratagem by which Gottfried's Isolde is able to survive her trial by ordeal.) When Dieterich contracts leprosy, the cure for which is a bath in innocent blood, the way is open for a reciprocal demonstration of unqualified friendship. After much soul-searching Engelhard murders his two young children, and their blood effects the cure. His actions, which were inspired by an angel of God, receive a retrospective stamp of divine approval when the children are miraculously restored to life. Thus, a deed that, when viewed objectively, seems reprehensible is validated by the overriding ethos of the work. Engelhard is also exemplary in another respect, for he demonstrates that, despite the lack of financial means, social mobility based on inherent nobility of disposition and character is possible – after all, Engelhard shows himself to be a worthy partner for a princess. The same nexus of motifs touching social status and innate virtues (or their absence) is found in some of the *Sprüche* and in *Partonopier und Meliur.*

The 588-line *Das Herzmaere* is another narrative that occupies a place in a widespread medieval tradition. The central image – the dead lover's heart that is eaten, by mistake or deliberately, by the beloved – is a motif that can be traced at least as far back as the middle of the twelfth century. Of those versions in which the lover is killed by the jealous husband, the best known is the story of Guardastagno in Giovanni Boccaccio's *Decamerone* (1351–1353); others include the *Lai d'Ignaure,* the novella that tells of Ariminimonte in the *Cento novelle antiche,* and the *Meisterlied Der Bremberger.* Within the other strand of the tradition, in which the lover dies in foreign parts, Konrad's tale is the earliest known; the *Roman du Châtelain de Couci* belongs here too. As in *Engelhard,* the prologue and epilogue assert the superiority of the past as compared with Konrad's times, which in this instance are characterized by the absence of true love, and the story is offered as an exemplum of the commitment lovers should show to one another. By mentioning Gottfried von Straßburg in the prologue and using his central concept of the *edel herze* (noble heart) in the last line Konrad pays homage to his masterly predecessor, and in the story he sets up a deliberate parallel with the situation and the ethos of *Tristan und Isolde.* A knight and a lady love one another, but since she is married the way is open for a demonstration that love is inevitably the source of both delight and sorrow. To counter the husband's suspicions the lover goes on a pilgrimage to the Holy Land, where he dies of a broken heart. He had instructed his servant that after his death the heart is to be cut from his body, embalmed, and brought back to the lady. The servant is intercepted by the husband, who has the heart prepared as a dish for his wife. On being told what she has eaten she is distraught, her heart splits within her, and she too dies, in obedience to the demands of absolute love. The tale is told as elegantly as one expects of Konrad, though an element of the grotesque is present in the gruesome central idea of the eating of the heart and in the account of the death of the lady with blood gushing from her mouth.

The contempt for the world shown by the 274-line *Der Welt Lohn* is much more conventional for an exemplum than the worldliness of *Das Herzmaere.* Here too there are parallel Latin versions; here, too, the exact relationship of these to Konrad's work has still to be clarified. The opening lines address the tale to "Ir werlte minnære" (you lovers of this world) and are followed by a description of a knight sitting in his chamber and reading a romance. He is given the name of a literary predecessor of Konrad, the poet Wirnt von Grafenberg. The reason for the use of a historical figure seems to be that the prologue and epilogue to Wirnt's romance *Wigalois* (circa 1210–1215 or circa 1235) show a transition from commitment to the world to scorn for it. This historicizing trait is offset by a highly idealized portrayal of Wirnt's chivalrous qualities that is reminiscent of Hartmann von Aue's portrait of Heinrich. Wirnt is astonished when a woman, Frau Welt (Dame World), enters his room. Even though her beauty is described as literally radiant (a motif that

Konrad shares with Wolfram von Eschenbach and that recurs in his descriptions of Meliur and of Helen in *Der Trojanerkrieg*), she is presented throughout the conversation, in which she asserts that Wirnt has long been one of her most faithful servants, as a real woman. The play with these differing levels of reality takes an abrupt turn to the allegorical when she offers to the already infatuated Wirnt a foretaste of the reward of such service by presenting her back to him. The sight of a mass of festering sores crawling with vermin converts Wirnt from worldly interests: forsaking the courtly life and his wife and children, he journeys to the Holy Land to earn the salvation of his soul by fighting the heathen. (The work may have had a role in encouraging support for the crusading ideal in Basel in the 1260s.) The epilogue reinforces the exemplary function, exhorting the readers to avoid the risk to their souls that is caused by love of this world. The somewhat slight narrative line is less important than the spiritual implications of the vivid contrast between the front and rear views of Frau Welt. Walther von der Vogelweide had employed the motif earlier, and in the later thirteenth century it was a popular iconographical element in the cathedral sculpture at Strasbourg, Freiburg, and Basel.

Die Klage der Kunst (The Indictment of Art, circa 1260?) mentions Konrad only in the persona of the narrator, Cuonze, but there is no doubt that he is the author. It stands out from his other works both in form (it seems to have consisted of thirty-two eight-line stanzas with alternating rhyme, of which the twenty-third is missing) and mode (the allegory that is introduced into an otherwise realistic setting in *Der Welt Lohn* here occupies the entire work). Frou Wildekeit (Dame Wildness) leads the narrator to the edge of a wood. Here he finds Frou Gerehtekeit (Dame Justice), assisted by a jury of eleven other virtues, presiding over a trial in which Milte (Largesse) is accused by Kunst (Art) of rewarding poets who do not deserve it. The judgment is that the generous man who does not reward good art is to be shunned – an outcome that Cuonze is to make known. *Die Klage der Kunst* is connected with other works of Konrad by an interest in juristic procedures, the proclaimed desire to restore a previous ideal state – here, one in which true poets were rewarded – and the theme of such reward. This theme could suggest that Konrad was still a nonestablished poet when writing the poem or that it falls into a gap between the earlier commissions and his success in Basel.

The 770-line *Heinrich von Kempten* is another work that Konrad claims to have taken from a Latin version; its anecdotal material is found in Godfrey of Viterbo's *Pantheon* and several German chronicles. On minimal provocation a steward kills a young boy at the court of Emperor Otto (his characteristics suggest Otto II). The outraged Heinrich von Kempten kills the steward, incurring the wrath of the emperor. By threatening and humiliating his overlord Heinrich is able to leave in safety, but if the emperor ever lays eyes on him again, Heinrich is to be put to death. Ten years later in Apulia, where Otto is waging war, Heinrich observes the emperor being ambushed; despite the danger of the situation and the threat that still hangs over his head, he dashes naked from his bath and rescues him. Such loyalty leads to reconciliation and reward. The story ends with the recommendation that any knight should follow Heinrich as a model of the chivalrous fearlessness he has thus twice demonstrated. If it must be admitted that the first instance involved behavior of a kind that no subject should display toward his emperor, it is equally true that Otto is a better ruler because he is no longer as impetuous and aggressive as he once was. Although Konrad does not draw explicit attention to the interconnected themes of power, loyalty, and justice, they are important for an understanding of the text.

The saints' legends *Silvester* (5,222 lines), *Alexius* (1,412 lines), and *Pantaleon* (2,158 lines) also draw on Latin sources. *Silvester* is based on a text that resembles the so-called *Normalfassung* (normal version) of the *Actus Silvestri,* compiled in Rome perhaps as early as the latter part of the fifth century. *Alexius* has Syrian origins, again possibly fifth-century ones, with a Western tradition establishing itself in Rome by the end of the tenth; Konrad's version belongs to the "papal" version, so called because at the end of the legend the pope, rather than Alexius's bride, takes the letter from the dead saint's hand. The Pantaleon legend is also oriental in origin; there is a Latin tradition from the fifth century, two texts within which (Munich clm 18546 and clm 9516) have a wording that is close to Konrad's *Pantaleon*. All three of his texts consist in the demonstration of the virtues and miracles that determine sanctity.

Silvester encapsulates the life of the first pope of the Roman Empire in a brief series of episodes representing encounters with unbelief: he rescues Rome from a dragon; he cures Constantine of leprosy (a symbol of and punishment for the paganism that led him to persecute the Christians) by invoking divine intervention rather than the bath in innocent blood the emperor's heathen doctors had suggested; and (taking up almost half the text) he dis-

putes with twelve Jewish scholars, defeating them by returning to life a bull that one of them, Zambri, has killed. There are also brief accounts of his important work as an organizer of the early western Church.

Alexius represents the ascetic life. Deserting his bride on their wedding night in Rome, he spends the next seventeen years as a destitute beggar in Edessa, followed by a further seventeen in Rome under the staircase in the house of his father, Euphemian, as the anonymous object of well-intentioned charity from his family and malicious bullying from the servants. After his death a heavenly voice leads the people to find the *homo dei* (man of God) in Euphemian's house, and a letter in which he has recorded the events of the last thirty-four years becomes the basis for his sanctity.

Pantaleon is a martyr. As a young doctor attached to the house of Emperor Maximian he converts to Christianity, is denounced by jealous heathen rivals, and, when called upon to sacrifice to the gods, refuses. There follows a series of five attempts to kill him by such means as drowning and throwing him into boiling lead, from all of which he is rescued by Christ. Still refusing to recant, he is executed with a sword stroke; his death is accompanied by miracles.

Pantaleon, patron of doctors and one of the Fourteen Holy Helpers, enjoyed an enthusiastic cult in the Basel area at the time. On the other hand, Konrad says in the prologue that Alexius's name is unfamiliar to many. Silvester's place in Church history assures him lasting veneration. All three legends, as adaptations from Latin sources, may be seen against the background of an upsurge in the use of the vernacular in legal documents in Basel in the 1270s.

Die goldene Schmiede is perhaps Konrad's most impressive work: a sustained series of images and theological concepts that describe the Virgin Mary and extol her role in the salvation of humanity. No other work by Konrad has survived in so many manuscripts – an indication of its popularity – and no other had such a direct influence on other poets, as can be seen in the work of Heinrich Frauenlob, Eberhard von Sax, Konrad Harder, Hugo von Langenstein, Peter Suchenwirt, Heinrich von Mügeln, Hermann von Sachsenheim, and Bruder Hans and in the existence of a partial translation into Middle Dutch prose, *Marien Voerspan of Sapeel*. The compiler of the catalogue of poets in the *Colmar Annals* must have been thinking of this poem when writing that Konrad composed "rhitmos Theutonicos de beata Virgine preciosos" (precious poems about the blessed Virgin in German); and where a vernacular poet such as Suchenwirt singles out a particular aspect of Konrad's oeuvre for praise, it is the Mariological poetry that comes to his mind: "Seins hertzen smitt waz dir berait" (The smithy of his heart was at your [Mary's] service). A more appropriate title might be *Das goldene Geschmeide,* suggesting an elaborate piece of jewelry rather than a smithy. Edward Schröder's edition (1926) prints the text in two thousand lines, a number that has a pleasing roundedness, but nowhere in the manuscript tradition can support be found for it.

When Konrad says in the prologue that the task of adequately praising the Virgin is one that Gottfried could have carried out much better, one feels that he is combining genuine respect for the master of a previous generation of poets with conventional modesty, for he goes on to provide a dazzlingly varied sequence of symbols and typological associations, epithets, metaphors, and allegories in fulfillment of his purpose. Admittedly, the images and concepts are for the most part the commonplaces of the exegetical and Mariological traditions: Mary is the morning star, a honeycomb, a mirror, a pane of glass undamaged by the light that shines through it, Ezekiel's gate, Gideon's fleece, the tabernacle of God or his chaste bride, the virgin who catches the unicorn, and the mother of Christ in his typological-allegorical guises as lion, leopard, panther, pelican. What impresses the reader, therefore, is not the originality of the ideas but the accumulation of motifs and rhetorical figures, the elegance with which they are strung together, and the unusual rhymes themselves – the "seltsên rîm" to which Hugo von Trimberg refers, the "wilder rime kriuter" (herbs of strange rhymes) that Konrad himself advocates in his prologue. In the mannered "geblümte Rede" (flowery speech), as Konrad calls his style, can be found something of the Latinity that Hugo saw as an impediment to an understanding of Konrad's poetry; and in the knowledge of the Mariological tradition lies the evidence of the book learning that Rumelant von Sachsen praised. *Die goldene Schmiede,* however, represents no mere victory of form over content, for particular concerns and recurring motifs can also be discerned: light in its many forms (including the image of the divine sun), polemics against Jews and heretics, the concept of the sea of sins with which the work opens and closes, and Mary's central role in the Incarnation and thus in the Redemption.

Konrad's thirty-two lyric poems can be divided, though not without some problems, into leiche (lays), *Lieder* (songs), and series of *Sprüche.* Of his two *Leiche* the religious one of 244 lines follows a well-established tradition in taking the Trinity, Mary, and Christ as its themes, but it differs in treating Mary and Christ together in one section and in giving more attention to the latter. In common with several of Konrad's short narrative works, the 138-line secular *leich* takes as its point of departure his dissatisfaction with the supposed contemporary state of affairs: Mars rules the land; Amor is oppressed by war and rapine. That men are so concerned with pillage and arson is not in the interests of women, whose desire is to be the objects of *Minne* (love). And so Amor and Venus are called on to bring about a change, to ensure that henceforth only the arrows of love will be loosed.

Both the concern with social conditions (however far removed from genuine social reality) and, to a lesser extent, the preoccupation with moral or spiritual matters also underlie many of the *Sprüche.* Religious themes range from further reflection on the Trinity, Christ, and Mary to the Eucharist and a meditation on death. In contrast to many other writers Konrad does not, with the exception of one stanza in praise of Rudolf von Habsburg, comment in his secular *Sprüche* on politics. Much more important for him are material concerns, above all the status and financial rewards of the poet. He berates the miserly, praises generosity as the true basis for honor, and expresses resentment of those inferior poets who are nevertheless able to attract the patronage of the nobility. In their misdirected liberality these latter show themselves to be "edelen tumben" (noble fools). And the concept of *nobilitas mentis,* the idea that nobility resides not in breeding but in inherent virtues, which was a theme in *Engelhard,* recurs here.

Konrad's *Minnelieder* (love songs) combine aspects of conventionality and repetitiveness with a readiness to experiment. Almost all comprise three stanzas, while the stanza shows a strong liking for a three-stanza pattern and three-line stanza – features that in some respects set him off against his predecessors, but which he repeats inexhaustibly. Generally, his rhymes do not show great originality or variety, but at times they are handled with a virtuosity that, if mannered, is nevertheless impressive:

Gar bar lît wît walt,
kalt snê wê tuot: gluot sî bî mir.
gras was ê, clê spranc
blanc, bluot guot schein: ein hac pflac ir.

(The broad wood lies quite bare,
the cold snow hurts: may warmth surround me.

Illustration in a fifteenth-century paper manuscript for Konrad's Der
Trojanerkrieg *(Berlin, Staatsbibliothek,*
ms. germ. fol. 1, f.236v)

There used to be grass, glossy clover
sprang up, blossoms gleamed beautifully: a hedge gave
   them cover.)

There are nine summer songs, ten winter songs,
and two dawn songs. Except in the dawn songs, the
standard opening is a *Natureingang* (description of
nature in fairly conventional terms), followed by
praise of a lady or, more often, reflections on the
nature of love; the impression of repetitiveness is
reinforced by no fewer than seven of the winter
songs and one of the summer songs beginning with
the word *jârlanc* (at this time of year).

Konrad's lyric output is noteworthy for the
way in which it questions the traditional boundaries
between genres. It has been claimed that, strictly
speaking, only two of his songs are genuine
Minnelieder. The readiness to reflect on love leads

away from the fiction of the suffering individual
that sustained *Minnesang* for so long and toward the
depersonalization of a highly personal genre. One
poem uses the dawn-song situation as a basis for a
Spruch-like reflection on covert love, and it does so
in a highly mannered form in which alternate lines
rhyme syllable by syllable with one another. Other
poems begin with a *Natureingang* but instead of continuing in *Minnelied* style go into the social or moral
comment characteristic of the *Spruch*. These comments can take the form of criticism of the "ver-
schamten rîchen tugentlôsen" (shameful and vicious
rich); the grounds for the accusation are not objectively moral but aesthetic and economic: the rich
have patronized worthless poets. It has frequently
been suggested that such poems must belong to an
early period in Konrad's career, but themes of economic insecurity and rivalry with other poets are

also present in the prologues to *Partonopier und Meliur* and *Der Trojanerkrieg,* which have always been seen as late works of the successful Basel period. In these prologues he claims that Schaler and Dieterich an dem Orte, in appreciating and supporting the work of fine poets, are exceptions to the philistinism that is all too prevalent among the nobility.

The French source for the 21,784-line *Partonopier und Meliur* to which Konrad refers in the prologue is the anonymous text *Partonopeu de Blois* from the second half of the twelfth century, yet another text with counterparts in several vernacular traditions. Partonopier, only thirteen years old but possessing already all the virtues and qualities required for ideal knighthood, is transported to a deserted castle by the magic powers of Meliur, heiress to the empire of Constantinople, who has long loved him. She slips into his bed, and they become lovers without his having seen her. She declares that she will marry him, but not for two and a half years, within which time he must prove his chivalric prowess and may not look upon her. In a tournament he demonstrates his chivalry in fighting the noble heathen king Sornagiur. Persuaded by his mother and the archbishop of Paris that Meliur may be a diabolical emanation and is not to be trusted, he looks at her one night by means of a magic lantern. The spell is broken, and Partonopier is banished from her sight. In this catastrophe, brought upon the hero through a defect of his character, the work corresponds to the demands of romance, though it differs from romance in that the woman took the initiative in the relationship. He spends the next year in despairing separation from her until chance leads Irekel, Meliur's sister, to him. Discovering his wretched state, she urges Meliur, who still loves Partonopier, to bring him comfort, but it has already been determined that a tournament will decide who her husband will be. Partonopier's qualities bring him victory in the tournament and, thus, the hand of Meliur and the crown of Constantinople. The work breaks off as a battle between the hero and the sultan of Persia initiates a new series of events, which one may suppose would have shown Partonopier, no longer the unthinking young man of the early episodes, tenaciously defending his new status and interests.

Supernatural and fairy-tale motifs may have provided the point of departure for the work, and its graphic battle scenes may remind one of the chanson de geste, but, taken as a whole, *Partonopier und Meliur* is a courtly romance, set in and aimed at courtly circles; indeed, it is the first courtly romance written for a sophisticated public, with the possible exception of Gottfried's *Tristan und Isolde.* The love that lies at its heart comes into conflict with family and religion, for they have a competing claim on Partonopier's *triuwe* (loyalty); and loyalty is also central to the episodes involving Mareis and Phares, which have often attracted scholarly attention. These men are peasants by birth, deceitful and treacherous by nature, and, when promoted to positions of power, they apply their vicious characteristics in their own interests and to the disadvantage of their masters and rivals. The vigorous criticism of them expressed by other characters and by the narrator may reflect social tensions in Basel, though critique of the parvenu is less pronounced in Konrad's work than in the source. As in *Engelhard,* however, there is also an example of the positive social climber in that Partonopier himself, the son of a count, wins a Byzantine princess.

The massive *Der Trojanerkrieg* (the Trojan War was a popular theme in medieval Europe) comprises 40,424 lines by Konrad, with a 9,412-line continuation by an anonymous writer. Even at that length Konrad only covers about one-third of the material of his principal source, the *Roman* [or *Estoire*] *de Troie,* written around 1160 by Benoît de Sainte-Maure. The prologue refers to this work as a "welsch" (French) version of "daz alte buoch von Troie" (the old book of Troy) and mentions Dares as a further source. Konrad shows a readiness to deviate from Benoît by starting the work with a long account of the birth and early life of Paris. In addition, the influence of Ovid's *Heroides, Metamorphoses,* and *Amores;* Statius's *Achilleis;* the *Ilias latina;* the *Excidium Troiae;* and (for the continuation) Dictys can be traced. The bringing together of so much material is compared in the prologue to the way in which many rivers run into the sea; the work's attempt at a kind of epic totality has been linked to a late medieval "encyclopedic" tendency (Konrad outlived Saint Thomas Aquinas, who compiled vast summaries of theology, by thirteen years). The complex manuscript tradition indicates that the popularity of the work, in various forms, stretched over several centuries. Konrad also treats the Trojan material in the second *leich* and in several *Sprüche.*

Among the episodes in *Der Trojanerkrieg* are Paris's youth, including the Apple of Discord; Achilles with Chiron; Jason and Medea; the destruction of Troy by Hercules; Achilles and Deidamia; the rebuilding of Troy; Paris and Helen; the preparations of the Greek and Trojan armies; and the first three battles, interspersed with the fetching of Achilles by Ulysses and Diomedes, a truce, and Achilles' mourning of Patroclos. Within this narrative framework – and despite the historical status the Middle Ages ascribed to the material – the traditional central concerns of the romance genre are developed: love and battle. Scenes of warfare are described in extensive detail, while sexual relationships are depicted with a degree of explicitness unusual in the Middle Ages. The erotic and military strands of action interact to produce much of the dynamic of the work: there is a recurrent narrative structure whereby a hero falls in love, offends by deceiving the beloved, and dies. Within Konrad's fragment the structure is fulfilled only in the cases of Jason and Hercules, but it can be assumed that Achilles and Paris would have repeated the pattern. The prologue suggests a more general exemplary function for the work in providing "ein bilde ûf tugentrîchez leben" (a model for virtuous living), and it has been observed that, in contrast to many other medieval writers, Konrad is not on the side of the Trojans but records the exemplary qualities of both Trojans and Greeks. The work is also notable for his emotional involvement in the individual fates of his characters; these fates are set, however, against the background of an all-embracing fatality, heightened by the dreams and prophecies of Hecuba, Cassandra, and others, which suggests that the downfall of Troy is inescapable. It has been suggested that *Der Trojanerkrieg* is the only thirteenth-century courtly romance to have been commissioned by a cleric; while it is courtly in its elegant scenes of chivalrous jousting and its concentration on love and while it appropriates the standard virtues of courtly literature, it seems to be less aimed at the vindication of a courtly ethos, less anchored in a sense of a courtly class, and more concerned with working out the idea of fate than is a work such as Hartmann's *Iwein* (circa 1203) or Konrad's own *Partonopier und Meliur*.

Among his contemporaries and successors Konrad was regarded above all as a *meister*, that is, a learned professional poet. This title is associated with his name by Rumelant von Sachsen, Hermann der Damen, Hugo von Trimberg, Boppe, Peter Suchenwirt, and Hermann von Sachsenheim; in entries preceding *Die Klage der Kunst* and following *Die goldene Schmiede* in the *Hausbuch* of Michael de Leone; and above the picture of him in the Manesse manuscript. The *Meistersänger* included him among the "Zwölf alte Meister" (twelve old masters), and he is titled a *magister* (master) in the Basel document of 1290 or 1295. Hermann der Damen praises him in general terms: "der Mîsner und meister Conrât, / die tzwêne sint nû die besten" (the Meißner and Master Konrad, / these two are now the best). In his more precise, lengthy, and detailed encomium Frauenlob says: "gewidemet in dem boume künste rîches lobes / hielt wipfels gunst / sîn list, durchlîljet kurc" (upon the tree of that renown which is granted to rich art was honored / with a place on the topmost branch / his genius, decorated with lilies for all to see); Hugo von Trimberg's praise in his *Der Renner* (circa 1295), on the other hand, is not unqualified: the language of "Meister Cuonrâdes meisterlîchez tihten" (Master Konrad's masterly poetry), Hugo says, betrays too much of its Latin origins to be easily understood by the laity, even if he is popular with the clergy; Konrad is accused, moreover, of ignoring the mean between too low and too high a style. The praise of other poets touches little on the content of his works; and where they mention subject matter, as do Heinrich von Mügeln, Peter Suchenwirt, and Hermann von Sachsenheim, it is to say that the poetic gift Konrad brought to the task of praising Mary was aesthetically superior to their own – just the compliment Konrad himself had paid to Gottfried. And even if he occasionally overuses formulaic phrases to fill out his metrical schemes, Konrad's style is rarely less than elegant. It is characterized by all kinds of anaphoric and parallel forms – especially synonymous pairs and alliteration, but also antitheses; in addition, he employs a wide range of epithets and an inventive stock of similes and metaphors, many of them drawn from nature.

These stylistic qualities are apparent in the work of those whom he influenced, a list that includes Frauenlob; Suchenwirt; Eberhard von Sax; Konrad Harder; Heinzelin von Konstanz; Hugo von Langenstein; Heinrich von Mügeln; Hermann von Sachsenheim; Bruder Hans; Dieterich von der Glesse; Egenolf von Staufenberg; Der Kanzler; Muskatplüt; Heinrich von Laufenberg; Walther von Rheinau; Johann Hadloub; the authors of the *Jüngeres Marienlob, Reinfried von Braunschweig* (circa 1300), *Virginal*, and *Der Sælden Hort* (circa 1300); and those who appropriated his strophaic forms. Further evidence for the impact of Konrad can be seen in the Middle Dutch prose versions of *Die goldene Schmiede,* the prose adaptation of *Alexius,* the brief prose treatise *Von der welt valscheit* (1393), the continuation of *Der Trojanerkrieg* and its inclusion in chronicles, and in his general effect on the development of heraldic poetry, allegory, and Swiss lyric poetry. Of the works that have at some time been attributed to him the most important are the *Nikolauslegende,* an *Ave Maria,* and *Die halbe Birne* (The Half Pear).

Scholars have emphasized his debt to Gottfried. There *was* a debt, and he happily presented himself as the pupil of the master from the classical generation, but more recent scholarship has moved away from the idea of the mere epigone toward a more differentiated understanding of Konrad and his work based on his own artistic concerns and the possible interests of his patrons. Moreover, he is no longer seen as a slavish translator of his sources but as an adapter who either remains close to the original or shows independence and creativity as he wishes: in the *Trojanerkrieg* prologue he says of the old story of Troy "daz ich ez welle erniuwen / mit worten lûter unde glanz" (that I wish to make it new / with pure and radiant words). He was long regarded as a prototype of the bourgeois writer, but this view, too, based on such diverse elements as his utilitarian moralizing, a tendency toward realistic portrayal, and the inclusion of realistic details such as travel and trade in the description of Schiefdeire in *Partonopier und Meliur,* has been rejected in favor of an urban perspective: Konrad wrote, at least during his time in Basel, for the small social and political elite of a town. There is now more discussion as to whether this elite was relatively homogeneous or whether it was characterized by tensions of the kind known to have existed between individuals such as Johannes von Arguel and Peter Schaler and between groups such as the Psitticher and Sterner.

It has frequently been said that Konrad lacked an ethically or ideologically unifying perspective, that he carried out commissions with consummate poetic skill but little concern for their content. It is, in fact, difficult to discern enduring moral interests of the kind that preoccupied Hartmann and Wolfram. It follows that, since the chronology of his works remains unclear, it is impossible to trace any development of his interests as his oeuvre progresses. Certain general features, however, emerge from an overall consideration of his work. Several times Konrad claims an edifying function for his legends; this claim is not just an expression of the principle of *imitatio* that is integral to the saint's life as a genre but also relates to many other works for which a similar moral-exemplary value is explicitly asserted or implicitly understood. Again and again – for example, in both *Das Herzmaere* with its tale of illicit love and the martyr legend *Pantaleon* – terms such as *bilde* and *bîschaft* (exemplum, precept) recur, and short exempla are used to make didactic points: one *Spruch* sees the beaver as a model of generosity in biting off its tail to satisfy the pursuing hunter, and the prologues of the legend *Silvester* and the romance *Partonopier und Meliur* use the exemplum of the tree bearing both flower and fruit to represent the pleasure and instruction the story will bring. The utilitarian attitude is expressed in the use of *nütze* (useful) in the first lines of *Pantaleon* and *Partonopier und Meliur.*

Literature, however, is about more than moral improvement, and the *Trojanerkrieg* prologue discusses poetry as a rare gift that cannot be learned but is granted by God to chosen individuals and that differs from other "künste" (crafts) such as tailoring or shoemaking in requiring no tools other than "zungen unde sinnes" (a tongue and a wise mind). In the presentation of his material Konrad shows a distinctive poetic personality that is at once linked to the past and eager to break new ground. He delights in descriptions of physical reality, be it the elegance of court dress or the radiant beauty of his heroines (occasionally with a hint of eroticism, as in the reference to Engeltrud's breasts gleaming through a diaphanous garment). Constant components of this idealizing descriptive method are light and color, which clearly tie him to an earlier tradition but have also been seen as linking him to the developing imagery of mystical writing. A quite different tendency takes him in the direction of the grotesque: the descriptions of Dietrich's leprosy, the back of Frau Welt, the death of the bull in *Silvester,* Kalchas's epileptic fit in *Der Trojanerkrieg,* or the horrors of hell in *Partonopier und Meliur.* At times his depiction of physical reality or character shows a desire to intensify the emotional appeal of the material – through the sentimentalizing physical description of a saint, the pathos of a mother as she mourns her dead son, or the emphasis on physical or mental suffering. Yet another mode reveals a more psychological approach to characterization, or at least a more detailed and analytical description of emotional states such as love or mental conflicts. This interest is often expressed in one of Konrad's most distinctive features: his obsessive examination of the relationships of outer and inner, physical and psychological, concrete and abstract. In these ways Konrad points forward from medieval romance to the modern novel.

References:

David M. Blamires, "Konrad von Würzburg's Verse *Novellen,*" in *Medieval Miscellany. Festschrift for Eugene Vinaver,* edited by Frederick Whitehead and others (Manchester, U.K.: Manchester University Press / New York: Barnes & Noble, 1965), pp. 28–44;

Rüdiger Brandt, *Konrad Von Würzburg* (Darmstadt: Hirzel, 1987);

Horst Brunner, "Konrad von Würzburg," in *Die deutsche Literatur des Mittelalters: Verfasserlexikon,* volume 5, edited by Kurt Ruh and others (Berlin & New York: De Gruyter, 1985), cols. 272–304;

Brunner, ed., "Konrad von Würzburg: Seine Zeit, sein Werk, seine Wirkung (Tagung Würzburg 1987)," *Jahrbuch der Oswald von Wolkenstein Gesellschaft,* 5 (1988–1989): 1–442;

Christoph Cormeau, "Quellenkompendium oder Erzählkonzept? Eine Skizze zu Konrads von Würzburg 'Trojanerkrieg,'" in *Befund und Deutung: Festschrift für Hans Fromm,* edited by Klaus Grubmüller and others (Tübingen: Niemeyer, 1979), pp. 303–319;

Trude Ehlert, "in hominem novum oratio? Der Aufsteiger aus bürgerlicher und aus feudaler Sicht: Zu Konrads von Würzburg 'Partonopier und Meliur' und zum altfranzösischen 'Partonopeus,'" *Zeitschrift für deutsche Philologie,* 99, no. 1 (1980): 36–72;

Peter Ganz, "Nur eine schöne Kunstfigur: Zur 'Goldenen Schmiede' Konrads von Würzburg," *Germanisch-Romanische Monatsschrift,* new series 29, no. 1 (1979): 27–45;

Regina Renate Grenzmann, *Studien zur bildhaften Sprache in der "Goldenen Schmiede" Konrads von Würzburg* (Göttingen: Vandenhoeck & Ruprecht, 1978);

Walter Haug, *Literaturtheorie im deutschen Mittelalter: Von den Anfängen bis zum Ende des 13. Jahrhunderts* (Darmstadt: Wissenschaftliche Buchgesellschaft, 1985);

Timothy R. Jackson, *The Legends of Konrad von Würzburg: Form, Content, Function* (Erlangen: Palm & Enke, 1983);

Gerhard P. Knapp, *Hector und Achill: Die Rezeption des Trojastoffes im deutschen Mittelalter. Personenbild und struktureller Wandel* (Bern & Frankfurt am Main: Lang, 1974);

Hartmut Kokott, *Konrad von Würzburg: Ein Autor zwischen Auftrag und Autonomie* (Stuttgart: Hirzel, 1989);

Inge Leipold, *Die Auftraggeber und Gönner Konrads von Würzburg: Versuch einer Theorie der "Literatur als soziales Handeln"* (Göppingen: Kümmerle, 1976);

Wolfgang Monecke, *Studien zur epischen Technik Konrads von Würzburg: Das Erzählprinzip der wildekeit* (Stuttgart: Metzler, 1968);

Peter H. Oettli, *Tradition and Creativity: The "Engelhard" of Konrad von Würzburg. Its Structure and Its Sources* (New York, Bern & Frankfurt am Main: Lang, 1986);

Ursula Peters, *Literatur in der Stadt: Studien zu den sozialen Voraussetzungen und kulturellen Organisationsformen städtischer Literatur im 13. und 14. Jahrhundert* (Tübingen: Niemeyer, 1983);

Christian Schmid-Cadalbert, ed., *Das ritterliche Basel: Zum 700. Todestag Konrads von Würzburg* (Basel: Öffentliche Basler Denkmalpflege, 1987);

Stephen L. Wailes, "Konrad von Würzburg and Pseudo-Konrad: Varieties of Humour in the 'Märe,'" *Modern Language Review,* 69 (January 1974): 98–114;

Gisela Werner, *Studien zu Konrads von Würzburg Partonopier und Meliur* (Bern & Stuttgart: Haupt, 1977).

Der Marner

(before 1230 – circa 1287)

Will Hasty
University of Florida

MAJOR WORKS: *Songs* (circa 1230–circa 1267)

Manuscripts: Of the five Latin songs, three are contained in an addition to the *Carmina Burana* manuscript in the Bayerische Staatsbibliothek in Munich (clm 4660, 55^r, Carm. Bur. 3*; clm 4660, 105^r/104^v, Carm. Bur. 6*; and clm 4660a, Bl. II^{rv}, Carm. Bur. 9*). The first two were written down in the latter half of the thirteenth century, the third around 1250. The fifth strophe of the first song, presumably written down before 1250, is also preserved in Klagenfurt (Perg.-Hs. 7, 6^r); the entire first song is preserved with a fourth song in the Sterzinger Miszellaneen manuscript in Innsbruck (29^v and 16^r) under the title "Marnarii"; the fourth song is also preserved in the Große Heidelberger Liederhandschrift from the early fourteenth century (Heidelberg, cpg 848, 354^v). A fifth song is preserved in the annals of Heinrich von Heimburg in Berlin (Stiftung Preußischer Kulturbesitz, ms. Lat. fol. 136, 22^r) and in the Landesbibliothek in Stuttgart (HB I 91, 80^r). German works include seven didactic songs and eight love songs in the *Minnesang* tradition, preserved in eighty-one strophes in the Große Heidelberger Liederhandschrift C (cpg 848, 349^r–354^v). Single strophes are also in the Jenaer Liederhandschrift in Jena (Pergament 133 Bll.), in Bern (Burgerbibliothek, cod. 260, 234^r), and in the Niederrheinische Liederhandschrift in Leipzig (Universitätsbibliothek, Rep. II fol. 70^a, 96^{rv}, and 102^v). Hans Ulrich Schmid has discovered verses by Der Marner in the margins of a collection of sermons produced around 1300 in Oberaltaich (clm 9690). A few melodies are also preserved in the Jenaer Liederhandschrift.

First publications: German songs in *Sammlung von Minnesingern aus dem schwaebischen Zeitpuncte, CXL Dichter enthaltend,* 2 volumes, edited by Johann Jakob Bodmer and Johann Jakob Breitinger (Zurich: Orell, 1758–1759), II: 166–177; Latin songs in *Carmina Burana,* edited by Johann Andreas Schmeller (Stuttgart: Literarischer Verein, 1847).

Standard editions: *Der Marner,* edited by Philip Strauch (Strasbourg: Trübner, 1876; reprinted, Berlin: De Gruyter, 1965); *Die Sangesweisen der Colmarer Handschrift und die Liederhandschrift Donaueschingen,* edited by Paul Runge (Leipzig: Breitkopf & Härtel, 1896), pp. 119–122, 125; *Deutsche Lieder des Mittelalters,* edited by Hugo Moser and Joseph Müller-Blattau (Stuttgart: Klett, 1968), pp. 155–158; *The Art of the Minnesinger,* 2 volumes, edited by Ronald J. Taylor (Cardiff: University of Wales Press, 1968), I: 39–42, 118–119; II: 63–69, 180; *Carmina Burana,* volume 1, edited by Alfons Hilka and Otto Schumann (Heidelberg: Winter, 1970).

An itinerant poet-singer dependent on the favor of many patrons during his career, Der Marner composed an impressively wide variety of songs in Latin and German, combining in an often unique way themes popular in Latin poetry with those of vernacular court literature. His relationship with his literary contemporaries was anything but congenial: he made bitter attacks on Reinmar von Zweter in some of his songs and was himself an object of criticism and ridicule for other poets. Der Meißner and Rumelant von Schwaben, poets of a younger generation in the latter part of the thirteenth century, called him senile and distanced themselves, as German poets, from the Latin component of his didactic program. The dangers linked to a life of wandering may have led sometime before 1287 to a violent death, which was reported by Rumelant: "schentlicher mort der wart noch nie begangen / an eime kranken, blinden, alten manne" (a more hideous murder was never committed against a sick, blind, old man). Der Marner is considered, along with Freidank and Reinmar, one of the significant

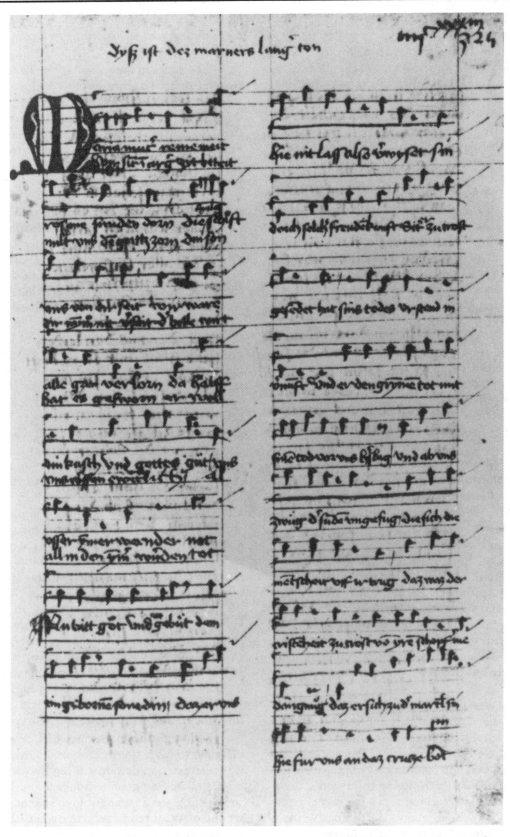

*A song by Der Marner in the "long melody" form, with musical notation, in a fifteenth-century manuscript
(Munich, Bayerische Staatsbibliothek, cgm 4997, f.447r)*

authors of *Spruchdichtung* (didactic poetry) in the thirteenth century.

Rumelant calls Der Marner a "Swabe" (Swabian), while Der Meißner says that he is either Swabian or Bavarian. It is impossible to say anything with certainty about his social background, but it is clear that his life was spent wandering from one powerful patron to another, a situation that characterizes the careers of many other contemporary poets of not-very-high social standing (the most notable example being Walther von der Vogelweide). Among the probable patrons for his Latin works were Heinrich von Zwettel and Bruno von Holstein-Schauenburg, bishop of Olmütz in Mähren. His earliest datable song praises the former on the occasion of his election as bishop of Seckau in 1230 or 1231. The German works of Der Marner were produced for a lay, courtly audience, and among their patrons were Hermann von Henneberg; a Herr von Heinberg, who has not been identified; and the Hohenstaufen Konradin (Duke Konrad of Swabia), all of whom are praised in Der Marner's didactic poetry. The last datable song, a didactic work in honor of Konradin, was composed in 1266 or 1267. On the basis of his Latin works, it is clear that Der Marner experienced a thorough education. In the Heidelberger Liederhandschrift (Heidelberg Song Manuscript) the poet is pictured drinking beside a fire in the company of a servant; the coat of arms he bears is presumably fictitious.

The Latin component of Der Marner's oeuvre consists of five songs in the style of the *Carmina Burana*: a lament of the onset of winter, a praise of Heinrich von Zwettel, a polemic against the mendicant orders, a praise of Bishop Bruno of Olmütz, and a catalogue of the liberal arts that vastly expands the traditional number of seven. Burghart Wachinger has suggested a division of the German songs, which are the most significant in Der Marner's oeuvre, into three generic groups: two groups of didactic songs, which comprise Der Marner's central literary interest, and a group of love songs.

The songs in the first group are relatively closed and thematically consistent from strophe to strophe; examples are songs 1, 6, and 11. The first deals with God's omnipotence, the redemptive power of his love, and the necessity of preparing for the Last Judgment by performing good works. Song 6 is interpreted by Wachinger as a harangue, reminiscent of Walther von der Vogelweide's "ungefüges doenen," of those in Der Marner's audience who are too foolish to be receptive to the poet's message. Song 11 deals with *gît* (greed) and *nît* (hatefulness) at court and includes a bitter attack on Reinmar, who is, according to Der Marner, only too full of these qualities.

The songs in the second group have a wide variety of themes and often lack a clear organizing principle. Here interpretation must be based on individual strophes, and Wachinger has suggested that Der Marner's frequently employed technique of placing special emphasis on final lines may provide information about the meaning of a given strophe. In the fifteenth strophe of song 15, for instance, the relationship of six species of animals to their progeny is described in the tradition of the *Physiologus*. The strophe is purely descriptive except for the final line: "mit der bezeichenunge sîn wir von der helle erloeset hie" (these symbolic meanings save us from hell). Strophe 2 of song 13 and strophe 8 of song 14 are prayers that praise God and the redemptive power he has demonstrated in the past, turning in the final lines to a request for divine assistance in the future. Strophe 14 of song 10 presents a mixture of prayer and social criticism, beginning with a reproach of God for allowing less righteous men than the poet to obtain a greater amount of wealth than he. The last line revokes this reproach, saying that he has arranged things well after all: better to be without wealth than to be rich and live a Godless life. Strophe 5 of song 14 is an implicit request for the financial favor of a patron: the dead can be embalmed, but only "guot behügde" (honor after death) is of help to rich men after they have died. The poet's implicit request comes at the end of the strophe: God gives to the giving; only through generosity can the rich man assure that he will obtain honor, and therefore salvation, after his death. Another example is strophe 16 of song 14, which emulates a song by Walther von der Vogelweide. But in contrast to Walther's verses, which base the *fröude* (joy) associated with singing on an ethical distinction between good and evil, Wachinger observes that this joy is contingent in Der Marner's verses on a favorable moment that cannot be controlled. This differing emphasis corresponds to a shift characteristic of late court literature from moral reflection to transitory amusement.

Although the love songs of Der Marner are marginal to his major interest in didactic poetry, he was interested in demonstrating his proficiency in several *Minnesang* genres. Songs 2 and 3 are dawn songs; song 4 is a standard love lament with the introductory nature imagery characteristic of Neidhart von Reuenthal; songs 7, 8, 9, and 10 couple subjective laments with didactic elements. Song 5 combines, according to Wachinger, a more religiously toned portrayal of love as a natural power that tends toward *unstaete* (inconstancy) with a courtly appraisal of it as an ethical principle; this innovative mixing of Middle Latin and vernacular literary traditions involving reflection on love is made possible only by viewing love as a not-too-serious diversion.

Although Der Marner has not received a great deal of attention from modern readers and scholars, the popularity of some of his melodies ensured that he would remain a popular figure for several centuries after his death. The "golden melody" of song 1, the "short" or "court melody" of song 14, and the "long melody" of song 15 were used by others throughout the late Middle Ages and in the sixteenth and seventeenth centuries came to be part of the repertoire of the *Meistersänger,* who considered Der Marner one of the Twelve Old Masters.

References:

Weibke Freitag, "Zum allegorischen Konzept einer Fabel des Marners (XIV.6)," in *Die mittelalterliche Literatur in der Steiermark: Akten des internationalen Symposions 1984,* edited by Alfred Ebenbauer (Bern: Lang, 1984), pp. 87–102;

John L. Riordan, "Additional Notes to a Spruch of Der Marner," *Modern Language Quarterly,* 3 (December 1942): 605–610;

Riordan, "Additional Notes to the Marner's 'Tagelieder,' " *Modern Language Quarterly,* 7 (September 1946): 329–336;

Riordan, "More Notes to Marner's 'Minnelieder,' " *Modern Language Quarterly,* 11 (June 1950): 146–155;

Hans Ulrich Schmid, "Verse Freidanks und des Marners in einer lateinischen Predigt aus Oberaltaich (clm 9690)," *Zeitschrift für deutsches Altertum,* 118, no. 3 (1989): 176–180;

Burghart Wachinger, "Anmerkungen zum Marner," *Zeitschrift für deutsches Altertum,* 114, no. 1 (1985): 70–87;

Wachinger, "Der Marner," in *Die deutsche Literatur des Mittelalters: Verfasserlexikon,* volume 6, edited by Kurt Ruh (Berlin: De Gruyter, 1987), pp. 70–79.

Mechthild von Magdeburg

(circa 1207 – circa 1282)

Margit M. Sinka
Clemson University

MAJOR WORK: *Das fließende Licht der Gottheit* (circa 1250–circa 1282)

Manuscripts: The original Middle Low German manuscript has been lost. The complete work, consisting of seven books, is preserved in an Alemannic version prepared circa 1343 to 1345 by the Basel religious community Friends of God (Stiftsbibliothek, Einsiedeln, manuscript 277). Manuscripts for fragments of the work, in various dialects and in which the order of individual chapters or blocks of chapters have been rearranged, have been preserved at Colmar (Bibliothèque de la ville, manuscript 2137), Würzburg (Franziskanerkloster, manuscript I,110), and Budapest (Országos Széchényi Könyvtár, Cod. Germ. 38). Excerpts, usually consisting of one chapter, have been found in manuscripts for various other works of the medieval period. The manuscript for the Latin translation of the first six books, prepared shortly after Mechthild's death, has been lost, but the Latin translation itself survives in two manuscripts in Basel (Universitätsbibliothek, Cod. B IX, 11 and Cod. A VIII, 6).

First publication: *Offenbarungen der Schwester Mechthild von Magdeburg, oder Das fließende Licht der Gottheit, aus der einzigen Handschrift des Stiftes Einsiedeln,* edited by P. Gall Morel (Regensburg: Manz, 1869; reprinted, Darmstadt: Wissenschaftliche Buchgesellschaft, 1980).

First publication of the Latin manuscript: *Liber specialis gratiae accedit sororis Mechtildis ejusdem ordinis Lux divinitatis,* edited by the Benedictines of Solesmes (Paris: Oudin, 1877).

Standard edition: *"Das fließende Licht der Gottheit": Nach der Einsiedler Handschrift in kritischem Vergleich mit der gesamten Überlieferung,* 2 volumes, edited by Hans Neumann and Gisela Vollmann-Profe (Munich: Artemis, 1990, 1993).

Edition in modern German: *Das fließende Licht der Gottheit,* edited by Margot Schmidt and Hans Urs von Balthasar (Einsiedeln, Zurich & Cologne: Benziger, 1955).

Editions in English: *The Revelations of Mechthild of Magdeburg (1210–1297); or, The Flowing Light of the Godhead,* translated and edited by Lucy Menzies (London & New York: Longmans, Green, 1953); *The Flowing Light of the Divinity,* translated by Christiane Mesch Galvani, edited by Susan Clark, Garland Library of Medieval Literature, volume 72, series B (New York: Garland, 1991).

Due to the poetic power of her only work, *Das fließende Licht der Gottheit* (The Flowing Light of the Divinity, circa 1250–circa 1282), Mechthild von Magdeburg ranks not only among the most admired German spiritual writers of the thirteenth century but also among the most innovative authors of medieval Germany. It can be argued that *Das fließende Licht der Gottheit* is the first extant work to use German prose to express original thought; before Mechthild, German prose was used almost exclusively for translations, mainly from Latin.

To document what she believed to be her soul's mystical journeys to God, Mechthild blends religious and secular language in unprecedented ways. She justifies her soul's yearning for spiritual union with God by means of both the Neoplatonic emanationist doctrine and courtly models of love and also draws on a wide range of motifs from biblical exegesis and from folk-song traditions. Coining many compound words and creating images suggestive of both the secular and the spiritual realms, Mechthild tends to transform whatever she uses. Matters of the spirit become sensualized; physical actions become spiritualized. Her bold linguistic combinations seem to be formed without awareness of potential limitations, in concert with her Godhead's spontaneous outpourings of love unmarked by either a beginning or an end. Though not lacking analytical material from the speculative mystical tradition represented by writers such as Saint Augustine, Origen, or Bernard of Clairvaux, Mechthild's nuanced, vivid writings concentrate on her own affective experiences. At the forefront of experiential mysticism, her book is also the first work in any European vernacular containing largely autobiographical material – though this material consists of fragments pertaining to her inner life rather than of biographical episodes in the conventional sense.

As is the case for many other authors of her era, the details of Mechthild von Magdeburg's life remain conjectural; most of the conjectures are based on the sparse references in her own writing, above all in the second chapter of the fourth book of her work. Still, the various attempts to reconstruct her life have resulted in consensus about the approximate dates of her birth, her call to the spiritual life, her arrival in Magdeburg, her joining of the convent of Helfta, and her death. The scrupulous investigations of Hans Neumann, the foremost Mechthild scholar, seem to have convinced most other critics; only Ursula Peters strongly challenges his dates, arguing not for alternate ones but for the impossibility of establishing any factual information at all from Mechthild's formulaic references to time. Yet it is unlikely that Mechthild's temporal allusions will be disregarded, especially since comments enumerating elapsed years in later portions of her book seem to confirm previous references.

Thus it remains generally accepted that Mechthild was born around 1207 in the diocese of Magdeburg, a prosperous area east of the river Elbe. Though differing on whether her parents belonged to the nobility, scholars agree that they must have been wealthy and sufficiently aware of courtly ideals and courtly language to be able to impart them to their daughter. Mechthild's repeated descriptions of herself as unlearned and uneducated are regarded as reflective of the humility topos characteristic of spiritual writings. Her confident adaptation of courtly material, as well as her biblical and liturgical knowledge, indicates that she probably enjoyed pronounced educational privileges, though these in all likelihood did not include either the study of Latin, of which she claims to be ignorant, or the kind of systematic theological training associated with elitist convent schools reserved for girls of noble birth. The passage on her brother Baldwin in the Latin version of her work, which mentions his education and subsequent status as a Dominican friar in Halle, lends additional support to the assumption that Mechthild, too, had obtained a good education.

According to her own testimony, Mechthild received "gottes gruos" (God's greeting) – that is, the call to the spiritual life – at age twelve. In the dialogue between *minne* (Lady Love) and the soul initiating her mystical writings, she says that her first call ended the happy days of her childhood and her carefree behavior among friends and relatives. God's summons did not, as was generally the case in males, lead to an abrupt break from familiar surroundings and the assumption of a radically different kind of life. Although she insists that God thereafter repeated his "greeting" on a daily basis, she did not leave her family until about eleven years after her first call – that is, around 1230.

Choosing the kind of voluntary exile often associated with those committed to the spiritual life, Mechthild moved to the town of Magdeburg. She feared, however, that her only friend in Magdeburg, an unidentified man, might influence her to abandon the spiritual path she had chosen. The identity of that person has intrigued critics. The most forceful arguments focus on Wichmann von Arnstein and Heinrich von Halle, but neither would have been likely to dissuade her from a life of poverty. At any rate, she says her fears proved unfounded, for God fortified her against earthly temptations by repeatedly blessing her with visions and other inconceivable wonders.

On the basis of Mechthild's reference to herself as a Beguine in the town of Magdeburg, many critics – especially feminists – have investigated the European Beguine movement, hoping to supply more definitive data on her life. Most scholars agree that the Beguines constituted the first European women's movement. Starting in Belgium and the Netherlands and spreading to most parts of Europe, the Beguine communities were among the alternative forms of religious life that proliferated in Europe in the twelfth and thirteenth centuries. Whereas women could previously pursue religious vocations only by entering convents, they could now stake out a spiritual life in a great variety of newly formed communities, many of them dedicated to leading lives of poverty. While *Beguine* gradually came to refer to all holy women who were not nuns, at first it signified women who formed small communities in towns and cities and frequently devoted themselves to evangelical lives. They did not take vows, they renounced worldly riches, and they strongly upheld ideals such as chastity. Many supported themselves through weaving or tending the sick; but many others, to the consternation of church and civic authorities, roamed city streets and the countryside, begging for their subsistence.

The theory that they came mainly from poor backgrounds has been discredited; most often, as is assumed of Mechthild, they seem to have come from the upper bourgeoisie or the lower nobility. For a long time it was supposed that there was a surplus of women in both secular and religious life, partly because the increasingly high dowries women were expected to bring into marriage, and the equally escalating cost of contributions demanded for admittance to the convents became prohibitive, even for the moderately wealthy. Other arguments hold that husbands could not be found for many women and that the Cistercian convents, already filled, refused to expand to accommodate more women. According to such "surplus" theories, women turned to the only option left for them – the Beguine life.

Feminists have strongly objected to this line of reasoning. Caroline Walker Bynum contends that the Beguine life probably appealed to many women as a novel and attractive alternative to cloistered life. The lack of hierarchical structures in the Beguine communities may also have drawn enthusiastic adherents. Mechthild's book lends no support to any of these conjectures, though her expression of fear that her friend in Magdeburg would interfere with her commitment indicates that her decision to pursue a religious life without the comforts of worldly riches was her own choice.

Das fließende Licht der Gottheit contains many passages indicative of a Beguine existence, particularly references to ministering to the sick, offering spiritual counsel, rejecting worldly wealth, and renouncing physical pleasures in favor of spiritual rewards. The tribulations Mechthild repeatedly mentions may have been merely the hardships necessarily associated with a life of poverty, as Peters seems to believe, or they may have been connected with the peripheral status of the Beguines. Mechthild's accounts of her spiritual experiences may have been assailed by her detractors – who remain unnamed in her work – precisely because she was a Beguine, an outsider. She may, in addition, have been one of the "isolated" Beguines Joanna Ziegler considers so prevalent in northern Germany (isolated in contrast to the cloistered Flemish Beguines or the collective and corporate Beguines enjoying power and respect in the Netherlands). It was such isolated Beguines who were most often criticized for heretical notions. By the time of the Council of Lyon in 1274 they had become so irritating to church authorities that they were publicly chastised for shockingly inept Bible

exegeses and for their quest for theological novelties. To categorize Mechthild as an isolated Beguine living on the periphery of society seems, however, unwarranted. In prayers interspersed throughout her work she demonstrates familiarity with the Dominican order, which was responsible for offering spiritual guidance to many Beguine communities of the thirteenth century.

Mechthild's visions constitute the first written manifestation of experientially based mysticism in Germany. The affective, experimental knowledge claimed by many female mystics proved to be far more immediate than the speculative mysticism that characterized most male writings and even the prophetic visions of Mechthild's female predecessor, Hildegard von Bingen. Thus, Mechthild may have been criticized for the subjective tone of her recorded visions. Her many references to enemies remain vague, restricted to phrasings such as "als mich mîn viende jagent" (when my enemies pursue me), but she probably incurred the wrath of clerics for her unrelenting criticism of their worldly ways. Mechthild does not attack the institution of the church, though she does promote its reform so vigorously that she has been considered the female precursor of Martin Luther. Twice in her work, in the prologue to book 1 and in book 5, chapter 34, God says that the book is addressed to all spiritual people, both evil and good, "wand wenne die súle vallent, so mag das werk nút gestan" (for if the pillars fall, the building cannot stand). Mechthild directs her criticism most of all at the corrupt members of the clergy, though she does not spare the pope or the emperor.

Mechthild might also have incurred enmity because of the religious doctrines her revelations challenge, directly and indirectly. People lacking theological expertise, as Kurt Ruh points out, easily succumbed to heretical thought; and Mechthild makes statements directly in conflict with church teachings, generally as if she were the first one to utter such "truths." Her claim that the nature of the human soul is identical with the nature of the Deity might have led to the tribulations she mentions; there is, however, no record of Mechthild's being brought to trial for heretical statements or having to justify her stances before church authorities. Yet it remains likely that her orthodoxy was questioned particularly regarding her commitment to the practice of Christian virtues. In chapter 44 of book 1 she says that the soul needs to refresh itself after dancing ecstatically in praise of Christ. Rejecting suggestions to cool herself in the tears of Mary Magdalene, in the blood of martyrs, in the wisdom of the

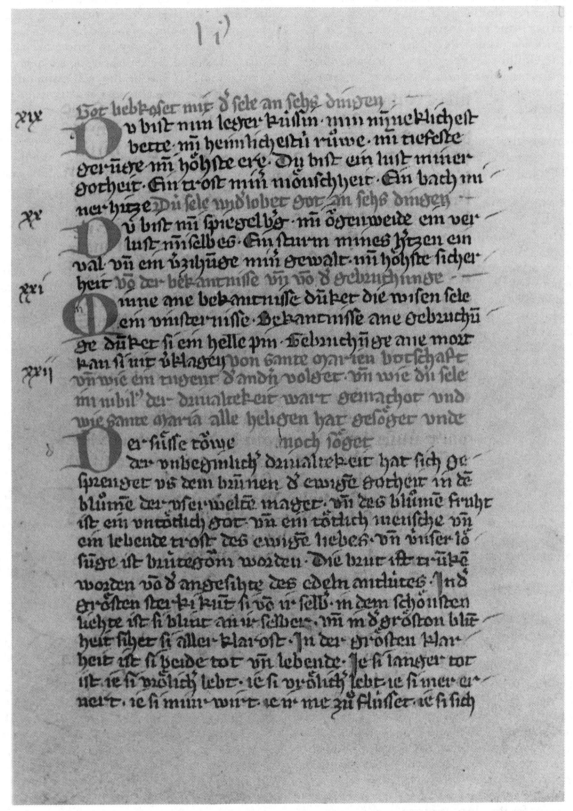

Page from the fourteenth-century manuscript for the Alemannic version of Mechthild von Magdeburg's Das fließende
Licht der Gottheit *(Einsiedeln, Stiftsbibliothek, ms. 277, f.8r)*

Apostles, or in the hard life of John the Baptist – all of these expressions representing the practice of the virtues – the soul insists on drinking the *ungemengeten win* (undistilled, pure wine) of union with the Godhead. Such passages have brought accusations that Mechthild advocated bypassing the hard work related to the spiritual life.

Likewise, her references to the soul's *ze nihte werden* (becoming annihilated) – the ecstatic end phase of mystical union with the Deity – may have caused consternation. Annihilation of the soul, which became a popular but controversial theme in later western European mysticism, was also connected with what was perceived as attempts of mystics to place themselves above the need to practice the virtues in this life. Modern critics easily dispel the applicability of this charge to Mechthild by pointing to the prominent role of the virtues in all seven books of *Das fließende Licht der Gottheit,* yet her contemporaries may have perceived the work as diminishing or even eliminating the importance of Christian virtues. Also, the widespread suspicion that mystics emphasized their unitive experiences with the Godhead in part to eliminate the necessity of ecclesiastical mediators could have led Mechthild's "enemies" to take offense at passages in her work emphasizing the Godhead's impatient desire for the soul – a motif that she introduced into mystical literature.

Whatever the objections to Mechthild's work, they surfaced soon after she started writing. The concluding section of book 2 mentions threats that if Mechthild does not stop writing, her book will be burned. Turning to God for advice, she receives a vision in which God holds her book in his right hand and counsels her not to worry, for no one is capable of burning truth. Still, Mechthild continues to worry. In the first chapter of book 3 she says: "Nu voerhte ich got, ob ich swige, und voerhte aber unbekante lúte, ob ich schribe" (I fear God if I keep silent, but fear uncomprehending people if I write). Yet, firmly believing God's word that "Das buoch ist drivaltig und bezeichent alleine mich" (the book is triune and refers only to me) and convinced by her continuing visions that she cannot do otherwise, she continues writing. As the book progresses, she seems to become less fearful of her enemies. In book 6, chapter 3, she derides the secular clergy for reeking of the same impurity as goats. In chapter 36, after calling one of her detractors a Pharisee incapable of differentiating between physical appearances and spiritual truths, she vehemently ridicules priests for their hypocrisy and hatred.

As Mechthild's criticism of the corrupt clergy became more forceful in the course of her writing, the enmity of the clergy toward her could also have increased. There is a consensus among the critics that she entered the convent of Helfta, in the vicinity of Eisleben in Saxony, to escape her enemies. This view should, however, remain a hypothesis because it seems to rest on the tacit assumption that her *multas tribulationes* (many tribulations), a phrase appearing in the prologue of the Latin version of her work, caused her to seek refuge in the Helfta convent. Perhaps these tribulations refer only to her life of poverty. It is, at any rate, clear from several passages in book 7 that Mechthild's enemies continued their verbal attacks even after she became a nun at Helfta.

Though other critics agree with Neumann that Mechthild went to Helfta around 1270, most have rejected his conjecture that she did not move directly from the Magdeburg Beguine community to the Helfta convent. Neumann suggests that Mechthild may not have spent forty years in Magdeburg, as is generally assumed on the basis of the Latin prologue to the German manuscript, but that she returned to her home after thirty years in Magdeburg because she was suffering from a severe illness and was convinced of her impending death. On the basis of several observations in book 6 pertaining to Mechthild's renewed inner battles in regard to settling on a life of wealth and worldly comforts or continuing on the spiritual path she had chosen thirty years earlier, Neumann hypothesizes that these deliberations would have been far more likely to occur in her home environment than in Magdeburg. Instead of returning to Magdeburg after leaving home the second time, Mechthild may have immediately entered the convent of Helfta. From her account in book 7, chapter 27, of a visit to her at the convent by relatives and friends, it is reasonable to assume that Helfta was close to her birthplace.

While the possibility remains that Mechthild turned to the cloistered life to flee her enemies, it is just as likely that she sought an environment offering greater security and more receptivity to her revelations. The Cistercian convent of Helfta, which was advised by Dominicans, would have been the ideal spiritual retreat for the embattled, ailing Mechthild. She was warmly received by Abbess Gertrud von Hackeborn, who was known for her insistence on the rigorous study of the Scriptures and the liberal arts. Gertrud's sister Mechthild von Hackeborn, respected for her musical talents and called "the nightingale of the Lord," was also at Helfta, along with the scholar Gertrud von Helfta, who later became known as Gertrud die Große (Gertrude the Great). Highly regarded by both clergy and laity, who frequently consulted them on spiritual matters, these nuns held Mechthild von Magdeburg in the highest esteem and were influenced by her work.

Though Mechthild von Magdeburg is the author of the earliest writing associated with Helfta, the works of other Helfta nuns seem to have enjoyed more renown in the fourteenth century. This disparity might be partly attributable to the continued criticism leveled at Mechthild even while she was a revered member of the deeply spiritual environment of Helfta. On Mechthild's death, generally dated around 1282, Gertrud von Hackeborn prayed for divine signs to silence Mechthild's critics. These signs never came, but both she and Gertrud die Große interpreted Mechthild's death in their own writings as the earthly pilgrim's arrival at God's heavenly court. While Mechthild von Magdeburg was not canonized, her fellow Helfta nuns clearly considered her a holy woman.

There is no doubt that Mechthild wrote book 7, the last of the books comprising *Das fließende Licht der Gottheit,* at Helfta. All critics agree on the circumstances under which book 7 was written, and none disputes that its chapters are organized in the order in which they were conceived. Critics also concur in the belief that chapter 27, which reports that visiting relatives and friends complained about losses of material possessions, was probably written in the midst of war years, around 1281 or 1282. Since Mechthild died soon afterward, this chapter has proven helpful in pinpointing the earliest possible date for her death.

The single manuscript in German containing all seven books of Mechthild's work, discovered by Carl Greith in 1861 in Einsiedeln, includes a Latin prologue specifying that Mechthild started writing in 1250 and continued for approximately fifteen years. The prologue also contains an index of main topics treated in her work. Since the index pertains to only five of the seven books, critics arrived at the conclusion that books 1 through 5 were written between 1250 and 1265. Agreement that book 7 originated at Helfta was also easily attained. Thus book 6 became the focus of controversy. Some doubted that there had originally been a separate sixth book and suggested that the one in the Einsiedeln manuscript had been compiled from chapters extracted from the first five, thereby maintaining that the sixth book, too, had been written between 1250 and 1265. This theory lost adherents when tested against the two Latin manuscripts of Mechthild's work discovered in Basel. Though not containing the seventh book, the Latin version did have a sixth book along with a Latin prefix referring to contents pertaining to all six. This finding convinced most critics that there had been an independent sixth book, but it was difficult to date it. Thus many resorted to the simplest conclusion, however imprecise: that Mechthild started to write in 1250 and finished her entire work in a span of somewhat more than thirty years.

This conclusion remained unsatisfactory to those concerned with discovering the stages of Mechthild's spiritual life. The reliability of both Latin prologues was also questionable, since neither seemed to indicate close acquaintance with the circumstances of Mechthild's life. Critics returned, therefore, to the bodies of the German and Latin manuscripts to determine a more secure chronology. It was generally concluded that books 1 through 4 in particular belonged together thematically and in their choice of imagery. Substantial evidence indicates later revisions of these books, mainly through the addition of excerpts. Even the autobiographical chapter – book 4, chapter 2 – might contain some of these additions.

Again, it was book 6 that proved to be the most difficult to categorize, but studies of its scattered allusions to historical personages and historical events indicated that it extended from 1260 to at least 1271. In all likelihood, because of references characteristic of convent life, the last chapters of book 6 were written after Mechthild entered the convent at Helfta. According to Neumann, the thirty-third chapter indicates Mechthild's relief at separating herself from family bonds and rejoining a spiritual community united in the cultivation of poverty. Further, the prayer constituting chapter 37 definitely reflects a convent setting, and chapter 43, the concluding one of book 6, speaks of Mechthild as a *swester* (sister). That the time between the writing of some sections of book 6 and the writing of some sections of book 7 could not have been very long is evident from Mechthild's complaint in book 6, chapter 4, that she is worse off than thirty years before and from her claim in book 7, chapter 36, that she is just as unworthy of writing God's book as she was thirty or more years before.

Just when it seemed that the debates surrounding the time frames for the writing of the first six books had subsided, new doubts surfaced. Some feminist critics argued that the chronological divisions of those books had been determined on the basis of unreliable, stock references to time characteristic of the medieval period. Noting that the convent of Helfta initiated, in a highly supportive atmosphere, a considerable amount of women's religious writing, they suggest that much more of Mechthild's book was written at Helfta than had been assumed previously. This suggestion seems far less tenable, however, than conclusions based on historic references in Mechthild's work.

Residual doubts about chronology seem more justified on other grounds. The view that Mechthild jotted down her visions on loose sheets, which were compiled into chapters and books by her spiritual adviser, is largely based on a reference in book 5, chapter 12, of the Latin version to Heinrich von Halle as the one who gathered her writings into a single volume and divided them into six books; added to this passage is the comment that Mechthild outlived him and, after his death, saw him in a dream holding her book in heaven as a reward for having written it down. In contrast, the sole function of the unidentified Heinrich in book 5, chapter 12, of the extant German manuscript is to express amazement at Mechthild's surprising words. In book 4, chapter 22, the German manuscript mentions that a Heinrich has died, but it neither reveals his identity nor does it grant him any credit for the production of Mechthild's book.

On the other hand, the German version contains its own confusing reference to the writing of the book. Discussing the threats to burn her work, Mechthild intercedes with God on behalf of "dîne schribere, die das buoch na mir haben geschriben" (your writers, who have written the book according to me). Nowhere else in the German version does Mechthild mention receiving writing help, and the Latin manuscript mentions only Heinrich. With Heinrich in mind, Neumann and Margot Schmidt have reluctantly followed Hubert Stierling's suggestion that the text be emended to indicate a single writer, consistent with the single writer mentioned in the Latin prologue to the German manuscript.

The question then arises whether the other writer, if there was one, simply copied down what Mechthild said or altered Mechthild's formulations. Even if one eliminates the possibility of a collaborative writer, the question of Heinrich's role in the production of the original Middle Low German manuscript remains: whether he edited it considerably, rearranged material within individual chapters, and reorganized the whole, or simply collated Mechthild's writings in the order he received them, limiting his contribution to the division of the chapters into books.

Neumann's carefully argued view that Heinrich's contribution was limited to encouragement, collation, and dissemination seems to be gaining

adherents. Neumann notes Mechthild's repeated assurances that she is the medium for God's truth and that the book is actually God's, not hers; surely Heinrich would not have wanted or dared to emend God's words. Neither would he have interfered with the chronology of the visions determined by God, nor would Mechthild have tolerated his interference, as she makes clear in response to his objection in book 5, chapter 12, to her surprising words. To be sure, she considers herself an inadequate vehicle for God's truths, but she does not doubt that God has chosen her to convey them in her own words, irrespective of the level of erudition they reflect. In book 2, chapter 26, her Godhead expresses the same belief in a particularly memorable manner: "Das ist mir . . . ein gros êre . . . das der ungelerte munt die gelêrte zungen . . . lêret" (it is for me . . . a great honor . . . that the unlearned mouth . . . teaches the learned tongues).

Against the claim that Heinrich rearranged the writings, thus creating his own organization of them, Neumann remarks that there is no discernible organization: the writings are not arranged according to themes, specific religious messages, or any other logical principle. They seem to be collated in the order in which the visions occurred to Mechthild from the time she started writing. Those defending Mechthild as the only author of the work tend to believe that the chapters are indeed presented in the order in which she wrote them.

There is agreement that whoever prepared the Latin translation did tamper substantially with both the content and organization of the original. That *Das fließende Licht* was translated into Latin at all attests to its high standing in ecclesiastical circles. Perhaps to increase its instructional value for clerics acting as religious mentors for women in Beguine communities and convents, the Latin translation eliminated particularly erotic passages, rephrased or left out questionable theological tenets, and rearranged sections to emphasize moral lessons.

For a long time the Latin translation was attributed to Heinrich; but one wonders why he would have altered the Latin version so drastically if he did not change the German and, conversely, if he did change the German, why he would have elected totally different changes for the Latin. These questions have become moot since it has been conclusively determined that the Latin translation originated after Mechthild's death and that Heinrich died before Mechthild. The Latin translation must have existed by the 1290s since Dietrich of Apolda's *Life of Saint Dominic* (circa 1298) contains long passages from it. Today it is assumed that the Latin translation was prepared by more than one person, in all likelihood by Dominicans in the Halle cloister that Mechthild's brother Baldwin had joined.

Conclusive answers to questions about editorial changes in the writing and organization, which could have provided information on Mechthild's spiritual growth and the development of her singular language usage, are unattainable because both the original Middle Low German copy and the original Latin translation have been lost. The only extant manuscript of the entire work, in the monastic library at Einsiedeln, is an Alemannic version prepared around 1343 to 1345 in Basel by the Friends of God, a group formed around the secular priest Heinrich von Nördlingen. Like the Latin version, which is preserved in two manuscripts also prepared in Basel – one in the middle of the fourteenth century and one around 1500 – the Alemannic version is not a direct translation of the original. It is probable that several Middle High German and even other Alemannic translations preceded it, each of them eliminating passages from Mechthild's text or adding to it.

Heinrich von Nördlingen has usually been credited with the Alemannic translation produced in Basel, but this assumption has been discredited by Neumann. He notes that excerpts from *Das fließende Licht* in one of Heinrich's letters from 1345 are written in language that departs substantially from that of the manuscript. Perhaps Heinrich translated from another manuscript, deliberately altered his first translation, or wrote the excerpts from memory; but, on the basis of Heinrich's letters and other writings, Neumann concluded that the Alemannic manuscript shows no evidence of Heinrich's Swabian vocabulary or the style characteristic of his writings at that time. Heinrich could not have finished the translation much earlier than the date of his letter, since another of his letters testifies that his first acquaintance with *Das fließende Licht* could have occurred no earlier than 1343.

In spite of the lack of clarity surrounding the authorship and editing of the original manuscript, as well as later transcriptions and translations of it, including those into Latin, the manuscript at Einsiedeln is generally considered a close approximation of Mechthild's original. The Latin translation has proved to be a reliable source for clearing up corruptions of the German version and for solving some of its riddles, such as the identities of the Baldwin and Heinrich mentioned in its pages. Fragments recovered in the twentieth century, as well as short excerpts from Mechthild's work sprinkled liberally throughout other medieval spiritual writings

– mostly without crediting Mechthild as the source – also confirm the reliability of the manuscript at Einsiedeln. It is now accepted that it maintains the sequential organization of the original and that linguistically it is more a recasting of the original than a re-creation of it.

At the same time it is likely that the original German version was often taken apart as various segments were arbitrarily chosen for devotional literature in spiritual houses or for chapters in the mystical anthologies that proliferated in the thirteenth century. Nonetheless, intact German manuscripts must have reached the Friends of God in Basel. Their Alemannic version assured the wide dissemination of Mechthild's work in what was then considered the southern part of Germany – for example, to spiritual women living in hermitages, such as Margaretha Ebner, and to clerics in the Rhineland.

Almost all branches of Mechthildian influence can be traced to the manuscript tradition represented by Basel, including the extensive use of passages from *Das fließende Licht* in *Der Minne Spiegel* (The Mirror of Love), a popular work of the fifteenth century. Attempts to identify a north German manuscript tradition have been futile, but because of the discovery of a Budapest manuscript representing approximately one-tenth of the original work, an East High German tradition and, thus, a wider sphere for Mechthild's influence than had been presumed can be stipulated. Speculation that Mechthild's influence extended to Italy has been abandoned since it was proved that Dante did not pattern the figure of Matilda in the *Purgatory* part of his *Divine Comedy* (completed 1321) after Mechthild. It is more likely that Mechthild influenced speculative German mystics such as Meister Eckhart – for example, in the matter of God and the soul sharing an identical nature – but no conclusive proof can be found for this argument, just as no evidence supports the hypothesis that women mystics influenced their spiritual advisers far more than had previously been realized. All the trails of influence Mechthild may have left had disappeared by the early part of the sixteenth century, and the work that Heinrich von Nördlingen had praised as "das lustigistz tützsch" (the most marvelous German) and "das innerlichst rürend minenschosz" (the most moving tribute to love) was rediscovered in Einsiedeln only in the second half of the nineteenth century.

Since then Mechthild's sparkling poetic language has stunned readers. As Ruh points out, there were many other female mystics during her era, especially in southern Germany, but Mechthild's poetic gifts remain unparalleled. Like other medieval spiritual writers, Mechthild herself seems unaware of her literary talent and is concerned only with convincing others of the trustworthiness of her writings. Throughout her work she stresses the reality of her experiences and the reliability of her spiritual senses in recording them – most emphatically, perhaps, in chapter 13 of book 4: "Ich enkan noch mag nit schriben, ich sehe es mit den ougen mîner sele und hoere es mit den oren mînes ewigen geistes und befinde in allen lîden mînes lichamen die kraft des heiligen geistes" (I cannot nor do I wish to write unless I see it with the eyes of my soul and hear it with the ears of my eternal spirit and feel the power of the Holy Spirit in all limbs of my body). In book 6, chapter 36, she warns against equating the knowledge grasped by the physical senses with the spiritual truths conveyed to the soul in divine visions: "Man mag gotliche gaba mit menschlichen sinne nit begrifen. . . . Das man mit vleischlichen ougen mag gesehen, mit vleischlichen oren mag gehoeren, mit vleischlichem munde mag gesprechen, das ist also ungelich der offenen warheit der minnenden sele als ein wachs lieht der claren sunnen" (One cannot comprehend divine gifts with human senses. . . . Whatever one can see with the eyes of the flesh, hear with the ears of the flesh, say with the mouth of the flesh is as unequal to the open truth of the loving soul as candlelight is to the clear sun). Here, as in other passages, Mechthild touches on a major problem for all mystics who believe that they have been directed by God to convey to others the mystical union they have experienced: how to communicate the ineffable. By its very nature knowledge of the divine is supposed to be incommunicable through human means; no earthly language can reveal its essence. On the other hand, affective mystics are incapable of remaining silent: having experienced God's overspilling, fecund love, they themselves overflow with abundant love demanding expression. In the recording of their visions, assurances of the necessity of communicating their insights despite their own inadequacy are considered obligatory. In Mechthild's case, however, the humility topoi might have seemed particularly unconvincing, for her vivid use of language by no means suggests verbal inadequacy. Perhaps for this reason she repeatedly insists that it is God himself who is speaking through her book. In the prologue to chapter 1 of book 1, Mechthild has her Godhead announce that he produced the book because he could not curtail his diffusive plenitude. At the same point the Godhead even declares the title of the book. Her book is a divine work, Mechthild remarks em-

phatically elsewhere; it is the Godhead's book, not hers, she says at every opportunity.

Her self-deprecatory comments might have spared Mechthild from criticism, but passages such as one in book 3, chapter 15, practically call for it: "Ich muos mich selber melden, sol ich gottes guete werlich moegen verbringen" (in order to spread God's goodness, I have to announce my own self). Here Mechthild seems to stress her own responsibility in assuring that the message of God's goodness is communicated to others and thus, perhaps inadvertently, points to her own importance. Despite her self-chastisement and emphasis on humility throughout her work, she projects a joyous, self-confident attitude that may have prompted and increased clerical antagonism toward her.

Perhaps one of the reasons for her choosing to write in prose – though a prose that spills easily into poetry and dramatic dialogues – was to hinder others from questioning the veracity of her visions: prose was the medium associated with religious writing. It was, however, expected to be Latin prose. Mechthild's fellow nuns at Helfta, who were younger than she, conformed to this expectation, as her predecessor Hildegard von Bingen had. Lyric forms and the German vernacular were, on the other hand, associated with courtly literature – that is, with fictitious works representing at least some authorial individualism. Thus Mechthild's use of German may have automatically subjected her writings to suspicion. Possibly to deflect criticism, Mechthild repeatedly apologizes for not being able to express herself in Latin, implying that she recognizes the limits of her Middle Low German vernacular in conveying the nature of her mystical experiences. Likewise, she apologizes for being unlearned in scriptural knowledge. Since she does, however, resort to Latin terms more than thirty times in the work and liberally uses scriptural material – though only once specifically quoting from the Bible – her statements probably refer to her lack of formal theological training.

Earlier criticism stressed the bridal mysticism prominent in Mechthild's work, undoubtedly influenced by Saint Bernard's eighty-six sermons on the Song of Songs, circulated among Dominicans in Magdeburg by Wichmann von Arnstein. Bernard's spiritual interpretations of the eroticism in the Song of Songs and his exegeses making the lover of the poem Christ and the beloved – for the first time in the history of Christianity – the soul rather than the Virgin Mary or the church probably inspired and enriched Mechthild's bridal mysticism. In turn, Mechthild changed the genderless soul in Bernard's writing into a female one. Thus the soul as bride in Mechthild's book dances, hops, runs, and flies to heaven. It hunts and is hunted. In heaven, inebriated, it continues to play and dance; only union with God can quench its resulting thirst. Its longing is rewarded with victory again and again. Mechthild's is not the immobile Godhead far removed from humanity and impervious to the latter's frenzied attempts to approach him but an active Godhead whose longing for union with the soul matches the soul's longing for union with the divine. Mechthild thus introduced into German mystical literature the notion of the Godhead's impatient desire for the soul, a somewhat heretical tenet that would play an important role in Meister Eckhart's mysticism and in the papal allegations against him.

In the first five chapters few vestiges remain of the twenty years of tiredness and illness that were Mechthild's lot before she started writing down her visions in 1250, but abundant proof occurs of the eight joyous years she experienced afterward. In unconcealed delight she synthesizes the most disparate traditions, such as folklore and liturgy. Her bridal mysticism joyously fuses spiritual and courtly vocabulary or courtly and scriptural situations – for example, the courtly greeting and the heavenly summons or the courtly and heavenly dance. Although the speculative mysticism of such predecessors as Saint Bernard or Saint Victor is by no means absent from Mechthild's writings – paradoxes, antitheses, and allegorical explications recur in her work – emotive aspects clearly dominate. Mechthild evokes especially the symbolic power of images. Since the infinite and the finite were thought to coincide in symbols, many medieval mystics wishing to manifest the divine in matter availed themselves of the evocative capacities of symbols. Drawing most of her symbols – the mirror, the globe, the stone, the mountain – from biblical sources or from other religious writings, Mechthild infuses them with abundant spiritual content accessible mainly through the senses.

With her highly developed sense of symbolism Mechthild is able to discern Trinitarian principles in all creation. Her Trinitarian Godhead is characterized by a fecund plenitude of being; as in Neoplatonic emanationist theory, he necessarily diffuses his essence; he must spontaneously overflow with the fullness of his Love. It is the humanity of Christ incarnate, rather than the triune Godhead or even Christ as Logos, who helps Mechthild the most in penetrating the mysteries of human and divine love.

Religious ardor kindled by Christ's humanity was already circulating in Europe. Mechthild could easily have absorbed and interrelated material transmitted to her by her spiritual guide (or guides), read in the circular letters of Dominican spiritual directors, or heard at devotional services. In addition to Saint Bernard, Mechthild's Christological concern could have been inspired by several sources. As her emphasis on *gebundene minne* (bound love) throughout her work indicates – even her Godhead experiences it in book 2, chapter 25 – she must have been informed of Victorine mysticism and its stress on *amor ligans,* gathering the mind into the unity necessary for developing the kind of wonder that enables the soul to catch fire and bind it to Christ. She was, moreover, well acquainted with the Franciscan dedication to imitating Christ in the material world, with the Dominican emphasis on exemplary behavior through imitating Christ also, and with the cult of the Eucharist so common among Beguines.

In Mechthild's work the emanationist, flowing light of the Trinitarian Godhead interrelates with everything else that flows: nourishing milk, fertilizing water, and inebriating wine. But she penetrates the ineffable mysteries of active Trinitarian love by means of Christ. Much as the Christ of Dante's end vision archetypically contains the whole universe, Mechthild in book 4, chapter 2, sees the entire Trinity in Christ: "Do sach ich mit mîner selen ougen in himmelscher wunne die schoenen menscheit únsers herren Jhesu Christi, und ich bekante an sînem heren antlútte die heligen drivaltekeit, des vatter ewekeit, des súnes arbeit, des heligen geistes suessekeit" (In heavenly bliss, I then saw with the eyes of my soul the beautiful humanity of our Lord Jesus Christ, and I recognized in his splendid countenance the holy Trinity, the Father's eternity, the son's travails, and the Holy Spirit's sweetness). In book 6, chapter 16, she is surprised by how prominently the Trinity features Christ, who then hastens to inform her that his is a soul just like hers.

It is, however, the blood of Christ incarnate, shed in love to absolve humanity of sin, that most often leads to Mechthild's mystical experiences. Mechthild may be the first German mystic to mention Christ's Sacred Heart, relating its flowing blood to the wound in the crucified Jesus' side inflicted by the centurion's spear. By imitating the Passion of Christ in all its stages – the assumption of humility, suffering, the acceptance of derision, alienation from God, and the torture of the body – the soul becomes worthy of the mystical union implied by Christ's Resurrection.

Mechthild's stress on the "dark night of the soul," on actively seeking alienation from God, has caused critics to remark that hers is not the prototypical upward journey of the soul or the traditional mystical journey consisting of the purgative, illuminative, and unitive stages. Mechthild herself comments in book 6, chapter 20, that "der minne nature ist, das si allererst vlússet von suessekeit, dar nach wirt si rîche in der bekantnisse, zem dritten male wirt si gîrig in der verworfenheit" (It is love's nature to flow in the beginning with sweetness, after that it will become rich in knowledge, and in the third stage it will be yearnful in depravity). Here Mechthild divides the mystical journey into illuminative, unitive, and alienated stages. In her *imitatio christi* she places the greatest emphasis on Christ's descent into the abyss of his *gottes vroemdunge* (alienation from God), the most important precondition of his redemption. When the soul has reached its most abysmal state, it is subject to the greatest temptations and must prove itself by choosing the most severe renunciations: the rejection of the Godhead's gifts and his offer of divine union. Before it has repeated the entire cycle involved in imitating the path of the crucified Christ, the soul considers union with the Godhead premature and, therefore, futile: it would be doomed to being another of the short, temporary unions the soul has previously experienced rather than the eternal one it seeks. Thus, Mechthild accents the downward, sinking aspect of emanationist thought. Paradoxically, the descent ultimately turns into an ascent, ending in the merger of the soul's nature with God's nature.

The imitation of Christ's Passion Cycle, depicted in considerable detail in the tenth chapter of book 3, seems to gain increasing importance with Mechthild's advancing age. In books 6 and 7 the weakness that had plagued her before she started writing set in again, heightened by the infirmities of old age and seldom relieved by unitive experiences with the divine. Mechthild longs more and more for the physical death that will finally free her soul from the prison of her body. Contrary to Saint Bernard, who had urged the soul to obtain final rest in Christ's wounds, represented by the crevices of a rock, Mechthild demands in book 7, chapter 58, that Christ lie down in her wounds. Then, instead of receiving only the love she can bear, she would finally receive the full measure of Christ's love – the precondition to her departure from earth. Clearly Mechthild has come to the end of the *via affirmativa* and is ready for nothingness, the last stage of the *via negativa* advocated by Pseudo-Diony-

sius the Aeropagite. Yet modern readers may find it difficult to imagine Mechthild in nothingness because of her incisive descriptions of hell, purgatory, and heaven. It seems more appropriate to picture her in heaven, partaking of the fecund, creative plenitude of the Trinity intimated by her writings.

Mechthild von Magdeburg deserves to be remembered for the first spiritual autobiography in the German language and the first German account of a life spent in the imitation of Christ. Her work still effectively conveys the abundant attractions of the inner life and the strengths it can harness for social and humanitarian concerns. Her sparkling, inventive language has survived the test of time. Even today it reveals the power of symbolism to convey affective experiential knowledge.

Bibliography:

Gertrud Jaron Lewis, "Mechthild von Magdeburg," in *Bibliographie zur deutschen Frauenmystik des Mittelalters* (Berlin: Schmidt, 1989), pp. 164–183.

References:

Caroline Walker Bynum, *Jesus as Mother* (Berkeley: University of California Press, 1982);

Bynum, "Religious Women in the Later Middle Ages," in *World Spirituality: An Encyclopedic History of the Religious Quest,* volume 17: *Christian Spirituality: High Middle Ages and Reformation,* edited by Jill Raitt (New York: Crossroads, 1987), pp. 121–139;

Eric Colledge, "Mechthild of Magdeburg," *Month,* 25 (June 1961): 325–336;

Joan Gibson, "Mechthild von Magdeburg," in *A History of Women Philosophers,* volume 2: *Medieval, Renaissance and Enlightenment Women Philosophers, A.D. 500–1600,* edited by Mary Ellen Waithe (Boston: Kluwer, 1989), pp. 115–140;

Alois Maria Haas, "Schools of Late Medieval Mysticism," in *Christian Spirituality: High Middle Ages and Reformation,* edited by Raitt, pp. 140–175;

Haas, "Die Struktur der mystischen Erfahrung nach Mechthild von Magdeburg," *Freiburger Zeitschrift für Philosophie und Theologie,* 22 (1975): 3–34;

John Howard, "The German Mystic: Mechthild of Magdeburg," in *Medieval Women Writers,* edited by Katharina M. Wilson (Athens: University of Georgia Press, 1984), pp. 153–185;

Niklaus Largier, " 'in einicheit und in der wüestunge': Entfremdung und Selbsterkenntnis bei Mechthild von Magdeburg und Hadewijch," in *Begegnung mit dem "Fremden":*

Grenzen – Traditionen – Vergleiche. Akten des VIII. Internationalen Germanisten-Kongresses, Tokyo 1990, volume 9, section 15: *Erfahrene und imaginierte Fremde,* edited by Yoshinori Shichiji (Munich: Iudicium, 1991), pp. 268–280;

Grete Lüers, *Die Sprache der Deutschen Mystik des Mittelalters im Werke der Mechthild von Magdeburg* (Darmstadt: Wissenschaftliche Buchgesellschaft, 1966);

John Margetts, "Latein und Volkssprache bei Mechthild von Magdeburg," *Amsterdamer Beiträge zur älteren Germanistik,* 12 (1977): 119–136;

Hans Neumann, "Beiträge zur Textgeschichte des 'Fließenden Lichts der Gottheit' und zur Lebensgeschichte Mechthilds von Magdeburg," *Nachrichten der Akademie der Wissenschaften in Göttingen,* no. 3 (1954): 27–82;

Neumann, "Problemata Mechthildiana," *Zeitschrift für deutsches Altertum und deutsche Literatur,* 82 (December 1948): 143–172;

Wilhelm Oehl, ed., *Deutsche Mystikerbriefe des Mittelalters 1100–1550* (Darmstadt: Wissenschaftliche Buchgesellschaft, 1972);

Ursula Peters, *Religiöse Erfahrung als literarisches Faktum: Zur Vorgeschichte und Genese frauenmystischer Texte des 13. und 14. Jahrhunderts* (Tübingen: Niemeyer, 1988);

Kurt Ruh, "Beginenmystik: Hadewijch, Mechthild von Magdeburg, Marguerite Porets," *Zeitschrift für deutsches Altertum und deutsche Literatur,* 106, no. 3 (1977): 265–277;

Margot Schmidt, "Mechthilde de Magdebourg," in *Dictionnaire de Spiritualité, Ascetique et Mystique: Doctrine et Histoire,* edited by M. Viller and others (Paris: Beauchesne, 1980), pp. 880–882;

William Seaton, "Transformation of Convention in Mechthild von Magdeburg," *Mystics Quarterly,* 10 (June 1984): 64–72;

Margit M. Sinka, "Christological Mysticism in Mechthild von Magdeburg's *Das Fließende Licht der Gottheit:* A Journey of Wounds," *Germanic Review,* 60 (Fall 1985): 123–128;

Hubert Stierling, "Studien zu Mechthild von Magdeburg," Ph.D. dissertation, Nuremberg University, 1907;

Philipp Strauch, "Kleine Beiträge zur Geschichte der deutschen Mystik," *Zeitschrift für deutsches Altertum und deutsche Literatur,* 27 (1883): 368–381;

Petrus W. Tax, "Die grosse Himmelsschau Mechthilds von Magdeburg und ihre Höllenvision: Aspekte des Erfahrungshorizontes, der Gegenbildlichkeit und der Parodierung," *Zeitschrift für deutsches Altertum und deutsche Literatur,* 108, no. 2 (1979): 112–137;

Johannes Thiele, "Die religiöse Frauenbewegung des Mittelalters. Eine historische Orientierung," in *Die Religiöse Frauenbewegung des Mittelalters in Porträts,* edited by Thiele (Stuttgart: Kreuz, 1988), pp. 9–34;

José de Vinck, "Mechthild of Magdeburg," in *Revelations of Women Mystics from the Middle Ages to Modern Times* (New York: Alba House, 1985), pp. 3–23;

Elizabeth Wainwright-deKadt, "Courtly Literature and Mysticism: Some Aspects of their Interaction," *Acta Germanica,* 12 (1980): 41–60;

Friedrich-Wilhelm Wentzlaff-Eggebert, *Deutsche Mystik zwischen Mittelalter und Neuzeit: Einheit und Wandlung ihrer Erscheinungsformen,* third edition (Berlin: De Gruyter, 1969);

Joanna Ziegler, "Women of the Middle Ages: Some Questions Regarding the Beguines and Devotional Art," *Vox Benedictina: Women and Monastic Spirituality,* 3, no. 4 (1986): 338–357;

Emilie Zum Brunn and Georgette Epiney-Burgard, "Mechthild of Magdeburg," in *Women Mystics in Medieval Europe,* translated by Sheila Hughes (New York: Paragon House, 1989), pp. 36–68.

Neidhart von Reuental

(circa 1185 – circa 1240)

William E. Jackson
University of Virginia

MAJOR WORKS: *Poems* (circa 1210 – circa 1240)

Manuscripts: Poems under Neidhart's name are transmitted in twenty-two manuscripts; the earliest is the *Carmina Burana* Manuscript M of Austria from the mid thirteenth century, now at the Bayerische Staatsbibliothek in Munich. The earliest – and only parchment – manuscript to preserve melodies to Neidhart's poems is the Frankfurt Manuscript o from the early fourteenth century, which is also the only transmission from a Low German area. The main manuscript sources of text editions have been the Riedegg Manuscript R of Austria, probably from the late thirteenth century, now in Berlin; Manuscript c from the fifteenth century, now in Berlin; and, to a lesser degree, the Große Heidelberger (Manessische) Liederhandschrift from the early fourteenth century, now in Heidelberg.

First publication: In Melchior Goldast, ed., *Paraeneticorum veterum pars I* (Lindau: Brem, 1604), pp. 384–385, 437.

Standard editions: *Neidhart von Reuenthal,* edited by Moriz Haupt (Leipzig: Hirzel, 1858); revised by Edmund Wießner as *Neidhartslieder* (Leipzig: Hirzel, 1923) revised edition, edited by Hanns Fischer (Tübingen: Niemeyer, 1963; revised, 1968).

Edition in modern German: *Die Lieder Neidharts,* edited and translated into modern German by Siegfried Beyschlag (Darmstadt: Wissenschaftliche Buchgesellschaft, 1975).

Editions in English: Translated by Frank C. Nicholson, in *Old German Love Songs* (London: Unwin, 1907), pp. 99–107; translated by M. F. Richey, in *Medieval German Lyrics* (Edinburgh: Oliver & Boyd, 1958), pp. 84–85; *The Songs of Neidhart von Reuental: 17 Summer and Winter Songs Set to Their Original Melodies with Translations and a Musical and Metrical Canon,* translated by A. T. Hatto and R. J. Taylor (Manchester, U.K.: Manchester University Press, 1958);

Miniature of Neidhart von Reuental in the fourteenth-century Große Heidelberger Liederhandschrift (Heidelberg, Universitätsbibliothek, cpg. 848, f.272r)

translated by J. W. Thomas, in *Medieval German Lyric Verse* (Chapel Hill: University of North Carolina Press, 1968), pp. 126–144; translated by Frederick Goldin, in *German and Italian Lyrics of the Middle Ages* (Garden City, N.Y.: Anchor Doubleday, 1973), pp. 151–173.

The name Her Nithard van dem Ruwenthal appears for the first time in Eberhard von Cersne's *Der minne Regel* (1404). Prior to that occurrence, the names Nîthart, Nithard, and Neithart appear with-

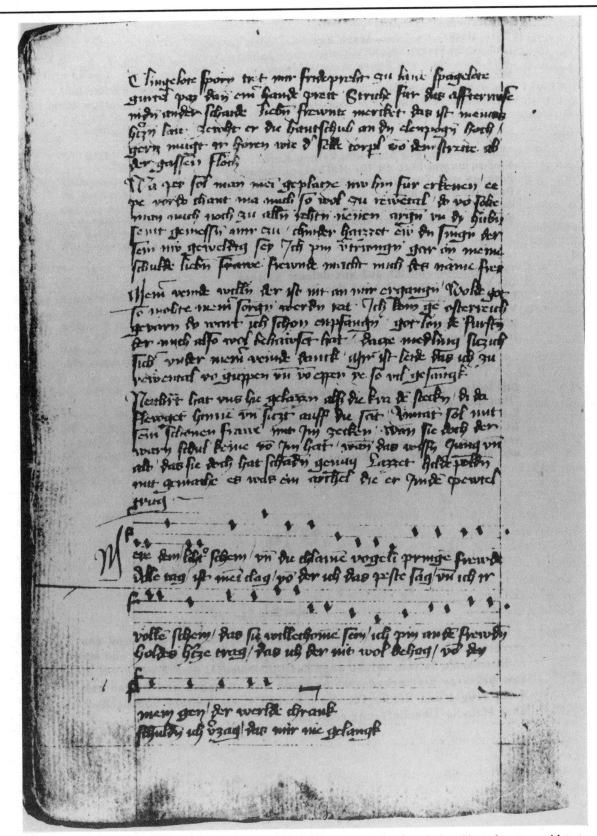

Page from the Austrian Riedegg Manuscript R, on parchment and probably dating from the late thirteenth century, with text and musical notation for Neidhart's song "Meie dîn liechter schîn" (Berlin, Staatsbibliothek Preußischer Kulturbesitz, Mgf. 1062, f37v)

out connection with Reuental. The name *Riuwental* occurs several times in Neidhart's poetry as the (fictional) home of the poet-lover. However, there is no longer general agreement that it is the name of the poet's actual home. Wolfram von Eschenbach refers to the poet in his *Willehalm* as "her Nîthart." Since this work has usually been dated between 1210 and 1220, Neidhart seems to have become an established poet early in the thirteenth century. It has been assumed that he was born in or around Landshut in Bavaria, where he was presumably in the service of Duke Ludwig I of Bavaria, although Karl Bertau has suggested that the area that includes Salzburg, Berchtesgaden, Hallein, and Reichenhall should also be considered.

Several of Neidhart's poems indicate participation in a Crusade. Some scholars have doubted whether he ever actually became a crusader, suggesting that he adopted the crusader persona for purposes of poetic creation. It has also been thought that Neidhart may have been a professional entertainer of low status and not the landed nobleman that a few of his poems seem rather vaguely to suggest. If Neidhart did go on a Crusade, the question remains whether it was that of 1217 to 1219, with Duke Leopold of Austria, or that of 1228 to 1229, with Austrian Emperor Friedrich II. The current scholarly consensus favors the former alternative. It has usually been thought that he moved from Bavaria to Austria around 1230. Based on some stanzas of one of his *Winterlieder* (winter songs), the move is thought to have been provoked by a falling out with his lord, presumed to be Ludwig I. There are indications, however, that Neidhart may have been popular at the Austrian court long before 1230. This suggestion could raise questions about the presumed course of Neidhart's career; on the other hand, it could indicate that Neidhart's presumed move to Austria was smoothed by prior contacts.

There is general agreement that after about 1230 Neidhart was a resident of Austria and in the service of Duke Friedrich II. In several of his poems this ruler is either praised or petitioned for economic support. One other point of general agreement is that Neidhart probably died around 1240, perhaps as late as 1242.

Neidhart is the best-documented poet of the Middle Ages, with about 150 poems and songs, totaling more than fifteen hundred stanzas, preserved in manuscripts and early printed texts over the better part of four centuries. It is difficult, however, to determine how many of the poems attributed to Neidhart were actually composed by him. Some

surely were not: some poems diverge so drastically in style and diction from others that a single authorship is unlikely; in addition, the poems seem to diverge in date of composition by more than the span of a lifetime. The Haupt-Wießner-Fischer edition of Neidhart's works (1968) includes only 66 poems as authentic and relegates 39 others to the appendix as spurious; the edition by Siegfried Beyschlag (1975) includes 90 poems. Beyschlag's edition also dispenses with the separation into summer songs and winter songs, classifications into which some of the included poems do not fit.

In the summer songs, "der von Riuwental" (the man of Reuental) is portrayed as the basically passive object of the affection of peasant girls and, in a few cases, of old women. In the poems involving young admirers, frequently the infatuated girl's mother gets wind of the situation and confronts her daughter. The confrontation leads to conflict, which in a few instances becomes physical. The words of such poems are, thus, often not the words of the man from Reuental but those of an infatuated girl or old woman. Some of the texts take the form of dialogue, either between the mother and daughter or, in a few cases, between girlfriends. Thus, in Neidhart's summer songs – indeed, in his poetry in general – the theme of *minne* (courtship) is not addressed in the form of effusions from a single speaker but from a multiplicity of perspectives and in a multiplicity of dictions. They include a substantial amount of epic and even dramatic discourse. Even the Crusade songs, which one might hear at first as lyrical expressions of strong sentiments, turn out to be formulated at least in part as instructions to a messenger and are, therefore, essentially dialogic.

This aspect of Neidhart's poetry is by no means an innovation on his part: there are strong epic and especially dramatic strains in medieval German *Minnesang* (love poetry) going back to Der Kürnberger and Dietmar von Eist and including all of the other known vernacular poets who preceded Neidhart in Bavaria and Austria. These strains are connected with a tradition of poetry in which the woman takes the initiative in expressing affection for a basically passive man. There may also be precedents in the poetry of Neidhart's vernacular predecessors for his portrayal of conflict between mother and daughter. A *Frauenlied* (woman's song) by Reinmar der Alte makes express reference to tensions between an infatuated woman and her relatives, and in a *Frauenlied* by Hartmann von Aue, objections to the woman's wishes – formulated as an ultimatum – are raised by *vriunde*. This term, which means "friends," was often used to refer to or at least include relatives, as seems to be the case here. Neidhart also uses *vriunde* to refer to his supporters, who seem to be or include relatives; the family-minded Wolfram singles out this term as a characteristic one for Neidhart's poetry.

In the winter songs only the voice of the male singer-lover is heard. The speaker still refers in a few cases to Reuental, but in a way noticeably different from the summer songs. There Reuental is the much-desired goal of its occupant's female admirers and, in a few cases, the subject of stern (and fruitless?) maternal warnings about this lover's questionable intentions. In the winter songs Reuental appears as a poverty-stricken lair where the speaker wishes to take women who do not at all seem inclined to go there. The Reuental of the winter songs also appears as a refuge from the hostility of the peasants who are the speaker's rivals for the affections of his love interests. Finally, the hibernal Reuental is also pictured as the target of intense hostility on the part of these rivals, who threaten destruction of it and bodily harm to its occupant.

This divergence between summer song and winter song in its view of the man of Reuental as, on the one hand, passive object of female desire and, on the other, devoted and unrequited lover of unresponsive women is precisely the divergence between *Frauenlied* and *Manneslied* (man's song) in the poetry of such Austrian predecessors of Neidhart as Der Burggraf von Rietenburg, Dietmar von Eist, and Reinmar. In their works, also, poetry featuring the woman's voice and the woman as aggressor contrasts with poetry featuring the man's voice and unrewarded *Frauendienst* (love service). The same three poets also provide striking passages anticipating Neidhart's use of the *Natureingang*, the formulaic nature scene that opens both his summer and winter songs. To note these similarities is not to rule out the French *pastourelle* or Latin goliardic poetry as possible influences on Neidhart, but one should not overlook the considerable evidence that he was a creative continuator of the traditions that preceded him in his Bavarian and Austrian homeland. It would seem that Neidhart took over important motifs from his predecessors and reworked them in a dramatic style that is very much his own.

The division of Neidhart's poems into summer songs and winter songs, though not exhaustive, influenced younger poets, particularly Gottfried von Neifen and Ulrich von Winterstetten. Also important for future generations was Neidhart's strik-

ing brand of self-fictionalization. In the summer songs he has his audience view the singer-lover through the eyes of others. This is also true of the verse tales featuring Neidhart in the main role which are fairly numerous in some of the song manuscripts. And if the so-called *trutzstrophen* (defiance stanzas) of the winter songs, which the Haupt-Wießner-Fischer edition banishes to the appendix as suspect, were indeed composed by Neidhart, as they surely were, then here, too, Neidhart has implemented a special kind of self-fictionalization. In so doing, he laid the groundwork for future portrayals of the fictional Neidhart by (himself and?) others, culminating, on the one hand, in the Neidhart of the *Fastnachtspiel* (Shrovetide play) and, on the other, in that late medieval bane of the peasants, Neidhart Fuchs.

References:

Ingrid Bennewitz-Behr, *Original und Rezeption* (Göppingen: Kümmerle, 1987);

Karl Bertau, "Neidharts 'Bayrische Lieder' and Wolframs 'Willehalm,'" *Zeitschrift für deutsches Altertum und deutsche Literatur*, 100 (1971): 296–324;

Helmut Birkham, ed., *Neidhart von Reuental* (Vienna: Braumüller, 1983);

Horst Brunner, ed., *Neidhart* (Darmstadt: Wissenschaftliche Buchgesellschaft, 1986);

Hildegard Janssen, *Das sogenannte "genre objectif"* (Göppingen: Kümmerle, 1980);

Erhard Jöst, *Bauernfeindlichkeit: Die Historien des Ritters Neidhart Fuchs* (Göppingen: Kümmerle, 1976);

Hugo Moser and Helmut Tervooren, eds., *Des Minnesangs Frühling*, 2 volumes (Stuttgart: Hirzel, 1977);

Hans-Dieter Mück, "Walthers Propaganda gegen Neidharts Publikum," in *Zur gesellschaftlichen Funktionalität mittelalterlicher deutscher Literatur* (Greifswald, 1984), pp. 89–103;

Ulrich Müller, "Die Kreuzfahrten der Neidharte," in *From Symbol to Mimesis*, edited by Fränz H. Bäuml (Göppingen: Kümmerle, 1984), pp. 35–68;

Eckehard Simon, *Neidhart von Reuental* (Boston: Twayne, 1975);

Burghart Wachinger, "Die sogenannten Trutzstrophen zu den Liedern Neidharts," in *Formen mittelalterlicher Literatur*, edited by Otmar Werner and Bernd Naumann (Göppingen: Kümmerle, 1970), pp. 99–108.

Der Pleier

(flourished circa 1250)

J. Wesley Thomas
University of Kentucky

MAJOR WORKS: *Garel von dem blühenden Tal* (circa 1250)

Manuscripts: The adventures of the Arthurian knight Sir Garel are recorded in a well-preserved paper manuscript of the late fourteenth century in Linz (Oberösterreichisches Landesarchiv, Archiv Schlüsselberg Hs. 96) and in a fragment of an early-fourteenth-century parchment manuscript in Berlin (Staatsbibliothek Preußischer Kulturbesitz, mgf 923, Nr. 18).

First publication: *Gârel von dem Blühenden Tal,* edited by Michael Walz (Vienna: Privately printed, 1881).

Standard editions: *Garel von dem blühenden Tal: Ein höfischer Roman aus dem Artussagenkreise von dem Pleier,* edited by Walz (Freiburg: Wagner, 1892); *Garel von dem blünden Tal von dem Pleier,* edited by Wolfgang Herles, Wiener Arbeiten zur germanischen Altertumskunde und Philologie, no. 17 (Vienna: Halosar, 1981).

Edition in English: "Garel of the Blooming Valley," in *The Pleier's Arthurian Romances: Garel of the Blooming Valley, Tandareis and Flordibel, Meleranz,* translated, with an introduction, by J. W. Thomas (New York: Garland, 1992), pp. 1–196.

Tandareis und Flordibel (circa 1260)

Manuscripts: The romance appears in four paper manuscripts of the fifteenth century and a fourteenth-century parchment fragment. The most important manuscripts are those in Munich (Bayerische Staatsbibliothek, Cgm. 577) and Heidelberg (Universitätsbibliothek, Cod. pal. germ. 370); one that was in Hamburg has been missing since World War II.

First publication and standard edition: *Tandareis und Flordibel: Ein höfischer Roman von dem Pleiaere,* edited by Ferdinand Khull (Graz: Verlags-Buchhandlung Styria, 1885).

Edition in English: "Tandareis and Flor-dibel," in *The Pleier's Arthurian Romances: Garel of the Blooming Valley, Tandareis and Flordibel, Meleranz,* translated, with an introduction, by J. W. Thomas (New York: Garland, 1993), pp. 197–366.

Meleranz (circa 1270)

Manuscript: This adaptation of a fairy tale is extant in a single paper manuscript that was prepared in 1480 by Gabryel Lindenast and is now in Donaueschingen (Fürstliche Fürstenbergische Hofbibliothek, Hs. Nr. 87). Sixty of the large red, blue, and black capital letters that introduce the separate sections of the story are distorted to depict caricatures of faces.

First publication and standard edition: *Meleranz,* edited by Karl Bartsch (Stuttgart: Litterarischer Verein, 1861; republished, with an appendix by Alexander Hildebrand, Hildesheim & New York: Olms, 1974).

Edition in English: "Meleranz," in *The Pleier's Arthurian Romances: Garel of the Blooming Valley, Tandareis and Flordibel, Meleranz,* translated, with an introduction, by J. W. Thomas (New York: Garland, 1993), pp. 367–490.

Der Pleier's narratives appear to have been quite popular during the second half of the thirteenth century and the late Middle Ages. Their influence is seen in the writings of Albrecht von Scharfenberg, Konrad von Stoffeln, Ulrich von Türheim, the anonymous author of *Wigamur* (circa 1250?), the Albrecht who wrote *Der jüngere Titurel* (The Later Titurel, circa 1275), and especially Ulrich Füetrer, who borrowed extensively from *Garel von dem blühenden Tal* (circa 1250; translated as "Garel of the Blooming Valley," 1993) and *Meleranz* (circa 1270; translated, 1993) for his *Flordimar* (circa 1490), took over some characters from *Garel von dem blühenden Tal* for his *Lancelot,* and prepared an abridgment of *Meleranz.* Three Czech versions of *Tandareis und Flordibel* (circa 1260; translated, 1993) and a Czech abridgment of *Meleranz* show that Der Pleier's fame was not limited to the German-speaking lands. But perhaps the most significant confirmation of his popularity in the Middle Ages came about 1400 when Nikolaus Vintner added a wing to Runkelstein Castle in Alto Adige and had one of the two new halls decorated with frescoes that portrayed episodes in *Garel von dem blühenden Tal;* twenty of the original twenty-three have been preserved. A salient characteristic of Der Pleier's work is the emphasis on customs and manners.

Almost nothing is known of the man who referred to himself as "der Pleier." Since he composed his verse romances in a Bavarian-Austrian dialect, some scholars have attempted to connect him with a county near Salzburg, a family of Salzburg minor nobility, or a family of Styrian counts – all with names similar to Pleier. Others have suggested that *Pleier,* which could mean one who blows glass or smelts metallic ores, may indicate a family trade or even be a descriptive pseudonym for an artist who creates something of value from raw materials. One theory makes the author an employee or protégé of a certain Wimar Frumesel, who resided in or near Schärding in Upper Austria. This theory is based on a passage at the end of *Meleranz* in which the author thanks and praises a patron whom he calls "der frum edel Wîmar" (the noble, esteemed Wimar), but it is quite likely that Der Pleier was only comparing his benefactor to the generous merchant of that name in Wolfram von Eschenbach's *Willehalm* (circa 1210–1220). In any event, the author's apparent ignorance of Latin and his failure to identify himself by a place-name probably means that he was neither a clergyman nor a nobleman but a member of the middle class. The approximate period of his productivity, between 1240 and 1280, has been determined by taking note of the literature with which he was familiar and which was influenced by him, but there is little agreement with respect to the order in which his works appeared. The sequence *Garel von dem blühenden Tal – Tandareis und Flordibel – Meleranz* is plausible because certain deeds of the hero of the first work are mentioned in the second and the prosody of the third work is superior to that of the other two.

Writing some fifty years or more after the first Arthurian romances appeared in Germany, Der Pleier strove to preserve the Arthurian literary tradition he had inherited from Hartmann von Aue, Ulrich von Zatzikhoven, Wirnt von Grafenberg, and, above all, Wolfram. He carefully fits his heroes and their adventures into the framework that the older writers had created and presents his works as authentic chapters of Arthurian lore rather than as original compositions. He validates them with the familiar, chatty narrator and by using well-known knights as his supporting cast, referring to episodes in earlier works, employing a traditional overall structure, and adopting to a considerable extent the language and style of his predecessors. Der Pleier also frequently borrows adventures from those predecessors, producing variations of familiar themes and situations.

Yet in one important respect his works, like those of all the later authors, differ from their chief models. Hartmann and Wolfram have imperfect heroes who err and pay dearly for their errors, and their adventures are less the result of exterior circumstances than expressions of their states of mind. These characters are interesting in a way that the idealized knights of a later time could not be – not only because they are less predictable but also because their failings, like the tragic flaws of William Shakespeare's heroes, are universal. Der Pleier compensates for his knights' infallibility by concentrating on the adventures themselves, providing logical exterior motivations for them, and lending their outcomes general social significance. The teachings that are implicit in the actions of the early romances appear in Der Pleier's works as digressions by the narrator.

Der Pleier's high regard for the courtly literature of the past may have led to the composition of *Garel von dem blühenden Tal,* whose chief source, as the title suggests, is Der Stricker's *Daniel von dem blühenden Tal* (1210–1225; translated as *Daniel of the Blossoming Valley,* 1990), the most unknightly and unorthodox Arthurian romance of medieval Germany. Its hero has an untraditional Old Testament name, gains his ends by cunning rather than pure valor, and cares nothing about courtly love; Arthur is portrayed as a crafty and bold warrior rather than as a passive model of generosity and honor. Der Pleier employs the basic plot of *Daniel von dem blühenden Tal* but uses only two of its adventures, and these are drastically altered. His goals seem to be to build a proper Arthurian romance on Der Stricker's foundation and to correct what he apparently considered a rather shocking corruption of a revered art form.

Ekunaver, king of far-off Kanadic, sends a messenger to Arthur to declare that Ekunaver will launch an invasion in a year's time. The knight Garel advises Arthur to attack Ekunaver in the latter's own land, then rides forth to spy out the enemy territory. Along the way he has a series of adventures during which he frees noble families from oppression and thereby wins promises of military support for a campaign against Ekunaver. In the last of these contests he not only slays a dreadful monster that has caused widespread devastation but also marries the queen of the country.

Garel raises an army from his newly acquired vassals, calls on his allies, and invades Kanadic without waiting for Arthur. After several bloody battles that are described in realistic, gory detail, the hero defeats Ekunaver and takes him as a prisoner to Arthur's court, where the two kings make peace. Garel returns to his own realm, which under his wise rule once again becomes prosperous and happy.

Garel von dem blühenden Tal is a tale of adventure that includes a love affair; *Tandareis und Flordibel* is a love story that is embellished and complicated by adventures. The bare outline came from one of the most popular narratives of the Middle Ages, versions of which appeared from Greece to Iceland, which tells of the love of a young Saracen prince for a captive Christian maiden at his father's court, of their separation and many trials, and of their joyous reunion and marriage. Der Pleier probably knew it from Konrad Fleck's *Flore und Blanscheflur,* composed about 1220.

Flordibel, an Indian princess staying at Arthur's court, asks the king to protect her virtue from the men of his retinue by condemning to death whoever should seduce her; he promises to do so. After several years she and Tandareis, a young prince who is serving as a page at the court, fall in love and flee to his father's kingdom, where he is knighted. Determined to keep his vow, Arthur invades the land with a mighty army. When a truce is arranged, Flordibel saves her lover's life by denying that she has been seduced; but Tandareis is forced into exile to atone for having offended Arthur by his flight.

Two series of adventures follow. First there are struggles with robbers and giants that end with Tandareis becoming lord of Mermin, a country that he has rid of a cruel tyrant. But his longing for Flordibel makes the hero restless, and he sets forth again. His adversaries now are uncourtly knights, and his experiences include freeing a mysterious mountain kingdom from the oppression of a neighbor, a lengthy imprisonment in the ladies' quarters of a castle, and several incognito appearances at tournaments held by King Arthur. Learning Tandareis's identity, Arthur welcomes him back to the court. Three maidens lay claim to Tandareis, but he declares that he will wed no one but Flordibel. There is a festive marriage, and the couple live joyfully and in splendor to the end in their prosperous and happy kingdom.

Meleranz, too, is primarily a story of young love. The nucleus of the work probably came directly or indirectly from the well-known Breton lay "Graelent," but Der Pleier makes many changes and additions. In his version the boy Meleranz, son of the king of France, encounters Tydomie, a maiden queen, in a remote forest clearing while on the way to become a page at the court of his uncle, King Arthur. The two fall in love. Several years later Meleranz, now a knight, sets out to find her. On the way he frees a large group of people from wretched captivity by slaying an evil king in single combat, and the lords of the land choose him as their monarch. Having promised one of the captives that he would go to the aid of her mistress, a queen whose land is threatened by a heathen despot, the knight places his country under the temporary control of one of its noblemen, leads the queen's troops against the invaders, slays their lord, and routs his army.

In the meantime, Meleranz learns that his ladylove's uncle has threatened to drive her from her land if she does not marry a certain king. The latter has seized the forest clearing where Meleranz and Tydomie met and has issued a general challenge to single combat. Meleranz defeats the king, sends him as a prisoner to Arthur, and rides to Tydomie's land to protect it from invasion. But as soon as the uncle discovers that his niece is to marry the son of the king of France and the nephew of King Arthur, hostilities cease. Arthur and his court come for the wedding, and there is a splendid celebration. Thereafter Meleranz and Tydomie wear the crowns of two kingdoms and reign wisely and in splendor till their deaths.

Der Pleier was not greatly talented, but he was a skillful craftsman. His plots are well constructed with no loose ends, and the individual adventures are either connected by a common goal or evolve logically out of one another. Despite his admiration for Hartmann, Wirnt, and Wolfram, the younger author clearly belonged to a new generation and composed for an audience with different interests from those that marked the literature of his masters. The three romances portray gracious living at its best while stressing piety and fine manners. Courtesy and propriety are of the utmost importance at all courts worthy of the name, and their lords display lavish generosity. Receptions, greetings, seating arrangements, farewells, and other ceremonies are described so frequently and at such length that the works have been praised as a source of cultural history. Good breeding and correct behavior are attributes of most of the characters, whether they are friends or foes of the hero. Etiquette is in effect equated with morality, for those who have no manners also have no morals.

Der Pleier's works achieve continuity and gain substance from his social consciousness, which expresses itself not only in his keen interest in customs that facilitate the interactions of courtly life but also in his conviction that great deeds do not merely bring fame to the hero but also benefit society as a whole. While saving individuals from distress, the heroes free entire lands from oppression; and, in addition to being trustworthy and brave, they turn out to be competent, conscientious rulers who could well serve as models for such noblemen as might learn of their deeds.

An unusual feature of the three romances is the sympathetic treatment that most of the hero's adversaries receive from the kindhearted author. They are shown to be victims of circumstance whose offenses are due to misunderstanding, need, or the tyranny of their masters, and they welcome the opportunity to lead peaceful, law-abiding lives. For all the violence he depicts, Der Pleier's optimism with respect to human nature remains unshaken.

References:

Helmut de Boor, "Der Daniel des Stricker und der Garel des Pleier," *Beiträge zur Geschichte der deutschen Sprache und Literatur,* 79 (1957): 67–84;

Karel Brušák, "Some Notes on *Tandariáš a Floribella,* a Czech 14th Century Chivalric Romance," in *Gorski vijenac: A Garland of Essays Offered to Professor Elizabeth Mary Hill,* edited by R. Autry and others (Cambridge: Modern Humanities Research Association, 1970), pp. 44–56;

Danielle Buschinger, "Die Widerspiegelung mittelalterlicher Herrschaftsstrukturen im 'Garel' des Pleier," in *Ergebnisse der XXI. Jahrestagung des Arbeitskreises "Deutsche Literatur des Mittelalters"* (Greifswald: Ernst-Moritz-Arndt-Universität, 1989), pp. 21–31;

Karin R. Gürttler, *"Künec Artûs der guote": Das Artusbild der höfischen Epik des 12. und 13. Jahrhunderts* (Bonn: Bouvier, 1976);

Walter Haug, "Paradigmatische Poesie: Der spätere deutsche Artusroman auf dem Weg zu einer 'nachklassischen' Ästhetik," *Deutsche Vierteljahrsschrift für Literaturwissenschaft und Geistesgeschichte,* 54 (1980): 204–231;

Alfred Karnein, "Minne, Aventiure und Artus-Idealität in den Romanen des späten 13. Jahrhunderts," in *Artusrittertum im späten Mittelalter: Ethos und Ideologie,* edited by Friedrich Wolfzettel (Giessen: Schmitz, 1984), pp. 114–125;

Petra Kellermann-Haaf, *Frau und Politik im Mittelalter: Untersuchungen zur politischen Rolle der Frau in den höfischen Romanen des 12., 13., und 14. Jahrhunderts* (Göppingen: Kümmerle, 1986);

Peter Kern, *Die Artusromane des Pleier: Untersuchungen über den Zusammenhang von Dichtung und literarischer Situation* (Berlin: Schmidt, 1981);

Kern, "Eine Handschrift von Pleiers *Tandarios und Flordibel* im historischen Archiv der Stadt Köln," *Zeitschrift für deutsches Altertum und deutsche Literatur,* 104, no. 1 (1975): 41–54;

Kern, "Der Pleier," in *Die deutsche Literatur des Mittelalters: Verfasserlexikon,* volume 7, edited by Kurt Ruh (Berlin: De Gruyter, 1989), cols. 728–737;

Ann G. Martin, *Shame and Disgrace at King Arthur's Court: A Study in the Meaning of Ignominy in Arthurian Literature to 1300* (Göppingen: Kümmerle, 1984);

Dorothea Müller, *"Daniel vom blühenden Tal"* und *"Garel vom blühenden Tal": Die Artusromane des Stricker und des Pleier unter gattungsgeschichtlichen Aspekten* (Göppingen: Kümmerle, 1981);

Horst P. Pütz, "Pleiers *Gârel von dem blühenden Tal:* Protest oder Anpassung?," in *Literatur und bildende Kunst im Tiroler Mittelalter,* edited by Egon Kühebacher (Innsbruck: Institut für Germanistik, 1982), pp. 29–44;

John L. Riordan, "A Vindication of the Pleier," *Journal of English and Germanic Philology,* 47 (1948): 29–43;

Werner Schröder, "Das *Willehalm*-Plagiat im *Garel* des Pleier oder die vergeblich geleugnete Epigonalität," *Zeitschrift für deutsches Altertum und deutsche Literatur,* 114, no. 2 (1985): 119–141;

Günter Zimmermann, "Die Verwendung heldenepischen Materials im *Garel* von dem Pleier: Gattungskonformität und Erweiterung," *Zeitschrift für deutsches Altertum und deutsche Literatur,* 113, no. 1 (1984): 42–60;

Manfred Zimmermann, "Ritter Garel von dem blühenden Tal: Arthurische Idealität aus der Steiermark," in *Die mittelalterliche Literatur in der Steiermark,* edited by Alfred Ebenbauer and others (Bern: Lang, 1988), pp. 337–356.

Reinmar der Alte

(circa 1165 – circa 1205)

William E. Jackson
University of Virginia

MAJOR WORK: *Six Songs* (circa 1195)

Manuscripts: Songs and strophes attributed to Reinmar are transmitted mainly in four major *Minnesang* manuscripts: 70 strophes in A (Kleine Heidelberger Liederhandschrift, Universitätsbibliothek, Heidelberg; cpg 357), 115 strophes in B (Weingartner Liederhandschrift, Württembergische Landesbibliothek, Stuttgart; cod. HB XIII 1), 262 strophes in C (Große Heidelberger [or Manessische] Liederhandschrift, Universitätsbibliothek, Heidelberg; cpg 848), and 164 strophes in E (Würzburger Liederhandschrift, Universitätsbibliothek, Munich; 2 Cod. ms. 731). Isolated strophes are preserved in Bu (Széchényi-Nationalbibliothek, Budapest; cod. Germ. 92, 4 strophes), i (Die Rappoltsteiner Parzival-Handschrift, Fürstlliche Fürstenbergischen Hofbibliothek, Donaueschingen; cod. perg. 97, 1 strophe), M (*Die Carmina Burana,* Bayerische Staatsbibliothek, Munich; clm 4660, 3 strophes), p (Sammelhandschrift der Bürgerbibliothek, Bern, cod. 260, 3 strophes), s (Die Haager Liederhandschrift, Königliche Bibliothek, The Hague; 128E2, 1 strophe), G^2 (Bayerische Staatsbibliothek, Munich; Cgm. 5249/74, 4 strophes), and x (Berliner Liederhandschrift, mgf. 922, 5 strophes). The order of the strophes differs from one manuscript to another. Different manuscripts attribute the same strophes to different poets. A source of particular perplexity has been the poems attributed in some manuscripts to Reinmar and in others to Heinrich von Rugge.

First publication: In *Proben der alten schwäbischen Poesie des dreyzehnten Jahrhunderts: Aus der Maneßischen Sammlung,* edited by Johann Jakob Bodmer and Johann Jakob Breitinger (Zurich: Heidegger, 1748), pp. 46–63.

Standard edition: In *Des Minnesangs Frühling,* thirty-sixth edition, revised by Hugo Moser

Miniature of Reinmar der Alte in the fourteenth-century Große Heidelberger Liederhandschrift (Heidelberg, Universitätsbibliothek, cpg 848, f98r)

and Helmut Tervooren, volume 1 (Stuttgart: Hirzel, 1977), pp. 285–403.

Edition in modern German: *Lieder: Nach der Weingartner Liederhandschrift (B) Mittelhochdeutsch/Neuhochdeutsch,* edited and translated by Günther Schweikle (Stuttgart: Reclam, 1986).

Editions in English: Translated by Frank C. Nicholson, in *Old German Love Songs* (London: Unwin, 1907), pp. 51–59; translated by Jethro Bithell, in *The Minnesingers,* volume 1 (New

York: Longmans, 1909), pp. 45–49; translated by M. F. Richey, in *Medieval German Lyrics* (Edinburgh: Oliver & Boyd, 1958), pp. 55–58; translated by Angel Flores, in *An Anthology of Medieval Lyrics* (New York: Modern Library, 1962), pp. 417–420; translated by J. W. Thomas, in *Medieval German Lyric Verse* (Chapel Hill: University of North Carolina Press, 1968), pp. 102–106; translated by Frederick Goldin, in *German and Italian Lyrics of the Middle Ages* (Garden City, N.Y.: Anchor Press, 1973), pp. 84–95; women's songs *(Frauenlieder)* translated by William E. Jackson, in *Reinmar's Women* (Amsterdam: Benjamins, 1981), pp. 1–42.

Except in manuscript C, where Reinmar is given the sobriquet *der Alte* (the Old) – apparently to distinguish him from younger authors of the same name – his only historically attested name is simply Reinmar (spelled variously). The name Reinmar von Hagenau is a creation of nineteenth-century scholarship based on a passage in the literary review in Gottfried von Straßburg's *Tristan und Isolde* (circa 1210; translated as *The Story of Tristan and Iseult,* 1889). There Gottfried, while discussing the lyric poets of his age metaphorically as nightingales, laments the passing of one who has been their "leitevrouwe" (leader) up to now as "diu von Hagenouwe" (the one from Hagenau). Since Hagenau is an Alsatian city north of Strasbourg, where the imperial Hohenstaufen family had important estates, Gottfried's praise of the nightingale of Hagenau has been seen as a eulogy to a fellow Alsatian. A few scholars view Reinmar as an Austrian and possibly a member of the Austrian Hagenau family mentioned in Adalbert Stifter's novel *Witiko* (1865–1867), one of the noble families superseded by the Babenbergs on their road to rule.

The reigning assumption has been that Reinmar was an Alsatian who moved to Austria, presumably to assume the position of court poet in Vienna. Günther Schweikle has raised well-founded objections to this assumption: there is, he says, no basis for seeing Reinmar as court poet in Vienna or, for that matter, for assuming that there existed such a position at all in Reinmar's lifetime. On the other hand, there is just as little basis for Schweikle's assumption that Reinmar was a traveling entertainer. In the poems of Reinmar's contemporary Walther von der Vogelweide (whose eulogy to Reinmar reveals some apparently intense bad feelings between the two poets) there are many indications of the needs, exigencies, and hardships with which the traveling performer had to cope; there is no such indication in Reinmar's opus, indicating that Reinmar perhaps knew no such life of hardship.

Furthermore, the assumption that Reinmar was an Austrian better fits the nature of his opus and proves helpful for understanding it. Even the scholarly tradition that has favored the Alsatian thesis has assumed Austrian birth or, at least, Austrian youth for Reinmar. A group of Reinmar's poems that feature a woman openly expressing affection for a man has generally been viewed as poems of Reinmar's youth; in these poems have been found clear signs of the influence on Reinmar of the so-called *Donauländische Minnesang* (Danubian love poetry), a poetic tradition that preceded him in earlier-twelfth-century Austria. Helmut de Boor even refers to these *Jugendlieder* (youthful songs) as a Danubian heritage. In so doing, he contradicts his own depiction of Reinmar in the same discussion as an Alsatian: it does not seem strange to de Boor that Reinmar should have grown up in Rhineland Alsatia composing poems in the old Austrian style of his future home.

Gottfried von Straßburg characterizes the poetry of the nightingale of "Hagenouwe" in terms that seem to indicate great variety: sealed in the tongue of this nightingale was "aller doene houbet list" (a great range in melody), and Gottfried is amazed by the "wunder . . . so maneger wandelunge" (marvel . . . of variety or modulation). Reinmar's opus as transmitted in the manuscripts can certainly lay strong claim to these characterizations.

In the genre of *Wechsel* (alternation), inherited from the Danubian past, stanzas formulated in the words of a man *(Mannesstrophe)* and stanzas formulated in the words of a woman *(Frauenstrophe)* are composed in the same meter; the man and woman address one another without engaging in direct dialogue. In the standard edition of Reinmar's work (1857; revised, 1977) there are six *Wechsel* plus a seventh poem that has a *Frauenstrophe.* In all except two cases the *Mannesstrophen* outnumber the *Frauenstrophen.* The same imbalance in favor of *Mannesstrophen* is a feature of the *Wechsel* of Reinmar's Danubian predecessor (and, perhaps, model) Dietmar von Eist. In Reinmar's version, as in the *Wechsel* of the older generation, the man and woman speak differently about the amorous relationship: hers is the language of erotic longing and of suffering from the lover's absence; his is the language of service and of exalted claims of devotion.

The *Frauenlieder* (women's songs) of Reinmar also show clear links to the Austrian past. The standard text includes five, plus an unusual composition in which the first stanza features an anonymous voice introducing the woman's monologues of the five following stanzas. One of the *Frauenlieder,* the widow's lament *Si jehent, der sumer der sî hie* (They say that summer is here), is important for the dating of Reinmar's poetry: Jeffrey Ashcroft has made a strong case that the "herre Liutpolt" lamented by the widow is Duke Leopold V of Austria, who died in 1195. He also makes a strong case for hearing in the poem Reinmar's support for that beleaguered ruler, who was banned by the pope for imprisoning Richard the Lion-Hearted. There is nothing in the poem, however, to merit the label "Panegyrik höfischen Herrschertums" (panegyric of courtly rulership) that Ashcroft ascribes to it. For one thing, there is no mention of, and indeed not even so much as an allusion to, ruling power or knightly deeds – a striking omission since Duke Leopold was an accomplished ruler and valiant crusader. Nor are there expressions of deference or any of the other features that one would expect in a poem addressed by a professional poet to a powerful and valiant former patron. "Liutpolt" is eulogized exclusively as lover: the widow remembers him as the "spiegel mîner vröiden" (mirror of my joy), a phrase of visual eroticism that reminds one of the woman's longing look of love in poems by Dietmar and Meinloh von Seveling. The widow's lament is to some degree a typical Danubian *Frauenlied.* Less typical are the dialogue poem *Sage, daz ich dirs iemer lône* (Tell me and I shall reward you) and a similar *Frauenlied, Lieber bote, nu wirp alsô* (Dear Messenger, now proceed like this). In both, a woman in a position of authority tries to enlist the help of a messenger in her attempt to conduct a relationship with an apparently troublesome suitor. In the dialogue poem she engages in a battle of wits with the curiously high-handed messenger and loses: he reduces her to incoherence. In the *Frauenlied,* in which the messenger only listens but still seems to exert considerable influence, she decides rather belatedly (in the last line) to cancel her strikingly indecisive message of six strophes. In *Sage, daz ich dirs iemer lône* a woman confides that her cold and unresponsive behavior toward her suitor contrasts strongly with her real feelings, which she dares not show openly out of concern for her honor. The three remaining *Frauenlieder* portray women who have apparently abandoned such caution and are now enduring the consequences. The woman in the poem *Dêst ein nôt* (It is distressful) finds herself under the power of her beloved to such an unsettling degree that she wishes for *huote,* the surveillance of lovers that is usually hated and maligned. The stress of frustrated infatuation has affected the physical appearance of the woman in a manner that reminds one of Sigune in Wolfram von Eschenbach's *Parzival* (circa 1200–1210). In the poem *Âne swaere* (with-

out care) a woman recommends submission to the beloved man as a matter of moral principle: she will give him anything he wants, she will sacrifice anything for his sake, and she wants others to follow her example. Finally, the poem *Zuo niuwen vröuden stât mîn muot* (My mind is joyful anew) is a woman's jubilant song of joy over an experience of erotic pleasure.

Thus Reinmar not only composed more poetry in the persona of the woman than any other male medieval poet, but he also composed the most unusual and the most profound of such poetry. He creates, from the woman's point of view, a world in which the amorous relationship is somehow connected with fears of deceit and the struggle for power, a world in which the woman assents to the man's wishes at the risk of succumbing to domination. In this light, the fact that the *Carmina Burana,* the Latin collection of erotic poems, contains more poems by Reinmar than by any other vernacular poet does not seem at all surprising.

The portrayal of the man in Reinmar's poetry is dominated by complaints about unrequited love. These laments are by no means monotonous, as traditional scholarship would have it, but quite varied; and they are interspersed with comments on *minne* (amorous love) that are clearly not plaintive. In rough order of frequency of occurrence, the most prominent themes in Reinmar's *Mannesstrophen* are: he is satisfied with meager rewards (the opposite is proclaimed in *Als ich werbe und mir mîn herze stê* [As I woo and as my heart now feels], where the speaker has never bowed in gratitude for such a paltry reward); he thinks admiringly of the successful lover; he is in great spirits and confident that things will go his way; he remembers a previous time when he himself was a more successful lover; he admits that people get tired of his endless complaining; exasperation over unrequited love makes him consider giving up; he proclaims his faithfulness to the beloved; he is concerned about the effect of love on the aging process; he decides that it would be silly for him to claim amorous successes he has never had; and he cannot blame his beloved for his suffering because he is bringing it on himself.

In only one passage in Reinmar's opus is there any indication that *minne* is supposed to provide some kind of moral uplift or betterment for the male courtly lover: in *Sô vil sô ich gesanc nie man* (No man ever sang as much as I) the speaker says that he would not serve another day if he did not know that his beloved could make him "wert" (worthy). Love, courtly or otherwise, as some kind of ethical elevation of the man who serves, is not a major theme in Reinmar's poetry.

Page from the Carmina Burana *manuscript, written in the first half of the thirteenth century, with the song "Sage, daz ich dirs iemer lône," attributed to Reinmar (Munich, Bayerische Staatsbibliothek, clm. 4660, f.60v)*

The scholarly tradition has found Reinmar to exemplify consistently the courtly lover's service to the beloved lady. There is, indeed, considerable talk in Reinmar's opus about service, but the same is true of the older Danubian *Minnesang:* the man in the poems of Meinloh von Sevelingen, the Burggraf von Rietenburg, and Dietmar also brags about his service. In addition, however, the man rewards the woman for her service in two stanzas of Reinmar's poem *Wie ist ime ze muote, wundert mich* (I wonder how he feels); in the second passage the reward is for her *staete* (faithfulness). Here also the old Danubian *Minnesang* provided the model: the woman in a poem by Meinloh has become her lover's principal beloved through service; her counterpart in *Ich bin mit rehte staete* (with genuine constancy am I), by the Burggraf von Regensburg, is "einem guoten rîter undertân" (in subservience to a good knight). In *Der winter waere mir ein zît* (The winter would be for me a time), by Dietmar, a woman seems unsure of her service capability – "dem will ich dienen, obe ich kan" (I will serve him if I can) – but will die if she cannot reap the fruits of her service, whatever its quality; in Dietmar's *Sich hât verwandelt diu zît* (The season has changed) one identified as "der aller beste man" (the best man of all) has rewarded a woman according to her wishes for her "staete" and her "grôzer arbeit" (great effort). Thus Reinmar is again the creative continuator of the Danubian tradition in which both man and woman serve as well as reward.

Many of these motifs are mutually contradictory, and that is undoubtedly the point: Reinmar was a practitioner of the *revocatio,* the juxtaposition of contradictory and mutually canceling assertions. The poems *Ich lebte ie nach der liute sage* (I would live as people tell me) and *Niemen seneder suoche an mich deheinen rât* (No person in anguish should seek my advice) provide examples of *revocatio* that extend through a whole stanza: every claim has its nullifying counterclaim. Contradiction is an artistic tool that Reinmar uses effectively to create an aura of mystification and intrigue. These incoherent and contradictory motifs are woven kaleidoscopically into a poetic tapestry within which it is difficult to determine the exact confines of individual units: at times stanzas composed in the same metrical pattern constitute an artistically unified poem; at other times they do not. Those which clearly constitute unified poems include all of the *Frauenlieder,* the Crusade poems *Durch daz ich vröide hie bevor ie gerne pflac* (Since I used to enjoy being happy) and *Des tages dô ich daz kriuze nam* (On the day that I took the cross) (which, as Schweikle notes and as Marie-Luise Dittrich had pointed out years before, are not pro-Crusade propaganda poems but bitter anti-Crusade poems), and the falcon song *Ich waene, mir liebe geschehen wil* (I think something nice is going to happen). Otherwise, the strophes in Reinmar's opus seem to be quite autonomous in content. There are also cases where a passage in one meter clearly constitutes a cross-reference to a passage in a different meter: the woman in the dialogue poem *Sage, daz ich dies iemer lône,* for example, refers pointedly to words of the man in the poem *Mich hoehet, daz mich lange hoehen soll* (I am gladdened by what should long since have made me glad).

Most of Reinmar's poetry is composed in the tripartite canzone form. Exceptions include the magnificent falcon song *Ich waene, mir liebe geschehen wil* (156,10), in which a returning traveler frolics with joy in anticipation of a blissful reunion with his beloved. The poem is a powerful tour de force whose penultimate line quotes the fifth line of *Der winter waere mir ein zît* by Dietmar and whose metrical form is reminiscent of Dietmar's falcon song *Es stuont vrouwe alleine* (A woman stood alone). Both falcon songs are composed in rhymed couplets of four metrical feet (with different cadences), and both feature a driving, almost frenetically surging rhythm. Another exception, which looks vaguely like a canzone without actually being one, is the widow's lament *Si jehent, der sumer der sî hie;* it is metrically most similar to Dietmar's poem *Urloup hât des sumers brehen* (The summer's brightness has taken leave). Both poems open with comments about summer and continue with reminiscences on amorous joys of the past. Both are composed in iambic lines of four beats – except for the three opening lines of Dietmar's poem, where the anacrusis is missing. All the other strophes in Reinmar's opus are in canzone form.

> Sô wol dir, wîp, wie rein ein nam!
> wie sanfte er doch z'erkennen und ze nennen ist!
> ez wart nie niht sô lobesam,
> swâ dûz an rehte güete kêrest, sô du bist.
> Dîn lop mit rede nieman volenden kan.
> swes dû mit triuwen pfligest wol, der ist ein saelic man
> und mac vil gerne leben.
> dû gîst al der welte hôhen muot:
> maht ouch mir ein wênic vröide geben!

> (So bless thee, woman, how pure a name!
> How sweet it is both to hear and to say!
> There was never anything so praiseworthy
> As you are, when you put your mind to good.
> No one can ever speak your praise in full.
> Whoever knows your loving care is truly a blessed
>   man
> And can rightly rejoice in his life.
> You give all the world high spirits:
> You can also give me a little joy!)

The first two lines of this stanza constitute a *Stolle* (prop). They are mirrored by the next two lines of matching rhyme scheme, which form another *Stolle* and in which, when performed musically, the melody of the opening *Stolle* would be repeated. The two *Stollen* form the *Aufgesang*. The remaining lines of the strophe, with their different rhyme scheme, form the *Abgesang* and would, in musical performance, have a different melody from the *Aufgesang*.

This structure is varied in Reinmar's poetry with a range that is breathtaking. Earlier Danubian poetry also contained strophes in canzone form, but Reinmar's development of this structure is peculiarly his own. This development runs generally in the direction of extension and elaboration, but it does not provide a basis for a chronology of Reinmar's works: there is no reason to assume a linear development in his career. Reinmar may, for instance, have waxed archaic from time to time.

Three of Reinmar's compositions stand out in the length of strophe and line. The poem *Daz beste, daz ie man gesprach* (The best that a man ever spoke) features a stanza fifteen lines long; there are a few poems with longer stanzas in the opus of Walther von der Vogelweide, but no other canzone comes close to Reinmar's poem in its majestic length. The other two poems stand out in the length of a single line. Here lines of seven or eight metrical beats come in midstrophe and form a kind of middle axis. This structure looks like a variation of the old Danubian long closing line, found in the *Nibelungenlied,* and the poetry of Kürenberg. Reinmar also uses this extended line quite often in its more traditional location at the end of the strophe.

Reinmar der Alte was not the paragon of courtly love that scholars have continually made him out to be. He was first and foremost a master of psychological portrayal, depicting men and women caught up in a struggle to cope with the stresses and complexities of amorous relationships which seem, at times, to have been entered into foolishly. Both men and women are plagued by indecision, uncertainty, incoherence, and contradiction, and both tend to make assertions that, while intended to allay doubt and suspicion, seem likely to arouse them. This impression is clearly intended by the author, and, to make certain that the audience did not miss the point, Reinmar wrote from time to time a *revocatio* full of contradictions that are particularly obtrusive and blatant.

References:

Jeffrey Ashcroft, "Der Minnesänger und die Freude des Hofes: Zu Reinmars Kreuzliedern und Witwenklage," in *Poesie und Gebrauchsliteratur im deutschen Mittelalter,* edited by Volker Honemann and others (Tübingen: Niemeyer, 1979), pp. 219-238;

Reinhold Becker, *Der altheimische Minnesang* (Halle: Niemeyer, 1882);

Helmut de Boor and Richard Newald, *Geschichte der deutschen Literatur,* volume 2: *Die höfische Literatur: Vorbereitung, Blüte, Ausklang (1170-1250)* (Munich: Beck, 1969), pp. 282-292;

Marie-Luise Dittrich, "Reinmars Kreuzlied (MF 181,13)," in *Festschrift für Ludwig Wolff,* edited by Werner Schröder (Münster: Wachholtz, 1962), pp. 241-264;

William E. Jackson, *Reinmar's Women: A Study of the Woman's Song of Reinmar der Alte* (Amsterdam: Benjamins, 1981);

Carl von Kraus, *Die Lieder Reinmars des alten* (Munich: Bayerische Akademie der Wissenschaften, 1919);

Friedrich Maurer, *Die "Pseudoreimare"* (Heidelberg: Winter, 1966);

Silvia Ranawake, "Walthers Lieder der *herzeliebe* und die höfische Minnedoktrin," in *Minnesang in Österreich,* edited by Helmut Birkhan (Vienna: Halosar, 1983), pp. 109-152;

Walter Salmen, *Der Spielmann im Mittelalter* (Innsbruck: Helbing, 1983);

Wiebke Schmaltz, *Reinmar der Alte: Beiträge zur poetischen Technik* (Göppingen: Kümmerle, 1975);

Günther Schweikle, "Kommentar," in Reinmar, *Lieder: Mittelhochdeutsch/Neuhochdeutsch,* translated by Schweikle (Stuttgart: Reclam, 1986), pp. 303-390;

Schweikle, "War Reinmar 'von Hagenau' Hofsänger zu Wien?," in *Gestaltungsgeschichte und Gesellschaftsgeschichte,* edited by Helmut Kreuzer (Stuttgart: Metzler, 1969), pp. 1-31;

Manfred Stange, *Reinmars Lyrik: Forschungskritik und Überlegungen zu einem neuen Verständnis Reinmars des Alten* (Amsterdam: Rodopi, 1977);

Helmut Tervooren, *Reinmar-Studien: Ein Kommentar zu den "unechten" Liedern Reinmars des Alten* (Stuttgart: Hirzel, 1991);

Friedrich Wilhelm, "Zur Frage nach der Heimat Reimars des Alten und Walthers von der Vogelweide," *Münchener Museum,* 3 (1917): 1-15;

Eva Willms, *Liebesleid und Sangeslust: Untersuchungen zur deutschen Liebeslyrik des späten 12. und frühen 13. Jahrhunderts* (Munich & Zurich: Artemis, 1990).

Reinmar von Zweter

(circa 1200 – circa 1250)

Albrecht Classen
University of Arizona

MAJOR WORKS: One *leich* (lyrical lay), 311 *Sprüche* (didactic poems)

Manuscripts: The most important manuscript, containing 193 stanzas by Reinmar von Zweter in the "Frau-Ehren-Ton" and 22 stanzas in the "Neue Ehrenweise," is the Heidelberger Liederhandschrift D (Universitätsbibliothek Heidelberg, cod. pal. germ. 350). The Große Heidelberger Liederhandschrift C (Universitätsbibliothek Heidelberg, cod. pal. germ. 848) contains Reinmar's Leich, 2 stanzas in the "Meister-Ernst-Ton," and 217 stanzas in the "Frau-Ehren-Ton." Reinmar's Leich can also be found in the "Wiener Leichhandschrift" manuscript W (Österreichische Nationalbibliothek, Vienna, cod. 2701); manuscript l in the same library (cod. 2677); manuscript k[1], (Universitätsbibliothek Heidelberg, cpg 341); manuscript k[2], the socalled Kaloczaer manuscript (Genf-Cologny, Bibliothèque Bodmeriana, cod. Bodmer 72); a manuscript in Kassel (Gesamthochschulbibliothek, 2° Ms. poet. et roman. 30 [1]); and a manuscript in Marburg (Staatsarchiv, No. 9/3). A few fragments are included in manuscript Mainz, Staatsbibliothek, cod. I 15. Additional manuscripts with some of Reinmar's songs are manuscript Zurich, Zentralbibliothek, Z XI 302 (nos. 335, 336, and 341) and the "Niederrheinische Liederhandschrift" (Leipzig, Universitätsbibliothek, CCCCXXI, Rep. II 70[a]). Recently two fragments were discovered in Los Angeles (University of California Research Library AIT 36s Reinmar von Zweter) that include fourteen of Reinmar's songs, one of them previously unknown to Reinmar scholarship. All manuscripts were written in the late thirteenth and fourteenth centuries.

Miniature of Reinmar von Zweter dictating his poetry to two young women, in the fourteenth-century Große Heidelberger Liederhandschrift (Heidelberg, Universitätsbibliothek, cpg. 848, f.323)

First publication and standard edition: *Die Gedichte Reinmars von Zweter: Mit einer Notenbeilage,* edited by Gustav Roethe (Leipzig: Hirzel, 1887; reprinted, Amsterdam: Rodopi, 1967).

Reinmar von Zweter was one of the most highly praised didactic poets in the period between

Walther von der Vogelweide and Heinrich Frauenlob. The Meistersinger of the fourteenth century idealized him as one of the Twelve Old Masters (who allegedly laid the foundation for their art) because of the sophistication of his melodies and meters (among those were counted Walther, Wolfram von Eschenbach, Der tugendhafte Schreiber, Biterolf, Heinrich von Ofterdingen, Regenbogen, and especially Heinrich Frauenlob). As a professional goliard in southern Germany he frequently participated in public disputes and openly expressed his opinions on religious and political issues in many of his *Sprüche* (didactic poems). He attacked the pope for assuming worldly power and meddling in German politics, criticized the clergy for immorality and greediness, and mocked traditional courtly love poetry for its hollowness and formality. He strongly advocated a centralized empire on German soil, headed by the Hohenstaufens, who, however, had already begun to lose influence by that time. Walther was the first German lyric poet to incorporate political topics in his songs, but Reinmar developed this interest much further and created a wide range of stanzas supporting or opposing rulers and governments.

Reinmar's name appears in the earliest and most important manuscripts containing his work; various manuscripts give his name as "der von Zweter," "Reymar von tzweten," "Reinmar von Zwetel," "Reinhart von Zweten," or "Reynhard von zcwetzen." The late-medieval Meistersinger changed the name to "Römer von Zwickau" and "Ehrenbote" (vom Rhein).

He was probably born around 1200; except for a few fleeting references in his *Spruch* "Von Rîne sô bin ich geborn" (I was born near the Rhine) about his childhood and early upbringing, nothing is known about his early life. He might have learned his art from Walther at Duke Leopold VI's court in Vienna, but no solid evidence can be cited to confirm this hypothesis. He began to compose didactic poetry between 1227 and 1230, when he polemicized against Pope Gregory IX. The superscript of his portrait in the Große Heidelberger Liederhandschrift (Large Heidelberg Codex) gives him the title *her* (Sir), but no inference about his social status can be drawn from the use of that term. The miniature shows him resting his cheek on his left hand while sitting on a bench with eyes closed, obviously dictating to two female scribes. This was a well-known pose and had been used by various illuminators in antiquity and the Middle Ages. Reinmar is here modeled like Heinrich von Valdeke and Walther in various manuscripts. Rudolf Losse, the fourteenth-century secretary to Archbishop

Baldewin of Trier, included some of Reinmar's poems in a collection and characterized him as "Reymarus cecus dux nacione" (the blind Imperial Duke Reinmar); the miniature in manuscript C might corroborate his blindness. Losse's statement, however, was not based on historical documentation. In addition, the stereotypically meditative posture the poet assumes in his portrait does not necessarily indicate that he was blind.

References to political figures in Reinmar's poetry provide the basis for a picture of his activities between 1235 and 1241. In several *Sprüche,* including the so-called *Kurfürstenspruch* (didactic poem on the prince electors), he praises and defends Emperor Friedrich II against his opponents; but he changes his attitude after Friedrich's excommunication by the pope in 1239 (song 146). The poet also seems to have spent some time at the court of Duke Friedrich II der Streitbare (the Bellicose). That the poet went to Prague around 1237 to join the entourage of King Wenzel I is reflected in a panegyric on Wenzel and in an autobiographical poem. Reinmar repeatedly emphasizes Wenzel's interest in the arts. Obviously, the poet enjoyed a good reputation in Bohemia, but he had to change his political orientation once again because of Wenzel's emerging opposition to the Hohenstaufen emperor. Reinmar was the first major German poet to live in Prague, indicating the rise of Bohemia as a political power and cultural center.

The poet both chided and glorified emperors, kings, and princes. In song 148 he praises King Erik IV of Denmark, who, instigated by Wenzel I, competed with Friedrich II for the royal crown of Germany. In his *Spruch* 143 Reinmar appeals to God to assist the alliance against the emperor, who is now perceived as the Antichrist. Previously Reinmar had declared the nation to be identical with the emperor; now he separates the latter from his empire and accuses him of wrongdoings that do damage to the well-being and peace of the country.

That Reinmar spent time at the courts of Mainz and Sayn during the late 1240s can be inferred from his praise of certain patrons. Repeatedly the poet argues that rulers should be qualified not on the basis of birthright but by their character and abilities. He threatens to expose slanderers in his poetry; in song 153 he admonishes lords to dismiss egoistic cowards and to give preference to loyal servants; in song 154 he criticizes the influence of flatterers; in song 155 he attacks liars and cowards; and in 156 he laments the inability of great poets such as himself to fight back against buffoons and to retain the

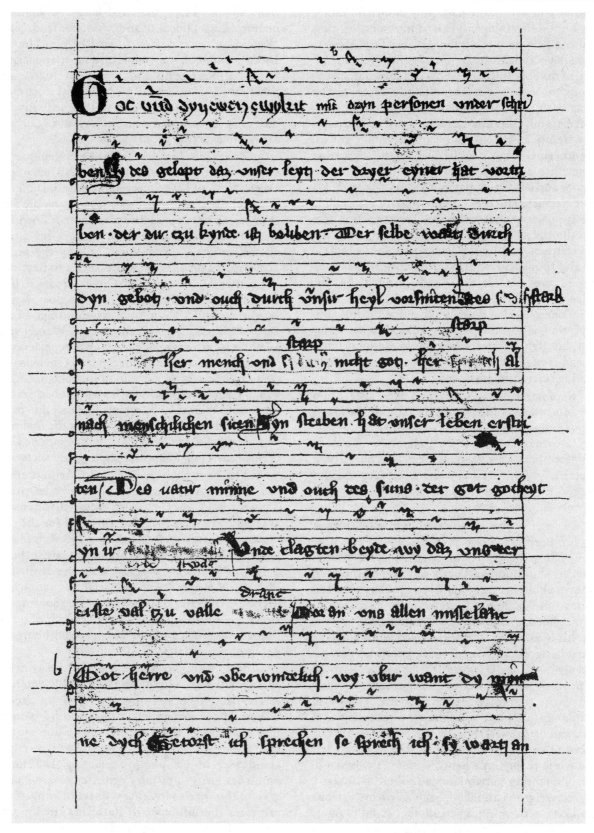

Part of Reinmar's Leich, *in a parchment manuscript dating from the first half of the fourteenth century (Vienna, Österreichische Nationalbibliothek, cod. vindob. 2707, f.2r)*

audience's goodwill. Finally he asks the dukes and kings to be guardians of Christianity, to protect the empire and maintain peace, to be fair judges, and to uphold honesty.

Reinmar seems to have died around 1250. He was buried in Eßfeld, near Würzburg. Later poets such as Hermann Damen, Der Rubin, Frauenlob, Hugo von Trimberg, and Lupold Hornburg included Reinmar in their catalogues of great composers from the past. Others, however, such as Der Marner, harshly criticized him – although unjustly – for having copied his tunes from other poets, for being a flatterer of his patrons, and for exaggerating. But in general he was highly admired for his didactic poems, and his *Töne* (melodies) were copied by the late medieval Meistersinger.

His religious *leich* (lay) does not differ remarkably from other *leiche* written in the thirteenth century; it deals with the Holy Trinity, the Virgin Mary, Christ, and God's love for humanity and concludes with an appeal to all Christians to remain pious, to refrain from sin, and to trust in Mary as a safeguard against damnation. In his large corpus of *Sprüche* Reinmar covers a broad spectrum of themes that do not break new ground but reiterate the standard concepts of German *Minnesang* and didactic poetry.

Reinmar also composed religious *Sprüche*. In song 235 he interprets each letter of Mary's name in spiritual terms: *M* stands for *Medjâtrix,* "the one who atones for us"; *A* stands for *Auxiliatrix,* "the one who helps us"; and so on. In song 229 he ridicules the importance attributed to this world and downplays its relevance for the human soul. Reinmar reminds people that they are made from dust and will return to dust.

Apart from his religious concerns, the range of his themes is wide; he discusses courtly love and service to courtly ladies; he praises the beloved lady and outlines a catalogue of virtues of good lovers. On the other hand, following the misogynistic tendencies of the Middle Ages, Reinmar warns men that women are evil, pointing out what happened to Adam, Samson, and Solomon. In the same poem, however, he makes a valiant attempt at rectifying this stereotypical impression by stressing that good women can inspire men to strive for virtue. In fact, *minne* (love) proves to be the decisive instrument in teaching people the values necessary for courtly society:

diu Minne lêret grôze milte,
diu Minne lêret grôze tugent,

diu Minne lêret, daz diu jugent
kan ritterlîch gebâren under schilte. (song 31, lines 9–12)

(love teaches great generosity,
love teaches great virtue,
love teaches that young people
can acquire chivalrous behavior.)

In his didactic poems Reinmar deals with the social structure of his time; he examines honor, poverty, virtue, true nobility of the soul (especially in songs 81, 82, and 255), and modesty; he provides an overview of the various dangers to virtues, such as alcohol and gambling (songs 107, 108, 109, 111, 115); and he praises intelligence. He describes the decline of tournament culture (song 106), as well as many other aspects of the noble lifestyle that have lost their traditional idealism. For him, honor should be one's highest goal, which implies: "Triuwe, Staete, reine Site, / Sorge unt Schame, Kiusche, Milte unt Manheit vert ir mite, / Dêmuot, Wârheit, Gehôrsam [song 71, lines 4–6]" (loyalty, constancy, good manners, / concern about one's proper behavior, chastity, generosity, and manliness go along with her, / modesty, truth, obedience). Observing superficiality and falsity, Reinmar stresses the relevance of a profound understanding of all things, emphasizing that beauty requires honor and that love must emanate from the heart (song 93).

Criticizing the downfall of his society, the poet appeals to the Antichrist to arrive earlier than scheduled and punish people who are entirely given to the pursuit of money. If Christ were alive today, Reinmar notes, the Christians themselves would sell him: "ez ist ir allez veile: sô gar stêt nû nâch guote ir herzen gir" (the whole world has become for sale: their hearts are craving so much for profit). Reinmar repeatedly describes the fickle character of fortune, warning people against placing their trust in it, as in song 91: "Gelückes rat ist sinewel; / im loufet maneger nâch, doch ist ez vor im gar ze snel" (Fortune's advice is round; / many people run after it, but it is too fast for them). He laughs at people who are never content with themselves and want to be something else. On the other hand, he advises young men to examine themselves in a mirror, to shed evil habits, and to follow good models (song 255).

Reinmar demonstrates familiarity with some of the major literary texts of the day, such as Wolfram von Eschenbach's *Parzival* (circa 1200–1210) and the anonymous *Herzog Ernst* (late twelfth or early thirteenth century). Both the broad panorama of Reinmar's themes and his pragmatic, didactic approach to many questions of his time made him an attractive poet for later generations.

References:

Franz H. Bäuml and Richard H. Rouse, "Roll and Codex: A New Manuscript Fragment of Reinmar von Zweter," *Beiträge zur Geschichte der deutschen Sprache und Literatur,* 105, no. 2 (1983): 192–231;

Hans-Joachim Behr, *Literatur als Machtlegitimation: Studien zur Funktion der deutschsprachigen Dichtung am böhmischen Königshof im 13. Jahrhundert,* Forschungen zur Geschichte der älteren deutschen Literatur, no. 9 (Munich: Fink, 1989);

Karl H. Bertau, "Über Themenanordnung und Bildung inhaltlicher Zusammenhänge in den religiösen Leichdichtungen des 13. Jahrhunderts," *Zeitschrift für deutsche Philologie,* 76, no. 2 (1957): 129–149;

Edgar Bonjour, *Reinmar von Zwetel als politischer Dichter: Ein Beitrag zur Chronologie seiner politischen Sprüche,* Sprache und Dichtung, no. 24 (Bern: Haupt, 1922);

Horst Brunner, *Die alten Meister: Studien zur Überlieferung und Rezeption der mittelhochdeutschen Sangspruchdichter im Spätmittelalter und in der frühen Neuzeit* (Munich: Beck, 1975);

Brunner, "Reinmar von Zweter," in *Die deutsche Literatur des Mittelalters: Verfasserlexikon,* revised by Kurt Ruh and others, volume 7 (Berlin & New York: De Gruyter, 1989), cols. 1198–1207;

Joachim Bumke, *Mäzene im Mittelalter: Die Gönner und Auftraggeber der höfischen Literatur in Deutschland 1150–1300* (Munich: Beck, 1979);

A. E. Cooke, "The Political Songs of Reinmar von Zweter: A Re-examination of Their Content and Chronology in Light of Recent Scholarship," Ph.D. dissertation, University of London, 1974;

Herta Gent, *Die mittelhochdeutsche politische Lyrik: 17 Längsschnitte,* Deutschkundliche Arbeiten, no. 13 (Breslau: Maruschke & Berendt, 1938);

Christoph Gerhard, "Reinmars von Zweter 'Idealer Mann' (Roehte Nr. 99 und 100)," *Beiträge zur Geschichte der deutschen Sprache und Literatur,* 109, no. 1 (1987): 51–84; no. 2 (1987): 222–251;

Wolfgang Jaeger, "Die Darstellung von Blinden in der Manessischen Liederhandschrift," *Heidelberger Jahrbuch,* 32 (1988): 119–128;

Ulrich Müller, *Untersuchungen zur politischen Lyrik des deutschen Mittelalters,* 2 volumes (Göppingen: Kümmerle, 1974);

Dietmar Peil, "'Im selben Boot': Variationen über ein metaphorisches Argument," *Archiv für Kulturgeschichte,* 68, no. 2 (1986): 269–293;

Olive Sayce, *The Medieval German Lyric 1150–1300: The Development of Its Themes and Forms in Their European Context* (Oxford: Clarendon Press, 1982);

Ursula Schulze, "Zur Vorstellung von Kaiser und Reich in staufischer Spruchdichtung bei Walther von der Vogelweide und Reinmar von Zweter," *Stauferzeit: Geschichte, Literatur, Kunst,* edited by Rüdiger Krohn and others, Karlsruher kulturwissenschaftliche Arbeiten, no. 1 (Stuttgart: Klett, 1979), pp. 206–219;

Volker Schupp, "Reinmar von Zweter, Dichter Kaiser Friedrichs II.," *Wirkendes Wort,* 19 (July-August 1969): 231–244;

Helmut Tervooren and Thomas Bein, "Ein neues Fragment zum Minnesang und zur Sangspruchdichtung: Reinmar von Zweter, Neidhart, Kelin, Runzlant und Unbekanntes," *Zeitschrift für deutsche Philologie,* 107, no. 1 (1988): 1–26;

Burghart Wachinger, *Sängerkrieg: Untersuchungen zur Spruchdichtung des 13. Jahrhunderts* (Munich: Beck, 1973).

Rudolf von Ems

(circa 1200 – circa 1254)

Adrian Stevens
University College London

MAJOR WORKS: *Der guote Gêrhart* (circa 1221)

Manuscripts: There are two extant manuscripts: *A* from the late thirteenth or early fourteenth century (Vienna cod. 2699) and *B* from the late fifteenth century (Vienna, cod. 2793).

First publication: *Der gute Gerhard: Eine Erzählung von Rudolf von Ems,* edited by Moriz Haupt (Leipzig: Weidmann, 1840).

Standard edition: *Der guote Gêrhart,* edited by John A. Asher (Tübingen, 1971).

Edition in modern German: *Der gute Gerhard,* translated by Karl Tober, edited by Eugen Thurnher (Bregenz: Russ, 1959?).

Barlaam und Josaphat (circa 1222–1232)

Manuscripts: Fourteen complete manuscripts and thirty-three fragments from the thirteenth to the fifteenth centuries have been recorded.

First publication: *Barlaam und Josaphat von Rudolf von Montfort, mit einem Wörterbuch versehen,* edited by Friedrich Karl Köpke (Königsberg: Nicolovius, 1818).

Standard edition: *Barlaam und Josaphat von Rudolf von Ems,* edited by Franz Pfeiffer (Leipzig, 1843); revised edition, edited by Heinz Rupp (Berlin: Weidmann, 1965).

Alexander (circa 1230–circa 1254)

Manuscripts: The work survives in one fragment from the thirteenth or fourteenth century and two manuscripts from the first half of the fifteenth century: *M* (Munich, cgm. 203, containing lines 1–21643) and *B* (Brussels, Bibliothèque Royale, ms. 18232, containing lines 1–21623).

First publication and standard edition: *Alexander: Ein höfischer Versroman des 13. Jahrhunderts,* 2 volumes, edited by Victor Junk (Leipzig: Hiersemann 1928, 1929).

Willehalm von Orlens (circa 1235–1243)

Manuscripts: Seven parchment manuscripts from the thirteenth and fourteenth centuries, twelve paper manuscripts from the fifteenth and sixteenth centuries, and fourteen frag-

Miniature of Rudolf von Ems dictating to a scribe, in the Wernigerode Manuscript (Wernigerode, Fürstliche Bibliothek)

ments are currently recorded.

First publication and standard edition: *Rudolfs von Ems Willehalm von Orlens: Herausgegeben aus dem Wasserburger Codex der Fürstlich Fürstenbergischen Hofbibliothek in Donaueschingen,* edited by Victor Junk (Berlin: Weidmann, 1905).

Weltchronik (circa 1243–circa 1254)

Manuscripts: The work survives in more than one hundred manuscripts and fragments from the thirteenth to the fifteenth centuries.

First publication and standard edition: *Ru-

dolfs von Ems Weltchronik: Aus der Wernigeroder Handschrift, edited by Gustav Ehrismann (Berlin: Weidmann, 1915).

Rudolf von Ems is one of the most important figures in the literary history of thirteenth-century Germany. Like his predecessors Heinrich von Veldeke, Hartmann von Aue, and Gottfried von Straßburg, whose work of accommodating the classical heritage to the vernacular he saw himself continuing, Rudolf was skilled in the school-based techniques of rhetorical and dialectical composition. His work shows that he had received a thorough grounding in the subjects that comprised the trivium and that he was well versed in the fundamentals of theology. He was a self-consciously literary author who was regarded by his contemporaries and successors as a master, and his texts continued to be read and copied in unusually large numbers for more than two centuries after his death.

According to his own account in *Willehalm von Orlens* (circa 1235–1243), he was a *ministeriale* (members of the unfree nobility) in the service of the counts of Montfort. His full name is given by the writer who completed his *Weltchronik* (Chronicle of the World, circa 1243–circa 1254) as Ruodolf von Ense. The Ems family to which Rudolf is thought to belong took its name from Hohenems, near Bregenz in the Vorarlberg region of Austria. The family had built a castle at Hohenems toward the end of the twelfth century; its members had established themselves as imperial *ministeriales,* and the counts of Montfort were their immediate neighbors. It is not known what functions Rudolf performed in the counts' service, and he does not name them among the patrons of his work; but his clerical education could have been put to a variety of practical uses. On the available evidence, it made him upwardly mobile, eventually affording him the opportunity to pursue a prestigious literary career at the court of Emperor Friedrich II's younger son, King Konrad IV.

Rudolf's beginnings were comparatively modest, and he was dependent initially on local contacts and patronage. His first known work, *Der guote Gêrhart* (The Good Gerhart, circa 1221), was composed at the prompting of Rudolf von Steinach, a *ministeriale* who between 1209 and 1221 held an influential position in the service of the bishop of Constance and who had lands and a castle adjoining the territories of the Ems family and the counts of Montfort. The close link between Rudolf von Steinach and the bishop of Constance suggests that *Der guote Gêrhart* may initially have been read at the bishop's court to and by a mixed audience of lay people and clerics. It must have been favorably received, for Rudolf von Ems was given the chance to compose his second work for another important figure connected with the bishop of Constance: Wido, abbot between 1222 and 1232 of the Cistercian monastery of Cappel near Zurich, who supplied the Latin text on which Rudolf based his *Barlaam und Josaphat* (1222–1232). Cappel formed part of the diocese of Constance, and there are good reasons for thinking that Rudolf wrote his narrative in the expectation that it would be read and performed not only in the monastery but also at the bishop's court. The monastery and the bishop's court would also be plausible settings for the version of the Eustachius legend that Rudolf claims in *Alexander* (circa 1230–circa 1254) to have composed after *Barlaam und Josaphat* but that has not survived.

It seems that after finishing *Eustachius* he began work on *Alexander,* presumably still for the bishop's court, but broke off the project when he received a prestigious commission to compose the romance *Willehalm von Orlens.* His new patron, Konrad von Winterstetten, was one of the most powerful men in Germany. Appointed procurator of the duchy of Swabia by Emperor Friedrich II, he was one of a small group of advisers entrusted with the upbringing of Friedrich's son Konrad IV, who in 1237, just before his ninth birthday, was elected king of Germany and designated his father's successor. Konrad had been brought to Germany by Friedrich in 1235 following the rebellion of Friedrich's older son, Heinrich VII. Having secured Heinrich's deposition as king and Konrad's election, Friedrich returned to Italy in 1237, never to set foot in Germany again. The composition of *Willehalm von Orlens* can plausibly be located at the court of Konrad IV, and there is strong internal evidence that it was written with the young king in mind. In this case, it is unlikely that Rudolf began it before Konrad's arrival in Germany in 1235, and he must have finished it by 1243: Konrad von Winterstetten died in that year, and Rudolf's elaborate acknowledgment of him in the epilogue as his patron makes plain that he was still living when *Willehalm von Orlens* was completed.

Rudolf retained his position at the royal court after 1243, evidently attracting the active support of the king. It was on the personal instructions of Konrad IV that he undertook the long and expensive labor of composing the *Weltchronik,* and the likelihood is that the king charged him to resume work on *Alexander* at the same time. Rudolf's main source for the early part of *Alexander* (to line 5014) is the tenth-century *Historia de preliis;* he then switches abruptly to adapting the history of the Roman author Quintus Curtius Rufus, which had clearly not been available to him during the initial phase of composition. Not only does he acquire a new principal source and other secondary sources, but he also arranges *Alexander* into a clearly designated sequence of books, thereby bringing it into line with the model established in *Willehalm von Orlens* and adopted also in the *Weltchronik*. The king's commission would have given him the time and the resources necessary to produce two large-scale works in chronicle form. Rudolf was able to incorporate into *Alexander* material originally intended for inclusion in the *Weltchronik,* indicating that the two works were written in tandem. Add to this point the fact that both employ typological models of historical interpretation to support the political cause of Konrad, and there can be little doubt that *Alexander,* too, was composed for the king.

The eulogy Rudolf addresses to Konrad in the prologue to the fifth book of the *Weltchronik* (lines 21556-21740) could not have been written before 1251, since it makes reference to the death of Friedrich II; although Friedrich died in December 1250, news of his death did not reach Germany until February 1251. Konrad, forced to fight for his inheritance, left for Italy in October 1251, but he seems to have instructed Rudolf to remain behind in Germany and continue work on the *Weltchronik* (lines 21711-21740). Rudolf added some twelve thousand verses after his address to the king. The *Weltchronik* and *Alexander* break off abruptly, in the middle of narrative sequences. It is possible that Rudolf was forced to abandon both projects because, after the death of Konrad in Italy in 1254, he could find no other patron; but according to the continuator of the *Weltchronik,* Rudolf himself died "in welschen richen" (in Italian regions, line 33483). Whether Konrad had summoned him to Italy to bring further installments of the works he had been commissioned to write for the royal court and whether Rudolf's death in Italy occurred before or after the death of the king remain matters for conjecture.

What does seem certain is that he had become famous and that his art was widely admired by the time of his death. The continuator of the *Weltchronik* remarks of Rudolf, "sîn name ist iu wol bekant" (his name is well known to you, line 33495), clearly confident that his audience will share his high opinion of his illustrious predecessor. The esteem in which the *Weltchronik* was held may be judged by the fact that it survives in more than a hundred manuscript copies and fragments, as compared, for instance, with eighty-six for Wolfram von Eschenbach's *Parzival* (1200-1210) and seventy for Wolfram's

Willehalm (circa 1210-1220). And Rudolf's *Willehalm von Orlens* appears to have been as widely disseminated in the Middle Ages as Hartmann von Aue's *Iwein* (circa 1203) and Gottfried von Straßburg's *Tristan und Isolde* (circa 1210): thirty-three manuscript copies and fragments are currently recorded for *Willehalm von Orlens,* thirty-two for *Iwein,* and twenty-seven for *Tristan und Isolde,* while the forty-seven copies of Rudolf's *Barlaam und Josaphat* compare favorably with the eleven of Hartmann's *Gregorius* (circa 1187).

The audiences for whom Rudolf wrote valued his ability to accommodate Latin-based clerical learning to secular aristocratic culture within the genre of vernacular narrative. The extended literary excursuses incorporated into *Alexander* (lines 3063 to 3298) and *Willehalm von Orlens* (lines 2143 to 2334) presuppose readers and listeners with a detailed knowledge of German authors and their works. Konrad IV himself may well have shared that interest: it seems that through Konrad von Winterstetten and his circle the king became acquainted with German court literature at an early age, and his retention of Rudolf as a court author would have enhanced not only Rudolf's personal prestige but the prestige of the art of vernacular writing in general.

Rudolf makes his mastery of that art a central part of his self-presentation in his works. In composing his two literary excursuses he continues a generic form introduced into German vernacular narrative by Gottfried in *Tristan und Isolde.* Like Gottfried before him, Rudolf implies that the German vernacular court literature of the modern age is a renewal of classical literature. It is validated on the general grounds of its indebtedness to classical Latin models and gains distinction specifically through the ability of those modern clerical authors who are masters of their craft to fuse words and ideas in the manner of the ancients. The eulogy on Gottfried that forms a central part of the literary excursus in *Alexander* documents Rudolf's clerical concepts of both the art of writing and the nature of the literary relationship between past and present:

> . . . der wîse Gotfrit
> von Strâzburc der nie valschen trit
> mit valsche in sîner rede getrat.
> wie ist sô ebensleht gesat
> sîn vunt, sô rîch, sô sinneclîch!
> wie ist sô gar meisterlîch
> sîn Tristan! swer den ie gelas,
> der mac wol hœren daz er was
> ein schrôter süezer worte
> und wîser sinne ein porte. (lines 3153-3162)

Page from a late-fourteenth-century manuscript of Rudolf's Weltchronik, *with a miniature depicting Lot and his wife fleeing from the burning city of Sodom (Donaueschingen, Fürstliche Fürstenbergische Hofbibliothek, ms. 79)*

(. . . the wise Gottfried
von Straßburg, who never took a wrong step
by mistake in his speech.
How smoothly and evenly sown
is his invention, so rich, so brilliant and considered!
What artistic mastery there is
in his Tristan! Anybody who has ever read it
can easily hear that he was
a tailor of sweet words
and a gateway of wise ideas.)

Gottfried's *Tristan und Isolde* is the work of a master, a cleric schooled, like Rudolf, in the arts of the trivium. In avoiding all mistakes in his speech Gottfried demonstrates his mastery of grammar — the science, according to the standard medieval-school definition, of speaking correctly. His implied facility in dialectic — the technique of reasoning from opinions that commend themselves, according to the accepted Aristotelian formula, to all or to the majority or to the wise — is attributed to Gottfried's rich invention; and his skill in rhetoric is attested by his talent for dressing in pleasing language the ideas his invention enables him to find. Behind this characterization, too, stand the lines from Horace's *Ars Poetica* that provided medieval commentators with an enduring and authoritative definition of the function of poetry:

Aut prodesse volunt aut delectare poetae
aut simul et iucunda et idonea dicere vitae . . . (lines 333–334)
. . . .

omne tulit punctum qui miscuit utile dulci,
lectorem delectando pariterque monendo (lines 343–344)

(Poets aim either to benefit or to delight,
or to utter words both pleasing and proper to life . . .
. . . .
He has won every vote who has blended profit and pleasure,
at once delighting and instructing the reader.)

A mixture of pleasure and profit is precisely what, on Rudolf's reading, *Tristan und Isolde* provides. Its language is pleasing (Rudolf's *süeze* [line 3161] echoes, perhaps intentionally, Horace's *dulce*), and to the extent that it presents the reader with wise ideas, its effect can be said to be beneficial. But to suggest, as Rudolf does, that Gottfried fulfills Horace's ideal of the function of literature is by implication to make an ambitious claim for *Tristan und Isolde*: that by meeting the standards of composition associated in the schools with the works of the Latin authors of antiquity it has earned the status

of a modern classic. Just as Rudolf reads Gottfried, so Gottfried himself claims to read and value Hartmann von Aue, Bligger von Steinach, and Heinrich von Veldeke for their ability to fuse words and ideas, eloquence and wisdom. And when the continuator of the *Weltchronik* seeks to summarize the essential features of Rudolf's literary art, he, too, cites the classical-clerical ideal of matching words to ideas:

Der dis buoch getihtet
hat unze her uns verrihtet
wol an allen orten
an sinnen und worten. . . . (lines 33479–33482)

(The man who composed this book
has done it correctly
and properly everywhere for us
with regard to ideas and words. . . .)

Bernard Silvestris declares in his commentary on Virgil's *Aeneid* that "prius enim non debet aliquis nomen magistri praesumere quam possideat sapientiam et eloquentiam" (nobody should lay claim to the title of master before he comes to possess wisdom and eloquence). It is the combination of wisdom and eloquence that they were thought to achieve in their works that entitled Rudolf and Gottfried to be seen, from the clerkly perspective of their contemporaries and successors, as masters. But the project of renewing the classic within the context of vernacular court literature has nothing to do with mere antiquarianism or pedantry. Rudolf sees himself as a modern writer producing modern texts for modern audiences. The problems he addresses are the problems of his society; the old forms are adapted to new ends and are renewed and made more widely accessible by being accommodated to the vernacular. Rudolf's intertexts are many and varied: classical, theological, biblical and hagiographic, legal and historical, fictional and non-fictional, Latin and vernacular. His works bring into productive dialogue with one another a wide variety of the languages and ideologies of the Germany of his time, and this richness and immediacy of reference helps to explain his appeal to the broad spectrum of lay and clerical groups from which the court audiences of the thirteenth century were drawn.

In *Der guote Gêrhart* the tenth-century emperor Otto I, having instituted the archbishopric of Magdeburg, asks God to reveal to him what his reward will be in heaven for his pious deed. An angel reproaches him for his presumption and cites as an example of goodness and humility the merchant Gerhart. The emperor hurries to Cologne, where Gerhart tells him his story. During a successful trade voyage he was driven ashore in Morocco. There he discovered that the Norwegian princess Erene, having been shipwrecked while on her way to marry King Willehalm (William) of England, was being held captive together with a group of Christian noblemen. Gerhart used the entire profit from his voyage to buy their release and took Erene back to Cologne with him. For two years he attempted to discover the whereabouts of Willehalm, who had been shipwrecked at the same time as Erene, but without success. Assuming Willehalm to be dead, he arranged for Erene to marry his son, but Willehalm appeared unexpectedly at the wedding feast. Gerhart returned Erene to him and accompanied Willehalm to England to help him reclaim his throne. Leaving Willehalm on the ship, Gerhart made his way to London. The English, having had no news of Willehalm since his shipwreck and believing him to be dead, offered Gerhart the crown, but Gerhart declined. Having restored Willehalm to his rightful inheritance, he was content to return to Cologne and resume his life as a merchant. As he listens to Gerhart, Otto realizes that his endowment of the archbishopric of Magdeburg is not as conspicuously generous as he had assumed. He acknowledges that in renouncing a queen for his son and a kingdom for himself Gerhart has shown both greater self-denial and greater goodness. Otto does penance for his complacency and presumption in anticipating a heavenly reward for what now seems to him an overvalued act of charity, and he orders Gerhart's story to be recorded in writing for the spiritual benefit of the Christian community.

In presenting Gerhart's story, Rudolf is in an obvious sense extending its spiritual benefit to the court of the bishop of Constance. But the appeal of *Der guote Gêrhart* at the bishop's court appears not to have been solely a matter of its moral content. As Rudolf makes explicit in the epilogue, he has set himself the task of meeting demanding expectations in respect to form and genre, and in the process demonstrating his skill in the art of literary composition. Rudolf von Steinach asked him not merely to produce a vernacular version of Gerhart's story but to write it using the correct verse form. According to the literary excursus in *Alexander,* the correct verse form for court narrative was introduced into German by Heinrich, "der rehter rîme alrêrst began" (who first began to use right rhymes, line 3114) and was consolidated by Hartmann, Wolfram, and Gottfried. Rudolf assumes that there will be present among his audience at the bishop's court

people sufficiently familiar with the works of his predecessors and the criteria according to which they were composed to judge his art against theirs. He is writing for a court at which court literature is known and read, and he is eager to show that he commands both its linguistic registers and its rhetorical forms. With this goal in mind he takes the works of his predecessors, most notably Gottfried's *Tristan und Isolde,* as intertexts. Rudolf's is an art of allusion and imitation: he even goes so far as to quote phrases from Gottfried, but he does so in a way calculated to demonstrate his own ability to accommodate words to ideas, to fuse dialectical and rhetorical invention. In deliberately imitating an author acknowledged to be a master, Rudolf's aim is not, as used to be assumed, to plagiarize but to display his own mastery, to draw attention to his command of the same registers and techniques of literary composition as Gottfried.

Der guote Gêrhart was written, Rudolf says, for a mixed audience of noble men and noble women (lines 6834–6835). To be worthy of such an audience, his art must project a noble message in a noble form. The narrative turns on the definition of nobility and on the paradoxical sense in which it is possible for a merchant to be more noble than an emperor. Gerhart, in his humility and self-denial, serves as a model for Otto, as Otto is obliged to recognize. From the Christian perspective the emperor is less noble than his subject, although in the end, by humbling himself sufficiently to learn a lesson in humility from a merchant, Otto becomes Gerhart's spiritual equal. The figure of Gerhart is sometimes taken to symbolize the rise in importance of the urban merchant class in thirteenth-century Germany; yet if Gerhart is exemplary, it is not because he is a merchant but because he has assimilated so completely the mentality and manners of a nobleman as to shame an emperor. He is a model of conduct because of his generous and self-denying acts but also because of his refined and elegant self-presentation in terms of speech, dress, and gesture. Otto himself admires Gerhart from the outset for his style and refinement, exclaiming in praise of the merchant that "er ist sô hovelich [line 810]" (he is so courtly). Gerhart is both a perfect Christian and a perfect gentleman, and it is these qualities that lend him his initial credibility in Otto's eyes. His story enacts a dialogue between aristocratic and Christian values, between the secular language of the court and the spiritual language of the church. Gerhart makes plain that the way to success and esteem is

Page from the Wernigerode Manuscript of the Weltchronik, *with illustrations depicting events in the life of David (Wernigerode, Fürstliche Bibliothek, f.178r)*

through the pursuit of both spiritual and secular nobility; in the case of Rudolf himself, it is through the literary presentation of that pursuit before the court of the bishop of Constance.

In *Barlaam und Josaphat* Rudolf again presents a dialogue between spiritual and courtly values. His source, procured for him by Abbot Wido, was a Latin version of John of Damascus's Greek adaptation of an Indian legend of the Buddha. Josaphat, the son of Avenier, the pagan king of India, is converted to Christianity by the hermit Barlaam. After failing to persuade Josaphat to renounce his belief, Avenier gives Josaphat half his kingdom, which Josaphat governs as a Christian ruler, and Avenier is eventually himself converted by his son to Christianity. After the death of Avenier, Josaphat renounces his kingdom and the world and rejoins his master Barlaam to live the life of a saintly hermit. Rudolf says of the story that "ez ist der welte widerstrît [line 1610]" (it is the enemy of the world), and its elegant presentation of Christian doctrine certainly accounts for its appeal at the monastery of Cappel; yet it is not a monastic work. It accommodates the liturgical and sermon rhetoric of Latin ecclesiastical tradition to the secular verse form of German vernacular literature, and although it may have been read at Cappel it was designed to be read, too, at the more worldly court of the bishop of Constance, where women were in the audience. In Rudolf's source the magician Theodas counsels Avenier to tempt Josaphat away from Christianity by surrounding him with beautiful and seductive women, but in Josaphat's unworldly eyes women are the devil. Rudolf interrupts the narrative at this point (line 11735), inserting an elaborate digression in praise of courtly ladies and the joy they bring to men, like himself, who are less hostile to secular pleasures than the hero of his legend. Although he presents the Christian life as exemplary and stresses the moral benefit to be derived from his work, the type of spirituality he promotes is not confined to the monastic ideal. *Barlaam und Josaphat* is a heteroglot text in a way that its uncompromisingly ascetic Latin source is not, and in finding a place for the language and values of polite society it significantly relaxes the generic constraints normally associated with the writing of hagiography.

The romance *Willehalm von Orlens* has a secular theme. The orphaned Willehalm is raised by Jofrit of Brabant, who sends him to the court of the king of England. There he falls in love with the English princess Amelie. The two become secretly engaged after Willehalm promises Amelie that he will prove

himself by serving her as her knight. After returning home and being invested, Willehalm distinguishes himself at a series of tournaments. Meanwhile, the king of England promises Amelie in marriage to the king of Spain. Willehalm returns to England and attempts to abduct her, but they are caught. Willehalm is banished and forced to promise that he will not speak again until Amelie gives him permission. Keeping his vow of silence, he journeys to the court of the king of Norway, in whose service he performs heroic feats of arms. The abbess Savine, sister of the king of England, learning of her niece's love for Willehalm, takes Amelie to the Norwegian court. There Amelie releases Willehalm from his vow of silence. He and Amelie, having remained constant to one another through their separations and tribulations, are married. Returning to England, they are reconciled to the king. Willehalm succeeds to the duchy of Brabant and later to the throne of England. Among his descendants is Godfrey of Bouillon, the first king of Jerusalem.

Through his mother, Isabella of Brienne, the second wife of Friedrich II, Konrad IV was heir to the kingdom of Jerusalem. In linking the young king so deftly to his hero, Rudolf turns Willehalm into a special kind of role model. The work, which is almost entirely the story of Willehalm's formative years, is designed as a mirror for a prince close to him in age. Willehalm is introduced into the essential legal, diplomatic, military, and social functions of kingship; he also undergoes a long and strenuous sentimental education. But if Rudolf wrote his romance with Konrad in mind, the king was not its only addressee. The lost French source of *Willehalm von Orlens,* Rudolf says, was procured by Johannes von Ravensburg, a Swabian *ministeriale* in the imperial service, who requested Rudolf to produce a German version for the delectation of Johannes's lady, in the hope "Das ouch si im den sînen pîn / senfterte und den kumber sîn [lines 15623–15624]" (that she might be moved / to alleviate his anguish and grief). A similar motive is attributed to Rudolf's actual patron, Konrad von Winterstetten, who is said to have commissioned the work "Ze dienste sîner vrowen [line 15655]" (In the service of his lady). The stylized linguistic registers of courtly love were apparently not, at the court of King Konrad, confined to fiction but were used to define relationships that existed outside it. The lives of Willehalm and Amelie are exemplary in that the public and private roles they play, and the languages and values by which those roles are defined, were essential elements of the self-understanding of the aristocratic society from which the members of

Rudolf's audience were drawn. The young King Konrad could be expected to try out the world-making roles assigned to the royal hero of Rudolf's romance and to assimilate and use the languages by which those roles were constituted.

In rewriting the story of Alexander the Great, Rudolf's main concern was to present Konrad with an attractive model of the duties of kingship and the ways in which they were properly fulfilled. Rudolf does not hesitate to modernize his principal sources, the *Historia de preliis* and (from line 5015) Curtius Rufus. Whereas Curtius Rufus presents an urbane and colorful account of Alexander that details his vices as well as his virtues, Rudolf refuses to admit any negative traits into the presentation of his hero. Rudolf's Alexander is heavily idealized; every incident recounted from his life and career is designed to demonstrate how a thirteenth-century king ought to act out the roles that define the royal office. But just as important as the new social and cultural perspective that informs Rudolf's work is the changed understanding of history within which the achievements of the central figure are judged and evaluated. Rudolf's Alexander is seen within the context not of pagan but of Christian history; his deeds acquire a prefigurative, typological significance that has no equivalent in Curtius Rufus. The implicit moral and political invitation that Rudolf's text offers to Konrad is to become a new, Christian Alexander and thereby surpass the ruler in whose life his life is prefigured.

The typological relationship between Alexander and Konrad plays a vital part in Rudolf's apocalyptic view of the destiny of Konrad and of the history of the empire. Friedrich II had been excommunicated by Pope Gregory IX in 1239 and deposed by supporters of Gregory's successor, Innocent IV, in 1245. In 1247 Wilhelm of Holland was elected king of Germany at Innocent's instigation, even though Konrad still claimed the title. The war between the papal and Hohenstaufen parties continued after Friedrich's death. Each side sought to justify its cause by making polemical use of the prophecies of pseudo-Methodius concerning the coming of the Antichrist, the Last Emperor, and the end of the world. These prophecies are reinterpreted by Rudolf in his *Alexander* in the interests of King Konrad (lines 17320–17576). Alexander conquers the evil descendants of the Ishmaelites and of Gog and Magog (lines 17219–17319) and imprisons them in an inaccessible mountain fastness (lines 17301–17318). Their descendants escape in modern times and conquer most of Africa, Asia, and Europe, including Germany, France, Rome (where it is

to be inferred that they form the papal party), and Jerusalem. But on Rudolf's reading of pseudo-Methodius it is ordained that, just as their predecessors were conquered by Alexander, the new Ishmaelites will be conquered before the world ends by Alexander's modern antitype, the Last Emperor. Rudolf identifies the Last Emperor as Konrad IV, acting in fulfillment of his eschatological and historical role as the new Alexander, the rightful Christian ruler of both Rome and Jerusalem. This chiliastic scheme is reinforced by being accommodated within the traditional doctrine that the history of the world is encompassed by the succession of four great empires: the Babylonian, Persian, Macedonian, and Roman. Just as the Roman Empire supersedes the Macedonian, so it is the divinely conceived destiny of Konrad, the last legitimate Roman emperor, to supersede Alexander.

Rudolf continued his prophetic efforts in support of Konrad in the *Weltchronik,* integrating them into his ambitious task of setting before the king and his court God's purpose as revealed in the history of the world from the Creation to the present. History in the *Weltchronik* is the working out of God's plot; divine time presses constantly upon mundane time. God, for Rudolf, is the master storyteller, the ultimate referent of every event, the significance of which can be discerned by taking bearings back upon the sacred past recorded in the Bible, and forward upon doomsday and the kingdom to come. To judge from the unusually large number of manuscripts in which it is preserved, the *Weltchronik,* which introduced the ecclesiastical genre of the world chronicle into the vernacular, was one of the most popular and highly esteemed works of the German Middle Ages. Rudolf's principal sources were the Vulgate and the *Historia Scholastica* of Petrus Comestor. In rewriting those sources, he abridges, adapts, and reinterprets them: the truth of history he undertakes to reveal to Konrad and his court is not only factual but spiritual, accessible through figurative understanding and typological interpretation. Whereas in *Alexander* he had made use of the tradition that divided history into four empires, in the *Weltchronik* he appropriates the alternative exegetical practice of allotting to the world six ages in figurative parallel with the six days which, according to Genesis, God took to create it. In Rudolf's scheme the first age begins with Adam and ends with Noah; the second begins with Noah and ends with Abraham; the third begins with Abraham and ends with Moses; the fourth begins with Moses and ends with David; the fifth begins with David and ends with the Incarnation; and the sixth age, which is the present age, begins with the Incarnation and will end when the world ends.

Within each age Rudolf briefly leaves what he calls "der rehtin mere ban" (the highway of the true story, line 3786) which is Christian biblical history, to follow the "biwege" (byways, line 3782) of pagan history. This division of history and the narrative procedures that it entails are evidently influenced by Saint Augustine's distinction between the city of God and the city of the world. But Rudolf differs from Augustine in one important particular. In Rudolf's account pagan history starts not with the sin of Cain, as it does in Augustine's *De civitate Dei* (The City of God), but with the building of the Tower of Babel (lines 1287–3065), after which the descendants of the three sons of Noah, deprived of a common language, scatter across Asia, Europe, and Africa. Since for Rudolf it is axiomatic that the truth of all history is a product of Christian revelation, pagan history is of interest only insofar as it can be accommodated to Christian history. The events of pagan history are inserted in the biblical master narrative according to the age of the world within which they are deemed to have occurred and are interpreted in relation to God's larger design, which it is the aim of the *Weltchronik* to explicate. Africa, settled by the descendants of Ham, the son cursed by Noah, has no prestigious part to play in Rudolf's rendering of the divine plot, and so is relegated to the margins of his narrative. But Asia and Europe, settled respectively by the descendants of Shem and Japheth, the two sons blessed by Noah, are given positive roles in Rudolf's exposition of God's design. Noah prophesies that God will enlarge Japheth and that Japheth will dwell in the tents of Shem; Rudolf offers a figurative interpretation of his words (lines 957–1007), according to which Jesus is one of the descendants of Shem, and the children of Japheth are the Christian peoples of Europe who dwell with Jesus in the new tents of salvation. The elect among the descendants of Shem are "Gotis burgere" (the citizens of God, line 3755); and from the children of Japheth, under the old dispensation "der welte burgere" (citizens of the world, line 3780), are descended the Greeks

(lines 3354–3365), the Trojans, and the Romans, whose empire has continued into the sixth age – the age of Rudolf and his audience and the age of grace. Konrad IV, as "rœmeschin keisirs kint" (the child of the Roman emperor, line 21617), is the rightful heir to Rome and a child of Japheth; but he is also the rightful heir to the kingdom of Jerusalem and, as such, both a child of Shem and the royal descendant of David, Solomon, and Jesus chosen by God to be ruler over all his people (lines 21556–21710). In Konrad, according to the *Weltchronik,* as the sixth age of the world draws to its appointed close, the highway and the byways of history converge and are completed.

Bibliography:

Angelika Odenthal, *Rudolf von Ems: Eine Bibliographie* (Cologne: Gabel, 1988).

References:

Helmut Brackert, *Rudolf von Ems: Dichtung und Geschichte* (Heidelberg: Winter, 1968);

Joachim Bumke, *Geschichte der deutschen Literatur im hohen Mittelalter* (Munich: Deutscher Taschenbuch Verlag, 1990);

Xenja von Ertzdorff, *Rudolf von Ems: Untersuchungen zum höfischen Roman im 13. Jahrhundert* (Munich: Fink, 1967);

D. H. Green, "On the Primary Reception of the Works of Rudolf von Ems," *Zeitschrift für deutsches Altertum,* 115 (1986): 151–180;

Joachim Heinzle, *Geschichte der deutschen Literatur von den Anfängen bis zum Beginn der Neuzeit,* volume 2, part 2: *Wandlungen und Neuansätze im 13. Jahrhundert (1220/30–1280/90)* (Königstein: Athenäum, 1984);

Adrian Stevens, "Zum Literaturbegriff bei Rudolf von Ems," in *Geistliche und weltliche Epik des Mittelalters in Österreich,* edited by David McLintock, Stevens, and Fred Wagner (Göppingen: Kümmerle, 1987), pp. 19–28;

Wolfgang Walliczek, "Rudolf von Ems," in *Verfasserlexikon der deutschen Literatur des Mittelalters,* volume 8 (Berlin: De Gruyter, 1991), cols. 322–345.

Der Stricker

(circa 1190 – circa 1250)

Michael Resler
Boston College

MAJOR WORKS: *Daniel von dem blühenden Tal* (1210-1225)

Manuscripts: The work is transmitted in four manuscripts dating from the late fifteenth century; a fifth – m (Bayerische Staatsbibliothek, Munich; cgm 429) – has been missing since World War II. MS h (Stadt- und Universitätsbibliothek, Frankfurt am Main; Ms. germ. qu. 111) is thought to be closest to the original. MS b (Biblioteka Jagiellońska, Krakow; Ms. germ. qu. 1340) contains forty-six illustrations.

First publication: *Daniel von dem blühenden Tal: Ein Artusroman von dem Stricker,* edited by Gustav Rosenhagen (Breslau: Koebner, 1894; reprinted, Hildesheim & New York: Olms, 1976).

Standard edition: *Der Stricker: Daniel von dem blühenden Tal,* edited by Michael Resler, Altdeutsche Textbibliothek, no. 92 (Tübingen: Niemeyer, 1983).

Edition in English: *Der Stricker: Daniel of the Blossoming Valley (Daniel von dem blühenden Tal),* translated by Michael Resler, Garland Library of Medieval Literature, no. 58 (New York & London: Garland, 1990).

Karl der Große (1217-1225)

Manuscripts: *Karl der Große* is abundantly transmitted in forty-one manuscripts (twenty-three complete and eighteen fragmentary). As many as a dozen of the older manuscripts may date from the thirteenth century. Two distinct branches in the transmission are represented by MS A (Stadtbibliothek, Saint Gall; A 8 [14]) and MS K (Bayerische Staatsbibliothek, Munich; cgm 5154).

Standard edition: *Karl der Große,* edited by Karl Bartsch (Quedlinburg & Leipzig: Basse, 1857; reprinted, Berlin: De Gruyter, 1965).

Die Schwänke des Pfaffen Amîs (after 1225–circa 1250?)

Manuscripts: This work survives in nine nearly complete manuscripts and two fragments. The oldest – R (Staatsbibliothek Preußischer Kulturbesitz, Berlin; Ms. germ. fol. 1062) – may date from as early as the late thirteenth century. Based on the sequence and the number of episodes in the various manuscripts, two distinct transmission branches have been identified; some scholars believe that Der Stricker himself may have authorized both "versions" of his story.

First publication: "Der Pfaffe Amîs," in *Erzählungen und Schwänke,* edited by Hans Lambel (Leipzig: Brockhaus, 1872).

Standard edition: *Des Strickers Pfaffe Amis,* edited by Kin'ichi Kamihara (Göppingen: Kümmerle, 1978).

Kleindichtung (after 1225–circa 1250?)

Manuscripts: Der Stricker's *Kleindichtung* (short poetry) is preserved in approximately forty manuscripts, which date from as early as several decades after the poet's death to as late as the first half of the sixteenth century. Of these, MS A (Österreichische Nationalbibliothek, Vienna; Codex Vindob. 2705) and MS H (Universitätsbibliothek, Heidelberg; cpg 341) are superior to the others in terms of their reliability, their proximity to the original texts, and the large number of poems they contain.

Standard edition: *Die Kleindichtung des Strickers,* 5 volumes, edited by Wolfgang Wilfried Moelleken and others (Göppingen: Kümmerle, 1973-1978).

Der Stricker is most noted as a major transitional figure from the rarefied courtly world of the *Blütezeit* (golden age of German medieval literature, 1180 to 1230) to the more mundane, everyday arena of postclassical literature. His two early poems – the Arthurian romance *Daniel von dem blühenden Tal* (1210-1225; translated as *Daniel of the Blossoming Valley,* 1990) and the heroic epic *Karl der Große* (Charlemagne, 1217-1225) – give way to the less sublime verse narratives and fables of the poet's later years. It was in this latter field that Der Stricker discovered his true literary prowess and established his enduring reputation as a poet.

Little is known about the lives of even the most renowned of the German poets of the Middle Ages, and Der Stricker is no exception. An early scholar, Karl Goedeke, attempted to associate the name *Stricker* with the verb *strîchen* (to wander, to rove about) in line with the belief that the poet was a *vagus* (traveling poet). Subsequent research, however, has led to the consensus that this nom de plume was meant to indicate a weaver or knitter and not an itinerant. In this case the poet, by dubbing himself "the weaver," clearly meant to refer to his poetic role as a weaver of stories. At the same time, other evidence suggests that the name might not have been a pseudonym at all but an authentic patronymic; at least two documents from the period confirm the existence of a person by that name. While there is no conclusive proof that *Der Stricker* was either a family name or a pseudonym, most scholars incline toward the latter possibility.

Der Stricker must have spent a considerable portion of his life in Austria. Certain of his later poems contain references to events in that part of the German-speaking world; among these is "Die Klage" (The Lament), in which the poet notes:

> min chlage ist ein ursprinc,
> dar uz manic chlage fliuzet
> und so grozlich begiuzet,
> daz min chlage wirt erchant
> noch verrer denne in osterlant. (lines 40–44)

> (My lament is a fountain
> from which many a lament flows
> and [which] pours forth so much water
> that my lament is recognized
> much farther than in Osterlant.)

The place name *Osterlant* refers to eastern lands in general but also specifically to an area comprising parts of present-day Austria. To be sure, this passage need not necessarily be interpreted to indicate that Der Stricker was actually speaking from within Austria, but other allusions argue for the notion that Der Stricker did live there. In the poem "Die Gäuhühner" (The Chickens Paid in Tribute) he speaks of a castle at *chirchelinge* – the present-day Kierling, which is near Vienna in the vicinity of Klosterneuburg. Furthermore, Der Stricker's story of the blind Duke Heinrich through various allusions points unmistakably to Austria. And the poem "Die Herren

zu Österreich" (The Lords of Austria) makes unequivocal reference to Austria.

There is a considerable body of evidence that Der Stricker was born elsewhere and later traveled to Austria. Scholars such as Gustav Rosenhagen and Karl Bartsch have uncovered compelling textual proof that he was a professional traveling poet. For instance, in the poem "Die Frauenehre" (The Honor of Women) a foe of Der Stricker claims that a fitting reward for the latter's poetic efforts would be "ein pfert und alt gewant" (a horse and an old piece of clothing). The two objects mentioned here are thought to be typical of what was offered such professional itinerants. Additional evidence is found in a passage near the end of *Daniel von dem blühenden Tal* in which Der Stricker complains "daz nû die herren sint sô karc / und er an gebene was sô starc" (that the lords nowadays are so miserly / and he [King Arthur] was so generous). Just this sort of lament might be imagined on the lips of an itinerant poet subject to the largesse of the patrons at whose courts he performed. Thus, if Der Stricker was a wandering poet, he may have journeyed to Austria from somewhere else within the German-language region of Europe.

It was Rosenhagen who first dealt critically with this question and debunked the long-held assumption that Der Stricker was a native Austrian. In his examination of the dialect of *Daniel von dem blühenden Tal*, Rosenhagen unearthed certain Middle German peculiarities that point to a central German region north of Austria. More-recent scholars have taken the further step of linking Der Stricker to the Franciscan Lamprecht von Regensburg, who lived and wrote in eastern Franconia, a region well within Rosenhagen's "Middle Germany." Any conclusion that Der Stricker was born in eastern Franconia or that his language shows traces of the dialect of that specific area remains premature, but Rosenhagen's localizing of the language of *Daniel von dem blühenden Tal* within the Middle German dialect region yields persuasive evidence that Der Stricker was born in that area. Since *Daniel von dem blühenden Tal* was among the poet's initial works (probably his first), it was far more likely than the later stories to bear the original dialect traits of the poet's birthplace. Seen in this light, it appears highly implausible that Der Stricker could have been Austrian by birth. The whole issue of Der Stricker's dialect, and thus of his birthplace, however, is greatly confounded by the fact that none of the major extant manuscripts is in the dialect of the original work. Scholars have, therefore, been forced to rely largely on rhyme analysis in probing the many uncertainties surrounding Der Stricker's locale and dialect.

Der Stricker is noted as the author of a rather large corpus of works – by one count, approximately 170 – in a strikingly wide variety of genres. The longer works are the Arthurian story *Daniel von dem blühenden Tal;* the epic *Karl der Große,* a version of the French *Chanson de Roland; Die Schwänke des Pfaffen Amîs* (The Funny Tales of Parson Amîs, after 1225–circa 1250?); and "Die Frauenehre," a panegyric on women. Among his many shorter poems are prayers, beast fables, a large body of didactic poems, and sixteen *mæren* (stories or tales).

There is every reason to believe that – at least within the relatively narrow literary circles of the day – Der Stricker was a recognized practitioner of his art. His *Karl der Große* is preserved in more than forty manuscripts – a credible barometer of its popularity during medieval times – and he is acknowledged as one of the pioneers of the *mæren,* a popular form of literature in Germany. One can surmise that such a poet must have been welcome at the courts of eminent patrons; yet in contrast to many of his fellow poets, Der Stricker never directly names any such benefactors. This omission seems particularly odd when one considers that his longer works almost surely could not have been completed without outside sponsorship. It has been suggested – based largely on the presence of many religiously oriented works in his oeuvre – that Der Stricker may have been in the service of some unnamed ecclesiastical patron, and possible links have been surmised between Der Stricker and the Franciscans and between him and the Dominicans. By the same token, however, Der Stricker's nonreligious works might just as well be cited as an argument for his sponsorship by a secular patron.

There is somewhat more certainty surrounding Der Stricker's period of florescence: those few poems of his that can be dated stem from the first half of the thirteenth century; it would follow that Der Stricker was born near the end of the twelfth century. Aside from a consensus that *Daniel von dem blühenden Tal* and *Karl der Große* were probably composed first and the shorter fables and verse narratives later, the question of the chronology of the works remains formidable. A few poems are roughly datable on the basis of allusions to historic events or persons, but on the whole, Der Stricker's works – though broadly assigned to the second through fifth decades of the thirteenth century – can neither be assigned a definitive date of composition nor be arranged in a chronological sequence.

Some of the early attempts to establish a chronology among Der Stricker's shorter stories were based on the rather illusory notion that the humorous stories – by virtue of their frivolity – must have been products of Der Stricker's youth and that the more pious tales must have been composed by an older and more meditative poet. It is far more likely that Der Stricker composed his works according to the differing tastes of his various patrons. Hence, his religious poems and his comic stories might have been written concurrently.

The question of dating is much less difficult for *Daniel von dem blühenden Tal* and *Karl der Große.* On the basis of cross-references with other contemporary works, it has been established that *Daniel von dem blühenden Tal* was composed between 1210 and 1243. Using similar logic and with the added recourse to certain internal historical allusions, *Karl der Große* has been placed within the time span from 1217 to 1225. Scholars were long in disagreement as to which was earlier, but recent stylistic examination has demonstrated that *Daniel von dem blühenden Tal* was likely written first; and if it predates *Karl der Große,* then *Daniel von dem blühenden Tal* must have been composed prior to 1225. In sum, it appears that *Daniel von dem blühenden Tal* was written between 1210 and 1225, *Karl der Große* between 1217 and 1225, and most of the shorter works after 1225.

In contrast to many of the other German poets of the courtly age, Der Stricker appears not to have been a member of the chivalric order. Unlike the romances of such poet-knights as Hartmann von Aue and Wolfram von Eschenbach, which abound with the real-life particulars of chivalry, *Daniel von dem blühenden Tal* betrays little intimate acquaintance with the daily minutiae of knighthood.

By the time Der Stricker set about writing his sole Arthurian romance, German Arthurian poets – following the example of Hartmann, whose *Erec* (circa 1185) was modeled on the Old French *Erec et Enide* of Chrétien de Troyes – had for several decades been basing their stories on French sources. Der Stricker made a dramatic break with this convention. Scholars are virtually unanimous that the 8,483-line *Daniel von dem blühenden Tal* was the first original Arthurian story in German. Perhaps even more intriguing than Der Stricker's innovativeness is the compulsion he apparently felt to disavow his creativity by making a false appeal to a French source. Early in his prologue he asserts that a French story about Daniel by Alberich de Besançon has come to his attention and that he has set about translating it for his German audience. The trouble with this claim is that no such romance is known to

Diſz buchlein ſagt von dem ofenturlichē man genant
pfaf Amyſz/was er wunders hat volbzacht ſein tag ·

Je voz hat froide vnd ere / geliebet allo
rechte ſere · So ein hubſch mann zu hofe
kam/das man gern von im vernam · Bey⸗
ten ſpil ſingen vnd ſagen/dis was gemein
in den tagen · Das iſt nu ſo gar vnwert/dz
ſein nyman me begert · Er kunde dan ein mere/ die gut
den leuten were · Voz ſozgen vnd voz armut/ ſo dunck
et eſz vil ſelten gut · Was er mit woztē kunſte kan/ wie
ſol dann ein hofelich man · Zu hofe nu geboze/ das
enkan ich mit ofenbozen · Ich hab gefuget wozte vil/
das beiwere ich wer ſy hozen wil Wo man der zu hofe
nit gert/ ſo byn ich eins tozen wert

Vhozent was hie voz beſchach/ do freude fur
die ſorge bzach · Vnd man ere fur ſchande ent⸗
pfieng / vnd miltekeit fur karckept ging · Vnd
trew fur vntrewe ee ſchreit / vnd fromkeit fur die boſ⸗
heit · One kummer wol genaſz/ vnd wozheit fur die lu
gen was · Do was die zucht geneme/ vnd vnzucht wiſz
zeme · Vnd beſaſz die tugent alle lant / das man vntu⸗
gent nyergent fant · fur das boſze ging die gute/ vnd
fur truren hoch gemute · Vnd ging das recht fur das
vnrecht/ demutikeit was des friden knecht · Diſz was
in den ſtunden / ee liegen vnd tryegen wart funden ·

Vſeit vns der dichtere/ wer der erſte man were
Der liegen triegen anfing/ vnd wie ſein wil fur
ſich ging Weſz er ſich dan vnder want/ vnd wie er was
auſz engelant · Von ein er ſtat genant dranyſz /er hieſz
pfaf amyſz Vnd waz 8 buch ein weiſze man/ er vergab
ſo gar wz er gewan Durch ere vnd durch got/ daz er 8

Pages from a manuscript dating from the 1480s, with a woodcut illustration for Der Striker's Die Schwänke des Pfaffen Amîs
(Munich, Staatsbibliothek, Rar 422, f. 1v-2r)

¶ Die begeret der byschof von pfaf
amylz das er den esel lere lesen .

Der bischof sprach ir kunnent vil/ dozumb ich
mit enberen wil Ir mussent mich do mit eren
vnd einen esel die buch leren · Seyt ir dē him
el gemessen hant/ vnd die wege die dar gant · Dozu dz
mete vnd die erden/ nu wil ich innen werden · Wie ich
euch kunne wider ston/ habent ir das alles gethon ·
Das ir mir hie hant vor erzelt/ so thunt ir wol was ir
welt · Nu wil ich schowen ouch do by/ ob dz ans alles
war sy · Leret ir dē esel wol/ so nym ich alles dz fur vol
Das ir mir hant geseit ee/ vnd mercke dz esz recht stee ·

have been written by Alberich, who is best known for his romance *Alexander.* Further discrediting Der Stricker's contention is the suspicious circumstance that the passage in which he propounds his claim is borrowed almost verbatim from the *Alexanderlied* (Song of Alexander, circa 1130–1150) of Pfaffe Lamprecht. Appeal to a source – particularly to a French source – had become nearly canonical among German poets of the courtly age, even to the point of their fabricating a false one.

Daniel arrives at the Arthurian court, proves his mettle in combat against several of the knights, and is received into King Arthur's fellowship. The story is set in motion by the arrival of an unnamed giant who, as an emissary of King Matur of Cluse, brazenly demands that King Arthur swear fealty to Matur. The giant embellishes his challenge with fantastic descriptions of the land of Cluse, where the ladies are supreme in their beauty, sweetly warbling birds provide shade from the sun, and elephants are strapped together to carry whole palaces on their backs.

Unwilling to wait while King Arthur musters an army to meet this challenge, Daniel slips out in secret and journeys alone to Cluse. As he is about to confront the messenger's equally enormous brother at the entrance to the kingdom, Daniel is diverted by a plea for help from the Maiden of the Dark Mountain. Her land is being terrorized by a dwarf named Juran, who is able to hold all challengers at bay with his magic sword. It is during this adventure that Daniel first deviates from the bearing of the conventional Arthurian knight: only by tricking Juran into putting aside his sword does Daniel defeat the evil dwarf. Physical strength and fighting prowess are, thus, subordinated to guile and cunning – a pragmatic posture that is also found in many of Der Stricker's nonchivalric works.

Anxious to return to his anticipated bout with the second giant and oblivious to an implicit offer of the maiden's hand as reward for his efforts, Daniel sets out again. But once more he is diverted from his journey: the Countess of the Bright Fountain and forty of her maidens seek his help against a demon, the mere sight of whose Medusa-like head dispatches his victims, whereupon he sucks the blood from their bodies. As before, Daniel relies on cunning to defeat the creature: using a mirror so as to avoid gazing directly at the lethal head, he slays the demon. Daniel possesses all of the more conventional Arthurian virtues such as bravery and fortitude, yet it is his use of cunning that repeatedly saves the day.

The grateful Count of the Bright Fountain offers to assist Daniel in Cluse, but just as the two are about to take on the second giant, an unknown knight abducts the count. This new adversary cuts off the pursuing Daniel by means of a boulder that drops down in his path and unleashes a flood. As before, Daniel is faced with conflicting responsibilities: should he search for the count or journey on alone to Cluse? Since Arthur's planned march into Cluse is imminent, Daniel decides to travel there first. Arriving in advance of Arthur's army, he subjugates the second giant as much by virtue of the magic sword he took from Juran as by dint of his own strength.

King Arthur's arriving knights initiate battle with the first of King Matur's seven armies by removing a banner from the mouth of a golden beast under a lime tree; once the banner is withdrawn, the beast raises a deafening wail so powerful as to buffet all the knights from their horses. This scene is reminiscent of the adventure at the perilous fountain in Hartmann's *Iwein* (circa 1203). Of all the German works of the day, Hartmann's romance appears to have left the most pervasive imprint on *Daniel von dem blühenden Tal;* but as Rosenhagen and Bartsch have pointed out, a wide range of other contemporary works – Pfaffe Konrad's *Rolandslied* (Song of Roland, circa 1170), Hartmann's *Erec,* Wirnt von Grafenberg's *Wigalois* (circa 1210–1215 or circa 1235), Heinrich von Veldeke's *Eneit* (circa 1185), and Ulrich von Zatzikhoven's *Lanzelet* (circa 1194–1203) – as well as sources from antiquity, including Homer's *Odyssey* and the myth of Medusa, have left their stamp on Der Stricker's Arthurian romance. Thus, while Der Stricker made a significant break with tradition by inventing the plot for *Daniel von dem blühenden Tal,* the individual episodes and motifs are replete with reminiscences of other literary works.

At this juncture Der Stricker introduces an element that is quite alien to classical Arthurian romance: he has King Arthur assume a combat role by challenging King Matur to the first duel. The monarch of Chrétien's romances and of the German adaptations of Chrétien is an older, far more passive figure. Once Arthur has slain his opponent, their armies engage one another in mass battle. This, too, is atypical of classical Arthurian romance, in which the fighting is one-on-one combat.

Due in large part to Daniel's magic sword, the messenger giant and the first army of Cluse are defeated. While Arthur's men rest in anticipation of the arrival the following morning of the second army, Daniel slips off to resume the search for the

Count of the Bright Fountain. He finds himself involved in yet another adventure when he is entrapped in an invisible net by the Maiden of the Green Meadow. Her country is beset by a devilish creature who is killing off all the men; the demon is afflicted by an illness that can be alleviated only by his bathing weekly in human blood. Daniel is destined for this bloodbath, and so too, it turns out, is the abducted count. Daniel ransoms himself by promising to help against the beast. Despite the paralyzing effect of the creature's voice on all who hear him speak, Daniel inexplicably manages to venture close enough to decapitate him, thereby freeing the land and at the same time liberating the count. With newly acquired volunteers from the Land of the Green Meadow, Daniel and the count set out for King Arthur's encampment.

They arrive prior to the resumption of the next battle, which King Arthur's forces win. On the following day they win a third skirmish. On the fourth day, however, the remaining four armies of Cluse join forces. The battle is singularly fierce and protracted; after a full day of ferocious fighting, an overnight truce is finally called. At council with Arthur and the other knights, Daniel proposes a plan: prior to the resumption of fighting the next morning they shall all plug their ears, then withdraw the banner from the mouth of the wailing beast. Once again, guile takes precedence over brute strength: while King Arthur's knights are spared the effects of the deafening din, the men of Cluse are knocked senseless and surrender.

After the dead have been buried and a conciliation is established between King Arthur and Queen Danise, Matur's widow, the queen agrees, after a token protest, to accept Daniel as her husband. This hurriedly arranged marriage is reminiscent of the union between Iwein and the newly widowed Lunete in Hartmann's romance, but the utter lack of any amorous sentiment between Daniel and Danise is characteristic of Der Stricker: in none of his works — whether early or late — does this poet depict with conviction any positive effects of romantic love on any of his characters. The absence of love is all the more striking in the context of Arthurian romance, in which the love of a knight for a lady typically serves as the prime motivating force.

The coronation of Daniel as King of Cluse and the wedding of Daniel and Danise, a splendid Whitsuntide festival in the finest Arthurian tradition, is interrupted by the father of the two slain giants. Enraged over the loss of his sons, he abducts Arthur and Parzival and deposits them high on a dangerous cliff. Daniel approaches this final adventure with the same pragmatic single-mindedness that characterizes his other feats: seeing the impossibility of overcoming the giants' father by traditional chivalric means, he goes to the Land of the Green Meadow and convinces the maiden to return to Arthur's campsite with her invisible net. For one last time, cunning wins the day: Daniel lures the intruder into the magic net, forcing him to capitulate and to release Arthur and Parzival. The festival resumes, several hundred of Arthur's men marry and remain behind with King Daniel in Cluse, and the story concludes on the positive note characteristic of Arthurian romance.

Early scholarship was harsh in its evaluation of *Daniel von dem blühenden Tal,* labeling it an inferior work of a marginally gifted epigone. More recent critics, such as Ingeborg Henderson, have been more positive in their assessment of the work's merits. The sparse manuscript transmission of *Daniel von dem blühenden Tal* hardly attests to the work's widespread popularity among Der Stricker's contemporaries; on the other hand, at least one contemporary applauds him. In *Willehalm von Orlens* (circa 1235–1243) Rudolf von Ems praises *Daniel von dem blühenden Tal,* and in his *Alexander* (circa 1230–circa 1254), he says: "swenn er wil der Strickære / sô macht er guotiu mære" (whenever he wishes to, Der Stricker / puts together a good story). Modern scholarship would generally concur with such an assessment of *Daniel von dem blühenden Tal.*

Der Stricker's creativity is far less in evidence in *Karl der Große.* This 12,206-line epic is little more than a stylistic reworking of the twelfth-century *Rolandslied* of Konrad, which is itself a German version of the Old French *Chanson de Roland.* The story is that of the military campaign waged by Charlemagne against the Spanish infidels in 778. The crusading fervor that pervaded much of Europe during Der Stricker's lifetime gave such tales renewed popularity.

The bulk of Der Stricker's story consists of deliberative councils prior to the fighting and the battles themselves. The plot does not differ dramatically from that of the *Rolandslied;* and when Der Stricker does choose to make his own imprint upon the story, poetic cohesion does not always prevail. Following his prologue, Der Stricker inserts a brief account of Karl's youth that is lacking in the *Rolandslied* and in which several characters are introduced — Karl's half brothers Rapot and Wineman and Karl's later adversary Marsilies, the leader of the heathen forces — who in the *Rolandslied* appear only much later. The problem is that when these figures reemerge much later in *Karl der Große,* they are introduced as though they were appearing for the first time – which in the *Rolandslied* was precisely the case. It is clear from this example that Der Stricker had little talent for transmuting or augmenting the tale as he had inherited it from Konrad. He saw his chief role as that of polishing the story's rhyme, meter, and vocabulary to correspond more closely to the expectations of his courtly audience. Scholars such as Rüdiger Schnell and Udo von der Burg have demonstrated that political motives may have dictated some of the minor alterations Der Stricker made in composing *Karl der Große,* but the work represents far more a stylistic updating of the *Rolandslied* than a transformation or rethinking of the story.

At the outset Der Stricker says that he wishes to renew "ein altez mære" (an ancient tale) for the sake of those who cherish courtly art. He tells of Karl's youth: his father, Pippin, is mentioned, as is the legend that one of Karl's brothers would later become Pope Leo; Marsilies's sister falls in love with the young Karl, who is reported as having spent time in Spain during his youth. God sends his angel to bid Karl to journey to Spain and spread the Christian faith. The angel gives Karl a horn called Olivant and a sword called Durndart and prophesies the valiant role Karl's nephew, Roland, will play in the conquering of lands for the empire. In addition to Roland, the emperor Karl is surrounded by the finest of warriors, among them Archbishop Turpin, the valiant Olivier, and Genelun.

Karl mobilizes a vast army and defeats the infidels in their first encounter. Those of the enemy forces who survive agree to accept Christianity, and for six years Karl holds power in Spain. Der Stricker now shifts his focus to the camp of Marsilies, the heathen king, who commands a powerful army. The aged warrior Blanschandiez suggests that the Christians might be tricked into leaving only a minimal force in Spain if Marsilies and his men promise to convert; once Karl is back at Aachen, the infidels can retake the territory. Blanschandiez delivers the proposal to the Christians. Of Karl's twelve paladins, only Genelun advocates accepting Blanschandiez's plan. At Roland's urging, Genelun is chosen as emissary to the heathen side. Thinking himself doomed by this assignment, Genelun harbors deep enmity toward Roland. On the way to the heathen camp, Genelun – "der ungetriuwe bote" (the treacherous messenger) – is won over by Blanschandiez's offer of one hundred thousand marks in gold. He promises to see to it that Karl will depart Spain, leaving behind a re-

duced fighting force under Roland's command. Genelun proposes that once Karl is back home in Aachen, the heathens should attack and kill Roland; the emperor will be so devastated by the news that he will never return to Spain. Der Stricker likens the treacherous Genelun to Judas.

Marsilies mobilizes an enormous army as Genelun returns to Karl with the counterproposal, which includes an offer of hostages and gold. Genelun assures himself of personal revenge by urging that Roland be left behind to command the Christian army in Spain. Karl assents to the plot, though during the night he is troubled by three premonitory dreams – a compellingly crafted passage in which Der Stricker displays a rare flash of poetic mastery. Despite heavy misgivings, the emperor departs for his court at Aachen.

Soon thereafter Marsilies attacks. This segment of the story is dominated by the depiction of battles. Der Stricker repeatedly employs contrastive depictions of the two sides to underscore the moral disparity between Christians and heathens: the former enter piously into confession prior to battle, while the latter consume their final hours "mit tanze unt mit spil" (dancing and carousing) and worshiping false deities (seven hundred in all). Lengthy battle preparations are portrayed on both sides. Each army boasts hundreds of thousands of fighters, all of whom exhibit a burning zeal to enter the fray.

In the first engagement, the Battle of Runceval, the Christian forces are vanquished after a protracted and bloody fight. Their defeat is due in large part to Roland's failure to summon help by signaling the departing Charlemagne with a blast on the horn Olivant. By the time Roland gives the signal Karl is still barely within earshot, but it is too late. Roland's death on the battlefield is heralded by a bright light from the heavens, an earthquake, and a thunderstorm; many of those present take these phenomena as a sign that Judgment Day has come. This scene is a memorable one, but Der Stricker derived much of his imagery from the *Rolandslied.*

Arriving on the battlefield, Karl finds his compatriots slain and the enemy in flight. God causes the setting sun to rise back into the sky, affording Karl sufficient daylight to pursue the fleeing heathens. Many drown as they are chased into the sea. The wounded Marsilies returns to Saragossa, where he is offered reinforcements by the Persian king Paligan. Despite being outnumbered two hundred to one, the Christians are victorious. Karl slays Paligan, and Marsilies dies of grief; Roland's death has been avenged.

Queen Pregmunda, the widow of Marsilies, willingly embraces Christianity. In a lengthy and poignant passage – again, mostly derivative of the *Rolandslied* – Karl laments over the body of Roland. Before departing, Karl establishes a hospital at Runceval and a church on the spot where Roland lies buried. In Aachen, Roland's fiancée, Alite, falls dead with grief at the news of his demise and that of her brother, Olivier. The traitor Genelun escapes but is recaptured. His fate is debated; finally it is decided that a close kinsman of Genelun and one of Roland shall face off against one another. The much smaller Dietrich, Roland's relative, overpowers Genelun's representative, Pinabel. The will of God is seen in Pinabel's defeat; Genelun's arms and legs are tied to four wild horses, which tear him apart. Only Judas himself, Der Stricker reiterates, was a more wicked traitor than Genelun. In a brief epilogue Der Stricker petitions God for eternal salvation, expressing the wish that all follow in the footsteps of "sante Karle" (Saint Karl).

The popularity of *Karl der Große* is reflected in the rich manuscript transmission. It was this version of the battle against the Spanish infidels, not the more celebrated *Rolandslied,* with which later generations of medieval audiences were most familiar.

Only a handful of Der Stricker's other poems are of sufficient length to be considered independent works. The most noted is *Die Schwänke des Pfaffen Amîs,* the story of a roguish cleric who exploits the gullibility of his fellow human beings. The 2,510 lines of this poem consist of twelve droll anecdotes held together primarily by the persona of Amîs, "der erste man . . . / der liegen und triegen an vienc" (the first man who practiced falsehood and deceit). The satiric portrayal of a world populated largely by fools suggests a didactic aim on the part of Der Stricker, yet the story's chief purpose seems to have been the entertainment rather than the moral betterment of its audience. Consequently, the moralizing voice in *Die Schwänke des Pfaffen Amîs* is – compared with that in many of Der Stricker's other poems – more implicit than explicit.

The story begins in Amîs's home parish in England, where the wealthy priest practices a lifestyle of lavish generosity. So grandiose are Amîs's ways that his jealous bishop subjects him to a test of his knowledge of theology by posing a series of unanswerable questions. Amîs's deft replies are characteristic of the mental agility that carries the clever priest through life. The bishop asks him, for instance, how many days have elapsed since the Creation; only seven responds Amîs, but these seven have been repeated many times over. Called on to state the distance between heaven and earth, Amîs replies that it is the same distance in which his voice is audible; go up into heaven, he says to the bishop, and listen as I shout. If you cannot hear me, then I was mistaken, and you may return and take my parish from me. The bishop then orders Amîs to teach a donkey to read. Amîs places oats between the pages of a book; the donkey quickly learns to turn the pages with his nose to get at the oats. Unable to prove that the donkey is not actually reading the book, the bishop concedes defeat.

Eventually Amîs squanders all his wealth. Aware that he can apply his innate cleverness for monetary gain, he embarks on a journey that takes him to the Continent, on to the Orient, and finally home again. During his travels priests, knights, merchants, peasants, and princes all fall prey to his trickery. As Rosenhagen was the first to note, Amîs's farcical adventures are strung together much like the series of heroic adventures that a typical Arthurian knight undergoes on his journeys through unknown lands. Unlike the chivalric heroes, of course, it is not Amîs's physical prowess but his mental adroitness that helps him to triumph in his trials. For example, he insists that he will accept contributions for an imaginary church only from women who have been faithful to their husbands; eager not to appear adulterous, all the women flock to contribute whatever they can afford to give. In Paris Amîs claims the ability to paint pictures that are visible only to those who are of legitimate birth; though he leaves the canvas empty, his painting is praised by all, including the king. In Lorraine the wily priest heals the ill by asking for the sickest person to step forward and sacrifice his blood as a remedy for the others; unwilling to face certain death, all present declare themselves cured.

The conclusion of the story is marked by a devout turnabout on the part of its protagonist. Thirty years after returning to England, Amîs is converted to a true belief in God, forswears deceit and trickery, and enters a monastery. On the death of the abbot, Amîs is chosen to lead the brothers. By the time of his own death Amîs has sufficiently atoned for his earlier knavery "daz im daz ewige leben / nach disem libe wart gegeben" (that he was granted eternal life / following this earthly existence). It is only in the last few lines that Amîs's conversion to a life of probity is revealed. Some critics have seen incongruity in Der Stricker making Amîs into the epitome of a clerical impostor while lecturing in certain of his religious poems about the evils of simony. But there is no discrepancy, for Amîs the deceitful charlatan in the end becomes Amîs the venerable abbot.

Page from a late-fourteenth-century manuscript for Pfaffe Amîs *(Gotha, Forschungsbibliothek, Cod. Chart. A 823, f. 104r)*

Many features of this poem derive from narrative material that was already long in circulation; it has been suggested that Der Stricker may have worked from a French original, though no such work has been uncovered. Certainly the temperament of *Die Schwänke des Pfaffen Amîs* shares a great deal of common ground with that of the fabliaux that were then in fashion in France. It appears that Der Stricker's real contribution lies chiefly in his skilled collation of and humorously engaging retelling of the individual stories that make up his work. One telling measure of the popularity of *Die Schwänke des Pfaffen Amîs* during the Middle Ages is the fact that several of the individual *Schwänke* were incorporated into the early sixteenth-century chapbook *Till Eulenspiegel*.

In the nearly universal judgment of critics, the shorter poems that make up the remainder of Der Stricker's work constitute his true literary achievement. These poems, roughly 170 in all, range in length from 8 to 1,902 lines and include prayers, *mæren*, *bîspel* (fables), *Schwänke*, and didactic poems. They are often consolidated under the rubric *Kleindichtung* (Short Poetry, after 1225–circa 1250?).

Der Stricker's *Kleindichtung* is populated by the full spectrum of medieval life – kings and peasants, citizens and priests, husbands and wives, knights and workers, innkeepers and princes – and the topics of the poems are equally diverse. Common to most of the short poems is Der Stricker's droll exposure of ubiquitous human failings and weaknesses.

Any attempt to classify Der Stricker's *Kleindichtung* into genres is complicated by the fact that many of the poet's favorite literary forms overlap with one another. For example, one *mære* might have a primarily comic function, while another might make a serious moral point. Similarly, one *bîspel* may contain a religious message, whereas another may speak to a more worldly issue. The most useful classification might be between those with a primarily narrative function and those with a primarily didactic function. Many of Der Stricker's *Kleindichtungen* consist of a story (the narrative portion) and a moral explication of that story (the didactic segment). Depending on which segment is accorded greater prominence, the poem will tend toward one or the other pole along a continuum between narrative and didactic. Many of the *Schwänke* and *mæren* have a chiefly narrative function and probably served more as entertainment than as teaching, while many of the *bîspel* and virtually all of the religious poems are predominantly didactic and were intended more to instruct than to entertain. The didactic element is rarely altogether lacking in

this body of poems but is almost always at least implicitly present, even in the most amusingly burlesque *Schwänke*.

The prominent form among Der Stricker's didactic poems – the form for which this poet is particularly noted as both originator and master practitioner in the German literary tradition – is the *bîspel*. This type of story, which is rooted both in the biblical parables and in the Aesopian tradition, was also widely cultivated in medieval sermon writing. Der Stricker's *bîspel* characteristically contain both a narrative and a didactic component. In the *bîspel* tradition it is this latter part which is the more crucial – so much so that in some instances the narrative makes little sense if read without the commentary.

Many of Der Stricker's *bîspel* are so-called *tierbîspel* (beast fables) that employ familiar animals to personify human vices and virtues. Probably the most commonly recurring beast in Der Stricker's *tierbîspel* is the wolf, whose frequent setbacks in life are emblematic of human folly. Der Stricker is also fond of depicting in his *bîspel*, frequently with an implicit sense of resignation, the unalterable ways of the world. For instance, in "Der Esel" (The Donkey) the title beast runs away to a land where his ilk is hitherto unknown and where he will, he hopes, no longer be called upon to carry heavy sacks. Initially, all goes just as the donkey has planned; he even becomes an object of fear among the inhabitants of this land. Eventually, however, the donkey is captured and is once more put to work doing what he had always done before. Der Stricker's message is a simple one: donkeys are meant to be beasts of burden; this is the natural order of things, and no one should tamper with such matters.

Der Stricker frequently uses his *Kleindichtungen* as a forum from which to preach a wide variety of virtues. In "Das wilde Roß" (The Wild Horse) he shows that it is foolish and dangerous to tie oneself to a headstrong horse that others have already tried – and failed – to tame. In the explicatory segment of this *bîspel* the poet links his narrative with the virtue of constancy, explaining that such a horse is like a beautiful but faithless woman who will drag down to ruin any man who is foolish enough to attach himself to her. The notion of strength in numbers is the theme of "Der Turse" (The Giant), in which a monster entraps a band of twelve men and requires them to hand over one after another of their number for him to devour. At each successive demand they relinquish the weakest member of the group until only one of the captives is left. Der Stricker then imparts the moral of his story through the monster, who discloses to his last remaining captive that, had the men but joined forces, they could have held him at bay.

Humility also has its place among the virtues Der Stricker singles out in his *Kleindichtung.* "Der wunderbare Stein" (The Wondrous Stone) features a young king whose arrogance has cost him the affection of his people. The king is redeemed when a sagacious adviser tells him that the young man's father had always worn a hat with a precious stone mounted on it; this stone, the counselor claims, had the power of winning the devotion and respect of all who beheld it. The counselor arranges for such a hat to be made for the son, who is instructed to bow his head when wearing it so that the stone will be visible. The people interpret this gesture as a sign of humility, gain renewed trust in their sovereign, and begin appearing before him with their concerns and petitions. At this point the counsellor cautions his king that the stone will lose its powers if its bearer fails to ensure that justice is always carried out in his land, and the young king fashions his reign in accordance with this advice. In "Der wunderbare Stein" Der Stricker delineates a social order that comprises justice not only for the privileged few but for those of all social strata. Inasmuch as Der Stricker lived and wrote in the very midst of the High Middle Ages, it is rather striking that his worldview was sufficiently broad as to encompass so "democratic" an outlook. Yet once again, this poet was a transitional figure, and it is in poems such as "Der wunderbare Stein" that the shift away from the literary elitism of the *Blütezeit* is most palpably felt.

This same broad-based weltanschauung is apparent in the many *mæren* that focus on the theme of marital conflict, for in place of the knight and lady, whose relationship forms the core of so much of the high courtly literature, Der Stricker frequently depicts peasant couples. Their interchanges with one another – set not in the rarefied air of the court but in the mundane world of the village – most often center not on lofty questions of love but on the petty antagonisms of married life. In "Der begrabene Ehemann" (The Buried Husband) the husband is so wholly under the thumb of his overbearing wife that he fulfills her every command – even to the point of permitting the local priest, who happens to be the woman's lover, to bury him alive. While Der Stricker spares no group his biting ridicule, a whiff of misogyny – seen here in the domineering wife – is evident in some of his work. A similar air is evoked by "Das Ehescheidungsgespräch" (Talk of Divorce), where a man plucks up his courage to announce to his repulsive and spiteful wife

the end of their marriage. In his resolve to terminate their unhappy union, the man gradually pushes the divorce date forward from "in a year's time" to "this very day." The wife seems to agree to the dissolution. But in her overbearing fashion she nudges the date farther and farther back, ending finally with "never" and with a threat to deal harshly with her husband if he should voice so much as a word of protest. Utterly cowed, the man begs her forgiveness and proceeds to extol her as a model of beauty and virtue. Der Stricker injects a further note of comedy into his tale by having the husband employ many of the rhetorical conventions of high *Minnesang* in his praise of this uncomely and surly woman.

Despite his frequently unfavorable portrayal of women and of marriage, Der Stricker leaves no doubt about his aversion to extramarital love. In "Der kluge Knecht" (The Shrewd Servant) a woman has taken a priest as her lover. One day the husband comes home unexpectedly, and the priest has to take refuge beneath a bench. During dinner a servant who is aware of the affair relates an experience he once had had with a wolf that slipped off into a hiding place. Alerted by the servant's anecdote, the husband drags his wife's lover out from his place of concealment and agrees to free him only after extracting a large ransom. Der Stricker concludes by praising the deft manner in which the servant exposed the woman's adulterous affair. A similar note is struck in the *bîspel* "Der Krämer" (The Merchant); in this instance, however, it is faithfulness on the part of the husband that is emphasized. Two merchants offer their goods: the first sells wares of gold, which, albeit expensive, will retain their value; the second merchant peddles copper goods, which, though they have the color of gold and are readily affordable, lose their shine over time. A wise woman, Der Stricker asserts, will understand that a steadfast man, like the gold of the first merchant, will endure in his faithfulness.

In contrast to the German *Minnesang,* in which a knight sues – though typically without success – for the love of a married lady, Der Stricker champions a type of love that is rooted in social reality rather than in literary posturing. In this regard it is telling that Der Stricker, despite his chronological proximity to the *Minnesang* period – indeed, despite his own wide-ranging literary versatility – wrote not a single poem in that still-popular tradition. In fact, in "Die Minnesänger" (The Minnesingers) he actually ridicules the poets of *Minnesang* with biting irony. These *Minnesänger,* Der Stricker contends, ought to remain beneath their linden trees and off in their forests and glades – the recurrent locales of courtly love songs. But with a caustic allusion to the favorite songbird of the *Minnesänger,* he goes on to assert that such poets have no place in the real world, for "ein sou und ein nahte gal, / die singent ungelichen sanc" (a sow and a nightingale / sing quite different songs).

In light of this poem and of Der Stricker's vaguely misogynistic propensities, it is somewhat surprising that the longest of the poems to fall under the broad rubric of *Kleindichtung,* "Frauenehre," is a panegyric to women. It offers a grand and rather long-winded praise, almost in the courtly style, of the many ways in which women's goodness and love gladden and ennoble the world. "Der Weidemann" (The Huntsman) offers an allegorical discourse on the essence of knightly honor. And "Die Königin vom Mohrenland" (The Queen of the Moorish Land) tells of the sorrow that ensues when courtly values and the courtly way of life are no longer practiced. Poems such as these are anomalies among Der Stricker's *Kleindichtung,* but itinerant poets had to tailor their writings to the tastes and expectations of the patrons under whose sponsorship they worked.

More in line with the overall spirit of the *Kleindichtungen* are poems in which Der Stricker holds up to ridicule various weaknesses and vices. Drunkenness is a favorite such fault, finding its way into many of the *Schwänke.* In "Die Martinsnacht" (Saint Martin's Night) a farmer becomes intoxicated, leaving himself open to the wiles of a swindler who purports to be Saint Martin himself and proceeds to steal the poor man's cattle. In "Der durstige Einsiedel" (The Thirsty Hermit) the title character resolves to mend his drunken ways by living as a recluse; later he returns to the city and goes to the taverns to preach to his former fellow imbibers. Yet old ways are hard to change, and the man ends up slumped over and thoroughly inebriated. Here, as in many of Der Stricker's poems on drunkenness, the tone is one of disapproval but not of strident, moralistic condemnation.

The same might be said of many of the poems that focus on clerical misbehavior. More often than not, the particular form of misconduct here is of a sexual nature: the priest, for example, who fails to obey his vow of chastity. Yet at times the poet issues a more stern and unsympathetic reprimand: in "Die Pfaffendirne" (The Priest's Whore) Der Stricker directs his censure primarily at women who would sexually tempt members of the clergy. The theft of any holy vessel from a church, he reminds his audience, is punishable by death; by the same token, a woman guilty of stealing God's own vessel, a priest, is culpable of a far more serious offense. Such a theft can never be atoned for, since the priest's very soul would have been corrupted in the process. Der Stricker reserves equally harsh condemnation for homosexuality in "Die gepfefferte Speise" (The Peppered Meal) and in "Gegen Gleichgeschlechtlichkeit" (Against Homosexuality).

By and large, however, Der Stricker is content to stand back and induce his audience to smile more or less benignly as he exposes human foibles. This attitude may be nowhere in better evidence than in the well-known poem "Die drei Wünsche" (The Three Wishes). Human foolishness, a favorite theme of Der Stricker's, is on full display in this story, which has been retold many times by poets of various epochs. A man and wife lament their joyless lot in life, voicing the wish that God might intervene and alleviate their poverty. Finally God sends his angel to them with an offer of three wishes. The woman wishes for and promptly receives a beautiful dress. Exasperated that she would so foolishly squander one of their three wishes, her husband also forgets himself and wishes for the dress to end up in the woman's stomach – a wish that is likewise fulfilled. The man now has little choice but to use the final wish to free his wife from her unbearable plight. The three wishes are frittered away, and the two are left in as cheerless a predicament as at the beginning. As he so often does, Der Stricker relates this story more with a wry smile than with a tone of stern condemnation.

The final major thematic group within Der Stricker's *Kleindichtung* are the poems focusing on religious or theological issues. Some of these works are simple prayers; others deal with the liturgy and other articles of faith. "Die Messe" (The Mass) is a theological treatise on the significance of the Mass for salvation. Another major concern of Der Stricker which comes to light in such poems as "Das weiße Tuch" (The White Cloth) and "Der ernsthafte König" (The King Who Never Laughed) is the depth of God's compassion for mankind. And many of the religious poems deal with sin and atonement. In the *bîspel* "Die Buße des Sünders" (The Sinner's Penitence) Der Stricker relates penance and the question of free will: a sinner asks God not to permit him to die until he has atoned "mit sinem libe" (on his own) for his misdeeds; despite all his earnest attempts, the man remains unable to achieve full penance, since he never gives himself over fully into God's hands. The centrality of penitential theology in Der Stricker's religious poems has led scholars to surmise that the poet was familiar with the proceedings of the Fourth Lateran Council of 1215, which dealt with the notion of penance. The Lateran influence appears plausible, though it does not necessarily follow that Der Stricker pursued any formal study of theology. It is more likely that, as Helmut de Boor and Richard Newald have suggested, the poet was able to deal with such issues with the help of patrons who were versed in the theological niceties of the day.

A handful of poems from among the *Kleindichtung* stand apart in terms of their content. Political poetry is nowhere to be found except in the *mære* "Die Herren zu Österreich" (The Lords of Austria), the tale of a glutton who devours food in such excess that he vomits up all that he eats. He then undergoes a change of heart, fasting with the same passion that had once distinguished his eating habits. Such a man is emblematic of the Austrian nobility, whose members had once been excessively generous but are now as miserly as they had been charitable. As a consequence of such parsimony, Der Stricker laments, the courts in Austria are devoid of the tournaments, the songs, and the joy that had previously lent them so elegant a sparkle. In the *bîspel* "Die Gäuhühner" Der Stricker also does something he does nowhere else in his works: he alludes directly to a contemporary historic event, a peasant uprising against the nobility. While scholars have not been able to identify the incident to which Der Stricker refers, he speaks of it as having occurred at *chirchelinge.* The uniqueness of this allusion underscores the sparseness of real-life, historic anchors in the poetry of Der Stricker.

A further poem that is sui generis among the works of Der Stricker is "Die Klage," a work of 708 lines in which the poet regards with a bitter sense of resignation the world in which he lives. In twenty-four segments, each of which begins with the formula "ich klage" (I lament) or "ich wil klagen" (I wish to lament), Der Stricker casts a plaintive glance at a litany of evils: the decline of love toward God and toward women, lawlessness in the land, the weakened position of the emperor, lack of moral probity, dishonesty, the subversion of courtly values, material deprivation and greed, homosexuality, heresy and devil worship, and the withholding from God of one's earthly possessions. The highly personal tone of the opening lines has led some critics to regard this poem as the late work of an aged poet gazing back on his earthly existence with a sense of grizzled melancholy. The introspective ring of these verses is undeniable, yet – as so often in medieval literature – it is equally plausible that Der Stricker was writing not from personal experience but from an assumed poetic posture that may have had nothing to do with autobiographical fact.

Der Stricker was neither a preeminent poetic genius nor a fundamental innovator. Yet he was not without other, quite formidable achievements. He was sufficiently in step with popular tastes to compose an Arthurian romance – and, in so doing, to make a major break with the convention of adapting from a French source. He displayed a keen sense of style in polishing for contemporary expectations the rough-hewn *Rolandslied;* indeed, his was the version of the story that was to achieve fame among subsequent generations. And Der Stricker stood as a highly versatile transitional figure between the glittering, chivalric High Middle Ages and the more down-to-earth postcourtly era; in that pivotal role he helped to usher in the literature of the later Middle Ages. Perhaps most significantly, Der Stricker was the first major German author to suffuse didactic poetry with an animated and engaging narrative timbre.

References:

Erhard Agricola, "Die Prudentia als Anliegen der Stricker'schen Schwänke," *Beiträge zur Geschichte der deutschen Sprache und Literatur,* 77 (1955): 197–220;

Helmut de Boor and Richard Newald, *Geschichte der deutschen Literatur von den Anfängen bis zur Gegenwart,* seventh edition (Munich: Beck, 1966): II, 192–195, 416–417; III/1, 231–247;

Helmut Brall, "Strickers *Daniel von dem Blühenden Tal:* Zur politischen Funktion späthöfischer Artusepik im Territorialisierungsprozeß," *Euphorion,* 70, no. 3 (1976): 222–257;

Joachim Bumke, "Strickers 'Gäuhühner': Zur gesellschaftlichen Interpretation eines mittelhochdeutschen Textes," *Zeitschrift für deutsches Altertum,* 105, no. 3 (1976): 210–232;

Udo von der Burg, *Strickers Karl der Große als Bearbeitung des Rolandsliedes: Studien zu Form und Inhalt,* Göppinger Arbeiten zur Germanistik, no. 131 (Göppingen: Kümmerle, 1974);

Danielle Buschinger, "Parodie und Satire im 'Daniel von dem Blühenden Tal' des Stricker," in *Parodie und Satire in der Literatur des Mittelalters,* edited by Edine Breier (Greifswald: Ernst-Moritz-Arndt Universität, 1989), pp. 15–23;

Albrecht Classen, "Misogyny and the Battle of Genders in the Stricker's Maeren," *Neuphilologische Mitteilungen,* 92, no. 1 (1991): 105–122;

Classen, "Transformation des arthurischen Romans zum frühneuzeitlichen Unterhaltungs- und Belehrungswerk: Der Fall 'Daniel vom blühenden Tal,'" *Amsterdamer Beiträge zur älteren Germanistik,* 33 (1991): 167–192;

Thomas Cramer, "Normenkonflikte im 'Pfaffen Amîs' und im 'Willehalm von Wenden': Überlegungen zur Entwicklung des Bürgertums im Spätmittelalter," *Zeitschrift für deutsche Philologie,* special issue, 93 (October 1974): 124–140;

Ingrid Hahn, "Das Ethos der *kraft:* Zur Bedeutung der Massenschlachten in Strickers *Daniel von dem Blühenden Tal,*" *Deutsche Vierteljahrsschrift,* 59 (June 1985): 173–194;

Thomas Elwood Hart, "An Afterword in Response," *Colloquia Germanica: Internationale Zeitschrift für germanische Sprach- und Literaturwissenschaft,* 13, no. 2 (1980): 156–159;

Hart, "'Werkstruktur' in Stricker's *Daniel:* A Critique by Counterexample," *Colloquia Germanica: Internationale Zeitschrift für germanische Sprach- und Literaturwissenschaft,* 13, no. 2 (1980): 106–141;

Barbara Haupt, "Der *Pfaffe Amîs* und *Ulenspiegel:* Variationen zu einem vorgegebenen Thema," in *Till Eulenspiegel in Geschichte und Gegenwart,* edited by Thomas Cramer, Beiträge zur älteren deutschen Literaturgeschichte, no. 4 (Bern, Frankfurt am Main & Las Vegas: Lang, 1978), pp. 61–91;

Ingeborg Henderson, "Stricker's *Daniel* in the Recently Found *Ms. Germ. 1340,*" *Journal of English and Germanic Philology,* 86 (July 1987): 348–357;

Ludwig Jensen, *Über den Stricker als Bîspel-Dichter, seine Sprache und seine Technik unter Berücksichtigung des "Karl" und "Amîs,"* (Marburg: Universitäts-Buchdruckerei, 1885);

Barbara Könneker, "Strickers *Pfaffe Amîs* und das Volksbuch von *Ulenspiegel,*" *Euphorion,* 64, nos. 3–4 (1970): 242–280;

Walter Köppe, "Grundherrlichkeit versus Kaufmannschaft: Versuch einer sozio-ökonomischen Analyse des *Pfaffen Amis,*" *Acta Germanica,* 14 (1981): 39–50;

Köppe, "Ideologiekritische Aspekte im Werk des Stricker," *Acta Germanica,* 10 (1977): 139–211;

Albert Leitzmann, "Das chronologische Verhältnis von Strickers Daniel und Karl," *Zeitschrift für deutsche Philologie,* 28 (1896): 43–47;

Robert E. Lewis, "The Devil as Judge: The Stricker's Short Narrative 'Der Richter und der Teufel,'" in *The Dark Figure in Medieval German and Germanic Literature,* edited by Edward R. Haymes and Stephanie Cain Van D'Elden, Göppinger Arbeiten zur Germanistik, no. 448 (Göppingen: Kümmerle, 1986);

John Margetts, "*Der durstige Einsiedler* des Strickers: Ein Deutungsversuch," *Neuphilologische Mitteilungen,* 82, no. 2 (1981): 122–136;

Hans Mast, *Stilistische Untersuchungen an den Kleinen Gedichten des Strickers mit besonderer Berücksichtigung des volkstümlichen und des formelhaften Elementes* (Basel, 1929);

Wolfgang W. Moelleken, "Minne und Ehe in Strickers 'Daniel von dem blühenden Tal': Strukturanalytische Ergebnisse," *Zeitschrift für deutsche Philologie,* special issue, 93 (October 1974): 42–50;

Moelleken, "Der Pfaffe Amis und sein Bischof," in *In hôhem prîse: Festschrift Ernst S. Dick,* edited by Winder McConnell, Göppinger Arbeiten zur Germanistik, no. 480 (Göppingen: Kümmerle, 1989), pp. 279–293;

Moelleken and Ingeborg Henderson, "Die Bedeutung der *liste* im 'Daniel' des Strickers," *Amsterdamer Beiträge zur älteren Germanistik,* 4 (1973): 187–201;

Elke Müller-Ukena, "Rex humilis – rex superbus: Zum Herrschertum der Könige Artus von Britanje und Matur von Cluse in Strickers 'Daniel von dem blühenden Tal,'" *Zeitschrift für deutsche Philologie,* 103, no. 1 (1984): 27–51;

H. Niewöhner, "Strickerhandschriften," *Beiträge zur Geschichte der deutschen Sprache und Literatur,* 77 (1955): 495–496;

Ursula Peters, "'Bürgertum' und Literatur im 13. Jahrhundert: Probleme einer sozialgeschichtlichen Deutung des 'Pfaffen Âmîs,'" *Zeitschrift für Literaturwissenschaft und Linguistik,* 7, no. 26 (1977): 109–126;

Hedda Ragotzky, *Gattungserneuerung und Laienunterweisung in Texten des Strickers,* Studien und Texte zur Sozialgeschichte der Literatur, no. 1 (Tübingen: Niemeyer, 1981);

Ragotzky, "Das Handlungsmodell der list und die Thematisierung von guot: Zum Problem einer sozialgeschichtlich orientierten Interpretation von Strickers 'Daniel vom blühenden Tal' und dem 'Pfaffen Amîs,'" in *Literatur – Publikum – historischer Kontext,* edited by Gert Kaiser (Bern, Frankfurt am Main & Las Vegas: Lang, 1977), pp. 183–203;

Johanna Reisel, *Zeitgeschichtliche und theologisch-scholastische Aspekte im "Daniel von dem blühenden Tal" des Stricker,* Göppinger Arbeiten zur Germanistik, no. 464 (Göppingen: Kümmerle, 1986);

Michael Resler, "Zur Datierung von Strickers *Daniel von dem Blühenden Tal,*" *Euphorion,* 78, no. 1 (1984): 17–30;

Gustav Rosenhagen, "Der Stricker," in *Die deutsche Literatur des Mittelalters: Verfasserlexikon,* volume 4, edited by Karl Langosch (Berlin: De Gruyter, 1953), pp. 292–299;

Rüdiger Schnell, "Strickers 'Karl der Große': Literarische Tradition und politische Wirklichkeit," *Zeitschrift für deutsche Philologie,* special issue, 93 (October 1974): 50–80;

Werner Schröder, "*und zuckte in úf als einen schoup:* Parodierte Artus-Herrlichkeit in Strickers 'Daniel,'" in *Sprache und Recht: Beiträge zur Kulturgeschichte des Mittelalters. Festschrift Ruth Schmidt-Wiegand,* edited by Karl Hauck and others (Berlin & New York: De Gruyter, 1986), pp. 814–830;

Johannes Singer, "Der Eingang von Strickers 'Karl dem Großen': Text und Anmerkungen," *Zeitschrift für deutsche Philologie,* special issue, 93 (October 1974): 80–107;

Wolfgang Spiewok, "Parodie und Satire im 'Pfaff Amis' des Stricker," in *Parodie und Satire in der Literatur des Mittelalters,* pp. 5–15;

Dieter Vogt, *Ritterbild und Ritterlehre in der lehrhaften Kleindichtung des Stricker und im sogenannten Seifried Helbling,* Europäische Hochschulschriften, no. 845 (Frankfurt am Main, Bern & New York: Lang, 1985);

Stephen L. Wailes, "Heresy in Austria," *Neuphilologische Mitteilungen,* 79, no. 2 (1978): 97–101;

Wailes, "Immurement and Religious Experience in the Stricker's 'Eingemauerte Frau,'" *Beiträge zur Geschichte der deutschen Sprache und Literatur* (Tübingen), 96, nos. 1–2 (1974): 79–102;

Wailes, "Stricker and the Virtue *Prudentia:* A Critical Review," *Seminar,* 13, no. 3 (1977): 136–153;

Wailes, *Studien zur Kleindichtung des Stricker,* Philologische Studien und Quellen, no. 104 (Berlin: Schmidt, 1981).

Thomasîn von Zerclære

(circa 1186 – circa 1259)

Michael Resler
Boston College

MAJOR WORK: *Der welsche Gast* (1215–1216)

Manuscripts: The work is transmitted in twenty-four manuscripts predating 1500. Most include illustrations (a total of 120 in the various manuscripts) believed to have been authorized by Thomasîn himself. No single manuscript contains either the complete text or all of the illustrations. The transmission falls into two main branches, which are represented by *G* (Forschungsbibliothek, Gotha; Membrana I 120) and *A* (Universitätsbibliothek, Heidelberg; cpg 389). The latter is the oldest, dating from the second half of the thirteenth century.

First publication: *Der wälsche Gast des Thomasin von Zirclaria,* edited by Heinrich Rückert (Quedlinburg & Leipzig: Basse, 1852; reprinted, with an introduction and index by Friedrich Neumann, Berlin: De Gruyter, 1965).

Standard edition: *Der welsche Gast,* 4 volumes, edited by Friedrich W. von Kries (Göppingen: Kümmerle, 1984–1985).

Thomasîn von Zerclære's renown as a poet rests solely on his long didactic work *Der welsche Gast* (The Italian Guest, 1215–1216). Over the course of the more than fifteen thousand lines of his poem Thomasîn sets forth a comprehensive set of societal norms for men and women living within the courtly world of the High Middle Ages.

Perhaps just as noteworthy as the content of this poem is the fact that it was composed in Middle High German. Thomasîn's native tongue was Italian – his real name was Tommasino dei Cerchiari – and Middle High German was for him a second language. Thomasîn says (line 681 in the Friedrich W. von Kries edition [1984–1985]) that he is a native of Friuli, a margravate in northeastern Italy not far from the present-day border with Slovenia. Since 1077 Friuli had been a part of the patriarchate of Aquileia, and Thomasîn occupied a position of some responsibility at the court of the patriarch of Aquileia, Wolfger of Erla. Because Aquileia was on the fringes of the German empire and German was the chief language of the court, it is not surprising that Thomasîn acquired a knowledge of Middle High German; on the other hand, that he gained such proficiency as to compose a major work in the language is remarkable.

In contrast to most other German poets of the High Middle Ages, Thomasîn's life can, as Hans Teske first established, be reconstructed in considerable detail. Much of what is known about him stems from what he says in *Der welsche Gast.* He says in lines 11123 to 11129 that he was in the entourage of the patriarch Wolfger in October 1209, when Otto IV was crowned emperor by Pope Innocent III in Rome. In addition, certain allusions in *Der welsche Gast* make it likely that Thomasîn accompanied Wolfger to Rome in November 1215 for the Fourth Lateran Council. Moreover, Thomasîn even divulges his age at the time he was writing *Der welsche Gast:* in line 3047 he claims to be not yet thirty.

Because the poem can be precisely dated, it is possible to calculate Thomasîn's year of birth. In book 8 Thomasîn appeals to the young Hohenstaufen Friedrich II to recapture the Holy Land from the Muslim infidels. In the same passage he says of the grave of Christ: "ez sint wol acht und zwenzic iar, / daz wirz verlorn, daz ist war" (In truth, it has been a good twenty-eight years since we lost it). Since the news of that loss – Saladin's capture of Jerusalem in December 1187 – reached Europe early in 1188, it can be deduced that Thomasîn wrote this passage in 1215. This information allows *Der welsche Gast* to be dated with far greater preci-

Page from a late-thirteenth-century manuscript of book 5 of Thomasîn von Zerclære's Der welsche Gast
(Heidelberg, Universitätsbibliothek, cpg. 389, f.100v)

Page from a manuscript written circa 1340 for book 7 of Der welsche Gast *(Gotha, Forschungsbibliothek, Mbr. I no. 190, f. 130)*

sion than the vast majority of works of the age, but Thomasîn provides another chronological anchor for his poem: at the beginning of book 9 (lines 12877–13004) the poet engages in a dialogue with his own writing instrument, which has grown weary of the task of recording Thomasîn's words and begs him for a respite. I have served you faithfully all winter long, asserts Thomasîn's pen, toiling more than ten hours a day; but you have become a hermit, and you shun all the pastimes that once brought us both such pleasure: tournament and dance and the good company of knights and ladies. Thomasîn replies that he produced the first eight books in eight months; furthermore, since (as Thomasîn has already set forth in his prologue) the entire work is to encompass ten books, "du mûst zwene manode wachen" (you [Thomasîn's pen] shall have to remain on call for another two months, line 12936).

Assuming that Thomasîn's avowed timetable for composing *Der welsche Gast* can be taken at face value, he completed his work during a ten-month period centered on the winter of 1215-1216. In other words, *Der welsche Gast* was written between July or August 1215 and, perhaps, May of the following year. If he was twenty-eight or twenty-nine when he wrote *Der welsche Gast,* then Thomasîn must have been born between about 1186 and 1188.

As regards the date of his death, however, there is considerably less certitude. A Thomasinus de Cerlara Canonicus is recorded in the *necrologium* of the church at Aquileia; while there is no apparent cause to believe that this person is anyone other than Thomasîn, the document neglects to record a year. Thus, it is impossible to say how long Thomasîn may have lived beyond the composition of *Der welsche Gast.* The word *canonicus* (canon regular) indicates that by the time of his death the poet held a fairly high position of authority in the church.

As to the period 1215-1216, it is difficult to say what Thomasîn's duties were at Wolfger's court. It appears that he was a secretary or adviser to the politically astute patriarch, perhaps (given his linguistic talent) a translator and interpreter. That he was a member of the clergy is, in light of his title *canonicus,* beyond question, though a certain worldliness (or at least an openness to the pleasures of courtly life) shines through the didactic verses of *Der welsche Gast* and belies any notion of fanatical or rigid asceticism on Thomasîn's part.

Contemporary documents corroborate the existence of a line of aristocrats named de Circlaria (with widely divergent spellings) in Cividale, a town in Friuli near Aquileia, around 1200. The family appears to have been among the landed nobility; such a patrician family – perhaps of knightly stock and equal in standing to the members of the German nobility then resident in Aquileia – might well have produced a son who became a *clericus* and entered the service of the patriarch.

One requires little more than a cursory reading of *Der welsche Gast* to appreciate Thomasîn's erudition. While no single literary influence plays a dominant role in shaping *Der welsche Gast,* scholars have uncovered a broad range of writings that left their imprint on his thinking. Chief among these works are the Bible and the writings of Boethius, Cicero, Seneca, Horace, Saint Augustine, John of Salisbury, Isidor of Seville, and Ambrose of Milan, as well as the works of other important though less widely celebrated thinkers, such as Hildebert of Lavardin, Honorius Augustodunensis, Petrus Alfonsi, Guillaume de Conches,

and Alain de Lille. Certain of these sources were part of the general body of knowledge current among the ranks of the educated during the High Middle Ages; others are sufficiently arcane as to attest to a high level of erudition on Thomasîn's part. On but one occasion does Thomasîn explicitly cite another author to make his point: in lines 5431 to 5438 he refers to the commentary on Job by Pope Gregory I, a work known as *Moralia*. On the other hand, Thomasîn alludes on many occasions to exemplary figures from the then-popular chivalric romances; whether he knew these stories in their German versions or, as is more likely, in the Old French or Provençal originals is a point of controversy. At any rate, what emerges is the portrait of a young scholar and poet with a broad knowledge of philosophical, theological, and literary writings.

Thomasîn's writing of *Der welsche Gast* in what was for him a foreign tongue has long attracted the attention of scholars. Thomasîn himself is aware of his possible shortcomings in the German language: in the prologue he notes (lines 677- 679) that his audience ought not to find it odd should he make mistakes in his German, "wan ich vil gar ein wælich bin" (for I am very much an Italian). The Middle High German noun *wælich* was used to indicate any person of Romance heritage and was frequently applied to both French and Italian foreigners; given Thomasîn's own ancestry, the word is most conveniently translated in context as "Italian."

The general consensus among scholars, ushered in by the work of Friedrich Ranke, is that Thomasîn's German is technically quite good. Not unexpectedly, given the proximity of Friuli to present-day Carinthia, his language shows distinct characteristics of the Carinthian dialect spoken south of the Alps in the early thirteenth century. Any egregious infelicities of expression appear to be lacking, to the extent that such features can still be detected eight centuries later. Scholars have raised certain criticisms of Thomasîn's German: a limited vocabulary, a certain monotony in his rhymes, and a lack of metrical sophistication. Yet such objections are more poetic than linguistic and might be brought against any native German whose skills as a poet were imperfect but whose command of the language was beyond reproach. At the very least, there is every reason to concur with Friedrich Neumann's assessment that Thomasîn possessed an "extraordinary linguistic talent."

While Thomasîn's literary language was Middle High German, his mother tongue was a dialect of northeastern Italian. In addition, he was surely well grounded in both Latin and Provençal. The former was de rigueur for any literate person during the Middle Ages, and at many of the northern Italian courts in Thomasîn's day Provençal stood alongside Latin as a chief vehicle for literature since Italian had not yet fully developed into a literary language. The only other work Thomasîn is known to have composed, an earlier didactic poem on the nature of courtly love, was written, as Thomasîn himself says "in welhischer zünge" (in Provençal tongue, line 2156). Though the adjective *welhisch* ("Romance," that is, French or Italian) contains the same ambiguity as its companion noun *wælich,* scholars are in agreement that this poem must have been composed in Provençal, not in Italian. The work in question, which probably dates from shortly after 1200, is not transmitted in any extant manuscript and lives on only in Thomasîn's references to it in *Der welsche Gast.*

As regards the social status of his intended audience, Thomasîn makes it clear at several junctures that he is addressing himself exclusively to the world of the court, to "früme ritter und güte vrowen / und wise pfaffen" (valiant knights, noble ladies, and learned priests, lines 15349–15350). Typically for his age, there is no room in Thomasîn's worldview for peasants or city dwellers, nor does he speak charitably of the nascent merchant class. It is, then, only within his own rather narrow social sphere that Thomasîn seeks a public for his work.

By choosing to write in German, Thomasîn was consciously restricting the potential audience for his work within his native region of northeastern Italy; he apparently anticipated a much broader public beyond the borders of Italy, in the German-speaking areas of Europe. The title of the work literally means "The Italian Guest," and in two passages Thomasîn expressly refers to his book in just such terms. In the first reference, which occurs in the prologue (lines 697–700), he speaks directly to the question of his public:

> Tütsche lant entphahe wol,
>   als ein güt hüsfrowe sol,
> disen dinen welehischen gast,
>   der din ere minnet vast.

> (German soil, welcome warmly,
>   as a fine hostess should,
> this your Italian guest,
>   who greatly cherishes your good name.)

Thomasîn unambiguously casts his work as a "guest" from Italy, bearing a set of teachings intended to preserve the *ere* (good name) of German-speaking lands. In a passage near the end of his book (line 15335) Thomasîn explicitly affixes a title to his treatise: "Min büch heizet der Welsche Gast" (My book is called the Italian Guest) and proceeds (line 15339) to send it on its journey: "nü var hin min Welscher Gast" (be off on your way now, my Italian Guest), expressing the hope that it will find lodging only with persons receptive to its prescripts. From these passages it is evident that Thomasîn envisioned an audience that significantly transcended the German-speaking court at Aquileia.

Der welsche Gast is composed, as are virtually all German works of the age, in rhymed couplets of mostly four-stress lines. It consists of 15,406 verses in the von Kries edition; the earlier edition, by Heinrich Rückert (1852), comprises only 14,742 lines (miscounted as 14,752). The difference in number of lines between the two editions is accounted for by a fairly extensive prose synopsis of the poem that is transmitted in most of the manuscripts and is widely believed to be by Thomasîn himself; Rückert relegates the prose summary to his critical apparatus, but von Kries breaks it up into 610 lines and places it at the beginning of his critical text.

The prose summary affords Thomasîn an opportunity to set forth the structure of his work: the poet declares that his treatise is divided into ten parts (generally referred to by scholars as books); most of the parts have ten chapters, though some contain fewer and others more; and each chapter consists of an irregular number of what Thomasîn calls *liumde,* each of which appears to be the amount of text intended to be read or heard at a single sitting.

In his prologue proper (lines 611–754) Thomasîn names himself and reveals that he is writing in a foreign tongue. He also discloses the intended function of his poem, saying that good literature ought to have an ameliorative effect on its audience. He addresses book 1 (lines 755–2308) to the younger members of his public – to the "iunchherren unde vrovelin" (squires and maidens, line 830) – for whom he proposes as role models real and fictional characters from ancient and contemporary literature. The young maidens in Thomasîn's noble audience ought to follow the examples of Andromache, Enide, Penelope, and Blanscheflor, while the noble youths should take their cue from such figures as Charlemagne, King Arthur, Gawein, Erec, Iwein, Tristan, and Alexander. The tales of such characters, Thomasîn notes, are suitable for those who have not yet reached intellectual maturity – though not, he declares, for adults. Thomasîn then quotes from his own lost Provençal treatise on love and courtliness, a work he had composed at the behest of an unnamed lady.

In book 2 (lines 2309–3164) Thomasîn widens his perspective to encompass all members of his audience. In typically medieval fashion he declares that it is the princes and lords who must act as a moral compass for the rest of society. In view of the tumultuous age in which Thomasîn lived – an age characterized by uncertain leadership within the empire and by the struggle between emperors and popes – it is not surprising that Thomasîn declares *stete* (constancy) to be the fundamental societal virtue. Book 3 (lines 3165–4782) begins with the question of why humans are so lacking in *stete*. Thomasîn's answer is that God has endowed humans with the capacity to exercise free will; as a result, they all too frequently opt not to practice the constancy with which God has also endowed them.

The relationship between constancy and virtue is the centerpiece of book 4 (lines 4783–6328). Inconstancy is indigenous to all vices, Thomasîn argues; conversely, its antithesis, *stete,* informs all virtues; therefore, it is the consummate virtue. In book 5 (lines 6329–7436) Thomasîn examines the natures of good and evil and their relationship to human salvation. As in book 1, he links literature and learning to the betterment of society; here he enumerates well-known figures from the Bible and from ancient and contemporary literature as role models for his public. In the rather bleak fashion that typifies Thomasîn's view of his changing world, the poet questions why such fine heroes as Erec, Gawein, Parzival, and Iwein are no longer present in his own degenerate age. The way out of this dilemma, Thomasîn posits, is to shun worldly urges such as the desire for wealth, power, and fame.

In book 6 (lines 7437–9122) Thomasîn urges the knights among his audience to lead a sort of allegorical battle against the army of vices. Knights and priests are called upon to set an example for others in word and in deed; they ought to practice humility and to stand before God in fear, hope, and love. Book 7 (lines 9123–10502) serves as a showcase for Thomasîn's erudition as he probes the natures of and the relationship between the body and the soul in a fashion reminiscent of the "psychologies" that were then in vogue. Furthermore, he makes the seven liberal arts coextensive with learning and expresses the Socratic notion that learning furthers virtue.

Book 8 (lines 10503–12876) is by far the longest of the ten because Thomasîn digresses from the central thesis of the book – the effect of immoderation on the human condition – to comment on pressing political issues of the day. He accuses Otto of Brunswick, one of the two imperial candidates in the bitterly contested double election of 1198, of immoderation and champions the cause of Otto's opponent and successor, the young Hohenstaufen, Friedrich II. Then, in the most frequently cited passage from *Der welsche Gast,* Thomasîn reproaches Walther von der Vogelweide, the great contemporary German lyric poet who had, in a series of songs, savagely accused Pope Innocent III of greed, of treachery, and even of complicity with the devil:

> nu wie hat sich der gûte chnecht
>   an im gehandelt ane reht,
> der da *sprach* durh sinen hohen mût,
>   daz der pabest wold mit tûtschem gût
> fullen sinen welschen schrin.
>   het er gehabt den rat min,
>   er het daz wort gesprochen niht (lines 11843–11849).

> (How is it now that this good fellow [Walther]
>   has treated him [the pope] unjustly –
> this fellow who, in all his arrogance, has claimed
>   that the pope sought to fill
> his Italian shrine with German wealth.
>   Had he but had my advice,
>   he would not have spoken such words.)

Walther's anti-Innocent songs are not only insolent and intemperate, contends Thomasîn, but they have also had a grave impact on popular opinion:

> wand er hat tûsent man betôret,
>   daz si habent uberhôret
>   gotes und des papstes gebot (lines 11875–11877).

> (For he [Walther] has misled a thousand men,
>   such that they have failed to hear
>   both God's and the pope's commandment.)

Thomasîn never mentions Walther by name, referring to him ironically as "der gute chnecht" (the good fellow) and addressing him in line 11883 as "lieber friunt min" (my dear friend). Neumann has suggested that Thomasîn and Walther were personally acquainted; whether they were or not, it is clear that the two poets stood on opposite sides of the conflict between the papacy and the empire. (The patriarch Wolfger, at this point Thomasîn's patron, had in 1203, while still bishop of Passau, given Walther money for a fur coat – a circumstance widely believed to indicate that Walther had himself been in the service of Wolfger at this earlier date.)

In the final segment of Thomasîn's political excursus in book 8, he addresses the German knights generally and the young Friedrich specifically in support of the upcoming Crusade, which had been promoted by the Fourth Lateran Council of November 1215. Thomasîn's crusading fervor follows logically from his criticism of Walther, who had derided the pope's measures to collect revenues for the Crusade.

All in all, the political digressions of book 8 reveal Thomasîn as a young poet who, from his vantage point in Aquileia, was not merely a passive witness to the great events of his day. Instead, as a key member at the court of the influential and politically astute Wolfger, Thomasîn showed no hesitation in taking a stand on many of those issues. And, not surprising, Thomasîn's positions are quite in line with those of his powerful patron.

Book 9 (lines 12877–14218) begins with the colloquy between the poet and his pen, in which Thomasîn sketches his timetable for *Der welsche Gast*. The major portion of the book is dedicated to a learned reflection on justice, both secular and divine. Book 10 (lines 14219 – 15406) includes a discourse on generosity, which Thomasîn calls (line 14348) "der tugende frowe" (the mistress of virtues). In the spirit of generosity, Thomasîn presents his finished work as a gift. In the concluding lines (which are structurally part of book 10 but form a sort of freestanding epilogue) Thomasîn names his book and dispatches it on its journey to German lands.

Thomasîn's stated purpose in writing *Der welsche Gast* is not to entertain but to enlighten; his faith in the educative effect of literature is unshakable. In the discourse with his pen he concedes that he would much rather be out in the courtly world, where he could observe knights and ladies; as he contends in lines 12977– 12978, however, he can achieve more good "daz ich spreche wol, / daz in beiden frûmen sol" (by speaking well, / in ways that shall be of benefit to both [knights and ladies]). And yet it is not with a preaching, moralizing voice that Thomasîn seeks to educate his public. His message is more philosophical than religious, and he speaks as a socially conservative observer intent on preserving intact the world in which he has come of age and which he sees endangered by unwelcome forces of change.

Near the end of the final book (line 15281) Thomasîn expresses his hope that "Min bûch sol lange wern" (My book should endure for a long time). His hope was not in vain: while major portions of this lengthy poem appear dry and repetitive by modern standards, *Der welsche Gast* was well received and widely read not only during its own age

but – judging by the many extant manuscripts from the late fifteenth century and beyond – by later generations as well.

References:

Bruno Boesch, *Lehrhafte Literatur: Lehre in der Dichtung und Lehrdichtung im deutschen Mittelalter* (Berlin: Schmidt, 1977);

Judith A. Davidson, "The Two Exemplars of Manuscript D of *Der welsche Gast* (Dresden, Sächs. Landesbibl. M.67)," *Neuphilologische Mitteilungen*, 83, no. 2 (1982): 132–149;

Klaus Düwel, "Lesestoff für junge Adlige: Lektüreempfehlungen in einer Tugendlehre des 13. Jahrhunderts," *Fabula*, 32, no. 1, 2, 3 (1991): 67–93;

Karl-Heinz Göttert, "Thomasin von Zerclaere und die Tradition der Moralistik," in *Architectura poetica: Festschrift Johannes Rathofer,* edited by Ulrich Ernst and Bernhard Sowinski, Kölner Germanistische Studien, 30 (Cologne: Böhlau, 1990), pp. 179–188;

Christoph Huber, "Höfischer Roman als Integumentum?: Das Votum Thomasins von Zerklaere," *Zeitschrift für deutsches Altertum,* 115, no. 2 (1986): 79–100;

Fritz Peter Knapp, "Integumentum und âventiure: Nochmals zur Literaturtheorie bei Bernardus (Silvestris?) und Thomasin von Zerklaere," *Literaturwissenschaftliches Jahrbuch,* 28 (1987): 299–307;

Friedrich W. von Kries, *Textkritische Studien zum Welschen Gast Thomasins von Zerclaere* (Berlin: De Gruyter, 1967);

Kries, "Zur Überlieferung des 'Welschen Gasts' Thomasins von Zerclaere," *Zeitschrift für deutsches Altertum,* 113, no. 2 (1984): 111–131;

Friedrich Neumann and Ewald Vetter, *Der Welsche Gast des Thomasîn von Zerclaere: Codex Palatinus Germanicus 389 der Universitätsbibliothek Heidelberg* (Wiesbaden: Reichert, 1974);

Adolf von Oechelhäuser, *Der Bilderkreis zum Wälschen Gaste des Thomasin von Zerclaere* (Heidelberg: Koester, 1890);

Friedrich Ranke, *Sprache und Stil im Wälschen Gast des Thomasin von Circlaria,* Palaestra, no. 68 (Berlin: Mayer & Müller, 1908; reprinted, New York & London: Johnson Reprint, 1970);

Catherine Teresa Rapp, *Burgher and Peasant in the Works of Thomasin von Zirklaria, Freidank and Hugo von Trimberg,* Studies in German, no. 7 (Washington, D.C.: Catholic University of America, 1936);

Dieter Richter, "Zur Überlieferung von Thomasîns 'Welschem Gast,'" *Zeitschrift für deutsches Altertum,* 96, no. 1 (1967): 149–153;

Daniel Rocher, *Thomasin von Zerclaere: Der Wälsche Gast (1215–1216)* (Paris: Champion, 1977);

Rocher, "Thomasin von Zerclaere, Innocent III et Latran IV ou La véritable influence de l'actualité sur le *Wälscher Gast,*" *Le moyen âge,* 79, no. 1 (1973): 35–55;

Werner Röcke, *Feudale Anarchie und Landesherrschaft: Wirkungsmöglichkeiten didaktischer Literatur. Thomasin von Zerklaere "Der Wälsche Gast"* (Bern, Frankfurt am Main & Las Vegas: Lang, 1978);

Ernst J. F. Ruff, *"Der wälsche Gast" des Thomasin von Zerclaere: Untersuchungen zu Gehalt und Bedeutung einer mittelhochdeutschen Morallehre,* Erlanger Studien, no. 35 (Erlangen: Palm & Enke, 1982);

Manfred Günter Scholz, "Die 'Hûsvrouwe' und ihr Gast: Zu Thomasin von Zerclaere und seinem Publikum," in *Festschrift für Kurt Herbert Halbach,* edited by Rose Beate Schäfer-Maulbetsch, Manfred Günter Scholz, and Günther Schweikle, Göppinger Arbeiten zur Germanistik, no. 70 (Göppingen: Kümmerle, 1972), pp. 247–269;

Hans Teske, *Thomasin von Zerclaere: Der Mann und sein Werk* (Heidelberg: Winter, 1933);

Ursula Winter and Heinz Stănescu, "Ein neuentdecktes Fragment aus dem Welschen Gast des Thomasin von Zerclaere," *Beiträge zur Geschichte der deutschen Sprache und Literatur* (Halle), 97 (1976): 291–298.

Ulrich von Liechtenstein

(circa 1200 – circa 1275)

Klaus M. Schmidt
Bowling Green State University

MAJOR WORKS: *Frauendienst* (circa 1255)

Manuscript: The work is preserved in one almost complete manuscript (Munich, Bayerische Staatsbibliothek; cgm. 44). It consists of 129 pages of parchment (18.5 by 12.5 centimeters); one double sheet is missing between pages 99 and 100, causing a gap between song 37/2 and stanza 1400. Moreover, songs 57 and 58 are missing. There are also two fragments of lost manuscripts: the first is a 17.3-by-11.8-centimeter sheet of parchment (Augsburger Stadtbibliothek; fragm. germ. 10) containing stanzas 560/5 to 574/4; the other fragment consists of parchment sheets (Stadtarchiv Landshut; Pergamentfragmente) containing parts of stanzas 849 to 894. All manuscripts are dated circa 1300, and their language is traced to the Bavarian/Austrian region. Since *Frauendienst* originally had all of Ulrich's songs integrated with the narrative stanzas, the missing lines from song 37 and the complete songs 57 and 58 are added to the editions from the collection of *Minnesangs,* Die Große Heidelberger (or Manessische) Liederhandschrift (Heidelberg, Universitätsbibliothek; cpg 848), which was assembled shortly after 1300.

First publication: *Frauendienst, oder: Geschichte und Liebe des Ritters und Sängers Ulrich von Lichtenstein, von ihm selbst beschrieben. Nach einer alten Handschrift bearbeitet und herausgegeben,* edited by Ludwig Tieck (Stuttgart: Cotta, 1811).

Standard editions: "Vrouwen Dienest," in *Ulrich von Lichtenstein,* edited by Karl Lachmann and Theodor von Karajan (Berlin: Sander, 1841; reprinted, Amsterdam: Rodopi, 1974); *Ulrich's von Liechtenstein Frauendienst,* 2 volumes, edited by Reinhold Bechstein, volumes 6–7 of *Deutsche Dichtungen des Mittelalters,* edited by Karl Bartsch (Leipzig: Brockhaus, 1888); *Ulrich von Liechtenstein Frauendienst,* edited by Franz Viktor Spechtler, Göppinger

Arbeiten zur Germanistik, volume 485 (Göppingen: Kümmerle, 1987).

Edition in modern German: *Narr im hohen Dienst,* edited and translated by Walter Zitzenbacher (Graz: Stiasny, 1958).

Edition in English: *Ulrich von Liechtenstein's "Service of Ladies,"* translated by J. Wesley Thomas, University of North Carolina Studies in the Germanic Languages and Literatures, no. 63 (Chapel Hill: University of North Carolina Press, 1969).

Fifty-eight Songs (circa 1255)

Manuscripts: Although the songs are integrated with the narrative of the *Frauendienst,* they have always been treated as separate entities as well. The majority of the songs are also preserved in Die große Heidelberger (or Manessische) Liederhandschrift (Universitätsbibliothek Heidelberg; cpg 848), in which, with the exception of songs 22, 23, 25, 49, 51, and 56, which are either preserved only in part or are missing altogether, the songs appear in the same sequence as in *Frauendienst.* In addition, song 12 is preserved under the heading "Niune," and the first stanza of song 40 is preserved under anonymous songs in Die kleine Heidelberger Liederhandschrift (Universitätsbibliothek Heidelberg; cpg 357), assembled toward the end of the thirteenth century.

First publication: In *Frauendienst, oder: Geschichte und Liebe des Ritters und Sängers Ulrich von Lichtenstein, von ihm selbst beschrieben. Nach einer alten Handschrift bearbeitet und herausgegeben,* edited by Ludwig Tieck (Stuttgart: Cotta, 1811).

Standard editions: In *Ulrich von Lichtenstein,* edited by Karl Lachmann and Theodor von Karajan (Berlin: Sander, 1841; reprinted, Amsterdam: Rodopi, 1974); in *Ulrich's von Liechtenstein Frauendienst,* 2 volumes, edited by Reinhold Bechstein, volumes 6–7 of *Deutsche Dichtungen des Mittelalters,* edited by Karl Bartsch (Leipzig: Brockhaus, 1888); "Die Lie-

The character Ulrich, in his guise as Lady Venus, in Ulrich von Liechtenstein's Frauendienst *(Große Heidelberger Liederhandschrift, Heidelberg, Universitätsbibliothek, cpg 848, f. 237a)*

der Ulrichs von Liechtenstein," in *Deutsche Liederdichter des 13. Jahrhunderts,* volume 1, edited by Carl von Kraus, second edition, edited by Gisela Kornrumpf (Tübingen, 1978), pp. 428–494; in *Ulrich von Liechtenstein Frauendienst,* edited by Franz Viktor Spechtler, Göppinger Arbeiten zur Germanistik, volume 485 (Göppingen: Kümmerle, 1987).

Edition in modern German: *Sechs Lieder,* translated by J. Strobl (Vienna: Holzhausen, n.d.).

Frauenbuch (circa 1256–1260)

This work is preserved only in the Ambraser Heldenbuch (Österreichische Nationalbibliothek, Vienna; ser. nova 2663) under the heading "Ditz puech haysset der Ytwitz" (This book is called the Reproach). The large parchment manuscript contains twenty-five narrative works, of which fifteen are preserved exclusively in that volume. It was commissioned

by Emperor Maximilian I and written down by Hans Ried of Bozen between 1504 and 1516.

Standard edition: *Ulrich von Liechtenstein Frauenbuch,* edited by Franz Viktor Spechtler, Göppinger Arbeiten zur Germanistik, volume 520 (Göppingen: Kümmerle, 1989).

Ulrich von Liechtenstein is by far the best-documented author of the high courtly period of medieval German literature. What is known about his life, however, seems not at all compatible with what one learns about him from his work. His main work, the *Frauendienst* (Service of Women, circa 1255), is the first epic in the German vernacular written in the first person. For that reason many scholars — especially in the nineteenth century — have wanted to see the work as an early forerunner of Johann Wolfgang von Goethe's *Dichtung und Wahrheit* (Poetry and Truth, 1811–1813; translated as *Memoirs of Goethe,* 1824) — that is, as a kind of autobiography treated with a high degree of poetic freedom. Such a comparison has caused much confusion, which is heightened by the clear identification of the "I" in the work with the author's own name as well as by his frequent references to names, places, and events that can be historically documented. At the same time, the first half of the work tells about such outrageous behavior of the hero that it has been difficult to identify the highly respectable Ulrich von Liechtenstein with the fool who appears in his narrative under the same name. The dearth of historical information about the majority of writers from the period has forced scholars to glean biographical data mainly from their writings; Ulrich makes that approach highly questionable should the biographical information in his works turn out to be historically untenable, as seems to be the predominant opinion among scholars today.

Whether the *Frauendienst* is placed in the context of the medieval genre of the confession in the line of Saint Augustine and Boethius or the tradition of the dream report reaching from Cicero's *Dream of Scipio* to Guillaume de Lorris's *Romance of the Rose* (circa 1230) is of less importance than that it shows that the medieval epic may deal with the auctorial point of view in a flexible way, as does the modern novel. Thus the information given about the first-person narrator may be an early use of the narrative device of creating an atmosphere of intense verisimilitude around fictitious subject matter. If Ulrich's *Frauendienst* does use such a technique, Ulrich reveals himself not only as a remarkable historical personality but also as an innovator in the history of literature comparable to Dante, who reinvented a similar form for his *Vita nova* about fifty years later.

Ninety-four documents bearing Ulrich's name or seal are known. They span dates from 17 November 1227 to 27 July 1274 and show him issuing, witnessing, and guaranteeing contracts and acting as a high judge and negotiator. Accordingly, he must have been one of the most respected personalities of the courtly society in the triangular region bounded by Salzburg, Venice, and Vienna. The most extensive rhymed chronicle of the time on Austria was written around 1300 by Ottokar of der Geul (today Gaal, near Knittelfeld), a vassal of Ulrich's son Otto II. In that work Ulrich is characterized as highly intelligent and a forceful personality.

Ulrich was born between 1200 and 1210 into a Styrian family belonging to the class of *ministeriales*. Originally that was an unfree class of functionaries and officials serving the higher courts, but Ulrich is one of the best examples of the extreme upward mobility of that class, members of which frequently managed to gain positions of influence and power that surpassed by far those of some members of the originally freeborn nobility. Ulrich's father was Dietmar III, who married a Gertrud from the free house of Treisen-Freistritz in Lower Austria. Ulrich had three brothers: Otto, who became a priest in Graz; Hartnid, who became a priest in Pöls and later bishop of Gurk; and Dietmar IV from Offenburg, who married Gertrud from Wildon. One of Ulrich's two sisters, Hedwig, married Dietmar von Steyr; the other sister, whose name is not known, married the Austrian chamberlain Heinrich von Waßerburg.

From information given in the *Frauendienst* it is conceivable that Ulrich was sent away from home at an early age, like most young noblemen, to be educated and brought up with courtly manners under the tutelage of a patron lady at a court of high esteem. Speculation that this woman may have been Beatrix, daughter of Otto II of Burgundy and granddaughter of Emperor Friedrich I (Barbarossa), cannot be confirmed. It is known that in 1208 she married Otto I, Duke of Andechs-Meran, becoming the sister-in-law of Henry, Margrave of Istria, at whose court Ulrich may have served as an esquire. Through such connections he may have gained his obvious familiarity with the French and Italian troubadour tradition. The *Frauendienst* reports that the young esquire was called home from the court of the margrave of Istria when his father died, which must have occurred between 1219 and 1221. The

work also says that Ulrich was knighted in Vienna at the wedding of the daughter of Duke Leopold IV of Austria to a prince of Saxonia, an event that is historically documented as having occurred in 1222. Between 1225 and 1230 Ulrich married Perchta von Weissenstein. They had two sons and two daughters: Ulrich II, who married Kunigunde von Goldegg; Otto II, who was married three times – to Agnes von Wildon, to Diemut von Liechtenstein-Nikolsburg, and to Adelheid von Pottendorf; Diemut, who married Wulfing von Trennstein in 1250; and Perchta, who married Herrand II von Wildon, the well-known Styrian poet, in 1260.

Ulrich's extraordinarily long life – for medieval conditions – spanned the reigns of Duke Leopold IV, who died in 1230, and Duke Friedrich II, the last ruler of the house of Babenberg. Friedrich's death in the battle on the Leitha, a small river marking the border between Austria and Hungary, in 1246 is the other major event in the *Frauendienst* that is historically confirmed. According to the work, this tragic event marks a turning point in the history of Austria and Styria. Documents confirm that Ulrich's relationship with Friedrich II was a close one: in 1241 Ulrich is mentioned as "dapifer Stirie" (lord high steward in Styria); in 1245 he settled a legal case in the name of Friedrich II that had been raised by the monastery of Admont. The Interregnum following Friedrich's death was marked by a power struggle between the king of Hungary and King Ottokar of Bohemia over the reign in Austria and Styria that was not settled until Rudolf von Hapsburg was elected king of Germany in 1273. The struggle between Bohemia and Hungary was, however, temporarily settled in 1254 by the peace treaty of Ofen. It may have been this grudgingly accepted peace settlement that led Ulrich to take some time off from public life to devote his energies to the composition of the *Frauendienst,* followed by his *Frauenbuch* (Book of Women, circa 1256–1260).

Ulrich must have experienced those years of uncertain government and political struggle as a period of decay and decadence, against which he wrote his message of true chivalry based on an honest and balanced relationship between men and women of the courtly society. Since he wanted to keep Austria and Styria united under one rule, he favored Ottokar of Bohemia, who gained the reign over both dukedoms in 1260. Several documents of the king of Bohemia show Ulrich von Liechtenstein as a witness during those years, and in 1272 Ottokar appointed his faithful servant as marshal and *iudex provincialis Styrie* (supreme provincial judge of Styria), making him governor of the province.

Ich hozte sagen ein meist' gut
waer ze potzen dar reit ich
Man riost des endelichen mich
vn chom ich kurzelichen dar
Er machte mir den ving' gar
Mit sin' meist'schaft gesunt
Ich reit zu in sa an d' stunt

Do ich dar vf dem wege reit
von gedanchen mir min leit
Swant ein teil ich gedaht also
Ich mac wol immr wesen vro
Daz ich d' werden dienen sol
Daz tut mir inneclich wol
Min hze singen mir do riet
von min vrowen disiu liet.

Ein tanz wise vn est diu sehste wise
Iue daz mir div gute so verret

Ulrich died around 1275 and was succeeded in office by his eldest son, Otto II.

Ulrich's grave must be sought in or around Saint John's Chapel of the canonical convent of Seckau, the spiritual center of his parental stronghold, Treisen-Freistritz. Despite the wishful thinking of the area chamber of commerce and a long-lasting scholarly dispute, the gravestone at the Frauenburg near Unzmarkt, one of Ulrich's castles in the vicinity of Murau and Judenburg, does not mark the famous Ulrich's tomb. The inscription "Hie leit Uolrich.dises.houses.rehtter erbe" (Here rests Ulrich, lawful heir to this house) probably refers to Ulrich III, the grandson of Ulrich von Liechtenstein. It would be unlikely that the children of one of the most important personalities of the area and the era might have seen the need to have engraved on his tombstone that he was "the lawful heir" to his own castle.

The *Frauendienst* is a revolutionary literary work not only for its use of the first-person narrator and for its content but also because it unites the most common genres of courtly literature into one work. The epic narrative, in iambic tetrameters rhymed in pairs, consists of 1,850 eight-line stanzas; interspersed are fifty-eight songs that follow the most elaborate and intricate canzone and other stanzaic patterns of the high courtly *Minnesang*. Also integrated into the narration are three pieces in the genre of the *büechlin*: longer treatments of the topic of *minne* (courtly love) in rhymed pairs of iambic tetrameters that are sent to the beloved lady at crucial points throughout the service relationship as allegorical messengers. Moreover, there are letters in rhymed verse as well as in prose, and one *leich* (lay), a longer and metrically more intricate lyric genre.

The narrative portion of the work uses elements from the courtly romance and the epic elements contained in the song sequences of troubadours and minnesingers. Ulrich joins them into a plot that revolves around the relationship between a noble lady and her serving knight. The work exhibits the bipartite structure of the developmental Arthurian romance, which follows the hero from his youth through a fast ascent to a high point in his career, followed by a sudden fall into ignominy; then there is a gradual recovery and a renewed ascent to even greater heights. About three-fourths of the narration is devoted to the first part and only one-fourth to the second, which means that the demonstration of failure and folly is much more prominent than that of reassertion and achievement. The *Frauendienst* is especially revolutionary in that it transposes these elements from the fantasy realm of dragons, fairies, sorcerers, dwarfs, giants, and encounters with mysterious opponents in dark forests into the real world. There is not a series of *aventiure* (adventures) but the continuous struggle of the hero to prove his prowess through jousts at tournaments that he organizes in honor of his beloved lady. Some events to which the hero submits himself to prove his steadfastness may appear bizarre, but they are conceivably real. Ulrich, the hero of the work, first experiences *hohe minne* (courtly love), a relationship with a high-ranking lady that is marked by the lady's refusal to bestow sexual favors in return for the knight's service. That type of love leads Ulrich into a state of deep frustration, depression, and despair, until he finds a new relationship, *ebene minne* (plain love), that is based on mutual respect and satisfaction, a form of the love ideal that was promoted by Walther von der Vogelweide.

The first service of Ulrich, the hero, begins as a youthful infatuation with his patron lady, under whose tutelage the lad has spent his formative years. Thus Ulrich, the writer, places the origin of *hohe minne* clearly within the hothouse atmosphere of juvenile sexuality. In this context it does not seem bizarre for the boy to find excitement simply by imagining the lady touching the bunch of flowers he has picked for her at the same place his sweaty hand had held it or for him secretly to drink water from the bowl in which she washed her white hands (lines 24–25). He adds that in his childish ways he did many things in her service that he might best not talk about (line 26). One can imagine audiences hearing these lines, presented in the appropriate musical and histrionic fashion, rolling their eyes in amusement at such juvenile folly, which, to a more moderate degree, they could observe among the young pages and squires at their courts on a daily basis. The author skillfully employs the most effective techniques for creating comedy, exaggerating and distorting things just a few degrees beyond the level of reality. Wolfram von Eschenbach's description of the first clumsy steps of his young hero Parzival into courtly society may have served as Ulrich's model.

When his father takes him away from his lady's court to have him trained as a young esquire under the tutelage of a fatherly patron, Ulrich's amorous excitement for his lady reaches almost fever pitch:

daz was ein wunderlîch geschiht,
daz man den lîp von danne treip
und daz mîn herze aldâ beleip;
daz was bî ir naht und tac,
daz es vil selten ruowe pflac. (lines 27–31)

(that was a strange thing,
that the body was driven away
and the heart stayed behind;
it stayed with her day and night,
so that it never came to rest.)

Heinrich von Isterrich, Ulrich's first male mentor, introduces him to the rules of *hohe minne*, the selfless service of a lady that involves composing lyrical eulogies in the form of letters and songs and performing feats of chivalry in her name. The problem is that Heinrich tells Ulrich to serve only *guoten wiben* (good women). A misunderstanding about that instruction turns out to be the central dilemma of the work: a lady who is of the highest nobility and great beauty and who enjoys the best reputation for virtue is not guaranteed to belong to the category of *guoten wiben;* she may be ruled by vanity and caprice, not by the idea of having her lover prove himself before she enters with him into a relationship of mutual respect and fulfillment. Nobody warns young Ulrich about the pitfalls of choosing the wrong object of desire.

The gist of the story is the conversion of a sick lover – Ulrich – who will suffer any degree of humiliation his beloved lady imposes on him, into a lover who will lead a healthy and fulfilled sex life based on mutual respect. In principle, this plot is not radically different from that of the typical Arthurian epic; it is similar to the stories of tragic lovers such as Sigune and Schionatulander and Anfortas and Orgeluse and happy ones such as Erec and Enite, Laudine and Iwein, and Parzival and Condwiramurs. The difference is that Ulrich is just an ordinary knight who tries to win his lady not by heroic adventures involving supernatural beasts but by organizing one tournament after the other. Although always victorious, he never pleases and never gets his reward in accordance with the *hohe minne* ideal. Consequently, he makes a fool of himself.

The state of overheated and unsatisfied desire is unhealthy for the frustrated hero. When the lady accuses him of having lied to her, since he had not really lost a finger in her service in a joust (it was just permanently stiff), he chops it off and sends it to her in an elaborate miniature casket. He submits himself to painful surgery after she complains about the ugly shape of his mouth. He sleeps and eats among lepers on her instructions.

In keeping with the erotic metaphors associated with jousting, Ulrich sets out dressed as Lady Venus. In that role he defeats a knight dressed as a monk and another fighting as a Slavic woman. He has to be convinced that the former challenger is in reality a knight in disguise before he consents to raise his lance against a monk; similarly, he has to be convinced that he is not facing a real female before he jousts against the "Slavic woman." Ulrich von Liechtenstein leaves no doubt that the joust is a metaphor for sexual intercourse when he has his hero say:

"Swâ ich noch ie bî mînen tagen
getyostirt hete wider diu wîp,
dâ waer gar harnaschblôz mîn lîp
gegen ir aller tyost gewesen
und bin doch vor ir wol genesen;
Ir tyost tuot herzenlîchen wol,
gegen in sich nieman wapen sol." (688, lines 2–8)

("Whenever I jousted against women
I did so totally without protective armor
against all of their jousts.
Yet, I was never harmed.
Their joust is a pleasure that goes to the heart
and no man should arm himself against it.")

In an anticlimactic episode Ulrich steps into a basket to be hoisted to his lady's bedroom. He makes it to her bed, but when her attendants appear, she persuades him to step back into the basket until they leave. As a guarantee of her "honest" intentions she lets him hold her hand. Then she unexpectedly invites him to embrace her from that position. The excited lover lets go of her hand and crashes to the ground, tumbles down a gully, and lands in an ice-cold lake, where he wants to cool off his ardent desire forever. But his messenger arrives with yet more encouraging lies from the capricious lady. She suggests that if he goes on a Crusade in her service, she will grant him his reward. Actually, she hopes that he will never return. But by now he has become wiser through his ordeals, and he makes her entangle herself in her own web of intrigue. He tells her that he will be exclusively *her* pilgrim and, consequently, will have to receive his cross and blessing directly from her; a truly Christian pilgrimage could not be abused for blasphemously erotic purposes. She has to back away from her plan under such ethical pressure.

It takes an even more serious blow to the lover's ego before he finally calls off this silly and sickly service. Contrary to his counterparts in thirteenth- and fourteenth-century French literature, however, Ulrich does not take drastic revenge on his lady. He even apologizes, in a few songs that – in the traditional *Minnesang* fashion – do not mention her by name, for having vented his anger against her. Ultimately he comes to the realization that

Swer dienest dâr die lenge tuot,
dâ man im niht gelônen chan,
der ist ein gar unwîser man. (1365, lines 4–7)

(Whoever does long service,
to someone who cannot reward him,
he is a total fool.)

Ulrich does not say what the final indignity inflicted on him by the lady was. This silence may be a clever trick by the writer to force the audience to invent even more bizarre events. On the other hand, it may be an allusion to the only loose end that seems deliberately left dangling in the otherwise clearly structured epic. Two almost identical humorous episodes take place during the hero's jousting trip when he is disguised as Lady Venus. In the first episode three tokens of love – a belt, a wreath, and a clasp – and a love letter from an unknown lady are wrapped in a skirt and smuggled among his women's clothes. In the second episode he is surprised in the bathtub by a page who covers the room with rose petals and then forces on him the same love tokens, a similar letter, plus a ring with a red ruby. In both cases Ulrich is trapped in a situation where he cannot reject the gifts, and both times his own pages witness that he received them – although he kept them with the intention of returning them as soon as he learned the identity of the sender. To an audience familiar with the meaning of erotic rituals involving love tokens, the hero has formally become guilty of unfaithfulness to his chosen one. But the audience could guess that his own capricious lady has staged these episodes to have something to hold over him. This explanation fits perfectly into the pattern of intrigue and flirtation that has fooled the inexperienced lover repeatedly.

In the second part of the poem Ulrich finds another lady, one who has all the right qualities and with whom he develops a harmonious and mutually satisfying relationship, and they live happily ever after. In her service he organizes the *Artusfahrt* (Arthur Journey), a jousting trip during which Ulrich plays the role of King Arthur and all other participants, except for Duke Friedrich II, take as pseudonyms well-known names from the Arthurian romances. That the real Ulrich was no stranger to such activities is evidenced by the meticulous descriptions, down to the minutest details, of equipment, horsemanship, and all other aspects of the tournament. The *Frauendienst* is the literary work that has been used most frequently by historians as a source of information about such events.

Besides the *Artusfahrt,* the major event in the second part of the *Frauendienst* is the death of Friedrich II during the battle near the river Leitha, and Ulrich's account of the death of his beloved Friedrich is one of the most gripping and realistic descriptions in medieval literature. Its most remarkable aspect is its simplicity and total lack of heroic pathos. Death comes unexpectedly and suddenly as the result of a simple mistake: as the duke is trying to lead his people in an attack, no one notices that a stray group of enemies is galloping up from behind. According to Ulrich's report, Friedrich must not even have had time to defend himself: he was simply ridden down, since his body showed no trace of a battle wound. Thus the great leader falls to his death unnoticed by friend or foe. Stripped to his linen undergarment and his breastplate, with one shoe missing and with bruises on his cheek and one leg, he is found by his scribe while the battle is still raging. So as not to jeopardize their victory by demoralizing the troops, the scribe throws the body across his horse, covers it with his cloak, and takes it to a simple home of burghers in a nearby town, where it is left until the battle is over. A prayer to God to take care of Friedrich's soul ends the account. Ulrich probably did not participate in the battle himself, but he reports that a Heinrich von Liechtenstein acted as a decisive force in winning it for the Austrians. No such person is historically documented; Ulrich may be using a fictitious name. Be that as it may, it is obvious that his report of Friedrich's death is deliberately submitted to all the restraints of realism. There is no stylization or heroic and tragic exaggeration according to the memento mori tradition or the traditional courtly romance that places its heroes either in a distant past or the never-never land of the fairy tale.

Ulrich's *Frauendienst* is a reaffirmation of the medieval *minne* service, but of that service stripped of all the decadent aspects that are degrading to both men and women. He upholds true love, as opposed to the type of glassy-eyed puppy love that drives men and women to antisocial behavior. He would have the irresistible force of the sex drive channeled so that it leads to harmonious relationships of mutual satisfaction and serves a public function as well. The ultimate purpose of the "service of ladies" is to maintain meaningful courtly activities in the form of tournaments and festivals; such activities create the proper erotic atmosphere in which mutually satisfying sexual relationships can thrive. The wealthy have a strong incentive to organize and finance these events, which provide poor knights with a stable source of income; in this way the threat of rampant highway robbery during peacetime, when scores of armed and highly skilled fighters found themselves without income, is lessened. Such civilized courtly activities become meaningless when the "service of ladies" reveals itself as a wild-goose chase of bloodless and pining lovers who earn nothing but frustration.

Such views are compatible with the forceful yet responsible personality of Ulrich that is revealed through the historical documents. Of course, Ulrich the author intentionally subjected Ulrich the fictional antihero of the first part of the work to ridicule so as to expose love service gone awry; had he not used his own name as the narrative *I,* the message would have had much less impact. By no means are the adventures of the fictional Ulrich an autobiographical report. On the other hand, when the work has Ulrich the protagonist, weary from his arduous service of his capricious lady, interrupt his journey and rest at his castle in the care of his beloved wife, this situation is quite plausible: a harmonious marriage was totally compatible with the service of ladies; both relationships, if they were working well, fulfilled important social and political functions. In that respect Ulrich's ideas differ considerably from the views promoted in most courtly works, especially in those by Wolfram and Hartmann von Aue, in which love service invariably leads to a happy marriage or to tragedy.

The second part of the *Frauendienst* has frequently been criticized as lacking in dramatic tension, but then a truly harmonious relationship is characterized by the absence of tension. To tell about the relationship in detail would indicate both the beginning of doubt and dissatisfaction and a lack of respect for the privacy of the relationship and would only satisfy voyeuristic instincts. Instead, he transposes the satisfaction of such instincts to the more anonymous level of the love poems that are interspersed in the narrative text and that become increasingly erotic in the second part. Only by balancing the first part and the highly sensuous lyric poetry of the second part can the work deliver its most important message without being received as unbearably preachy. A large portion of the second part is devoted to detailed didactic explanations of what constitutes virtuous men and good women, leading into transcendental speculations about how a life spent in the service of ladies may ultimately be as beneficial and important in the eyes of God as one devoted to spiritual service.

Although the love songs are an integral part of the *Frauendienst,* they have been dealt with separately from early times. That most of the songs appear in the well-known anthology of poetry, the Manesse, or Große Heidelberger, Liederhandschrift (Large Heidelberg Codex, circa 1300), means that Ulrich must have been considered a great lyrical poet by his contemporaries.

The formal patterns and motifs of earlier songs in the cycle constitute a retrospective of the "classical" type of *Minnesang,* following the models of Reinmar der Alte, Hartmann, Heinrich von Morungen, Walther, and Wolfram. Then the patterns and motifs switch over to the modern model of Gottfried von Neifen, and there are several innovative patterns and styles that Ulrich points out as his own inventions. But even where he deliberately alludes to his traditional models through the use of familiar motifs and stanzaic forms, a strong creative tendency can be observed. Ulrich characterizes the majority of the songs as *tanzwisen* (dance tunes), a form that was probably the most popular one for courtly entertainment: rhythmically supporting the dances with full instrumental accompaniment, they were the perfect alternative to the more monotonous recitation of epic stanzas. As an occasional variation to that alternation Ulrich also uses two *sincwisen* (song tunes) with little musical accompaniment and two *uzreisen* (marching tunes) that were probably accompanied by drums and wind instruments. The *leich* (lay) serves as a lyrical centerpiece. Its lengthy and complicated poetic and musical patterns underscore the turning point of the narration from outbursts of anger about the terrible behavior of the first lady to the expression of hope for a new and satisfying relationship. An extremely skillful master can be seen at work in each genre and each individual poem.

Many scholars have been inclined to see in Ulrich's *Minnesang* cycle the work of a great lyrical poet, around which he later decided to build the *Frauendienst.* Against that theory one can point out that the fifty-eight songs are so intricately interwoven into the epic narration that it is hard to imagine that most of them were not composed at the same time as the rest of the work. That the sequence of the songs has not been altered by the collector of the Manesse anthology also suggests that they were taken directly from the *Frauendienst* and not from a separate source.

The songs are not distributed evenly throughout the epic narrative; strong lyrical outbursts alternate with long stretches from which lyric poetry is absent. For example, the accounts of the two major jousting trips, the *Venusfahrt* and the *Artusfahrt,* contain hardly any lyrical verse. Ulrich must have wanted to suggest that during such periods of intense chivalric activity his hero would not have had the leisure to compose highly sophisticated music and poetry. The song cycle can be divided into three major parts: service to the capricious lady (songs 1 to 19), a period without service (songs 20 to 31), and service to the "good" lady (songs 32 to 58). The first part spans almost three-fourths of the narration (1,362 epic stanzas), the second consists mostly of songs (27 epic stanzas), and the third takes up almost the last fourth of the work (488 epic stanzas). The three parts of the cycle can be further subdivided: songs 1 to 13 express intense desire and pleas for fulfillment; songs 14 to 19 tell of extreme frustration; songs 20 to 25 are songs of anger; songs 26 to 31 speak of new hope and expectation; songs 32 to 44 sing of bliss and sexual fulfillment; songs 45 to 50 deal with support in times of crisis, and songs 51 to 58 praise good men and women or love as paradise on earth.

It is difficult to assess fully the many formal innovations Ulrich made; they are closely tied to their musical elements, about which not enough information has been preserved. As far as the poetic motifs are concerned, however, one innovation stands out above all others: Ulrich's contribution to the genre of the *tagewise* (dawn song) in songs 36 and 40. Usually called *tagelied* (or *alba* in Provençal poetry), the genre had been popularized especially by Wolfram. It tells of a couple whose lovemaking is interrupted by the first rays of the sun and by a watchman who warns them of the approaching day and the danger of their discovery. It usually peaks in a tableau of painful leave-taking and the male lover's promises to return. Ulrich applies to the genre the same principle of verisimilitude that underlies his entire work: he suggests that if the couple was really surprised by daybreak and if it was dangerous for the lover to leave his lady's bedroom, she could simply hide him there during the day, and they could spend another night of lovemaking. Moreover, in the introductory epic stanzas to the second *tagelied* Ulrich claims that the idea of having a watchman enter a lady's bedroom is not plausible, because watchmen were normally of peasant origin and no proper lady would admit such an uncouth fellow to her private chamber. Therefore Ulrich has the lady's closest maid fulfill that role.

Ulrich and his female audiences must have felt that the message of his radically altered courtly romance was still not strong and clear enough. That feeling evidently led to the composition of another radically new form, at least for the German-speaking areas: the *Frauenbuch,* a dispute between an anonymous courtier and a lady on matters of social and sexual relations. The form is close to that of a dramatic dialogue, with a prologue, epilogue, and introductory and linking passages narrated by Ulrich under his own name. The setting is even more direct, contemporary, and realistic than that of the *Frauendienst.* Not even a hint of fictional distancing can be perceived in the *Frauenbuch,* which expresses an even deeper sense of frustration about the loss of coherence and high-spirited enterprise among the courtly society of Ulrich's time. Again, Ulrich uses his own name to heighten the level of verisimilitude, functioning as the referee in this battle between the sexes.

The lady begins the debate by observing that courtly society is in a crisis; the knights seem to have lost all their love for life and just hang around the court like morons. She encourages her opponent to be completely open and frank with her and to give her all the reasons he can think of that might have led to this low point in the relationship between men and women. In return she will tell him bluntly what she thinks is wrong with the men of Austria and Styria. The courtier replies that women sit around like their own portraits, giving the men no smiles, no greetings, no encouragement. Even worse, they dress like nuns, scaring off the men with the crucifixes dangling from their necks. Instead of going dancing, they spend day and night in church. They no longer take care of themselves, and they look like hags.

The lady counters that men no longer show women any sign that they find the women attractive, through neither gestures, words, nor knightly activities. Anything the women do – smile, kiss, choose nice clothes, wear makeup – is immediately interpreted by the gossiping males as an attempt to entice strangers. At least the women go to church; the men neither have fun nor care for their souls (lines 597–606). Sexually active women seem to bother men: they evade the women's kisses and caresses instead of responding in kind. What else should women do but abandon sex altogether? Some men leave the house in the morning and spend the entire day hunting with their dogs; they seem to love their dogs more than their women. Instead of at least blowing kisses toward their ladies, they blow their hunting horns all day. Only nightfall drives them home, where they plop down at a table and play games and drink until all their potency is drained away. Only after midnight do they finally make it to the bedroom, where their women have been waiting for them in loving expectation. Without muttering a word they drop onto the bed and fall asleep until morning, when the routine starts all over again. What can a woman do under such circumstances but turn pious (lines 606–609)? And, she continues, there is the other type: men who spend their entire day and night drinking with their friends. In their alcoholic stupor they brag about their great feats of prowess in jousting and their adventures with women – all of it nothing but hot air (lines 609–611).

The man responds that today's women are all for sale: it is gifts, gifts, gifts – the bigger the better – in return for sexual favors, where once all that would have been required were small tokens of love. Besides, many ladies have sex slaves who are members of the lower classes and who are always at their disposal (lines 612–613). The lady retaliates that while there are a few sluts – and she would not mind if someone killed them – most women are not for sale. But what about all those men, nowadays, who do with each other something not even animals would do (lines 614–615)?

He agrees with her, launching into a long tirade against homosexuals. During the final rounds they try to explain to each other what constitutes real good men and women. The courtier finally agrees that any woman – wife or concubine – has the right to leave her man if he cannot give her sexual satisfaction. Each claims to the end that there are many good members of his or her sex who are not like the terrible examples to which the other has been referring.

When the character Ulrich is called in to judge the outcome of the bout, he renders a clear decision in favor of the lady. It is conceivable that Ulrich's works were composed primarily for a female courtly audience in Austria, women who were suffering from boredom and the lack of a civilized erotic atmosphere.

The male misogynist reaction came soon, and its intensity increased with the growing degree of literacy in male urban society during the fourteenth century. Sexual literature for insecure males deteriorated into the sort of crude attack on female sex objects that is manifested in the enormously popular continuation of the *Romance of the Rose* (circa 1275) by Jean Chopinel de Meun. In such an atmosphere the messages of Ulrich fell on deaf ears. Furthermore, the rich city burghers had little sympathy for the woes of courtly society. For those reasons, and because his main work, the *Frauendienst,* is complex and difficult, Ulrich found no widespread reception among his immediate posterity.

References:

Hans Arens, *Ulrichs von Lichtenstein "Frauendienst": Untersuchungen über den höfischen Sprachstil,* Pa-laestra, volume 216 (Leipzig: Akademische Verlagsgesellschaft, 1939);

Anton Becker, "Der Weg der Venusfahrt Ulrichs von Liechtenstein in Niederösterreich," *Monatsblatt des Vereins für Landeskunde von Niederösterreich,* 24 (1925): 34–43;

Reinhold Becker, *Wahrheit und Dichtung in Ulrich von Liechtensteins Frauendienst* (Halle: Niemeyer, 1888);

Hans-Joachim Behr, "Frauendienst als Ordnungsprinzip: Zum Verständnis von Wirklichkeit und derer Bewältigung im 'Frauenbuch' Ulrichs von Liechtenstein," in *Die mittelalterliche Literatur in der Steiermark,* edited by Alfred Ebenbauer, Fritz Peter Knapp, and Anoton Schwob (Bern: Lang, 1988), pp. 1–13;

Elke Brüggen, "Minnelehre und Gesellschaftskritik im 13. Jahrhundert: Zum 'Frauenbuch' Ulrichs von Liechtenstein," *Euphorion,* 83, no. 1 (1989): 72–97;

Marie-Luise Dittrich, "Die Ideologie des 'guoten wîbes' in Ulrichs von Lichtenstein 'Vrowen dienst,'" in *Festschrift für William Foerste,* edited by Friedrich Hofmann and Willy Sanders, Niederdeutsche Studien, volume 18 (Cologne & Vienna: Böhlav, 1970), pp. 502–530;

Heinz Dopsch, "Der Dichter Ulrich von Liechtenstein und die Herkunft seiner Familie," in *Festschrift für Friedrich Hausmann,* edited by Herwig Ebner (Graz: Akademische Druck- und Verlagsanstalt, 1977), pp. 93–118;

Carolyn Dussère, "Humor and Chivalry in Ulrich von Lichtenstein's 'Frauendienst' and Gerhard Hauptmann's 'Ulrich von Lichtenstein,'" *Colloquia Germanica,* 16, no. 4 (1983): 297–320;

Urs Herzog, "Minneideal und Wirklichkeit: Zum 'Frauendienst' Ulrichs von Liechtenstein," *Deutsche Vierteljahrsschrift,* 49 (July 1975): 502–519;

Otto Höfler, "Ulrichs von Liechtenstein Venusfahrt und Artusfahrt," in *Studien zur deutschen Philologie,* edited by Richard Kienast (Heidelberg: Winter, 1950), pp. 131–152;

Wernfried Hofmeister, "Minne und Ehe im 'Frauenbuch' Ulrichs von Liechtenstein," in *Die mittelalterliche Literatur in der Steiermark,* pp. 131–142;

Dieter Kartschoke, "Ulrich von Liechtenstein und die Laienkultur des deutschen Südostens im Übergang zur Schriftlichkeit," in *Die mittelalterliche Literatur in Kärnten,* edited by Peter Krämer (Vienna: Halosar, 1981), pp. 103–143;

Fritz Peter Knapp, *"Chevalier errant" und "fin amor": Das Ritterideal des 13. Jh. in Nordfrankreich und im deutschsprachigen Südosten. Studien zum "Lancelot en prose," zum "Moritz von Craûn," zur "Krone" Heinrichs von dem Türlin, zu Werken des Strickers und zum "Frauendienst" Ulrichs von Liechtenstein*, Schriften der Universität Passau, Reihe Geisteswissenschaften, volume 8 (Passau: Passau Universitätsverlag, 1986);

Karl Knorr, *Über Ulrich von Lichtenstein: Historische und litterarische Untersuchungen*, Quellen und Forschungen zur Sprach- und Literaturgeschichte der germanischen Völker, volume 9 (Strasbourg: Trübner, 1875);

Jürgen Kühnel, "Zu den Tageliedern Ulrichs von Liechtenstein," *Jahrbuch der Oswald von Wolkenstein Gesellschaft*, 1 (1980-1981): 99-138;

Maja Loehr, "Die Grabplatte auf der steirischen Frauenburg und die Ruhestätte Ulrichs von Liechtenstein," *Mitteilungen des Instituts für österreichische Geschichtsforschung*, 65 (1957): 53-69;

W. J. McCann, "Wertsystem und Weltbild in Ulrichs von Liechtenstein 'Frauendienst' und 'Frauenbuch,' " in *Geistliche und weltliche Epik des Mittelalters in Österreich*, edited by David McLintock, Adrian Stevens, and Fred Wagner (Göppingen: Kümmerle, 1987), pp. 41-56;

Timothy McFarland, "Ulrich von Lichtenstein and the Autobiographical Form," in *Probleme mittelhochdeutscher Erzählformen*, edited by Peter F. von Ganz and Werner Schröder (Berlin: Schmidt, 1972), pp. 178-196;

Humphrey Milnes, "Ulrich von Lichtenstein and the Minnesang," *German Life and Letters*, 17, no. 1 (1963): 27-43;

Cola Minis, "Ulrich von Lichtenstein," in *Die deutsche Literatur des Mittelalters: Verfasserlexikon*, volume 5, edited by Karl Langosch (Berlin: De Gruyter, 1955), pp. 1098-1099;

Georg Misch, "Das Verhältnis von Lyrik und Autobiographie: Ulrich von Lichtenstein – Guillaume de Machault – Adam de la Halle – Juan Ruiz," in his *Geschichte der Autobiographie*, volume 4: *Das Hochmittelalter in der Vollendung*, edited by Leo Delfoss (Frankfurt am Main: Schulte-Bulmke, 1967), pp. 492-537;

Jan Dirk Müller, "Lachen – Spiel – Fiktion: Zum Verhältnis von literarischem Diskurs und historischer Realität im 'Frauendienst' Ulrichs von Lichtenstein," *Deutsche Vierteljahrsschrift*, 58 (March 1984): 38-73;

Müller, "Ulrich von Liechtenstein," in *Deutsche Dichter*, volume 1: *Leben und Werk deutschsprachiger Autoren*, edited by Gunter E. Grimm and Frank Rainer Max (Stuttgart: Reclam, 1989), pp. 329-335;

Friedrich Neumann, "Ulrich von Lichtensteins Frauendienst: Eine Untersuchung über das Verhältnis von Dichtung und Leben," *Zeitschrift für Deutschkunde*, 40 (1926): 373-386;

Max Ortner, "Ulrich von Liechtenstein und Steinmark," *Germania*, 32 (1887): 120-125;

Ursula Peters, *Frauendienst: Untersuchungen zu Ulrich von Lichtenstein und zum Wirklichkeitsgehalt der Minnedichtung*, Göppinger Arbeiten zur Germanistik, volume 46 (Göppingen: Kümmerle, 1971);

Michael Pieper, *Die Funktionen der Kommentierung im "Frauendienst" Ulrichs von Liechtenstein*, Göppinger Arbeiten zur Germanistik, volume 351 (Göppingen: Kümmerle, 1982);

Hermann Reichert, "Exzentrität als Zentralgedanke: Ulrich von Liechtenstein und seine Artusfahrt von 1240," *Österreich in Geschichte und Literatur*, 27, no. 1 (1983): 25-41;

Reichert, "Vorbilder für Ulrich von Lichtenstein Friesacher Turnier," in *Die mittelalterliche Literatur in Kärnten*, pp. 189-216;

Ingo Reiffenstein, "Rollenspiel und Rollenentlarvung im Frauendienst Ulrichs von Liechtenstein," in *Festschrift für Adalbert Schmidt*, edited by Gerlinde Weiss, Stuttgarter Arbeiten zur Germanistik, volume 4 (Stuttgart: Akademischer Verlag H. D. Heinz, 1976), pp. 107-120;

Helga Reuschel, "Ulrich von Lichtenstein," in *Die deutsche Literatur des Mittelalters: Verfasserlexikon*, volume 4, edited by Langosch (Berlin: De Gruyter, 1953), pp. 583-587;

Elisabeth Schmid, "Verstellung und Entstellung im 'Frauendienst' Ulrichs von Liechtenstein," in *Die mittelalterliche Literatur in der Steiermark*, pp. 181-198;

Klaus M. Schmidt, *Begriffsglossare und Indices zu Ulrich von Lichtenstein*, 2 volumes (Munich: Kraus International Publications, 1980);

Schmidt, "Der Kampf im Schlafzimmer – Erwartungen und Realität in sexuellen Beziehungen: Ulrich von Liechtenstein," in *Sprachspiel und Lachkultur: Beiträge zur Literatur- und Sprachgeschichte*, edited by Angela Bader, Irene Erfen, Ulrich Müller, and Alois Eder (Stuttgart: Heinz, 1993), pp. 1-23;

Schmidt, "Späthöfische Gesellschaftsstruktur und die Ideologie des Frauendienstes bei Ulrich von Liechtenstein," *Zeitschrift für deutsche Philologie*, 94, no. 1 (1975): 37-59;

Schmidt, "Tendenzen zum Realismus in der ritterlichen Epik der nachklassischen Periode: Untersuchungen zu Ulrichs von Lichtenstein 'Frauendienst,' " Ph.D. dissertation, University of Michigan, 1972;

Karl Ludwig Schneider, "Die Selbstdarstellung des Dichters im Frauendienst Ulrichs von Liechtenstein: Bedeutung und Grenzen des Autobiographischen in der älteren deutschen Dichtung," in *Festgabe für Ulrich Pretzel,* edited by Wolfgang Bachofer, Wolfgang Dittmann, and Werner von Simon (Berlin: Schmidt, 1963), pp. 216–222;

Anton Schönbach, "Zum Frauendienst Ulrichs von Liechtenstein," *Zeitschrift für deutsche Philologie,* 28 (1896): 198–226;

Franz Viktor Spechtler, "Probleme um Ulrich von Liechtenstein: Bemerkungen zu historischen Grundlagen, Untersuchungsaspekten und Deutungsversuchen," in *Österreichische Literatur zur Zeit der Babenberger,* Wiener Arbeiten zur germanischen Altertumskunde und Philologie, volume 10, edited by Alfred Ebenbauer, Fritz Peter Knapp, and Ingrid Strasser (Vienna: Halosar, 1976), pp. 218–232;

Spechtler, "Ulrich von Liechtenstein bei Gerhart Hauptmann und Hugo von Hofmannsthal," in *Mittelalter-Rezeption,* edited by Jürgen Kühnel, Hans-Dieter Mück, and Ulrich Müller, Göppinger Arbeiten zu Germanistik, volume 286 (Göppingen: Kümmerle, 1979), pp. 347–364;

Spechtler, "Ulrich von Liechtenstein: Literarische Themen und Formen um die Mitte des 13. Jahrhunderts in der Steiermark," in *Die mittelalterliche Literatur in der Steiermark,* pp. 189–217;

J. Wesley Thomas, "The Minnesong Structure of Ulrich von Liechtenstein's 'Frauendienst,' " *Zeitschrift für deutsches Altertum,* 102, no. 3 (1973): 195–203;

Thomas, " 'Parzival' as a Source for 'Frauendienst,' " *Modern Language Notes,* 87 (April 1972): 419–432;

David F. Tinsley, "Die Kunst der Selbstdarstellung in Ulrichs von Lichtenstein 'Frauendienst,' " *Germanisch Romanische Monatsschrift,* 40, no. 2 (1990): 129–140;

Anthonius H. Touber, "Der literarische Charakter von Ulrich von Lichtensteins 'Frauendienst,' " *Neophilologus,* 51 (July 1967): 253–262;

Touber, "Ulrichs von Lichtenstein 'Frauendienst' und die Vidas und Razos der Troubadours," *Zeitschrift für deutsche Philologie,* 107, no. 3 (1988): 431–444;

Touber, "Ulrichs von Lichtenstein unbekannte Melodie," *Amsterdamer Beiträge zur älteren Germanistik,* 26 (1987): 107–118;

Mary F. Wack, *Lovesickness in the Middle Ages: The "Viaticum" and Its Commentaries* (Philadelphia: University of Pennsylvania Press, 1990), pp. 163–165;

Alois Wolf, "Komik und Parodie als Möglichkeiten dichterischer Selbstdarstellung im Mittelalter: Zu Ulrich von Liechtensteins 'Frauendienst,' " *Amsterdamer Beiträge zur älteren Germanistik,* 10 (1976): 73–101;

Manfred Zips, "Frauendienst als ritterliche Weltbewältigung: Zu Ulrich von Liechtenstein," in *Festschrift Otto Höfler zum 75. Geburtstag,* edited by Helmut Birkhan (Vienna: Braunmüller, 1976), pp. 742–789;

Zips, "Ulrich von Lichtenstein 'Das Frauenbuch': Herausgegeben von Manfred Zips," in *Wiener Neudrucke Ankündigungsband,* edited by Herbert Zeman (Vienna: Bundesverlag, 1970), pp. 20–27;

Walter Zitzenbacher, "Einleitung," in *Ulrich von Liechtenstein: Narr in hohem Dienst,* edited by Karl Lachmann (Graz & Vienna: Stiasny, 1958), pp. 5–31.

Ulrich von Zatzikhoven

(before 1194 – after 1214)

Kathleen J. Meyer
Bemidji State University

MAJOR WORK: *Lanzelet* (circa 1194–1203)

Manuscripts: This work has survived in two complete manuscripts with minor gaps and in three fragments. The oldest complete version, from the early fourteenth century, is found in Vienna (#2698). A later manuscript, dated 1420, is in the codex palatinus in Heidelberg (cpg 371). Two fragments from a fourteenth-century manuscript are preserved, one at Harvard (Houghton Library, MS Ger. 80) and one in Klagenfurt (G-Klagenfurt; perg. hs. 47). A third fragment, the earliest to be preserved, is from an early-thirteenth-century manuscript and is at Oxford (Bodleian Library, MS. Germ. b3, ff. 9–10). A fragment from the late thirteenth or fourteenth century at Strasbourg was destroyed, but copies exist.

First publication: *Lanzelet de Lac: Aus dem dreizehnten Jahrhundert,* volume 1 of *Altdeutsche Gedichte aus den Zeiten der Tafelrunde: Aus Handschriften,* edited by Felix Franz Hofstaeter (Vienna: Schaumburg, 1811).

Standard edition: *Lanzelet: Eine Erzählung,* edited by K. A. Hahn (Frankfurt am Main: Brönner, 1845; reprinted, with afterword and bibliography by Frederick Norman, Berlin: De Gruyter, 1965).

Edition in modern German: *Altdeutsche Gedichte aus den Zeiten der Tafelrunde: Aus handschriften der k.k. Hofbibliothek in die heutige Sprache ubertragen,* translated by Felix Franz Hofstaeter (Vienna: C. Schaumburg, 1811).

Edition in English: Translated by Kenneth G. T. Webster, revised and edited by Roger Sherman Loomis, as *Lanzelet: A Romance of Lancelot* (New York: Columbia University Press, 1951).

Ulrich von Zatzikhoven occupies an uncertain place in medieval German literature of the late twelfth and early thirteenth centuries. Overshadowed by the works of such monumental figures as Hartmann von Aue, Gottfried von Straßburg, and Wolfram von

Portrait of Ulrich von Zatzikhoven in a circa 1420 manuscript of his Lanzelet *(Heidelberg, Universitätsbibliothek, cpg 371)*

Eschenbach, Ulrich's *Lanzelet* (circa 1194–1203) has variously been characterized by early critics as insignificant, mediocre, shallow, morally degenerate, a compilation, a good story, a relic, an imitation, and a latecomer. Though later critics have softened and in some cases reversed these assessments, Ulrich can be granted only secondary importance. His only known work is *Lanzelet,* and the extent to which it is his own work is an unresolved question. The author says that it is a translation of a "welschez buoch" (*welsch* in Middle High German generally means French, in this case probably Anglo-Norman), "so enist dâ von noch zuo geleit" (and nothing has been added or subtracted). Whether that claim is true is unclear, since the original has never been found. Early scholars found the significance of this work largely in its preservation of a Lancelot tradition quite different from that of Chrétien de Troyes's *Chevalier de la charrete* and the prose works derived from it and in its richness of Celtic motifs that figure in the development of the Arthurian romance. Structurally it does not conform to the bipartite model of Arthurian romance found in the works of Chrétien, Hartmann, and Wolfram; in this model the hero first achieves honor through a series of adventures but loses it because of some flaw, and in a final series of more purposeful adventures he regains and surpasses his original honor. This difference has led to many of the negative appraisals by literary scholars who have measured *Lanzelet* against the works of these other authors or have tried to force it into the bipartite structure. More recently scholars have attempted to deal with the structure of *Lanzelet* on its own terms: James A. Schultz sees Ulrich's accomplishment in his development of a static, symmetrical structure that reflects the static perfection of the hero and the theme of political stability; Barbara Thoran defines the structure as two parallel, intertwining actions dominated by the motif of loss and recovery. Nevertheless, Ulrich does not exhibit the literary ability or the thematic complexity of Hartmann or Wolfram. Furthermore, the focus is not on the ethical development of the protagonist, as it is in Hartmann's and Wolfram's works; hence, the hero's moral stance is seen to be defective, particularly in regard to his relationships with women. It is perhaps here, most of all, that the author fails to integrate or motivate the actions of the hero, so that they seem capricious and impulsive.

Little is known of Ulrich or the production of *Lanzelet* outside of what Ulrich himself says in the work. He received the manuscript of the book from "Hûc von Morville," who had been a hostage to Duke Leopold of Austria and later to Emperor Henry VI in exchange for King Richard the Lion-Hearted of England. At the urging of friends, Ulrich says, he undertook the translation of the manuscript into German. The exchange of hostages took place in 1194, thus dating the composition of the German *Lanzelet* sometime after that year. The only historical record of Ulrich's existence is found in a 1214 document given to the monastery of Saint Peterszell by Count Diethelm von Toggenburg, where Ulrich is mentioned as a parish priest of Lommis in the Swiss canton of Thurgau ("capellanus Uolricus de Cecinhoven plebanus Loumeissae"). Hûc von Morville is probably Hugh of Morville, known to have been a forester in Burgh on Sands in Cumberland and possibly the Hugh of Morville who took part in the murder of Saint Thomas Becket in Canterbury in 1170. The likelihood of this identification is increased by the fact that the Cumberland forester had both a mother and a daughter named Ada, a name that is borne by Lanzelet's second "wife" and that has been characterized by Roger Sherman Loomis as "un-Arthurian."

The dates of composition of *Lanzelet* and its debt to other literary works of the time have been subjects of much debate. Most critics feel that Ulrich knew Hartmann's *Erec* (circa 1180), but not his *Iwein* (circa 1203), and at least the first six books of Wolfram's *Parzival* (circa 1200–1210). It is also possible that Wolfram was acquainted with *Lanzelet,* because certain names that appear in the later portions of *Parzival* are found in *Lanzelet.* This would mean that the latest possible date of composition for the latter would be around 1204. Scholars have also noted similarities in the discussion of *minne* (love) to Heinrich von Veldeke's *Eneit* (circa 1185) and Eilhart von Oberge's *Tristrant und Isalde* (circa 1170) and feel that Ulrich must have been acquainted with those works.

The number of manuscripts of and contemporary allusions to *Lanzelet* would indicate that the work enjoyed a modest popularity among medieval audiences. Rudolf von Ems mentions Ulrich briefly in his *Willehalm von Orlens* (circa 1235–1243) and somewhat more extensively and positively in his *Alexander* (circa 1230–circa 1254). In 1462 Jacob Püterich von Reicherzhausen in his "Ehrenbrief" mentions five Lancelot manuscripts, of which one is by Ulrich:

Sam hat auch Lantzilot, von Säzenhouen
Ausz welisch ulrich gedichtet
Das mag man leszen schon in allen hofen.

(Likewise there is also Lanzelet,
composed from the French by Ulrich von Zatzikhoven,
which one can read at every court.)

Lancelot figures in other Arthurian romances as the lover of Arthur's wife, Queen Guinevere. Here, however, Lanzelet has no illicit liaison with the queen and is merely a minor player in her rescue from her abductor, Valerîn. Lanzelet is, nevertheless, remarkable for his effect on women and acquires no fewer than four wives. The work is a mixture of realistic courtly, political, and social elements mingled liberally with the fantastic world of fairies and magicians. Early literary critics concerned themselves by and large with investigations of the sources, both literary and legendary, of the various episodes in *Lanzelet*. Werner Richter's book-length study (1934) traces motifs and episodes to their Irish roots and studies the influences of Hartmann, Heinrich, Eilhart, Wolfram, and the *Minnesang* while holding that there is little literary merit in the work. Loomis brings out the Celtic origins of the story in his introduction and footnotes to the English translation by Kenneth G. T. Webster (1951).

Beginning in the late 1960s, the efforts of literary scholars to "rehabilitate" Ulrich focused primarily on the structure of the work – especially on that of the first half, where the author structured the episodes in a series of increasingly more courtly encounters for Lanzelet. This pattern of progression can also be found in the second half, though not to the same degree. At the same time, efforts were made to discover the underlying moral dimension of the work.

Lanzelet's father, Pant, is the tyrannical monarch of Genewîs whose rule is tempered only by the generosity and kindness of his wife, Clarîne. In an uprising of nobles, Pant is killed, and Clarîne is taken prisoner. The one-year-old Lanzelet, who remains unnamed for the first half of the romance, is spirited away by a *merfeine* (sea fairy) to be raised in the crystal castle in her island realm, which is also inhabited by ten thousand ladies who have never known a man. Mermen are brought in to teach the young Lanzelet sporting games, hunting, and the use of sword and buckler, but he is kept innocent of horsemanship and armor.

At the age of fifteen, desiring to learn the ways of knights, Lanzelet asks the sea fairy for permission to journey forth from the island; he also inquires as to his real name. She tells him that he will find out his name only when he has avenged her by killing Iweret, who, it is revealed later in the story, had taken land from her own son, Mâbûz. Then she equips Lanzelet as befits a courtly knight and has him transported across the sea. Because he has never had instruction in horsemanship, he rides wildly and without reining the horse. His first encounter is with the dwarf of Plûrîs, who lashes him with a whip. Not knowing how to react and being unable to control his horse, he suffers the insult; but he notes the name of the castle and plans to take his revenge later. After a brief encounter with the young Jôhfrît, who instructs him in the art of riding and whose mother affords him the chance to prove himself in a tournament, Lanzelet sets forth on his adventures.

The similarity to Parzival's upbringing has been pointed out by many scholars. It is, however, only superficial. Though Lanzelet is raised by women, he is thoroughly instructed in courtly ways – the sea fairy has every reason to want Lanzelet to learn the ways of knighthood so that he can avenge her – whereas Parzival is kept ignorant of such behavior and, as a consequence, blunders badly. Furthermore, the *Dümmling* (innocent youth) motif – Lanzelet's lack of riding ability and failure to understand certain customs – is only sparsely developed. Jôhfrît's instruc-

tions to Lanzelet on riding are so abbreviated that he can hardly be comparable to Gurnemanz, Parzival's tutor. In fact, as Schultz has pointed out, Lanzelet is for all practical purposes the best knight there is at the time he departs from Jôhfrît.

The major episodes of the first half are Lanzelet's fights with Galagandreiz and Lînier and his participation in the tournament at Djoflê. Lanzelet kills Galagandreiz after being discovered in bed with the latter's love-hungry daughter, who first tried unsuccessfully to seduce Lanzelet's two companions. Lanzelet thus falls heir to the land and the daughter. Lanzelet soon grows restless, leaves her, and comes upon Lînier's castle. There he fails to comply with the custom of approaching the castle with an olive branch as a sign of peace, thus provoking an attack by Lînier's knights. Lanzelet acquits himself well in an exceedingly lopsided fight with the knights and is given safe passage by Lînier's niece, Ade. Lînier, who was away, returns to find many of his best men killed and angrily imprisons Lanzelet. Ade persuades him to let Lanzelet stand the test of fighting, successively, a giant, two ferocious lions, and, if he survives, Lînier himself. Lanzelet kills Lînier, again winning both land and lady. Accompanied by Ade and her brother, Lanzelet journeys to Djoflê. There he participates in a tournament, appearing anonymously on three successive days in three different colors and defeating all comers. By now Lanzelet's renown has reached Arthur's court, and Arthur sends the knight Wâlwein (Gawein) to invite him to join the Round Table. But Lanzelet steadfastly refuses to be diverted from his main goals: the discovery of his identity and the recovery of the honor he lost in the encounter with the dwarf from Plûrîs.

On his way to Plûrîs, Lanzelet comes to the castle of Mâbûz der bloede (Mâbûz the timid), the son of the sea fairy, who was destined to be cowardly. Because of this fate, the sea fairy had fashioned a magical castle for him, Schatel le Mort, in which the cowardly become brave and the brave cowardly. Lanzelet, the bravest of knights, becomes the most abject coward when he crosses the drawbridge, and he is taken prisoner by Mâbûz. Ade leaves Lanzelet and disappears from the story. As it turns out, Iweret is the ruler of the nearby kingdom of Dôdône and is the archenemy of Mâbûz, frequently laying waste to the latter's lands. Since Mâbûz becomes cowardly when he leaves the castle, he convinces Lanzelet to fight Iweret for him and releases the knight from custody for this purpose.

The abbot of a nearby monastery over which Iweret is lord tells Lanzelet of Iweret's adventure.

Iweret has offered his beautiful daughter Iblis to any knight who can defeat him at the spring. By striking three times a cymbal which is hanging there, a knight can summon Iweret to battle. The many knights who have died there are buried at the monastery, which has become rich with the booty of Iweret's victories.

Lanzelet proceeds to the spring and strikes the cymbal. Iblis, who had seen Lanzelet in a dream and fallen in love with him, has vowed to marry no man but this knight and thus rushes to the spring whenever the cymbal is struck. Finding this time the very knight she had seen in her dream, she tries to persuade him to run away with her and give up the adventure lest he be killed. He refuses and kills Iweret in the subsequent fight. Fearing the reaction of her father's men, Iblis leaves with Lanzelet but sends a message to her liegemen that she is leaving her lands in their hands to hold faithfully until she finds the right time to return. At nearly the mathematical center of the work a messenger from the sea fairy announces Lanzelet's identity and his relationship with Arthur: Lanzelet's mother was Arthur's sister. In addition, the sea fairy has sent the gift of a magical tent with a mirror which shows the reflection of the person most loyal to the one looking into the mirror. When Iblis and Lanzelet enter the tent and look into the mirror, each sees only the reflection of the other.

Now that Lanzelet knows his identity, he is eager to accept the invitation to Arthur's court. Before he can find Wâlwein, he learns that Valerîn has claimed Queen Ginover by right of a previous engagement. Wâlwein is preparing to fight Valerîn, but Lanzelet takes Wâlwein's place, wins the battle, and spares Valerîn's life. At long last Lanzelet can take a seat at the Round Table.

Lanzelet then goes to Plûrîs to avenge the insult he had received at the beginning of the romance. The castle is ruled by a queen who will take as her husband the man who can defeat in one day all of the one hundred knights whose shields adorn her tent. Lanzelet beats them all, and

dô muose aber bruiten
der wîpsaelige Lanzelet.
ich enweiz, ob erz ungerne tet,
wan diu künegin was ein schoene maget.
si müeste wol sîn behaget
eim man der halbtôt waere.

(Then Lanzelet, lucky with women,
had to consummate another marriage.
I do not know if he did it unwillingly,
for the queen was a beautiful maiden.

She would certainly have been pleasing
even to a man who was half dead.)

The queen takes away his weapons and puts a guard on him so that he cannot run away. Iblis, in the meantime, is proving her worth in the *Mantelprobe* (cloak test) episode: she is the only woman at Arthur's court whom the cloak, a gift from the sea fairy, fits exactly, thus demonstrating her virtue.

The rescue of Lanzelet from Plûrîs is undertaken by four of Arthur's knights, Karjet, Erec, Tristan, and Wâlwein, who outjoust sixty-five, seventy-three, eighty-nine, and ninety-nine of the one hundred knights, respectively. Since Wâlwein lost only to the one hundredth man on a technicality (Wâlwein's spear knocked off the knight's helmet but did not unhorse him), Lanzelet begs the queen for weapons to avenge the honor of her knights. Arthur's four knights flee in mock terror as Lanzelet attacks, and he effects his escape by pretending to chase them.

The Plûrîs episode has troubled literary scholars, who can dismiss Lanzelet's first two liaisons as merely prefatory to his true love but have difficulty explaining his marriage to the queen of Plûrîs after he has won Iblis. Some scholars have contended that because he is sorrowful and does not forget Iblis, he has exhibited a kind of male fidelity. Others see the Plûrîs episode as a parallel to the capture of Queen Ginover, whose rescue, like Lanzelet's, is carried out by the cooperative actions of the best knights of the Round Table. Schultz sees this episode as corresponding to that of Ade and Lînier: both involve Lanzelet's captivity, his accomplishment of an adventure, and the aggressive actions of a woman; thus both function to show the reaction Lanzelet provokes in women.

On their return to the court of Arthur, the knights learn that Ginover has been kidnapped by Valerîn. Because Valerîn lives in an enchanted castle, the only possibility of rescue is to enlist the aid of Malduc, the magician. Malduc, however, agrees to help only if Erec and Wâlwein, who had slain his father and brother, are turned over to him. Malduc casts a spell on Valerîn's castle, causing the dragons to fall asleep, and the knights kill Valerîn and rescue Ginover. Kurt Ruh regards the minor role Lanzelet plays in this episode as a sign of growth on Lanzelet's part: here Lanzelet works in cooperation with other knights to restore order to society, a less self-centered act than his earlier adventures. Lanzelet then leads an expedition to rescue Wâlwein and Erec in which the band of one hundred knights, with the help of the giant Esêalt, kills Malduc.

Lanzelet's final adventure occurs following the celebration of Ginover's return. Hearing of a dragon in the forest who implores passing knights to kiss it, he sets forth and kisses the beast, and it turns back into a beautiful lady; she had been under a spell because of an indiscretion in love. Lanzelet brings her to Arthur's court, where she becomes a judge in matters of love etiquette.

In the final section, which extends for more than fourteen hundred lines – nearly 15 percent of the total work – Lanzelet is eagerly accepted as king by the nobles of Dôdône and Genewîs because his renown is so great. W. H. Jackson suggests that this part of the work reflects twelfth-century conflicts between monarchs and nobles in Germany: the lords of the realm wanted to have a say in the choice of the king, as the nobles in Dôdône and Genewîs do. The work is critical of rulers such as Pant, Galagandreiz, Lînier, and Iweret who fail to protect the established rights and customs of the nobles and whose vassals, as a result, justifiably rebel. But Lanzelet's accession to the throne of his father also makes a strong statement for the hereditary right of kings.

The terms *saelde* (luck, fortune, blessedness, salvation) and its adjective form, *saelic,* appear sixty-five times in *Lanzelet,* in most instances referring to the main character. He is the knight destined to win glory, the one who cannot lose. Though he occasionally suffers, he rarely does so for long and certainly without any inner turmoil. Lanzelet is thus a relatively static hero whose life story consists less of inner growth than of the actualization of already-present potential greatness.

References:

Rosemary N. Combridge, "Lanzelet and the Queens," in *Essays in German and Dutch Literature,* edited by W. D. Robson-Scott (London: Institute of Germanic Studies, University of London, 1973), pp. 42–64;

R. W. Fisher, "Ulrich von Zatzikhoven's *Lanzelet:* In Search of 'Sens,' " *Archiv für das Studium der neueren Sprachen und Literaturen,* 217 (1980): 277–292;

Walter Haug, *"Das Land, von welchem niemand wiederkehrt": Mythos, Fiktion und Wahrheit in Chrétiens "Chevalier de la Charrete," im "Lanzelet" Ulrichs von Zatzikhoven und im "Lancelot"-Prosaroman* (Tübingen: Niemeyer, 1978);

Stefan Hofer, "Der *Lanzelet* des Ulrich von Zatzikhoven und seine französische Quelle," *Zeitschrift für romanische Philologie,* 75 (1959): 1–36;

W. H. Jackson, "Ulrich von Zatzikhoven's *Lanzelet* and the Theme of Resistance to Royal Power," *German Life and Letters,* 28 (April 1975): 285–297;

Teresa Kinnear and Carl Lofmark, eds., *A Word Index to Ulrich von Zatzikhoven's "Lanzelet"* (Lampeter, 1972);

Patrick M. McConeghy, *"Aventiure* and Anti-*Aventiure* in Ulrich von Zatzikhoven's *Lanzelet* and Hartmann von Aue's *Iwein,"* *Germanic Review,* 57 (Spring 1982): 60–69;

René Pérennec, "Artusroman und Familie: 'Daz welsche buoch von Lanzelet,' " *Acta Germanica,* 11 (1979): 1–51;

Werner Richter, *Der 'Lanzelet' des Ulrich von Zazikhoven* (Frankfurt am Main: Diesterweg, 1934);

Kurt Ruh, "Der *Lanzelet* Ulrichs von Zatzikhofen: Modell oder Kompilation?," in *Deutsche Literatur des späten Mittelalters,* edited by Wolfgang Harms and L. Peter Johnson, Hamburger Colloquium 1973 (Berlin: Schmidt, 1975), pp. 47–55;

Klaus M. Schmidt, "Frauenritter oder Artusritter? Über Struktur und Gehalt von Ulrichs von Zatzikhoven *Lanzelet,"* *Zeitschrift für deutsche Philologie,* 98, no. 1 (1979): 1–18;

James A. Schultz, "*Lanzelet:* A Flawless Hero in a Symmetrical World," *Beiträge zur Geschichte der deutschen Literatur* (Tübingen), 102, no. 2 (1980): 160–188;

Helga Schüppert, "Minneszenen und Struktur im *Lanzelet* Ulrichs von Zatzikhoven," in *Würzburger Prosastudien, II; Untersuchungen zur Literatur und Sprache des Mittelalters,* edited by Peter Kesting (Munich: Fink, 1975), pp. 123–138;

Ernst Soudek, "Die Funktion der Namensuche und der Zweikämpfe in Ulrich von Zatzikhovens *Lanzelet,"* *Amsterdamer Beiträge zur älteren Germanistik,* 2 (1972): 173–185;

Barbara Thoran, "Zur Struktur des *Lanzelet* Ulrichs von Zatzikhoven," *Zeitschrift für deutsche Philologie,* 103, no. 1 (1984): 52–77;

Dieter Welz, "Lanzelet im *schoenen walde:* Überlegungen zu Struktur und Sinn des *Lanzelet*-Romans (mit einem Exkurs im Anhang)," *Acta Germanica,* 13 (1980): 47–68.

Walther von der Vogelweide

(circa 1170 – circa 1230)

Hubert Heinen
University of Texas at Austin

MAJOR WORKS: A religious *leich* (lay) and 110 strophic "songs" (clusters of strophes)

Manuscripts: There are four extensive collections of Walther von der Vogelweide's songs on parchment: A (Small Heidelberg Song Codex, Universitätsbibliothek Heidelberg, cpg 357), from the late thirteenth century, includes 151 strophes ascribed to Walther and 38 strophes elsewhere ascribed to him but here to other singers or in an anonymous appendix; B (Weingarten Song Codex, Württembergische Landesbibliothek Stuttgart, HB XIII pg 1), from the early fourteenth century, includes 112 strophes ascribed to Walther and 8 differently ascribed or anonymous strophes ascribed elsewhere to him; C (Manesse or Große Heidelberger Liederhandschrift, Universitätsbibliothek Heidelberg, cpg 848), from the first half of the fourteenth century, includes the *leich* (also transmitted in a variant form in the closely related k [Universitätsbibliothek Heidelberg, cpg 341, first third of the fourteenth century], k^2 [Kálocsa Middle High German Miscellany, Bibliotheca Bodmeriana Genf Cologny, Dod. Bodm. 72], and 1 [Österreichische Nationalbibliothek, Vienna, cvp 2677, first half of the fourteenth century]), 447 strophes ascribed to Walther, and 27 strophes ascribed elsewhere to him but here to other singers; E (Würzburg Codex, 2° Cod. Ms. 731 der Universitätsbibliothek Munich), from the mid fourteenth century, a commonplace book, includes 212 strophes ascribed to Walther and 18 ascribed to Reinmar der Alte that are ascribed elsewhere to Walther (10 with scant plausibility). In addition, there are five considerable fragments on parchment: G (Bayerische Staatsbibliothek, Munich, cgm 5249/74), from the mid fourteenth century, includes 21 anonymous strophes, of which 12 are ascribed elsewhere to Walther; O (Berlin Fragments, Biblioteka Jagiellonska, Krakow), from the end of the thirteenth century, includes 44 anonymous strophes ascribed elsewhere to Walther; U^x/U^{xx} (Wolfenbüttel Fragments, Landeskirchliches Archiv Brunswick, H 1a), from the end of the thirteenth century, includes 42 anonymous strophes, of which 35 are ascribed elsewhere to Walther; w^x/w^{xx} (Walther Fragments [w^x in the Landeskirchliches Archiv Brunswick, H 1a; w^{xx} in the Biblioteka Jagiellonska, Krakow]), from the late thirteenth century, includes 11 anonymous strophes, of which 9 are elsewhere ascribed to Walther; Z (Münster Fragment, Staatsarchiv Münster, Ms. VII, 51), from the mid fourteenth century, includes 26 strophes ascribed to Walther. One paper manuscript, F (Weimar Song Codex, Nationale Forschungs- und Gedenkstätten der klassischen deutschen Literatur Weimar, Q564), from the second half of the fifteenth century, includes 49 contiguous anonymous strophes, 43 of which are ascribed elsewhere to Walther (an additional 5 strophes, 3 of which are ascribed elsewhere to Friedrich von Hausen, may represent Walther's adaptation of Friedrich's song). Strophes can also be found in three parchment codices: s (Hague Song Codex, Koninklijke Bibliotheek, The Hague, Cod. 128 E 2), includes 8 contiguous strophes ascribed to Walther and 6 contiguous and 2 scattered anonymous strophes ascribed elsewhere to him; D/H (Middle High German *Spruchdichtung*/Early Mastersongs, Universitätsbibliothek Heidelberg, cpg 350), from the end of the thirteenth century and the fourteenth century, respectively, include 18 contiguous anonymous strophes ascribed elsewhere to Walther in D and 5 unique anonymous strophes with the words *ich Walther* in the last in H; N (Kremsmünster Codex, Stiftsbibliothek Kremsmünster, Cod. 127), from the early fourteenth century, includes 7 contiguous

Miniature depicting Walther von der Vogelweide in the early-fourteenth-century Große Heidelberger Liederhandschrift (Heidelberg, Universitätsbibliothek, cpg 848, f.124r)

anonymous strophes ascribed elsewhere to Walther. In three other parchment manuscripts or fragments, scattered songs or strophes are ascribed to Walther: m (Möser's Fragments, Staatsbibliothek Preußischer Kulturbesitz, Berlin, mgq 795), from the late fourteenth or early fifteenth century, includes 11 strophes ascribed elsewhere to Reinmar and Hartmann von Aue; q (Universitätsbibliothek Basel, B. XI. 8), from the fourteenth century, includes 1 unique strophe; r (Zentralbibliothek, Zurich, Ms. Z. XI. 302), from the early fourteenth century, includes 1 unique strophe. Scattered anonymous or otherwise ascribed strophes ascribed elsewhere to Walther can be found in eleven codices, most

notably M (Codex Buranus, Bayerische Staatsbibliothek, Munich, clm 4660), from the early to mid thirteenth century, includes 3 anonymous strophes attached to Latin songs. Facsimiles of almost all extant manuscripts are found in Horst Brunner, Ulrich Müller, and Franz Viktor Spechtler, eds., *Walther von der Vogelweide: Die gesamte Überlieferung der Texte und Melodien. Abbildungen, Materialien, Melodietranskriptionen* (Göppingen: Kümmerle, 1977).

First publication: *Die Gedichte Walthers von der Vogelweide,* edited by Karl Lachmann (Berlin: Reimer, 1827).

Standard editions: *Walther von der Vogelweide,* volume 2, edited by Wilhelm Wilmanns, fourth edition, revised by Victor Michels (Halle an der Saale: Buchhandlung des Waisenhauses, 1924); *Die Lieder, unter Beifügung erhaltener und erschlossener Melodien,* 2 volumes, edited by Friedrich Maurer (Tübingen: Niemeyer, 1955, 1956); *Die Gedichte Walthers von der Vogelweide,* edited by Lachmann, revised by Carl von Kraus, thirteenth edition, revised by Hugo Kuhn (Berlin: De Gruyter, 1965); in *Mutabilität im Minnesang,* edited by Hubert Heinen (Göppingen: Kümmerle, 1989).

Editions in modern German: *Die Gedichte Walthers von der Vogelweide,* translated by Hans Böhm, third edition (Berlin: De Gruyter, 1964); *Werke,* translated by Joerg Schaefer (Darmstadt: Wissenschaftliche Buchgesellschaft, 1972); *Gedichte,* translated by Peter Wapnewski (Frankfurt am Main: Fischer, 1984).

English editions: Translated by Frank C. Nicholson, in *Old German Love Songs* (London: Unwin, 1907); translated by Jethro Bithell, in *The Minnesingers,* volume 1 (New York: Longmans, 1909); translated by Edwin H. Zeydel and Bayard Quincy Morgan, in *Walther von der Vogelweide: The Poems* (Ithaca, N.Y.: Thrift, 1952); translated by M. F. Richey, in *Medieval German Lyrics* (Edinburgh: Oliver & Boyd, 1958); translated by Barbara G. Seagrave and J. W. Thomas, in *The Songs of the Minnesingers* (Urbana: University of Illinois Press, 1966); translated by Frederick Goldin, in *German and Italian Lyrics of the Middle Ages* (New York: Norton, 1973).

Walther von der Vogelweide was the most important medieval lyric poet in the German language. His songs include religious, moral-didactic, political, and erotic themes. References in his songs show him repeatedly seeking acceptance at the Viennese court, where, he says, he learned to sing and express himself (L.32,14 – although many editors have attempted to replace the cumbersome method of citing Walther's songs according to the page and line number in Karl Lachmann's 1827 first edition of them, no alternative manner of citation has superseded it). In presenting his persona as a quarrelsome and demanding petitioner for favor and an arbiter of proper courtly behavior, he also demonstrates a peripatetic acquaintance with a wide variety of rulers and areas within the German-speaking realm. Uncertainty reigns about his birthplace and social status. A document of 1203 refers to him as a

cantor (singer) richly rewarded by Bishop Wolfger of Erla. An early consensus that he was of noble birth gave way in the third quarter of the twentieth century to the assumption that he was a professional performer with no claim to nobility. Scholars have posited a dichotomy between minnesingers and singers of didactic songs and strophes, with the former group having greater prestige; Walther, more than any other German singer, belonged, on the evidence of the diversity of his oeuvre, to both groups. Internal evidence of a clerical education suggests that he identified himself and was identified by others with the secular clergy (there is no reason to assume that he had taken orders), and highly educated clerics, serving as administrators and messengers, traveled as widely as did lords and minstrels. A second contemporary document identifies one such cleric as *dominus Walterus;* he may be the poet. In terming himself "von der Vogelweide" (of the bird meadow) Walther may be referring to a family landholding; there are "bird meadows" (hunting reserves) scattered from South Tirol to Franconia. On the other hand, the equation of singers with birds was commonplace. The familiar manner Walther uses with his audience of courtiers would speak for his having a status not all that disparate from theirs; in any case, the audience for *Minnesang* was probably restricted to a coterie of cognoscenti in relatively few courts (most important for Walther was the Viennese court).

Received opinion about the basic outlines of Walther's life and artistic development achieved a certain stability in the late nineteenth and early twentieth centuries, and though it has been challenged in almost all details, it probably contains considerable truth. Some scholars see in Walther's comments on political and social matters his efforts as a spokesman for whatever faction supported him, while others argue that he is presenting his own opinions. A similar dichotomy occurs in regard to his *Minnelieder* (courtly love songs): whereas most scholars see in them Walther's personal views on love, others place more weight on the influence of literary fashions at various courts. According to received opinion, Walther began to sing *Minnelieder* in a conventional style at the Viennese court during the 1190s. On the death of his patron, Duke Friedrich of Austria, in 1198, Walther had to leave the court; from that time on he traveled widely, with connections to courts throughout the south and central portions of the empire, and added political and gnomic songs and strophes to his repertoire. At first he supported the claim of Philip of Swabia to be emperor of the Holy Roman Empire;

on Philip's assassination he began to support Philip's successor, Otto. Even before Otto's death Walther shifted his allegiance to Friedrich II, who became king of the Romans in 1212 and of the Germans in 1215 and Holy Roman emperor in 1220; Friedrich eventually granted him a fief. For several decades after 1203 Walther made repeated attempts to return to the Viennese court, but his exclusion from it exposed him to a variety of modes of *Minnesang* and spurred him to turn from the high style of songs lamenting unrequited love and create songs of love for a simple maiden and, eventually, songs of mutual love in a high and refined courtly style. In his later years retrospective songs, lamenting the loss of former glory, made up a greater part of his oeuvre.

Some of Walther's *Minnelieder* parallel those by older minnesingers, especially Reinmar der Alte, to whom there are many direct and indirect references in Walther's works. The consensus of several generations of scholars was that Reinmar was a mentor with whom the younger singer broke and that the two engaged in a running literary feud based on Walther's having developed a divergent concept of love. More recent scholars, who do not deny that Reinmar had a significant influence on Walther, have reassessed the evidence and suggested that the similarities outweigh the differences and that much of what has been regarded as antagonism may be regarded as a development of typical themes of rivalry common to many medieval lyrics. In questioning the pertinence of internal evidence for biographical information, the "antifeud" scholars also reject earlier attempts to create a developmental scheme for the songs. An approximate chronology of many of the didactic songs and strophes can be worked out on the basis of specific references, however, and songs containing retrospective reflections are doubtless late.

A good example of a fairly traditional (and possibly early) song is L. 119,17, often regarded as a double *Wechsel* (exchange between two speakers, usually the lady and her would-be lover). Although editors and critics have almost always rearranged the order of the four strophes to create a more unified song, the relationship among them remains tenuous. As in a typical *Wechsel,* the two speakers do not speak directly to each other but present monologues on related topics. Thus, though a reordering of strophes might make for a somewhat more logical development of thought or bring similarities into proximity, the overwhelming autonomy of each strophe obviates a tight unity. The second strophe is usually read in the woman's voice (signaled in the

editions by the use of single quotation marks); although this reading is probable, it is not certain. In the first strophe the suitor laments that although his lady says she loves him, he has reason to think otherwise and suffers "ein senfte unsenftekeit" (a comforting discomfort; the oxymoron is a rhetorical device prevalent in twelfth-century Latin poetry and theological writings that became increasingly important in later *Minnesang*). In the second strophe he (or the lady) laments that he (or she) must be sad since all others are; were it not that he/she would be plagued by the scorn of others, he/she would not wish to eschew joy. He/she suggests, however, that his/her joy will merely remain hidden. An understanding of this strophe is complicated both by its slightly skewed use of traditional motifs (which the editors changed into conventional clichés) and by a lack of certainty as to who is speaking. It is not unusual for the sex of the speaker of a given strophe to be indeterminate; the scribe of manuscript C apparently understood this strophe to be in the male voice, whereas recent editors and critics have preferred the ambiguous reading of manuscript E and assign the strophe to the lady. The four strophes would be better balanced if the lady were the persona of this one; there are, however, several *Wechsel* in which a solitary woman's strophe is set off against several in the man's voice. It is somewhat disconcerting that it does not make all that much difference who is speaking here.

In the third strophe, which begins, as does the first, with the word *Got* (God), the lady rejoices in her choice of lovers, details the favors she has bestowed on him (kissing and embracing), and declares that she is so inflamed by love for him that she would grant him all he desires if the opportunity should arise. This forthrightness on the part of the lady does not square well with the recalcitrant reception that the suitor in the typical *Minnelied* laments, but the same paradox is typical of most *Minnelieder* up to and including Walther's: the lady as seen by the man denies his pleas hard-heartedly, but when she is given a voice she reveals herself as more eager to enter a physical relationship than is the suitor himself.

In the fourth strophe the man ignores his lady's impassioned wish for mutual fulfillment, of which he may not have been apprised. He continues the lament of the first strophe (with which verbal echoes link this one) and expands on the sentiments of the second (whether they were his or his lady's) and, indirectly, of the third. In a traditional *laudatio temporis acti* (praise of bygone days) he reports that in earlier times, as he knows from personal experi-

Poems by Walther in the Große Heidelberger Liederhandschrift (Heidelberg, Universitätsbibliothek, cpg 848, f. 144b)

ence, people (that is, courtiers) were happy and a man could, given the fulfillment of his desires, be happy and behave properly. The inference is that in the poet's day people are sad (as in the second strophe) and that he must eschew fulfilled love. Only the reference to the mirthful season reflects a potential love relationship in this strophe; its speaker makes general, remarkably abstract, and indirect assertions. After the mounting intensity and specificity of the relationship between the suitor and his lady in the first three strophes, the sententious concern of the fourth with public behavior, and the self-absorption of the strophe's persona, strikes one as a lame conclusion. As an exercise in the stereotypical manner of much of Reinmar's poetry, with its hapless suitor and its lady eager for what the suitor dares not expect, the song is, however, quite successful.

Although both manuscripts connect the first four strophes with a fifth – L. 120,16 – no editor has ever followed their lead. The first to suggest that the five might be read together is Christoph Cormeau, and there is much to recommend his suggestion. The meter of the final section of the fifth strophe differs from that of the first four, and scholars have tended to link L. 120,16 with MF 214,34, a song variously ascribed to Walther and to Hartmann von Aue that is transmitted as Walther's in manuscript E immediately before 119,17. The scribe of the exemplar of C and E may have erred in placing it where it now is (its formal flaws suggest that he paid little attention to its structure); E and this section of C reflect a North German Walther renaissance of the later thirteenth century, and the addition may have been made by a singer of Walther songs in this context. In general, scholars have insisted that all strophes of a song must have an identical metrical form; the manuscripts are, however, replete with examples of the first or last strophe deviating in form from the others. If L. 120,16 is, in fact, Walther's conclusion for 119,17, then he has changed literary masters: instead of ending, in the manner of Reinmar, in an inconclusive lament, he demands, in the manner of Hartmann – albeit less forcefully than in some of Hartmann's and his own (later?) songs – that the lady whom he serves with feudal obeisance should treat him as befits a proper vassal and reward him for service rendered.

Heinrich von Morungen is as noted for striking imagery and pointed conclusions as Reinmar is for intellectual musings largely devoid of imagery; the latter poet also has a tendency to dampen rhetorical climaxes with extended reflective denouements. Thus Walther's use of techniques derived from Heinrich (though he seldom uses such original images or attempts Heinrich's intensity of expressed feeling) is often seen as a developmental stage, and it is suggested that Walther did not encounter Heinrich's songs until well into his mature period; the dichotomy between the two earlier poets is not as clean as scholars would have it, however, and there is no reason to assume that Walther could not have borrowed from both simultaneously (Reinmar also, in songs earlier scholars often considered spurious, emulates Heinrich). Even the common view that Walther introduced new modes of love into *Minnesang* reflects a reductionist reading of earlier minnesingers. Nevertheless, many of Walther's songs do display an insouciant attitude toward love like that sometimes found in Heinrich's and a stress on the necessary mutuality of love that is not immediately apparent in the songs of his predecessors in Germany (although it is in those of his Provençal forerunner Bernard de Ventador, for example). Some of Walther's songs demonstrate his melding of the conventions of Provençal and, especially, of German love songs with those of goliardic Latin songs.

The notion that many of Walther's songs are *Mädchenlieder* (songs of unmarried peasant girls) has been called into question; in most cases the girls are not necessarily unmarried, and there is never any direct indication that they are peasants. For that matter, the lady of traditional *Minnesang* need not, as has commonly been asserted, be a mature woman rather than a young girl, be of high social rank, or be married. In any case, many of Walther's songs, such as L. 50,19, seem fresher than the laments of a hapless suitor that dominate the songs of most of those before and after him. The attitude toward the lady or girl seems freer; the stance of the suitor is not that of abject subservience. The most appealing version of 50,19 is in manuscript C. Here the suitor playfully turns the lady's ignoring him into a declaration of her love. His ploy for evading detection – he recommends that she signal her love by continuing to avoid looking at him directly – echoes earlier *Minnesang* (in the considerably different version in E *she* probably makes the recommendation to *him,* since the unique following strophe in E has the singer exclaim that now everyone is looking at his lady's feet). He then details, with considerable condescension, how he has chosen her above all others despite her excelling them only in goodness. In the last strophe he extols mutuality in love and stresses that true love must not only be mutual but also exclusive. What especially endears such songs to modern readers is that they downplay the brittle artificiality so prevalent in medieval love poetry and seem

Words and music for the song "Allerêrst lebe ich mir werde," ascribed to Walther, in the mid-fourteenth-century Münster Fragment (Münster, Staatsarchiv, ms. VII, 51, f. lr–lv)

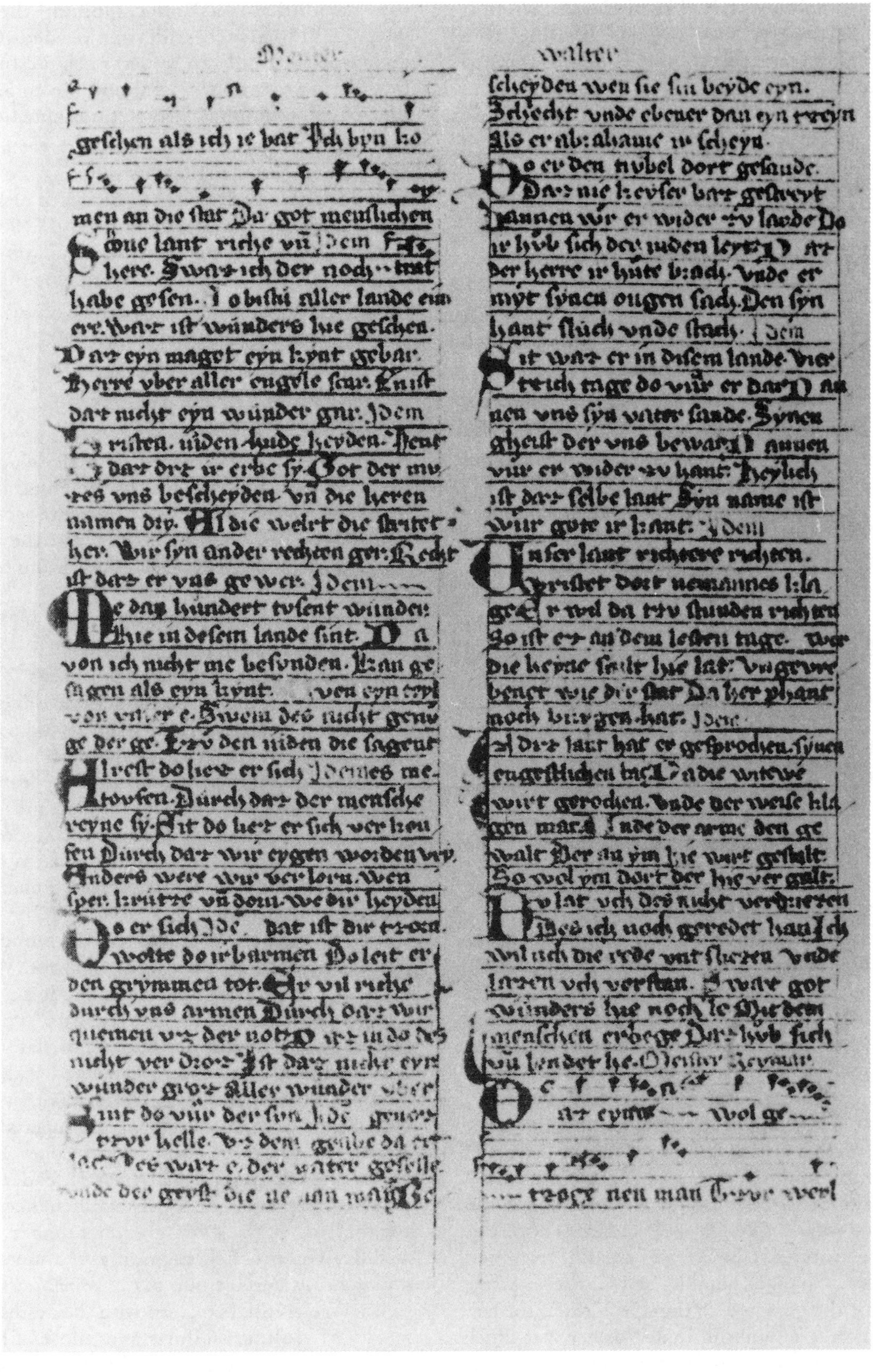

both simple and heartfelt. The modern reaction is probably partly based on a misunderstanding: even when Walther seems direct, he is using ambiguity to create an artful simplicity. His distinction in L. 46,32 between *hôhe* (lofty) and *nidere minne* (base love) has shaped scholarly concern far more than its relevance for his own songs warrants; the distinction had little contemporary resonance and does not seem to be consistently maintained even in Walther's songs.

Walther would have been a notable minnesinger even if he had restricted himself to love songs; his preeminence, however, is based on his not only excelling in these but also, as far as is known, his being the originator in German of gnomic songs for topical, especially political, purposes (there were precursors for religious and moral-didactic songs). What may be his first political song is also one of the best known: L. 8,4. In the century after his death this set of three strophes was considered characteristic of Walther; an illustrator of a collection of his songs used its initial image to portray him: the portraits in manuscripts B and C clearly derive from a common exemplar in which this song began the collection. The initial strophe is also the most general; it deals with the disorder resulting from the emperor Heinrich VI's having died suddenly in 1197 without the succession of his son, Friedrich II, having been secured.

The singer sits on a rock with his legs crossed; his elbow rests on his leg, and his chin and cheek rest against his hand. This position, the typical posture of the contemplative sage, lends his reflections authority. The three values thought to be necessary for a nobleman – honor, wealth in the form of movable property, and God's grace – seem to be incompatible, he says. Without honor – that is, a good reputation – one was lost; no vassal would serve a dishonored lord, and no lord would reward a dishonored servant. The only sources of wealth for the nobility were freely given rewards for services and rents and fees from land or benefices; Walther does not refer to these specifically, since they were the precondition for those forms of wealth one could carry: jewels, coins, clothes. But such wealth could be and often was obtained in dishonorable ways – through theft and extortion. The excessive search for honor and wealth, however, was contrary to pious humility and Christian asceticism; thus the person who thought himself (or herself, though it is doubtful that Walther was much concerned here with the plight of women) most noble might well incur God's wrath rather than his benevolence. For there to be the slightest chance

that the difficult task of combining these three goods could be successful, one needed the peace and justice that only an emperor could establish. As the other two strophes point out, the empire at the time of composition lacked an undisputed emperor.

Though the three strophes each refer to a specific point in the intrigues surrounding the selection of a German emperor upon the death of Heinrich VI, with two of them being timely in 1198 and the third (9,16) reflecting the state of affairs in 1201, Walther may have decided to combine them into a unit that downplayed their disparity of topical reference in favor of a broader discussion of the role of the emperor as the guardian of secular and ecclesiastic order. Their unity is underscored by striking formal and thematic parallels. Neither of the two versions transmitted, however, makes a satisfactory whole. The "Papal" strophe, L. 8,28, which would best culminate the series, lacks the initial four lines in manuscript A; in B and C it is in the second position. Thus, one cannot be sure that the splendid three-strophe song found in many anthologies was ever performed as such.

The tradition of gnomic didacticism of Walther's day (and afterward) made the individual strophe an autonomous vehicle of pithy sentences. Though a fair number of Walther's didactic strophes appear to cluster in multistrophic groups comparable in their loose, associative coherence to his *Minnelieder,* most of them were probably not only initially created for a specific occasion but also subsequently performed, collected, and transmitted as monostrophic *Sangsprüche* (didactic songs). It is likely that Walther was influenced by the Provençal model of the multistrophic didactic *sirventes* and the monostrophic didactic *coblas* (as well as the indigenous monostrophic *Spruch* tradition) in creating both types. Walther's influence on later peripatetic didactic singers was far greater than that he exercised on later minnesingers, for whom he was but one of many models. Among the diverse topics broached in his single strophes and multistrophic songs, Walther's consistent allegiance to the antipapal, proimperial factions stands out. The large number of strophes addressed to specific secular and ecclesiastic leaders urging private preference (be it reward, benefice, or fief) for the singer, the even greater number deriding such leaders for their niggardly treatment of him, and the considerable number of *Minnelieder* devoted to a self-referential concern with the aesthetic superiority of Walther's efforts over those of his rivals would seem too personal to have found a sympathetic hearing among the courtiers who made up Walther's audience. All of his self-conscious songs, however, allow the listening courtiers to compare the depicted struggle for recognition with their own constant efforts to maintain or attain status.

An extraordinary strophe, L. 19,29, combines all these strains; its striking imagery has elicited erudite and perceptive modern commentary (though almost all critics base their remarks on the text as rewritten by Lachmann):

Dô Friderîch ûz Œsterrîch alsô gewarp,
daz er an der sêle genas und im der lîp erstarp,
do fuort er mînen krenechen trit in die erde.
do gieng ich slîchent als ein pfâwe, swar ich gie,
daz houbet hanht ich nider unz ûf mîne knie:
nû riht ich ez ûf nâch vollem werde.
ich bin wol ze fiure komen:
mich hât daz rîch und ouch diu krôn an sich genomen.
wol ûf, swer tanzen welle nâch der gîgen!
mir ist mîner swære buoz:
êrste wil ich eben setzen mînen fuoz
und wider in ein hôhgemüete sîgen.

(When Frederick of Austria acted in such a manner
that he saved his soul as his body perished,
he cast down my cranelike step.
Then I went slinking like a peacock wherever I went;
I hung my head down all the way to my knees:
Now I'll pick it up in full dignity.
I have indeed gained a place at the hearth:
the empire and also the crown have accepted me.
Arise, whoever wishes to dance to the fiddle!
I have recompense for my tribulation:
first I will place my foot evenly
and against that droop in high spirits.)

Though the strophe deals with matters far removed from the usual pastoral setting of dances, Walther is using an underlying image of the dance in a consistent ironic manner to make a sociopolitical comment. Walther's depiction of his cranelike haughtiness having been transformed, on the death of his patron, to peacocklike humility reflected in his dipping of his head uses both traditionally skewed emblems and observations from nature. Walther, on remarking how his proud obsequiousness has earned him service and a warming hearth, comments that now he can bear himself haughtily. As the oxymoronic *sîgen* (droop) clearly suggests, however, dancing to the fiddle (and singing for the dance) will not necessarily insure one's acceptance at court, with its attendant high spirits; what is raised high will fall. But just as his humility is suspect, his final dashed hopes will not remain depressed; by paralleling the gestures of this strophe to those of a dance, Walther has created a perfect parallel to the maneuvering in which courtiers must engage to prevail at court. Far from giving a deeply felt report of his personal fate, something that would be of little interest to his audience, he presents a model of *urbanitas* (courtly decorum), a quality without which the court would collapse.

One of the consistent targets of Walther's songs is papal power and even the pope himself. Throughout the history of the German Empire there were tensions between the pope and the emperor; in Walther's day the popes repeatedly sought to influence the choice of emperor or the actions of the emperor, and wherever possible Walther sides with those opposed to the pope. One strophe in Walther's *Unmutston* (Song of Displeasure, L. 34,4) illustrates his bitter sarcasm:

Ahî, wie kristenlîche nû der bâbest lachet,
swanne er sînen Walhen seit: "ich hân's alsô gemachet!"
daz er da seit, des solt er niemer hân gedâht.
er gihet: "ich hân zwêne Allamân under eine krône brâht,
daz si daz rîche suln stœren unde wasten.
ie dar under müez i'n in ir kasten:
ich hân si an mînen stoc gemenet, ir guot ist allez mîn:
ir tiutschez silber vert in mînen welschen schrîn.
ir pfaffen, ezzent hüenr und trinkent wîn
unde lânt die tiutschen – vasten."

(Hey, in what a Christian manner the pope now laughs,
whenever he tells his Wops: "I've managed it just right!"
What he says there he should never have thought.
He maintains, "I brought two Krauts under one crown
so that they should destroy and demolish the empire.
In the meantime I have to get into their [treasure] chests:
I have yoked them to my offering box; their wealth is all mine:
Their German silver goes into my Italian coffer.
You priests, eat chickens and drink wine
and let the Germans – fast.")

One of Walther's most impressive songs, L. 66,21, by its own words a late one, puts the splendors of courtly life and the worthiness that the singer has acquired with his singing in stark contrast to the fate ordained for those eager to serve Dame World. The final two strophes of version A illustrate the contrast that permeates the whole song.

Lât mich an eime stabe gân
und werben umbe werdekeit
mit unverzageter arebeit,
als ich von kinde hân getân,
sô bin ich doch, swie nider ich sî, der werden ein
gnuoc in mîner mâze hô.
daz müet die nideren. ob mich daz iht swache? nein.
die biderben hânt mich deste baz.
der werden wirde ist so guot,
daz man in daz hôhste lop sol geben.

ez enwart nie hovelîcher leben,
swer sô dem ende [rehte] tuot.

Welt, ich hân dînen lôn wol gesehen:
swaz dû mir gîst, daz nimest du mir.
wir scheiden alle blôz von dir.
schame dich, sol mir alsô geschehen.
ich hân lîp unde sêle (des was gar ze vil)
gewâget tûsent stunt dur dich:
nû bin ich alt und hâst mit mir dîn gampelspil:
ist mir daz zorn, so lachest dû.
nu lache uns eine wîle noch:
dîn jâmertac wil schiere komen
und nimet dir, swaz du uns hâst benomen,
und brennet dich dar umbe iedoch.

(Let me take up the wanderer's staff
and earn worthiness
with fearless travail
as I have done since childhood;
then I am, however low I may be, one of the worthies,
high to the extent it befits me.
That causes the base ones grief. Does that disgrace me?
    No.
The honorable esteem me all the more.
The worthiness of the worthy is so good
that one ought to give them the highest praise.
A more courtly life never came into existence
than if someone acts properly toward the end.

World, I have indeed seen your reward:
What you give me you take from me.
We all part naked from you.
Be ashamed, if such a thing befalls me.
I have dared body and soul [there was far too much of
    that]
on your account a thousand times:
Now I am old and you play your silly games with me:
If I grow angry about that, you laugh.
Now go ahead and laugh at us for a while:
your day of lamentation will soon arrive
and take from you all that you have taken from us
and burn you for all that because of it.)

Even a minimal list of Walther's "greatest hits" would have to include the *Palästinalied* (Palestine Song, L. 14,38); the "Elegy" (L. 124,1); the *Preislied* (Song of Praise, L. 56,14); the *Mailied* (May Song, L. 51,13); the *Traumliebe* (Love Vision, L. 74,20); "Aller werdekeit ein füegerinne" (Arbitress of all worthiness, L. 46,32); and "Under der linden" (Under the lime tree, L. 39,11). Walther's songs reflect many facets and some new nuances in the definition of love; his *Minnelieder* share with most of those before and after him a concern for singing of love as a model for living a proper courtly life, with decorum and elegance. His political, moral, and religious songs range from praise to lament to scolding; some are concerned with petty quarrels, and others

touch on profound problems of imperial power. Almost all his songs show his skill in shaping complex contents in an attractive manner so as to engage his audience and bring them to accept the views he expresses.

Bibliographies:
Kurt Herbert Halbach, *Walther von der Vogelweide* (Stuttgart: Metzler, 1965; fourth edition, revised by Manfred Günter Scholz, 1983);
Scholz, *Bibliographie zu Walther von der Vogelweide* (Berlin: Schmidt, 1969).

References:
Thomas Bein, "Walther von der Vogelweide: *Nû sol der keiser hêre*," in *Gedichte und Interpretationen: Mittelalter,* edited by Helmut Tervooren (Stuttgart: Reclam, 1993), pp. 409–424;
Siegfried Beyschlag, ed., *Walther von der Vogelweide* (Darmstadt: Wissenschaftliche Buchgesellschaft, 1971);
Susan L. Clark, " 'ein schoenez bilde': Walther von der Vogelweide and the Idea of Image," in *From Symbol to Mimesis: The Generation of Walther von der Vogelweide,* edited by Franz H. Bäuml (Göppingen: Kümmerle, 1984), pp. 69–91;
Christoph Cormeau, "Zur textkritischen Revision von Lachmanns Ausgabe der Lieder Walthers von der Vogelweide: Überlegungen zur Neubearbeitung am Beispiel von MF 214,34/L. 120,16," in *Textkritik und Interpretation: Festschrift für Karl Konrad Polheim zum 60. Geburtstag,* edited by Heimo Reinitzer (Bern: Lang, 1987), pp. 53–68;
Trude Ehlert, *Konvention – Variation – Innovation: Ein struktureller Vergleich von Liedern aus "Des Minnesangs Frühling" und Walther von der Vogelweide* (Berlin: Schmidt, 1980);
Gerhard Hahn, *Walther von der Vogelweide* (Munich: Artemis, 1986);
Hubert Heinen, "Clothes Make the Man: Walther 62,6 and the Status of the Poet/Performer," in *Word and Deed: German Studies in Honor of Wolfgang F. Michael,* edited by Thomas E. Ryan and Denes Monostory (Bern: Lang, 1993), pp. 67–84;
Heinen, "Performance Dynamics and the Unity in the Diversity of Walther's Elegy," in *in hôhem prîse: A* Festschrift *in Honor of Ernst S. Dick,* edited by Winder McConnell (Göppingen: Kümmerle, 1989), pp. 153–161;
Heinen, "Walther's 'Under der linden,' Its Function, Its Subtexts, and Its Maltreated Maiden," in *Medieval German Literature: Proceedings from*

the 23rd International Congress on Medieval Studies, edited by Albrecht Classen (Göppingen: Kümmerle, 1989), pp. 51–73;

Heinen, "When Pallor Pales: Reflections on Epigonality in Late 13th-Century Minnesongs," *Medieval Perspectives*, 4–5 (1989–1990): 53–56;

George F. Jones, *Walther von der Vogelweide* (New York: Twayne, 1968);

James V. McMahon, *The Music of Early Minnesang* (Columbia, S.C.: Camden House, 1990);

Hans-Dieter Mück, ed., *Walther von der Vogelweide: Beiträge zu Leben und Werk* (Stuttgart: Stöffler & Schütz, 1989);

Jan-Dirk Müller and Franz Josef Wortbrock, eds., *Walther von der Vogelweide: Hamburger Colloquium 1989 zum 65. Geburtstag von Karl-Heinz Borck* (Stuttgart: Hirzel, 1989);

Alfred Mundhenk, *Walthers Zuhörer* (Würzburg: Königshausen & Neumann, 1993);

Theodor Nolte, *Walther von der Vogelweide: Höfische Idealität und konkrete Erfahrung* (Stuttgart: Hirzel, 1991);

Oxford German Studies, 13, special Walther von der Vogelweide issue (1982);

Hermann Reichert, *Walther von der Vogelweide für Anfänger* (Vienna: WUV, 1992);

Olive Sayce, *The Medieval German Lyric 1150–1300* (Oxford: Clarendon, 1982);

Günther Schweikle, *Minnesang* (Stuttgart: Metzler, 1989);

Heike Sievert, "Walther von der Vogelweide: *Unter der linden*," in *Gedichte und Interpretationen: Mittelalter,* edited by Tervooren (Stuttgart: Reclam, 1993), pp. 129–143;

Burghart Wachinger, "Die Welt, die Minne und das Ich: Drei spätmittelalterliche Lieder," in *Entzauberung der Welt: Deutsche Literatur 1200–1500,* edited by James F. Poag and Thomas C. Fox (Bern: Francke, 1989), pp. 107–118;

Eva Willms, *Liebesleid und Sangeslust: Untersuchungen zur deutschen Liebeslyrik des späten 12. und frühen 13. Jahrhunderts* (Munich: Artemis, 1990).

Wernher der Gartenaere

(flourished circa 1265 – 1280)

Linda B. Parshall
Portland State University

MAJOR WORK: *Helmbrecht* (circa 1265–1280)

Manuscripts: *Helmbrecht* is preserved in two manuscripts. The more recent is A in the Ambras Heldenbuch (Vienna, Österreichische Nationalbibliothek, Cod. Vind. Ser. nova 2663), a costly parchment manuscript produced between 1504 and 1515 for Emperor Maximilian I in Bolzano and Innsbruck by Hans Ried. It includes, in addition to *Helmbrecht,* twenty-four literary works of varying genres. *Helmbrecht* was copied in 1514, along with two texts from the Styria region in Austria (*Herrand von Wildonie* and *Ulrich von Liechtenstein*). All three were possibly transcribed from a single source that is now lost but presumed to date before 1300. The second manuscript is B, the Leombach Manuscript (Berlin, Staatsbibliothek Preußischer Kulturbesitz Manuscript germ. 2⁰ 470), written on paper in Upper Austria around 1413 by a scribe of Swabian descent in the employ of Leonhard Meurl of Leombach Castle. This manuscript contains only Albrecht's *Der jüngere Titurel* and Wernher's *Helmbrecht.* Though closer in time to Wernher's original, this scribe took more liberties with his source than did Ried. The model for this version of *Helmbrecht* was written down before 1320.

First publication: *Von dem Mayr Helmprechte: Eine poetische Erzählung,* edited by Joseph Bergmann (Vienna: Gerold, 1839).

Standard edition: *Meier Helmbrecht, von Wernher dem Gartenaere,* edited by Friedrich Panzer (Halle: Niemeyer, 1902); revised by Kurt Ruh as *Helmbrecht,* Altdeutsche Textbibliothek, no. 11 (Tübingen: Niemeyer, 1974).

Edition in modern German: *Helmbrecht,* edited and translated by Fritz Tschirch (Stuttgart: Reclam, 1974; revised, 1978).

Editions in English: Translated by Clair Hayden Bell in *Peasant Life in Old German Epics: Meier Helmbrecht and Der arme Heinrich* (New York: Columbia University Press, 1931; reprinted, New York: Octagon Books, 1965), pp. 35–89; translated by J. W. Thomas as "Helmbrecht," in *German Medieval Tales,* edited by Francis G. Gentry (New York: Continuum, 1983), pp. 125–147; translated by Linda B. Parshall as *Helmbrecht* (New York & London: Garland, 1987).

In the closing line of *Helmbrecht* (circa 1265–1280) the narrator and implied poet identifies himself as Wernher der Gartenaere (the Gardener). This name has been accepted by scholars, even though the last twelve lines of the poem appear only in manuscript A (1514) and were probably added by a copyist preceding Hans Ried, who produced that manuscript. Wernher's life is otherwise undocumented in contemporary records and the testimony of fellow writers, and no other works have been attributed to him. Yet this relatively short piece of 1,934 lines in rhymed couplets has been a major focus of scholarly attention and has inspired many attempts to seek out the author's vanished tracks. Speculation was particularly rampant in the nineteenth century, when the author of *Helmbrecht* was identified with various individuals named either Wernher or Gärtner, with ecclesiastics or wandering minstrels, with gardeners, with *ministeriales* (lower-ranking knights without land of their own), with landed knights, and even with aging peasants. None of these identifications has proved persuasive.

Wernher's influence has been only slightly less difficult to trace than his existence. Some have seen reflections of *Helmbrecht* in the works of Der Pleier, a poet active around 1260 to 1280, and in *Seifried Helbling* (circa 1282–1283), but the first definite allusion to *Helmbrecht* occurs in Ottokar von Steiermark's *Österreichische Reimchronik* (Austrian Rhymed Chronicle, circa 1310–1315), where cer-

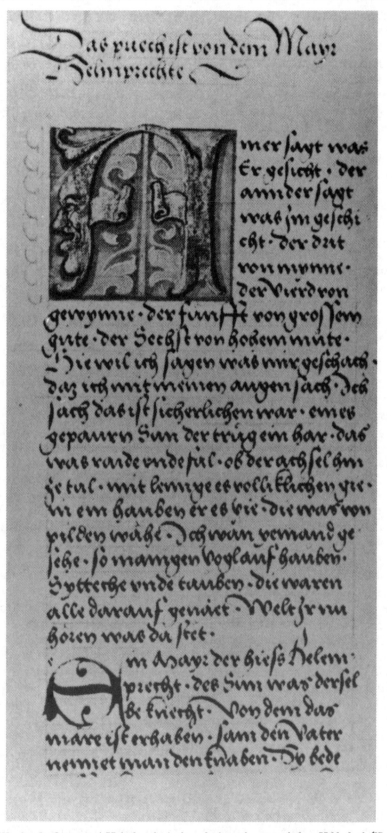

The beginning of Wernher der Gartenaere's Helmbrecht *in the early-sixteenth-century Ambras Heldenbuch (Vienna, Österreichische Nationalbibliothek, Cod. Vind. Ser. nova 2663)*

tain peasants justify their refusal of military service by recalling the teachings of Father Helmbrecht. A broader response is suggested by some related words that occur in fourteenth-century Bohemia and Vienna: *helmbrecht,* meaning bon vivant; *helmbrechtice,* loose woman; and the adjective *helmbrechtny,* dissolute. Though it is difficult to document the early success of *Helmbrecht,* the copious scholarly literature since the nineteenth century attests to its continuing popularity (Ulrich Seelbach's bibliography, published in 1981, includes 450 entries). From 1839 to 1994 almost twenty separate editions of the entire text appeared, with still more abridged editions. There have also been at least twenty-five translations, including Russian and Japanese, and in the early twentieth century several theatrical versions appeared.

The work's title has been cause for speculation. Each of the two extant manuscripts includes a title, but both titles are clearly later additions. Manuscript A reads: "Das puech ist von dem Mayr Helmprechte" (This book is about the farmer Helmbrecht); manuscript B is more informative: "hie hebt sich ain mar von dem helmprecht / der war ain nar vnd auch ain gauglar amen" (Here begins a tale about Helmbrecht / who was a fool and also a trickster. Amen). Early editions adopted the version of A and used *Meier Helmbrecht* as the title, but this choice seemed unsatisfactory because it ignored the son. Alternatives were suggested, including a plural form, *Die Helmbrechte;* the resolution now accepted by scholars is simply *Helmbrecht,* ambiguously encompassing both father and son.

The text remains the only reliable source of information about the author, and it makes clear that Wernher was an educated person who was familiar with much of the literature of his predecessors. Though he does not boast of this knowledge, there are specific allusions in *Helmbrecht* to Neidhart von Reuental, to tales of the Trojan War and of Aeneas, to the *Karlssage,* to *Herzog Ernst* (Duke Ernst, circa 1190), and to several stories concerning the hero Dietrich von Bern (Theodoric the Great). It seems clear that Wernher was also familiar with other Middle High German works he does not specifically name, including Hartmann von Aue's *Gregorius* (circa 1187), Gottfried von Straßburg's *Tristan und Isolde* (circa 1210), Wolfram von Eschenbach's *Parzival* (circa 1200–1210), and works by Der Stricker and Der Marner. His familiarity with both peasant customs and courtly behavior, along with the worldly perspective of the poem, suggests that its author was a layman, perhaps a wandering minstrel, though he may have enjoyed a more settled position as occasional poet in the service of a patron.

For all his allusions to other works, Wernher's sympathetic and richly detailed rendering of peasant life is virtually without precedent in the medieval period. No prototype has been identified for the *Helmbrecht* story, though Hannes Kästner has suggested the parable of the prodigal son as a possible paradigm. Among Wernher's more immediate predecessors, Neidhart most conspicuously breaks with the courtly tradition by including in his poetry many representatives of the lower orders, though for him peasants are still colorful and humorous rustics and not to be taken seriously. It seems to have been Neidhart who supplied the model for Wernher's upstart, overdressed peasant, since one of his short poems tells of a young peasant fop named Hildemar who decks his blond curls with a gaudy cap. Both the hair and its decorative covering are identified as signs of Hildemar's unseemly aspiration to rise beyond his station, and like Helmbrecht he ultimately loses his cap along with his pride. Wernher, far from disguising any debt to Neidhart, openly defers to him as a masterful writer (lines 217–220).

The higher estates are not represented in *Helmbrecht,* nor are urban dwellers, artisans, or the small tradespeople who were transforming late-medieval society and economy. Instead, the status and mores of the peasantry make up the subject matter of the poem, with peasants accounting for both its heroes and its villains. Yet the tale is stylistically sophisticated, full of the kind of structural intricacies, literary allusions, parodies, and subtle ironies that require an experienced audience to be fully appreciated. Scholars agree that *Helmbrecht* was designed for a noble audience that was able to benefit from its didacticism and enjoy its poetic refinement.

The sparse evidence offered by the language of the two manuscripts helps to place its author and audience in the southern part of Germany and in Austria. Both manuscripts were written in the Bavarian-Austrian language area, one in the Tirol (Bolzano and Innsbruck), the other in Upper Austria. The original language of Wernher's poem cannot be uncovered, however, for both copyists tended to modernize the spelling, grammar, and occasionally even the vocabulary of their respective models. Yet regional traces survive in vocabulary and in descriptions of customs and legal practices, and three localities are identified by name. Unfortunately, the manuscripts differ on the latter point: whereas manuscript A extols the luxury of young Helmbrecht's costume, calling it unmatched from

Hohenstein to Haldenberc (line 192), B makes the same assertion but refers to Wels and Traunberg. Similar problems arise in the location of incomparably fine springwater, which is in Wanckhûsen in A but in Leubenbach in B, indicating, respectively, the Innviertel in southern Bavaria or the Traungau in Austria, about seventy miles to the east. These references to specific places have sent scholars exploring the Bavarian and Austrian countryside in search of the story's origins. The most ambitious claims were made by Friedrich Keinz in the 1860s: following clues in manuscript A, he investigated the area around the Austrian village of Gilgenberg and announced his discovery not only of the spring but also of the Helmbrecht family farm, the robber knights' castle, and even the pine slope of line 1427. Though his identifications have been discounted, Keinz was correct to trust the place-names in manuscript A, since they may represent the original version of *Helmbrecht;* the references in B are known to have been added to honor a later owner of the manuscript. Even if genuine, the place-names can lead one closer only to Wernher der Gartenaere and his patrons, not to Helmbrecht and his son as historical figures.

Most scholars agree that Wernher's poem was composed around 1280, though Seelbach has suggested that it may have been read in 1268 at the court of Heinrich XIII in Burghausen in Lower Bavaria. A reference to the death of Neidhart establishes a terminus a quo of 1237, but no satisfactory terminus ad quem exists. The text includes no other specific historical references, and there are no clear outside allusions to *Helmbrecht* before the early fourteenth century. Nor have other traces of the text been preserved: no fragmentary lines, no page discovered in the binding of some missal, no detached illustrations. Yet it survived long enough to spark interest many generations after the original composition, inspiring two noble patrons to have it copied as part of collections of early works. Its appeal to the antiquarian fascinations of the German Renaissance is not surprising; the unusual subject matter perhaps provided a compelling lesson, in an era of unrest, on the virtues of social stability.

The vivid rendering of a farmer's life – a station rarely represented in medieval literature – and Father Helmbrecht's character seems disarmingly true to life, as do the richly visual descriptions of dress, the arguments about class, and the legalities embedded in scenes of weddings or hangings. In fact, the story is so unusual and the incidental detail so compelling that many have assumed *Helmbrecht* to be more fact than fiction, an assumption the poet encourages in his opening lines:

> Hie wil ich sagen waz mir geschach
> daz ich mit mînen ougen sach. (lines 7–8)

(Now I want to tell of what happened to me, something I saw with my own eyes.)

Protestations of truthfulness are common enough in medieval prologues, but rarely does a narrator claim to be an eyewitness to events. This unusual authorial stance complements the impression of credibility in the story itself and may have helped convince many readers of the poem's factuality. Much of what Wernher describes can be historically corroborated, including legal restrictions on arms, costume, hairstyle, and food that imply that the peasant class was displaying its increasing wealth and its independence in these matters; yet the story is not a chronicle, and current scholarship has abandoned the idea that texts such as Wernher's offer a completely realistic portrayal of medieval life. Even so, *Helmbrecht* provides some of the best information available on certain aspects of daily life in thirteenth-century Germany and Austria. The reader learns about local customs such as the practice of one year of mourning, of burying criminals at crossroads, of a groom's gift to a bride, and of the payment of minstrels; about superstitions such as children inheriting traits from their godparents, illicit sex investing a fetus with characteristics of a "second" father, and sheriffs being inescapable; and about laws such as the peasant class not being allowed to bear arms or wear blue except on certain days. These details are woven into a story of surprising richness that, through the milieu of peasant culture, addresses general conflicts of the day.

The opening section of *Helmbrecht* exemplifies Wernher's attention to the background of his tale, for he offers a lengthy description (223 lines) detailing the accoutrements of a peasant's son and how these have been prepared for him by his sister, Gotelind; his mother; and a wayward nun. Readers are told that the young man is named Helmbrecht after his father, are offered an amazing view of his ludicrously elaborate clothes, and are informed that he is as foolish as his attire is inappropriate. It is only gradually revealed that the lad is about to abandon his family and their farm for the court (line 227). The father tries to dissuade him but finally yields and acquires a horse as his contribution to the son's preparations, though he continues to warn of the hardships of life at court, the dangers of trying to escape one's allotted station in life, and the folly of ignoring a father's advice – to no avail. It becomes apparent that the court to which young Helmbrecht aspires is not one of gallant knights and their ladies but rather one appropriated by a band of brigands. As the son explains his aspirations, their distance from an idealized notion of chivalry becomes clear: he speaks of the pleasure he will derive from dragging peasants through hedges by the hair (lines 372–373) and of his ambition to spend every day plundering (line 379). The father counters with arguments extolling the comfort and respectability of a peasant's life (lines 453–460). For Father Helmbrecht, correct behavior is not the prerogative of a particular social stratum but is a question of individual responsibility. This judgment is central to the ethos of *Helmbrecht*. By this point all of the tale's major themes have been introduced. The litany is repeated as the foolish son is about to depart: his father tries once more to dissuade him by retelling four ominous dreams presaging a horrible end for the young upstart. Young Helmbrecht pays no heed and rides off without ceremony (lines 646–648).

The next forty-four lines summarize his first year as a brigand. By the time he becomes homesick and decides to return to the family farm for a brief visit, he has become an arrogant, debased robber knight. Blindly self-satisfied, he has no ability to reflect or judge and no concern for censure, as becomes patently clear in the following 758 lines describing his seven-day sojourn at home. As in many passages in *Helmbrecht,* there is considerable irony in the description of his initial encounter with the household. He greets each person in turn, showing off his newly acquired sophistication by using a flowery mixture of foreign phrases – so much so that he is thought to be a foreigner. Yet his attempts are riddled with errors; he is no more a master of these tongues than he is of the ethos of knighthood. Later, in discussion with his father, he boasts at length about the uncouth behavior of his companions, blithely offering counterexamples to his father's reminiscences of the noble life that he witnessed when he visited the court in his own youth. The contrast between the morally sound life of the farmer and the corrupt one of the renegade knight is reinforced throughout their exchanges. Father Helmbrecht is aware that the exemplary world he recalls, a world familiar from the literary conventions of earlier German romances, no longer exists; but he holds to its ideals. His son, however, scorns the old values. While his stupidity may provoke laughter, his attitude is deeply disturbing: his adventures are revealed as exploits of violence, his companions as villains; his deeds are shocking:

> Leider tuon ich in noch:
> dem ich daz ouge ûz drucke,

disen hâhe ich in den rucke,
disen bind ich in den âmeizstoc,
enem ziuhe ich den loc
mit der zangen ûz dem barte,
dem andern rîz ich die swarte,
einem mülle ich die lide,
disen henc ich in die wide
bî den sparâdern sîn.
Daz die gebûren hânt deist mîn. (lines 1242–1252)

(I do even worse things to [farmers]:
I put that one's eye out,
this one I hang in the chimney flue,
another I tie up on an anthill,
I yank the hairs out of that one's beard
with pincers,
I rip the scalp off the next one,
I crush that one's limbs,
this one I string up by his heels
in a noose.
Whatever the farmers have is mine.)

The stable social hierarchy recalled by Father Helmbrecht cannot be retrieved; the new order is deplorable, but its seductiveness for the younger generation is illustrated further when young Helmbrecht convinces Gotelind to steal away with him to marry one of his band. The wedding festivities (lines 1470–1611) are interrupted by a sheriff and his posse, who find the robbers guilty and summarily execute the other nine but spare young Helmbrecht. He is blinded and mutilated as punishment for his ill-treatment of his parents. The end of young Helmbrecht's story is related in a little more than two hundred lines. He returns to the family home but is turned away by his father, who scornfully refuses to acknowledge him; his mother presses a bit of bread into his hand. He departs and wanders for a year – blind, lame, and taunted – until he is hanged by vengeful peasants.

Helmbrecht is related with an engaging vitality that hovers between lighthearted humor and bleak tragedy. Images of violence appear early, but at first they seem part of the comedy. The narrator indulges in amusing asides but refrains from overt judgment, generally allowing his characters to carry the show in direct discourse. The initial description of the young buffoon being outfitted as a knight (lines 9–402) is additionally humorous as a parody of literary convention: an account of the preparation of a young knight's attire had been de rigueur in medieval German courtly literature since the classic period, yet what Wernher offers is topsy-turvy. Young Helmbrecht is not dressed and coached by a seasoned knight but dresses himself with the help of his mother, his sister, and the nun; he pays no heed to the advice offered by his peasant father. His flowing hair and the clothes he dons point up his lack of decorum: his coiffure is beyond the pale for either knight or peasant, his headgear impossible, and the rest an overpriced clash of exaggerated elegance and coarse or ill-chosen material. The result is sartorial proof that this young man is a misfit in any society.

The most prominent aspect of young Helmbrecht's attire is his elaborate cap, and a good deal of scholarly ink has been spilled on the subject. The cap is sewn together in several sections, each covered with an embroidered depiction of courtly life drawn from known epics or romances. Overwhelmed by a profusion of detail, the reader is unable to picture the whole. The cap description, based partly on contemporary fashion and partly on the Neidhart poem, may be a late addition by Wernher; it is not an actual cap but rather a collage of possibilities that is being described. The newly made cap opens the story; its destruction concludes it. In the body of the tale it is not mentioned after the initial argument between father and son, but it remains emblematic of a central moral premise. The cap's immoderate decoration reflects both young Helmbrecht's misguided notion of courtliness and his outrageous behavior as a "knight." It is a sign of the impropriety of his life, of the conflict between outward show and essence, and its reappearance at the end of the narrative effectively concludes the moral lesson being drawn. Young Helmbrecht refused to heed his father's initial warning, "sô hüete dîner hûben" (Watch out for your cap, line 429); when he hears these words again (line 1879), it is too late: the cap is torn to bits by his executioners.

The clash between young Helmbrecht's "modern" aspirations and the conservative values imparted by his father represents a fundamental issue for the later Middle Ages: *ordo* (the order of society) had long been seen to reflect God's inviolable plan, to which change was inimical. Yet change was taking place, and the stability of the old order was being undermined. In *Helmbrecht* this conflict is presented both straightforwardly by the plot and more discreetly through Wernher's use of language. The cap embodies the confusion of values: the scenes depicted on it show heroes of epic sagas and graceful knights and ladies from courtly romances, yet they are crowded together haphazardly on a garment sewn by a defrocked nun and sported by a fool turned brigand for whom the scenes can have no real meaning.

Wernher uses parody to point up aspects of the conflict in the family debates but also in subtler ways. Occasionally he applies a courtly term in a far-from-courtly context; overt parodies of the *Minnesang* tradition occur at several points and are especially obvious in the wedding scene. This use of parody and humor and the balance of coarse subject matter with formal sophistication disguise the increasing sobriety of the poem's message.

In *Helmbrecht* the old order is dead in everything but memory. The new world is reduced to a few simple relationships where good and evil are not difficult to judge. In the end a semblance of justice prevails at horrible cost. Yet this conclusion is not a triumphal resolution but only a temporary staying of violence by violence.

At first it appears that the message of *Helmbrecht* is an essentially conservative justification of the old hierarchy and of reliance on the tradition of chivalric conduct in which transgressions against the social order are met with uncompromising punishment. Father Helmbrecht insists that peasants must remain peasants and be content with the virtues of their God-given lot, but his views are already obsolete: his maxims are undermined by the ravenous world beyond his farmyard. Yet there is also a progressive note in his insistence that nobility of spirit be set above nobility of birth (lines 503–507), that neither virtue nor villainy is guaranteed by one's birthright. By choosing the peasantry as the milieu of his tale, the author could challenge the aristocratic preconceptions of his audience in a subtle and oblique way: there is an amazing incongruity in a farmer's using courtly language to characterize his own honor; yet as the tale unfolds, any feelings of condescension toward him give way to a realization that the system that allows such condescension is being undermined. The narrator has played a game of seduction. His skill at entertainment lures his listeners into a position of moral superiority until they find the spotlight that seemed focused on young Helmbrecht's folly turned on them as well – on society and its inability to cope with change. What begins as a breach of decorum matures into a caustic parody of conventional values and is finally resolved in the gruesome vengeance taken by the poor and weak on the rich and powerful.

This clash between old and new orders takes place within a text bound up in literary convention. Yet salient features of contemporary life are there: social unrest, political disruption, and spreading lawlessness. Signs of political instability became evident in Germany in 1197 with the death of Emperor Henry VI and increased steadily in the second half of the thirteenth century, a period of major crises in much of western Europe. The years of the

Interregnum (1254-1274) saw German-speaking areas in disarray, especially in the south. As the feudal system faltered, local princes fought over land and influence. The economic situation improved for farmers but deteriorated drastically for many noble families; some found their power and holdings eroded to such an extent that they were forced to turn to pillaging to support their lifestyles. The robber baron who houses Helmbrecht's band and hires them to fight his battles is such a failed nobleman.

One should be cautious about supposing that a work almost certainly composed under court patronage could harbor revolutionary sentiments. Not surprisingly, there is considerable disagreement about the object and extent of Wernher's social critique. Some see the text as an unwavering condemnation of the peasantry and its disruption of the status quo. Others find Wernher merely disturbed by the rising power of the peasants, a change for which he finds no political solution. Still others discern a consistently anticourtly attitude. Whatever the political verdict, much of the complexity of the story, its peasant setting, and its inversion of romantic conventions becomes more meaningful and consistent if the text is regarded as a reflection on the conditions of its time. At the least, *Helmbrecht* seems set on leading the audience to question its own preoccupations about literature and about life.

Bibliography:

Ulrich Seelbach, *Bibliographie zu Wernher der Gartenaere,* Bibliographien zur deutschen Literatur des Mittelalters, no. 8 (Berlin: Schmidt, 1981).

References:

Hermann Bausinger, "Helmbrecht: Eine Interpretationsskizze," in *Studien zur deutschen Literatur und Sprache des Mittelalters: Festschrift für Hugo Moser zum 65. Geburtstag,* edited by Werner Besch (Berlin: Schmidt, 1974), pp. 200-215;

Bruno Boesch, "Die Beispielerzählung vom Helmbrecht," *Der Deutschunterricht,* 17 (May 1965): 36-47;

Helmut Brackert, "Helmbrechts Haube," *Zeitschrift für deutsches Altertum und deutsche Literatur,* 103, no. 3 (1974): 166-184;

Peter Göhler, "Konflikt und Figurengestaltung im 'Helmbrecht' von Wernher dem Gartenaere," *Weimarer Beiträge,* 20, no. 8 (1974): 93-116; reprinted in *Das Märe: Die mittelhochdeutsche Versnovelle des späteren Mittelalters,* edited by Karl-Heinz Schirmer, Wege der Forschung, no. 558

(Darmstadt: Wissenschaftliche Buchgesellschaft, 1983), pp. 384-410;

Sieglinde Hartmann, " 'siteche unde tûben' – Zur Vogelsymbolik im 'Helmbrecht,' " in *Deutschfranzösische Germanistik: Mélanges pour Emile Georges Zink,* edited by Hartmann and Claude Lecouteux, Göppinger Arbeiten zur Germanistik, no. 364 (Göppingen: Kümmerle, 1984), pp. 143-159;

Barbara Haupt, "*durch iuwer liebe sagte ich daz* – Eine literarhistorische Studie zum *Märe vom Helmbrecht,*" *Euphorion,* 68, no. 3 (1974): 229-251;

William E. Jackson, "Das Märe von *Helmbrecht* als Familien-Geschichte," *Euphorion,* 84, no. 1 (1990): 45-58;

Hannes Kästner, "Der 'Helmbrecht' und die 'Proverbia Salomonis': Bildmuster, Argumentationsweisen und didaktische Intentionen bei Wernher dem Gartenaere," *Zeitschrift für deutsche Philologie,* 98 (1979): 407-420;

Friedrich Keinz, *Meier Helmbrecht und seine Heimat* (Munich: Fleischmann, 1865);

Walter Köppe, "Überlegungen zur textadäquaten Interpretation des *Helmbrecht,*" *Acta Germanica,* 9 (1976): 111-122;

Peter Krahé, "*Slintezgeu Helmbrecht,*" *Euphorion,* 73, no. 1 (1979): 106-120;

Joachim Kuolt, "Theater um Helmbrecht: Anmerkungen zu sechs Beispielen literarischdramatischer Mittelalter-Rezeption in der ersten Hälfte des 20. Jahrhunderts," in *Ist zwîvel herzen nâchgebûr: Günther Schweikle zum 60. Geburtstag,* edited by Rüdiger Krüger and others (Stuttgart: Helfant, 1989), pp. 273-289;

Günter Lange, "Das Gerichtsverfahren gegen den jungen Helmbrecht: Versuch einer Deutung nach dem kodifizierten Recht und den Landfriedensordnungen des 13. Jahrhunderts," *Zeitschrift für deutsches Altertum und deutsche Literatur,* 99 (August 1970): 222-234;

Ernst Erich Metzner, "*Râte iu wol ein tumbe!:* Zu Titel, Thema, Textbestand und Textgestalt der Beispielerzählung vom Helmbrecht," *Zeitschrift für deutsches Altertum und deutsche Literatur,* 107, no. 4 (1978): 276-297;

Ernst von Reusner, "Helmbrecht," *Wirkendes Wort,* 22 (March/April 1972): 108-122;

Anton Schwob, "Die Kriminalisierung des Aufsteigers im mittelhochdeutschen Tierepos vom 'Fuchs Reinhart' und im Märe vom 'Helmbrecht,' " in *Zur gesellschaftlichen Funktionalität mittelalterlicher deutscher Literatur* (Greifswald: Ernst-Moritz-Arndt Universität, 1984), pp. 42-67;

Ulrich Seelbach, *Späthöfische Literatur und Rezeption: Studien zum Publikum des "Helmbrecht" von Wernher dem Gartenaere* (Berlin: Schmidt, 1987);

Seelbach, "Die werdent ouch Helmbrehtel . . . Zu den Prager und Wiener Helmbrechten im Spätmittelalter," *Beiträge zur Geschichte der deutschen Sprache und Literatur,* 109, no. 2 (1987): 252–273;

Bernhard Sowinski, *Wernher der Gartenaere, Helmbrecht: Interpretation* (Munich: Oldenbourg, 1971);

Horst Wenzel, " 'Helmbrecht' wider Habsburg: Das Märe von Wernher dem Gärtner in der Auffassung der Zeitgenossen," *Euphorion,* 71, no. 3 (1977): 230–249;

Edmund Wiessner, "Helmbrecht und Neidharts Strophen über Hildemar," *Beiträge zur Geschichte der deutschen Sprache und Literatur,* 49 (September 1924): 152–158.

Wirnt von Grafenberg

(circa 1170? – circa 1235?)

Ernst S. Dick
University of Kansas

MAJOR WORK: *Wigalois* (circa 1210–1215)

Manuscripts: A relatively large number of manuscripts, dating from the early thirteenth to the late fifteenth centuries, have been preserved: thirteen complete manuscripts, some with minor gaps, and twenty-nine fragments. The earliest are the manuscript A (Cologne) and the fragment E (Vienna), both from early-thirteenth-century Bavaria.

First publication: *Wigalois, der Ritter mit dem Rade,* edited by George Friedrich Benecke (Berlin: Reimer, 1819).

Standard edition: *Wigalois, der Ritter mit dem Rade, von Wirnt von Gravenberc,* edited by Johannes Marie Neele Kapteyn, *Rheinische Beiträge und Hülfsbücher zur germanischen Philologie und Volkskunde,* volume 9 (Bonn: Klopp, 1926).

Edition in English: Translated by John Wesley Thomas as *Wigalois, The Knight of Fortune's Wheel* (Lincoln: University of Nebraska Press, 1977).

Wirnt von Grafenberg's fame as an author of Arthurian romance rests on *Wigalois* (circa 1210–1215 or circa 1235). A courtly epic of nearly twelve thousand lines, it exceeds the length of Hartmann von Aue's *Erec* (circa 1180) and *Iwein* (circa 1203), the two major earlier works in the "classical" form of the genre, as well as Ulrich von Zatzikhoven's *Lanzelet* (circa 1194–1203), the first of the so-called postclassical Arthurian romances. Compared with epic works such as Wolfram von Eschenbach's *Parzival* (circa 1200–1210) or Gottfried von Straßburg's *Tristan und Isolde* (circa 1210), which clearly transcend the genre conventions, its size and scope appear modest; within the confines of the genre, however, it stands out as a major example of the postclassical group that departs from the structural conventions of the narrative form introduced by Chrétien de Troyes and embraces a new model of romance construction, with a new type of hero inspired by the fairy tale and Christian legend. In *Wigalois* the otherworldly Christian realms of purgatory and hell are presented on the same level of reality as the terrorist rule of a pagan usurper. At the same time the work is open to the concerns of the actual world. In its emphasis on the fantastic, *Wigalois* has much in common with the work in which this tendency culminates, Heinrich von dem Türlîn's *Diu Crône* (The Crown, circa 1230). To achieve its serious moral purpose, however, *Wigalois* creates a new model in which Arthurian ideality is found side by side with remarkable political and social realism.

Little is known about the author. His name is attested in several places in his own work (lines 141, 5755, and 10576) as well as in references by such contemporary authors as Konrad von Würzburg and Rudolf von Ems. Grafenberg (*Gravenberc* or

Illustration of the hero slaying the dragon Pfetan from a manuscript of Wirnt von Grafenberg's Wigalois *produced in the workshop of Diebold Lauber in Hagenau between 1427 and 1467 (Donaueschingen, Fürstliche Fürstenbergischen Hofsbibliothek, Ms. 71, f. 199)*

Gravenberg in the manuscripts) has been identified as Gräfenberg, located in Bavaria between Nuremberg and Bayreuth.

The dates of Wirnt's birth and death are unknown. No event of his life has been established with certainty, and the dating of his work has proven unusually difficult – in older scholarship it was given as 1204–1206; now it is usually dated 1210–1215 but also as late as after 1234. Wirnt belongs roughly to the same generation as his two great models, Wolfram and Hartmann; judging from his work, he seems younger than either. A legal document from the monastery of Weißenohe, south of Gräfenberg, which records a Wirrito de Greuenberc in 1172, must refer to an earlier member of Wirnt's family rather than to the poet himself.

Konrad's verse narrative *Der Welt Lohn* (The World's Reward, circa 1270–1280) includes a rare fictional portrayal of another author. It has always been tempting to fill the vacuum in Wirnt's biography with some of the information in Konrad's sketch of "von Grâvenberc her Wirent." Although this picture must be dismissed as completely stereotyped, in keeping with the design of the story, one point remains noteworthy: Wirnt is referred to as *her,* which indicates that he was a free knight rather than a knight in service; the title probably reflects his social status, since Konrad is not the only author to use this designation for Wirnt. Konrad's story, which features the ambivalent death-in-life figure of Frau Welt (Dame World) as a temptress, depicts the hero's spiritual renewal and ends with his taking part in a Crusade. The theme may have been suggested by Wirnt's emphatic use of *laudatio temporis acti* (praise of past times) and his highly critical stance regarding the state of the world in general and the decline of chivalry in particular. Given the strong religious disposition reflected in the narrator's comments in *Wigalois,* Wirnt may actually have taken part in a Crusade. Certainly the descriptive detail he includes about the Orient suggests familiarity with the locale of the Crusades. He might have joined the Crusade of 1217–1218, in which many nobles from his region took part. But a strong case has also been made for the Crusade of Friedrich II in 1228–1229.

An affiliation with a major regional court is indicated by places and events referred to in his composition, such as the Sant south of Nuremberg (line 8447), a popular place for tournaments, and especially the allusion to the grief caused by the death of a "fürst" (prince) of Meran

(lines 8063–8064). The title *Herzog von Meran* (Duke of Meran) was carried by the count of Andechs; the more loosely used designation *fürst* could, however, according to Albert Schreiber, also refer to a prominent member of the duke's family. Depending on whether the "prince" in question was Count Berthold IV of Andechs (Berthold I of Meran), who died in 1204; Count Otto VII (Otto I of Meran), who died in 1234; or Margrave Heinrich IV of Istria, who died in 1228, *Wigalois* has been dated after 1204, after 1234, and after 1228, respectively. The locations of the Meran family's residences in southern Bavaria – at Andechs and later at Dießen on the Ammersee, southwest of Munich – fit into what is known about Wirnt's language, which has been identified as South Bavarian, and also about the earlier manuscript tradition, which likewise points to the southern part of Bavaria. But while the Andechs family must have played an important role in Wirnt's life, at least one further connection merits consideration: given the traditional ties between Wirnt's hometown of Gräfenberg and the Zollern family in Nuremberg, his reference to the Sant of Nuremberg may reflect a closer relationship with, if not employment by, the counts of Nuremberg, who were also called the "Herren vom Sant."

Wirnt's work also provides the only clues to his education. Although he was a literate knight, who knew some French and apparently also some Latin, it is not certain whether he received any formal education in a monastery school. He certainly had a good knowledge of contemporary German literature, especially of the epic works of his time. The eponymous heroes of *Erec, Iwein,* and *Lanzelet,* along with Gawein, the hero's father, form the group of four Arthurian knights who join the festivities at Wigalois's wedding and later take part in the campaign against Count Lion of Namur. Whether Wirnt had firsthand knowledge of French works in the genre of Arthurian romance remains uncertain. In *Wigalois* he says that he heard the story from a squire (lines 11687–11690). While immediate French sources have not been identified, there are obvious plot parallels with the verse epic *Le Bel Inconnu* (The Handsome Stranger, circa 1185–1190; also known as *Guinglain*) of Renaut de Beaujeux.

A verse adaptation of *Wigalois* was prepared by Ulrich Füetrer in Munich around 1480. By including it in his *Buch der Abenteuer* (Book of Adventures), a vast compilation of Arthurian romance, Füetrer made the Wigalois story part of the cultural heritage that he reconstructed for an aristocratic audience of a new era. The story was reworked in a prose version and printed in Augsburg in 1493. The most unusual adaptation, however, is *Artushof* (Arthur's Court; also known as *Ritter Widuwilt* [Knight Widuwilt]), a Yiddish version in verse printed in Amsterdam by Josel von Witzenhausen in 1683. The three extant manuscripts of this work are from the sixteenth century, but the adaptation itself could be much older. Scenes and comments that were not suited to the new audience have been eliminated, as Robert G. Warnock has shown. In any case, it is, as Christoph Cormeau points out, the only known Arthurian text in a Yiddish adaptation.

The reception of *Wigalois* also extends to the pictorial arts. Apart from the manuscript illustrations, the frescoes of the castle of Runkelstein in Tirol, north of Bozen, have been the subject of scholarly attention. Among figures and scenes from heroic legend, from *Tristan und Isolde*, and from Der Pleier's *Garel von dem blühenden Tal* (Garel of the Flowering Valley, circa 1250), they originally featured a cycle of about forty pictures from *Wigalois*. While the castle was built soon after the composition of *Wigalois* in the first half of the thirteenth century, the frescoes date from around 1400. Owing to the interest of Emperor Maximilian I they were renewed early in the sixteenth century, but some were later destroyed.

Wirnt's aesthetic orientation is reflected in his prologue to *Wigalois*. The emphasis is, as is usual in epic poetry, on the pursuit of truth, but there is also a new interest in didacticism. By linking epic poetry with teaching, Wirnt's aesthetic implies less an actual search for truth than an application of given models of truth and of pre-established ideals of human perfection. Where Hartmann, Gottfried, and Wolfram were deeply committed to finding a utopian ideal or defining a new form of humanity, Wirnt proceeds from ideals that already exist; the renewal of the human community is to be achieved by reactivating time-honored models of universal appeal. His emphatic criticism of the social and moral conditions of his time shows that he was seeking the reestablishment of a spiritual and legal order that existed in an idealized past. Wirnt's ideal past is a fictional product, a conglomerate of ideals from history, religion, and fiction. From history is derived the Carolingian model of justice, "Karles reht" (Charlemagne's legal order, line 9554); from religion comes the Redeemer's victory over the forces of Satan in hell; from fiction is taken the Arthurian model of an ideal society. "Karles reht" is introduced by Wigalois when he becomes king; Christ's descent to the underworld is re-created in the protagonist's successful fight against Roaz, an otherworldly opponent in league with the forces of the devil; and the society of the Round Table is reestablished by the protagonist's being the son of Gawein, by the important role played by four of the best-known Arthurian knights, and by the suggestion of a translation of the Arthurian world to the realm of Wigalois; while at the beginning Wigalois's challenge consists in proving himself another Gawein, at the end Gawein seems to grow increasingly into the world of his son.

Wirnt's poetics may not be as strikingly inventive as those of his more experimentally inclined contemporaries. It is, nevertheless, an essentially experimental poetics in its own right. Werner Schröder had ample reason to call Wirnt's approach "syncretistic." It is no doubt eclectic, as are the experimental constructions of his contemporaries. Wirnt's accomplishment was to mold diverse traditional components into a coherent aesthetic of romance that, as Max Wehrli suggests, creates the impression of an aesthetic of the modern novel.

The construction of the story is remarkably straightforward. It differs from other Arthurian romances in that it has a Gawein section at the beginning and also ends with a section in which Gawein plays a prominent part. He is the knight whom a stranger, King Joram, who comes to Arthur's court, has singled out as the husband for his niece in his otherworldly mountain kingdom. Defeated by the visitor, who has the help of a magic girdle, Gawein must follow Joram to his realm and marry the beautiful Florîe. But he soon abandons her and returns to the pleasures of the Round Table. There, however, his love for Florîe causes Gawein to reverse his decision, but he discovers that he cannot find the way back to her realm without the help of the magic girdle. So he resigns himself to an unhappy future and returns to the Round Table. In the meantime, his son Wigalois is born and grows up at Florîe's court to become a splendid knight. He sets out to find his father and eventually arrives at Arthur's court, where he is welcomed as a perfect knight – a magic stone on which he happened to rest has proved him to be as immaculate as no other knight except Arthur himself. He gives his name as "Gwî von Galois" (line 1574). He and Gawein do not recognize each other as father and son. Gawein becomes his mentor.

Queen Amena giving Wigalois the hand of Princess Larie in the Lauber manuscript (Donaueschingen, Fürstliche Fürstenbergischen Hofbibliothek, Ms. 71)

The main part of the story starts with the appearance of another figure from a strange place in need of a suitable hero. This time the task is to liberate the land of Korntin, and the messenger, a woman named Nereja, has Gawein in mind as the hero. The land is held by the usurper Roaz, who has slain King Lar and his followers. Lar's widow, Queen Amena, and their daughter, Princess Larie, have survived and are in exile at the castle of Roimunt. When, instead of Gawein, Wigalois takes on this adventure, Nereja is outraged by his youthful appearance and his presumable lack of prowess. Ignoring her resistance, Wigalois persistently adheres to his mission. His success in a series of five adventures on the way to Korntin leads Nereja to accept him. When they reach Roimunt he immediately falls in love with Larie.

At this point the story takes a turn toward the supernatural. The spirit of King Lar appears in the shape of a fantastic animal – half leopard, half stag – to guide Wigalois to the castle of Korntin and prepare him for the dangers ahead. The setting at Korntin contains motifs of the traditional picture of Purgatory but also a "paradise" where Lar periodically regains his human form. From Lar Wigalois learns that Gawein is his father. Equipped with a blossom from the paradise tree and a lance from heaven, he starts out to fight the dragon, Pfetan, that terrorizes the land. After killing the dragon and saving the life of one of its intended victims, Count Moral, he falls unconscious. A fisherman and his wife find him lying by the lake and rob him of his armor. When he regains consciousness, he does not remember who he is. Moral's wife, Beleare, discovers him and gradually restores his memory of his identity. As he continues on his way to Glois to battle Roaz, his life is repeatedly threatened by various demonic creatures; but in each crisis he turns to God, who never fails to save him. This second sequence of adventures contains five such incidents that lead up to the culminating event, the encounter with Roaz. The fierce fight against the satanic knight, carried out in the presence of Roaz's wife Japhite and twelve of her maidens, takes place after midnight. The defeat of Roaz causes Japhite to die of grief. Roaz is carried away by a band of devils, and his pagan followers are converted to Christianity.

Wigalois's victory is followed by his coronation as king of Korntin and his wedding with Larie. These events take place at Moral's castle at Joraphas. Four Arthurian knights, including Gawein, join the festivities. Just when the end of the story seems near, the appearance of yet another messenger pleading for help starts a new chapter. One of the wedding guests, King Amire of Libya, has been killed on his way by Count Lion of Namur, who hoped to win the love of Amire's beautiful wife, Liamere. After a siege of six weeks Lion is defeated by Gawein. On the way to a brief visit at Arthur's court Gawein and Wigalois receive the news of Florîe's death. After the visit Wigalois returns to Korntin, where he and his wife spend the rest of their lives in happiness. The story concludes with a reference to the untold story of their son, Lifort Gawanides.

Wigalois is the story of a knight under the special protection of *sælde* (fortune). His heraldic emblem, a golden wheel derived from the Wheel of Fortune in the castle of his mother's otherworldly mountain realm, accounts for his epithet, *der Ritter mit dem Rade* (the Knight with the Wheel).

The otherworldly background on Wigalois's mother's side is balanced by the Arthurian component represented by his father. Gawein is a key figure in the story: before being aware of Wigalois's identity, he provides the model for his son's chivalrous education. Gawein is the only hero believed capable of undertaking the central adventure, the delivery of Korntin; finally, he plays the most decisive role in the final campaign against Lion. In these diverse functions Gawein exceeds by far the mere role as the hero's father, which should be confined to the *Vorgeschichte* (background material preceding the main story). The *Vorgeschichte* in *Wigalois,* in fact, seems to be designed to introduce the story of Gawein rather than that of his son.

To an extent, then, *Wigalois* is also a story about Gawein. It is the first German Arthurian romance to start out as a story of Gawein as a hero in his own right. Furthermore, Wirnt appears to view Wigalois as a hero of the type represented by Gawein, and this choice has consequences for the narrative form he uses. The French romances about Gauvain, for example, although clearly influenced by Chrétien's classic type of romance, tend to favor new narrative strategies, such as compilation instead of composition, or a tendency toward realism. The German romances featuring Gawein or similar icons of chivalric success likewise depart from the classic structure established by Chrétien. Once regarded as mere products of epigonism or unimaginative imitation, they are now recognized as respectable and even innovative attempts at a different form of romance. *Wigalois* shares many of the distinctive features of this new form. At the same time, the work's theme and structure are unique.

Perhaps the most characteristic feature of postclassical romance, as represented by *Wigalois,* consists in the new concept of the hero. In contrast to the typical hero of classical romance, Gawein and Wigalois are perfect from the beginning. Thus, they experience no spiritual crisis followed by inner rebirth. Unlike Iwein or Parzival, this type of hero pursues his chivalric career in the form of a linear ascent toward a predictable goal rather than in two contrasting phases reflected in a bipartite narrative structure. Since the challenges faced by the postclassical knight do not constitute serious threats to his spiritual integrity and perfection as a knight, they simply serve as tests that allow the hero to prove himself. Gawein's role in *Wigalois* is that of a universally recognized paragon of chivalry, while Wigalois starts out as someone whose superiority, although not yet in evidence to the outside world, has already been established for those at the Round Table through the testimony of the magic stone. In the end his absolutely flawless character clearly surpasses the moral standing of his father, the standard against which he is at first measured.

What distinguishes *Wigalois* from other romances of its kind is the author's experiment with a new form of multisegment composition. The hero's progress, although conceived of as an essentially linear ascent, is carried out in three distinct stages. In the first section the protagonist, setting out to deliver the kingdom of Korntin from its evil usurper, proceeds through two clearly distinguished sequences of adventures: five chivalrous encounters on the way to Korntin, which prove his readiness as a knight and lead to his confirmation for the major adventure; and the continuation of his journey from the first destination, Korntin, to the residence of the usurper Roaz at Glois. The transition to the second section is marked by the fight with the dragon and accentuated by the hero's symbolic death. The second section, also made up of a sequence of five adventures, differs from the first on account of its emphasis on the demonic and supernatural; its goal is the victory over the usurper, who, through his association with the devil, embodies the power of evil. Instead of concluding the romance in the classical fashion with the delivery of the land and the wedding of Wigalois and Larie, the narrative strategy takes a completely new and unparalleled turn with a third section: the elaborate campaign against Lion. Once more the forces of evil threaten the order of society, but this time they are completely dissociated from any otherworldly context. Only after Wigalois, decisively aided by Gawein, defeats Lion and his forces does the romance end on a more conventional note: a reunion at Arthur's court and the final return of Wigalois to his new kingdom of Korntin.

By adding a third part, Wirnt clearly goes beyond the scope of Arthurian romance. A military campaign at the height of a hero's career is neither Arthurian nor particularly suitable for the genre of romance. Wigalois's transformation at the end into a military leader is hard to dismiss as a mere extension of the plot to demonstrate the hero's qualifications as a ruler; the focus appears to shift from the hero as an individual to society as a whole. In promptly responding to a particularly heinous act of violence (the killing of a king to win his queen), Wigalois certainly acts as a responsible king. But by forming an impressive alliance of western and eastern vassals and friends, including Gawein and three other knights of the Round Table, Wigalois more than matches his opponent's international connections, thus prevailing in the battle of politics and strategy even before the physical defeat of the evil ruler. His accomplishment in terms of realpolitik goes far beyond a token demonstration of his ability to live up to the ideal of a Christian king: he restores the critically disturbed order of the international community. To have one's hero triumph not only in adventures in the otherworld but in a conflict in the historical reality of courts, cities, and kingdoms is a new element in the romance genre. The campaign not only involves the Arthurian world but also draws on the international dynastic network outside the fictional realm of the Round Table. By having the protagonist pursue the cause of justice, conciliation, and lasting peace, *Wigalois* reflects actual political concerns of the time. Little of the final part of the work has its roots in the genre of romance; it is more reminiscent of the heroic epic, the chanson de geste, or the Crusade epic. Wirnt's reason for combining incompatible genres must be sought in his deep concern with the cultural decline of society in the feudal world, a concern that is emphatically reflected in comments by the narrator. By employing literary forms more suited to the message of restoring the ideal of social order than to redefining a fictional hero's individual moral and spiritual constitution, Wirnt von Grafenberg contributes a new sense of social realism to the genre of romance.

References:

Christoph Cormeau, "Die jiddische Tradition von Wirnts *Wigalois*: Bemerkungen zum Fortleben einer Fabel unter veränderten Bedingungen," *Zeitschrift für Literaturwissenschaft und Linguistik*, 8, no. 32 (1978): 28–44;

Cormeau, *'Wigalois' und 'Diu Crône': Zwei Kapitel zur Gattungsgeschichte des nachklassischen Aventiureromans* (Munich: Artemis, 1977);

Carola L. Gottzmann, *Deutsche Artusdichtung*, volume 1: *Rittertum, Minne, Ehe und Herrschertum: Die Artusepik der hochhöfischen Zeit* (Frankfurt am Main: Lang, 1986);

Klaus Grubmüller, "Artusroman und Heilsbringerethos: Zum 'Wigalois' des Wirnt von Gravenberg," *Beiträge zur Geschichte der deutschen Sprache und Literatur* (Tübingen), 107, no. 2 (1985): 218–239;

Walter Haug, "Paradigmatische Poesie: Der spätere deutsche Artusroman auf dem Weg zu einer 'nachklassischen' Ästhetik," *Deutsche Vierteljahrsschrift für Literaturwissenschaft und Geistesgeschichte*, 54 (1980): 204–231;

Haug and others, eds., *Runkelstein: Die Wandmalereien des Sommerhauses* (Wiesbaden: Reichert, 1982);

Ingeborg Henderson, "Dark Figures and Eschatological Imagery in Wirnt von Gravenberg's *Wigalois*," in *The Dark Figure in Medieval German and Germanic Literature*, edited by Edward R. Haymes and Stephanie Cain Van D'Elden (Göppingen: Kümmerle, 1986), pp. 99–113;

Henderson, "Selbstentfremdung im *Wigalois* Wirnts von Grafenberg," *Colloquia Germanica*, 13, no. 1 (1980): 35–46;

Gert Kaiser, "Der *Wigalois* des Wirnt von Grâvenberc: Zur Bedeutung des Territorialisierungsprozesses für die 'höfisch-ritterliche' Literatur des 13. Jahrhunderts," *Euphorion*, 69, no. 4 (1975): 410–443;

Gisela Lohbeck, *Wigalois: Struktur der* bezeichenunge (Frankfurt am Main: Lang, 1991);

Volker Mertens, "Iwein und Gwigalois – der Weg zur Landesherrschaft," *Germanisch-Romanische Monatsschrift*, new series 31 (1981): 14–31;

Friedrich Neumann, "Wann verfaßte Wirnt den 'Wigalois'?," *Zeitschrift für deutsches Altertum*, 94 (1964): 31–62;

Albert Schreiber, "Über Wirnt von Graefenberg und den Wigalois," *Zeitschrift für deutsche Philologie*, 58 (1933): 209–231;

Werner Schröder, "Der synkretistische Roman des Wirnt von Gravenberg: Unerledigte Fragen an den *Wigalois*," *Euphorion*, 80, no. 3 (1986): 235–277;

Neil Thomas, *A German View of Camelot; Wirnt von Gravenberg's* Wigalois *and Arthurian Tradition* (Frankfurt am Main: Lang, 1987);

Thomas, "Literary Transformation and Narrative Organization in Wirnt von Gravenberg's *Wigalois*," *Modern Language Review*, 80 (April 1985): 362–371;

Thomas, *The Medieval German Arthuriad: Some Contemporary Revaluations of the Canon* (Frankfurt am Main: Lang, 1989), pp. 105–157;

Robert G. Warnock, "Wirkungsabsicht und Bearbeitungstechnik im altjiddischen 'Artushof,'" *Zeitschrift für deutsche Philologie*, 100 (1981): 98–109;

Max Wehrli, "Wigalois," *Der Deutschunterricht*, 17, no. 2 (1965): 18–35; republished in his *Formen mittelalterlicher Erzählung: Aufsätze* (Zurich & Freiburg: Atlantis, 1969), pp. 223–241.

Wolfram von Eschenbach

(circa 1170 – after 1220)

Marianne Wynn
University of London

Seven Songs (circa 1200?)

Manuscripts: The songs are extant in three major manuscripts that date from the turn of the twelfth to the thirteenth century. There are four strophes in A, the Kleine Heidelberger Liederhandschrift (Heidelberg, Universitätsbibliothek, cpg 357), and three songs in B, the Weingartner Handschrift (Stuttgart, Württembergische Landesbibliothek, HB XIII, 1). Nine songs are attributed to Wolfram in C, the Manessische or Große Heidelberger Liederhandschrift (Heidelberg, Universitätsbibliothek, cpg 848), and two songs in G, the Munich manuscript of *Parzival* (Munich, Bayerische Staatsbibliothek, cgm 19).

First publication: Two songs in *Auswahl aus den Hochdeutschen Dichtern des dreizehnten Jahrhunderts: Für Vorlesungen und zum Schulgebrauch,* edited by Karl Lachmann (Berlin, 1820).

Standard edition: In *Die Lyrik Wolframs von Eschenbach: Edition Kommentar Interpretation,* edited by Peter Wapnewski (Munich: Beck, 1972).

Edition in modern German: In *Titurel; Lieder: Mittelhochdeutscher Text und Übersetzung,* edited and translated by Wolfgang Mohr (Göppingen: Kümmerle, 1978).

Editions in English: Translated by Arthur T. Hatto, in his *Eos: An Enquiry into the Theme of Lovers' Meetings and Partings at Dawn in Poetry* (London, The Hague & Paris: Mouton, 1965), pp. 448–455; translated by Olive Sayce, in *The Medieval German Lyric 1150–1300* (Oxford: Clarendon Press, 1982), pp. 211–216; translated by Marion E. Gibbs and Sidney M. Johnson, in their *Wolfram von Eschenbach: Titurel and the Songs. Texts and Translations with Introduction, Notes and Comments* (New York & London: Garland, 1988), pp. 70–111.

Parzival (circa 1200–1210)

Manuscripts: The work has been handed down in more than eighty manuscripts, sixteen of which give the complete version; no other court romance has been transmitted in so many manuscripts. The main manuscripts on which the standard edition is based are D (Saint Gall, Stiftsbibliothek, 857) and G (Munich, Bayerische Staatsbibliothek, cgm 19).

First publication: *Parzival* (Strasbourg: Printed by Johann Mentelin, 1477).

Standard edition: In *Wolfram von Eschenbach,* edited by Karl Lachmann (Berlin: Reimer, 1833; revised, edited by Moriz Haupt, 1854).

Editions in modern German: *Parzival,* translated by Wolfgang Mohr (Göppingen: Kümmerle, 1977); *Parzival,* 2 volumes, translated by Wolfgang Spiewok (Stuttgart: Reclam, 1981).

Editions in English: Translated by Helen M. Mustard and Charles E. Passage as *Parzival* (New York: Vintage, 1961); translated by Arthur T. Hatto as *Parzival* (Harmondsworth, U.K.: Penguin, 1980).

Willehalm (circa 1210–1220)

Manuscripts: The transmission of this unfinished work comprises more than seventy manuscripts, twelve of which include as much of the work as Wolfram completed. The earliest of the latter, the Saint Gall manuscript (Saint Gall, Stiftsbibliothek, 857) dates from the thirteenth century and forms the basis for the three standard editions of the work. The oldest of the fragments can be dated to the first half of the thirteenth century (Munich, Bayerische Staatsbibliothek, cgm 193 III).

First publication: *Wilhelm der Heilige von Oranse: Zweyter Theil von Wolfram von Eschilbach, einem Dichter des schwäbischen Zeitpuncts,* edited by Wilhelm Johann Christian Gustav Casparson (Cassel, 1784).

Standard editions: In *Wolfram von Eschenbach,* edited by Karl Lachmann, sixth edition, edited by Eduard Hartl (Berlin & Leipzig: De Gruyter, 1926); in *Wolfram von Eschenbach,* edited by Albert Leitzmann, volumes 4–5, Altdeutsche

Illustration for Wolfram von Eschenbach's Parzival *in the Große Heidelberger Liederhandschrift (Heidelberg, Universitätsbibliothek, cpg 848, f. 149v)*

Textbibliothek (Tübingen: Niemeyer, 1963); *Willehalm,* edited by Werner Schröder (Berlin & New York: De Gruyter, 1978); *Willehalm,* edited by Joachim Heinzle (Frankfurt am Main: Bibliothek deutscher Klassiker, 1991).

Edition in modern German: *Willehalm, aus dem Mittelhochdeutschen übertragen,* translated by Reinhard Fink and Friedrich Knorr (Jena: Diederichs, 1941).

Editions in English: Translated by Charles E. Passage as *The Middle High German Poem of Willehalm by Wolfram von Eschenbach* (New York: Ungar, 1977); translated by Marion E. Gibbs and Sidney M. Johnson as *Willehalm* (Harmondsworth, U.K.: Penguin, 1984).

Titurel (circa 1217)

Manuscripts: The work is extant in three manuscripts. The *Parzival* manuscript G (Mu-

nich, Bayerische Staatsbibliothek, cgm 19) contains both fragments. The first sixty-eight strophes of the first fragment are preserved in H, the Ambraser Heldenbuch (Vienna, Östereichische Nationalbibliothek, 2663), and forty-eight strophes of the same fragment are in M (Munich, Universitätsbibliothek, Ms 154).

First publication: *Titurel* (Strasbourg: Printed by Johann Mentelin, 1477).

Standard edition: In *Wolfram von Eschenbach,* edited by Karl Lachmann, sixth edition, revised by Eduard Hartl (Berlin & Leipzig: De Gruyter, 1926) in *Wolfram von Eschenbach,* edited by Albert Leitzmann, volume 5, Altdeutsche Textbibliothek (Tübingen: Niemeyer, 1963).

Edition in modern German: In *Titurel; Lie-*

der: Mittelhochdeutscher Text und Übersetzung, edited and translated by Wolfgang Mohr (Göppingen: Kümmerle, 1978).

Editions in English: Translated by Charles E. Passage, in his *Titurel: Wolfram von Eschenbach. Translation and Studies* (New York: Ungar, 1984); translated by Marion E. Gibbs and Sidney M. Johnson, in their *Wolfram von Eschenbach: Titurel and the Songs. Texts and Translations with Introduction, Notes and Comments* (New York & London: Garland, 1988).

One of the great poets of all time, Wolfram von Eschenbach was conscious of his stature and emphasizes it unashamedly in one of his major works: "ich bin Wolfram von Eschenbach unt kan ein teil mit sange" (114, 12–13 [all citations refer to the standard edition of Wolfram's works by Albert Leitzmann, 1963]: I am Wolfram von Eschenbach and do know a thing or two about poetry). Many of his contemporaries agreed with this self-assessment. Wirnt von Grafenberg, for example, maintained that "leien munt nie baz gesprach" (no layman's tongue has ever uttered finer poetry). His great rival, Gottfried von Straßburg, on the other hand, assigned Wolfram to the meretricious practitioners of literature, the paid hacks and obscurantists. Gottfried's crushing verdict did not gain wide currency. Wolfram was held in great reverence both by contemporary and later authors who refer to him or show themselves to have been influenced by him. Moreover, all three of his main works were seized on eagerly by poets who continued and enlarged them. That his works enjoyed widespread admiration among listeners and readers is borne out by the unusually large number of manuscripts that have been handed down.

Despite his fame, everything that is known about him has to be inferred from his work, from references to him in other works of literature, and from general information about his time. There is no direct documentary evidence about him. But at least one can be certain of his name, for he gives it several times, and other writers also mention it. His homeland was Franconia; he mentions several places in the vicinity of the Frankish town of Eschenbach (now Wolframs-Eschenbach), among them Abenberg, Nördlingen, and the Sant near Nuremberg. During his lifetime Eschenbach was a hamlet; like every other village in central Europe it cannot have consisted of more than a few wattle and daub cottages. There was a church, consecrated in the eleventh century, which means Wolfram would have had regular contact with a priest. A

community like Eschenbach, however, could hardly have hoped to have the services of a learned clergyman. At some point Wolfram left the village, but he never traveled far. There is no evidence that he went on a pilgrimage to Rome or to the Holy Land, two of the main destinations of the medieval traveler, or that he joined a Crusade. It would appear that he never left the German-speaking territories.

One of the greatest magnates of his time, Hermann, Landgrave of Thuringia, seems to have been his patron for a while. The Thuringian court rivaled that of the emperor. The Wartburg at Eisenach was no mere castle; it was a palace. In a commanding position, high on a mountain promontory, it dominates the surrounding forests and valleys. Hermann kept a lavish court and was known to be an open-handed patron of the arts. At the Thuringian court Wolfram would have met the learned clerks of a first-rate chancery; great ladies, well versed in literature; political schemers; cavalrymen; foot soldiers; free lances; and entertainers of every conceivable sort – jesters, singers, and conjurers but also serious artists. Hermann's court had a reputation for rowdiness, yet it was also a cultural center, rather like the Babenberg court of Vienna. It is not difficult to recognize the ambience of this court in Wolfram's works – for example, in his portrayals of the court of King Arthur in *Parzival* (circa 1200–1210). Wolfram had connections with lesser courts as well. He was familiar with Wildenberg Castle, an imposing stronghold on a spur in the Odenwald near Amorbach owned by the rich lords of Durne. It was one of the finest castles of the Hohenstaufen period, though not as grand as the Wartburg. Wolfram's relationship with this family is unknown. The same is true of his connection with Count Wertheim, whose castle stood on the river Main. The Wertheims were neighbors of the Durnes and also had property in Eschenbach. Wolfram mentions Count Wertheim in a manner that leaves it unclear whether the two men knew one another. Wolfram also speaks of a patroness, whose name he does not reveal, three times in *Parzival;* he describes her as a *wîp* (woman), not as a *vrouwe* (noblewoman).

Wolfram, thus, had patrons, but he would hardly have been able to make a regular living from his poetry. A patron would commission a work, offer board and lodging to the poet while it was being composed, pay for the vellum, and supply a secretary for dictation. The poet might also receive a gift, but it would not be enough for him to live on, let alone to support a family. Wolfram begins to plead poverty early in his career, and although such hard-luck claims were a cliché among the beggar-

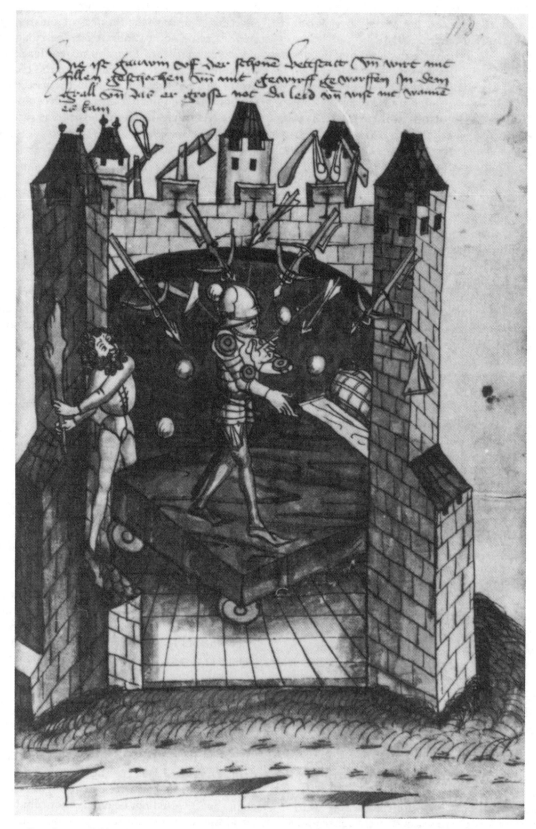

Page from a mid-fifteenth-century manuscript for Parzival, *with an illustration depicting Gawan in his struggle with the magic bed at Schastel Marveile (Bern, Stadtbibliothek, COD. 91, f. 118r)*

poets of the Middle Ages, there is no reason to dismiss Wolfram's statements as nonautobiographical. The same applies to his mention of a wife and a daughter.

Proud as he was of his achievement as a poet, Wolfram was prouder still of his vocation as a soldier. He claims that he is a military man and offers the opinion that only a silly woman will love him for his poetry: love must be won in a passage of arms. His remark "schildes ambet ist min art" (115, 11) is ambiguous; its meaning could mean either "the office of the shield is my vocation" or "the office of the shield is mine by heredity." At any rate, he introduces himself as a shield-bearing man-at-arms. It has been argued that he assumes the guise of a knight for his persona as a narrator and that his self-description need bear no relation to his life. As the context in which this statement appears is neither ironic nor humorous, however, there seems little ground for disbelieving him.

He would not have been a foot soldier; they were the lowest social group among the fighting men, and Wolfram could hardly have expressed pride at belonging to their ranks. As a cavalryman he could have been a mercenary, a vassal, or a member of a magnate's household troop. His pride in his profession as a soldier points to the last possibility: mercenaries were considered unreliable because they followed the highest bidder, while vassals owed only forty days of military service a year and ignored the liege lord's summonses whenever they could. The elite group among the mounted shock troops in medieval warfare was a landowner's private army, and Wolfram may well have belonged to one. His knowledge of fighting techniques is considerable; throughout his works there are many descriptions of jousts, but unique in the literature of the time are his battle descriptions in his later epic, *Willehalm* (circa 1210–1220). They represent the first detailed strategic battle descriptions in medieval German literature.

He knew the work of Heinrich von Veldeke, Hartmann von Aue, Gottfried, Walther von der Vogelweide, and Neidhart von Reuental and was familiar with the *Kaiserchronik* (Emperor Chronicle, circa 1135–1150), the *Rolandslied* (Song of Roland, circa 1100) and the *Alexanderlied* (Song of Alexander circa 1130–1150) of Pfaffe Lamprecht, the *Nibelungenlied* (Song of the Nibelungs, circa 1200), and an early version of the Tristan story by Eilhart von Oberg. That he knew French is clear from his use of the source books for his two major narratives. He twice denies quite vehemently that he had any book learning, yet the disclaimer "ine kan decheinen

buochstap" (115, 27: I cannot make out a single letter) is an exact rendering of the phrase in Psalm 70:15, "non cognovi litteraturam," and his use of it as a reverse-modesty topos shows that he understood its double meaning. Moreover, he betrays extensive knowledge of theology, the natural sciences, cosmology, astronomy, and medicine. A fair amount of such knowledge could have been picked up by sitting in on conversations among those who were better educated than he, so that Wolfram could have gathered a good deal of learning without knowing much Latin. Although there is some dispute as to whether Wolfram could read, it is extremely unlikely that he could have constructed narratives on so grand a scale, and of such detailed complexity, as *Parzival* and *Willehalm* if he were illiterate.

With the death of the emperor Heinrich VI in 1197, the Hohenstaufen and Welf dynasties embarked on a power struggle that lasted for two decades. For some of this period Germany had two rival kings, the Hohenstaufen Philip II and the Welf Otto IV. By the time the Hohenstaufen Friedrich II was crowned emperor in 1220 there had been twelve royal and imperial elections and coronations in the Holy Roman Empire. Twice the head of state was excommunicated, for the Holy See also claimed its share of political power. The civil wars meant destruction of villages and crops, burning and looting, and perpetual fear. In 1217 famine began in the northern German regions, moved southward to Bavaria and Austria, and finally spread as far as Bohemia and Hungary. Corpses in towns and fields would have been a familiar sight. Although Wolfram does not comment on these events, he shows himself acutely aware of their results. He is the poet of compassion par excellence, with a supreme understanding of human misery.

Wolfram also composed his works in an age of faith. Heresies, Crusades, the expansion of the Cistercian order, and the rise of a religious movement among women were all part of it, and much of this preoccupation with religion is reflected in his narratives. He portrays the personal dilemmas in which people find themselves trapped through their religious beliefs, and he also meditates on complex theological questions.

The German Wolfram wrote is Frankish, with some Bavarian characteristics. Often his syntax is emotional rather than grammatical, suggesting the impulsiveness and casual incoherence of spoken language. His imagery is extravagant and frequently obscure. His vocabulary embraces bold coinages of his own invention, loan words from French, and ter-

Two of the four full-page illustrations in the early-thirteenth-century Munich Parzival Manuscript: (left, top to bottom) a banquet at King Arthur's court, the fight between Parzival and Feirefiz in the forest, the reconciliation of Parzival and Feirefiz; (right, top to bottom) Parzival and Feirefiz arriving at Arthur's camp, Cundrie pleading before the Round Table, Cundrie leading Parzival and Feirefiz to the Grail Castle (Munich, Bayerische Staatsbibliothek, cgm 19)

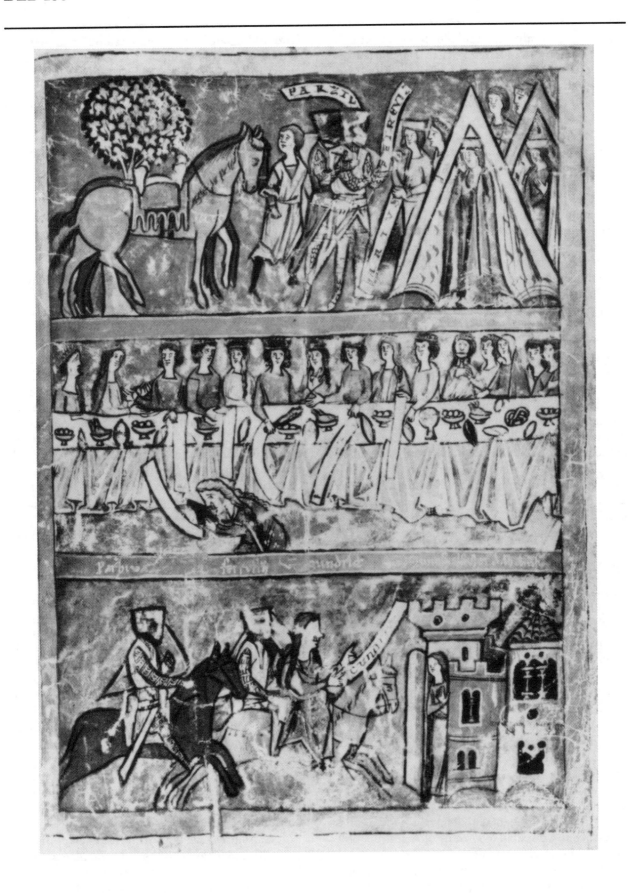

minology generally encountered in the heroic epic rather than in the courtly romance. He constructed his longer narratives on the basis of a unit of thirty lines of rhymed couplets, with verses of three or four beats. Their division into books (chapters) may have been introduced by scribes.

Wolfram's first major work of fiction, *Parzival,* is based on the unfinished court romance by Chrétien de Troyes, *Perceval le Gallois ou Le Conte du Graal* (Perceval the Gaul; or, The Tale of the Grail, circa 1180), whose plot accounts for books 3 to 13. Wolfram completed and expanded Chrétien's work and added a long introductory section and a conclusion, but on the whole he follows the action as set out by Chrétien. Even while adopting some of Chrétien's stylistic devices and structural patterns, however, he changes the French romance fundamentally. Many of his changes can be categorized as closer narrative definition; thus, he gives proper names to figures not named in his source, such as the hero's cousin, Sigune, and his mentor, Trevrizent. Altogether there are 222 named characters in the German work, against a mere handful in the French source. Many of these characters he links with one another in a network of two great families, the Grail dynasty and the Arthurian clan. The mere belonging of a figure to one or the other family characterizes his or her fundamental nature. In addition, Wolfram gives place-names to his settings, creating a full-fledged fictional geography consistent within itself and endowing certain backgrounds with symbolic significance. This world of fiction is set in contrast, and at the same time linked, with the world of reality. Furthermore, while the hero of the French work is introduced as a boy, the German work begins before his birth and gives a detailed prehistory – including the biographies of the hero's parents, particularly that of the father, establishing a pattern of inherited characteristics that will come to the fore in his hero's development. Taken from Chrétien is the double-hero structure, which Wolfram enhances through immense elaboration and subtle annotation.

The most momentous change Wolfram effects is to give the narrative an overriding theme. He announces in his introduction that the story he is about to unfold has the leitmotiv of *triuwe* (loyalty or faithfulness), which he links with true femininity and manliness. The basic meaning of *triuwe* is a capacity for loving in total selflessness, with a love that is wholly directed toward its object. It denotes the bond between humanity and God and declares itself as maternal and paternal love, love in marriage, love among siblings, love between friends, feudal allegiance, and compassion. Its archetypal and perfect manifestation is God. Many of the characters in *Parzival* exhibit this capacity. Parzival possesses it as his birthright, loses it, and must recover it. The poet says in the first words of the prologue that life will lead his hero through suffering, doubt, and despair but that by dint of single-mindedness and persistence he will find happiness and salvation.

The prologue is one of the most opaque passages in the work. Any interpretation of it will be controversial. It would appear that Wolfram was being deliberately cryptic: he speaks of a winged example that is much too quick for fools. He goes on to describe his style and the way in which it has been received by his public. Special instructions for women are given: they are to guard their honor and dignity and to bestow their love with care; outward beauty is less important by far than the beauty of character and soul. It is clear that Wolfram has his critics in mind, and one would assume, therefore, that this part of the prologue was written after large sections of the work had been made public. It seems reasonably certain that the instructions for women were aimed at the heroine of Gottfried's *Tristan und Isolde* (circa 1210). Gottfried sharply and brutally attacked Wolfram and his work, and Wolfram's counterattack pays Gottfried back in like coin. Gottfried's assault on Wolfram was couched in as mysterious a language and imagery as is Wolfram's response to it.

The third part of the prologue is the introduction proper to the narrative, stating its theme and introducing the hero. The story is as yet, however, not concerned with him.

The first two books are devoted to the hero's father, Gahmuret. When Gahmuret's father, the king, dies, the law of primogeniture leaves Gahmuret landless, and he becomes a free lance. He seeks his fortune in Europe, Asia, and Africa, achieving high distinction as a warrior. Reaching the besieged capital of a kingdom in Africa, he lifts the siege for its queen, Belakane. He falls in love with her, and they marry. Belakane conceives a son, but before he is born, Gahmuret grows restless. He leaves her by stealth, boarding a ship under cover of darkness. While he is at sea his son is born, a child of singular appearance, with checkered black and white skin, and hair colored like the feathers of a magpie. Belakane names him Feirefiz.

Gahmuret reaches Europe and makes his way to Seville and Toledo and then to the fictional kingdom of Waleis. The kingdom is in need of a ruler, and the young queen, Herzeloyde, has arranged a tournament to select one: she will marry the winner. Gahmuret enters the city in an eye-catching procession that proclaims his riches. He takes part in the exercises preliminary to the tournament and emerges clearly as the most skilled fighter among the participants. Herzeloyde claims him in marriage, but Gahmuret advances three excuses to escape this unsought wedlock: he is married already, the queen of France has a prior claim on him, and he is in mourning, having just had news of his brother's death. When Herzeloyde brushes his excuses aside – pointing out in response to the first one that a Christian marriage supersedes marriage to a pagan – Gahmuret lights on yet another escape clause: the tournament proper has not taken place, so the rule regarding its outcome cannot be applied. Neither will give way, the matter is referred to a jury, and the verdict is in the queen's favor. They marry, but not long after the wedding Gahmuret leaves for the East, where he falls in battle. When the news of his death is brought to Herzeloyde, she faints in shock and hovers on the brink of death. But she rallies and proclaims to her people that she is carrying in her womb the heir to the kingdom. Shortly afterward, Parzival is born.

Herzeloyde's lands are overrun by a robber baron, and she flees with her son and a group of retainers into the magic wasteland of Soltane. Here Parzival is brought up in total ignorance of chivalry. One day, however, he meets a group of knights in the forest and learns about King Arthur. The knights' description kindles in him the desire to present himself at Arthur's court and become a knight himself. Herzeloyde lets him go, then dies of a broken heart. In the forest of Brizljan, the forest of Arthurian adventure, Parzival has a series of encounters, each of which will impinge decisively on his career and development. He stumbles on Jeschute, asleep alone in her pavilion; kisses her; and robs her of her ring. She is later accused of adultery by her husband. He next finds Sigune, his cousin on his mother's side and a member of the Grail family, cradling in her arms her lover, who has just been killed in a joust. She tells Parzival of his own lineage and his great inborn capacity for compassion. At Arthur's court Parzival kills the Red Knight in a joust, takes possession of the Red Knight's charger and accoutrements, and sets out again. Not being able to control the powerful horse, he rides on for two days in full armor until he comes to a castle. Its lord is Gurnemanz, who takes it upon himself to educate Parzival in horsemanship, fighting techniques, and rules of behavior, in-

cluding one that will prove fatal – that he should not ask too many questions.

After leaving Gurnemanz, Parzival comes upon a kingdom under siege; its inhabitants are starving. He offers assistance to the young queen, Condwiramurs; defeats the opposing army; and marries her. After some time he takes leave of her to return to his mother, not knowing that she is dead.

On his way Parzival arrives at the Grail Castle. Its inhabitants are careworn and melancholy, and the Grail King, Anfortas, suffers from a crippling illness; huge fires and immense fur wrappings cannot allay his chill. Parzival witnesses the display of a bleeding lance accompanied by loud weeping and lamenting, followed by a mysterious procession of young women, one of whom is holding the Grail. The Grail possesses the magical quality of being able to supply any kind of sustenance in any quantity. Finally, a dazzling treasure, Anfortas's sword, is presented to Parzival as a gift from his host. Parzival accepts it, not understanding that by doing so he is acknowledging a close link with the giver. It should prompt him to inquire into the wretched fate that has befallen Anfortas, but, because of the reticence instilled in him by Gurnemanz, he does not do so. When he leaves the next morning, the castle is deserted. Riding through the forest he comes upon Sigune, who hails him as the Grail king-elect. When he confesses that he did not ask the healing question, she hurls violent abuse at him and refuses to have anything further to do with him. He next meets Jeschute, fights a joust with her husband, and reconciles husband and wife by testifying to her innocence. He takes his oath at Fontane la salvatsche, Trevrizent's hermitage.

Parzival's travels now take him out of Grail territory and back to the Arthurian world. Three drops of blood on the snow from a bird injured by a falcon remind him of the colors of Condwiramurs, and he falls into a trance of longing. Gawan, the most distinguished member of the Round Table, breaks the spell and takes him to Arthur's encampment, where he is received by the king and the nobles as an equal. Almost immediately, however, the Grail messenger, Cundrie, arrives and humiliates him before the assembled company for not having asked the vital question at the Grail Castle. Arthur and his court are degraded, she says, by his presence. Devastated by this public disgrace, Parzival despairs. He casts doubt on God's omnipotence, thereby committing the cardinal sin of *superbia* (pride). He and Gawan leave the court.

Page from the Kleine Heidelberger Liederhandschrift, including four strophes by Wolfram (Heidelberg, Universitätsbibliothek, cpg 357, f. 30v)

The secondary hero, Gawan, now moves into the foreground of the narrative. His first exploit takes him to a castle that is to be attacked by a large army because its lord's elder daughter has rejected the marriage proposal of a young king. The younger daughter, Obilot, still a child, captivates Gawan by her charm, and he agrees to fight in their defense. He captures the king, hands him over to Obilot, and she hands him over to her sister. They marry, and Gawan leaves.

At the next castle Gawan meets the irresistible Antikonie. Left alone with her, he makes immediate advances, to which she responds; they are, however, interrupted by a knight, who raises the alarm. At this point the story turns into farce. Gawan, who is unarmed, uses a chessboard as a shield, while Antikonie hurls chess pieces in their defense. A settlement is reached that obliges Gawan to seek the Grail.

The narrative returns to Parzival. He is once again on Grail territory, where he stumbles upon Sigune. This time he finds a sympathetic response from her, and she shows him the way to the Grail Castle. After winning a horse in a joust with a Grail knight, he loses his way and moves out of Grail country. Weeks later he is back. A group of pilgrims tells him that it is Good Friday and advises him to seek Trevrizent, the hermit, who turns out to be his maternal uncle. God guides him to the hermitage, where, in long and detailed discussions structured with great complexity, he is taught about love, mercy, the grace of God, and the sin of *superbia* and is led to sincere penitence and confession. He learns also of the secrets of the Grail and of his mother's death.

Meanwhile, Gawan reaches yet another country, whose beautiful and spirited liege lady, the duchess Orgeluse, treats him with disdain but accepts his offer to serve her. They ride on together, Orgeluse intent on testing Gawan's qualities as a knight, Gawan determined to carry his courtship of her to a successful conclusion. As they approach a river, beyond which rises a magnificent castle with ladies at every window, Gawan is challenged by a knight who is a rival for Orgeluse's favors. She leaves but promises to meet Gawan again, should he defeat his opponent. Gawan is victorious and spends the night in the ferryman's house.

The next morning Gawan is eager to hear about the castle he saw the day before. Gawan plies the ferryman and his daughter with questions and discovers that in the castle, Schastel Marveile, stands the great bed, Lit Marveile. A spell lies on the castle, and he who breaks the spell will become the castle's lord. Gawan enters the castle and faces the extraordinary bed, which charges about like a warhorse. He jumps on the bed, and as he rides it he has to protect himself against a shower of arrows and stones and kill a lion. The spell is broken, and Gawan, though wounded, survives. This episode also has elements of farce: that the womanizer Gawan should be riding a bed as if it were a horse and should be responsible for freeing four hundred women is a joke that would hardly be lost on the contemporary audience.

On the following morning Gawan inspects the castle and discovers a magic pillar in which the surrounding countryside may be seen. He catches a glimpse of Orgeluse, hurries to join her, and defeats her escort. Orgeluse offers her love if he will fight King Gramoflanz. To do so he must take a branch from the king's garden, which can only be reached by jumping a dangerous ravine on horseback. Gramoflanz appears the moment Gawan has picked the branch, declares himself to be in love with Gawan's sister, and announces that he nurses an unremitting hatred against Gawan. After they arrange a duel, Gawan returns to Orgeluse, who asks his forgiveness. The two ride back to Schastel Marveile.

The next day great celebrations take place at Schastel Marveile. Among the inhabitants of the castle are Gawan's two sisters, his mother, and his grandmother, but he has not revealed his identity to them. The festivities culminate in Gawan and Orgeluse's being led to their nuptial chamber. In the meantime Gawan has sent a messenger to ask Arthur to bring the court to Joflanze, where his joust with Gramoflanz is to take place. Gawan then sets out with the court of Schastel Marveile, as does Orgeluse with her own ducal court. The integration of the three courts is an important achievement, the more so because it allows Gawan to reunite the king with members of his family who had been imprisoned at Schastel Marveile.

Before the duel Gawan rides out to exercise his charger. On the plain he meets a knight who wears a garland made of branches from Gramoflanz's tree. Gawan takes him to be Gramoflanz and begins the joust. Soon it becomes clear that Gawan has found a dangerous opponent. He is, in fact, Parzival, who shows himself to be the superior fighter. Gawan is close to defeat when some passing pages call out his name. Parzival, in deep distress at having engaged in a duel with so close a friend, immediately reveals his identity and flings aside his sword, and they rejoin Arthur's court. Gawan's duel with Gramoflanz does not take place. Several weddings follow, among them the formal nuptials of Gawan and Orgeluse.

Witnessing the good fortune and happiness of those around him, Parzival concludes that his destiny is otherwise: "got wil miner freude niht" (733,8: God does not want happiness for me). With this thought he lays down defiance and rebellion and accepts what fate has decreed for him. He has moved from *superbia* to *humilitas,* from one of the cardinal sins to one of the cardinal virtues, and he can now be called to the Grail. He leaves Arthur's court and sets out alone.

The Gawan story is now at an end. Almost half the work is allotted to it, indicating its importance. Gawan is carefully contrasted with Parzival in personality, career, and fate. His conduct is without blemish; his faith never wavers; his actions are marked by courage and his thoughts by maturity. While Parzival's life is portrayed as exceptional, Gawan's is exemplary. Apart from its serious function, the Gawan story also introduces humor into the work. Witty and occasionally bawdy, it is entertaining in itself and serves, in addition, to throw Parzival's loneliness and misery into sharp relief.

Riding toward a large forest, Parzival meets a luxuriously accoutred pagan knight. Without speaking, they begin to fight. Parzival's sword splinters, and the stranger magnanimously throws his own aside and reveals his identity: he is Feirefiz, Parzival's half brother, and has arrived with an army to search for his father, Gahmuret. Overjoyed, the brothers exchange the kiss of peace, and Parzival takes Feirefiz to Arthur's court. Arthur makes Feirefiz a member of the Round Table and arranges a banquet in his honor. The festivities are interrupted by the arrival of the Grail messenger, Cundrie, who proclaims Parzival king of the Grail. Parzival and Feirefiz take leave of the court and, guided by Cundrie, ride to the Grail Castle.

Anfortas, in his agony, pleads for death but is kept alive by the Grail. Parzival, greatly moved, now asks the long-awaited question of pity: "oeheim, was wirret dier?" (795, 29: Uncle, what ails you?), and Anfortas is released from his misery. Parzival, now king of the Grail, rides out to meet Condwiramurs and sees his twin sons for the first time. There is one further meeting with Trevrizent, and on the return journey to the Grail Castle he passes Sigune's dead body. Feirefiz falls in love with the young woman who leads the Grail procession; after his baptism they marry and leave for the East. Parzival's son Loherangrin, a knight of the Grail, is sent to Brabant to help its liege lady against her enemies. He marries her on the condition that she never ask him who he is. She does ask the forbidden question, and he returns to the Grail. In a brief epilogue Wolfram names himself once more and concludes that a life led doing justice to both God and the world is a great achievement.

Alongside his epic work, Wolfram also composed seven songs. An eighth song handed down under his name is generally not considered genuine but may contain some strophes by him. Four of the songs are dawn songs, the standard subject of which is the parting of illicit lovers at daybreak. The genre is found in many civilizations, and a substantial corpus of it was developed in medieval Provençal. In Germany only two poets are known to have chosen this lyrical category before Wolfram. Dawn songs are miniature dramas, and in Wolfram's four examples the atmosphere is particularly highly charged. The yearning of the lovers for one another, the pain of parting, the fear of loss, and the menace of discovery make up a powerful poetic blend. The danger is ever present, and the suspense is sustained throughout.

Wolfram's dawn songs vary greatly in structure. In two of the songs only the lovers appear; in the others a third figure – the castle guard – enters the scene. Two of the songs are cast chiefly in dialogue; two are introduced by a monologue. One is a dispute between the woman and the castle guard; a large part of another is taken up by the castle guard's considering his function as protector of the lovers. This figure is given an important role. As he takes a considerable risk by waking the lovers at sunrise and thus enabling the knight to leave undetected, Wolfram makes him a friend of the lovers. The poet indicates this relationship by the use of the second-person singular, *du,* in the dialogue between the guard and the woman.

The identities of the lovers in the four songs are left vague. They could be married (though clearly not to one another), unmarried, young, or older. He could be a lord, a vassal, or a free lance living by his wits; she could be the lord's wife, one of the lord's legitimate or illegitimate daughters, or a cherished concubine of the lord. The constellation of identities in the songs, subtly left to the audience's imagination, makes for a variety of dramas.

These songs are distinguished by great artistic daring: in all of them Wolfram portrays the act of love. Descriptions of nudity, physical intimacy, and sex in serious literature constituted a breathtaking novelty. In all four dawn songs the lovers embrace in a last farewell before parting. This juxtaposition of union and separation invests the scene with maximum pathos.

Wolfram also composed an anti–dawn song in which the lovers' friend is not needed, for the lovers are married and are not forced to meet in secret. As regards poetic quality, the song is not to be compared with the dawn songs proper; it is probably a parody. Of the remaining songs, one ridicules the clichés of the conventional contemporary love lyric, referring to a song by Walther that, in turn, had as its target a song by Reinmar der Alte. The last song, a plea for love, is remarkable chiefly for the eccentric images the poet uses to describe the setting. Unusual also is the masterful stance the speaker of the poem takes in his wooing: in the opening section of the lyric his plea is a scarcely disguised command. It then dissolves in the second half into the standard begging attitude of the traditional courtly love song.

Wolfram's later verse narrative, *Willehalm,* is quite different from *Parzival.* While the central concern of the early work may be said to be the problem of the relationship of humanity to God, the main thrust of *Willehalm* is the disastrous nature of war. While the early work is a simple biography of two individuals, hero and counterpart, *Willehalm* is a highly elaborate, episodic work with a huge cast of characters. The action in *Willehalm* is diffuse, even confusing, and the work is, therefore, not as accessible as *Parzival.* The war in *Willehalm* involves not only the soldiers but also civilian men, women, and children. It is also a war of religion between Christianity and Islam, in which faith fuels fanaticism and barbarity. The subject was highly topical at the time; by the end of the first decade of the thirteenth century four Crusades had been fought. In the first the religious fervor of the Christians had spilled over almost immediately into mindless brutality: in 1096 pogroms took place in the Rhineland, and hundreds of Jews were put to the sword in Mainz, Speyer, Worms, and Cologne; the Crusade was successful in that Jerusalem was captured, but the victory was a bloodbath – soldiers, it was said, waded through blood up to their knees – and even the Christians were appalled at the massacre. The Second Crusade, in 1147, was a fiasco, and the Third Crusade, in 1187, led by Friedrich Barbarossa, disintegrated on Barbarossa's death, with most of the German crusaders returning home and much of the Holy Land remaining in Muslim hands. With the sack of Constantinople in the Fourth Crusade, in 1204, war reached a new level of horror. For three days the crusaders committed murder, rape, and torture and looted or destroyed the city's artistic treasures. Constantinople's catastrophic fate reverberated throughout the world. So when audiences listened to a recitation of *Willehalm,* his portrayal of a war of religion and its implications held awesome meaning for them.

The war at the center of Wolfram's narrative has another dimension, also a deeply tragic one: it is a war between two great families that should be at peace because they are bound together by the marriage of the Christian margrave Willehalm and the Muslim Giburc, who has become a Christian. Members of the two families murder one another relentlessly. Their unremitting hostility reveals the pattern of a Germanic blood feud, in which the killing must go on until only one protagonist is left. More than half of *Willehalm* is devoted to war: books 1 and 2 are taken up with the portrayal of the first battle, and the last three, books 7, 8, and 9, with that of the second. The work is incomplete; several narrative strands are not followed to a proper conclusion. It is not known why Wolfram did not finish it, but the story is so full of problems that are unlikely ever to find a solution that he may have lost heart. The mood of resignation that pervades the work makes it unlikely that he would have ended it with the same confident optimism that marks the conclusion of *Parzival.*

The enmity between the warring families is counterbalanced by the love of Willehalm and Giburc. In two love scenes the strength of their emotional bond transcends the gloom cast by war and devastation. Yet their past constitutes one of the many problems that beset the epic: Willehalm abducted Giburc, the wife of the Muslim king Tybalt, whose territory he invaded and devastated; she accepted baptism out of love for Willehalm but also out of conviction. The twofold treachery – the abduction and the apostasy – provides the Muslims with a just grievance and a desire for revenge.

Wolfram's characterizations of Willehalm and Giburc are full of irony. While Willehalm, the Christian warrior, has a violent temper, is brutally vindictive, and gives no quarter to the enemy, refusing even to heed the pleas of the maimed, Giburc, the onetime "infidel," proclaims the Christian message of tolerance and pity in an impassioned speech that forms the ideological core of the work.

There are more than one hundred named characters in *Willehalm,* and they each attain a certain measure of individuality. Yet more important than their often sketchy individual identities is the mass they make up, for Wolfram's objective is to transmit the impression that hundreds upon hundreds suffer and are massacred in this war.

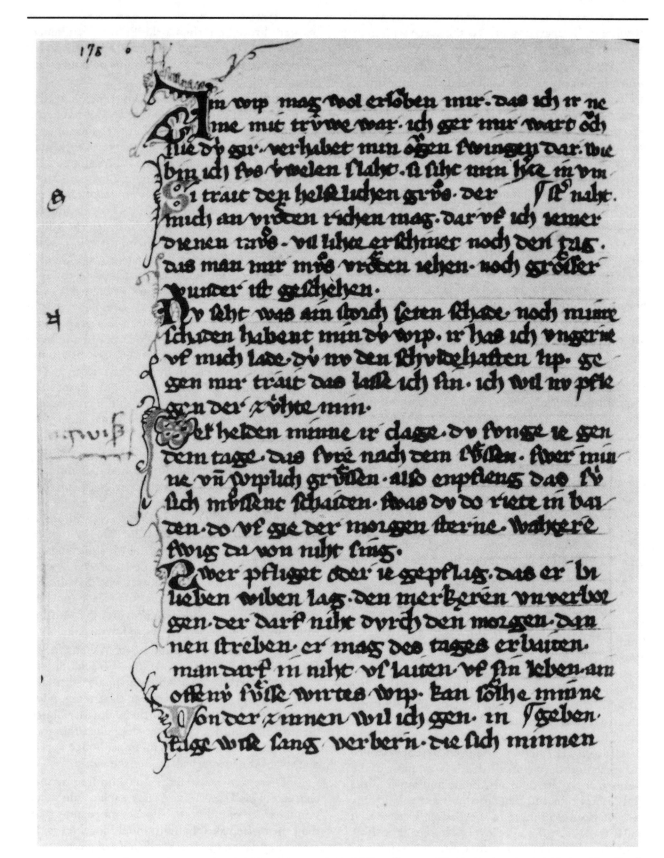

Pages from the Weingartner Handschrift with three strophes by Wolfram (Stuttgart, Württembergische Landesbibliothek, HB XIII, 1)

regenliche vñ obe si priſe ir minne wer n.
ſ gedenke ſere an ſine lere den lip vñ ere
ergeben ſin.per mich des bere deſwar ich
gere ime gŭte rete. vñ hette ſchin ritter
wache hie dir.

Mihr ver trenken wil ich aller wahtere
triwe an werden man dv enſolt denken an
ſchadens triwe vſ kvnte win. es were vn
wege ſwer minne pflege das vſ ine lege
melden laſt. am ſener bringet. ſwas min
mvnt ſinget. dvrch wolken dringet. a in
tagender glaſt. wache vñ hŭte dich lieber
Er mis ehe dannen der ſi clagen ſ gaſt.
Vngerne horte do ſprach ſin mvnt. allen
mannen triwen nie ſo gar zer ſtorte ir ṽch
den kvnt. ſwie balde es tagete der vnverza
gete. an ir belagete. das vorge ṽ flach. vn
vrōmedes rvchen. gar haimlich ſprachen
ir brvſtel druchen vñ ine darnach vrlop
gap des pris was hoch.

Willehalm has remote historical roots. In 793 Count Guillaume of Toulouse, a grandson of Charles Martel, fought against the Saracens in the area between Narbonne and Carcassonne; in 801 he fought them again, this time in Spain. In 804 he founded the monastery Gellone near Montpellier, entered it in 806, and died there six or seven years later. Gellone was renamed Saint Guilhem-le-Désert, the name it bears today.

Guillaume's courage and his saintly later life became the stuff of legend. In oral poetry, exploits of other warriors as well as fictitious episodes came to be linked with his name, and so the figure of real life gradually developed into a hero of fable. In the twelfth century a series of chansons de geste was composed on Guillaume and members of his family. The series grew into a cycle of more than twenty poems, of which *La Bataille d'Aliscans* (The Battle of Aliscans) forms the source of Wolfram's *Willehalm*. *La Bataille d'Aliscans* has been handed down in thirteen manuscripts, of which twelve are cyclic – that is, they also contain other epics of the Guillaume cycle. A comparison of the manuscripts has led to the view that the version from which Wolfram worked was close to manuscript M (now at Saint Mark's, Venice), the only extant noncyclic manuscript of *La Bataille d'Aliscans*.

According to Wolfram's own testimony it was the landgrave Hermann of Thuringia who made the story known to him. *La Bataille d'Aliscans* is believed to have been composed between 1180 and 1190; Wolfram worked on *Willehalm* between 1210 and 1220. No manuscripts of *La Bataille d'Aliscans* from that period have been handed down, and it is doubtful that any existed at that time: the chansons de geste were then still largely disseminated orally.

The prologue begins with a prayer in which the poet invokes God's help in telling the story of Willehalm. He refers to his source and then asks Saint Willehalm to save him from perdition. He mentions his own name and invites the audience to listen to his new work.

Willehalm's father has disinherited his sons. Willehalm, the eldest, has sought his fortune in the East and has carried off the Muslim queen Arabel, who has converted to Christianity and been baptized in the name Giburc. A huge Muslim army commanded by her father, King Terramer, and her former husband, King Tybalt, has arrived in Provence to exact vengeance. On the field of Alischanz the twenty thousand Christians are vastly outnumbered by the Muslims, who inflict a crushing defeat on them. Willehalm's beloved nephew Vivianz is mortally wounded; an archangel speaks to

him and protects his soul from the devil, and as he dies in Willehalm's lap, a miraculous fragrance rises, as if from a scented fire. Willehalm breaks away with his last fourteen men and tries to make his way to his castle at Oransche. In a final skirmish the other fourteen are killed, but Willehalm escapes into the mountains. Here he finds Vivianz, who briefly comes back to life and makes his confession. Willehalm holds vigil by the body throughout the night. The next day he meets eighteen Muslim kings and slays ten, among them Giburc's uncle, Arofel. From Willehalm's grief over Vivianz springs unbridled vengefulness. He cuts off Arofel's leg; helpless, Arofel, one of the richest and most powerful of the Muslim kings, offers untold treasure and pleads for his crippled life. In answer, Willehalm slaughters him in the most ignominious manner, cutting off his head and stripping the corpse. The scenes of Vivianz's death and the killing of Arofel are both intensely moving, and Wolfram clearly meant them to be considered together. Both episodes end with the same gesture of resignation on the part of the narrator: "waz hilfet, ob ichz lange sage?" (69, 17: What is the use, if I dwell on it any longer?) concludes the Vivianz episode, and "war umme solde ichz lange sagen?" (81, 11: What is the point of saying any more?) ends the Arofel scene. Willehalm spares Giburc's son, Ehmereiz. Wearing Arofel's armor and riding Arofel's charger, he reaches Oransche, where he has difficulty convincing Giburc of his identity. The poet is here implicitly condemning Willehalm's gratuitous cruelty to Arofel: his own wife takes him to be a heathen, not a Christian. The Muslim army besieges Oransche, and Willehalm leaves under cover of darkness to seek help at the court of the French king. As he speaks Arabic and is taken for Arofel by the Muslims, he rides unscathed through their lines.

Giburc has been left behind to defend Oransche. In a dialogue with her father he tells her that he despises the Christian faith and intends to heap dishonor on Jesus by giving his daughter a shameful death: he offers her the choice of being drowned, burned, or hanged. She refuses to surrender, although most of her men have been killed. In the meantime Willehalm, exhausted and unkempt, arrives at the French court. He is not made welcome: his sister, the queen, gives orders not to admit him, and Willehalm is forced to find lodgings with a merchant. The next day he enters the great hall fully armed and publicly upbraids the king, reminding him that he, Willehalm, has been the kingmaker. Despite Willehalm's insults and threats, the king is conciliatory, but the

Page from a manuscript for Wolfram's Willehalm, *dating from the second quarter of the thirteenth century. The illustrations show Willehalm accepting money from his mother, the poet speaking of Willehalm's reconciliation with the Roman queen and of the dead at the battle of Alischanz, and the poet describing Willehalm's concern about the plight of Giburc in the besieged castle at Oransche (Munich, Bayerische Staatsbibliothek, cgm 193 III, f. 1r)*

queen refuses to give him any help. Willehalm, in an uncontrollable rage, tears the crown from her head, seizes her by the hair, and raises his sword to decapitate her, but their mother separates them. In the end Willehalm's father offers military support, and his mother puts her fortune at his disposal. Willehalm's anger is calmed by the appearance of his niece, Princess Alice, who begs forgiveness for her mother's harshness.

When the queen learns of the many dead among her kin she decides that Willehalm must be helped, and she intercedes for him with the king. When the king is reluctant, Willehalm angrily threatens to return his fiefs. The king finally gives way, and a summons for military aid is proclaimed throughout the kingdom.

Willehalm notices a boy working in the kitchen, a Muslim who has refused to be baptized. He is Rennewart, Giburc's brother, but their kinship is not disclosed until later. Willehalm offers to equip Rennewart with arms, but he wants only a club. Rennewart is presumably introduced to relieve some of the tragedy and gloom that burden the narrative. He appears as a clumsy clown, but much of the humor associated with him is black humor; the farcical situations in which he is shown are mingled with cruelty. When he is teased by some young squires, he seizes one of them and hurls him against a pillar, bursting him open like rotten fruit. Later, when some of them knock over his club, he picks it up and hits out with such force at a boy who is hiding behind a pillar that although he misses the squire the club striking the stone sends flames flaring up to the roof. While he is asleep in the kitchen, the cook purposely singes his beard; on discovering his disgrace Rennewart ties up the cook and throws him alive into the kitchen fire. There is humor in Rennewart's uncouth bearing, but there is none in his menacing strength.

The king makes Willehalm supreme commander of the army. At this point the war against Islam takes on a new importance: the safety of the kingdom is at stake. Oransche is under siege. In a second conversation with Giburc, Terramer tries to win her back to Islam; this time he shows himself to be grief-stricken, declares his love for his daughter, and claims that he has been forced to join the campaign against her. He is, however, adamant that Giburc must reconvert, but he is unable to persuade her to surrender. In a massive assault the town is set on fire, and the Muslims return to their fleet. The inner part of the castle is spared, and Willehalm arrives with the French army. A banquet is arranged to welcome the relief forces,

during which Giburc reveals her deep distress to Willehalm's father. She tells him that, of her kin, twenty-three kings and countless other nobles have been killed. She is devastated by the loss of life on both sides and by the hatred shown to her by her countrymen and her kin: even her ten brothers had joined the attack.

A council of war is called; Willehalm outlines his desperate straits, but the French princes decline to help until a plea is made to them in the name of Christ. The scene culminates in Giburc's great speech: facing the all-male assembly, whose discussion has centered on fighting and revenge, she pleads for mercy. Should victory in the forthcoming struggle and, therefore, eternal salvation be theirs, let it be earned fittingly, she urges: "Hœrt eines tummen wîbes rât, / schônet der gotes hantgetât" (306, 27–28: Listen to the counsel of a simple, untutored woman, / Spare the handiwork of God). Although she calls herself simple, she grapples with problems that were highly topical in contemporary theological debates. Not all infidels can be meant for perdition; every child is born an infidel, even when born to a Christian mother, and the examples of Noah, Job, and the three Magi show that God does not consign all heathens to hell. Jesus even forgave those who took his life. Charity should be the Christians' lodestar. God and humanity form a vast family of Father and children; this realization throws the kin-versus-kin feud of the war between Christians and Muslims into sharp relief. At the end of her speech, the longest in the work, Giburc breaks down in tears.

This call for tolerance of those of different faith and for compassion for a defeated enemy would be remarkable at any time in history; that it should have been made during the period of the Crusades is even more astonishing. An unambiguous affirmation of intensely demanding moral values, it stands out not only in the work but in the whole of Western literature. Throughout the epic Wolfram is at pains to demonstrate the high level of civilization achieved by the non-Christians; time and again he points to similarities in fighting techniques and behavior toward women between knights of the East and the West. Knights from the East, richer and more resplendent than their counterparts of the West, are knights nevertheless; the ideals of chivalry unite them all. This concern to isolate the features that link opponents and opposing views permeates *Willehalm* and rises to its climax in the speech of the onetime Muslim, but now Christian, Giburc. The endeavor to establish a basis for tolerance, and the ultimate proclamation of tol-

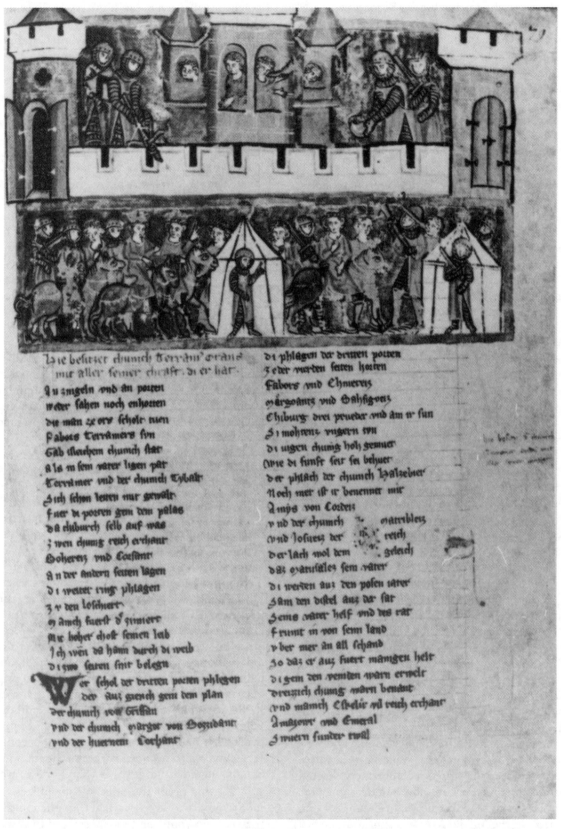

Page from a 1320 manuscript for Willehalm, *with an illustration depicting the siege of Willehalm's castle by Terramer (Vienna, Österreichische Nationalbibliothek, Cod. Vindob. 2670, f. 79r)*

erance as a guiding principle for human behavior, makes the work one of the great declarations of humaneness in Western culture.

Books 7, 8, and 9 are devoted to a detailed description of the second great battle, in which Rennewart plays a leading role. When the Christian troops reach a position close to the Muslim encampment and see the overwhelming force that confronts them, the French princes turn back; but they meet Rennewart, who kills many of them and forces the rest to return to the battlefield.

The portrayal of the battle represents the first detailed account of strategy and tactics in medieval German literature. References to place and time project a clear picture of the engagement. The Christian army is organized into six divisions, the Muslim army into ten. There are two parts to the battle: the first is dominated by the encounters of groups, the second by duels. The slaughter seems unending; Rennewart alone kills nine kings. When the bearer of the Muslim battle standard is cut down, Christian victory is assured. Many of the remaining Muslim soldiers are killed trying to flee. In individual combat between Willehalm and King Terramer, the latter is injured but is rescued by his men and carried to his ship. The victory the Christians celebrate has turned out to be a Pyrrhic one. There are countless dead, and Rennewart is missing. Among the twenty Muslim kings who have been taken captive is Matribleiz, a kinsman of Giburc. In a magnanimous gesture that contrasts favorably with Willehalm's initial stance toward the Muslims, he sets Matribleiz free and charges him to gather the bodies of the slain Muslim kings and have them buried according to the rites of their own faith. There the work breaks off.

Titurel (circa 1217), which was also left incomplete, is the first court romance cast in stanzas and the first not to be based on an earlier source. The work is preserved in two fragments. These fragments were enlarged in the latter half of the thirteenth century by a poet who calls himself Albrecht into a huge Grail narrative of more than 6,000 stanzas that is commonly referred to as *Der jüngere Titurel* (The Later Titurel). Wolfram's fragments consist of 131 and 39 stanzas, respectively. Stanzas were the metrical norm for the heroic epic and were traditionally of a rigid pattern. Wolfram seems occasionally to loosen the structure deliberately through the use of a mobile caesura; now and then this practice lends his stanzas a free-flowing rhythm. All stanzaic poetry in the Middle Ages was sung, but the melody for *Titurel* has not been preserved. The language Wolfram uses to tell his story displays an extrava-

gance unusual even for him; it abounds in metaphors, unorthodox usages, ambiguities (possibly deliberate), coined words, and invented compounds. The combination of the novel rhythm, the music, and the eccentric language makes the work one of extreme sophistication and elegance.

Titurel presupposes knowledge of *Parzival*. The fragments represent, in the main, a partial biography of Sigune before her first appearance in the earlier work. Of the thirty-two named characters in *Titurel*, twenty-nine can also be found in *Parzival*. The theme Wolfram explores here is selfless love between the sexes. In what appears to be the early part of the story, the Grail king Titurel maintains in his abdication speech that one outstanding characteristic will mark all his descendants: "wâre minne mit triuwen" (strophe 4: true love and loyalty). The later Sigune, as portrayed in *Parzival*, is the epitome of selfless loving and, in this way, a model after which the hero is to strive. In *Titurel* she is shown experiencing the awakening of love in childhood and its changed nature in adolescence. Love is assessed in authorial comment, examined in discussions among the characters, and demonstrated in the behavior of the lovers. In both fragments the frame of reference is the code of manners that was expected to govern a love relationship in medieval aristocratic society.

In the first fragment Titurel abdicates in favor of his son, who has five grown children. One of the son's daughters dies while giving birth, and her husband decides to become a hermit. The province with which his brother, King Tampunteire, enfeoffed him is transferred to the baby, who is named Sigune. Tampunteire also has a daughter, Condwiramurs, and Sigune is brought up with her. After Tampunteire's death Sigune is taken to her aunt Herzeloyde, who marries Gahmuret. The latter has a boy named Schionatulander in his retinue. Sigune and Schionatulander fall passionately in love but are soon parted when Gahmuret leaves for the East and Schionatulander accompanies him. Sigune and Schionatulander suffer torments of longing and begin to ail visibly. Gahmuret, noticing the change in Schionatulander, presses for an explanation; when he hears of the boy's love for Sigune, he promises to help Schionatulander in his courtship. Herzeloyde also becomes aware of Sigune's love for Schionatulander and gives her approval as well.

At this point the poet apostrophizes the immense power of love. He fears for the children, as they are too young and inexperienced to endure the agony of a great passion. The love of Schionatulander and Sigune is cast in a conventional mold; indeed, it involves two conventions superimposed on one another. They keep their love secret not only from others but also from one another; they exhibit the physical symptoms of lovesickness when they are separated; and Sigune displays the characteristic behavior of the woman waiting for her lover – standing in the window, watching from the battlements. All three features – the secrecy, the lovesickness, and the waiting woman – are part of the stockpile of motifs of the contemporary love lyric. Their love also bends to the conventional demand of the courtly romance that a man earn a woman's love through deeds of valor in jousts and on the battlefield. Sigune makes this demand, and Schionatulander immediately accepts the obligation. Gahmuret and Herzeloyde subscribe to this code of behavior as well: Gahmuret exhorts Schionatulander to win Sigune's love with a long career in fighting, and Herzeloyde assumes that Schionatulander will do so.

In the second fragment Sigune and Schionatulander no longer have to hide their love because it has been sanctioned by their elders. They are encamped on a clearing in the middle of a forest, chaperoned by ladies-in-waiting and other attendants, when they hear the baying of a hound that is racing in their direction. Schionatulander catches the animal, which is wearing a magnificently jeweled collar with an extraordinary leash that is twelve fathoms (seventy-two feet) long and also set with precious stones. The gems form letters; the inscription on the collar says that the hound's name is Gardeviaz, which means "mind the trail!" (a command used in hunting), and it admonishes that human beings might well heed this warning, too: men and women must watch their path through life so that they may find favor in this world and salvation in the next. The message on the leash is from a young queen who is sending the hound as a gift to her husband-to-be. It relates the fate of her sister, Florie, who denied the man she loved nothing except her body. He set out to earn her love by deeds of arms and was killed in a joust, whereupon she died as well. To read the rest of the inscription, Sigune must untie the leash from the tent pole. As she undoes the knot, Gardeviaz breaks free and races off into the forest, dragging the leash behind him. Obsessed with the desire to read the inscription to the end, Sigune promises Schionatulander all he desires if he will bring back the leash to her. The story of Florie as told on the leash parallels that of Sigune: both love and are loved in return, and both postpone the fulfillment of their love until their lover has proved himself; the fate of Florie foreshadows tragedy for Sigune. The message began with advice; it might end with more.

Sigune must have that ending. The urgency with which she clamors to have the leash restored to her, and the extravagant manner in which she expresses her need, clearly imply that she is filled with foreboding. Her demand is neither capricious nor unreasonable, as some scholars have labeled it. Neither in the two fragments nor in *Parzival* is such superficiality attributed to her. Wolfram, a master at consistent characterization, would hardly have been guilty of such a lapse. Anxiety drives her, not whim. Schionatulander agrees at once to retrieve the leash.

And so Sigune unwittingly sends Schionatulander to his death. When she makes her appearance in *Parzival,* he has just been killed in a joust while on this mission, and she is holding his dead body. When first shown in *Parzival* Sigune is still in the world of the Arthurian court; she later moves to Grail country, where she finally becomes an anchorite living with Schionatulander's embalmed body. In *Titurel* and *Parzival* Wolfram charts Sigune's progress from childish love through adult love to love of God.

Wolfram's works were enlarged, imitated, and copied for hundreds of years. Ultimately, however, there came a break in this continuity of appreciation as the German language changed and the age of feudalism passed. By the sixteenth century Wolfram's works were no longer being read. It was not until 1753, when the Swiss poet Johann Jakob Bodmer translated *Parzival* into hexameters, that interest in Wolfram's poetry began to revive. His second rise to fame gathered momentum in the nineteenth century as scholars recognized the outstanding qualities of his work and made it accessible to a wider public through editions, commentaries, translations, and adaptations, yet knowledge of his poetry has largely remained restricted to cognoscenti. His thoughts are often movingly, wittily, or dramatically expressed, and many of the themes he treats are universal. He is one of the great visionary poets of Western civilization.

Bibliography:

Ulrich Pretzel und Wolfgang Bachofer, *Bibliographie zu Wolfram von Eschenbach* (Berlin: Schmidt, 1968);

Joachim Bumke, *Die Wolfram von Eschenbach Forschung seit 1945: Bericht und Bibliographie* (Munich: Fink, 1970).

References:

David Blamires, *Characterization and Individuality in Wolfram's "Parzival"* (Cambridge: Cambridge University Press, 1966);

Joachim Bumke, *Wolfram von Eschenbach* (Stuttgart: Metzler, 1991);

Renate Decke-Cornill, *Stellenkommentar zum III. Buch des Willehalm Wolframs von Eschenbach* (Marburg: Elwert, 1985);

Dennis Howard Green and Leslie Peter Johnson, *Approaches to Wolfram von Eschenbach: Five Essays* (Bern, Frankfurt am Main & Las Vegas: Lang, 1978);

Erich Happ, "Kommentar zum zweiten Buch von Wolframs Willehalm," Ph.D. dissertation, University of Munich, 1966;

R. M. S. Heffner, ed., *Collected Indexes to the Works of Wolfram von Eschenbach* (Madison: University of Wisconsin Press, 1961);

Joachim Heinzle, *Stellenkommentar zu Wolframs Titurel* (Tübingen: Niemeyer, 1972);

Carl J. Lofmark, *Rennewart in Wolfram's "Willehalm"* (Cambridge: Cambridge University Press, 1972);

Ernst Martin, *Wolframs von Eschenbach Parzival und Titurel: Kommentar* (Halle: Waisenhaus, 1903);

Bodo Mergell, *Wolfram von Eschenbach und seine französischen Quellen,* 2 volumes (Münster: Aschendorff, 1936, 1943);

Benedikt Mockenhaupt, *Die Frömmigkeit im Parzival Wolframs von Eschenbach* (Darmstadt: Wissenschaftliche Buchgesellschaft, 1968);

Ingrid Ochs, *Wolframs Willehalm-Eingang im Lichte der frühmittelhochdeutschen geistlichen Dichtung* (Munich, 1968);

Linda B. Parshall, *The Art of Narration in Wolfram's "Parzifal" and Albrecht's "Jüngerer Titurel"* (Cambridge: Cambridge University Press, 1981);

Margaret Fitzgerald Richey, *Gahmuret Anschevin* (Oxford, 1923);

Richey, *Schionatulander and Sigune* (London, 1927; revised, 1960);

Richey, *Studies of Wolfram von Eschenbach* (Edinburgh & London: Oliver & Boyd, 1957);

Heinz Rupp, ed., *Wolfram von Eschenbach,* Wege der Forschung, no. 57 (Darmstadt: Wissenschaftliche Buchgesellschaft, 1966);

Hugh Sacker, *An Introduction to Wolfram's "Parzival"* (Cambridge: Cambridge University Press, 1963);

Ernst-Joachim Schmidt, *Stellenkommentar zum IX. Buch des "Willehalm" Wolframs von Eschenbach* (Bayreuth: University of Bayreuth, 1979);

Werner Schröder, *Die Namen im "Parzival" und im "Titurel" Wolframs von Eschenbach* (Berlin & New York: De Gruyter, 1982);

Schröder, ed., *Wolfram-Studien: Veröffentlichungen der Wolfram-von-Eschenbach-Gesellschaft* (Berlin: Schmidt, 1970–);

Marianne Wynn, "Book I of Wolfram von Eschenbach's *Willehalm* and Its Conclusion," *Medium Aevum,* 49 (1980): 57–65;

Wynn, "Orgeluse: Persönlichkeitsgestaltung auf Chrestienschem Modell," *German Life and Letters,* 30 (1977): 127–137;

Wynn, "Wolframs Dawnsongs," in *Festschrift Werner Schröder* (Tübingen: Niemeyer, 1989), pp. 549–558;

Wynn, *Wolfram's Parzival: On the Genesis of Its Poetry* (Frankfurt am Main, Bern, New York & Nancy: 1984).

Carmina Burana

(circa 1230)

Dennis M. Kratz
University of Texas at Dallas

Manuscripts: The *Carmina Burana* manuscript, known as the Codex Buranus (Munich, Bayerische Staatsbibliothek, clm 4660), consists of 112 vellum folios; portions of the manuscript, including the beginning and concluding leaves, are missing. The major portion of the manuscript was written in the first half of the thirteenth century and was primarily the work of two scribes. The original collection consisted of 228 works, but during the next two centuries at least twenty scribes added poems and commentaries and made corrections to the original text. In the fifteenth century the anthology, which by then included more than 300 works, was rearranged into its present form and bound. By the eighteenth century the manuscript had found its way to the monastery in Benediktbeuern, Bavaria, where it was trimmed and re-bound in leather. Johann Christoph, Baron of Aretin, the official in charge of secularizing monastic property, discovered the manuscript at Benediktbeuern in 1803. The manuscript was placed in the Bayerische Staatsbibliothek in Munich, where Christoph was appointed chief librarian in 1806. An additional seven folios were recovered later; they are known as the Fragmenta Burana (Ms. clm 4660a) and are also at the Bayerische Staatsbibliothek. Six of these folios originally came between folios 106 and 107 of the Codex Buranus.

First publication: *Carmina Burana: Lateinische und deutsche Lieder und Gedichte einer Handschrift des XIII. Jahrhunderts aus Benedictbeuren auf der K. Bibliothek zu München,* edited by Johann Schmeller (Stuttgart: Literarischer Verein, 1847).

Standard edition: *Carmina Burana,* 3 volumes, edited by Alfons Hilka, Otto Schumann, and Bernhard Bischoff (Heidelberg: Winter, 1930–1970).

Editions in modern German: *Carmina Burana: Lateinisch-Deutsch. Gesamtausgabe der mittelalterlichen Melodien mit den dazugehorigen Texten,* translated by René Clemencic and Michael Korth (Munich: Heimeran, 1979); *Carmina Burana: Texte und Ubersetzungen. Mit den Miniaturen aus der Handschrift und einem Aufsatz von Peter und Dorothee Diemer,* edited by Benedikt Konrad Vollmann (Frankfurt am Main: Deutscher Klassiker Verlag, 1987).

Editions in English: Sixty poems translated by John Addington Symonds, in *Wine, Women and Song* (London: Chatto & Windus, 1884); seventy-five poems translated by George F. Whicher, in *The Goliard Poets* (Westport, Conn.: Greenwood Press, 1949); sixty-three poems translated by David Parlett, in *Selections from the Carmina Burana* (New York: Penguin, 1986); sixty poems translated into prose by P. G. Walsh, in *Love Lyrics from the Carmina Burana* (Chapel Hill: University of North Carolina Press, 1993).

Carmina Burana (Songs from Benediktbeuern, circa 1230) is a somewhat misleading title for the best-known and most extensive collection of medieval Latin poetry. Though discovered in the monastery at Benediktbeuern, Bavaria, the manuscript was not compiled there. Moreover, while the majority of the texts in the anthology are lyric poems, many of which were clearly intended to be sung, it includes a broad spectrum of genres. Among its more than 315 texts are songs about subjects ranging from love to the Crusades; learned poetry; satires; parodies in prose and verse; debates; and six religious dramas. Furthermore, while most of the works are in Latin, forty-seven poems and portions of others are in Middle High German. The German compositions range in length from four to fourteen lines. In most cases the scribe has added the vernacular verses to the end of a Latin lyric. Some of the German poems deal with the same themes as, and are intended to extend or comment on, Latin texts.

tmpanum cum lyra. Do er zu der linden chom dui se
veamus. div minne couuch sere den nun ludum faciam.
Er graif mir an den wiven lip. non absq; timore. er sprah
ich mache dich ein wip dulcis es cum ore. Er war mir
uf daz hemdelin coepe detrecta. er rante mir in daz pur
gelin cuspide erecta. Ornam den chocher unde den bogen
vene venabatur. der selbe jerr mich betrogen ludus copleat.
Sospe flos florem quia flos designat amorem.

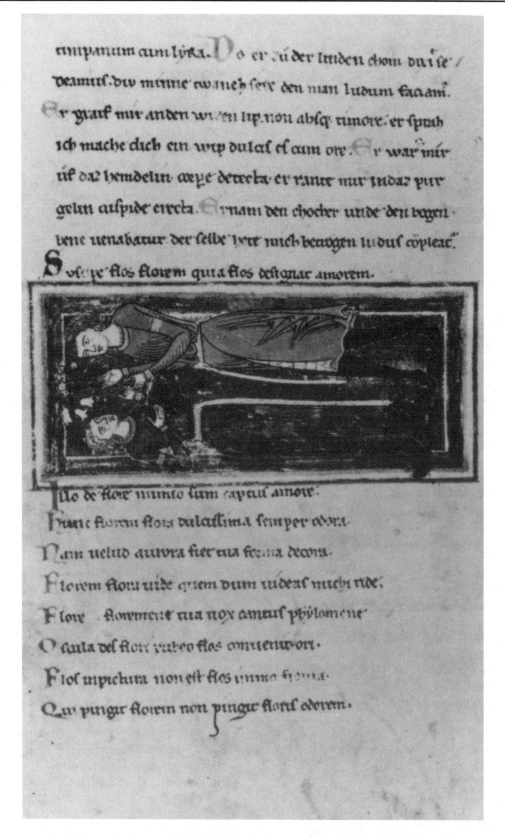

illo de flore munto sum captus amore.
Hunc florem flos dulcissima semper odora.
Nam velud aurora fier tua fecula decora.
Florem flora vide quem dum videas michi ride.
Flore florement tua nox cantus phylomene.
Oscula des flore rubeo flos omnemori.
Flos inpictura non est flos immo figura.
Qui pingit florem non pingit floris odorem.

Part of the text for a Pastourelle *from the* Carmina Burana *(Codex Buranus, Munich, Bayerische Staatsbibliothek, clm 4660, f.72v)*

In one instance the situation may be reversed: the Latin text of number 149, "floret silva nobilis," may be a translation of the German text "gruonet der walt allenthalben," which follows it.

The variety of genres is matched by the range of authors represented; the *Carmina Burana* is a truly international anthology. Most of the works, to be sure, are anonymous. Only two poets identify themselves: Der Marner, a German poet of the mid thirteenth century whose lyrics were added to the original collection, and Walter of Châtillon, one of the most renowned poets of the twelfth century, who composed at least four of the Latin poems (texts 3, 8, 41, and 123). Several other authors have been identified with relative certainty, including four of the other great masters of the medieval Latin lyric: the Archpoet, Hugo Primas of Orleans, Peter of Blois, and Philip the Chancellor. Among the authors of German verses are Reinmar der Alte, Heinrich von Morungen, and perhaps Walther von der Vogelweide.

The variety of the collection extends to the poetic forms found in it. Although a few of the Latin poems are in classical meters such as the dactylic hexameter, the majority are in rhythmic verse based on stress accents. The rhythmic meters employed range from simple forms intended for singing and dancing to highly complex patterns that demonstrate the virtuosity of the author. The rhythmic meter found most often is the goliardic, a line of seven trochees. The collection also includes many *iubili* (sequences), a variable verse form based on the pairing of stanzas that have the same pattern of accent and rhyme. There are nine poems for which a scribe has included neumes (musical notations in plainchant).

The circumstances that led to the creation of this extraordinary anthology are unknown. Bernhard Bischoff has argued that it must have originated in the area that is now Bavaria or Austria. The inclusion of so many secular poems, not to mention several religious parodies, argues against a monastic origin. It seems probable that the collection was ordered by a nobleman, or perhaps by a prelate who was enamored of contemporary literature. Many of the poems exist in other medieval manuscripts; four poems attributed to Peter of Blois, for example, also appear in another anthology, the Arundel collection from the twelfth century. Where comparable versions exist, the readings in the *Carmina Burana* are often inferior. The scribes may have been working from poor originals or writing down poems from memory.

Despite its diversity, the collection gives the impression of an overall guiding vision. The original 228 works fall naturally into four groups: texts 1 through 55 are primarily moralistic and satiric; poems about love dominate numbers 56 through 186, while 187 through 226 deal predominantly with drinking and gambling. Two religious dramas at the end of the collection are possibly intended to return the reader to the moral emphasis of the beginning section. In some cases poems composed in the same meter are grouped; poems written in classical meters tend to be placed after groups of poems that are linked thematically, as if to prepare the reader for a transition to a new category of works.

The first section begins with thirteen poems that criticize contemporary immorality, with emphasis on the vice of greed. It was a commonplace of medieval thought to associate concern for worldly goods with surrendering oneself to the power of fortune, and poems 14 through 17 depict the instability of a life governed by chance. Included in this section is the powerful hymn to fortune (17), with its compelling Boethian image of the Wheel of Fortune. Texts 18 through 45 present variations on the subject of moral correction.

Included in this section is a brilliant prose parody known as "the Gospel according to Mark" (44), the title referring to the measure of currency rather than the apostle. This learned satire on clerical venality uses allusions to and pointed alterations of biblical verses to make its points. Thus, when a cleric asks, "Et hoc quid est inter tantos?" (And what is this among so many?), he is complaining about the paucity of the bribe he has been offered. The satire ends with the grasping pope declaring, "exemplum enim do vobis ut quemadmodum ego capio ita et vos capiatis" (I give you the example that as I take so also you should take).

The most extensive section of the *Carmina Burana* (56 through 186) is devoted primarily to songs about love. Texts 97 through 102 are unhappy love stories, such as those of Dido and Aeneas and Helen and Paris, taken from classical sources. Other poems seem placed, if not haphazardly, at least according to a scheme not easily apparent to the modern reader. Inserted in the midst of the poems devoted to love, for example, is a sequence of thirteen poems (122 through 134) that, with one exception, have little to do with that subject. Most of the poems in this group are formal laments on political themes, two of them (122 and 124) lamenting the deaths of kings. Along with these apparently sincere laments appears the delightful mock lament (130) for a swan who once inhabited lakes but now sits on a plate, roasted and ready to eat.

An anthology as extensive as the *Carmina Burana* must have taken months, perhaps years, to complete, and the compilers obviously took many of the poems from other manuscripts. It has been suggested that a manuscript containing these thirteen poems came into the possession of the scribe as he was working on the section devoted to love. On the other hand, it may be that the poems are, indeed, part of a thematic fabric that simply escapes the modern reader. They may be intended to prepare the reader for a new series of thirteen poems lamenting unrequited love that begins with number 163.

Medieval Latin poetry is characterized by erudition: the art of the Latin lyric poet lies not in the candid expression of personal feelings or experiences but in the ability to employ with creative variation the conventions of a given genre. Hence, many of the poems in the collection treat the same theme in roughly the same manner. The learned and conventional nature of medieval Latin lyric often poses problems for the modern reader. Number 77, "si linguis angelicis" (If with the tongues of angels), one of the recognized masterpieces in the anthology, is a case in point. The poem is in part a celebration of love, in part a studied manipulation of literary motifs. The poet begins by using a scriptural allusion (1 Cor 13:1) to praise his beloved:

> Si linguis angelicis loquar et humanis
> non valeret exprimi palma, nec inanis
> per quam recte preferor cunctis Christianis
> tamen invidentibus emulis profanis.
>
> (If I were to speak with the tongues of angels and men,
> the prize could not be described, not a trifling one,
> through which I am rightly set above all Christians,
> while I am envied by jealous noninitiates.)

In language rich with religious allusions and images the poet describes his beloved and seeks her favor. Modern interpretations of this poem not only disagree but often contradict each other. It has been described as both a sincere vision of love that anticipates the *Roman de la Rose* (Romance of the Rose, 1230–1275) and as an ironic work using religious language to make fun of the pretensions of the lover. The use of the goliardic meter, usually associated with satiric or playful poetry, may provide a clue to the poet's intentions. The poem is placed immediately after an essentially bawdy poem about a young man's trip to a bordello (number 76), but it is not clear whether the editor made this placement because the poems are alike or to contrast them.

Many of the lyrics in this section are part of a popular genre that could be described as nature poems. The basic three-part design of such a poem was firmly established by the twelfth century, when almost all of the poems in the original collection were written. A poem in this genre begins with the poet's description of the arrival of spring, then celebrates (or at least discusses) the arousal of love brought on by the change of season. The poem may stop there or conclude with the confession or description of the desire felt by the speaker, who connects these personal feelings with the description of nature that began the poem.

A typical example is text 143, the lyric "Ecce gratum" (Behold delight). It consists of three stanzas and is in two carefully balanced parts. The first stanza and half of the second celebrate the return of "gratum et optatum ver" (delightful and desired springtime). The second half of the second stanza and all of the third are devoted to a celebration of the love that spring arouses in the human heart. In another poem that employs the same structure, number 136, the speaker tells his love that the coming of spring should remind her to remain faithful to him even though he is far away.

Several poems reverse the convention. For example, text 69, which has been attributed to Peter of Blois, devotes the first of its three stanzas to the bitter cold of winter rather than the warmth of spring. The second stanza speaks of the burning love that "nulla vis frigoris valet attenuare" (no power of cold can weaken), and the third describes the beauty of the lady for whom the speaker burns. Later in this section, three poems (111, 113, and 114) alter the conventional pattern by contrasting the joyful return of spring with the sadness of the poet.

The poems in this section express a wide range of attitudes toward passionate love. At one extreme are depictions of what Peter Dronke has called "the courtly experience," poems reflecting the literary interest in love that led to the rise of the romance genre in the twelfth century. In text 111, for example, the speaker mourns the difference in social status that keeps him from his beloved. Text 88 extols the superiority of *amor purus* (pure love) to *amor mixtus* (mixed love), passion leading to the *turpis voluptas* (shameful pleasure) of sexual intercourse.

At the other extreme are poems celebrating the joys of physical passion; text 76 is an unromanticized depiction of a young man's experiences in a brothel. Between these extremes are erotic poems such as texts 83 and 156, which describe the mutual pleasure of sexual union.

Passage, with musical notation, from the second Passion drama in the Carmina Burana *(Codex Buranus, Munich, Bayerische Staatsbibliothek, clm 4660, f.108r)*

Perhaps the crowning artistic achievement among the love lyrics is text 62, "Dum Diana vitrea" (When Diana's lantern), a haunting meditation on the blessings of sleep and the power of love that is preserved only in the *Carmina Burana*. It is a learned poem that employs both medical terminology and allusions to classical mythology. The poem begins with a description of nightfall and the rising of "Diana's lantern" – that is, the moon – then extols the blessings of sleep for the troubled lover and even compares the pleasure of sleep to that of love-making:

> O quam felix est antidotum soporis!
> quot curarum tempestates sedat et doloris!
> dum surrepit clausis oculorum poris,
> ipsum gaudio equiperat dulcedini amoris.

> (How blessed is the antidote of sleep!
> What storms of cares and pain it softens!
> As it creeps along the closed passages of the eyes,
> it equals in joy the sweetness of love.)

The fifth and sixth stanzas describe in technical terms the act of falling asleep, and the final two stanzas renew the comparison of the pleasures of sleep and love.

This section of the anthology also contains several examples of the medieval "debate" poem. In text 82 two young women, Thyme and Sorrel, weigh the relative merits of the knight and the cleric as lovers. By far the longest poem in the collection, text 92 presents the debate of Phyllis and Flora on the same issue. (This popular poem is also found in twelve other manuscripts.) Given that the poem, being in Latin, must have been written by a cleric, it comes as no surprise that the final stanzas declare clerics to be more suited to love than knights by virtue of both their knowledge and their way of life.

Two of the most compelling love lyrics in the *Carmina Burana* are written from the perspective of women. Text 126 presents the lament of a young pregnant woman whose lover has either abandoned her or been forced into exile by her father. In 185 a young woman sings of her seduction and betrayal in alternating lines of German and Latin.

The *Carmina Burana* also includes four examples (79, 90, 157, and 158) of the *pastourelle,* a lyric genre that emerged from folk traditions. The conventions of this genre are that a young man encounters a beautiful shepherdess in a *locus amoenus* (pleasant place); he attempts to seduce her, and she either rejects or accepts his advances. Three of the *pastourelles* in the *Carmina Burana* follow this conventional pattern exactly. In 157, however, the poet in-

troduces a new motif: a wolf appears in the *locus amoenus* and threatens the girl's sheep, and the young man kills it after she promises to marry the one who saves her flock. Some commentators read this poem as an allegory of salvation, others as just a charming variation of a popular genre.

Finally, in the midst of the poems about love is a parody of poems about love: in text 105 the poet writes of a dream vision in which a bedraggled cupid appears to him to complain about the debasement of the art of love by the current generation of lovers. The poem presupposes a reader with knowledge of both Ovid's verse and the precepts of proper conduct such as those laid down by André le Chapelain (Andreas Capellanus) in his treatise *De arte honeste amandi* (On the Art of Noble Love, circa 1185).

The third section of the *Carmina Burana* (texts 187 through 226) consists primarily of songs about drinking and gambling. This section is rich in parodies, and text 197, "Dum domus lapidea," is a parody of a poem that appears earlier in the collection, "Dum Diana vitrea." Among the parodies is one of the best-known Latin poems of the twelfth century, the so-called confession of the Archpoet (191), in which the poet celebrates the vices of which he claims to be repenting.

This section also includes subgroups of poems; texts 193 through 206, for example, deal with the pleasures of food and drink. Here the reader will also find several rousing songs celebrating the pleasures of the tavern, perhaps the finest and certainly the best known being text 196, "In taberno quando sumus" (When we are in the tavern). This group also includes a drinker's variation on the debate poem (193), in this case a debate on the relative merits of wine and water, in which wine emerges the victor.

After the poems on food and drink come four (texts 207 through 210) devoted to dice and chess. The poems that conclude this section seem to be something of a medley, although several call on students to give up their studies in favor of more immediate pleasures. The third section concludes with the poem "de mundi statu," which seems to belong more appropriately in the first section of moral and satiric poems. In a manuscript that begins with descriptions of the Wheel of Fortune, however, such a circular conclusion is appropriate, and the more serious tone of this poem prepares the reader for the religious dramas that follow.

Of the six religious dramas that appear at the conclusion of the *Carmina Burana,* four are among the later additions to the anthology. The two that formed part of the original manuscript (227 and 228) are passion dramas. The first, *Ludus breviter de Passione* (Shorter Passion Play), seems to have been intended as a prologue to a more elaborate dramatization of the Resurrection. It begins with the Last Supper and ends with the burial of Christ.

The longer play, *Ludus de Passione* (Passion Play), is both a superior work of art and an important document of intellectual history. Its 284 lines are mostly in Latin — partly prose, partly strophes — but include 73 lines of German verse. The drama is divided into six scenes. Sprinkled throughout the poetic lines of both languages are musical notations. This indication that the play was intended to be sung rather than recited, along with its episodic structure, led Karl Young to characterize the *Ludus de Passione* as an "episodic religious opera" rather than a drama.

The drama — or opera — begins with Christ's gathering of the Disciples and ends with his death. One notable feature of this play is its extended treatment of Mary Magdalene (lines 36 through 152): two scenes devoted to her conversion constitute a third of the entire play. First appearing on her way to a shop to buy cosmetics, she pauses to sing of earthly delights. This song begins with four strophes in German that seem to be an original composition rather than a translation of a Latin text. She then engages in a dialogue, also in German, with the merchant. In the next scene Mary Magdalene is warned three times by an angel who appears before her; the angel and the devil who accompany Mary Magdalene seem to represent the conflict in her soul. Young has suggested that they may also be "the precursors of the abstractions of virtue and vice which animate the moral plays of the later Middle Ages." Mary Magdalene rejects her former life, puts on a black shawl, and goes to Simon's house, where she washes Christ's feet. The importance given to Mary Magdalene in this play coincides with the rise of interest in her that began in the twelfth century and reached its greatest flowering in the thirteenth.

The *Carmina Burana* is one of the most important cultural documents of the European Middle Ages. Preserved only in this anthology are master-pieces of Latin lyric such as the "Dum Diana vitrea" and "si linguis angelicis," the *Ludus de Passione,* and many passages of twelfth-century German poetry. The anthology derives its importance also from the diversity of its contents: the reader of the entire collection will have encountered most of the genres, subjects, and poetic forms of the early thirteenth century. Mingled among works of artistic complexity are simple dance tunes, incantations, and even a versified list of animals and the sounds they make. Gathered together, and occasionally placed side by side, are celebrations of the spirit and the flesh. Given the inclusiveness of its contents and the attempt of the editors to organize that material into a coherent whole, the *Carmina Burana* should be regarded as far more than a book of songs: it is more appropriately described as a literary encyclopedia. In 1937 the composer Carl Orff set a selection of the texts to music.

References:

J. Ashcroft, "Venus Clerk: Reinmar in the *Carmina Burana,*" *Modern Language Review,* 77 (July 1982): 618–628;

B. A. Beatie, "Macaronic Poetry in the *Carmina Burana,*" *Vivarium,* 5 (May 1967): 16–24;

Peter Dronke, "Poetic Meaning in the *Carmina Burana,*" *Mittellateinisches Jahrbuch,* 10 (1975): 116–137;

Allison G. Elliott, "The Bedraggled Cupid: Ovidian Satire in *Carmina Burana* 105," *Traditio,* 37 (1981): 426–437;

D. W. Robertson, Jr., "Two Poems from the *Carmina Burana,*" in *Essays in Medieval Literature* (Princeton: Princeton University Press, 1980), pp. 131–150;

M. Rudick, "Theme, Structure and Sacred Context in the Benediktbeuern Passion Plays," *Speculum,* 49 (April 1974): 267–286;

Sandro Sticca, *The Latin Passion Play* (Albany: State University of New York Press, 1970);

P. G. Walsh, *Love Lyrics from the Carmina Burana* (Chapel Hill: University of North Carolina Press, 1993), pp. 13–35;

Karl Young, *The Drama of the Medieval Church,* volume 1 (Oxford: Clarendon Press, 1933).

Der jüngere Titurel

(circa 1275)

R. William Leckie, Jr.
University of Toronto

Manuscripts: *Der jüngere Titurel* survives in eleven more or less complete manuscripts; the oldest, Vienna, Cod. Vindob. 2675, designated "A," dates from around 1300. Some fifty fragments are also known to be extant. The manuscript transmission divides into two principal groups, I and II, with H (Heidelberg, cpg 141, mid fourteenth century) occupying a middle position. Group I appears to be the earlier version, while Group II constitutes a fourteenth-century vulgate redaction. The value of H for a putative Group I archetype has been hotly debated, and many issues remain contentious.

First publication: *Parzival; Der jüngere Titurel* (Strasbourg: Printed by Johannes Mentelin, 1477).

Standard editions: *Albrecht von Scharfenberg: Der jüngere Titurel,* edited by Karl August Hahn, Bibliothek der gesammten deutschen National-Literatur, volume 24 (Quedlinburg & Leipzig: Basse, 1842); *Albrecht von Scharfenberg: Der jüngere Titurel,* edited by Werner Wolf, Altdeutsche Übungstexte, no 14 (Bern: Francke, 1952); *Albrechts von Scharfenberg Jüngerer Titurel,* 4 volumes to date, edited by Wolf and Kurt Nyholm, Deutsche Texte des Mittelalters, volumes 45, 55, 61, 73 (Berlin: Akademie, 1955–).

Throughout the late medieval and early modern periods *Der jüngere Titurel* was universally regarded as perhaps the greatest work of Wolfram von Eschenbach. In his *Ehrenbrief* (1462), a versified honor roll, the bibliophile Jakob Püterich von Reichertshausen lavishly praised *Der jüngere Titurel* as the crowning achievement of German narrative. He took evident pride in the fact that his personal library contained a copy of so notable a work. Püterich also records his dissatisfaction with the texts in circulation: he claims to have seen some thirty exemplars, none of which was right. Both the manuscript transmission and the 1477 incunabulum edition bear witness to the demand for copies. It was

not until the early nineteenth century that August Wilhelm Schlegel and Karl Lachmann finally removed the work from the Wolfram canon.

As the title suggests, this late-thirteenth-century Grail romance is the more recent of two *Titurels.* Wolfram did compose 170 strophes, which fall into two unequal parts: first, Titurel's abdication speech followed by a depiction of the childhood love between Sigune and (as Wolfram spells the name) Schionatulander (1–131); second, the fateful capture and subsequent escape of the hound Gardevias, dragging a wondrously inscribed leash (132–170).

Although Wolfram's fragments provided an important stimulus and were incorporated into the composition, *Der jüngere Titurel* does not constitute a "continuation" in the usual sense of the common medieval practice of completing works left unfinished or of extending completed works beyond their original closure. Though sequential, the two fragments do not form a seamless narrative: the *Brackenseil* (hound's leash) episode begins abruptly, leaving an obvious gap in the chronology of events. Romancers composed in performable segments, and those segments need not have followed in exact order, especially if the outline of a tale were familiar; Wolfram's *Titurel* provides background for matters depicted in *Parzival,* and contemporary audiences could doubtless situate the scenes. That being the case, Wolfram may never have intended to compose a full romance around the fragments. There is no other example of this kind of experimentation in late-twelfth- and early-thirteenth-century vernacular narrative, but scholars have had trouble imagining where Wolfram intended to go with the fragments. There is certainly nothing to suggest the vast scope and monumental proportions of *Der jüngere Titurel,* a work of more than sixty-two hundred strophes.

Wolfram's *Titurel* fragments underwent significant alteration prior to inclusion in *Der jüngere Titurel.* The original strophic form is modified through the addition of caesural rhymes. The stanzaic pattern of the fragments is integrated with the composi-

Da ritter tempeleise.
als ist hie vor gesprochen.
uf strittlicher vreise.
voi helme schilt flugen von in zebrochen.
si cherten vnde iagtten sunder vlihen.
als in dw schrift, da sagtt.
den mans an dheiner herte sach di schihen.

Iostiren horttschluchen.
gestozen vnde vellen.
daz triben si taglichen.
vnd niht wan tage viere vnd gestellen.
als vns der magt, den heilant was geberend.
der ander do sin sterben.
vns ewich fröiden lebens was der werend.

o was der dritt genennet.
als er mit craft, vestendich.
ward von dem tod erchennet.
gar vnverzagt vnd an chranch gemeidich.
der vierde do di iunger sin onpfingen.
die chraft, des heren geistes.
da mit, si sunder vor dem tode gingen.

and peter vnrecht vorhte.
chvnd er do wol vermiden.
div im e zwivol vorhte.
div vorhte noch vil mangen chan versniden.
vnd vnrecht lieb als ich da vor was iehend.
war minn vnd rehte vorhte.
die müzz vns von der engel schar geschehen.

a stond ouch wol turniren
der iungen diet, zeleren:
durch strides conterwiren
ein heidenschaft, got vnd dem gral zo eren

Page from an early-fourteenth-century parchment manuscript for Der jüngere Titurel *(Munich, Staatsbibliothek, cgm 7, f. 10)*

215

tion as a whole, and various revisions move individual lines much closer to the mannered style so characteristic of *Der jüngere Titurel.* Completely new strophes are sometimes interpolated for elaboration and clarification. Sequence changes, as well as radical displacements, also occur. The fourteenth-century redactors of what are known as the Group II manuscripts of *Der jüngere Titurel* apparently regarded Wolfram's fragments as vestiges of an earlier, more authentic version. At least one and perhaps as many as four Group II redactors went back to Wolfram's *Titurel* for the original wording, undoing the homogenization of styles found in the earlier Group I manuscripts. Thus paradoxically, the earlier the version, the less it resembles Wolfram's work. The existence of the fragments seemingly failed to raise doubts concerning Wolfram's authorship of *Der jüngere Titurel:* the Middle Ages were all too familiar with the vagaries of transmission, and scribes regularly made changes of the order in question.

The mistaken attribution of *Der jüngere Titurel* stems from an audacious and highly successful authorial fiction. For much of the composition, the poet pretends to be Wolfram, repeatedly addressing the audience as "ich, Wolfram" (I, Wolfram). Shortly before the end, however, the poet identifies himself as Albrecht and lays claim to the entire composition, complaining that a loss of patronage has forced him to reveal his identity. The very success of his fictive stance had presumably become a liability, one which jeopardized his chances of finding new support: if *Der jüngere Titurel* were thought to be the work of a poet long dead, financial backing would hardly be forthcoming.

Although Albrecht unquestionably composed the whole, his posturing determined the work's attribution into the nineteenth century. His claim to authorship had surprisingly little impact, and the length of *Der jüngere Titurel* may have been a contributing factor: many readers probably never reached the crucial juncture in the text. Among those who did, some are known to have considered Albrecht a continuator in the strictest sense, responsible only for the concluding segments. Perhaps in anticipation of an imminent loss of support, the author quickens the pace of the narrative perceptibly even before he reveals his identity. He inserts whole blocks of material, including Arthuriana drawn from Geoffrey of Monmouth's *Historia regum Britanniae* (History of the British Kings, circa 1136), perhaps via Wace's *Roman de Brut* (Romance of Brute, 1155), with only the most perfunctory transitions. The final sections bear all the marks of a headlong rush toward closure. Because of the palpa-

ble shift, Albrecht could reasonably be thought responsible only for the less-than-satisfactory completion of an unfinished work by Wolfram.

The Albrecht who composed *Der jüngere Titurel* was almost certainly a cleric, possibly a Franciscan. Although he feigns illiteracy as part of the Wolfram fiction (68,2), his fondness for displays of learning bespeaks a considerable education. Such generalities can be inferred from the text, but identifying the poet with any precision has proven difficult. The name Albrecht has long been mentioned in connection with *Der jüngere Titurel,* and this association will inevitably continue. Werner Wolf, who undertook the monumental task of preparing a new edition (1955–   ), subscribed to the view that Albrecht was the author. Like Karl August Hahn (1842) before him, Wolf inscribed his belief on the edition's title page, but the identification is dubious at best.

Albrecht's name and condensed versions of two of his works, *Seifrid de Ardemont* and *Merlin,* appear in Ulrich Füetrer's *Buch der Abenteuer* (Book of Adventures), a late-fifteenth-century compilation of romance materials. Füetrer places Albrecht's stylistic achievement on a par with the artistry of Gottfried von Straßburg and Wolfram (17–18). A third title, *fraw Eren hof* (Dame Honor's Court), is later mentioned by Füetrer in the warmest terms and is also attributed to Albrecht. Scholarly debate has focused on two possibilities: that *fraw Eren hof* is a lost work, perhaps an allegory; or that the title refers to the work now known as *Der jüngere Titurel.*

If *fraw Eren hof* was a major romance, then its omission from the initial mention of Albrecht seems odd. The separate mention of *fraw Eren hof* accords much better with the notion of a genre distinction: it may have been out of place in a list of romances. On the other hand, Füetrer alludes to this apparently well-known work in the context of Schionatulander's demise; like the spelling of the name, the fatally flawed nature of his character comes directly from *Der jüngere Titurel* (3568–3569; 3573). According to Füetrer, the audience will have read often enough about the nature of proper moderation in *fraw Eren hof* (839,1–2). Although the example of Tschionatulander is undoubtedly taken from *Der jüngere Titurel,* this does not presuppose the identity of the two works: that the actions of the central figure in an enormously popular narrative should be cited in a didactic context is hardly without precedent. To judge from the title, *fraw Eren hof* might well have depicted a gathering of allegorical figures, each of which personified a particular courtly virtue. Well-known romances provided a frequently used store of illustrative materials for attendant discussions of behavioral modes. If Füetrer did equate *fraw Eren hof* with *Der jüngere Titurel,* he must have accepted Albrecht's claim of authorship in strophe H5883. Füetrer's words would imply that he alone among all his contemporaries had grasped the true situation and had identified the Albrecht in question, but this assumption is not reasonable. Furthermore, the manuscripts exclusively use the title *Titurel;* the expression "frou Eren hove" occurs only once in the entire textual tradition, and that in the hybrid manuscript H (strophe 682).

Apparently concerned that the Wolfram fiction threatened to efface his own creative identity, Albrecht belatedly attempted to clarify the situation by means of an addendum. In the so-called Heidelberg Verfasserfragment (author fragment) Albrecht dedicates the work to Ludwig II of Bavaria, evidently seeking to capitalize on Ludwig's candidacy for the imperial crown. These hopes came to nought with the election of Rudolf von Habsburg on 1 October 1273, an event to which Albrecht alludes in the text proper. Ludwig's interest seems to have cooled in the wake of the election, leaving Albrecht without needed patronage. Whether he interrupted the composition is difficult to say, but a lengthy break seems unlikely. A completion date around 1275 would allow for a brief period of indecision and poetic inactivity.

Neither *Seifrid de Ardemont* nor *Merlin* contains the kind of allusion that would facilitate accurate dating, but both could belong to the second half of the thirteenth century. *Der jüngere Titurel* and *Merlin* both attempt to reconcile Wolfram's account of the Grail's history with the Old French Joseph of Arimathea tradition, and it would seem highly improbable that two Albrechts were engaged simultaneously in such similar projects. On the other hand, as Kurt Nyholm has argued, there are significant differences in the sources that shaped *Der jüngere Titurel* and *Merlin,* discrepancies difficult to reconcile with the notion of unified authorship.

In the prologue to *Der jüngere Titurel* Albrecht declares his indebtedness to three princes whose names he refuses to divulge. When the composition had reached an advanced stage, these patrons apparently withdrew their support. Although Albrecht continues to shield their identities, he does place them in central Germany: "si sint der mitte wol vf devtscher terre" (H5768.3). Following Erich Petzet's lead, scholars have traditionally viewed the Heidelberg Verfasserfragment as a response to this loss of support — as an effort to rededicate the work to Ludwig II. That no extant manuscript incorporates the Verfasserfragment into the text seemingly attests to the short-lived nature of the attempted shift.

Helmut de Boor advanced the hypothesis that the three princes from central Germany were Heinrich III ("the Illustrious") of Meissen and his sons Albrecht, Landgrave of Thuringia, and Dietrich, Margrave of Meissen. Albrecht married Margaretha of Hohenstaufen, daughter of the emperor Friedrich II. Their second son bore the name of his maternal grandfather, and from 1269 to 1271 the hopes for a Hohenstaufen restoration rode on the young shoulders of Friedrich III. This brief campaign was brokered by Heinrich, Albrecht, and Dietrich, making *Der jüngere Titurel* part of an effort to recall both the political and literary glories of the Hohenstaufen ascendancy. De Boor's thesis has found widespread acceptance for at least three reasons: Margaretha and her son lived at the Wartburg Castle in Eisenach, the locale where the Wolfram fiction would have made the best sense; the family feuding that ended the campaign of Friedrich III in 1271 would have left Albrecht to fend for himself during the time when Ludwig II became a serious candidate for the imperial crown; and Ludwig, who had been the guardian of Konradin — the grandson of Friedrich II — was seen as the last hope of the Hohenstaufen cause, making Albrecht's shift politically consistent.

Joachim Bumke rejects de Boor's arguments out of hand: dialect traces in *Der jüngere Titurel* suggest that Albrecht was a Bavarian, and Bumke contends that Ludwig II had underwritten the work from the outset, at first with two other nobles and then alone. But even if the Wolfram fiction would have worked equally well at the Bavarian court, Bumke's thesis does not explain Albrecht's sudden compulsion to drop the mask. Ludwig's assumption of the entire burden of patronage for a work already being composed in Bavaria would hardly seem to require such a disclosure. Moreover, the language of the manuscripts points generally to central Germany, perhaps Meissen, with only vestigial Bavarian involvement. The linguistic evidence is consistent with the notion that Albrecht brought traces of his home dialect to a work composed and copied in a north-central location.

These views all presuppose that Albrecht is commenting on his own situation in his comments about his patrons in strophes 64 and H5767–5768 (strophe numbers preceded by *H* refer to the edition by Hahn, those preceded by *W* to the edition by Wolf [1952], and those without a letter to the edition by Wolf and Nyholm [1955–]). Peter Kern points out that Albrecht is an accomplished role player and seldom falls out of fictive character and that the first person tends to be reserved for utterances made using Wolfram's voice. Kern can see no reason to assume that Albrecht has stepped out from behind his mask at the junctures in question; thus, the three princes may have nothing to do with circumstances in Albrecht's day. On the other hand, it seems unlikely that the patrons are Wolfram's. The text implies audience familiarity with the three princes: Albrecht has no need to name them, since their identities are so well known. Even at the Wartburg, however, memorial transmission of patrons' names over a period of approximately fifty years is highly improbable. Kern proposes that the three princes refer to the Holy Trinity, a thesis that forces him into dubious emendation and far-fetched logic.

For all of Albrecht's posturing, his approach differs fundamentally from Wolfram's. In the prologue (19–21) he purports to answer those who have criticized the obliquity characteristic of *Parzival*. Although the poet derides Wolfram's detractors for their lack of perspicacity (19), the passage hardly constitutes a ringing defense; Albrecht's didactic purpose calls not for a dismissive attitude to the critics but for accommodation. The criticism was directed against the circuitous manner in which Wolfram approached the materials; Albrecht will eschew this tortuous route. Wherever a bend threatens to obscure the way, he intends to straighten it: "ich wil die krumb an allen orten slichten" (20,3). Rather than exclude audience members who might not be quick-witted enough to catch the import, Albrecht promises a form of assistance that he terms "worticlich bedûten" (50,2). Though certainly possible, the translation "to interpret literally" does not suit a work in which allegory figures prominently; a more accurate rendering would be "to spell things out," to make the meaning clear through explication and exegesis. He illustrates the approach with a commentary on selected images from the *Parzival* prologue. It is the primacy of didacticism that separates his work from that of Wolfram.

Der jüngere Titurel uses two Grail segments (86–668 and 5236–H6207) to bracket a massive core romance (669–5235). In the opening section Titurel's lineage is traced from Troy through Rome to the kingdom of the Franks (92–118). The line of descent moves inexorably toward the moment when God charges Titurel with custodial responsibility for the Holy Grail. Titurel undertakes the arduous journey to Salvaterre, where all is in readiness for his arrival. Salvaterre takes its name from *Salvator* (Savior), an indication of the land's special sta-

tus within the larger Christian context (322–324). Using a divinely revealed plan, Titurel presides over the construction of the Grail Temple on the summit of Munsalvaesche. The elaborate description of this edifice (329–439) and the subsequent allegorical interpretation of its architecture (514–586) mark the culmination of the opening section. The exegetical commentary forms part of Titurel's abdication speech, which also serves as a transition to the central tale of Sigune and Tschionatulander.

The core romance comprises nearly three-quarters (4,566 strophes in Wolf's edition) of *Der jüngere Titurel*. Tschionatulander, the squire of Parzival's father Gahmuret, does not stand in the line of succession for the throne on Munsalvaesche; except for Sigune, Titurel's great-granddaughter, he has little sustained contact with members of the Grail family. His activities remain within the temporal sphere, where capricious fortune and natural forces hold sway. When the hound Gardevias escapes, it is Duke Orilus of Lalander who chances upon dog and leash. Albrecht uses this change of possession as a motivational device. Sigune's obsession with the *Brackenseil* leads to confrontation and animosity between Schionatulander and Orilus. The wondrously wrought *Brackenseil* is actually a letter, sent by Clauditte to Ekunat, the brother of Tschionatulander's mother, Mahede. Clauditte, who reigns alone over Kanadic, lauds Ekunat for his many virtues, providing a portrait of the ideal ruler in the process.

Prior to the public reading of Clauditte's unconventional missive, emissaries arrive from the East with grave news of yet another Babylonian threat to the regional balance of power. Baruc Akerin of Baghdad, in whose service Gahmuret fought and died, appeals to Tschionatulander for help. The brothers Pompeius and Ipomidon, rulers of Babylon, have once again invaded the baruc's lands. Akerin cites the opportunity such a campaign will afford to take vengeance on Ipomidon for Gahmuret's death (1668). The lengthy account of this expedition dominates the remainder of the core. Akerin's emissaries bring costly gifts for Tschionatulander, including armor made from Tiger Gold (1675–1684) and the Salamander Shield (1696–1698). The former brings good luck to its owner, but misfortune if it is lost. The latter has a living salamander sealed within its boss. On the voyage to the East, Tschionatulander experiences a clash of elemental forces: sensing the salamander's presence, the sea rises up to extinguish the fire of which this creature is emblematic (2678–2715). Tschionatulander barely avoids catastrophe, but on the return voyage the shield and the armor are inadvertently sent back to Europe on the same cargo ship (4403–4410). Without Tschionatulander on board to intervene, the sea claims the vessel and its crew (4411–4415). When Akerin attempts to send Tschionatulander a replacement talisman made from Tiger Gold (4720–4727), it falls into Orilus's hands, with fateful consequences (4942–4977). Luck now rides with Orilus, and he slays Tschionatulander in knightly combat.

Working hastily, Albrecht brings the Grail's history to a resolution. When sin becomes rampant, God decides to remove the sacred object from an unworthy Europe (W6002–6048; H5964–5995 [there are seventeen additional strophes in Wolf's text]). The Grail is taken to India, where Prester John reigns over a fabulous kingdom. Parzival and his companions marvel at this easternmost bastion of Christianity (W6093–6142; H6031–6073 [seven additional strophes in Wolf's text]) but regret that the temple on Munsalvaesche could not have been erected here to provide a fitting sanctuary for the Grail. God responds by miraculously transporting Munsalvaesche and the Grail Temple to India (W6230–6235; H6160–6165). Confronted with such evidence of divine approbation, Prester John asks Titurel to apprise him of the nature of the Grail (W6236; H6166). The aged patriarch recounts how the chalice was carved from a stone and used at the Last Supper. Joseph of Arimathea later recognized the Grail and secretly kept it until the time of Titurel's guardianship (W6237–6246; H6167–6176). On hearing the story Prester John announces his intention to abdicate in favor of the current Grail king (H6189), but Parzival graciously refuses to accept this gesture by a ruler who is so obviously noble and virtuous (H6190–6201). Only when Parzival's name appears on the Grail (H6201,4) is the matter settled. God decrees that Parzival must first do penance for his sins and then be baptized anew with the name Prester John (H6202–6204). As Albrecht points out, similar preparatory steps are required of successors to the throne of Saint Peter (H6202,2). The analogy leaves little doubt that a vicar of God is to reign over the Grail's new home. Parzival is to be half prelate, half king. His accession has epochal significance, and eschatological expectations seem to lie just beneath the surface.

Bibliography:

Dietrich Huschenbett, "Bibliographie zum *Jüngeren Titurel*," *Wolfram-Studien*, 8 (1984): 169–176.

References:

Albrecht von Scharfenberg, *Merlin und Seifrid de Ardemont*, edited by Friedrich Panzer, Bibliothek des litterarischen Vereins in Stuttgart, no. 227 (Tübingen: Laupp, 1902);

Peter Jörg Becker, *Handschriften und Frühdrucke mittelhochdeutscher Epen* (Wiesbaden: Dr. Ludwig Reichert, 1977);

Helmut de Boor, "Drei Fürsten im mittleren Deutschland," *Festschrift für Ingeborg Schröbler zum 65. Geburtstag*, special issue of *Beiträge zur Geschichte der deutschen Sprache und Literatur*, 95 (1973): 238–257;

Joachim Bumke, *Mäzene im Mittelalter: Die Gönner und Auftraggeber der höfischen Literatur in Deutschland 1150–1300* (Munich: Beck, 1979);

Bumke, "Zur Überlieferung von Wolframs *Titurel*: Wolframs Dichtung und *Der jüngere Titurel*," *Zeitschrift für deutsches Altertum und deutsche Literatur*, 100 (1971): 390–431;

Alfred Ebenbauer, "Tschionatulander und Artus: Zur Gattungsstruktur und zur Interpretation des Tschionatulanderlebens im *Jüngeren Titurel*," *Zeitschrift für deutsches Altertum und deutsche Literatur*, 108 (1979): 374–407;

Hans Fromm, "Der *Jüngere Titurel*: Das Werk und sein Dichter," *Wolfram-Studien*, 8 (1984): 11–33;

Ulrich Füetrer, *Die Gralepen in Ulrich Füetrers Bearbeitung (Buch der Abenteuer)*, edited by Kurt Nyholm, Deutsche Texte des Mittelalters, no. 57 (Berlin: Akademie, 1964);

Joachim Heinzle, *Stellenkommentar zu Wolframs Titurel: Beiträge zum Verständnis des überlieferten Textes*, Hermaea: Germanistische Forschunge, new series 30 (Tübingen: Niemeyer, 1972);

Dietrich Huschenbett, "Albrecht, Dichter des *Jüngeren Titurel*," in *Die deutsche Literatur des Mittelalters: Verfasserlexikon*, second edition, volume 1 (Berlin & New York: De Gruyter, 1978), cols. 158–173;

Huschenbett, "Albrecht von Scharfenberg," in *Die deutsche Literatur des Mittelalters: Verfasserlexikon*, second edition, volume 1, cols. 200–206;

Huschenbett, "Der *Jüngere Titurel* als literaturgeschichtliches Problem," *Wolfram-Studien*, 8 (1984): 153–168;

Peter Kern, "Albrechts Gönner und die Wolfram-Rolle im *Jüngeren Titurel*," *Wolfram-Studien*, 8 (1984): 138–152;

Karl Lachmann, "Titurel und Dante," in his *Kleinere Schriften*, volume 1 (Berlin: Reimer, 1876), pp. 351–357;

R. William Leckie, Jr., "Albrecht von Scharfenberg and the *Historia de preliis Alexandri Magni*," *Zeitschrift für deutsches Altertum und deutsche Literatur*, 99 (1970): 120–139;

Hans-Georg Maak, "Zu Füetrers *fraw Eren hof* und der Frage nach dem Verfasser des *Jüngeren Titurel*," *Zeitschrift für deutsche Philologie*, 87 (1968): 42–46;

Volker Mertens, "Markgraf Heinrich III. von Meißen," in *Die deutsche Literatur des Mittelalters: Verfasserlexikon*, second edition, volume 3, cols. 785–787;

Nyholm, *Albrechts von Scharfenberg Merlin*, Acta Akademiae Aboensis, series A: Humaniora, 33/2 (Turku, Finland: Akademi, 1967);

Linda B. Parshall, *The Art of Narration in Wolfram's Parzival and Albrecht's Jüngerer Titurel*, Anglica Germanica, series 2 (Cambridge, New York & Melbourne: Cambridge University Press, 1981);

Erich Petzet, "Über das Heidelberger Bruchstück des *Jüngeren Titurel*," *Sitzungsberichte der philosophisch-philologischen und historischen Klasse der k. b. Akademie der Wissenschaften zu München* (1903): 287–320;

Jakob Püterich von Reichertshausen, *Der Ehrenbrief des Püterich von Reichertshausen*, 2 volumes, edited by Fritz Behrend and Rudolf Wolkan (Weimar: Gesellschaft der Bibliophilen, 1920);

Hans-Henning Rausch, *Methoden und Bedeutung naturkundlicher Rezeption und Kompilation im Jüngeren Titurel*, Microkosmos: Beiträge zur Literaturwissenschaft und Bedeutungsforschung, no. 2 (Frankfurt am Main: Lang, 1977);

Walter Röll, "Berthold von Regensburg und der *Jüngere Titurel*," *Wolfram-Studien*, 8 (1984): 67–93;

Röll, *Studien zu Text und Überlieferung des sogenannten Jüngeren Titurel*, Germanistische Bibliothek, Dritte Reihe: Untersuchungen und Einzeldarstellungen (Heidelberg: Winter, 1964);

August Wilhelm Schlegel, Review of B. J. Docen's *Erstes Sendschreiben über den Titurel*, *Heidelbergische Jahrbücher der Literatur*, 68–70 (1811): 1073–1075;

Werner Schröder, *Demontage und Montage von Wolframs Prologen im Prolog zum Jüngeren Titurel*, Abhandlungen der Marburger Gelehrten Gesellschaft, no. 19 (Munich: Fink, 1983);

Schröder, "Der Schluß des *Jüngeren Titurel*," *Zeitschrift für deutsches Altertum und deutsche Literatur*, 111 (1982): 103–134;

Schröder, "Textkritisches zum *Jüngeren Titurel*," *Wolfram-Studien*, 8 (1984): 34–48;

Schröder, *Wolfram-Nachfolge im Jüngeren Titurel: Devotion oder Arroganz*, Frankfurter wissenschaftliche Beiträge, Kulturwissenschaftliche Reihe, no. 15 (Frankfurt am Main: Klostermann, 1982);

Werner Wolf, "Wer war der Dichter des *Jüngeren Titurel*?," *Zeitschrift für deutsches Altertum und deutsche Literatur*, 84 (1953): 309–346;

Wolfram von Eschenbach, *Titurel and the Songs*, translated by Marion E. Gibbs and Sidney M. Johnson, Garland Library of Medieval Literature, Series A, no. 57 (New York & London: Garland, 1988).

Kudrun

(circa 1230 – 1240)

Winder McConnell
University of California, Davis

Manuscript: The only extant manuscript of *Kudrun* is in the Ambraser Heldenbuch (Vienna, Österreichische Nationalbibliothek, cod. Ser. nov. 2663, f.140ª–166ª). Emperor Maximilian I commissioned the collection, which includes twenty-five works; his secretary, Hans Ried, copied *Kudrun* from an earlier manuscript during the first quarter of the sixteenth century.

First publication: "Gudrun," *Deutsche Gedichte des Mittelalters*, 2 volumes, edited by Friedrich Heinrich von der Hagen and J. G. Büshing, volume 2, part 1: *Der Helden Buch in der Ursprache*, edited by von der Hagen and Alois Primisser (Berlin: Realschulbuchhandlung, 1820).

Standard editions: *Kudrun*, edited by Karl Bartsch (Leipzig: Brockhaus, 1865); revised edition, edited by Karl Stackmann (Wiesbaden: Brockhaus, 1965); *Kudrun*, edited by Bernd Symons (Halle: Niemeyer, 1883); republished, edited by Bruno Boesch, Altdeutsche Textbibliothek, no. 5 (Tübingen: Niemeyer, 1964); *Kudrun; Die Handschrift*, edited by Franz H. Bäuml (Berlin: De Gruyter, 1969); *Kudrun: Vollständige Faksimile-Ausgabe im Originalformat des Codex Vindobonensis Seria nova 2663 der Österreichischen Nationalbibliothek*, edited by Franz Unterkircher (Graz: Akademische Druck- und Verlagsanstalt, 1973).

Editions in modern German: *Kudrun: Ein mittelalterliches Heldenepos*, translated by Joachim Lindner, second edition (Berlin: Verlag der Nation, 1971); *Kudrun*, translated by Karl Simrock, edited by Friedrich Neumann (Stuttgart: Reclam, 1986).

Editions in English: Translated by Mary Pickering Nichols as *Gudrun: A Medieval Epic* (Boston & New York: Houghton, Mifflin, 1889); translated by Margaret Armour as *Gudrun* (London: Dent, 1928; New York: Dutton, 1928); *Kudrun*, translated by Brian O. Murdoch (London: Dent, 1987); *Kudrun*, translated by Marion E. Gibbs and Sidney M. Johnson, Garland Library of Medieval Literature, volume 79 (New York & London: Garland, 1992); *Kudrun*, translated by Winder McConnell, edited by Evelyn S. Firchow, Studies in German Literature, Linguistics, and Culture, vol. 73 (Columbia, S.C.: Camden House, 1992).

Kudrun is an epic of 1,705 four-line strophes, undoubtedly influenced by the *Nibelungenlied*, (Song of the Nibelungs, 1200–1210) with an *aabb* rhyme scheme throughout, arranged in thirty-two *aventiuren* (cantos). Nothing is known about the origins of the poet or of the circumstances that surrounded the genesis of the epic. The authorship of *Kudrun* as well as that of the *Nibelungenlied* will most likely continue to remain unknown, and anonymity may have been integral to the genre. Each work was probably composed for performance in song before an aristocratic audience over a period of several days, perhaps during or after a banquet at court. What is striking about both epics is the fascination on the part of the poets with the female protagonists, who, even though they may remain objects in the eyes of some of the male characters, are responsible for the negative or positive outcomes of their respective tales. The major protagonist in Kudrun is a woman who finds herself in a seemingly hopeless situation. Her sense of integrity, loyalty, and honor, combined with her will to persevere — that she is the granddaughter of the renowned and feared Irish king, Hagen, is stressed when Kudrun faces her greatest ordeals — insures that she will never compromise and give in to Norman demands so as to improve her lot while in captivity. She is a woman wronged, but, unlike Kriemhild in the *Nibelungenlied*, she never allows herself to become obsessed with a thirst for revenge.

The thirty-two *aventiuren* (normally rendered, somewhat freely, into English as "books" or "chapters") of *Kudrun* have been traditionally divided into

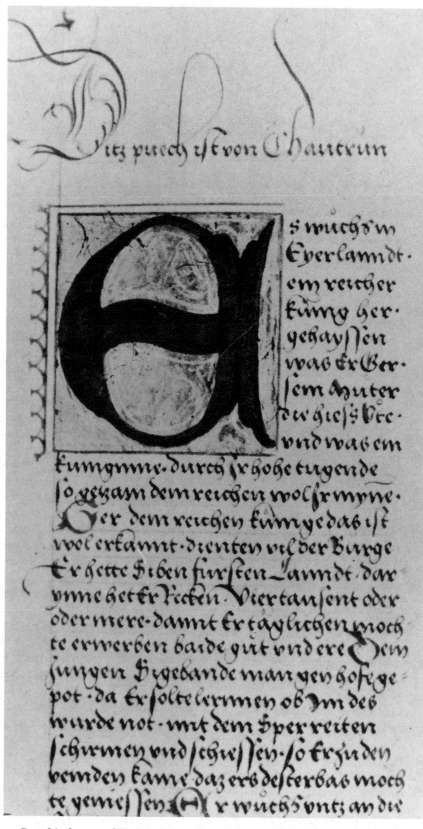

Part of the first page of Kudrun *in the early-sixteenth-century Ambraser Heldenbuch (Vienna, Österreichische Nationalbibliothek, Cod. Ser. nov. 2663, f.140ᵃ)*

three major sections: *Aventiuren* 1 through 4 deal with Hagen, prince and later king of Ireland; *Aventiuren* 5 through 8 with the "abduction" of his daughter, Hilde, and her marriage to King Hetel of Hegelingenland; and *Aventiuren* 9 through 32 with the kidnapping of Hagen's granddaughter, Kudrun, by Norman forces under the command of King Ludwig and his son, Hartmut, her captivity, and her rescue, engineered by the irascible Wate of Stormarn. Although it has been contended by some scholars that the Hagen section is a later addition to the epic and that the Kudrun section is simply an expanded version of the original "core" of the tale – the story of Hilde – the sense of unity that pervades the work is underscored by the familial associations and the harmonious conclusion to each section. *Kudrun* is concerned with continuity among several generations of the same family, beginning with the heroine's great-great-grandfather and concluding with the union between Kudrun and Herwig.

Analogues of Hagen, Hetel, and Wate occur as the names of leaders of prominent tribes in the eighth-century Old Saxon poem *Widsith,* which derives its material from the fourth through the sixth centuries. Furthermore, the name of Horand, who plays a prominent role in the Hilde section of *Kudrun,* also occurs in the seventh stanza of the eighth-century Old Saxon *Deor's Lament.* It has been conjectured that the story of Hilde lies at the core of the poem and that it originally contained a deeply tragic element in which Hagen meets his death at the hands of Hetel. A reflection of this earlier tragic outcome is to be detected in the allusion to the killing of Hagen by Wate, Hetel's liege man, in Pfaffe Lamprecht's *Alexanderlied* (Song of Alexander, circa 1130–1150).

Scholars have linked Wate with such Germanic deities as Wotan, Donar, and Aegir. Attempts to link episodes in *Kudrun* with actual historical events have been futile, although Brian Murdoch has pointed out that the overall "tenor" of the wooing and raiding expeditions underscores the "Viking presence" that is still much in evidence within the work.

While Stephen L. Wailes has labeled *Kudrun* a "Romance" and Theodor Nolte has designated it a "Frauenroman" (novel about women), most scholars seem to regard the work as a heroic epic that includes elements from diverse generic traditions. Young Hagen's fight against the *gabilûn* (lizardlike monster) that wishes to devour him and the increased strength he derives from skinning this mythological beast and drinking its blood are reminiscent of Siegfried's encounter with the dragon in the *Nibelungenlied.* The various wooing episodes and

the roles played by the artist Horand and the irascible, Brobdingnagian-like Wate have much in common with the German *Spielmannsepik* (minstrel epic) tradition, evincing parallels to both *Dukus Horant* and *König Rother,* in particular. The cyclical thematic structure (initial joy and harmony – period of crisis – successful rescue mission or overcoming of obstacles – restoration of joy and harmony) parallels that of courtly romance. The intentionally degrading "clothes washing" motif, which signals the lowest point of Kudrun's period of captivity among the Normans, is also to be found in the Judeo-Spanish ballad "Don Bueso y su hermana" (Don Bueso and His Sister), as well as in one of the legends from the island of Rügen in the Baltic, whose inhabitants were also familiar with the magnetic-mountain motif encountered during the second rescue mission of the Hegelings. This combination of elements does not, however, result in a lack of unity within *Kudrun:* the various episodes are linked by the common themes of productive leadership and continuity; the reader never gains the impression that the diversity of traditions that have gone into the constitution of *Kudrun* has in any way obscured the main focus of its poet.

Among works generally categorized as heroic epics in German medieval literature, *Kudrun* is an anomaly. While it conforms to the criteria that have been accepted as characteristic of the genre – anonymity of authorship, emphasis on mass battle scenes rather than individual combat, strophic form, and heroic landscape – the accent is on continuity and reconciliation, and it is the women of *Kudrun* who figure most prominently in the plot; the majority of listeners to recitations of the tale may have been noblewomen and their retinues. The poet offers in the two Hildes and Kudrun his image of the perfect partner for any king and in Gerlind, who has some parallels to the dark figure of Kriemhild, a graphic portrayal of what women should avoid. The independent nature of the female figures and the particularly heroic bearing of Kudrun could hardly have failed to impress the women of the court and made them well disposed toward the minstrel for such a positive portrayal of their sex.

Werner Hoffmann has shown that *Kudrun* was an "answer" to the *Nibelungenlied.* If the *Nibelungenlied* contains a message, it is to be found in its closing words: that all joy eventually turns to sorrow. Events in the *Nibelungenlied* proceed inexorably and in linear fashion to the cataclysmic, Armageddon-like conclusion, leaving the modern reader (and undoubtedly the medieval listener) with the sense of a moral void. This nihilistic view of the world, with no promise of consolation in the next, had no equal in the vernacular literature of the period. Given the genesis of *Kudrun* in written form – probably within forty years after the appearance of the *Nibelungenlied* – it seems to be an effort to counter the negativism of the earlier work through the promotion of a spirit of reconciliation, harmony, and restoration of order within society, showing that, in the end, all crises and sorrow can be transformed into peace and happiness. Marion E. Gibbs and Sidney M. Johnson have characterized *Kudrun* as "altogether more 'Christian' in its outlook" than the *Nibelungenlied;* the references to Christianity in *Kudrun,* however, do not leave the impression that its message is to be understood in terms of the orthodox theology of the time. It is significant that women consistently occupy pivotal roles as mediators and peacemakers in *Kudrun,* in contrast to the destructive proclivities of Kriemhild in the *Nibelungenlied.*

It was fashionable in the nineteenth and early twentieth centuries to compare the *Nibelungenlied* to Homer's *Iliad* and *Kudrun* to the *Odyssey.* The analogy is no longer made, but it was, in at least one respect, quite valid: even if the poet of *Kudrun* never read the *Odyssey,* there are aspects of the great classical work that the reader can also detect in the thirteenth-century epic. In a highly perceptive remark on the *Odyssey,* Camille Paglia has said: "The masculine glamour of the *Iliad* is gone. When we first see the hero of the *Odyssey,* he is weeping. The ruling virtues of this poem are female perception and endurance, rather than aggressive action." It would be wrong to suggest that there is no "aggressive action" in *Kudrun,* but, in contrast to the *Nibelungenlied,* it is not the "ruling virtue." "Female perception" is demonstrated in the concern for continuity, expressed through the desire for reconciliation among warring parties, and the capacity for "endurance" is embodied by the three princesses in the land of the griffins; by the younger Hilde, who, until her "abduction" by the Hegelings, lives in virtual captivity at the hands of her overprotective father, Hagen; and by Kudrun herself, who endures years of hardship and deprivation in Normandy as a prisoner of Gerlind, Ludwig, and Hartmut.

Kudrun spans five generations, culminating in the tale of the title figure. It is possible that a tempering of the spirit was intended by the poet as he moved from one generation to the next. For example, Wate embodies a different ethos from that of Kudrun or even Wate's fellow warrior Irold, who admonishes Wate for killing the Norman infants in their cribs during the taking of Kassiane. Yet it does not appear to have been the poet's aim to attack the more archaic ways of the older generations, for Wate plays an integral role in the process of reconciliation and bonding that follows the rescue of Kudrun and her return to Hegelingenland.

Common to each of the three major sections of the epic is the abduction motif. Hagen, Prince of Ireland, is carried off as a child by a demonic griffin, to be fed to its progeny. After escaping from the talons of one of the young griffins, Hagen spends several years in this otherworldly realm in the company of three princesses who have also been abducted by the predator. Although his salvation from the griffins – all of which he eventually kills – is initially attributed to God, references to the Almighty become fewer as the story progresses. Hagen's power and self-confidence increase radically, and while he serves as an exemplary protector of the three princesses, he also acquires some of the wilder and more primitive characteristics of this otherworld, of which he becomes master. He returns to Ireland and later assumes the kingship, and the harsh measures he metes out to suitors of his daughter as well as to lawbreakers – he kills them all – earn him the appellation "Vâlant aller künige" (devil-giant among all kings).

The "abduction" of Hagen's daughter, Hilde, by Hegelings disguised as merchants under the joint command of Wate and Horand, actually involves the connivance of Hilde, who thereby escapes from the semicaptivity in which she has been held by her father. While it has been conjectured that Hagen's severe treatment of suitors is a reflection of an archaic incest motif, it is more likely that it is overprotectiveness on the part of an individual who, as a child and an adolescent, came to appreciate the importance of independent strength and power in a highly unpredictable and dangerous world. Although he makes a valiant effort to retrieve his daughter, the Irish king is ultimately satisfied to know that she will be the wife of a monarch as powerful as Hetel.

The major section of the work relates the story of Hagen's granddaughter, the Hegeling princess Kudrun: her betrothal to King Herwig; her abduction by Prince Hartmut of Normandy; her years of humiliating captivity in the Norman stronghold of Kassiane; her eventual rescue after a disastrous initial attempt that claims the life of her father, Hetel; and, above all, her role as mediator in the reconciliation between the Normans and the Hegelings. The focus throughout this part of the epic is on the heroism of Kudrun during her years in bondage.

Part of a page from the manuscript for Kudrun, *on which appears a passage from the twenty-eighth* aventiur: *Herwig's killing of Ludwig (Vienna, Österreichisches Nationalbibliothek, Cod. Ser. nov. 2663, f. 161v)*

One of the most notable aspects of the major female figures in *Kudrun* is their ability to persevere under extremely adverse conditions. The three abducted princesses who share Hagen's plight in the realm of the gabilûn maintain their courtly bearing even in this wilderness. Hilde is subjected to a form of captivity by her father, who sees to it that neither sun nor wind may touch her and, through the brutal treatment to which he subjects suitors or their envoys, removes her from the marriage market – a nonproductive and unnatural situation that cannot continue. Kudrun spends many years as a prisoner of the Normans in Kassiane and refuses to better her lot by acquiescing to Hartmut's overtures of marriage. In all three instances the women are successful in preserving and asserting their independence. But it is not simply as quiet martyrs that women stand out in *Kudrun:* they are repeatedly the individuals who take the initiative in observing proprieties in society – as when Ute, Hagen's mother, encourages Sigeband, his father, to avoid falling into disrepute through "acedia" (sloth) and to sponsor a grand festival. Although some scholars see this suggestion as a reflection of a negative side of the Irish queen, it is much more indicative of the positive role as restorers of harmony and guarantors of balance assumed by female regents in courtly society. It is also Ute who is chiefly concerned about maintaining the honor of the Irish court after the abduction of Hagen: despite the catastrophe, invited guests must be accorded all due pomp and circumstance. Later Kudrun will be the one to initiate the sending of aid to Herwig by the Hegelings when her betrothed is attacked by one of her former suitors, Sîvrît of Morland. After Hetel's death in the fight against the Normans on the Wülpensand, Kudrun's mother, Hilde, will function as the strategist in the efforts to free her daughter and avenge the Hegeling losses.

There is, however, one woman in *Kudrun* who has a primarily negative impact on society: the Norman queen, Gerlind. From the moment she is introduced it is evident that Gerlind is the de facto ruler of Normandy and that her husband, Ludwig, occupies a subordinate role to his spouse. Gerlind's defiance of the order of feudal society leads to her death and the demise of Norman power. She is called "vâlandinne" (devil-woman) by the poet, but while she may share this description with Kriemhild in the *Nibelungenlied,* she does not match the latter in demonic intensity. On one level, Gerlind is simply an overzealous mother who will do whatever she can to insure the happiness of her son, Hartmut, as well as the continuity of the royal line. On another level, her denigration of Kudrun may be interpreted as a snubbing of the basic premises on which aristocratic society is founded. Gerlind is a paradox: she wishes fervently to secure the stability of Norman power through the marriage of Kudrun to her son, but she destroys her realm through her machinations; she wishes to teach Kudrun humility, to put an end to what she sees as the haughtiness of the Hegeling princess, while at the same time her own arrogance knows no bounds. Only a woman of stature, in Gerlind's eyes, would be worthy to rule next to her son, but she insists on denigrating Kudrun to the status of washerwoman. Gerlind becomes an archenemy of the basic order of medieval society and, consequently, a prime target of old Wate's wrath.

Marriage is a major motif in all of the subplots in *Kudrun,* reflecting a real concern of medieval aristocratic society. The selection of an appropriate spouse through deliberations with counselors and family members represents a high point in both the private and public life of a prince or king, who is ultimately incomplete without a female counterpart. A suitable and successful marriage by Hagen of Ireland to Hilde of Portugal had been followed by a similar union between Hetel of Hegelingenland and the Irish princess Hilde; in the case of Hartmut, it would appear that succession to the Norman throne is predicated on his marriage to an unwilling Kudrun. The epic concludes with the depiction of four unions: of Hartmut to Kudrun's lady-in-waiting, Hildeburg; of Ortwin, Kudrun's brother, to Ortrun, Hartmut's sister; of Herwig's unnamed sister to Siegfried, King of the Moors; and of Kudrun to Herwig. The four queens are crowned at the Hegeling court. The idea of wholeness appears to be underscored by the occurrence of the number four, the number most commonly employed in medieval literature to symbolize unity or completeness. Here, then, is one of the most striking contrasts to the *Nibelungenlied,* in which false marriages, based on deceit and self-deception, lead first to individual and ultimately to collective tragedy. With the successful overcoming of hurdles and crises in *Kudrun,* harmony, balance, and the natural order of things are restored, and the epic concludes on a highly optimistic note.

Although *Kudrun* shares the positive cyclical thematic pattern to be found in romance, it is also concerned with certain matters of state that have no role in that genre: individuals in *Kudrun* are linked to powerful societies or clans with specific pragmatic goals. Alliances, power, and the preservation and enhancement of honor and status, both personal and collective, are motivating factors in choosing a bride, deciding to go to war, or even sponsoring festivals.

If one were to choose a single word to express the major theme of the work, it would be *continuity:* the promise of a productive future that is symbolized by the multiple marriages that take place at the end of the epic could not represent a more decisive contrast with the apocalyptic outcome of its great predecessor, the *Nibelungenlied.* Moreover, in contrast to the *Nibelungenlied,* the bonds of kinship remain firm in the later epic. It is also primarily a work about women: *Kudrun* presents a view of women's role in aristocratic society that has no equal in medieval German literature. The individual characteristics of the women of *Kudrun* can be detected elsewhere, of course: Enite, in Hartmann von Aue's *Erec* (circa 1180), is as concerned about courtly propriety as is Ute; Kriemhild and Brünhild in the *Nibelungenlied* have traits that may be compared to those of Kudrun, albeit quite distinct ones in each case and with vastly different consequences for the individuals concerned and for society as a whole. What makes this epic unique with respect to the role of women is not only the manner in which the feminine element perseveres in the face of adversity but also how it consistently functions as the key factor in preserving the delicate bonds within society. The sense of "woman as an object" is replaced by that of "woman as guide." Woman is consistently at the forefront, sometimes in a negative capacity – as in the case of Gerlind – but primarily as the initiator of reconciliation between the warring parties and as the driving force behind the collective marriages at the conclusion of the work. Kudrun herself is no superwoman, and she exhibits understandable human emotions during her ordeal at the Norman stronghold. Her heroism lies in her perseverance and in her rejection of revenge for past wrongs.

In contrast to the women, the male figures in *Kudrun,* excepting Hagen, Wate, and Horand, scarcely leave a memorable impression on the reader. Although they are active participants in wars, feuds, and wooing expeditions, the delineation of their characters tends to be static. Hagen stands out as a consequence of his adventures in the land of the griffins and the effect this experience has on his role as king of Ireland. Horand's talent as a musician is integral to the successful wooing of Hilde for Hetel, but he has little to do for the rest of the work. Wate seems to enjoy the particular favor of the poet as a representative of a past less given to compromise; he is the closest thing in the epic to a Germanic hero. Apart from these three, the men of *Kudrun* are devoid of individual characteristics and

are appropriately regarded as type figures in a work that has deliberately laid emphasis on the female element.

Kudrun has not been as popular with readers or scholars as the *Nibelungenlied,* although scores of New High German translations appeared in the late nineteenth century and the first quarter of the twentieth. Since the late 1960s, however, interest in *Kudrun* has been rejuvenated through the work of scholars such as Hoffmann, Johnson and Gibbs, Murdoch, Franz H. Bäuml, Ian R. Campbell, Nolte, Donald J. Ward, and Roswitha Wisniewski, and much attention has been paid to the significance of the role played by women. *Kudrun* can stand on its own as a formidable work of art of the early thirteenth century, but its significance as a cultural and psychological document is more clearly delineated when it is compared with its great predecessor. The *Nibelungenlied* depicts the dissolution of empires, and its major female protagonist is a key factor in the process; *Kudrun* emphasizes preservation and intactness, and here women counter the aggressive male warrior ethos. In the *Nibelungenlied* the feminine element becomes alienated from society, as shown by Kriemhild's metamorphosis into a she-devil; in *Kudrun* that element is integrated into society, suggesting awareness on the part of the poet of the necessity of according it its due. Kudrun herself is the culmination of a line of independent women who defy the common perception of the female as a virtual nonentity in the medieval world.

References:

Franz H. Bäuml, "The Gabilûn-Episode in *Kudrun:* Some Palaeographic Implications," *Manuscripta,* 9 (July 1965): 67–78;

Adolf Beck, "Die Rache als Motiv und Problem in der *Kudrun,*" *Germanisch-Romanische Monatsschrift,* new series 6 (1956): 305–338;

Ian R. Campbell, *Kudrun: A Critical Appreciation* (Cambridge: Cambridge University Press, 1978);

Jean Carles, *Le Poème de Kûdrûn: Etude de sa matière,* Publications de la Faculté des Lettres et Sciences Humaines de l'Université de Clermont-Ferrand, 2e Série, Fasc. XVI (Paris: Presses Universitaires de France, 1963);

Alfred Haas, *Rügensche Sagen,* seventh edition (Stettin: A. Schuster, 1926);

Werner Hoffmann, "Die Hauptprobleme der neueren 'Kudrun'-Forschung," *Wirkendes Wort,* 14, nos. 3 and 4 (1964): 183–196, 233–243;

Hoffmann, "Kudrun," in *Mittelhochdeutsche Romane und Heldenepen,* edited by Horst Brunner (Stuttgart: Reclam, 1993), pp. 293–310;

Hoffmann, *Kudrun: Ein Beitrag zur nachnibelungischen Heldendichtung,* Germanistische Abhandlungen, no. 17 (Stuttgart: Metzler, 1967);

Eduard Huber, "Die Kudrun um 1300," *Zeitschrift für deutsche Philologie,* 100 (1981): 357–381;

Eckart Loerzer, *Eheschließung und Werbung in der "Kudrun,"* Münchener Texte und Untersuchungen zur deutschen Literatur des Mittelalters, volume 37 (Munich: Beck, 1971);

Helmut Maisack, *"Kudrun" zwischen Spanien und Byzanz: 5.-13. Jahrhundert,* Philologische Studien und Quellen, volume 90 (Berlin: Schmidt, 1978);

Winder McConnell, *The Epic of Kudrun: A Critical Commentary* (Göppingen: Kümmerle, 1988);

McConnell, "Hagen and the Otherworld in *Kudrun,*" *Res Publica Litterarum,* 6 (1983): 211–221;

McConnell, "The Passing of the Old Heroes: The *Nibelungenlied, Kudrun,* and the Epic Spirit," in *Genres in Medieval German Literature,* edited by Hubert Heinen and Ingeborg Henderson (Göppingen: Kümmerle, 1986), pp. 103–113;

McConnell, *The Wate Figure in Medieval Tradition,* Stanford German Studies, no. 13 (Bern: Lang, 1978);

Brian Murdoch, "Interpreting *Kudrun:* Some Comments on a Recent Critical Appreciation," *New German Studies,* 7 (1979): 113–127;

Theodor Nolte, *Das Kudrunepos – Ein Frauenroman?,* Untersuchungen zur deutschen Literaturgeschichte, volume 38 (Tübingen: Niemeyer, 1985);

Nolte, *Wiedergefundene Schwester und befreite Braut: Kudrunepos und Balladen* (Stuttgart: Helfant Edition, 1988);

Camille Paglia, *Sexual Personae: Art and Decadence from Nefertiti to Emily Dickinson* (New York: Vintage, 1990);

Friedrich Panzer, *Hilde-Gudrun: Eine sagen- und literargeschichtliche Untersuchung* (Hildesheim: Olms, 1978);

Hellmut Rosenfeld, "Die Kudrun: Nordseedichtung oder Donaudichtung?," *Zeitschrift für deutsche Philologie,* 81, no. 3 (1962): 289–314;

Heinz Rupp, ed., *Nibelungenlied und Kudrun,* Wege der Forschung, no. 54 (Darmstadt: Wissenschaftliche Buchgesellschaft, 1976);

Ursula Schulze, "Nibelungenlied und Kudrun," in *Epische Stoffe des Mittelalters,* edited by Volker Mertens und Ulrich Müller (Stuttgart: Kröner, 1984), pp. 111–140;

Barbara Siebert, *Rezeption und Produktion: Bezugssysteme in der "Kudrun"* (Göppingen: Kümmerle, 1988);

Hinrich Siefkin, *Überindividuelle Formen und der Aufbau des Kudrunepos,* Medium Aevum: Philologische Studien, volume 11 (Munich: Fink, 1971);

Karl Stackmann, "Kudrun," in *Die deutsche Literatur des Mittelalters: Verfasserlexikon,* edited by Kurt Ruh, second edition, volume 5, parts 1 & 2 (Berlin & New York: De Gruyter, 1984), cols. 410–426;

Stephen L. Wailes, "The Romance of Kudrun," *Speculum,* 58, (April 1983): 347–367;

Donald J. Ward, "The Rescue of Kudrun: A Dioscuric Myth?," *Classica Mediaevalia,* 26 (1965): 334–353;

Ward and Bäuml, "Zur Kudrun-Problematik: Ballade und Epos," *Zeitschrift für deutsche Philologie,* 88, no. 1 (1969): 19–27;

Inga Wild, *Zur Überlieferung und Rezeption des Kudrun-Epos: Eine Untersuchung von drei europäischen Liedbereichen des "Typs Südeli"* (Göppingen: Kümmerle, 1979);

Roswitha Wisniewski, *Kudrun,* second edition, Sammlung Metzler, 32 (Stuttgart: Metzler, 1969).

Minnesang

(circa 1150 – 1280)

Hubert Heinen
University of Texas at Austin

Manuscripts: The oldest song anthology with German texts, M (Codex Buranus [*Carmina Burana*], Munich, Bayerische Staatsbibliothek, clm 4660), dating from the early to mid thirteenth century, includes forty-five anonymous strophes (each concluding a Latin song). There are three extensive collections of medieval German love songs, organized by author, on parchment: A (Kleine Heidelberger Liederhandschrift, Heidelberg, Universitätsbibliothek, cpg 357), dating from the late thirteenth century, includes songs by 30 named singers who lived between 1180 and 1240 and an anonymous appendix; B (Weingartner Liederhandschrift, Stuttgart, Württembergische Landesbibliothek, HB XIII, pg 1), dating from the early fourteenth century, includes songs with 25 miniatures of the named singers, most of whom lived between 1170 and 1240; and C (Große Heidelberger [Manessische] Liederhandschrift, Heidelberg, Universitätsbibliothek, cpg 848), dating from the first half of the fourteenth century (the basic collection is dated 1300–1310), includes six thousand strophes of songs, with 138 miniatures of 140 named singers (some fictitious), who lived between 1150 and 1300 (it is the most extensive collection of German songs from the twelfth and thirteenth centuries). J (Jenaer Liederhandschrift, Jena, Universitätsbibliothek, Ms. El. f. 101), dating from the mid fourteenth century, includes works by twenty-eight authors, mostly from central Germany; many of the texts include music; this manuscript is an extensive anthology predominantly of *Sangsprüche* (didactic songs). Some strophes can also be found in other parchment codices: D/H (Middle High German Didactic Songs / Early Mastersongs, Heidelberg, Universitätsbibliothek, cpg 350), dating from the end of the thirteenth and beginning of the fourteenth centuries, is an extensive collection of didactic songs; Bu (Budapest Fragments, Budapest, Széchényi National Library, Cod. germ. 92), dating from the fourteenth century, includes twenty-one strophes and 3 miniatures; Gx (Munich Fragment, Munich, Bayerische Staatsbibliothek, cgm 5249/74), dating from the mid fourteenth century, includes twenty-one strophes; p (Bern Miscellany, Bern, Burgerbibliothek, cod. 260), dating from the mid fourteenth century, includes thirty-six strophes; s (Hague Song Codex, The Hague, Koninklijke Bibliotheek, Cod. 128 E 2), dating from around 1400, includes 115 songs. Paper manuscripts include x (Berlin Song Codex, Berlin, Staatsbibliothek Preußischer Kulturbesitz, Ms. germ. 2^0 922), dating from around 1410 to 1430, includes 86 songs; K (also t) (Kolmar Song Codex, Munich, Bayerische Staatsbibliothek, cgm 4997), dating from around 1470, comprises 856 leaves and includes mostly fifteenth-century *Meistergesang* but also some texts ascribed to Walther von der Vogelweide, Wolfram von Eschenbach, Neidhart von Reuental, and Tannhäuser, with melodies. Facsimiles or diplomatic editions of most of the manuscripts exist.

First publication: *Minnesinger: Deutsche Liederdichter des zwölften, dreizehnten und vierzehnten Jahrhunderts,* edited by Friedrich Heinrich von der Hagen, 5 volumes in 4 (Leipzig: Barth, 1838–1861; reprinted, Aalen: Zeller 1962–1963).

Standard editions: *Des Minnesangs Frühling,* edited by Karl Lachmann and Moriz Haupt (Stuttgart: Hirzel, 1857); revised by Hugo Moser and Helmut Tervooren (Stuttgart: Hirzel, 1988 [MF]); *Die Schweizer Minnesänger* edited by Karl Bartsch (Frauenfeld: Huber,

*Miniature depicting the minnesinger Heinrich von Morungen in the Große Heidelberger
Liederhandschrift (Heidelberg, Universitätsbibliothek, cpg. 848, f. 76v)*

1886); revised by Max Schiendorfer
(Tübingen: Niemeyer, 1990 [SSM]); *Der Dich-
ter Tannhäuser: Leben – Gedichte – Sage,* edited
by Johannes Siebert (Halle: Niemeyer, 1934
[ST]); *Deutsche Liederdichter des 13. Jahrhunderts,*
2 volumes, edited by Carl von Kraus and
Hugo Kuhn (Tübingen: Niemeyer, 1952,
1958 [KLD]); *Tannhäuser: Die lyrischen Gedichte
der Handschriften C und J,* edited by Helmut
Lomnitzer and Ulrich Müller (Göppingen:
Kümmerle, 1973); *Carmina Burana,* edited by
Benedikt Konrad Vollmann (Frankfurt am
Main: Deutscher Klassiker Verlag, 1987);
Mutabilität im Minnesang: Mehrfach überlieferte

Lieder des 12. und frühen 13. Jahrhunderts, edited
by Hubert Heinen (Göppingen: Kümmerle,
1989).

Editions in modern German: *Deutsche
Lyrik des Mittelalters,* translated by Max
Wehrli (Zurich: Manesse, 1955); *Die
Mittelhochdeutsche Minnelyrik I: Die frühe
Minnelyrik,* translated by Günther Schweikle
(Darmstadt: Wissenschaftliche Buchgesellschaft,
1977); *Gedichte von den Anfängen bis 1300,* trans-
lated by Werner Höver and Eva Kiepe (Mu-
nich: Deutscher Taschenbuch Verlag, 1978);
Minnesang, translated by Helmut Brackert
(Frankfurt am Main: Fischer, 1983); *Deutsche*

Gedichte des Mittelalters, translated by Ulrich Müller and Gerlinde Weiss (Stuttgart: Reclam, 1993).

Editions in English: Frank C. Nicholson, trans., *Old German Love Songs* (London: Unwin, 1907); Jethro Bithell, trans., *The Minnesingers,* 2 volumes (New York: Longmans, 1909); M. F. Richey, trans., *Medieval German Lyrics* (Edinburgh: Oliver & Boyd, 1958); Barbara G. Seagrave and J. Wesley Thomas, trans., *The Songs of the Minnesingers* (Urbana: University of Illinois Press, 1966); Frederick Goldin, trans., *German and Italian Lyrics of the Middle Ages* (New York: Norton, 1973).

Almost nothing is known about the lives of the minnesingers; that someone was a minnesinger did not warrant his mention in the documents of the time. The almost accidental reference to Walther von der Vogelweide as a singer is a rare exception; the travel expense account in which his name is mentioned was not, however, an official document. Any information about a singer's life or the time in which he lived must be deduced, through the haze of fiction and convention, from the songs themselves. Most of the minnesingers lived long before the extant manuscripts were written; their songs, however, appear to have been written down as, or soon after, they were created, rather than having been passed on for any considerable length of time in oral tradition.

The first minnesinger whose songs have been preserved is Der von Kürenberg. The fifteen strophes in manuscript C (the first nine of which are also in manuscript Bu) are archaic in form – most of them have much the same strophe as the *Nibelungenlied* (Song of the Nibelungs, circa 1200) and include slant rhymes, such as *fliegen / riemen,* that are common in rhymed couplets from the mid twelfth century – and they seem largely uninfluenced by the traditions of troubadour song. Dating them from 1150 must be based on such considerations, since they first appear around a century and a half later and are not attested in any of the thirteenth-century manuscripts. The first two strophes give an impression of the whole corpus:

'Vil lieber vriunt,   daz ist schedelîch;
swer sînen vriunt behaltet,   daz ist lobelîch
die site wil ich minnen.
bite in, daz er mir holt sî,   als er hie bevor was,
und man in, waz wir redeten,   dô ich in ze jungest sach.'

Wes manst dû mich leides,   mîn vil liebe?
unser beider scheiden   müeze ich geleben niet.
verliuse ich dîne minne,

sô lâze ich diu liute   wol entstân,
daz mîn vröide ist der minnest,   und alle andere man.
(MF7, 1–18)

('Many dear friends [lovers], that is harmful;
if someone retains his friend, that is praiseworthy.
I will admire those customs.
Ask him to cherish me as he did before
and remind him what we said when I last saw him.'

Why do you admonish me about shameful suffering,
      my darling?
May I never experience the parting of us both.
If I lose your love,
then I will certainly let the people at court,
and all other men, notice that my joy is the least.)

These strophes are somewhat anomalous within the Kürenberg corpus in having an unrhymed short line linking long-line couplets – lines with six to eight beats with fixed caesuras in the middle – two such couplets form the pattern of the other strophes – and some apparently defective half lines. It may be accidental that the short lines of the strophes rhyme; but linking strophes by having unrhymed lines within the strophe rhyme with the corresponding line in other strophes is a common practice in later lyrics. Whereas many of the Kürenberg strophes (as is the case with other early minnesingers) apparently formed monostrophic songs, these two are an example of the earliest known polystrophic type of German song, the *Wechsel* (alternation), in which the lady and her would-be lover speak, usually independently, about a common topic. This example is a more advanced variation (or a separate genre, as Manfred Günter Scholz has argued): the first strophe is a message – the lady gives instructions to the messenger in lines 4 and 5 – conveyed to the suitor, who then responds obliquely to his lady's remonstrances.

The early poets came from along the Danube. Although the Kürenberg songs, like those by the *Burggrafen* (barons) of Regensburg and Rietenburg (who may be the same person) and for the most part by Dietmar von Aist and Meinloh von Sevelingen, seem old-fashioned in comparison to those by Heinrich von Morungen, Albrecht von Johansdorf, Hartmann von Aue, Reinmar der Alte, and Walther, they are clearly part of a courtly ambience that was new and exciting in the last half of the twelfth century, a secular realm in which *hôher muot* (high spirits) and *vröide* (joy) were legitimate despite the contempt of worldly things preached by Christian ascetics. Many of the conventions of these songs are shared by Provençal and northern French songs, which may reflect either influence (medieval cour-

tiers and secular clergy were mobile) or similar societies. Outside this courtly sphere are the down-to-
earth didactic strophes of Spervogel (Sparrow), who
assumed a nom de plume that reflected his wanderings and lack of courtly or bourgeois status. Fifty
strophes, some of which may be clustered into polystrophic songs, are ascribed to him and to "der
jüngere Spervogel" (Sparrow, Junior), among them:

> Wan sol den mantel kêren, als daz weter gât.
> ein vrömder man der habe sîn dinc, als ez danne stât.
> sîns leides sî er niht ze dol,
> sîn liep er schône haben sol.
> ez ist hiute mîn, morne dîn: so teilet man die huoben.
> vil dicke er selbe drinne lît,   der dem andern grebt die
>   gruoben. (MF 22, 25–32)

(People ought to turn their coat according to the weather.
An outsider ought to accept things the way they are at
that time.
May he not be too upset about his misery;
he will have ample pleasure.
What's mine today is yours tomorrow: that's how the
plots of land are [or plot of land is] divided.
He who digs a hole for another quite often lies in it himself.)

Four aphorisms, each taking up a long line, surround a short-line couplet that is itself aphoristic.
Though the five aphorisms appear to make independent statements, a certain rough logical progression
may be inferred. The initial couplet with its six-beat
lines suggests that a wanderer (such as the singer himself) had best accommodate himself to his lot; the
short-line couplet adds that this lot, though it might
seem dismal, need not be so; the long-line couplet concludes that human destinies are similar. The struggle
for permanence (claiming a plot of land) and preference (scheming to lay a trap for another) is ultimately
futile. If *gruobe* (pit) is equated with *grap* (grave), then
the futility is absolute, and the joy to come promised
in the fourth line is a heavenly one. Most of
Spervogel's songs, however, are concerned with behavior in this life, and the vocabulary he uses here
does not support an eschatological reading. The intended message more likely approximates "To get
along, go along."

During the 1180s a Rhenish group of singers
came to the fore, including as a transitional figure Emperor Heinrich VI, to whom two pairs of archaic strophes and a "modern" four-strophe song are ascribed.
Heinrich von Veldeke, Rudolf von Fenis, and especially Friedrich von Hausen are remarkable not only
for the elegance of their poetry but also for the skillful
use they make of Provençal and northern French
models. Veldeke, who came from what is now Bel-

gium, was also strongly influenced by medieval
Latin lyrics. Beginning with these singers there are
new norms for *Minnesang* – which, to be sure, are not
always observed: thematically, an abject suitor's unrequited courtly service of an idealized and idolized
lady; formally, a strophe consisting of two or more
verse lines forming what is known as a *Stollen*, a repeat
of this *Stollen* – the two *Stollen* make up what is called
the *Aufgesang* – and another group of verse lines,
known as the *Abgesang*. Two or more strophes are
commonly linked together to form a polystrophic
song. A song by Friedrich illustrates this new style:

> Sich möhte wîser man verwüeten
> von sorgen, der ich manige hân.
> swie ich mich noch dâ von behüete,
> so hât got wol ze mir getân,
> sît er mich niht wolte erlân,
> ich naeme sî in mîn gemüete.
> joch engilte ich alse sêre ir güete
> und ouch der schoene, die si hât.
> lite ich durch got, daz sî begât
> an mir, der sêle wurde rât.
>
> Mich kunde niemen des erwenden,
> ich welle ir wesen undertân.
> den willen bringe ich an mîn ende,
> swie si habe ze mir getân.
> sît ich des boten niht enhân,
> so wil ich ir diu lieder senden.
> vert der lîp in ellenden,
> mîn herze belîbet dâ.
> daz suoche nieman anderswâ,
> ez kunde ir niemer komen ze nâ. (MF 51, 13–32)

(A wise man could go mad
with the sorrows of which I have so many.
However much I protect myself from that,
nevertheless God has treated me well
since he would not keep me
from taking her into my mind.
But I pay too much for her kindness
and also for her beauty.
If I were to suffer for God's sake what she does
to me, then my soul would be helped.

No one could keep me from wanting
to be subservient to her.
I'll have this desire to my end,
however she will have treated me.
Since I have no messenger,
I'll send her these strophes.
If my body travels in foreign lands,
my heart remains here.
No one should seek it elsewhere;
it could never come too near to her.)

Lines 1–4 form the *Aufgesang*. In the second
strophe every two lines form a sentence; that pat-

tern prevails in the first as well, with the striking exception of what would be the transition between the *Aufgesang* and the *Abgesang,* lines 4 and 5. The two strophes could well be independent; the links between the strophes, beyond the common form, are subtle indeed. The would-be lover is wholly absorbed in his sorrow – as is frequently the case, more attention is paid to the effects of love on the suitor than to the lady. His love has driven him to distraction, but he thanks God, who is the willing accomplice of lovers in many *Minnelieder* (medieval love songs), for her cruel treatment of him. He will serve her even from afar; when he is abroad his heart will be with her (love from afar and leaving the heart with the lady are motifs prevalent in Romance lyrics as well).

Beginning with Friedrich, some songs show an ironic distancing from the fervent supplications of the lovesick knights. Such distancing becomes more prevalent in the songs of singers who flourished slightly after the Rhenish group and were most accomplished in treating the traditional stances of the abject lover with formal and conceptual elegance and depth: Albrecht von Johannsdorf, Hartmann, Heinrich von Morungen, and Reinmar, as well as the somewhat later Walther and Wolfram von Eschenbach. An example of this playful treatment of matters dealt with elsewhere with apparent solemnity is Albrecht's dialogue song "Ich vant si âne huote" (I found her without a chaperone). The song is modeled on a Provençal one; since the extant Provençal version seems to be later, both may derive from a lost original. The song narrates how the speaker found his lady and began to woo her, but to no avail. In the first strophe the lady feigns ignorance of his intent. In each of the following six strophes the singer presses his suit in the first *Stollen,* and she rejects it in the second; after a brief interjection or question by the singer in the first line of the *Abgesang,* the lady makes a more general assertion in the seven-beat line that concludes it. It becomes increasingly clear that singer and lady are leading each other on, although one may accept as earnest her complaint "wert ich iuch, des hetet ir êre; so waere mîn der spot" (if I gave in to your entreaties, you would have acclaim; but I would be ridiculed). In the seventh and last strophe she seems to weaken, only to offer the suitor far less than he has been demanding (conventionally, double quotation marks enclose the male's speech, single marks the lady's):

"Sol mich dan mîn singen
und mîn dienst gegen iu niht vervân?"

'iu sol wol gelingen,
âne lôn sô sult ir niht bestân.'
"wie meinent ir daz, vrowe guot?"
'daz ir dest werder sint unde dâ bî hôchgemuot.' (MF 94, 9–14)

("Shall then my singing and my service of you avail me nothing?"
'You shall indeed succeed; you shall not remain unrewarded.'
"How do you mean that, kind lady?"
'That you are all the more worthy and high-spirited in addition.')

The last line, read in isolation, has repeatedly been cited to corroborate the notion that the goal of love service was to ennoble the suitor; certainly such an effect is mentioned occasionally, though as Stephen J. Kaplowitt and Eva Willms have demonstrated, its importance has been overrated. On the other hand, heightening of joy by all partaking in the courtly game of love service is what *Minnesang* is all about; it is advanced by the refinement with which the game is played rather than by any consistent spiritualization of love. Decorum demands discretion, and the practical poetic need to create tension precludes presenting carnal love as unproblematic; nevertheless, modern notions of courtly love that scholars have delighted in projecting onto *Minnelieder* find only sporadic support in them. The high lady, who may or may not be married, is exalted by the suitor, but she need not be his social superior. Frequently the love relationship is spiritualized and idealized; occasionally, consummated love is celebrated, though more commonly its thwarting is lamented. The lady is often recalcitrant and is always aware of the danger of damaging her reputation; on the other hand, sexual union is what her suitor almost always seeks, even when he deems it unachievable, and what the lady herself often desires when she is given a voice (by male poets). The varying portrayals of the love relationship and of the participants in it reflect the differing conventions of a considerable range of subgenres of medieval song; genre boundaries are fluid, however, and the poets allow few constraints on the violations of generic expectations.

Heinrich von Morungen utilizes intense light imagery and vivid motifs of perception to depict love as magic, as sickness, as irresistible power; the lady as goddess and as murderess: the hyperbolic themes of *Minnesang* are expressed to the extreme. In his thirty-four songs he uses the full panoply of images developed in praise of the Virgin Mary to imbue his praises of his secular lady with emphasis and seriousness. One of his rare monostrophic songs illustrates his fervor, though even here a wry sense of humor, which is more apparent elsewhere, may provide an ironic subtext:

> Vil süeziu senftiu toeterinne,
> war umbe welt ir toeten mir den lîp,
> und ich iuch so herzeclîchen minne,
> zwâre vrouwe, vür elliu wîp?
> waenent ir, ob ir mich toetet,
> daz ich iuch iemer mêr beschouwe?
> nein, iuwer minne hât mich des ernoetet,
> daz iuwer sêle ist mîner sêle vrouwe.
> sol mir hie niht guot geschehen
> von iuwerm werden lîbe,
> so muoz mîn sêle iu des verjehen,
> dazs iuwerre sêle dienet dort als einem reinen wîbe.
> (MF 147, 4–15)

> (Sweet soothing murderess,
> why do you want to kill me
> when I love you so heartily,
> in truth, lady, more than all other women?
> Do you think that if you kill me
> I will never again gaze at you?
> No, my love for you has forced me
> to accept your soul as the mistress of mine.
> If no good will befall me here
> from your worthiness [or worthy person; literally, worthy body],
> then my soul must proclaim to you
> that it will serve your soul there as that of a flawless woman.)

In her discussion of this song in *Gedichte und Interpretationen: Mittelalter* (Poems and Interpretations: Middle Ages, 1993), edited by Helmut Tervooren, Trude Ehlert observes that the reaction of the singer of the lady's recalcitrance is not a lament, as would be typical of Reinmar, but a renewed intensification of the promise of service, a promise that perpetuates the relationship between singer and lady into their life after death. Love lasts longer than earthly existence and, thus, also the earthly caprice of the lady. The vision of the singer is not mutuality of love in this world and love's fulfillment through physical union, as Hartmann and Walther demand in their songs, but complete devotion in service of the lady – even against her will and beyond imperfect earthly life. Heinrich von Morungen's trying out of courtly forms of life initially perhaps merely playful, gains a new dimension. The assertion that the love service that is fulfilled in *beschouwen* (gazing at the beloved) lasts beyond death connects it with notions of religious transcendence and thereby lends it a greater intrinsic value in this world as well. Ehlert does not find any humor in the singer's persistence despite the lady's wishes; she downplays the tensions between earnestness and irony in this fervid apostrophe of the femme fatale. It is certainly true that Heinrich von Morungen comes closer than any of the other minnesingers to assigning devotion to the lady a religious fervor, and perhaps he meant no ironic overtones.

The most prominent singer after Walther was Neidhart von Reuental. In most *Minnelieder,* especially of the thirteenth century, nature imagery tends to be stereotypical and is usually restricted to the beginnings of songs; but just as Walther did, Neidhart and a few others, such as Ulrich von Winterstetten and Tannhäuser, let nature become a major theme. Often such songs show an affinity to the *pastourelle,* a dialogue poem commonly depicting an encounter between a peasant girl and a higher-born man (a knight or a cleric). Among the didactic poets, Reinmar von Zweter and Der Marner stand out; most of the rest flourished in the last half of the thirteenth century. While Count Otto von Botenlauben may have been a contemporary of Walther and Wolfram, his dawn songs (laments of a lady and her lover forced to part by the coming of the day) seem more archaic than Wolfram's extravagant masterpieces.

Ulrich von Singenberg created parodies of Walther as well as writing both *Minnelieder* and didactic songs in Walther's manner; a pallid reprise of Albrecht's "Ich vant si âne huote" in "Hât ieman leit, als ich ez hân?" (Does anyone suffer as I do?); brief rejections of the typical courtly stance, such as "Ist si schoene und ist si guot, / deste wirs tuot mir versagen – : / waers alt, arm und ungemuot, / sô möhte ich si wol verclagen" (If she is beautiful and kind, / then rejection causes me all the more grief; / if she were old, poor, and grouchy, / then I could easily be done with lamenting her loss); and an extraordinary dialogue ostensibly between the singer and his son that concludes the otherwise conventional *Minnelied* "Funde ich vreide volgi, ich freute gerne mich" (If I were to find the consequences of joy, I'd gladly be happy):

> "Ich wil mînem vatir gerne wol
> râten, daz er hinnenvür sich sanges mâze.
> ez ist billich, daz ich in vurwesen sol
> und er sich an mînen dienest lâzze.
> ich wil vür in dienen frowen:
> habe er, daz er heime habe, und lâz uns jungen âventiure schowen!"

> "Rüedelîn, du bist ein junger blappenblap!
> dû muost dînen vater lâzen singen:
> er wil sîne hövescheit vüeren in sîn grap,

234

des müest dû dich mit virlornen dingen.
er wil selbe dienen sîner frowen:
du bist ein viereggot gebûr, des muost du holz an eime
reine houwen!" (SSM 22)

("I'll gladly advise my father
henceforth to moderate himself in singing.
It is only right that I should have precedence over him
and he should begin to serve me.
I want to serve ladies in his place;
may he keep what he has at home and let us youths see
adventure."

"Rudy, you are a young blabbermouth!
You have to let your father sing;
he'll bear his courtliness into his grave.
Therefore, you are struggling with a lost cause.
He wants to serve his lady himself.
You are a clumsy oaf; thus, you must chop wood at the
edge of the field!")

The last strophe is probably in the father's voice;
though there are no generic parallels for such a
conversation, it might have been created as an ana-
logue to Neidhart's dialogues between mother and
daughter. One might also imagine that it is the
mother reproaching her son and thus validating her
husband's gallivanting about serving high ladies. In
any case, the son comes closer than most contemporaries to finding some conflict in a married man's
wooing fair ladies in song. (Ulrich von Liechtenstein recounts spending a few days at home with his
wife, recuperating from the strain of declaring his
love for a recalcitrant lady.) Whether the father or
the mother reproaches the son, it is clear that in
placing him among the peasants he or she is referring to his behavior and not to his "true" social
standing, which would be that of the suitor who
aspires to courtesy and is presumably, therefore,
not baseborn.

Rubin, whose indebtedness to Reinmar der
Alte and Walther is striking, was probably Ulrich
von Singenberg's contemporary. A somewhat
later minnesinger, Burkhard von Hohenfels, is remarkable for the liveliness of his dance songs and
especially for his detailed imagery, for which he
draws on bestiaries, falconry, hunting lore, and
feudal customs. Susanne Staar points out in
Gedichte und Interpretationen: Mittelalter the probable
Romance influence on his marginally courtly *chanson de malmariée* (song of the ill-married woman)
"Ich wil mîn gemüete erjetten" (I want to free my
spirit), but she does not comment on discordant
details, such as the use of the rustic word *erjetten*
(to weed), that create a dissonance within the
courtly ambience.

Ulrich von Liechtenstein, Ulrich von Winterstetten, and Gottfried von Neifen flourished in the
second quarter of the thirteenth century. The songs in
Ulrich von Liechtenstein's *Frauendienst* (Service of Ladies, circa 1255) pale against the burlesque splendor
of his epic, though if the framework narrative had
been lost, the inventiveness of some of the songs
would have warranted notice. Ulrich von
Winterstetten's formal virtuosity is striking, though
the most remarkable feature of his songs is the frequent use of refrains, which are otherwise not common in the German tradition. Gottfried is a master of
formal elegance, though his incessantly repeated
themes and motifs, such as the praise of his lady's rosy
mouth, grow tedious. Amid the elegance are some
songs and passages that are so crude that they have
often, but probably incorrectly, been considered spurious. Even some of the refined songs have a hint of
bawdry, as in the fourth strophe in manuscript C of
"Sumer, dîner fr[ö]idebernden wunne" (Summer, at
your joy-bearing ecstasy). The third and fourth strophes read:

Sît ich bin gebunden mit den banden,
daz die senden heizent minnebant,
sô mac sî mich loesen mit ir handen,
sît si treit so helferîche hant.
frouwe ob allen frouwen mîn,
wendet mînen senden pîn;
durch iuwer reht lânt mich bî fröiden sîn.

Disiu liet wil ich der lieben singen,
der ich lange her gesungen hân.
sî kan beidiu dechsen unde swingen.
dur ir güete sol si mich erlân,
daz ich niht in sorgen sî,
sît ir wont diu fröide bî.
vil saelic wîp, nu tuo mich sorgen frî! (KLD II, 4–5)

(Since I am bound with the bonds
that lovers call the bonds of love,
she can release me with her hands,
since she has such a helpful hand.
My lady above all ladies,
relieve my lovesick pain;
by your authority, let me be joyful.

I want to sing these strophes to the dear lady
to whom I have sung for a long time.
She can really thrash flax.
Because of her kindness she ought to allow me
not to be sorrowful,
since joy dwells with her.
Blessed lady, now free me of sorrow.)

The use of grammatical rhyme in the third strophe is
an example of the sort of formal playfulness Gottfried
loves. Words such as *helferîche hant* (helpful hand) and

reht (authority) imply that the lady addressed is the speaker's feudal mistress; such implications are common in *Minnelieder* as an expression of the suitor's subservience and should not be taken as autobiographical. In the fourth strophe the singer makes a remark about his lady that is inappropriate to this sphere: "thrashing flax" is an image Gottfried uses elsewhere to intimate sexual activity. Here the song does not leave the courtly frame of reference, as most bawdy ones do; after the singer's salacious aside, he continues with stereotypical references to joy and sorrow and ends with an apostrophe to his lady. Another minnesinger, Steinmar, probably a younger contemporary who was influenced by Ulrich von Liechtenstein, alternates between dance songs and typical love songs but has an outrageous parody of the latter in "Ein kneht, der lac verborgen" (A farmworker lay concealed), in which the knight and the lady of a dawn song are transformed into peasants. His "Sît si mir niht lônen wil" (Since she does not want to reward me), which begins as if it were a *Minnelied,* is a striking German example of the common medieval Latin genre of songs in ostensible praise of gluttony. If he cannot have love, the singer says, he will eat and drink until his soul is forced to hop onto a rib to avoid drowning.

Among minnesingers flourishing in the third quarter of the thirteenth century, Konrad von Würzburg and Tannhäuser, who were also didactic poets, excel. Konrad is best known for his narratives, but his formal feats as a minnesinger surpass even Gottfried von Neifen's, though often at the cost of sacrificing salience and, especially, density of content to the demands of rhyme and meter. Tannhäuser's six *leiche* (sequences of disparate strophes) lack the prominent display of erudition that marks those of others, such as Walther and Konrad, but they are remarkable for their breadth of motifs and their vivacity. Tannhäuser introduces "Tanhusaer" as a figure in them in much the way Neidhart has "Nîthart" and "der von Riuwental" (he of the Vale of Sorrow) as figures in his songs. Both his *Minnelieder* and his didactic songs derive themes from Walther, but they are lighter and more frivolous in tone. Neidhart seems to have influenced his dance songs, though in some details he is closer to Ulrich von Winterstetten, from whom he probably borrowed the conceit of implying that he has to end two of his *leiche* because the fiddler's string or bow has broken. He goes beyond Neidhart in employing in a few poems foreign words and even (if the burlesque narratives ascribed to Neidhart are excluded) in the explicitness of his bawdry. In a winter song, "Gegen disen winnahten" (For this Christmas season) in which he describes his relationship to his dancing partner, he turns in the second strophe from third-person reference to second-person address:

Du liebez, du guotez,
tuo hin, la sten, du wunder wolgemuotez!
wol stent dine löckel,
din mündel rot, din öugel, als ich wolde.
rosevar din wengel,
din kelli blanc, da vor stet wol din spengel.
du rehtez sumertöckel!
reitval din har, rehte als ichs wünschen solde,
gedrat dine brüste.
nu tanze eht hin, min liebez, min gelüste!
la sitüli blecken
ein wenic dur den willen mîn,   da gegen muoz ich
                                       schrecken. (14c)

(You dear girl, you kind one,
put [it] away, let [it] be, you wonderfully cheerful girl!
Your little locks are pretty,
your little mouth, your little eyes, as I would [have them].
Your little cheeks are rosy;
your throat white; your brooch before it is attractive.
You true summer doll!
Your hair is blonde and curly, just like I'd wish it to be;
your breasts are firm.
Now dance on, my love, my delight!
Bare your derriere
a little for my sake; I must jump up startled at that.)

The speaker continues, mentioning all he sees, which is more than he asked for. His breaches of the etiquette of describing feminine pulchritude are lighthearted; neither he nor, in all likelihood, anyone in his audience would have thought that his voyeurism was debasing, though all would have appreciated that he was flouting convention. The only slight bow to decorum that he makes is to refer to the girl's buttocks with a pig-latin word. His reaction suggests that he is both aroused and frightened by the sensuality that he has evoked. The stance here, to be sure, is the superior one that characterizes the clerics' view of girls in many of the Latin songs of the *Carmina Burana* (Songs from Benediktbeuern, circa 1230), for example. The last two strophes, however, increasingly bear the hallmarks of courtly decorum. By the time the song ends he is celebrating a high lady.

One of the foremost didactic poets and composers of the last half of the thirteenth century was Meister Rumelant (Master Vacate-the-Country, a typical name for an erudite itinerant singer). Within the complex of strophes in his first song in manuscripts C and J is one with punning references to Der Marner; for this reason the song is probably an early one. Another of the strophes, which is the initial one in C and the fifth in J, illustrates the sort of learned allegorization that is characteristic of both the times and the works of the didactic poets (in J the strophe follows four strophes discussing how God appears in the four elements and relating each element to the human crafts of agriculture [earth], making music [air], smithing [fire], and cooking [water]; the corresponding strophes in C are transmitted under Walther's name, but nothing in their style or content is similar to Walther's other didactic songs):

> Der den zirkel tichte   sinewel umbe
> unde die linien durch die richte   sunder alle krumbe
> nâch der winkel mâze   zwîer wende schaft,
> wol sîn zirkel elle   dinc begrîfet,
> beide himel und die helle,   daz im nicht entslîfet.
> ganz in rechter sâze   vollichlîch sîn kraft
> gezirkelt hât sich selbe umb alle kêre.
> daz nicht ist ûzen, im des man gedenket.
> sîn linie durch den zirkel recht uns lêre
> der wîse geist, den uns der vater schenket,
> unde den sun gewaltich   kunde senden
> uns ein got, des name drîvaltich   ist, der in zwên
>   wenden
> zwîer ê gelâze   selbe ist winkelhaft. (5d)

(He who created the circle around the sphere
and drew lines through it directly without any curve,
forming two points with a right-angle rule,
indeed his compass includes all things,
both heaven and hell, so that nothing will slip away
from him.
In its totally correct place, its power has completely
described a circle in all directions.
That nothing is outside one has him to thank for.
May the wise Spirit the Father gave us properly teach
    us
his line through the circle,
and that God whose name is threefold
could send the mighty Son who at the two points
of the two Testaments' inheritance is himself angular.)

Not all of the obscurity of the strophe need derive from Rumelant; there may be spots where the scribe failed to understand his exemplar (for the most part J seems preferable to C in the few places where they differ). Rumelant, who was an adept at the arcane art of relating school learning to moral homilies, draws here from the quadrivium of the seven liberal arts – the advanced course, taken after the trivium, by those who studied in ecclesiastical schools and perhaps contemplated further study in theology. The intricacies of the singer's learning (which may not have been as thorough as his matter-of-fact cita-

tion of it would suggest) would have been foreign to almost all of his listening audience and to the scribes as well. The strophe may refer to scholastic efforts to elucidate the power of the Trinity by analogy to attempts to square the circle (such as by finding by use of a compass and straightedge a square whose area is equal to the inscribed area of a given circle) or to some other arcane mathematical manipulation. In any case, Rumelant clearly intends to impress his audience with his learning while instilling in them a sense of awe for the transcendent rationality of the Creator.

Not all the efforts of the didactic singers are this erudite; there are many references to proverbs, popular literature, and teachings of the Church derived from pastoral care. Proper behavior is central; admonitions recur to obey the dictates of the class into which one was born (perhaps a sign that many did not). Many songs, especially the more learned and ambitious *leiche,* are in adoration of the Virgin Mary. The most splendid of these is the *Marienleich,* from which – in addition to his other songs in praise of Mary – the didactic singer Heinrich von Meißen, who flourished around the end of the thirteenth and the beginning of the fourteenth centuries, got the name by which he is normally known: Frauenlob (praise of the lady). Although there are many *Minnelieder* collections that have a few didactic songs interspersed, the reverse is seldom the case; there may have been a tendency to discourage the possibly nonaristocratic didactic singers from participating in the courtly practice of *Minnelieder.* In the course of the thirteenth century this constraint must have been relaxed; Konrad, for example, though he wrote for an aristocratic audience (which would include the patrician and clerical upper class of the cities), was not born to this group. Hadlaub, a citizen of Zurich in the late thirteenth and early fourteenth centuries who had ties to the upper class, emulates all the traditions of courtly song and clearly understands the conventions; but he is also capable of making a travesty of them by resituating the themes into a middle-class milieu. Though he does not focus on class distinctions and the peculiar status of the emerging bourgeoisie, he seems to have more of a sense of them than did the Scholastics who wrote authoritatively of class, status, and mores in his time. Frauenlob and Hadlaub show that German song did not cease in 1270 or even 1300; it continued, changing forms and themes (less quickly than one might surmise), but retaining the close relationships between words and music and between performer and listening audience that characterized *Minnesang* until well into the fifteenth century (many of the manuscripts date from that century). Even as late as the early seventeenth century, though the typical themes had changed (more in the love poetry than in the didactic songs), songs to be sung and heard had not been completely replaced by poems to be read. If folk songs are included, the older traditions lasted at least until the nineteenth century.

Bibliography:

Helmut Tervooren, *Bibliographie zum Minnesang und zu den Dichtern aus "Des Minnesangs Frühling"* (Berlin: Schmidt, 1969).

References:

Gayle Agler-Beck, *Der von Kürenberg* (Amsterdam: Benjamins, 1978);

Franz H. Bäuml, ed., *From Symbol to Mimesis: The Generation of Walther von der Vogelweide* (Göppingen: Kümmerle, 1984);

Hugo Bekker, *Friedrich von Hausen: Inquiries into His Poetry* (Chapel Hill: University of North Carolina Press, 1977);

Bekker, *The Poetry of Albrecht von Johansdorf* (Leiden: Brill, 1978);

Gerald A. Bond, "*MF* 136,25 and the Conceptual Space of Heinrich von Morungen's Poetry," *Euphorion,* 70, no. 3 (1976): 205–221;

Peter Dronke, *The Medieval Lyric* (London: Cambridge University Press, 1968);

Trude Ehlert, *Konvention – Variation – Innovation: Ein struktureller Vergleich von Liedern aus "Des Minnesangs Frühling" und Walther von der Vogelweide* (Berlin: Schmidt, 1980);

Manfred Eikelmann, *Denkformen im Minnesang* (Tübingen: Niemeyer, 1988);

Peter Frenzel, "Contrary Forces and Patterns of Antagonism in Minnesang," in *Court and the Poet,* edited by Glyn S. Burgess (Liverpool: Cairns, 1981), pp. 141–154;

Frenzel, "Melody and Genre in German Courtly Singing in the Thirteenth Century," in *Genres in Medieval German Literature,* edited by Hubert Heinen and Ingeborg Henderson (Göppingen: Kümmerle, 1986), pp. 30–46;

Frenzel, "Minne-Sang: The Conjunction of Singing and Loving in German Courtly Song," *German Quarterly,* 55 (May 1982): 336–348;

Hans Fromm, ed., *Der deutsche Minnesang,* 2 volumes (Darmstadt: Wissenschaftliche Buchgesellschaft, 1961, 1985);

Jutta Goheen, *Mittelalterliche Liebeslyrik von Neidhart von Reuental bis zu Oswald von Wolkenstein* (Berlin: Schmidt, 1984);

Frederick Goldin, *Mirror of Narcissus in the Courtly Love Lyric* (Ithaca, N.Y.: Cornell University Press, 1967);

Arthur Groos, "Modern Stereotyping and Medieval Topoi: The Lover's Exchange in Dietmar von Aist's 'Ûf der linden obene,' " *Journal of English and Germanic Philology,* 88 (April 1989): 157–167;

Claudia Händl, *Rollen und pragmatische Einbindung: Analysen zur Wandlung des Minnesangs nach Walther von der Vogelweide* (Göppingen: Kümmerle, 1987);

Ann Harding, *An Investigation into the Use and Meaning of Medieval German Dancing Terms* (Göppingen: Kümmerle, 1973);

Hubert Heinen, "Guilhem IX and Der von Kürenberg: Their Beastly Views," in *Fide et amore: A Festschrift for Hugo Bekker,* edited by William C. McDonald and Winder McConnell (Göppingen: Kümmerle, 1990), pp. 157–172;

Heinen, "Making Music as a Theme in German Songs of the 12th and 13th Centuries," in *Music and German Literature,* edited by James M. McGlathery (Columbia, S.C.: Camden House, 1992), pp. 15–32;

Heinen, "When Pallor Pales: Reflections on Epigonality in Late 13th-Century Minnesongs," *Medieval Perspectives,* 4–5 (1989–1990): 53–68;

Christoph Huber, *Wort sint der Dinge zeichen: Untersuchungen zum Sprachdenken der mittelhochdeutschen Spruchdichtung bis Frauenlob* (Zurich: Artemis, 1977);

Stephen J. Kaplowitt, *The Ennobling Power of Love in the Medieval German Lyric* (Chapel Hill: University of North Carolina Press, 1986);

Ingrid Kasten, *Frauendienst bei Trobadors und Minnesängern im 12. Jahrhundert* (Heidelberg: Winter, 1986);

Rüdiger Krohn, ed., *Liebe als Literatur* (Munich: Beck, 1983);

James V. McMahon, *The Music of Early Minnesang* (Columbia, S.C.: Camden House, 1990);

Hugo Moser, ed., *Mittelhochdeutsche Spruchdichtung* (Darmstadt: Wissenschaftliche Buchgesellschaft, 1972);

Ulrich Müller, ed., *Minne ist ein swaerez spil* (Göppingen: Kümmerle, 1986);

Hans-Herbert Räkel, *Der deutsche Minnesang* (Munich: Beck, 1986);

Olive Sayce, *The Medieval German Lyric 1150–1300* (Oxford: Clarendon, 1982);

Sayce, *Plurilingualism in the Carmina Burana* (Göppingen: Kümmerle, 1992);

Max Schiendorfer, *Ulrich von Singenberg, Walther und Wolfram: Zur Parodie in der höfischen Literatur* (Bonn: Bouvier, 1983);

Manfred Günter Scholz, "Zu Stil und Typologie des mittelhochdeutschen Wechsels," *Jahrbuch für Internationale Germanistik,* 21, no. 1 (1989); 60–92;

Günther Schweikle, *Minnesang* (Stuttgart: Metzler, 1989);

David P. Sudermann, *The Minnelieder of Albrecht von Johansdorf* (Göppingen: Kümmerle, 1976);

Ronald J. Taylor, *The Art of the Minnesinger,* 2 volumes (Cardiff: University of Wales Press, 1968);

Helmut Tervooren, "Das Spiel mit der höfischen Liebe: Minneparodien im 13.–15. Jahrhundert," *Zeitschrift für Deutsche Philologie,* 104, special issue (1985): 135–157;

Tervooren, ed., *Gedichte und Interpretationen: Mittelalter* (Stuttgart: Reclam, 1993);

J. W. Thomas, *Tannhäuser: Poet and Legend* (Chapel Hill: University of North Carolina Press, 1974);

Frederic C. Tubach, *Struktur im Widerspruch: Studien zum Minnesang* (Tübingen: Niemeyer, 1977);

Burghart Wachinger, "Was ist Minne?," *Beiträge zur Geschichte der deutschen Sprach und Literatur,* 111, no. 2 (1989): 252–267;

Wachinger, "Die Welt, die Minne und das Ich: Drei spätmittelalterliche Lieder," in *Entzauberung der Welt: Deutsche Literatur 1200–1500,* edited by James F. Poag and Thomas C. Fox (Bern: Francke, 1989), pp. 107–118;

Stephen L. Wailes, "The Erotic Realism of the German Dawn Song," *Genres in Medieval German Literature,* edited by Hubert Heinen and Ingeborg Henderson (Göppingen: Kümmerle, 1986), pp. 1–15;

Peter Wapnewski, *Waz ist minne: Studien zur mittelhochdeutschen Lyrik* (Munich: Beck, 1975);

Eva Willms, *Liebesleid und Sangeslust: Untersuchungen zur deutschen Liebeslyrik des späten 12. und frühen 13. Jahrhunderts* (Munich: Artemis, 1990);

Alois Wolf, *Variation und Integration: Beobachtungen zu hochmittelalterlichen Tageliedern* (Darmstadt: Wissenschaftliche Buchgesellschaft, 1979);

Vickie L. Ziegler, *The Leitword in* Minnesang (University Park: Pennsylvania State University Press, 1975).

Moriz von Craûn

(circa 1220 – 1230)

J. Wesley Thomas
University of Kentucky

Manuscript: This anonymous work was transmitted only in the Ambras Heldenbuch (ser. nova 2663 of the Austrian National Library in Vienna), a large parchment manuscript that the Tirolese toll collector Hans Ried prepared from 1504 to 1516 for Emperor Maximilian I. Linguistic features indicate that the scribe copied it from an early manuscript.

First publication: "Ritter Mauritius von Erun und Gräfinn Beamunt," edited by H. F. Maßmann, *Hagens Germania,* 9 (1850): 103–135.

Standard edition: *Moriz von Craûn,* edited by Ulrich Pretzel and others, fourth revised edition (Tübingen: Niemeyer, 1973).

Editions in English: "Moriz von Craûn," translated by J. Wesley Thomas, in *The Best Novellas of Medieval Germany* (Columbia, S.C.: Camden House, 1984), pp. 4–8, 37–53; *Moriz von Craûn,* translated by Stephanie Cain Van D'Elden (New York: Garland, 1990).

Moriz von Craûn is one of the best novellas of medieval Germany and perhaps the most controversial. It has been interpreted as a model of courtly manners, a didactic poem, a loose collection of parodies, and an erotic anecdote; some studies have avoided strict categories and emphasized its varied content or stressed its incongruities. Actually the work is a tightly organized and consistent satire of a favorite *Minnesang* convention and certain elements of courtly narrative verse that were portrayed as requisites of knighthood. The work is, in fact, a realistic and amusing commentary on much of the romantic literature of the German High Middle Ages.

Little biographical information about the author can be gleaned from the work. Traces of Rhineland speech in the predominantly Bavarian-Austrian dialect of the manuscript indicate that the homeland of the author of *Moriz von Craûn* was somewhere between Strasbourg and Worms. Conjectures as to the approximate date of composition differ, but most scholars incline toward the immediate postclassical period, somewhere between 1220 and 1230. That would certainly be a favorable time to compose a work that ridiculed the fantasy of sentimental love lyrics and chivalric tales. All that can be added concerning the author is that he was well read, probably knew French, and composed for a sophisticated courtly audience that could appreciate his irony. His novella is not mentioned by any other medieval writer.

The names of the chief characters of the story are those of historical figures. The best known of several lords of Craon with the name Maurice was Maurice II, who died in 1196. He was an important vassal of Henry II of England and later of Richard the Lionhearted, whom he accompanied on the king's ill-fated crusade. If he is the hero of the narrative, then the wife of his neighbor, Viscount Richard de Beaumont, would be the heroine; but it is unlikely that the events described have any factual basis. Since five love songs have been attributed to Maurice II, he may deserve a place with Heinrich von Morungen, Wolfram von Eschenbach, Walther von der Vogelweide, Wirnt von Grafenberg, Reinmar von Brennenberg, and Tannhäuser among those poets who became heroes of medieval German literary works.

Moriz von Craûn begins with a history of chivalry. The narrator says that it originated in Greece, where it flourished during the Trojan War and declined after the conquests of Alexander; it then moved to Rome, reached its zenith with Julius Caesar, and fell into decadence and disrepute when Nero, simply for entertainment, had his troops set fire to Rome and attack its citizens. Chivalry thereupon went to France and prospered under Charlemagne, the narrator continues, but he adds ironically that present-day French chivalry is noble, that in France ladies are served for pay in a most refined manner, and that knights are better rewarded there than anywhere else. His medieval audience would not have missed the implied contrast between that service of ladies and the great deeds of Alexander, Caesar, and Charlemagne. It is the clear though unspoken message that the narrator considers chivalry to be in a period of decline at the time of his story.

That report is followed by a discourse on courtly love and an account of Sir Moriz's distress at not being rewarded for his lengthy service of the countess of Beaumont; coming after a history of famous warriors, his laments seem less than heroic. When he finally summons up the courage to complain to the lady, she promises to give him a lover's pay if he will hold a tournament close by her castle.

Delighted, he at once agrees. To arouse widespread interest in the affair, he has a splendid ship built on a large wagon that, together with the horses, is concealed by cloth. Apparently driven by oars and the wind, his galley moves across the fields of France to the lady's castle. Whereas warriors of the past had sailed across stormy seas to bloody battle, the counterfeit ship traverses peaceful meadows on the way to a make-believe conflict whose purpose is mere entertainment. The vessel is a colorful facade that represents all the empty pretense and ineffectiveness of chivalry as Moriz practices it: wasteful extravagance, combat that furthers no national ends, and generosity that neither satisfies the wants of the poor nor wins allies. At the journey's end the knight disembarks and lavishly entertains throngs of guests in a pavilion that has been set up. Most of those who come to enjoy his hospitality are vagrant minstrels, not nobles; but knights arrive the following morning to eat and drink in quantities that, since they are about to participate in a tournament, are certainly excessive.

Although Sir Moriz performs unparalleled feats of skill and valor on the field, striking several hundred opponents from their steeds, everything is recorded in a most perfunctory manner. It is clear that the narrator does not intend him to appear heroic. Moriz does seem generous, for whenever his charger becomes tired he gives it away, mounts another, and, at the end of the contest, offers gifts to all who want them. Then a disorderly rabble takes everything he has, including his armor; even the ship is dismantled and carried off.

Since he has demonstrated his chivalry and served his lady by inordinate expenditures, unprecedented success in jousting, and boundless munificence, Moriz is now ready to receive his reward. At nightfall a maiden in the lady's service leads him into the castle and to a splendid room that gleams like a cathedral and contains a wondrous bed of gold, ivory, and rare wood, covered by the finest cloth and furs. The lengthy description of the bed

and the reference to a cathedral make it obvious that the narrator is presenting an elegant symbol of the cult of courtly love.

The maiden then goes to bring the countess, but the latter has had a change of heart and will not come. In the following series of dialogues between the recalcitrant lady and the maiden, the maiden and the knight, and, again, the maiden and the lady, the preposterous arguments of the romantic young maiden are the chief sources of humor and satire. In a bizarre twist of reasoning she maintains that the lady would lose her honor if it became known that the latter had refused to go to bed with the knight, and she begs her mistress in the name of God to do what is right. For his part, Moriz insists that the lady's husband, as a man of courtly manners, would command her to pay him properly for his service.

At last, greatly exasperated, Moriz follows the maiden to the bedroom, where the lady lies with her sleeping husband. When Moriz noisily pushes open the door, the count springs up in fright and bumps his shin so hard that he faints – another reminder that the men of modern chivalry lack the hardiness of their forebears. The knight takes the count's place in the bed, and the lady decides to yield to him as the best way out of an awkward situation. This slapstick drama contrasts sharply with the veiled and elusive eroticism of the *Minnelied* (love song), especially since the bed in which she fulfills her pledge is not the fabulous bed of courtly love but a marriage bed that has been defiled by an act of simple adultery from which all romanticism has been stripped. Although he has received his reward, Moriz is not mollified and, on leaving, upbraids the lady for her duplicity and renounces his service to her.

Later, after Moriz has won extravagant praise and honor, the countess regrets having alienated him and is ashamed at having been reluctant to follow the conventions of courtly love. The last scene illustrates well the author's manipulation of traditional literary situations. The tableau is that of a type of early *Minnelied* known as the *Frauenstrophe* (lady's stanza): forsaken and lonely, the heroine stands by the window on a spring morning, looking out over the blooming roses and heather to the green forest while listening to the sweet singing of birds; the many joys of spring make her recall her own sorrow, and she bemoans the loss of her lover. Like the ladies of the *Frauenstrophe*, the countess is a sympathetic and poetic figure. But when she expresses the hope that the God who blots out her sin will send the knight back to her, the reader remembers that their relation was an adulterous one, and all the pathos turns to humor.

The author's story is better than his verse, which consists mainly of iambic tetrameter lines with couplet rhyme. There are relatively few obvious rhyme fillers, but the rhythm is frequently quite irregular. Like several courtly romances, *Moriz von Craûn* has a clearly defined five-part structure. After the introduction sets the stage, there is a story enclosed in a frame. The frame consists of an initial section that presents the hero and a discourse on courtly love and a final section that focuses on the heroine, who expounds on the same subject. In between are two sets of episodes: the ones associated with the ship ridicule by exaggeration certain traits that courtly epic verse connects with knightly behavior, while those linked to the symbolic bed form a burlesque of the lyric references to a lover's pay.

Although the novella exposes folly, it is not didactic in the usual sense because the folly is not of real life but only of literature. The story is simply a hilarious farce that lampoons popular literary conventions by presenting them in caricature, supporting them with ridiculous arguments, and emphasizing their incongruities. As the conceits of courtly literature were objects of parody almost from the time of their first appearance, it is difficult to assess the influence that the story may have had on subsequent narratives with the same targets. But at least one of these, the verse novel *Frauendienst* (Service of Ladies, circa 1255), by Ulrich von Liechtenstein, is sufficiently similar to make a direct relationship probable. A possible literary source for *Moriz von Craûn* is the fabliau *Du chevalier qui recovra l'amor de sa dame,* but it is generally assumed that the central plot was taken from a French tale that has not survived.

References:

Robert R. Anderson, *Wortindex und Reimregister zum Moriz von Craûn,* Indices Verborum zum altdeutschen Schrifttum, no. 2 (Amsterdam: Rodopi, 1975);

Hans Bayer, *"âne êre alse vihe:* Der 'Moriz von Craûn' und der 'Ligurinus' Gunthers von Pairis," *Mittellateinisches Jahrbuch,* 16 (1981): 180–211;

Karl Heinz Borck, "Zur Deutung und Vorgeschichte des 'Moriz von Craûn,' " *Deutsche Vierteljahrsschrift für Literaturwissenschaft und Geistesgeschichte,* 35 (1961): 494–520;

Albrecht Classen, "Das Spiel mit der Liebe – Leben als Spiel: Versuch einer Neuinterpretation des 'Morîz von Craûn,' " *Germanisch-Romanische Monatsschrift,* 71 (1990): 369–398;

Robert Folz, "L'histoire de la chevalerie d'après 'Moriz von Craûn,' " *Etudes Germaniques,* 32 (April–June 1977): 119–128;

Francis G. Gentry, "A Tale from a City: *Moriz von Craûn,"* in *Semper Idem et Novus: Festschrift für Frank Banta,* edited by Gentry (Göppingen: Kümmerle, 1988), pp. 193–207;

Ruth Harvey, *Moriz von Craûn and the Chivalric World* (Oxford: Clarendon, 1961);

A. T. Hatto, "Moriz von Craon," *London Medieval Studies,* 1, no. 2 (1938): 285–304;

Hartmut Kokott, *"Mit grossem schaden an eere* (V. 1718): Zur Minne-Lehre des 'Moriz von Craûn,' " *Zeitschrift für deutsche Philologie,* 107, no. 3 (1988): 362–385;

Heinrich Meyer, "Mauritius am Scheideweg," in *Die Bedeutung der Minne in "Moriz von Craûn,"* edited by Günther J. Gerlitzki (Bern: Lang, 1970), pp. 115–131;

Christa Ortmann, "Die Bedeutung der Minne im 'Morîz von Craun,' " *Beiträge zur Geschichte der deutschen Sprache und Literatur,* 108 (1986): 385–407;

Heimo Reinitzer, "Zu den Tiervergleichen und zur Interpretation des 'Moriz von Craûn,' " *Germanisch-Romanische Monatsschrift,* 27 (1977): 1–18;

Kurt Ruh, "Moriz von Craûn: Eine höfische Thesenerzählung aus Frankreich," in *Formen mittelalterlicher Literatur,* edited by Otmar Werber and others (Göppingen: Kümmerle, 1970), pp. 77–90;

Lothar George Seeger, "The Middle High German Epic *Moriz von Craon* and the 'New Morality,' " *Susquehanna University Studies,* 8 (June 1970): 259–269;

Heinz Thomas, "Zur Datierung, zum Verfasser und zur Interpretation des *Moriz von Craûn,"* *Zeitschrift für deutsche Philologie,* 103, no. 3 (1984): 321–365;

Tomas Tomasek, "Die mhd. Verserzählung 'Moriz von Craûn': Eine Werkdeutung mit Blick auf die Vor-Geschichte," *Zeitschrift für deutsches Altertum und deutsche Literatur,* 115, no. 4 (1986): 254–283.

The *Nibelungenlied* and the *Klage*

(circa 1200)

Henry Kratz
University of Tennessee

Manuscripts: The *Nibelungenlied* is extant in eleven complete manuscripts and some twenty-three fragments from the thirteenth century and later that fall into three groups. The leading manuscripts in these groups are A (the Hohenems-Munich manuscript, Munich, Bayerische Staatsbibliothek, Cod. germ. 34), written in the last quarter of the thirteenth century, with 2,316 strophes; B (MS 857, Saint Gall, Stiftsbibliothek), written in the middle of the thirteenth century, with 2,376 strophes; and C (the Hohenems-Laßberg or Donaueschingen manuscript, Donaueschingen, Fürstliche Fürstenbergischen Hofbibliothek), written in the first half of the thirteenth century, with 2,442 strophes. The first two of these manuscripts end with the words "daz ist der Nibelunge nôt" (that is the ordeal of the Nibelungs), while the third ends "daz ist der Nibelunge liet" (that is the song of the Nibelungs), so that the manuscripts are sometimes referred to as "nôt manuscripts" or "liet manuscripts," respectively. No satisfactory identification of an archetype or original has yet been made. Today MS B is generally preferred. The *Klage* is contained as a sequel to the *Nibelungenlied* in all the complete manuscripts except the "Piarist" manuscript k (Vienna, Österreichische Staatsbibliothek).

First publications: *Chriemhilden Rache, und die Klage: Zwey Heldengedichte aus dem schwäbischen Zeitpuncte,* edited by Johann Jakob Bodmer (Zurich: Orell, 1757); *Der Nibelungen Liet: Ein Rittergedicht aus dem XIII. oder XIV. Jahrhundert. Zum ersten Male aus der Handschrift ganz abgedruckt,* edited by Christoph Heinrich Myller (Berlin: Spener, 1782).

Standard editions: *Der Nibelunge nôt, mit der Klage, in der ältesten Gestalt mit den Abweichungen der gemeinen Lesart,* edited by Karl Lachmann (Berlin: Reimer, 1826; reprinted, Berlin: De Gruyter, 1960); *Die Klage, mit vollständigem kritischen Apparat und ausführlicher Einleitung,* edited by Anton Edzardi (Hannover: Rümpler, 1875); *Der Nibelunge Nôt, mit den Abweichungen von der Nibelunge Liet, den Lesarten sämmtlicher Handschriften und einem Wörterbuche,* 3 volumes, edited by Karl Bartsch (Leipzig: Brockhaus, 1870–1880); *Das Nibelungenlied: Paralleldruck der Handschriften A, B, und C nebst Lesarten der übrigen Handschriften,* edited by Michael S. Batts (Tübingen: Niemeyer, 1971); *Das Nibelungenlied nach der Handschrift C,* edited by Ursula Hennig, Altdeutsche Textbibliothek, no. 83 (Tübingen: Niemeyer, 1977); *Das Nibelungenlied,* edited by Bartsch, revised by Helmut de Boor and Roswitha Wisniewski (Mannheim: Brockhaus, 1988).

Edition in modern German: *Das Nibelungenlied: Heldehepos aus erster Hand,* translated by Karl Simrock, edited by Walter Hansen (Vienna: Ueberreuter, circa 1982).

Editions in English: *The Nibelungenlied,* edited and translated by Arthur Thomas Hatto (Harmondsworth, U.K.: Penguin, 1965); *The Lament,* translated by Winder McConnell (Columbia, S.C.: Camden House, 1994).

The *Nibelungenlied* (Song of the Nibelungs, circa 1200) is generally classified as a heroic epic or folk epic and is as close to being a national epic as any work of medieval German literature. Although it was not written down until about 1200, it is based on Germanic legend and folktales that must have been passed down through the centuries by oral tradition. Many of the central characters in the work are based on historical personages from the time of the Merovingians and the Ostrogoth kingdom in Lombardy. The ethics of the work are in large measure those of the pre-Christian Germanic world, but the work is also clad in the garb of the chivalric world of the High Middle Ages. It is an amalgamation of two stories that originally had no connection, to which several heterogeneous episodes have been added. Thus the work is replete with contradictions and inconsistencies. Versions that exist in Old Norse sources shed some light on the genesis of the poem but by no means explain all the difficulties.

In all the complete manuscripts except one, the poem is followed by another work, the *Klage* (Lament). This work begins where the *Nibelungenlied* leaves off, offering, as the title suggests, lamentations over the tragic fates of the characters in that poem but also summarizing the events in the *Nibelungenlied*. Aesthetically it is on a lower level than the *Nibelungenlied* – it is written in the usual rhymed couplets of the narratives of the day, and its style is best described as tedious – but it contains elements apparently from other sources, so that it does not lack interest.

The many extant manuscripts of the poem, together with the many references to it in contemporary sources, demonstrate that the *Nibelungenlied* was extremely popular in the medieval period. Since its rediscovery in 1755 by the Lindau physician Jakob Hermann Obereit, the work has been in the forefront of literary studies pertaining to the German Middle Ages. Karl Lachmann's edition of 1826 furnished a basis for the scientific study of the poem, and scholars have devoted considerable attention to it ever since. It has been translated many times, and many imitative novels and plays have been created. It has been subjected to the mystique of Wagnerian music drama (1874) and survived a horrendous two-part film version (1923–1924). It has often been viewed as the embodiment of Germanic heroic virtues that should stand as a model for all good Germans in the effete modern world. The association with national pride has invested the work with a sanctity that has caused many scholars to exaggerate its virtues and to rationalize away its defects.

The *Nibelungenlied* is anonymous, and there is little internal evidence to give clues to the identity of its author, his occupation, or his status in society. It was formerly believed that he was a minstrel; then the weight of scholarly opinion shifted, and he was believed to be a knight. Today he is generally considered a "cleric" in the medieval sense of the word – one connected with a religious order but not a monk or priest. The apparent familiarity of the author with place-names in Bavaria and Austria, together with the Bavarian dialect in which the poem is written, seems to place him in this area. The area around Passau seems to be the most likely area for his home, and it has been postulated that he resided at the court of Wolfger von Erla, bishop of Passau

from 1191 to 1204. This assumption is substantiated by the favorable portrait in the *Nibelungenlied* of Bishop Pilgrim, who seems to be modeled on Bishop Wolfger. Because of the association with Wolfger, because the *Nibelungenlied* shows the influence of Hartmann von Aue's *Iwein* (circa 1200), and because Wolfram von Eschenbach refers to the *Nibelungenlied* in *Parzival* (circa 1204), its likely time of composition is around 1200.

The *Nibelungenlied* is composed in four-line strophes, rhyming *aabb;* each line consists of two hemistichs, each of which has three beats except the last, which has four. This strophe is quite similar to that used by the twelfth-century Austrian lyric poet Der von Kürenberg in a poem involving a falcon; it is not easy, however, to determine in which direction the influence went. There has been much discussion as to whether the *Nibelungenlied* was sung, and it has become increasingly evident that it was. Musicologists have developed a melody for it, and the musician Eberhard Kummer has given performances of it to the accompaniment of a barrel organ or small harp.

The effect of a strophic narrative is, in general, to slow the pace of the story, and the extra beat in the last half line of the *Nibelungenlied* strophe intensifies this effect. The pace is further slowed by the frequent inclusion of epithets and other repetitive phrases. Characters are often described with such phrases long after they have been introduced – for instance, "Gêrnôt, ein riter küen' unt gemeit" (Gêrnôt, a knight bold and gallant) or "Kriemhilt der vil schœnen" (Kriemhild the very beautiful one). Such phrases often take the place of the name of the character, as "ein riter vil gemeit" (a very gallant knight) does for Siegfried. Such constructions have been viewed as indications of oral influence. Certainly the material must have existed in oral form for centuries, but if it came down in the form of verse, it was at some point transformed from the alliterative verse of the type found, for example, in the Old High German lay, the *Hildebrandslied* (circa 800).

There is much "epic foreshadowing" in the *Nibelungenlied;* thus the ending is never in doubt, but suspense and curiosity are aroused as to how that outcome will occur. In the first chapter there is a good example of foreshadowing (it is lacking in manuscript A): Kriemhild dreams that she had a falcon that was killed by two eagles (13, 1–4), and her mother interprets the dream (14, 3–4): "der falke, den du ziuhest, daz ist ein edel man. / in welle got behüeten, du muost in sciere vloren hân" (The falcon you are rearing is a noble man / who, unless God preserve him, will soon be taken from you). Al-

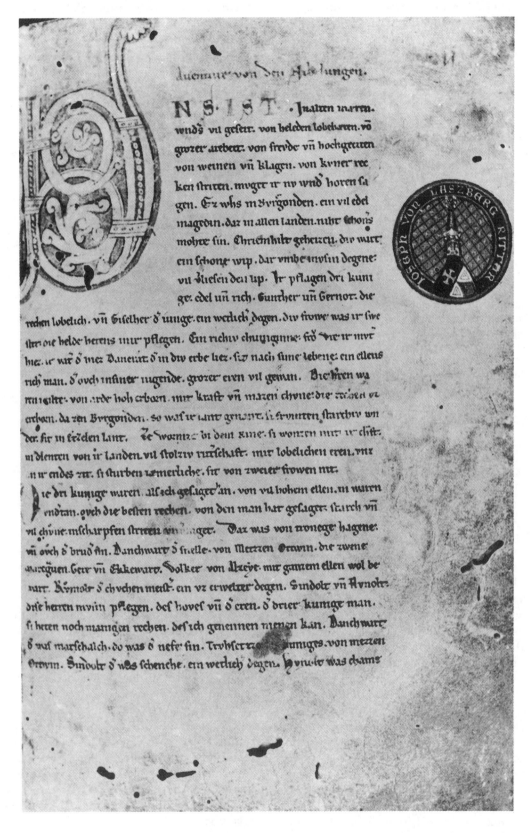

First page of the Nibelungenlied *in the Hohenems-Laßberg manuscript, dating from the beginning of the thirteenth century (Donaueschingen, Fürstliche Fürstenbergischen Hofbibliothek, Hs. 63, f. 1r)*

though Kriemhild protests that she will never marry, the chapter ends with a baleful prophecy:

Kriemhilt in ir muote　sich minne gar bewac.
sît lebte diu vil guote　vil manegen lieben tac,
daz sine wesse niemen,　den minnen wolde ir lîp.
sît wart si mit êren　eins vil küenen recken wîp.

Der was der selbe valke,　den si in ir troume sach,
den ir besciet ir muoter.　wie sêre si daz rach
an ir næhsten mâgen,　die in sluogen sint!
durch sîn eines sterben　starp vil maneger muoter kint.

(Kriemhild set all thought of love aside.
And after this conversation the good girl passed many a pleasant day
unaware of any man whom she would love.
Yet the time came when she was wed with honor to a very brave warrior,

to that same falcon whom she had seen in the dream,
which her mother had interpreted for her. What terrible vengeance
she took on her nearest kinsmen for slaying him in days to come!
For his one life there died many a mother's child.)

The *Nibelungenlied* contains many words that the chivalric poets seem to have regarded as old-fashioned or inappropriate, such as *recke*, *wîgant*, and *degen* (all of which mean warrior); *gêr* (spear); *brünne* (coat of mail); *ellen* (courage); *urliuge* (war); *march* (horse); *mære* (famous); *snel* (brave); and *veige* (doomed to die), which give the poem an antique flavor. There are also old-fashioned syntactic constructions, such as the postpositive position of the adjective in "der hêrre mîn" (*literally:* lord mine) and "ein riter guot" (*literally:* a knight good) and the end position of the finite verb in main clauses, as in "Des wirtes kameræere in becken vol golde rôt / daz wazzer für truogen" (*literally:* The host's chamberlains in bowls of gold / the water brought forth).

On the other hand, the poet has gone out of his way to bring the poem up to date by introducing much of the vocabulary of chivalry and chivalric customs such as tournaments, elaborate banquets, and knight-initiation ceremonies. Costly and elaborate clothing, viands, and gems are introduced to a much greater extent than they are in the chivalric epics. A good example is the five so-called *Schneiderstrophen* (tailor-strophes), where the clothing Kriemhild and her handmaidens make for the trip to Iceland is described.

Characters and events from Germanic antiquity form a historical nucleus for the *Nibelungenlied*. Brünhild's name reflects that of Brunichildus in Merovingian sources, although her nature seems to be derived from folktales or mythology. Names similar to Siegfried and Siegmund are found in Merovingian sources as well – for example, Sigibert I of Rheims; Siegfried, however, has often been equated with Arminius. The Burgundian kings Gunther and Gîselher in the *Nibelungenlied* reflect the names Gundaharius and Gislaharius, Burgundian kings of the fourth to fifth centuries mentioned in the *Lex Burgundionum* (circa 500). Etzel is based on the Hunnish king Attila, who is linked in tradition with Theodoric the Great, king of the East Goths, even though Theodoric was born around 454, the year after Attila died. There is a whole cycle of legends concerning Theodoric – who is called Dietrich von Bern in the *Nibelungenlied* – and his chief vassal, Meister Hildebrand, the hero of the *Hildebrandslied*. Theodoric's historical antagonist, Odoacer, is replaced in German legend by Ermenrich, based on Ermanaric, the fourth-century Ostrogothic king. Of the chief characters only Kriemhild and Hagen have no apparent historical counterparts; Hagen appears as Hagano in the tenth-century Latin poem *Waltharius manu fortis*, based on Germanic legends about Walter of Aquitaine, in which Gunther also appears as Guntharius. In the *Thidreks saga* (circa 1250) Hagen is said to be the bastard half brother of the three Burgundian kings, sired by a supernatural being, an *álfr*, in a garden. His name may well have meant "bastard" – literally, "one conceived in an open field" (an obsolete meaning of the German *Hag*).

All discussions as to the genesis of the *Nibelungenlied* have to take into account the evidence of Old Norse sources from the thirteenth century. The *Poetic Edda* (circa 1250), written down in Iceland, contains many heroic lays, many of them composed orally years before in Norway, that reveal a background of legend much older than the episodes recounted in the *Nibelungenlied*. The Icelandic *Volsunga saga*, based on the Eddic poems, contains material derived from poems that are lost. There is another version of the stories in the *Prose Edda* (circa 1220–1230) of Snorri Sturluson, likewise written down in Iceland. There is also an earlier version of most of the *Nibelungenlied*, often termed the *Niflunga saga*, included in a large compilation of tales about Theodoric, the *Thidreks saga*, written down in Norway and seemingly derived from the "Ältere Nôt" or a source closely related to it. By comparing the second part of the *Nibelungenlied* with the *Niflunga saga*, it is often possible to see the contributions of the final poet.

In 1816 Lachmann, influenced by then-current theories about the origin of the Homeric epics,

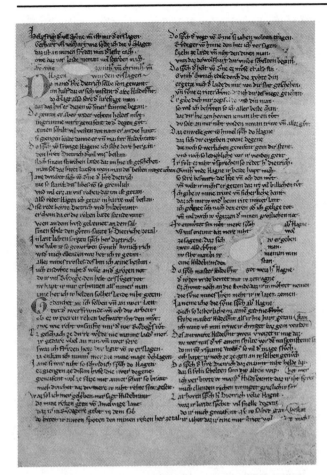
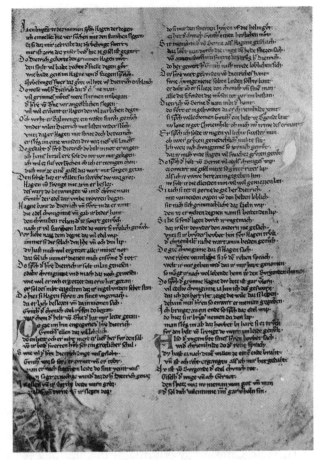

Pages from manuscript A for the Nibelungenlied, *dating from the last quarter of the thirteenth century (Munich, Staatsbibliothek, Cod. germ. 34, f. 92v–93r)*

postulated that the *Nibelungenlied* was a compilation of twenty heroic lays, more or less loosely sewn together. That hypothesis was questioned because of the apparent unity of the work. In 1921 Andreas Heusler postulated that the *Nibelungenlied* had been put together from two works: the second stage of the Brünhild-Siegfried legend, a poem he called the later *Brünhildenlied;* and the third stage of a Burgundian legend, which he called the older *Nibelungennôt.* The latter, Heusler contended, was of considerable size, but the former was short and was lengthened by a process of *Anschwellung* (introducing new elements into the text). Many variations of that hypothesis have been suggested, none of which has received universal scholarly applause.

The *Nibelungenlied* is divided into thirty-nine chapters or *âventiuren* (adventures). The first nineteen constitute the poem's first part, which is often called "Siegfrieds Tod" (Siegfried's Death). Siegfried is the only son of Siegmund, king of the Netherlands, whose capital is at Xanten. Siegfried is given the best chival-

ric upbringing and excels at all chivalric games and contests. This picture of Siegfried spending his youth at court is inconsistent with facts about Siegfried that later arise: in his youth he killed a dragon and bathed in its blood, making him invulnerable except for a spot between his shoulder blades where a leaf fell and kept the blood off his skin; also, he conquered a dwarf king, Alberich, and from this conquest held subject Alberich's people, the Nibelungs, as well as a tremendous treasure, the hoard of the Nibelungs, and a cloak (the *tarnhût* or *tarnkappe*) that makes the wearer invisible and gives him the strength of twelve men. Old Norse sources give Siegfried (or Sigurdr, as he is called there) a wild youth that contains many of these elements, so that it seems that the final redactor of the *Nibelungenlied* obscured them by making Siegfried the sort of model knight found in contemporary chivalric romances.

When Siegfried is told that he must get married, he decides that his bride must be Kriemhild, a Burgundian princess. She lives at the Burgundian capital, Worms, with her mother, Uote, and her three brothers, the kings Gunther, Gîselher, and Gêrnôt, and their retainer Hagen.

Siegfried comes to Worms alone – except, of course, for his servants. At first he acts strangely, challenging the Burgundian kings to a duel with their kingdoms as the prize. But he calms down, remembering his mission, and accepts the kings' invitation to be their guest. He stays there for a year without seeing Kriemhild, although she has been able to peek surreptitiously at him. When the Saxon king Liudegêr and the Danish king Liudegast declare war on the Burgundians, Siegfried leads the defense and saves the realm. As a reward for this service he gets to meet Kriemhild. Of course, it is mutual love at first sight. When Gunther declares that he wishes to woo the Icelandic queen Brünhild and solicits Siegfried's help, Siegfried offers his assistance if he is awarded Kriemhild's hand in return. The three brothers, Hagen, and Siegfried go to Iceland; Siegfried seems to know the way, although he could not ever have been there before. When they disembark, Siegfried plays the part of Gunther's vassal, holding his horse for him. When Brünhild hears their mission, she tells them that her suitor must engage in three athletic contests with her; he will claim her hand if he wins but forfeit his life if he loses. Gunther is fearful, but Siegfried helps him by donning his *tarnhût* and performing the feats while Gunther goes through the motions so that it appears that he is doing them. Siegfried catches a spear that Brünhild hurls at Gunther and throws it back, butt first, so that it knocks her down; he throws a huge rock farther than she does; and he jumps farther than she does even though he is carrying Gunther.

Brünhild returns with them to Worms, and the two couples are married. At the wedding feast Brünhild asks Gunther how Kriemhild could marry a vassal. (Although Brünhild's hostility to Siegfried allegedly comes from this disparity in rank between him and Kriemhild, in Norse sources she and Siegfried were lovers in earlier days; thus her hostility might result from jealousy.) When Gunther does not give her a satisfactory answer, Brünhild refuses to let him make love to her, trusses him up, and hangs him on a hook on the wall until daylight. The next day Gunther complains to Siegfried; the latter subdues Brünhild that night in his *tarnhût* so that Gunther can deflower her. Siegfried takes Brünhild's ring and girdle, which he apparently later gives to Kriemhild.

Siegfried and Kriemhild return to Xanten, where they have a child. Ten years after their departure Brünhild suggests that they be invited to Worms. Siegfried and Kriemhild accept the invitation, and all is joy for a while. Then, as they watch a tournament, Kriemhild and Brünhild argue over whose husband is the better man, Brünhild claiming that Siegfried must always be second to Gunther because he is Gunther's vassal. The women agree to meet at the cathedral door, and the one who is higher in rank will enter first. At the cathedral Kriemhild tells Brünhild that Siegfried, not Gunther, overcame her on their wedding night and sails triumphantly in ahead of her. After the service Brünhild demands proof of Kriemhild's claim, and Kriemhild produces the girdle Siegfried had taken from her.

This revelation provokes a crisis, but Siegfried solemnly swears that he did not tell Kriemhild that he had deflowered Brünhild. The three kings seem to be satisfied, but Hagen persuades them that Siegfried must die. The element of greed, perhaps paramount in older versions of the tale, is introduced:

Sin gevolgete niemen, niwan daz Hagene
geriet in allen zîten Gunther dem degene,
ob Sîfrit niht enlebte, sô wurde im undertân
vil der künege lande. der helt des trûren began.

(No one pursued the matter [of Siegfried's death] further, except that Hagen
kept impressing upon Gunther
that if Siegfried were not alive,
many of the kings' lands would fall into their hands.)

They pretend that the Saxon and Danish kings are again invading their realm, and Siegfried again offers his help. Claiming that he needs the information so that he can protect Siegfried in battle, Hagen tricks Kriemhild into revealing the location of Siegfried's vulnerable spot by sewing a small marker on his war shirt. The war threat is called off, and a hunting party is organized instead. After a successful hunt on an island in the Rhine, it is discovered that there is no wine to drink at the evening meal. Hagen tells of a spring where they can slake their thirst, and they race to it. As Siegfried drinks, Hagen drives a spear through the marker, and Siegfried dies eloquently.

Told that Siegfried was killed by robbers, Kriemhild is well aware of who actually perpetrated the deed. She eventually becomes reconciled with her brothers, but not with Hagen. Hagen, fearing that she will use the hoard of the Nibelungs to gain enough adherents to wreak vengeance upon him, steals it and sinks it in the Rhine at a place known only to him and Gunther.

The second part of the work, often called "Kriemhilds Rache" (Kriemhild's Revenge), now begins. Old Norse sources demonstrate that it was originally a completely independent story about the treachery of Attila, king of the Huns, who invited the Burgundians to his court to slay them for their land and treasure. This story presumably reflects an old hostility between Burgundians and Huns. In the *Nibelungenlied* Attila is called Etzel, and at his court resides Dietrich von Bern – the historical Theodoric of Verona – and Dietrich's legendary master-at-arms, Hildebrand.

Etzel's wife, Helche, dies, and Etzel, hearing that Kriemhild is a widow, sends messengers to woo her for him. After some hesitation she accepts and travels to Hunland to marry him. She lives there for thirteen years, becoming popular and acquiring adherents. She has a son, Ortliep. Now ready for vengeance, she persuades Etzel to invite her brothers and Hagen to visit them. The brothers accept over Hagen's opposition; Hagen is forced to go, lest he be dubbed a coward. He persuades the brothers to take an entourage of 1,060 knights and 9,000 squires and servants.

Oddly, the Burgundians are called Nibelungs in the second part of the poem. Their trip starts out ominously. While they are looking for a ferry to carry them across the swollen Danube, Hagen is told by some resident water sprites that no one of their contingent will return alive except the chaplain. Hagen slays the ferryman when he does not prove cooperative and tries to prove the prophecy wrong by casting the chaplain into the water to drown. When he beholds the chaplain swim to shore, Hagen realizes that the prophecy is true.

On the long trip through Bavaria the Nibelungs are pursued by Counts Else and Gelpfrât, who seek revenge for Hagen's killing of the ferryman. The Nibelungs repel them, killing Gelpfrât. A sleeping warrior, whose life Hagen spares, warns them that Kriemhild has hostile intent. At Bechelaren they stay for a time with Marchgrave Rüedeger, a vassal of Etzel's who is also amicably disposed toward the Nibelungs, and his wife, Gotelind. In an idyllic episode Gîselher becomes engaged to Rüedeger's daughter; her name is not given.

There is tension from the moment the Nibelungs arrive at Etzel's castle. Dietrich warns them that Kriemhild is up to no good, and when Kriemhild confronts them, she is friendly only to Gîselher and refuses to greet Hagen at all. She demands that the hoard be brought to her. Etzel, however, greets them warmly – especially Hagen, who as a young man had been a hostage at Etzel's court.

Before the evening banquet Hagen and his alter ego, Volker the fiddler, sit defiantly on a bench opposite Kriemhild's palace; Hagen has Siegfried's sword in his lap. Kriemhild comes toward them with a group of warriors, and the two refuse to rise to greet her. Hagen now for the first time admits to Kriemhild that he killed Siegfried. Kriemhild urges her men to attack them, but the warriors cowardly withdraw. After the banquet the Nibelungs are assigned to a large room for the night. Hagen and Volker keep watch by the door, Volker playing dulcet airs on his fiddle to lull his comrades to sleep. Again, the men Kriemhild sends to kill them withdraw in the face of Hagen and Volker's might.

After church the next day there are many jousts, in the course of which Volker kills a Hun. Etzel calms the people when a riot threatens to break out. That evening the Nibelungs are joined at dinner in the great hall of the castle by Kriemhild, Etzel, Ortliep, Dietrich, and some Hun warriors. Etzel suggests that the Nibelungs take his son back to Worms to further his education, but Hagen predicts that Ortliep will not live long. In the meantime Kriemhild persuades Blœdel, Etzel's younger brother, to slay the Nibelung squires and servants, who are quartered in another room under the supervision of Dancwart, Hagen's younger brother. All nine thousand squires and servants are killed, but Dancwart kills Blœdel, fights his way to the banquet hall, and delivers his news. Hagen responds by lopping off Ortliep's head. Dietrich gets free passage for himself, Etzel, Kriemhild, and Rüedeger, after which the Nibelungs slay the remaining Huns and cast their bodies out the door.

Îrinc of Denmark attacks the Nibelungs; he is killed, and the Danes and Thuringians seeking to avenge him are all slaughtered. The Huns attack the Nibelungs but are beaten back. Kriemhild has the hall set on fire; the Nibelungs ward off the falling beams with their shields and assuage their thirst by drinking the blood of the fallen.

In the ensuing battles the principal characters on both sides seem to search each other out, so that they are never killed by lesser warriors. Etzel demands that Rüedeger enter the fray, as he is Etzel's vassal, and after much soul-searching Rüedeger agrees to do so. Hagen asks Rüedeger to exchange shields, as his own is all hacked up, and when Rüedeger hands Hagen his shield, tears come to the eyes of the doughty warriors. Hagen and Volker agree not to fight against Rüedeger, but Gêrnôt kills him. Dietrich sends Hildebrand and Hildebrand's

Page from a manuscript for the Nibelungenlied, dating from the second quarter of the fifteenth century. The illustration depicts the murder of Siegfried by Hagen, who is using a bow and arrow rather than a spear, the weapon mentioned in the text (Berlin, Staatsbibliothek Preußischer Kulturbesitz, Ms. germ. fol. 855, f. 58v).

nephew, Wolfhart, to fetch Rüedeger's body. Wolfhart and Gîselher kill each other, and Hildebrand kills Volker. Dietrich subdues Hagen and Gunther and brings them in bonds to Kriemhild.

Kriemhild tells Hagen that he must either reveal the location of the hoard or lose his life. He replies that he cannot betray his lord, Gunther, as long as the latter is alive. Kriemhild has Gunther decapitated and brings his head to Hagen. Hagen laughs and says that he is the only one left who knows the whereabouts of the hoard, and he will never betray it. Kriemhild takes Siegfried's sword from Hagen's scabbard and lops off his head. This is too much for Hildebrand, and he puts Kriemhild to the sword. Thus there is a great purging that is reminiscent of the depiction of the end of the world in the *Poetic Edda*.

The *Klage* summarizes the entire *Nibelungenlied* plot and narrates the cleaning up of the battle site and the funerals of the warriors, Kriemhild, and Ortlieb. Messengers are sent to break the news to Gotelind, Detlind (Rüedeger and Gotelind's daughter, who is not named in the *Nibelungenlied*), Uote, and Brünhild. Gotelind and Uote swoon, and all lament their losses at great length. Gotelind and Uote die soon after. Gunther and Brünhild's son is knighted and crowned. Dietrich; his wife-to-be, Herrat; and Hildebrand leave Etzel's court and go home, visiting Bechelaren on the way. It is generally agreed that Hagen was responsible for the tragedy, although it could have been averted if the Burgundians had swallowed their pride and informed Etzel of what was going on.

The *Nibelungenlied* is a powerful work that has stirred the imaginations of generations of readers and can lay claim to being the German national epic. It contains many unforgettable incidents: the games in Iceland, the trussing up of Gunther on his wedding night and Siegfried's intervention the next night, the quarrel between Kriemhild and Brünhild, Siegfried's murder, Hagen's throwing the chaplain overboard, Hagen and Volker on guard in defiance of Kriemhild and her adherents, Hagen's killing of Ortlieb, the drinking of the blood of the slain to ward off the thirst caused by the fire, Hagen's tricking Kriemhild into killing Gunther so that she will never find the location of the hoard, and the killing of Hagen and Kriemhild.

Four central figures emerge from the work. Siegfried is a superhero who is too perfect to be realistic. Brünhild is remarkable principally for her obsession about Kriemhild's marriage to Siegfried, ostensibly because she thinks he is Gunther's vassal; it is, however, hard to escape the impression that she is motivated by jealousy. Kriemhild changes from a sweet maiden at the beginning of the work to a veritable demon intent on bloody revenge. Hagen is the most complex character of all. It is he who insists on Siegfried's death, although it is not clear why; a possible motive is his desire to appropriate Siegfried's wealth. In the second part of the poem Hagen emerges as a grim, ruthless warrior who kills without mercy and has no fear. He seems to be the embodiment of the Old Germanic ethos.

The *Nibelungenlied* includes many inconsistencies and impossibilities, such as the conflicting stories of Siegfried's youth, Siegfried's knowledge of a country he could not have seen, the marker that showed Siegfried's vulnerable spot miraculously transferring itself from his war shirt to his hunting shirt, Siegfried living for a year at the court of Worms without seeing Kriemhild, men surviving a fire by drinking blood, and a roomful of people allowing themselves to be killed. It also includes tedious descriptions of banquets, tournaments, and parties, as well as countless lines of empty rhetoric. It seems as if the final poet was more interested in the individual episodes than in consistency and did not scruple to include impossible elements, such as the wild youth of Siegfried, to advance his plot. He was also intent on including as much chivalric material as he could, hence the many parties, banquets, descriptions of clothing, and so on. He uses the same motifs again and again, as is most apparent in the bridal quests: Siegfried's for Kriemhild, Gunther's for Brünhild, and Etzel's for Kriemhild. The primary one seems to have been Etzel's quest for Kriemhild, which is essential to the plot; the two in the first half of the work seem imitative. This trait puts the final author on a level with the authors of the minstrel epics, such as *König Rother* ((King Rother, circa 1150) and *Orendel* (fifteenth century), where the same story is told over and over with slight variations. For all its flaws, however, the *Nibelungenlied* is superb entertainment, and that – not something profound, inspiring, or symbolic – is what it was intended to be.

Bibliography:

Willy Krogmann and Ulrich Pretzel, *Bibliographie zum Nibelungenlied und zur Klage,* fourth edition (Berlin: Schmidt, 1966).

References:

Theodore M. Andersson, "The Encounter between Burgundians and Bavarians in Adventure 26 of the *Nibelungenlied*," *Journal of English and Germanic Philology*, 82 (July 1983): 365–373;

Andersson, "The Epic Source of Niflunga Saga and the Nibelungenlied," *Arkiv för nordisk filologi*, 88 (1973): 1–54;

Andersson, *The Legend of Brynhild* (Ithaca, N.Y. & London: Cornell University Press, 1980);

Andersson, *A Preface to the Nibelungenlied* (Stanford, Cal.: Stanford University Press, 1987);

Andersson, "Why Does Siegfried Die?," in *Germanic Studies in Honor of Otto Springer,* edited by Stephen J. Kaplowitt (Pittsburgh: University of Pittsburgh Press, 1978), pp. 29–39;

Franz H. Bäuml, "The Oral Tradition and Middle High German Literature," *Oral Tradition,* 1 (1986): 398–445;

Bäuml and Eva-Maria Fallone, *A Concordance to the Nibelungenlied (Bartsch-de Boor Text)* (Leeds, U.K.: Maney, 1976);

Bäuml and Donald J. Ward, "Zur mündlichen Überlieferung des Nibelungenliedes," *Deutsche Vierteljahrsschrift für Literaturwissenschaft und Geistesgeschichte,* 41 (August 1967): 351–390;

Hugo Bekker, *The Nibelungenlied: A Literary Analysis* (Toronto: University of Toronto Press, 1971);

Karl H. Bertau, "Epenrezitation im deutschen Mittelalter," *Etudes Germaniques,* 20 (January-March 1965): 1–17;

Bertau and Rudolf Stephan, "Zum sanglichen Vortrag mhd. strophischer Epen," *Zeitschrift für deutsches Altertum,* 87 (1956-1957): 253–270;

Werner Betz, "Plädoyer für C als Weg zum älteren Nibelungenlied," in *Mediaevalia litteraria: Festschrift für Helmut de Boor zum 80. Geburtstag,* edited by Ursula Hennig and Herbert Kolb (Munich: Beck, 1971), pp. 331–341;

Siegfried Beyschlag, "Das Motiv der Macht bei Siegfrieds Tod," *Germanisch-romanische Monatsschrift,* 2, no. 2 (1951/1952): 95–108;

Kees H. R. Borghart, *Das Nibelungenlied: Die Spuren mündlichen Ursprungs in schriftlicher Überlieferung* (Amsterdam: Rodopi, 1977);

Helmut Brackert, *Beiträge zur Handschriftenkritik des Nibelungenliedes* (Berlin: De Gruyter, 1963);

Wilhelm Braune, "*Die Handschriftenverhältnisse des Nibelungenliedes,*" *Beiträge zur Geschichte der deutschen Sprache und Literatur,* 25 (1900): 1–222;

Jesse L. Byock, trans., *The Saga of the Volsungs* (Berkeley & Los Angeles: University of California Press, 1990);

Michael Curschmann, " 'Nibelungenlied' und 'Klage,' " in *Die deutsche Literatur des Mittelalters:*

Verfasserlexikon, edited by Wolfgang Stammler and Karl Langosch; second edition, edited by Kurt Ruh and others (Berlin & New York: De Gruyter, 1987), VI: 926–969;

Curschmann, " 'Nibelungenlied' und 'Nibelungenklage': Über Mündlichkeit und Schriftlichkeit im Prozeß der Episierung," in *Deutsche Literatur im Mittelalter: Kontakte und Perspektiven. Hugo Kuhn zum Gedenken,* edited by Christoph Cormeau (Stuttgart: Metzler, 1979), pp. 85–119;

Nelly Dürrenmatt, *Das Nibelungenlied im Kreis der höfischen Dichtung* (Bern: Lang, 1945);

Otfrid Ehrismann, *Nibelungenlied — Epoche — Werk — Wirkung* (Munich: Beck, 1987);

Ehrismann, *Das Nibelungenlied in Deutschland* (Munich: Fink, 1975);

Walter Falk, *Das Nibelungenlied in seiner Epoche: Revision eines romantischen Mythos* (Heidelberg: Winter, 1974);

Francis G. Gentry, "Trends in 'Nibelungenlied' Research since 1949: A Critical View," *Amsterdamer Beiträge zur älteren Germanistik,* 7 (1974): 125–139;

George T. Gillespie, " 'Die Klage' as a Commentary on the 'Nibelungenlied,' " in *Probleme deutscher Erzählformen: Marburger Colloquium 1966,* edited by Peter F. Ganz and Werner Schröder (Berlin: Schmidt, 1969), pp. 153–177;

Angelika Günzburger, *Studien zur Nibelungenklage: Forschungsbericht — Bauform der Klage — Personendarstellung,* Europäische Hochschulschriften, no. 685 (Frankfurt am Main: Lang, 1983);

Edward R. Haymes, "Dietrich von Bern im Nibelungenlied," *Zeitschrift für deutsches Altertum,* 114, no. 3 (1985): 159–165;

Haymes, *Das mündliche Epos: Eine Einführung in die "Oral Poetry" Forschung* (Stuttgart: Metzler, 1977);

Haymes, *Mündliches Epos in mittelhochdeutscher Zeit,* Göppinger Arbeiten zur Germanistik, no. 164 (Göppingen: Kümmerle, 1975);

Haymes, *The "Nibelungenlied": History and Interpretation,* Illinois Medieval Monographs, no. 2 (Urbana & Chicago: University of Illinois Press, 1986);

Haymes, trans., *The Saga of Thidrek of Bern* (New York & London: Garland, 1988);

Joachim Heinzle, *Das Nibelungenlied: Eine Einführung* (Munich & Zurich: Artemis, 1987);

Andreas Heusler, *Nibelungensage und Nibelungenlied,* sixth edition (Dortmund: Rohfus, 1921; reprinted, 1965);

Werner Hoffmann, "Die englische und amerikanische Nibelungenforschung 1959–1962: Überschau und Kritik," *Zeitschrift für deutsche Philologie*, 84, no. 2 (1965): 267–278;

Hoffmann, *Das Nibelungenlied* (Frankfurt am Main: Diesterweg, 1987);

Otto Höfler, *Siegfried, Arminius und die Symbolik* (Heidelberg: Winter, 1961);

Karl Heinz Ihlenburg, "Die gesellschaftliche Grundlage des germanischen Heldenethos und die mündliche Überlieferung heroischer Stoffe," *Weimarer Beiträge*, 17 (1971): 140–169;

Ihlenburg, *Das Nibelungenlied: Problem und Gehalt* (Berlin: Akademie, 1969);

Dietrich Kralik, *Die Sigfridtrilogie im Nibelungenlied und in der Thidrekssaga* (Halle: Niemeyer, 1941);

Dennis M. Kratz, ed. and trans., *Waltharius and Ruodlieb* (New York & London: Garland, 1984);

Henry Kratz, "The Etymology of the Name *Hagen* in the *Nibelungenlied*," *Names*, 10 (1962): 101–107;

Karl Lachmann, *Über die ursprüngliche Gestalt des Gedichts von der Nibelunge Noth* (Berlin: Dümmler, 1816);

August Lübben, *Wörterbuch zu der Nibelunge Nôt (Liet)* (Oldenburg: Stalling, 1876; reprinted, Wiesbaden: Sändig, 1966);

Winder McConnell, *The Nibelungenlied* (Boston: Twayne, 1984);

D. G. Mowatt and Hugh Sacker, *The Nibelungenlied: An Interpretative Commentary* (Toronto: University of Toronto Press, 1967);

Ulrich Müller, "Eberhard Kummer und die mittelhochdeutsche Sangversepik," *Österreichische Musikzeitschrift*, 5 (1989), 234–238;

Müller, "Überlegungen und Versuche zur Melodie des 'Nibelungenliedes,' zur Kürenberger-Strophe und zur sogenannten 'Elegie' Walthers von der Vogelweide," in *Zur gesellschaftlichen Funktionalität mittelalterlicher deutscher Literatur* (Greifswald: University of Greifswald, 1984), pp. 27–42, 136;

Bert Nagel, *Das Nibelungenlied: Stoff – Form – Ethos* (Frankfurt am Main: Hirschgraben, 1965);

Nagel, "Zur Interpretation und Wertung des Nibelungenliedes," *Neue Heidelberger Jahrbücher* (1954): 1–89;

Friedrich Neumann, *Das Nibelungenlied in seiner Zeit* (Göttingen: Vandenhoeck & Ruprecht, 1967);

Friedrich Panzer, *Das Nibelungenlied: Entstehung und Gestalt* (Stuttgart: Kohlhammer, 1955);

Panzer, *Studien zum Nibelungenlied* (Frankfurt am Main: Diesterweg, 1945);

Emil Ploss, *Siegfried-Sigurd, der Drachenkämpfer* (Cologne & Graz: Böhlau, 1966);

Hermann Reichert, *Nibelungenlied und Nibelungensage* (Vienna & Cologne: Böhlau, 1985);

Hellmut Rosenfeld, "Die Datierung des 'Nibelungenliedes' Fassung B und C durch das Küchenmeisterhofamt und Wolfger von Passau," *Beiträge zur Geschichte der deutschen Sprache und Literatur*, 91 (1969): 104–120;

Heinz Rupp, ed., *Nibelungenlied und Kudrun*, Wege der Forschung, no. 54 (Darmstadt: Wissenschaftliche Buchgesellschaft, 1976);

Werner Schröder, *Nibelungenlied-Studien* (Stuttgart: Metzler, 1968);

Schröder, "Die Tragödie Kriemhilts im Nibelungenlied," *Zeitschrift für deutsches Altertum*, 90 (1960–1961): 41–80, 123–160;

Karl Strecker, ed., *Waltharius* (Weimar: Böhlau, 1951);

Gottfried Weber, *Das Nibelungenlied,* revised by Hoffmann (Stuttgart: Metzler, 1982);

Werner Wunderlich, Ulrich Müller, and Detlef Scholz, eds., *"Waz sider da geschach": American-German Studies on the Nibelungenlied* (Göppingen: Kümmerle, 1992);

Jean I. Young, trans., *The Prose Edda of Snorri Sturluson* (Cambridge: Bowes & Bowes, 1954; Berkeley: University of California Press, 1973).

Ortnit and *Wolfdietrich*
(*circa 1225 – 1250*)

J. Wesley Thomas
University of Kentucky

Ortnit

Manuscripts: The work appears with *Wolfdietrich* in nine manuscripts and singly in one manuscript; two other manuscripts that contained both narratives were destroyed during the battle for Strasbourg in the Franco-Prussian War. The most important manuscripts with respect to *Ortnit* are a large parchment anthology of the early fourteenth century (cod. 2779) and the early-sixteenth-century Ambras Heldenbuch (Book of Heroes, cod. ser. nova 2663), both at the Austrian National Library in Vienna.

First publication: *Otnit,* edited by Franz Joseph Mone (Berlin: Reimer, 1821).

Standard edition: In *Ortnit und die Wolfdietriche,* volume 3 of *Deutsches Heldenbuch,* edited by Arthur Amelung and Oskar Jänicke (Berlin: Weidmann, 1871, 1873; reprinted, Zurich: Weidmann, 1968).

Edition in English: Translated by J. Wesley Thomas, in *Ortnit and Wolfdietrich: Two Medieval Romances* (Columbia, S.C.: Camden House, 1986).

Wolfdietrich

Manuscripts: The work appears with *Ortnit* in nine manuscripts and singly in three manuscripts. The most important manuscripts for *Wolfdietrich* are the Ambras Heldenbuch, a fifteenth-century paper manuscript in the Austrian National Library (cod. 2947), and a fifteenth-century paper manuscript in the Heidelberg University Library (cpg 373).

First publication: In *Der Helden Buch in der Ursprache,* volume 2, edited by Friedrich Heinrich von der Hagen and Alois Primisser (Berlin: Reimer, 1825).

Standard edition: *Ortnit und die Wolfdietriche,* volumes 3 and 4 of *Deutsches Heldenbuch,* edited by Arthur Amelung and Oskar Jänicke (Berlin: Weidmann, 1871, 1873; reprinted, Zurich: Weidmann, 1968).

Edition in English: Translated by J. Wesley Thomas, in *Ortnit and Wolfdietrich: Two Medieval Romances* (Columbia, S.C.: Camden House, 1986).

The anonymous *Ortnit* and *Wolfdietrich* (both circa 1225–1250) are among the best representatives of a tradition of noncourtly adventure novels in verse that began in the middle of the twelfth century and was still popular, though no longer productive, nearly three hundred years later. The two link the earlier works, known as *Spielmannsepen* (gleeman epics), to the later ones — especially those dealing with Dietrich of Verona and his companions — in that they exhibit characteristics of both groups. Although set in a remote Germanic past that recalls the Gothic presence in Macedonia and the Gothic and Lombard kingdoms of northern Italy, they reflect the conflicts and religious intolerance of the Crusades as well as the Alpine folklore of their day. Their graphic descriptions of bloody battles, their exploitation of the supernatural, and their burlesque humor are typical of the noncourtly narratives.

The language of *Ortnit* and *Wolfdietrich,* together with the detailed knowledge of the geography of northern Italy that they reveal, suggests that the authors of the two works were Austrian or Tirolese. There is nothing in the texts to indicate that they knew Latin or French or to connect them with any particular class, court, or town; they may have been professional entertainers who traveled from place to place. The authors appear to have been quite different from each other in their attitudes toward religion: *Wolfdietrich* includes religious miracles and many prayers and pious expressions, while *Ortnit* at times seems almost sacrilegious.

As with the *Spielmannsepen,* the principal action of *Ortnit* turns about the abduction of a bride. The young Ortnit, king of Lombardy, decides to marry a beautiful Saracen princess whose father, Machorel —

the heathen king of Jerusalem and Syria – plans to wed her himself and beheads the emissaries of all those who ask for her hand. While his friends and vassals are preparing for an invasion of Machorel's kingdom, Ortnit sets out alone in search of adventure. He comes upon what appears to be a beautiful four-year-old boy but is in fact Alberich, a mighty, five-century-old dwarf who is normally invisible and is seen by Ortnit only through the power of a ring that his mother gave him without explaining its true nature. After a violent struggle, Alberich reveals that he is the king's natural father, presents Ortnit with a splendid sword and hauberk, and promises to help him in time of need.

Ortnit returns to his castle at Garda. Several months later he leads a mighty force down to Messina, where they set sail for Tyre, Machorel's capital. The wiles of Alberich enable the invaders to enter the harbor and the gates of the city unopposed, but victory is won only after a fierce battle that claims many lives on both sides. Ortnit's army moves on to the mighty fortress of Mount Tabor, where Machorel and his daughter reside. A bloody struggle before the moat is indecisive.

During the night the invisible Alberich enters the stronghold and persuades the princess to flee with Ortnit. The invaders retreat hastily toward Tyre and their ships but are overtaken. The heathen army is destroyed; only Machorel escapes. Greatly reduced in number, Ortnit's forces set sail for Lombardy, where a splendid wedding festival takes place.

Not long afterward one of Machorel's huntsmen brings his lord two dragon eggs that he found in a wilderness. Seeking vengeance, the king sends them to Lombardy, where they hatch in a remote cave and are cared for by the huntsman until they can forage for themselves. The dragons then devour everything they encounter; they kill farmers, hunters, and any knights who dare to attack them. Ortnit decides that only he can rid the country of this plague and sets out to find the most troublesome of the dragons. After riding all day and all night, Ortnit sits down to rest and falls asleep. The dragon comes, seizes him in its jaws, and carries him off to feed its ravenous brood.

The author's sense of humor is evident in the role played by the invisible dwarf, who occasionally provides comic relief, but the prevailing atmosphere is one of somber foreboding. The casualties of the invading host are carefully recorded; as its number shrinks from thirty thousand to a mere one thousand, Ortnit's remorse at having led so many to their deaths increases. The subsequent devastation

Detail from a drawing in a 1418 manuscript, showing Ortnit riding out to do battle with the dragon (Heidelberg, Universitätsbibliothek, cpg. 373, f. 256)

of Lombardy by the dragons adds to his guilt, and he can free himself from it only by undertaking a quest from which he does not expect to return. Yet it is not the dragons themselves that he fears – his great strength, impenetrable armor, and irresistible sword will protect him – but providential retribution. And indeed, he succumbs not to a superior force but to his own weariness.

The author drew much of his material from current history and from other well-known adventure tales. His hero's expedition to Asia Minor to gain a queen may have been inspired by the marriage in 1225 of Emperor Friedrich II to Isabella of Brienne, heiress to the kingdom of Jerusalem, and it reflects reports of the Crusade of 1217 led by King Andreas of Hungary, Duke Leopold of Austria, and Duke Otto of Meran. Their army, which included many Austrians and Bavarians, unsuccessfully attacked the fortress on Mount Tabor that appears in *Ortnit*. It had been constructed a few years earlier by Malek al Adel, the Machorel of the story. The fictional account of the conquest of Tyre was apparently based on the seizure of the city by Christian forces in 1124. Ortnit's heathen supporter, Zacharis of Sicily, has been identified with an ally of Friedrich II with the same name.

The extant literature from which the author drew includes the older *Brautraub* (abduction of a bride) tales *König Rother* (King Rother, circa 1150) and

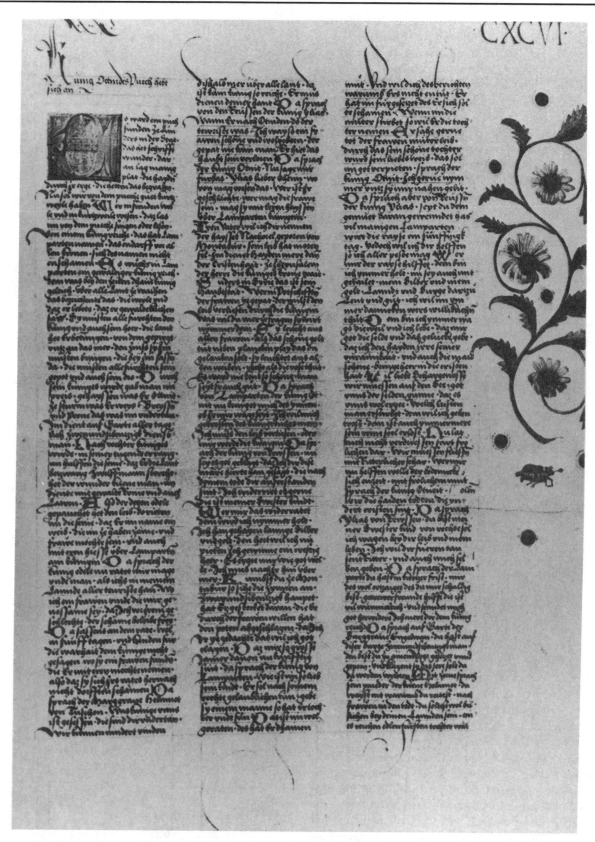

Page from the Ambraser Heldenbuch, an early-sixteenth-century manuscript that includes both Ortnit *and* Wolfdietrich *(Vienna, Österreichischen Nationalbibliothek, Cod. ser. nova 2663, f. 196r)*

Oswald, (twelfth century?) and perhaps *Orendel* (date unknown) and *Salman und Morolf* (late twelfth century?). He also borrowed from courtly narratives – the *Nibelungenlied* (circa 1200), Gottfried von Straßburg's *Tristan und Isolde* (circa 1210), Wirnt von Grafenber's *Wigalois* (circa 1204–1210), and Hartmann von Aue's *Iwein* (before 1205) – but did not imitate their speech and manners. There are no lengthy descriptions of fine clothing and grand festivals, no tournaments, and little consciously refined language or ethics. That all the warriors fight on foot is clear evidence that the poet was intentionally portraying a prechivalric culture, an age more primitive than his own.

Ortnit is basically theatrical. Nearly two-thirds of the verses consist of terse and lively dialogues; the narrator does not give his opinions about the action and almost never reveals the thoughts or feelings of the characters. The narrative parts – like other noncourtly adventure tales – use hyperbole to heighten suspense, portray violence, and arouse wonder. Another prominent stylistic device is repetition of words, phrases, and situations. Often this repetition is merely the result of formulaic composition, but occasionally it is used deliberately for emphasis or contrast. Most of the characters are the stock figures of such stories. Only Alberich is different, for he more closely resembles the mischievous kobold of the later fairy tale than the good or evil dwarfs of medieval German literature.

The work is extant in seven versions that differ mainly in their versification. Discrepancies with respect to the plot appear at the end, where medieval scribes or other adapters made such changes as were necessary to form a suitable accommodation with a particular variant of *Wolfdietrich*. In some cases Ortnit's death is foreseen in *Ortnit* but does not actually take place until well into *Wolfdietrich*.

Although each *Wolfdietrich* manuscript presents the story in a different form, the number of versions can be reduced to four if only major differences are considered. Three are designated according to the birthplace of the hero – "Wolfdietrich of Constantinople," "Wolfdietrich of Salonika," and the fragmentary "Wolfdietrich of Athens"; the fourth, a much longer work, is known as "the large Wolfdietrich." Each begins with a prologue that tells of the background of the hero, his birth, and his contact with wolves during infancy. Except for the correspondence between "Wolfdietrich of Salonika" and "the large Wolfdietrich," these accounts differ greatly, but there is generally agreement among the three complete variants with respect to the hero's subsequent experiences.

Like such anonymous works as *Herzog Ernst* (Duke Ernst, late twelfth century) and *Dietrichs Flucht* (Dietrich's Flight, late thirteenth century) and Der Pleier's *Tandareis und Flordibel* (circa 1240–1280), *Wolfdietrich* is the tale of an exile. It consists of a frame narrative dealing with Wolfdietrich's brothers and loyal vassals and an embedded story about the hero's relations with Emperor Ortnit and his wife. The events in Lombardy alternate with fantastic adventures that are only loosely connected to either the outer or the inner actions and their development; but they appealed to the medieval audience's interest in the supernatural.

The dying King Hugdietrich of Greece divides his kingdom among his three sons; he leaves Constantinople and the adjacent lands to the eldest, Wolfdietrich, whom he commends to the care of his vassal Duke Berchtung of Merano. Four years later, when Wolfdietrich's brothers seize his inheritance, the duke gathers an army and sails to Constantinople. But the attempt to retake the city fails, and Berchtung's forces are annihilated; he, ten of his sixteen sons, and Wolfdietrich are the only survivors. The young prince becomes separated from the others, and his wanderings begin.

Wolfdietrich first appears in Lombardy to keep a promise he made as a child. Soon after Hugdietrich's death, Ortnit, who here is an emperor – the plot requires it – had sent emissaries to demand tribute from Constantinople; Wolfdietrich had refused, declaring that, when he became a man, he would come to Lombardy and fight Ortnit. The single combat takes place below the castle, Ortnit is defeated, and the two take an oath of friendship. Wolfdietrich stays on at Garda for six months, during which he becomes well acquainted with Liebgart, the wife of his host.

He next comes through Lombardy while searching for Sigminne, the queen of Old Troy, whom he has married and who has been abducted. Out of loyalty to his friend, Ortnit insists on joining in the search. It is successful, and the three return to Garda together; then Wolfdietrich and his wife set out for their kingdom. She dies a short time later, and her grief-stricken husband gives up Old Troy to resume the life of a wanderer.

In the meantime, Ortnit's father-in-law has sent two fearful dragons into his land. Unable to endure the suffering of his people, the emperor tells Liebgart that he is riding forth to seek the monsters and advises her to marry Wolfdietrich if he should not return. In the forest he comes upon a struggle between an elephant and a dragon and intervenes, giving the latter three deep wounds that cause it to

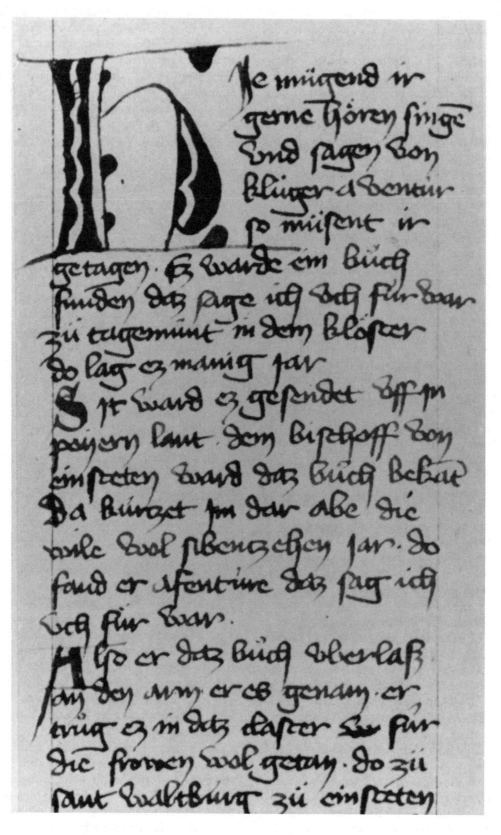

First page of Wolfdietrich, *from a fifteenth-century paper manuscript (Heidelberg, Universitätsbibliothek, cpg. 373, f. 25b)*

flee. Since the elephant will not leave him, Ortnit decides to take it back to Garda. On the way he dismounts under a linden to rest, but it is a magic tree: whoever goes to sleep under it will not wake for three days. Soon the dragon creeps near. The emperor's hound and steed try vainly to arouse their master while the elephant fights with the dreadful beast. At last the elephant is crushed, and the emperor is carried off to feed the dragon's hungry brood.

Roaming from land to land, Wolfdietrich comes to Lombardy and learns of Ortnit's fate. Determined to avenge his friend, he finds one of the dragons and attacks it. But his sword cannot pierce the horny skin of the monster and finally breaks. The dragon carries him to its den, throws him to its young, and lies down outside. In his shirt Wolfdietrich wears a saint's relic that protects him from the teeth of the whelps. After they lose interest in him, he looks about the cave and discovers Ortnit's famous sword that can cleave anything. With it the warrior quickly slays the young dragons and their huge dam, cuts out their tongues, and leaves for Garda.

A certain count hears the dragons are dead and hurries off with his men to their cave. Cutting off the heads, he brings them back to the castle as proof that he has slain the monsters. Thereupon, despite her reluctance, Liebgart is promised to him so that the empire might have a strong ruler. When the forest dweller with whom Wolfdietrich is staying tells the warrior of the betrothal, he goes to the wedding festival, displays the tongues, and shows the count to be an impostor. The latter's supporters attack the true dragon slayer; they are defeated, and the count is killed. The empress is then given to Wolfdietrich. The following morning, as he and Liebgart are examining the cave where Ortnit died, the second old dragon appears and is slain.

After establishing his authority over his newly won lands, Wolfdietrich raises an army and sails for Constantinople to regain his patrimony and learn what has happened to Berchtung and the latter's sons. Setting up camp near the city, he goes on alone after dark to reconnoiter and finds his faithful vassals – save the father, who has died – shackled together two by two and serving as watchmen. God causes their bonds to fall off, and they flee with Wolfdietrich. In the battle that follows, the army of Wolfdietrich's brother is defeated; but they are allowed to keep all that they had inherited. Wolfdietrich helps Berchtung's sons regain their heritage and also divides one of his kingdoms among them. Thereafter the brave warrior remains in Garda till his death.

Three interpolated adventures present supernatural events. In one, Wolfdietrich is driven mad by a hairy monster who wants him to marry her; when he finally agrees, she changes into the beautiful Sigminne, the queen of Old Troy. In another a sorceress torments the hero with fearful illusions: a meadow appears to become a stormy sea, he is attacked by devils that multiply as they are slain, and he is encircled by a ring of fire. In a third adventure Liebgart is abducted by a dwarf wearing a cloak of invisibility who leads her through a spring into a hollow mountain.

Although *Wolfdietrich* is episodic, an ever-present motif ties the parts together. That motif is loyalty: of Berchtung and his sons to Wolfdietrich; of Ortnit to Wolfdietrich; of Liebgart to Ortnit; of Wolfdietrich to Sigminne, Ortnit, and Liebgart; of men to beasts and beasts to men. But chiefly the story tells of the hero's loyalty to Berchtung and his sons, demonstrated by his oft-repeated prayer, "nu berât mir got ze Kriechen mîn eïnlif dienstman!" (May God care for my eleven vassals in Greece!) and at last by his freeing and rewarding them.

One conjecture about the work is that in its original form it was a deliberate attempt to alter history and create legend. Until he was seventeen, Theodoric the Great (known to literature as Dietrich of Verona) was a hostage at the court of the Eastern Roman emperor in Constantinople. Later he followed his father as leader of the Ostrogoths and, with the encouragement of the Eastern emperor, invaded Italy. Its king, Odoacer, surrendered after being defeated in battle and was treacherously slain by Theodoric, who then assumed the title of king of Italy. It has been argued that some song or ballad was composed soon thereafter, perhaps even during the king's lifetime, to throw a different light on these events by telling how Theodoric (Wolfdietrich) came to northern Italy to avenge the death of Odoacer (Ortnit) and remained there as his legitimate successor.

Other sources of *Wolfdietrich* are more obvious. The framework borrows liberally from *König Rother;* the influence of *Oswald* and Heinrich von Veldeke's *Eneit* (circa 1185) can also be seen. The inner story draws from *Iwein, Tristan und Isolde,* and *Wigalois,* while the interpolated adventures reflect certain elements in Ulrich von Zatzikhoven's *Lanzelet* (circa 1194–1203) and the anonymous Strasbourg *Alexander* (circa 1170).

With regard to narrative style, *Wolfdietrich,* like *Ortnit,* is highly dramatic. It emphasizes action above all and is made up largely of dialogue, and the depiction of extremes of feeling goes so far as to have the hero faint with intense emotion. It has considerable humor, mostly situation comedy such as is found in medieval *Schwänke* (amusing tales) and fabliaux. Repetition is more prominent than in *Ortnit;* it is found on all levels, from verse fillers to entire episodes. Among the examples of repeated but considerably varied action are two mass baptisms, two returns from the dead, two battles outside Constantinople, three struggles between a dragon and another beast, four conflicts in which a man and a beast are allies, and several recognition scenes. This structure suggests that the work may have grown by accretion and had a succession of authors.

Both *Ortnit* and *Wolfdietrich* are composed in four-line stanzas having six-stress verses with caesuras and couplet rhyme. The caesuras give the verses some resemblance to the Germanic long line and therefore produce an archaic tone in keeping with a setting in the remote past. Some presumably later versions have added rhyme at the caesuras, which produces trimeter lines that are not suitable for verse narratives.

If the two narratives are older than those of the Dietrich cycle, as they appear to be, they have provided the latter with considerable material. Other German verse novels that show their influence include Heinrich von dem Türlin's *Die Krone* (The Crown, circa 1230) and Ulrich von Etzenbach's *Alexandreis* (circa 1271–1287). The work that made the most use of material in *Ortnit* and *Wolfdietrich* is the Norse *Thidreks Saga* (circa 1250), but it is not clear whether the saga drew from them or shared a common source. Perhaps the greatest testaments to the popularity of the German stories are the two fourteenth-century murals at Runkelstein Castle in southern Tirol that portray Ortnit and a giantess from *Wolfdietrich*.

References:

Linde Baecker, "Die Sage von Wolfdietrich und das Gedicht *Wolfdietrich A,*" *Zeitschrift für deutsches Altertum und deutsche Literatur,* 92 (1963): 31–82;

Rolf Bräuer, *Literatursoziologie und epische Struktur der deutschen "Spielmanns-" und Heldendichtung* (Berlin: Akademie, 1970);

Wolfgang Dinkelacker, "Ortnit," in *Die deutsche Literatur des Mittelalters: Verfasserlexikon,* volume 7, edited by Kurt Ruh (Berlin & New York: De Gruyter, 1989), cols. 58–67;

Dinkelacker, *Ortnit-Studien* (Berlin: Schmidt, 1972);

Ruth Firestone, "A New Look at the Transmission of *Ortnit,*" *Amsterdamer Beiträge zur älteren Germanistik,* 18 (1982): 129–142;

Heino Gehrts, *Das Märchen und das Opfer: Untersuchungen zum europäischen Brüdermärchen* (Bonn: Bouvier, 1967);

Edward Haymes, *Mündliches Epos in mittelhochdeutscher Zeit* (Göppingen: Kümmerle, 1975);

Werner Hoffmann, *Mittelhochdeutsche Heldendichtung* (Berlin: Schmidt, 1974);

Bernd Kratz, "Gawein und Wolfdietrich: Zur Verwandtschaft der *Crone* mit der jüngeren Heldendichtung," *Euphorion,* 66, no. 4 (1972): 397–404;

Kratz, "Von Werwölfen, Glückshauben und Wolfdietrichs Taufhemd," *Archiv für das Studium der neueren Sprachen und Literaturen,* 211 (1974): 18–30;

Nils Lukman, "Der historische Wolfdietrich," *Classica et mediaevalia,* 4 (1941): 1–61;

Heinz Rupp, "Der *Ortnit:* Heldendichtung oder?," in *Deutsche Heldenepik in Tirol: König Laurin und Dietrich von Bern in der Dichtung des Mittelalters,* edited by Egon Kühebacher (Bozen: Athesia, 1979), pp. 231–252;

Dimitri Scheludko, "Versuch neuer Interpretation des Wolfdietrich-Stoffes," *Zeitschrift für deutsche Philologie,* 55 (1930): 1–49;

Christian Schmid-Cadalbert, *Der Ortnit AW als Brautwerbungsdichtung: Ein Beitrag zum Verständnis mittelhochdeutscher Schemaliteratur* (Bern: Francke, 1985);

Erich Seemann, "Wolfdietrichepos und Volksballade: Ein Beitrag zur Geschichte der mittelalterlichen Balladendichtung," *Archiv für Literatur und Volksdichtung,* 1 (1949): 119–176;

Jan de Vries, "Die Sage von Wolfdietrich," *Germanisch-Romanische Monatsschrift,* 39 (1958): 1–18.

Trierer Floyris
(circa 1170 – 1180)

Danielle Egan
University of Southern California

Manuscript: Fragments of 368 verses in rhyming couplets from the end of the narrative are in a manuscript in the Stadtbibliothek, Trier.

First publication: "*Floyris,*" edited by Elias von Steinmeyer and Max Roediger, *Zeitschrift für deutsches Altertum,* 21 (1877): 307–331.

Standard edition: "Die Trierer Floyris-Bruchstücke," edited by Gilbert de Smet and Maurits Gysseling, *Studia Germanica Gandensia,* 9 (1967): 157–169.

The *Trierer Floyris* is the earliest extant German rendering of the narrative of Flore and Blanscheflur; Konrad Fleck wrote another version around 1220. The popular tale first appeared in a song by the countess of Die in the 1150s. An Old French version, the "version aristocratique," dating from the 1160s, is now believed to be the source for the German poet. Scholars have considered another version, the "version populaire," as a possible source; but the "version aristocratique" and the "version populaire" differ widely, and it is today accepted that the "version aristocratique" is closest to the German fragment. Based on its syntactical structure and the dialect in which it is written, researchers believe that the poet lived in the Lower Rhine Valley and probably wrote the *Trierer Floyris* around 1170 to 1180.

The extant fragments narrate Floyris's travels to Babylon in search of his love, Blanscheflur. Floyris meets the helpful *Brückenpächter* (bridge leaseholder), who tells him how to win over the guardian of the tower in which Blanscheflur is being held prisoner by the amiral, the ruler of Babylon. The guardian is easily convinced to help Floyris, and the lovers are happily reunited. The amiral discovers them and wants to put them to death, but the pleas of his vassals persuade him to relent. The last fragment deals with Floyris's return to Spain. Contrary to Fleck's treatment of the love story, which borders on the sentimental, the poet of the *Trierer Floyris* feels no need to embellish the narrative. It is heavy on plot and leaves the protagonists without psychological depth.

References:

René Perennec, "Le Trierer Floyris: Adaption du Roman de Floire et Blanscheflur. A Propos d'une Etude de J. H. Winkelman," *Etudes Germaniques,* 35 (July–September 1977): 316–320;

Gilbert de Smet, "Der Trierer Floyris und seine französische Quelle," in *Festschrift für Ludwig Wolff,* edited by Werner Schroder (Neumünster: Wachholtz, 1962), pp. 203–216;

J. H. Winkelman, *Die Brückenpächter- und die Turmwächterepisode im Trierer Floyris und in der "Version Aristocratique" des altfranzösischen Florisromans: Eine vergleichende Untersuchung* (Amsterdam: Rodopi, 1977);

Winkelman, "Zum Trierer Floyris," *Neophilologus,* 66 (July 1982): 391–406.

Der Wartburgkrieg

(circa 1230 – circa 1280)

Alexander Mark Buckholtz
Yale University

Manuscripts: The strophes that make up *Der Wartburgkrieg* are transmitted in thirteen manuscripts and manuscript fragments, of which the most important are the Große Heidelberger Liederhandschrift (Heidelberg, Universitätsbibliothek; cpg. 848), including 91 strophes; the Jenaer Liederhandschrift (Jena, Universitätsbibliothek), including 119, of which 20 have been lost; and the Kolmarer Liederhandschrift (Munich, Bayerische Staatsbibliothek; cgm 4997), which, in addition to strophes included in the others, includes many later additions by the Meistersinger. Thirty-two strophes of the "Rätselspiel" are also transmitted in each of three manuscripts of the epic *Lohengrin* (circa 1280), where they serve as an introduction to the narrative material.

First publication: *Der Krieg auf der Wartburg, nach Geschichten und Gedichten des Mittelalters,* edited by August Zeune (Berlin: Blindenanstalt, 1818).

Standard editions: *Der Wartburgkrieg,* edited by Karl Simrock (Stuttgart & Augsburg: Cotta, 1858); *Der Wartburgkrieg,* edited by Tom Albert Rompelman (Amsterdam: Paris, 1939); "Meistergesänge astronomischen Inhalts," edited by Johannes Siebert, *Zeitschrift für deutsches Altertum und deutoche Literatur,* 83 (1951–1952): 181–235, 288–320; "Virgils Fahrt zum Agetstein," edited by Siebert, *Beiträge zur Geschichte der deutschen Sprache und Literatur,* 74, no. 1–2 (1952): 193–225; "Wolframs und Klingsors Stubenkrieg zu Eisenach," edited by Siebert, *Beiträge zur Geschichte der deutschen Sprache und Literatur,* 75, no. 3 (1953): 365–390.

For the literary historian the collection of song strophes known as *Der Wartburgkrieg* (The Contest at the Wartburg, circa 1230–circa 1280) remains of interest for the light it sheds on the growing self-consciousness of the professional *Spruchdichter* (poets of didactic and panegyrical lyrics). The strophes form an important link between the courtly lyric of the High Middle Ages and the *Meistersang* (lyric poetry written by Meistersinger, members of craft guilds organized into singing "schools") of the fifteenth and sixteenth centuries. For the general public *Der Wartburgkrieg* is best remembered for the role it played in nineteenth-century German culture, especially as the ultimate, albeit indirect, source of Richard Wagner's music drama *Tannhäuser und der Sängerkrieg auf Wartburg* (1845; translated as *Tannhäuser and the Tournament of Song on the Wartburg,* 1875). Rather than constituting a unified work of art, *Der Wartburgkrieg* is a heterogeneous complex of strophes composed in two distinct *Töne* (melodies). Although the major sections of the complex were composed over the course of some fifty years in the middle of the thirteenth century, additional strophes were added by later generations, including strophes composed by Meistersinger. Such a complicated and often confusing textual history is chiefly responsible for the lack of a satisfactory critical edition of the entire complex.

Standard histories of German literature rightly include *Der Wartburgkrieg* in their discussions of *Spruchdichtung* (didactic poetry), a genre that includes a great variety of poetic subjects and forms. Indeed, the term is used to cover all lyric poetry except *Minnesang* (courtly love lyrics). *Der Wartburgkrieg* reflects this diversity, including as it does examples of panegyric, riddles, laments for the dead, moral and religious allegory, social criticism, and literary debate.

Der Wartburgkrieg begins with the "Fürstenlob" (Praise of Princes), which depicts a contest of singers at the court of Landgrave Hermann I of Thuringia, who died in 1217. The fictitious nature of this contest is today generally recognized; the Wartburg castle only became the landgraves' regular residence during the reign of

Hermann's successor, Ludwig IV. Indeed, the "Fürstenlob" never mentions the Wartburg as the site of the event.

The terminus a quo for the "Fürstenlob" has been set at 1248 and the terminus ad quem at 1289. The strophes were most likely composed, however, between 1260 and 1280. The opening lines describe the singers' contest in terms appropriate to a trial by combat: the singers challenge each other while standing in a circle, and the loser must forfeit his life. Heinrich von Ofterdingen, probably a fictitious character, begins by praising his prince, the duke of Austria. Not to be outdone, Walther von der Vogelweide, Wolfram von Eschenbach, Reinmar von Zweter (included anachronistically, since he was of a later generation than Walther and Wolfram), der tugendhafte Schreiber (The Virtuous Scribe, who probably existed but whose identity is unknown), and Biterolf (probably fictitious) praise the virtues of Landgrave Hermann, before whom the action takes place. In the course of the contest Walther also praises the king of France and Biterolf praises the count of Henneberg. *Milte* (generosity) is the chief virtue for which the princes are praised – which is hardly surprising, since it is the one on which the life of a professional *Spruchdichter* (composer of didactic poetry) most depended. Other virtues, however, including fame, bravery, political influence, and piety, are not omitted. The princes are compared to noble beasts such as the lion, eagle, or falcon or historical figures such as Alexander the Great and are frequently praised using metaphors of light (for example, stars, sun, day). It is by means of the latter that Heinrich is tricked and defeated: Walther asks him, "Heinrîch von Ofterdingen, sage, wer mac der edele sîn, / des tugent vor allen vürsten kan der sunnen gelîche wesen?" (Heinrich von Ofterdingen, say, who can this nobleman be, who, because of his virtue, can be like the sun before all princes?). Ofterdingen naturally answers with the name of his prince, the duke of Austria. Walther then declares that the day itself is more praiseworthy than the sun, and that Landgrave Hermann alone is comparable to it: "der Düringe herre kan uns tagen" (the lord of Thuringia can dawn for us). The executioner, Stempfel of Eisenach, is sent for, but Heinrich feels that he has been cheated and asks that Klingsor, who excels in the art of the *Spruchdichter,* be brought from Hungary to be judge in the matter. The landgrave's wife intercedes for him, his request is granted, and his execution is postponed. The last two strophes of the "Fürstenlob" were apparently interpolated at a later date in

Miniatures illustrating Der Wartburgkrieg in the Große Heidelberger Liederhandschrift: (top) Landgrave Hermann of Thuringia and his wife on their thrones; (bottom) Walther von der Vogelweide, Wolfram von Eschenbach, Reinmar von Zweter (misidentified in the inscription as Reinmar der Alte), der tugendhafte Schreiber, Heinrich von Ofterdingen, Klingsor the magician, and (unnamed in the inscription) Biterolf (Heidelberg, Universitätsbibliothek, cpg. 848, f.219b)

order to form a connecting link with the so-called "Rätselspiel" and its character called Klingsor.

The "Fürstenlob" was probably written for the Thuringian court by a *Spruchdichter* who was familiar with the "Rätselspiel," the oldest portion of the *Wartburgkrieg* complex, and who counted himself among the class of itinerant singers whose stock-in-trade was the composition and performance of *Spruchdichtung* at such courts. He proclaims at the beginning that the strophes will be sung in "des edeln vürsten dôn" (the noble prince's melody), also known as the "thüringer-Fürsten-Ton" (Thüringian prince's melody), thus distinguishing his composition from the "Rätselspiel," which is composed in the "Schwarzer Ton" (black melody). This naming of a new *Ton* reflects the self-consciousness of a *meister* (a *Spruchdichter* who is distinguished both for his learning and for his skill in versification) who was required to invent a new *Ton* to prove his mastery of the *meisterkunst* (art of writing *Spruchdichtung* on learned topics). Indeed, it is clear that here one is dealing with *meisterkunst,* no longer with the courtly lyric of the High Middle Ages, since even the great figures of the *Blütezeit* (period of efflorescence) – Walther and Wolfram – are depicted as *meister.* Walther, in defeating Heinrich, relies on the authority of "wîse meister ... / ... die die biblien hânt gelesen" (wise masters ... / ... who have read the books) and thereby proves himself the wisest of *meister.* This outcome is fitting, since Walther was the first to unite *Minnesang* and *Spruchdichtung* in his repertoire. He was also considered the greatest exponent of each of these genres in the *Blütezeit.*

The "Fürstenlob" reflects the poet's consciousness not only of his art but of his social station as well. The itinerant *Spruchdichter* was dependent on a generous patron, and the choice of the right patron was, therefore, a serious matter. Yet the relationship was a symbiotic one: the best poet was he who best praised his patron, while the best patron was he who was best praised by the poets. In the "Fürstenlob" Hermann of Thuringia is praised as a patron of literature; *Der Wartburgkrieg* was intended, at least in part, to glorify his reign, thereby dignifying both his descendants and the *meister* at their courts.

The oldest section of *Der Wartburgkrieg,* the "Rätselspiel," follows the "Fürstenlob" in the manuscripts. The oldest strophes were probably composed between 1230 and 1239, but many strophes were added over a great period of time. It is even less unified structurally than the "Fürstenlob" and was originally independent of the latter. The two are related only through the figures of Wolfram and Klingsor, who appear or are mentioned in both. The "Rätselspiel" presents a contest between the two over the question of *meisterschaft* (mastery of the art of the *meister*). Klingsor appears in the role of a peddler who offers his "wares" (that is, his riddles) for sale. He poses a series of riddles, which Wolfram answers in turn. The riddles are mostly of a theological nature, presenting articles of Christian faith in an allegorical form: for example, sinful humanity is presented as a child asleep on a dam, unaware of the danger surrounding him and only awakened by his father's blows. Wolfram answers the questions correctly, proving himself as knowledgeable as Klingsor. Klingsor then sends a devil, Nasion, to pose astronomical questions that Wolfram is unable to answer: "vür wâr, ich weiz niht, waz dîn vrâge meinet" (in truth, I do not know what your question means), he says. The "Rätselspiel" ends with Wolfram calling on God and the Virgin Mary to help him and banishing Nasion by making the sign of the cross.

Due to the complexity of its textual history the "Rätselspiel," perhaps more than any other part of *Der Wartburgkrieg,* calls into question the concept of the autonomous literary "work." All attempts at reconstructing its original form have proved futile, and such a task now appears to exceed the possibilities of a historically grounded textual criticism. Rather than trying to reconstruct the "archetype" of the "Rätselspiel," scholars today stress the flexibility of its form and its ability to accept new riddles into its structure. The emphasis has shifted from a concern with the original order and number of the strophes to a concern with their original purpose. It seems clear that the origins of the "Rätselspiel" are closely bound up with the reception of Wolfram's works by his literary progeny. The central idea of the "Rätselspiel" appears to be the contrast between the pious *leie* (layman) Wolfram and the *meisterpfaffe* (one possessing a high degree of formal theological training) Klingsor. The figure of Klingsor is based on the magician Clinschor in Wolfram's own courtly epic *Parzival* (circa 1200–1210); at one point in that work Clinschor is referred to as a *pfaffe* (cleric). In the "Rätselspiel" Klingsor refers to himself as a *meisterpfaffe,* which in the literature of the thirteenth century carried a certain polemical weight: the term was used both to stress the inadequacy of a purely theoretical approach to religion and to hint at unchaste behavior among the clergy. The poet of the "Rätselspiel" radicalizes this concept by portraying Klingsor as an adept in the heathen sciences.

In contrast to the *meisterpfaffe,* the *leie* had the advantage of a practical, if simple, faith. Wolfram thus represents the ideal type of the pious layman. He can compete favorably with the *meisterpfaffe* in contests of Christian knowledge, but he remains undefiled by non-Christian learning. Klingsor himself expresses the opinion of Wolfram's followers when he paraphrases the epic poet Wirnt von Grafenberg: "man sagt von dem von Eschenbach / und gibt im prîs, daz leien munt nie baz gesprach: / her Wolferam, der tihtet guote maere" (one speaks of the man from Eschenbach / and gives him praise, for the mouth of a layman never spoke better: / Sir Wolfram, who writes good stories). The opposition between Wolfram and Klingsor appears to have been intended to strengthen the position of the lay *meister* as transmitter of religious truth. If his prototype, Wolfram, could solve riddles as an *illiteratus* (one who cannot read Latin), then the *Spruchdichter* could feel justified in spreading religious teachings by means of his vernacular songs and without the aid of a clerical education. It was this aspect of the work, combined with its flexible, open-ended form, that ensured its popularity for generations; it provided a model for the Meistersinger centuries later.

Der Wartburgkrieg contains other sections, of various ages and, for modern readers, of various degrees of interest. Their subject matter also varies greatly. "Aurons Pfennig" (Auron's Penny) was written in the "Schwarzer Ton" shortly after 1239. Auron is a fallen angel whose penny symbolizes the profit gained from selling the church's means of salvation. The strophes warn the layman of the dangers posed by such "pfaffen girikeit" (greed of the secular clergy). Many scholars believe that a dispute between the secular clergy and the newly formed mendicant orders over such practices forms the historical background of the strophes, and that they may have originated in Dominican circles.

The "Totenfeier" (Funeral Rite) was written between 1260 and 1280, also in the "Schwarzer Ton." It is thematically related to the "Fürstenlob" in that it eulogizes two dead princes, the landgrave of Thuringia and the count of Henneberg. The many attempts to identify the two princes and thereby date the poem have been unconvincing. The strophes also provide an account of the origin of the Grail stone featured in Wolfram's *Parzival*.

"Zabulons Buch" (Zabulon's Book) is of interest primarily because of the different image of Wolfram it presents from that of the "Rätselspiel." Composed in the "Thüringer-Fürsten-Ton," as is the "Fürstenlob," it describes a further contest between Wolfram and Klingsor in which Wolfram, too, displays the esoteric knowledge of a *meisterpfaffe;* it may reflect the changing self-image of the *meister* and their pride in their own erudition. Also in the "Thüringer-Fürsten-Ton" are two strophes directed against priests that are known as "Sprechen ohne Meinen" (Saying Something without Meaning It). In the "Schwarzer Ton" are two strophes in praise of the bishop of Cologne and a certain Johann von Zernin as well as additional riddles and strophes on astronomical topics by Meistersinger.

Despite its dubious value as a historical document, *Der Wartburgkrieg* served as the source for many chronicles and hagiographic writings in the later Middle Ages, beginning with the Latin *vita* of Saint Elizabeth by the Dominican Dietrich of Apolda in 1289. This work was soon translated into German prose and also served as the basis of a German poem in rhymed couplets written shortly after 1300 in which the singers' contest is brought into connection with Elizabeth by having Klingsor foretell her birth from the stars. The Wartburg is first mentioned as the scene of a singers' contest by Friedrich Ködiz in his life of Landgrave Ludwig (1314–1323), but there it is explicitly designated only as the meeting place of Wolfram and Klingsor; Heinrich and the rest of the cast of the "Fürstenlob" are reported to have met at Hermann's palace, which is not named. The use of the term *Wartburgkrieg* goes back only to the early fifteenth century, when the Eisenach town clerk, Johannes Rothe, wrote of "der krigk von wartberg" (the contest of the Wartburg) in his chronicles.

The nineteenth century brought a renewed interest in *Der Wartburgkrieg* and the theme of the singers' contest, as is attested to by the appearance of Novalis's novel *Heinrich von Ofterdingen* (1802; translated as *Henry of Ofterdingen*, 1964), E. T. A. Hoffmann's tale "Der Kampf der Sänger" (The Contest of the Singers, 1819), Friedrich de la Motte Fouqué's drama *Der Sängerkrieg auf der Wartburg* (1828), and, above all, by Wagner's *Tannhäuser und der Sängerkrieg auf Wartburg*. This interest is attributable both to the "rediscovery" of the Middle Ages by the Romantic generation and to the rise of German nationalism, for whose adherents the Wartburg came to symbolize all that was best in the German past.

References:

Hans Bayer, "Meister Klingsor und Heinrich von Ofterdingen: Die Zeitkritik der Wartburgkrieg-Dichtung und ihre literarischen bzw. geistesgeschichtlichen Quellen," *Mittellateinisches Jahrbuch*, 17 (1982): 157–192;

Helmut de Boor, *Das späte Mittelalter: Zerfall und Neubeginn, Erster Teil 1250–1350*, volume 3, part 1 of *Geschichte der deutschen Literatur*, fourth edition, edited by de Boor and Richard Newald (Munich: Beck, 1973);

Horst Brunner, *Die alten Meister: Studien zu Überlieferung und Rezeption der mittelhochdeutschen Sangspruchdichter im Spätmittelalter und in der frühen Neuzeit*, Münchener Texte und Untersuchungen zur deutschen Literatur des Mittelalters, no. 54 (Munich: Beck, 1975);

Joachim Bumke, *Geschichte der deutschen Literatur im hohen Mittelalter,* volume 2 of *Geschichte der deutschen Literatur im Mittelalter,* edited by Bumke, Thomas Cramer, and Dieter Kartschoke (Munich: Deutscher Taschenbuch Verlag, 1990);

Mary A. Cicora, "Aesthetics and Politics at the Song Contest in Wagner's Tannhäuser," *Germanic Review,* 67 (Spring 1992): 50–58;

Cicora, *From History to Myth: Wagner's* Tannhäuser *and Its Literary Sources* (Bern: Lang, 1992);

Thomas Cramer, ed., *Lohengrin: Edition und Untersuchungen* (Munich: Fink, 1971);

Gustav Ehrismann, *Geschichte der deutschen Literatur bis zum Ausgang des Mittelalters, Schlußband* (Munich: Beck, 1973);

Hubert Heinen, "Wartburgkrieg," in *Dictionary of the Middle Ages,* volume 12, edited by Joseph S. Strayer (New York: Scribners, 1989), pp. 573–574;

Joachim Heinzle, *Vom hohen zum späten Mittelalter: Wandlungen und Neuansätze im 13. Jahrhundert (1220/30–1280/90),* volume 2, part 2 of *Geschichte der deutschen Literatur von den Anfängen bis zum Beginn der Neuzeit,* edited by Heinzle (Königstein: Athenäum, 1984);

Willy Krogmann, "Heinrich von Ofterdingen," *Germanisch-Romanische Monatsschrift,* new series 15 (October 1965): 341–354;

Krogmann, "Studien zum Wartburgkrieg," *Zeitschrift für deutsche Philologie,* 80, no. 1 (1961): 62–83;

Krogmann, "Der Wartburgkrieg," in *Die deutsche Literatur des Mittelalters: Verfasserlexikon,* volume 4, edited by Karl Langosch (Berlin: De Gruyter, 1953), cols. 843–864;

Timothy McFarland, "Wagner's Most Medieval Opera," in *Richard Wagner's Tannhäuser,* Opera Guide Series, no. 39, edited by Nicholas John (London: Calder, 1988; New York: Riverrun, 1988), pp. 25–32;

Friedrich Mess, *Heinrich von Ofterdingen: Wartburgkrieg und verwandte Dichtungen* (Weimar: Böhlau, 1963);

Hedda Ragotzky, *Studien zur Wolfram-Rezeption: Die Entstehung und Verwandlung der Wolfram-Rolle in der deutschen Literatur des 13. Jahrhunderts,* Studien zur Poetik und Geschichte der Literatur, no. 20 (Stuttgart: Kohlhammer, 1971);

Paul Riesenfeld, *Heinrich von Ofterdingen in der deutschen Literatur* (Berlin: Mayer & Müller, 1912);

Stewart Spencer, "Tanhusære, Danheüser and Tannhäuser," in *Tannhäuser,* pp. 17–24;

Archer Taylor, *The Literary History of Meistergesang* (New York: Modern Language Association of America, 1937; London: Oxford University Press, 1937);

John Vincent Tillman, *An Edition of the Hort von der Astronomy from the Colmar MS (CGM 4997); With an Introduction on the History of the MHG Wartburgkrieg* (Chicago: Privately printed, 1941);

Burghart Wachinger, *Sängerkrieg: Untersuchungen zur Spruchdichtung des 13. Jahrhunderts,* Münchener Texte und Untersuchungen zur deutschen Literatur des Mittelalters, no. 42 (Munich: Beck, 1973);

Max Wehrli, *Geschichte der deutschen Literatur vom frühen Mittelalter bis zum Ende des 16. Jahrhunderts* (Stuttgart: Reclam, 1980);

Roswitha Wisniewski, "Wolframs Gralstein und eine Legende von Lucifer und den Edelsteinen," *Beiträge zur Geschichte der deutschen Sprache und Literatur,* 79 (1957): 43–66;

Herbert Wolf, "Zum Wartburgkrieg: Überlieferungsverhältnisse, Inhalts- und Gestaltungswandel der Dichtersage," in *Festschrift für Walter Schlesinger,* volume 1, edited by Helmut Beumann, Mitteldeutsche Forschungen, no. 74/1 (Cologne & Vienna: Böhlau, 1973), pp. 513–530;

Norbert Richard Wolf, "Die Gestalt Klingsors in der deutschen Literatur des Mittelalters," *Südostdeutsche Semesterblätter,* 19 (1967): 1–19.

German Drama 800–1280

Ralph J. Blasting
Towson State University

The story of theater in medieval Europe is the story of how religious drama became a defining element of the emerging urban culture from the tenth to the sixteenth centuries. The theater of the Middle Ages represents more than six hundred years of performance traditions that came to involve virtually every element of society. While particular theatrical traditions and styles varied among cities, dramatic genres and subjects achieved a commonality rooted in the Christian faith. Even when plays in the vernacular became prominent in the late thirteenth century, medieval drama remained reflective of a pan-European Roman Catholic culture. The disintegration of that culture in the sixteenth century, through the intellectual and political turbulence of the northern Renaissance and Reformation, led to the fragmentation of the medieval dramatic traditions. The German-speaking areas of Europe played a central role in the history of medieval drama, from the development of the tenth-century liturgical tropes at the monastery of Saint Gall to the last recorded performance of the great Passion Play of Lucerne in 1616. The influence of medieval performance traditions can be seen even today, perhaps the most familiar example being the Passion Play of Oberammergau.

The theater of a culture is its attempt to objectify – and thereby understand and control – its world. Performance implicitly reveals the worldview of a culture as the conflicts, struggles, fears, and expectations of a society are played out by and for its own members. This description is especially true of the theater of the Middle Ages. Medieval plays were sponsored, written, performed, and observed by the clergy, nobility, and citizenry of virtually every area of Europe. Archival research in Germany by Bernd Neumann has revealed rich traditions of performance even where no play texts have been preserved. But while religious drama achieved the central position in the theater of the Middle Ages, it was by no means the only type of performance undertaken. Germany provides the earliest literary evidence of classical influence on medieval drama in the plays of Hrotsvit of Gandersheim

(circa 930–980), a canoness in the Imperial Abbey of Gandersheim in Saxony. Itinerant professional entertainers, variously called mimes, minstrels, *histriones, joculatores,* or *Spielmänner,* performed before nobility, the clergy, and presumably the general public. Although they are said to have preserved Roman theatrical traditions, evidence regarding the nature of their performances is sparse. Folk traditions in the form of seasonal festivals and celebrations also contributed to the theater of the age. The relative importance of pre-Christian versus liturgical influences on the development of medieval drama has been debated at length, as discussed in Sandro Sticca's *The Latin Passion Play: Its Origins and Development* (1970), but it cannot be denied that the folk customs of procession, masking, and dancing have parallels in the religious drama. Courtly entertainments and spectacles, such as triumphal processions, royal entries, and jousts, also legitimately belong to the theatrical traditions of the age, since they were often carefully structured events in which mimetic performance – albeit allegorical – was central.

Theater from 800 to 1280 represents a confluence of classical, liturgical, secular, and civic modes of expression, but the predominant type of performance was religious drama. Perhaps the defining characteristic of the drama of the age is the predominant use of Latin as the language of performance until the mid thirteenth century. The growing popularity of the vernacular near the end of this period marked the transition to the great age of civic and religious drama which flourished from the mid fourteenth through the sixteenth centuries.

Little is known about theatrical performance in Europe after the fall of the Roman Empire. Although there are sporadic references to performers, and while it is fairly certain that they were welcome at noble courts (including that of Charlemagne), the records do not distinguish among actors, singers, reciters, acrobats, and other types of entertainers. It appears that performers were often welcomed into monastic houses and paradoxically used their observations there to satirize the clergy in their public performances, but beyond these glimpses almost nothing is known about the material they presented. It is a reasonable assumption that whatever professional theater existed was largely nonscripted.

While there has been extensive discussion of the degree to which Roman drama and theater practices survived or were known after the Fall of Rome, only one body of literature reveals a direct use of Roman models. Hrotsvit wrote six Latin plays in the style of Terence, "quo eodem dictationis genere, quo turpia lascivarum incesta feminarum recitabantur, / laudabilis sacrarum castimonia virginum" (so that in that selfsame form of composition in which the shameless acts of lascivious women were phrased / the laudable chastity of sacred virgins be praised). In her introduction to the most reliable English translation of the plays (1989), Katharina M. Wilson identifies Hrotsvit as "the first poet of Saxony, the first female German poet, the first dramatist of Germany, the first female German historian, and the first person in Germany to employ the Faust theme." Indeed, Hrotsvit is the first known female playwright in the Western tradition. Although she enjoyed an enthusiastic reception among German humanists after Conrad Celtis discovered the manuscript of her works in the Benedictine monastery of Saint Emmeram in 1494, her place in literary history later became somewhat ambiguous. In the latter half of the twentieth century revisionist influences, among them feminist criticism, have led to the beginning of a restoration of Hrotsvit's reputation not only as an important writer of the tenth-century Ottonian Renaissance (a term used to describe the flowering of the arts under the Saxon rulers Heinrich I, Otto I, Otto II, Otto III, and Heinrich II) but also, as Sue-Ellen Case argues, as an early medieval playwright who adapted Terentian drama to her own artistic purposes.

The plays comprise the second of the three books into which Hrotsvit organized her poetic works. In her prologue to the dramas the author confirms that the plays of Terence were read during the tenth century as models of Latin style and that she has imitated him, but nothing else is certain about the connections of Hrotsvit's plays to Roman theatrical traditions. While Richard Axton argues convincingly that Hrotsvit may have written her plays with the performances of professional itinerant mimes in mind, there is no scholarly consensus about how or even whether the plays were acted. Most commentators agree, however, that they are performable, and they have had occasional productions at least since the late nineteenth century.

Their strength lies in Hrotsvit's sophisticated literary sense and her expert use of a variety of dramatic techniques from tragicomedy to farce.

The six plays are clearly intended as a literary cycle. Correspondences of theme, action, and dramatic structure from one play to the next create a sense of interconnectedness and unity when the plays are read as a group. Although the question of their performance remains open, it is possible that if they were performed, the cycle may have been presented in its entirety. Each text could easily be performed in less than an hour, and in later medieval theatrical practice performances of several hours' duration became common. At the same time, the plays possess individual integrity and include an impressive variety of dramatic techniques.

The six plays, in their order in the manuscript, are *Gallicanus*, *Dulcitius*, *Calimachus*, *Abraham*, *Pafnutius*, and *Sapientia*. All deal with challenges to Christian virtue: two concern the martyrdom of Christian virgins; two depict the conversion of pagan men through the actions of Christian virgins; and two plays treat the redemption and conversion of prostitutes when they take the vow of chastity. Given the thematic restrictions, the plays reveal a fascinating versatility in treatment and dramaturgy.

Gallicanus is a militaristic history play of epic scope. When General Gallicanus experiences a battlefield conversion to Christianity, he renounces his claim on the emperor Constantine's daughter and vows to lead a life of chastity. The play moves forward to the time of Emperor Julianus, who forces Gallicanus into exile. John and Paul, the spiritual guides who effected his conversion, are killed by Roman soldiers under the direction of Terentius. When his son goes mad at the tombs of the martyrs Terentius converts, and the son is healed.

The title character of *Dulcitius*, a Roman governor under the emperor Diocletian, farcically becomes lost and confused as he attempts to make his way through a dark kitchen en route to seducing three imprisoned virgins. They watch through a crack in the wall as their captor makes love to the pots and pans, and when he emerges he is so sooty that the palace guards beat him, his own servants desert him, and he is a laughingstock. The virgins are martyred at the end of the play; but their souls triumph unharmed, reinforcing the futility of their oppressors' attempts to destroy them.

The action of *Calimachus* is melodramatic in the extremity of its dark images. To avoid seduction, Drusiana prays for death and is granted her wish. But Calimachus, obsessed, bribes the guard at her tomb to let him in to defile her body. As the guard leans over the corpse he is mortally stung by a serpent, and Calimachus dies of fright. Drusiana is resurrected, and she resurrects Calimachus, who converts to Christianity.

By contrast, *Abraham* is full of the poignant emotions of reunion, repentance, and salvation. Abraham, a religious hermit, ventures into the city to recover his young ward, Mary, from a house of prostitution. Posing as a potential client, he gains admission to the brothel, and Hrotsvit creates a memorable recognition scene as he rescues Mary from her sinful life (although modern audiences may wonder whether her penance – three years of solitary confinement – constitutes much of a rescue).

The final play of the cycle reaches heights of heroic passion and spectacle as Sapientia (wisdom) witnesses the cruel martyrdom of her three daughters, Fides (faith), Spes (hope), and Caritas (charity). A tragicomic mix of violence and miraculous preservation, the play presents scenes such as Fides frolicking in a vat of boiling pitch, to the frustration of her tormentors.

While Hrotsvit's classical learning is evident in the plays, they also possess a dramaturgical freedom that would not be seen for another two hundred years in medieval theater. Her language is spirited and sophisticated in the best tradition of Terence. There is a strong emphasis on science, mathematics, and rhetoric, as in the lesson on harmonics given by Pafnutius (in the play of the same name) before he sets out to convert the infamous harlot Thais. In *Sapientia* similar mathematical arguments are used by the title character in a bitter exchange with her captor, the emperor Hadrian. *Calimachus* strictly observes the unities of time, place, and action, but *Abraham* and *Gallicanus* use epic structures that span several years. Miraculous and spectacular events such as those in *Sapientia* would become commonplace in the drama of the fifteenth and sixteenth centuries. Although the plays are ideologically religious in their emphasis on the preservation of Christian virginity, they remain distinct from the liturgical and biblical drama that followed them and on which they apparently had no influence. Hrotsvit of Gandersheim remains singular among medieval authors. Her plays are the most sophisticated body of dramatic literature of the early Middle Ages, and they remained unequaled in Germany until the *Ludus de Antichristo* (Play of the Antichrist, circa 1160–1190) and Hildegard von Bingen's *Ordo Virtutum* (Service of the Virtues, circa 1136–1179).

By far the predominant form of drama in the period from 800 to 1280 was the religious drama, which had its beginnings in the liturgy of the Roman Catholic church. The vast majority of the surviving texts from this period revolve around the central events of Christian history – the birth, death, and Resurrection of Christ – and are consequently categorized as Christmas, Easter, and Passion plays. Most of the texts through the thirteenth century are written exclusively or primarily in Latin, although many exhibit a sophisticated mixture of Latin and German. The plays that were performed as a part of specific religious ceremonies are called liturgical dramas, and most works before the twelfth century seem to fall into this category. In the twelfth and thirteenth centuries longer and more complex works such as the *Benediktbeurer Passionsspiel* (Benediktbeuern Passion Play, circa 1200–1250) were performed independently of the liturgy, although their subjects were still religious. The development of drama should not, however, be viewed merely as an evolutionary process. While succeeding centuries brought more complex forms of Latin drama, the simpler versions are not always the earlier ones, and they were not superseded by the longer versions. In the same way, the later vernacular drama did not replace the Latin plays; a variety of forms – Latin and vernacular, liturgical, religious, and secular – coexisted into the seventeenth century.

The drama of the Middle Ages is unique in the history of Western theater in its form, function, and dramaturgy. It is the most closely connected with religious ritual of any surviving Western drama. Intimately related to the mysteries of the Catholic faith and initially performed in Latin by members of the clergy, the plays did not rely on classical ideas of dramatic form or technique; rather, they were perfectly suited to the purposes of medieval society. They tended to be epic in structure, freely traversing time and space as they presented the essential moments of sacred history, thereby reflecting the universal and timeless relevance of their action.

This new form of drama was grounded in the complex literary tradition of the Catholic liturgy. The liturgy includes two basic divisions: the Mass, which was performed at least once daily; and the Canonical Office, which included the eight daily devotional services (hours) of matins, lauds, prime, terce, sext, none, vespers, and compline. The Mass consists of texts that do not change (the Ordinary) and those that may vary with the days and seasons of the year (the Proper). Musical and textual elaborations to the liturgy – especially to the services for Easter – gave rise to the earliest religious drama. But there the specificity ends. While it is generally agreed that liturgical drama appeared sometime be-

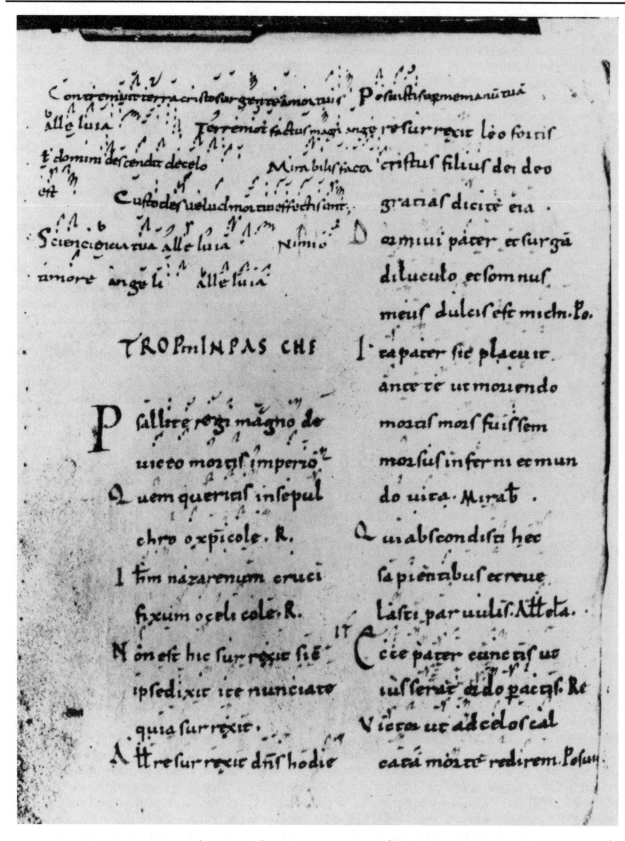

Page from the oldest surviving manuscript (circa 933–936) of a Quem quaeritis *trope (Paris, Bibliothèque Nationale, MS lat. 1240, f.30v)*

tween 800 and 1000, it remains difficult to identify a precise moment or method of origin. Questions of the definition of drama as opposed to ritual immediately present themselves. Most definitions of drama require that it include action and imitation, but these terms are not especially helpful. O. B. Hardison, for example, argues that the Mass itself was the drama of the Middle Ages and that attempts to distinguish it from later elaborations of the liturgy are pointless. His argument is in keeping with a view promulgated in the early ninth century by Amalarius, bishop of Metz, in his *Liber Officialis*. In "The Liturgical Context of the *Quem Quaeritis* Trope" (1974) and "The Roman Rite and the Origins of Liturgical Drama" (1974), C. Clifford Flanigan notes that the liturgical music-texts that were the foundations of the Christmas, Easter, and Passion plays were intentional additions to the official Mass or Office that served to strengthen the cultic experience of the ritual.

There is little agreement among English-speaking scholars about the precise distinction between liturgical drama and religious drama in Latin. The difficulty is also evident in the inconsistent understanding among German scholars of the terms *Osterfeier* (Easter office) and *Osterspiel* (Easter play). Hansjürgen Linke and Ulrich Mehler have attempted to establish definitive criteria in their discussion of *Osterfeiern* in the *Verfasserlexikon* (1989). *Osterfeiern,* they say, are dramatic texts that are sung in Latin and bound to the liturgy. When the priest who is conducting the liturgy relinquishes that function and plays the role of the resurrected Christ, the presentation has crossed over into true drama, the *Osterspiel*. While sophisticated in conception, this definition reveals the subtleties involved in distinguishing ritual from drama and the difficulties inherent in classifying the texts. David Bevington summarizes the difficulty when he says that "we are faced with a paradoxical distinction like that separating day from night: although ritual and drama differ profoundly from one another, the precise point of demarcation between the two is inherently obscure." Wherever the distinction lies, the German-speaking areas contributed significantly to the dramatic literature and activity that characterize the period. For example, of the nearly seven hundred extant texts of *Osterfeiern,* nearly three-quarters come from the German-speaking areas. Within these liturgical Easter ceremonies, the possible origins of the religious drama are to be found in the tropes.

Tropes are musical elaborations on standard parts of the liturgy, and they became especially numerous during the tenth century. They are not, in themselves, drama. One of the most popular was the *Quem quaeritis* (Whom do you seek?) trope of the Easter service. The two most important producers of texts were the Benedictine monasteries of Saint Martial in Limoges and Saint Gall in Switzerland. In its simplest form, the trope reads:

> Quem quaeritis in sepulchro, Christicolae?
> Jesum Nazarenum crucifixum, o caelicolae.
> Non est hic, surrexit sicut praedixerat; ite, nuntiate quia surrexit de sepulchro.

> (Whom do you seek in the sepulchre, O followers of Christ?
> Jesus of Nazareth who was crucified, O heaven-dwellers.
> He is not here, he has risen as he has foretold; go announce that he has risen from the sepulchre).
>   – translation by Bevington

The inherent drama of the trope lies in the described action of seeking and in an inferred reaction of joy by the seekers at the news of the Resurrection. The drama is actualized, according to William Smolden, when the parts are assigned to and acted out by individual singers, as described in the bishop of Winchester's *Regularis Concordia* (circa 965–975). This point is generally considered to be the beginning of medieval drama, when the *Quem quaeritis* trope became the liturgical drama called the *Visitatio Sepulchri* (Visit to the Sepulchre).

The earliest versions of this work in Germany can be dated to the late tenth or early eleventh century and remained fairly constant in form until the twelfth. The *Visitatio Sepulchri,* in which the three Marys visit the tomb, is classified as a Type 1 *Osterfeier*. In Germany, especially, it became common to portray the race between the apostles John and Paul to reach the tomb; these texts are designated Type 2. When the risen Christ appears to Mary Magdalene as a gardener (the *Hortulanusszene*), the text is classified as Type 3. All three types survive in texts from the thirteenth to the fifteenth centuries. Despite their classification, there is no distinguishable pattern of a chronological or evolutionary development from Type 1 to Type 3.

Other liturgical dramas were developed around the events of Christmas, with plays about the journey of the Magi and the slaughter of the innocents becoming popular in Germany. The texts which were apparently not bound to a liturgy are considered independent plays (*Spiele*) and are grouped according to their subject matter. Plays of the Easter season are either *Osterspiele* or *Passionsspiele* (Passion plays). Easter plays deal with events after the death of Christ, while the Passion plays

Relief, dating from circa 1130, depicting clerics performing the Visitatio Sepulchri, *in the church at Gustorf*

usually begin with scenes of Christ's ministry and end with his removal from the cross. *Weihnachtsspiele* (Christmas plays) can include a variety of seasonal stories concerning the shepherds, the Magi, and the slaughter of the innocents.

One of the most impressive single collections of such Latin play texts is the *Carmina Burana* manuscript (circa 1230), a collection of songs, lyrics, and plays from the Bavarian monastery of Benediktbeuern. The plays represent the greatest achievement of thirteenth-century medieval drama in Germany. In addition to a brief Easter play and a Passion play, the collection includes a Christmas play (*Benediktbeurer Weihnachtsspiel*) and a second Passion play (*Benediktbeurer Passionsspiel*) of considerable length and complexity. Unlike the liturgical drama, these plays were clearly considered independent artistic creations, as is reflected in the use of the word *ludus* (play) in their manuscript titles (*Ludus de Nativitate, Ludus de Passione*). Both plays rely extensively on music and were almost certainly performed in church by clergymen trained in singing and recitation. While they include many of the same episodes as the liturgical plays, they combine and adapt the material to the extent that they must be considered original works of drama.

The *Benediktbeurer Weihnachtsspiel* begins with the appearance of a series of Old Testament prophets who ensure that the birth of Christ is the fulfillment of their prophecies. This Procession of Prophets (*Ordo Prophetarum*) occurs also in the liturgical drama of the Christmas season. The play moves to an extensive debate between Saint Augustine and Archisynagogus, who represents the Jews. The debate is not only strong rhetorically but also sets up motifs that will recur later in the play. The "error" of the Jews is that they will not accept the possibility of events that defy natural law, such as the Virgin Birth. This disbelief will be contrasted with the Magi's faith in the star of the nativity, even though it defies their knowledge of astronomy. The Jews, as occurs often in medieval drama, are portrayed as the agents of evil; they will later be seen as advisers to Herod, who orders the slaying of the innocents at the end of the play.

The play continues with scenes of the Annunciation, the visit to Elizabeth and the Magnificat, the Nativity, the journey of the Magi, and a shepherds' scene. Shepherd and Magi plays were common liturgical topics, but here the Magi discuss the appearance of the star as a supernatural occurrence, and in the shepherds' scene a devil contradicts the heavenly proclamations of the angels, reminiscent of the earlier debate with Saint Augustine. There is a highly dramatic scene of the slaughter of the innocents (similar to the liturgical *Ordo Rachelis,* or Service of the Rachels, the name referring to the mothers of the children in Matthew 2:18), followed by a rather unusual conclusion in which Herod is gnawed by worms and taken away by devils.

The dramaturgy of the *Benediktbeurer Passionsspiel* is sophisticated in its presentation of the expansive story of Christ's ministry, betrayal, trial, and Crucifixion. Musical narratives by the choir serve as commentary on the action and help to unify the variety of scenes. Mary Magdalene becomes a focus of the play as more than one hundred lines are devoted to her conversion from a woman of worldly pleasures to a follower of Christ. She sings in German as she meets a merchant to buy cosmetics to attract young men. Later she repents and purchases the expensive ointment with which she will anoint Christ's feet. This theme has clearly been borrowed from that of the three Marys purchasing ointment on their way to Christ's tomb in the *Visitatio,* but here the merchant scenes signify her shift from secular pleasures to sacred devotion. The use of the vernacular supports the dramatic intent: Mary addresses the merchant twice in German, but the third time, after her repentance, the dialogue is in Latin.

As the play moves into the scenes of betrayal and trial, the simultaneous stage configuration (a series of platforms around a neutral playing area) is used expertly to weave multiple strands of action. Even as Christ conducts the Last Supper and proceeds to the Mount of Olives, Judas is betraying him and leading the soldiers to the arrest. The trial scene continually traverses the space as Christ is taken before the high priests, then Pilate, then Herod, then returned to Pilate, scourged, and brought before Pilate for the last time. As Christ is led to Calvary, Judas repents his betrayal and, accompanied by a devil, hangs himself.

German is used again as the Virgin Mary laments at the foot of the cross. The *Planctus Mariae,* or *Marienklage,* constituted a literary genre all its own, and versions of the lament are often found in medieval drama. Here both German and Latin versions are presented in a sequence that rivals the earlier scene of Mary Magdalene in its strength of characterization. Overall, the masterly use of text, music, and staging in the *Benediktbeurer Passionsspiel* attests to the achievement of the Latin religious drama.

In addition to the *Klosterneuburger Osterspiel,* which Linke identifies in the *Verfasserlexikon* (1983) as the earliest German Easter play, two other Latin dramas stand out in the corpus of German plays from the tenth to the thirteen centuries. The Tergernsee *Ludus de Antichristo* and Hildegard von Bingen's *Ordo Virtutum* date from the middle of the twelfth century, and neither fits easily into the categories of religious drama. Axton has called the two plays "poles of a tradition adapted [respectively] by statesman and mystic," and they have little in common other than their uniqueness.

The *Ludus de Antichristo* (circa 1160) seems to have been intended for a courtly audience and is perhaps the first medieval political allegory. In the context of the activities of Antichrist at the end of the world, the play reflects Emperor Friedrich Barbarossa's attempts to create a unified and holy Roman empire. The large cast includes the emperor; the kings of the Teutons, Franks, Greeks, Jerusalem, and Babylon; Ecclesia and Synagoga and their attendants; the pope; the followers of Antichrist, called Hypocrites; the prophets Enoch and Elijah; and, of course, Antichrist himself. Although all the kings except the king of Babylon pledge allegiance to Rome, they are all subdued by the forces of Antichrist. Enoch and Elijah denounce Antichrist and convert the Jews, but Antichrist has them all killed. The drama ends as Antichrist flees a thunderbolt from heaven and all the kings return to Ecclesia, the true faith. The play is an ambitious music drama that includes several battles in its stage action.

The *Ordo Virtutum* is an allegorical music drama of some 270 lines depicting a battle between the Virtues and the Devil for a human soul. Except for the music, this formula is typical for the medieval morality play, a genre that is not generally acknowledged to have appeared before the late fourteenth century. This is the only known drama written by the prolific Hildegard, a mystic and the abbess of Rupertsburg at Bingen who lived from 1098 to 1179, although its validity as a performance piece has been much discussed. There is no evidence that the text was staged; nonetheless, it is a highly imagistic work that includes Patriarchs and Prophets, a chorus of Virtues, a chorus of souls, the Devil, and the central character, Anima (soul). The Virtues engage in debate with the Devil (they sing; the Devil does not), and finally bind him in chains when he attempts physically to prevent Anima from returning to the Virtues. Hildegard is one of the two named writers of dramatic literature in Germany prior to the sixteenth century.

Plays about religious subjects – often performed on or around religious feast days – continued to dominate the theater of Europe well into the sixteenth century, and German practice was no exception. The latter half of the thirteenth century, however, saw the increasing popularity of plays that were performed in the vernacular and revealed a purpose fundamentally different from that of the Latin drama that had preceded them. Whereas the Latin plays were produced by the clergy and performed primarily in the church on liturgical occasions, the religious plays in German were produced by trade guilds, confraternities, and town councils. They were performed in the streets and marketplaces of cities by the people who lived and worked there, and they became an expression of the popular religious culture of the society. This is not to say that the vernacular drama had "outgrown" or otherwise freed itself from its clerical auspices; many of the anonymous texts appear to have been written by clerics and the church certainly had some control over what types of performances occurred on Catholic feast days. In fact, the church seems to have joined with the emerging urban bourgeoisie to create a participatory theater that was both celebratory and didactic and which generally supported the status quo.

While the late thirteenth century may be seen as a period of transition from Latin to vernacular drama as the dominant form, this should not be thought of as a linear development. The Latin drama did not cease to exist, nor were the early vernacular plays merely translations of Latin versions. The plays in German were a new form of drama: often staged outdoors, they usually involved larger casts, more expansive staging, less music (although it remained an important element), and more dialogue. Performances became major civic events that not only served to reinforce religious faith but could also bring considerable fame and profit to the sponsoring cities.

The vernacular plays continued to be associated with religious occasions and are usually categorized accordingly. In addition to the Christmas, Easter, and Passion plays, *Fronleichnamsspiele* grew up around the new Feast of Corpus Christi, which was instituted in 1264 but not ratified until 1311. *Heiligenspiele* and *Legendenspiele* (Saint or Martyr plays) were performed on the respective feast days of the religious figures. Other plays, such as those dealing with Old Testament stories or the Last Judgment, are more difficult to place in relation to the church calendar. Finally, certain quasi-dramatic forms have continued to resist clear definition. The *Marienklage* (Lament of Mary) was a popular form of lyric but also occurred regularly in Latin and German drama. It remains unclear which of the surviving texts should be considered dramatic literature and what the criteria for definition should be.

In addition to entries on individual plays in the revised *Verfasserlexikon* (1978–   ), edited by Kurt Ruh, two useful references for the study of the German religious drama of the thirteenth to sixteenth centuries appeared in the 1980s. Rolf Bergmann's *Katalog der deutschsprachigen geistlichen Spiele und Marienklagen des Mittelalters* (Catalogue of the German-language Religious Plays and Laments of Mary of the Middle Ages, 1986) lists 193 manuscripts of plays and 147 *Marienklagen*. Each entry describes the manuscript itself, summarizes its con-

tent, and lists editions and relevant literature. Neumann's *Geistliches Schauspiel im Zeugnis der Zeit* (The Religious Play in the Evidence of Its Time, 1987) is the first systematic attempt to research and publish archival records of performance in the German-speaking areas.

The chronological overviews provided by Bergmann and Neumann suggest only a tenuous existence of vernacular religious drama at the end of the thirteenth century. Bergmann lists only four texts prior to 1300 (one of which is the *Benediktbeurer Passionsspiel*), while Neumann finds only five references to performance (other than play scripts) for the same period. The mid-thirteenth-century *Himmelgartner Passionsspielfragment* (Himmelgarten Fragment of a Passion Play) is fewer than forty lines long, but Bergmann lists scenes of the flight into Egypt, the Magi, the temptation, the calling of the apostles, and the wedding at Cana. The late-thirteenth-century *Amorbacher Spiel von Mariae Himmelfahrt* (Amorbach Play of the Assumption of Mary) is a longer fragment that presents an extended debate between Ecclesia and Synagoga between scenes of the death and burial of Mary.

The most extensive vernacular script from the period before 1300 is the *Osterspiel von Muri* (Easter Play of Muri), dating from the middle of the century and usually called the first German medieval play written entirely in the vernacular. While its content is representative of the Easter plays, the format of the manuscript is unusual. The surviving fragments seem to have belonged to a roll of text some two hundred centimeters long, which was most likely used by a prompter or director during performance of the play. Only about six hundred lines remain of an original length estimated at eleven hundred to twelve hundred lines.

After five soldiers are placed at Christ's grave to guard the body, Pilate addresses the audience directly in a transitional speech before the Resurrection of Christ (represented by thunder and the reactions of the soldiers; no Christ figure is mentioned). On the advice of the Jews, Pilate pays the soldiers twenty pounds each to keep silent. In a continuation of that motif, a merchant offers Pilate the same fee for permission to sell his wares. He then has a long speech in which he describes his merchandise, presumably to the audience; the character is reminiscent of the ointment seller in the Latin Easter plays and a precursor to the quack doctor who later appeared in the secular drama, especially the Shrovetide plays. His speech is interrupted by a scene of Christ freeing the souls from hell, after which the merchant scene continues with Mary Magdalene buying ointment on her way to the grave. The visit to the sepulchre is followed by an appearance of Christ to Mary. After she praises him for nearly one hundred lines, Jesus assures her that she will be rewarded, and the fragment breaks off. Even though its structure is not entirely clear due to the gaps in the text, the *Osterspiel von Muri* marks the beginning of a tradition of religious drama that was spoken (not sung) in German, included representations of urban characters, and was intended for the enjoyment as well as the edification of the citizenry.

The vernacular religious drama flourished in Germany and throughout Europe for the next three centuries. Neumann's records reveal that virtually every urban area supported some type of play, although the scripts have not all survived. The communal, civic celebrations of the late Middle Ages coexisted with the Latin liturgical plays, each form influencing the other, so that the drama became, as Eckehard Simon asserts in his introduction to *The Theatre of Medieval Europe* (1991), "a pervasive, ubiquitous and tenacious form of popular culture" which survived for over six hundred years.

All historians are aware that the surviving evidence cannot tell the complete story of the activity of an era, and this lack is perhaps nowhere more keenly felt than in the study of theater. The texts, even when they do survive, offer only an outline of the live performance, and it is in the cultural event of the performance that the significance of these texts resides. For some performative events no texts have survived. While religious drama was dominant, professional entertainers were active throughout the period, performing in public, at court, and at the monasteries. It is unclear whether they "acted," but they certainly sang, recited poetry, told stories, danced, and performed acrobatics.

Folk customs, also not scripted, contributed to the theatrical heritage of the German-speaking areas. Celebrations often included processions, role-playing, mumming, dance, and music. While there is little evidence to connect these sorts of events to the religious drama, there is no reason to believe that they did not coexist. Axton offers a useful discussion of folk combat plays and dancing games, making connections to the Tegernsee *Antichrist* and to the (lost) *Ludus Prophetarum* from Riga. Finally, courtly spectacles such as jousts or processional entries of visiting dignitaries could become highly allegorical and almost certainly contributed to the ability of medieval audiences to appreciate sophisticated uses of emblems and symbols. A complete picture of the theater of the early Middle Ages must take into account the variety of theatrical and paratheatrical events and practices that were a part of the culture. The religious and secular spheres were closely linked through politics and economics; it would be shortsighted to believe that their arts, including performance, developed independently.

Although the history of theater relies on the preservation of play scripts and on other records of production, due to the transitory nature of performance the surviving artifacts can never give a complete picture of the dramatic traditions of a culture. This is especially true of the theater of medieval Europe. Records indicate that performances were widespread, but the archival evidence cannot always be tied to the relatively few play scripts that have survived. The archival records themselves are often incomplete, inconsistent, or ambiguous. There were no permanent theater structures; no properties, costumes, or set pieces are known to have survived; and pictorial evidence is rare. But the immediacy and communal involvement of live performance makes drama a crucial element of society, especially that of the Middle Ages. The period from 800 to 1280 is intriguing because it was during this time that a new theatrical tradition developed that has remained in many ways unique in the history of Western drama. Performances were intimately related to the religious and political life of medieval society, making theatrical events much more vital and significant than they are today. Perhaps second only to the pulpit, the theater was the mass medium of the Middle Ages. Through its close connections with the religious hierarchy and its increasing importance as a civic undertaking, the theater of medieval Germany offers important insights into the culture in which it was composed and performed.

References:

Richard Axton, *European Drama of the Early Middle Ages* (London: Hutchinson, 1974);

Rolf Bergmann, *Katalog der deutschsprachigen geistlichen Spiele und Marienklagen des Mittelalters* (Munich: Beck, 1986);

David Bevington, *Medieval Drama* (Boston: Houghton Mifflin, 1975);

Mary Marguerite Butler, R.S.M., *Hrotsvitha: the Theatricality of her Plays* (New York: Philosophical Library, 1960);

Sue-Ellen Case, *Feminism and Theatre* (New York: Methuen, 1988);

Fletcher Collins, Jr., *The Production of Medieval Church Music-Drama* (Charlottesville: University of Virginia Press, 1972);

Helmut de Boor, *Die Textgeschichte der lateinischen Osterfeiern* (Tübingen: Niemayer, 1967);

Peter Dronke, *Poetic Individuality in the Middle Ages. New Departures in Poetry 1000–1150* (Oxford: Clarendon, 1970);

Dronke, *Women Writers of the Middle Ages: A Critical Study of Texts from Perpetua (d. 203) to Marguerite Porete (d. 1310)* (Cambridge: Cambridge University Press, 1984);

Sabina Flanagan, *Hildegard of Bingen, 1098–1179: A Visionary Life* (New York & London: Routledge, 1989);

C. Clifford Flanigan, "The Liturgical Context of the *Quem Quaeritis* Trope," *Comparative Drama,* 8 (Spring 1974): 45–62;

Flanigan, "The Liturgical Drama and Its Tradition: A Review of Scholarship 1965–1975," *Research Opportunities in Renaissance Drama,* 18 (1975): 81–102; 19 (1976): 109–136;

Flanigan, "The Roman Rite and the Origins of the Liturgical Drama," *University of Toronto Quarterly,* 43 (Spring 1974): 263–284;

Anne Lyon Haight, ed., *Hroswitha of Gandersheim: Her Life, Times, and Works, and a Comprehensive Bibliography* (New York: Hroswitha Club, 1965);

O. B. Hardison, *Christian Rite and Christian Drama in the Middle Ages. Essays in the Origin and Early History of Modern Drama* (Baltimore: Johns Hopkins University Press, 1965);

Hildegard von Bingen, *Ordo Virtutum,* edited by Audrey Ekdahl Davidson (Kalamazoo, Mich.: Medieval Institute, 1985);

Rudolf Heym, "Bruchstück eines geistlichen Schauspiels von Marien Himmelfahrt," *Zeitschrift für deutsches Altertum und deutsche Litteratur,* 52 (1910): 1–55;

Hrotsvitha, *Hrotsvithae Opera,* edited by Helene Paderborn Homeyer (Munich: Schöningh, 1970);

Hrotsvitha, *The Plays of Hrotsvit of Gandersheim,* translated by Katharina M. Wilson, Garland Library of Medieval Literature no. 62 (New York: Garland, 1989);

Hansjürgen Linke, "Drama und Theater," in *Die deutsche Literatur im späten Mittelalter,* part 2, edited by Ingeborg Glier (Munich: Beck, 1987), pp. 153–233, 471–485;

Linke, Review of *Lateinische Osterfeiern und Osterspiele,* edited by Walter Lipphardt, *Anzeiger für deutsches Altertum und deutsche Literatur,* 94 (1983): 33–38;

Walther Lipphardt and Hans-Gert Roloff, eds., *Lateinische Osterfeiern und Osterspiele,* 9 volumes (Berlin & New York: De Gruyter, 1975–1981, 1990);

Rudolf Meier, ed., *Das Innsbrucker Osterspiel. Das Osterspiel von Muri* (Stuttgart: Reclam, 1962);

Bert Nagel, *Hrotsvit von Gandersheim* (Stuttgart: Metzler, 1965);

Alois Nagler, *Sources of Theatrical History* (New York: Theatre Annual, 1952);

Bernd Neumann, "Geistliches Schauspiel als Paradigma stadtbürgerlicher Literatur im ausgehenden Mittelalter," in *Germanistik: Forschungsstand und Perspektiven,* volume 2, edited by Georg Stötzel (Berlin: De Gruyter, 1985), pp. 123–135;

Neumann, *Geistliches Schauspiel im Zeugnis der Zeit. Zur Aufführung mittelalterlicher religiöser Dramen im deutschen Sprachgebiet,* 2 volumes (Munich: Artemis, 1987);

J. D. A. Ogilvy, "*Mimi, Scurrae, Histriones:* Entertainers of the Early Middle Ages," *Speculum,* 38 (October 1963): 603–619;

The Play of Antichrist, translated by John Wright (Toronto: Pontifical Institute of Medieval Studies, 1967);

Kurt Ruh, ed., *Die deutsche Literatur des Mittelalters: Verfasserlexikon,* second, revised edition, 9 volumes to date (Berlin & New York: De Gruyter, 1977–);

E. Sievers, "Himmelgartner Bruchstücke," *Zeitschrift für deutsche Philologie,* 21 (1889): 385–404;

Eckehard Simon, ed., *The Theatre of Medieval Europe. New Research in Early Drama* (Cambridge & New York: Cambridge University Press, 1991);

William Smoldon, *The Music of the Medieval Church Dramas,* edited by Cynthia Bourgeault (London: Oxford University Press, 1980);

Sandro Sticca, *The Latin Passion Play: Its Origins and Development* (Albany: State University of New York Press, 1970);

William Tydeman, *The Theatre in the Middle Ages. Western European Stage Conditions c.800–1576* (London: Cambridge University Press, 1978);

Karl Young, *The Drama of the Medieval Church,* 2 volumes (Oxford: Clarendon, 1933).

The Music of *Minnesang*

James V. McMahon
Emory University

Most scholars who have concerned themselves with the study of *Minnesang* agree that to understand it as a genre one must treat it as a unified art consisting of words and music and that to separate the text from the melody inevitably leads to an imperfect understanding of both. But so many good texts and so few authentic musical manuscripts for this genre survive that philologists have found it convenient to study the texts and more or less to ignore the music, and musicologists studying early music have tended to concentrate on more-fertile and more-easily accessible fields, such as liturgical music or early polyphony, leaving German secular monophony relatively untouched. Consequently, although to its practitioners it was a single, unified art, and although it would hardly have occurred to anyone in the twelfth or thirteenth century that poetry could be recited without music or even read silently, it is difficult for scholars today to get a good idea of the music of *Minnesang,* and even harder to understand how the texts and melodies came together in a single art.

The term *Minnesang* literally means "love song," but it is also used to designate all lyric poetry written in Middle High German. This article is limited to early *Minnesang* – the poets represented in Karl Lachmann's collection *Des Minnesangs Frühling* (Springtime of *Minnesang;* originally published in 1857 and reedited many times since) and Walther von der Vogelweide, or roughly the poetry of the period from 1180 to 1230. *Minnesang* was practiced into the fourteenth century and had an influence well into the sixteenth century, but the later music, starting with the works of Neidhart von Reuenthal, has received more scholarly attention because the sources are much richer.

Minnesang was an oral art, practiced by people who gave little or no thought to its theoretical foundations or to its preservation. The melodies extant for these songs were handed down in an oral tradition and not written until much later. But any attempt to reconstruct the art of *Minnesang* must start with the manuscripts, because the tradition in which the songs were produced is long dead.

There are no manuscript sources for either the words or the music that are contemporary with the makers of the songs. It is possible that earlier manuscripts once existed and are now lost, and it is also possible that there are manuscripts still waiting to be found. A manuscript containing one complete song and several fragments of songs by Walther was found in Münster in 1910, and there are many old books in libraries and monasteries that have not been examined in centuries. Most of the great collections of *Minnesang* texts are in manuscripts from the Renaissance. In her essay "Probleme um die Melodien des Minnesangs" (Problems Concerning the Melodies of *Minnesang,* 1967) Ursula Aarburg has suggested that those collections were made by or for lovers of a lost art – people who saw that art in decline and collected the songs to prevent their being lost, with the implication that before such time the songs were well enough known that there was little need to write them down. If such is the case, then even if there are any lost manuscripts, it seems unlikely that they will be any older than those currently known.

The most important text collections do not contain any musical notation. Various reasons have been given for this situation, but the most likely explanation is that those manuscripts were not intended to be used by singers as songbooks but were made for the persons who commissioned them. They may have survived precisely because they are beautiful rather than because they were practical. Books intended to be useful are soon worn out and are often lost or destroyed when their usefulness is past. In any case, if the tradition of *Minnesang* performance was an oral one, it is quite unlikely that there ever were "editions" for performers.

An oral tradition implies constant change in the form of both melody and text. Traditional philology, following Lachmann and his successors, proposed that it was possible by comparing enough manuscripts to make a critical edition that would reconstruct, if not the original, at least the archetype from which all later manuscript traditions derived. In this way one could approach an "authentic" text

First page of the Carmina Burana *manuscript, with staffless neumes — to indicate rising and falling pitch — above the lines of text. The illustration represents the Wheel of Fortune (Codex Buranus, Munich, Staatsbibliothek, Clm. 4660, f. 1r).*

of a song. Recent scholarship, however, has suggested that the very idea of an authentic text is illusory because the composers of the songs (unlike the modern composer or poet, whose work has a finished form when it is published), changed their songs from performance to performance, so that there was never a fixed form. Furthermore, the songs were freely copied, varied, and adapted by other composers and performers.

If it is impossible to establish an authentic text, it is equally impossible to establish an authentic melody. The manuscripts containing melodies are few and late, and even at best they do not contain all the elements necessary to reconstruct the melody.

The main problem is that every performer of a song learned it by hearing it and performed it as he thought it sounded best. He was under no obligation to reproduce exactly what he heard, and he felt free to perform it as he understood it. But the performers of *Minnesang* knew what they were doing and knew that they were part of a tradition. It is important to understand that absolute accuracy was less important in that tradition than fidelity to the spirit of the song and to accept the idea that the song, as it survives in a manuscript, represents what one scribe heard one performer sing or what the scribe thought the melody should be. In either case the song stands within the tradition; the medieval listener, unless he heard the composer perform the song, could not know what the original form had been and did not care to know. He enjoyed the song as he heard it, and the modern listener must be content to do the same.

There are four kinds of manuscript sources for these melodies. The first consists of texts by minnesingers along with staffless neumes, a system of musical notation intended primarily as a mnemonic device. The neumes indicate where the melody goes up and down in pitch and which notes are sung on which syllables, but they give no indication of what pitches are involved, what intervals exist between the notes, or what the rhythms might have been. There are two such manuscripts: one is in the library of the monastery of Kremsmünster in Austria, and the other is the *Carmina Burana* manuscript, now in Munich. Some attempts have been made to transcribe this notation into singable melodies, but they are conjectures at best.

The second type of source comprises texts by minnesingers with musical notes on musical staffs. There are two such manuscripts: the first is the Jena Manuscript, containing a song by Spervogel, and the second is the Münster Fragment mentioned above, containing one complete song (the *Palästina-lied* [Palestine Song]) and several fragments by Walther von der Vogelweide. Since the *Palästinalied* is thus the best-attested melody by the best known of all minnesingers, it appears in practically every modern collection of *Minnesang* and has been performed on many records.

Another group of manuscripts includes other texts with melodies attributed to Walther. There are nine later collections, from the fifteenth and sixteenth centuries, that contain various texts attached to five melodies attributed to minnesingers; all but one of them are said to be by Walther, and the one exception is attributed to Walther in other manuscripts. Three of these melodies are regarded as certainly not genuine, while the other two are probably genuine.

The final group is made up of those manuscripts containing French or Provençal texts and melodies that may have been copied or adapted by a minnesinger. These melodies, called "contrafactures," were borrowed by minnesingers, with suitable adaptations, from the works of trouvères and troubadours of northern and southern France, respectively. That this practice was followed is generally accepted; there are many references to it in the literature of the time, and there is some evidence for it in French manuscripts. Unfortunately, there is no extant German melody that can be proved by manuscript evidence to be a contrafacture of any French or Provençal song. So few melodies for German songs have survived that this absence is not surprising, but it would bolster the hypothesis of contrafacture considerably if such evidence could be found. The argument for contrafacture, apart from the references to the existence of the procedure, is a comparison of texts, revealing that some German minnesingers borrowed the theme, the format (meters and rhyme scheme), and sometimes even specific phrases and references from known models — and since they borrowed all these elements, it is reasonable to conclude that they borrowed the melody as well. But such conclusions should be viewed with caution since it is impossible to prove that any specific song is a contrafacture. The most one can claim for contrafactures is high probability and that only for songs which have the same content and form as their romance models and whose forms share some unusual characteristic with those of the models. Many formal structures are quite common in both romance and German songs, so songs with only such structures in common may well be similar by accident. Some themes, such as unrequited love, are also quite common in both areas, so sharing such a theme does not suffice to in-

*Miniature of the minnesinger and emperor Heinrich VI, from the
Große Heidelberger Liederhandschrift (Heidelberg,
Universitätsbibliothek, cpg. 848, f. 6r)*

dicate a contrafacture. But if two songs with similar themes share a strikingly unusual formal structure, an unusual rhyme scheme, or several specific idioms, the probability of contrafacture increases. Aarburg, in her essay "Melodien zum frühen deutschen Minnesang" (Melodies to Early German *Minnesang*; 1956), identified ten German songs that she called "sichere Kontrafakta" (certain contrafactures), but they might better be called "highly probable contrafractures."

There are no documents which describe factually an actual performance of *Minnesang*, and the songs themselves are not "self-conscious"; they do not refer to their own performance. Most books on the performance of early music concentrate on music after 1400 and have little to say about *Minnesang*. Modern recordings, of which there are several, are all based largely on conjecture; although they may be excellent performances, there is simply no way of knowing how close they come to

re-creating how the songs sounded in the twelfth or thirteenth century.

On the other hand, there are extant writings of some theoreticians of music from the early period, and even though they are concerned almost exclusively with liturgical music, such writings contain information useful to an understanding of *Minnesang*. Contemporary literary references are also of use, most important the *Tristan und Isolde* of Gottfried von Straßburg (circa 1210), which contains over seventy references to musical practice. Gottfried loved to show off his wide knowledge of various fields, gained not from formal education but from observation of the world. Gottfried's work never mentions music theory as it was taught in his day, nor is there any reference in his work to liturgical music, the "academic" music of the Middle Ages. His musical references are almost always to the sort of music that could be heard in the secular court environment, and that is precisely what makes his information so valuable. Although allowances must be made for the fact that *Tristan* is fiction and that it concerns times, places, and cultures with which Gottfried was not personally familiar, it is nevertheless quite likely that what he said about music reflected the practices he observed in the courtly society of his own time.

Anyone could sing a song, but not anyone could perform as a minnesinger. *Minnesang* was a social and courtly phenomenon, and only members of a court could be full participants. Nevertheless, the range of participants was quite extensive.

At the top were the emperor himself – the emperor Henry VI ("Kaiser Heinrich" in Lachmann's collection) was well known for his songs – and members of the high nobility, such as the counts of Rietenburg and Regensburg, Rudolf von Fenis, and Bligger von Steinach. Slightly lower were the *ministeriales*, landless knights, ranging from the emperor's counselors to the lowest retainer of the least important count. They usually had regular political, diplomatic, or military duties and composed songs on the side, though some of them – such as Friedrich von Hausen, Meinloh von Sevelingen, and Hartmann von Aue – became better known for their songs than for any other accomplishments.

There are also several examples of the "professional minnesinger," whose social status is uncertain. Reinmar der Alte, for example, seems to have been permanently attached to the court of Vienna, and Walther spent his life wandering from one patron to another until he was given land of his own by the emperor Frederick II. Walther is a most peculiar case. Many literary historians have assumed that he belonged to the class of *ministeriales*, but the evidence against that position is strong. Walther speaks often of himself but never refers to himself as a knight or a noble. The book of travel expenses of Bishop Wolfger of Passau, which contains the only nonliterary reference to Walther, calls him simply *cantor* (the singer). In several of his poems Walther complains about receiving poor treatment from others, which might also indicate low social status. Yet he is clearly of a higher status than the *spilliute* performers. The *spilliute* were wandering performers of all kinds: singers, dancers, instrumentalists, mimes, jugglers, storytellers, magicians, and animal trainers. They traveled in troupes, for the most part, and spent their lives on the road. They probably sang some of the same songs as the minnesingers, but not as part of the courtly ritual. *Spilliute* were commonly given used clothes as a reward for their performance, and Walther proudly declares in a poem: "getragene wât ich nie genan" (I never accepted used clothing). And indeed Bishop Wolfger's expense book says that he gave Walther money to buy a new coat; he was not given a used coat. In any case, Walther was careful to insist on a status above that of the *spilliute*.

All the minnesingers, from the emperor down, were travelers. The emperor traveled constantly and brought a large entourage wherever he went. Nobles who carried out political, diplomatic, or military missions also traveled widely. The professional minnesingers, such as Walther, moved from one patron to another. And, of course, the *spilliute* spent their lives on the road. These peregrinations account for the wide dissemination of the songs.

It took years of training and practice to become a minnesinger. Gottfried relates that Tristan's training took seven years and included learning to play seven instruments and sing in nine languages. Tristan is, of course, a paragon, an unusual case, but it is safe to assume that other performers of *Minnesang* spent much time learning their art.

Although there are at least twenty known female troubadours, no work by a woman minnesinger has been preserved. However, there are many songs that call for women's voices and that could have been performed by women, sometimes in dialogue with men. Gottfried's *Tristan* characterizes Isolde as an expert singer and musician.

The occasions for *Minnesang* range from the most public to the most private. The most public performances were probably those given at great festivals, such as that put on by the emperor Frederick Barbarossa at Mainz at Pentecost in 1184 to celebrate the knighting of his two sons. This festival apparently included more minnesingers, troubadours, and trouvères per acre than at any other time or place in history. One of the traditional bits of evidence for influence of one such person on another has been the presence of both at this festival, though such evidence is highly questionable.

Festivals were relatively rare, however, and normal life was less exciting. Courtly entertainment took place mostly in the courts themselves. From Gottfried it is known that people in a great court, such as King Mark's, expected entertainment after supper, especially if guests were present. Nothing shows the normality of having music after supper more clearly than the fact that many members of the court did not always attend the performances. Visits from traveling musicians are frequently portrayed as rare events eagerly awaited and much appreciated. This may have been true in smaller or out-of-the-way courts, but in the greater courts the performance of music was so common as to be

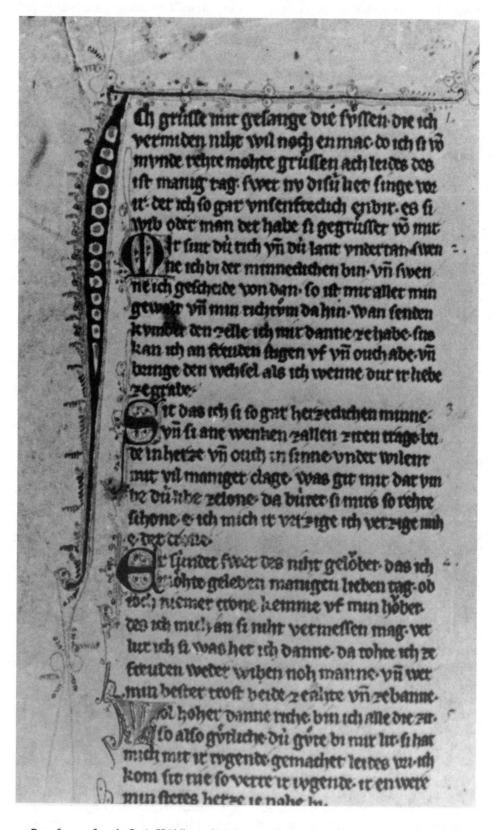

Part of a page from the Große Heidelberger Liederhandschrift with verses of Minnesang *by Heinrich VI
(Heidelberg, Universitätsbibliothek, cpg. 848, f. 6v*[a]*)*

taken for granted, and only unusually good performers drew large crowds. In Gottfried's romance, when Tristan first performs at King Mark's court, he takes over the harp from a minstrel who had been performing before him. When Tristan begins to play, the people in other parts of the castle hear him and, recognizing an unusually good performer, flock into the hall to hear him. If music had been unusual, they would doubtless have already been in the hall.

Even on less social occasions, when no guests were present or when no special performers were available, music still had a place in the social life of the court. The residents themselves would have performed. To the extent that *Minnesang* was the expression of courtly love, a set of social conventions, it was and could only be a social and courtly phenomenon. Thus, even with only the household present, *Minnesang* was a social or public event. In his "Minnesang als Gesellschaftskunst" (*Minnesang* as Social Art, 1954) Wolfgang Mohr points out that although it may be true that in the earliest forms of *Minnesang* the poet sang of his own love experience, he always did so to an audience. Furthermore, according to Mohr, "the medieval song, even when it is directed to a specific woman as a declaration of love, and even when it takes the form of a love letter or is sent by a messenger, is always also intended to be heard by the pubic as well."

These songs were sung by *spilliute* as well and were spread by them from place to place. But when the *spilliute* performed, it was only common entertainment; *Minnesang*, as courtly ceremony, required both courtly performers and a courtly audience.

It is important to understand that medieval monophony was essentially melodic, which means that the harmonic structure that underlies practically all modern Western music plays no part at all in it. (That is one of the reasons for the thesis that those songs were normally sung by one person.)

Medieval music sometimes sounds oddly "unfinished" to a modern listener, and there sometimes seem to be unusual or unexpected intervals in the melodies. That impression is due partly to the absence of any need to take harmony into consideration in composing such a melody and partly to the fact that the scales are usually not the same as those employed today.

Most musical scales that have ever been used can be thought of as ways of dividing up the intervals that can occur between one note and its octave. The octave as the limit is determined by the inescapable physical and mathematical fact that if the frequency of a note is doubled, the resulting note will be exactly one octave higher. But between one note and its octave there is a continuum, an infinite number of possible notes. Some instruments, such as the violin and the trombone, can slide up and down this continuum; but otherwise the octave is usually divided into specific intervals, and the series of intervals is a scale. The intervals can be of any size; for example, some scales are pentatonic, dividing the octave into five intervals. The black keys of a piano comprise a pentatonic scale.

Most Western music since Pythagoras has used a scale determined by dividing the octave according to a certain series of mathematical ratios: 2:1 for the octave, then 3:2 for the fifth, 4:3 for the fourth, 81:64 for the major third, 6:5 for the minor third, 9:8 for the whole tone, and 256:243 for the halftone. The combination of these ratios led to a division of the octave into seven intervals, of which five are whole steps and two are half steps. In theory the half steps, which are always a perfect fifth or perfect fourth apart, can begin on any position within the octave, but since about 1600 most Western music has used only two of the possible arrangements, which are now called the major and minor scales. The major scale consists of two whole steps, followed by one half step, three whole steps, and one half step; the minor scale follows the gradation of one whole step, then one half step, two whole steps, one half step, and finally two whole steps.

Before the major and minor scales came to predominate, Western music used many of the possible arrangements of intervals. The various arrangements are called modes. The medieval composers believed that each mode conveyed a particular mood or effect, and they used them with great skill. Over the years certain musical phrases or motives which occurred fairly often came to be associated with the modes in which they were written. Eventually there were so many of these characteristic motives that composers showed their virtuosity not by the originality of their compositions but by the skill and artistry with which they combined preexisting motives in new ways.

There has probably been more controversy over the rhythmic interpretation of these songs than over any other aspect. In modern music the notation used by the composer can indicate the rhythm. Also, modern music is usually written down or recorded at the time of composition, by the composer or by someone else. In either case, the rhythm is known from the beginning, and unless someone deliberately changes it, it will most likely be performed in the rhythm that the composer intended.

But medieval music was seldom, if ever, written down by the composer or even in the composer's lifetime. And there was no reason for performers to regard any performance they heard as definitive; they were free to alter or shape many of the musical elements to their personal tastes. When the songs were finally written down, the notation indicated nothing more than relative pitch; there was no possibility of indicating absolute pitch or rhythm. By the middle of the thirteenth century a mensural notation had been developed for polyphony to enable people singing from different pages of music to stay together rhythmically. If it had been necessary in this earlier period to indicate the rhythm of monophony, the scribes would have developed some appropriate system of notation.

The conclusion to be drawn from the situation is that the proper rhythmic interpretation of the songs was so clear – so standard and uniformly practiced – that it did not need to be indicated. Today, however, there is no way of knowing what the proper rhythmic interpretation was. Many theories have been proposed, but they all remain hypotheses, and unless some new evidence is found, none of them can ever be verified.

Each theory begins by emphasizing one aspect of the available data and then ignoring the rest of the data, building a structure of inferences and hypotheses upon the part emphasized. There are six main theories. The first proposes mensural rhythm, based on the fact that the manuscripts do indeed contain notes of different shapes. Manuscripts of polyphony use these different note shapes to indicate note length, and a few French manuscripts of monophony also use them in this way. But so far all attempts to prove that note shapes indicate rhythm in manuscripts of German monophony have failed. It is possible that scholars do not know how to read the notes properly, but if that is the case, they are not likely ever to learn, for the corpus of manuscripts is small and not likely to increase significantly.

The second theory bases rhythm on the text. It makes sense to base the musical rhythm on the metrical rhythm; but in practice it is impossible to say how that is to be done. Are some syllables held longer than others, and if so, by how much? Should notes be lengthened at the end of phrases? What should be done when there are many notes over one syllable? When and for how long should a singer pause for breath? The idea behind this approach makes sense, but further guidelines are necessary, perhaps an underlying principle for determining such practices. Several such principles have been proposed, but all of them are inadequate.

The third theory is one of free rhythm, based on the predominant interpretation of Gregorian chant today – that of the monks of Solesmes in France. In that system each note gets an unspecified unit of time; the rhythm is therefore free, not bound to any recurring pattern, flowing in groups of two and three, depending on where the accents fall in the Latin text. Unfortunately, German has a different accent pattern from Latin, and in any case there is no general agreement that that is the proper way to perform Gregorian chant; the method prevails not because of intrinsic merit but because the Catholic church approved it for liturgical use.

Like the idea of taking the musical rhythm from the text, the idea of free rhythm also makes sense. If all the notes have the same time value, then the word accents will determine the flow of the music. Ewald Jammers proposed in his essay "Untersuchungen über die Rhythmik und Melodik der Melodien der Jenaer Liederhandschrift" (Investigations of the Rhythmics and Melodics of the Melodies of the Jena Song Manuscript 1924–1925) an interpretation based on the idea that the melodies had to be in free rhythm while the texts had their own strict rhythm. He concluded that *Minnesang* had no definite, always-valid relationship between notes and syllables, and it is the interplay between the two rhythms, that of the text and that of the melody, that makes the performance interesting. That idea was later elaborated, by Jammers and by Hendrik Van der Werf, into a theory that Van der Werf called "declamatory rhythm," discussed below.

Fourth is isochronous rhythm, the simplest – and the least satisfactory – of the rhythmic theories. *Isochronous* means "of equal duration." That theory ignores the text completely and decrees that each note that stands alone is given the same unit of time, and all notes written in groups are given appropriate fractions of that unit of time. That approach provides an easy way to transcribe manuscripts, but that is its only advantage. When a musician tries to perform a song from such a transcription, its rhythmic absurdities immediately become obvious.

Modal rhythm is the fifth theory and the most controversial of the proposals. Oddly, though there has been controversy between the proponents and opponents of this theory, there has been much more conflict among its proponents. The case for modal rhythm was first advanced by Friedrich Ludwig, a professor of music at Strasbourg, who found justification for it in manuscripts of French polyphony. His students Jean Beck and Pierre Aubry each claimed to have been the first to apply it to monophony. Their conclusions were published in separate books in 1907: Aubry's *La Rhythmique musicale des troubadours et des trouvères* (The Musical Rhythm of the Troubadours and Trouvères) and Beck's *Die modale Interpretation der mittelalterlichen Melodien, besonders der Troubadours und Trouvères* (The Modal Interpretation of Medieval Melodies, Especially Those of the Troubadours and Trouvères). The animosity between them grew so great that case went to court; Beck won, and in 1910 Aubrey was forced to have all remaining copies of his book destroyed and to publish a second edition immediately, with a footnote on the first page acknowledging Beck's claim. Friedrich Gennrich was another student of Ludwig who applied the modal theory in his works. Beck claimed that some of his transcriptions had been plagiarized by Gennrich, who then published them as his own, and Gennrich in reply accused Beck of having stolen Aubry's work. The bitter strife ended only with the deaths of the combatants.

What Ludwig had discovered was that the manuscripts of some French motets used a notation that indicated relative note values in a set of triple rhythms. The notes and their equivalent values are

Mode	Notation	Modern Equivalent
1	▬ ■	♩ ♪
2	■ ▬	♪ ♩
3	■ ■ ■	♩. ♩ ♪
4	■ ■ ▬	♩ ♪ ♩.
5	▬ ▬	♩. ♩.
6	■ ■ ■	♪ ♪ ♪

Ludwig hesitated to apply his discovery beyond the area where it could be backed by manuscript evidence. Beck and Aubry, however, believed that it could be applied to all medieval French songs, and Gennrich went even further, claiming that it was applicable to all German secular songs as well — that it was, indeed, the universal rhythmic system of medieval monophony.

The problem faced by modalists was that they could not agree on which of the modal rhythms should be used for any given song. They transcribed the songs in many different ways, each individual insisting that his own interpretation was the only one possible. Obviously, a system that has such built-in inconsistencies seems not to be particularly well founded. Because of the enormous output and stature of people like Gennrich, most of the transcriptions of monophonic songs found today in music textbooks, histories of music, and scholarly treatments of all kinds are modal; the unwary

reader could easily assume that modal rhythms had been proven to be the correct way to interpret *Minnesang*. But there is not the slightest manuscript evidence for modal rhythm in *Minnesang*, and the "proof by analogy" is weak, being based primarily on the possible existence of German contrafactures of French songs that may or may not have been modal.

Finally, there is the theory of declamatory rhythm, based on the idea that the melody of a medieval song, unlike that of a modern song, was not intended to "interact" with the text or carry any particular emotional baggage. It was simply a means of conveying the message contained in the text. It should therefore be totally subordinate to the text, and the performer should be primarily concerned with "declaiming" the text by means of a melody.

The foundations of this theory were laid by Jammers in his 1924 article and, later, his book *Ausgewählte Melodien des Minnesangs* (Selected Melodies of *Minnesang*, 1963) and by Burkhard Kippenburg, who in his *Der Rythmus im Minnesang* (Rhythm *Minnesang*, 1962) agreed that although a song must have some rhythm, it need not have a fixed rhythm, nor need it have the same rhythm in every performance, since all performers were free to vary a song at will, and that in the long run the only significant criterion in determining the validity of a rhythmic interpretation is how it sounds when performed. An interpretation that is awkward today was probably awkward then, too. Jammers further proposed that the rhythm could not be precisely fixed because the performer's freedom was limited only by his art.

Hendrik Van der Werf of the Eastman School of Music coined the term *declamatory rhythm* and describes it in his article "Deklamatorischer Rythmus in den Chansons der Trouvères" (Declamatory Rhythm in the Chansons of the Trouvères, 1967) as "free, not only in the sense that stressed and unstressed notes, as well as stressed and unstressed syllables, can occur at irregular intervals, but also in the sense that there is not necessarily a simple ratio in the duration of one note compared to another (i.e. not necessarily 1:1, 1:2, 1:3). But this does not mean that a song cannot have binary or ternary passages, nor does it mean that the rhythm must differ from strophe to strophe: all these matters depended partly on the individual performer, and partly on the text and the tradition of the song in question." Fundamentally, he states in his book *The Chansons of the Troubadors and Trouvères* (1972), declamatory rhythm is "the rhythm in which one might declaim the poem without the music."

Miniature from the Große Heidelberger Liederhandschrift depicting the minnesinger Heinrich Frauenlob (seated at top) with a group of musicians playing typical medieval instruments: drum, flute, shawm, fiddles, psaltery, and bagpipe (Heidelberg, Universitätsbibliothek, cpg. 848, f. 399r)

It might be argued that there is no more hard evidence for that interpretation than for any of the others. But all the interpretations based on strict rhythm stumble over the fact that the notation did not indicate any such rhythm. Such being the case, an interpretation that rejects the idea of strict rhythm is at least in agreement with the notation that survives. In the end, for all the polemics and effort, scholars simply do not know what kind of rhythm was used in performing medieval German secular songs, and it is unlikely that they ever will. But since notations in the manuscripts shed little light on the subject, the interpretations that take this absence of useful information into account, and that do not try to find rhythmic systems where they do not exist, seem to be the most reasonable ones.

The evidence concerning instrumental accompaniment to *Minnesang* is scanty and contradictory. The songs themselves reveal nothing about how they were performed. Literary sources are suggestive, but either they are ambiguous or they require interpretation; they are never clear and explicit. Even Gottfried is not helpful. Evidence from pictures is also doubtful. Instruments were depicted as much for symbolic value as to illustrate reality. Pictures do reveal, to a certain extent, what the instruments looked like and how they were played (though details such as number of strings, number and position of finger holes, and position for playing are usually not reliable); but artists may have depicted large groups of musicians to symbolize a patron's wealth and largesse or to show off a painter's knowledge and versatility rather than to represent ensembles which actually existed. A common illustrative motif was a choir of angels playing trumpets, but that many trumpets playing together, given the technology of instrument making at the time, almost certainly could not have played in tune. And the frequent pictures in devotional books showing King David playing a harp accompanied by four other musicians in the four corners of the picture playing various other instruments do not imply, as Arnold Schering has concluded, that the typical instrumental ensemble in the Middle Ages was a quintet.

It is obvious that a singer accompanying himself could not have used a wind instrument. Furthermore, any instrument that was louder than the human voice would have been unsuitable. This leaves the harp and fiddle as the most likely instruments of the minnesinger. Medieval writers and modern historians agree that the most commonly used instrument was the fiddle, though the harp was a close second. Gottfried claims that Tristan could play seven instruments; but whenever the story describes him actually performing, he is always playing the harp.

As for the nature of the accompaniment, it is important to bear in mind again that medieval monophony was essentially melodic. Modern ideas about harmony simply did not exist in the twelfth and thirteenth centuries; there was no underlying chordal structure that could be used to accompany a melody. Accompaniment could consist of homophony (in which the instrument plays exactly what the voice sings), organum (in which the instrument plays the same melody a fixed interval above or below the voice), and the drone (in which the instrument plays one sustained note while the voice sings a melody). It is also likely that there were instrumental preludes, interludes, and postludes in which the melody was repeated or varied. Modern recordings, using elaborate instrumental ensembles and harmonic structures, make for excellent performances, but it is highly unlikely that they resemble anything heard by a medieval audience.

Little is known about the music of early *Minnesang*, and much of the information that is readily available to students of medieval literature is either false or is based on conclusions not justified by the evidence. Thus it is important to establish exactly what is known and to limit conclusions to those that can be supported by the manuscripts and common sense. The few songs that survive can be performed today in a satisfactory way, as long as both the performer and the audience understand that complete authenticity in such performance is probably an illusion.

References:

Ursula Aarburg, "Melodien zum frühen deutschen Minnesang: Eine kritische Bestandsaufnahme," *Zeitschrift für deutsches Altertum*, 87, no. 1 (1956): 24–45;

Aarburg, "Probleme um die Melodien des Minnesangs," *Der Deutschunterricht*, 19 (May 1967): 98–118;

Pierre Aubry, *La Rhythmique Musicale des troubadours et des trouvères* (Paris: Champion, 1907; revised edition, Paris: Alcan, 1910);

Jean Beck, *Die modale Interpretation der mittelalterlichen Melodien, besonders der Troubadours und Trouvères* (Strasbourg: LeRoux, 1907);

Siegfried Beyschlag, *Die Lieder Neidharts: Der Textbestand der Pergament-Handschriften und die Melodien* (Darmstadt: Wissenschaftliche Buchgesellschaft, 1975);

Horst Brunner, Ulrich Müller, and Franz Viktor Spechtler, *Walther von der Vogelweide: Die gesamte Überlieferung der Texte und Melodien* (Göppingen: Kümmerle, 1977);

Margot E. Fassler, "Accent, Meter and Rhythm in Medieval Treatises 'De rithmis,' " *Journal of Musicology,* 5 (1987): 164–190;

Ewald Jammers, *Ausgewählte Melodien des Minnesangs: Einführung, Erläuterungen und Übertragung* (Tübingen: Niemeyer, 1963);

Jammers, "Untersuchungen über die Rhythmik und Melodik der Melodien der Jenaer Liederhandschrift," *Zeitschrift für Musikwissenschaft,* 7 (January 1925): 265–304;

Burkhard Kippenburg, *Der Rhythmus im Minnesang. Eine Kritik der literar- und musikhistorischen Forschung mit einer Übersicht über die musikalischen Quellen,* (Munich: C. H. Beck'sche Verlagsbuchhandlung, 1962);

James V. McMahon, *The Music of Early Minnesang* (Columbia, S.C.: Camden House, 1990);

Wolfgang Mohr, "Minnesang als Gesellschaftskunst," *Der Deutschunterricht,* 6, no. 5 (1954): 83–107;

Carl Parrish, *The Notation of Medieval Music* (New York: Norton, 1978);

Arnold Schering, *Auffürungspraxis alter Musik* (Wilhelmshaven: Heinrichs-hofen, 1975);

Ronald Taylor, *The Art of the Minnesinger,* 2 volumes (Cardiff: University of Wales Press, 1968);

Hendrik Van der Werf, *The Chansons of the Troubadours and Trouvères. A Study of the Melodies and Their Relation to the Poems* (Utrecht: A. Oosthoek, 1972);

Van der Werf, "Deklamatorischer Rhythmus in den Chansons der Trouvères," *Die Musikforschung,* 20 (April–June 1967): 122–144.

The Medieval Arthurian Tradition in Its European Context

Will Hasty
University of Florida

Of special importance among the many European literary traditions contributing to the efflorescence of German literature from 1170 to 1280 was the so-called *Matière de Bretagne* (Matter of Britain, tales concerning King Arthur and the knights of the Round Table on which many of the great works of German court literature – such as Hartmann von Aue's *Erec* (circa 1180) and *Iwein* (circa 1203), Wolfram von Eschenbach's *Parzival* (circa 1200–1210), and Gottfried von Straßburg's *Tristan und Isolde* (circa 1210) – were based. Although the tales originated abroad, German literature played its own role in the shaping of a vast international Arthurian tradition that is best considered a collective product of the Western imagination. During the twelfth century Arthur ceased to be an obscure Celtic chieftain promising the future return to greatness of his oppressed people and became the embodiment of the international ideals of chivalry. For example, at the beginning of *Iwein* Arthur is presented as exemplary of chivalrous virtues:

Swer an rehte güete
wendet sîn gemüete,
dem volget saelde und êre.
des gît gewisse lêre
künec Artûs der guote,
der mit rîters muote
nâch lobe kunde strîten.
er hât bî sînen zîten
gelebet alsô schône
daz er der êren krône
dô truoc und noch sîn name treit.[1]

(Fortune and honor follow him,
who turns his mind
to just goodness.
A good example of this is provided
by the good King Arthur,
who often fought for praise
with knightly valor.
In his day he lived
in such a chivalrous fashion

that he wore the crown of honor
and his name still wears it today.)

By the twelfth century, Arthur and the stories surrounding him offered authors such as Hartmann a fertile combination of historical, legendary, mythical, and religious elements.

Arthur appears as a king for the first time in Geoffrey of Monmouth's *Historia regum Britanniae* (History of the British Kings, completed circa 1136). Arthur is presented as a model of authority and power with which medieval potentates could identify. Henry II of England seems to have derived some political benefit from comparisons made between his court and that of Arthur, who at one point subdues all Europe and reigns over a peaceful and magnificent courtly world.[2] Arthur, however, also served as a rallying point for resistance to Henry's rule, which may have led him to search for Arthur's body at Glastonbury, held by many to be the mythical Avalon.[3] Servants such as the *ministeriales*,[4] who hoped to receive from their own rulers the same *milte* (royal generosity) for which Arthur was known and who wished for the same relationship of equal status and mutual respect among subordinates that generally prevailed at the legendary king's court, could also find much in the Arthurian tales that reflected their own concerns.[5]

Besides his social and political associations, Arthur remained connected to an otherworldly, mythical realm to which his adviser and protector Merlin and his fairy sister Morgan le Fay still belonged. The Arthurian tradition rests on a substratum of mythical elements from Ireland, Wales, and Cornwall. The quest for the Holy Grail, for instance, may be related to an older tale recounted in an obscure and fragmentary Welsh poem, "The Spoils of Annwn," in which Arthur and his men raid a Celtic otherworld and steal a magic cauldron that will not cook meat for cowards. The Arthurian

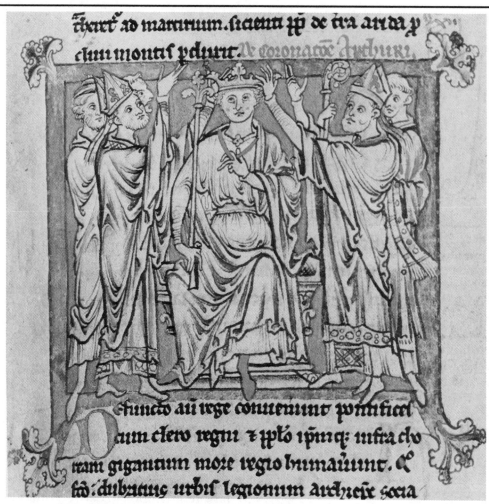

The coronation of Arthur in a miniature drawn circa 1230–1250, probably by Matthew Paris, considered one of the finest medieval English artists (Manchester, Chetham's Library, MS 6712, col. 185)

legend also offered models corresponding to changes in emotional life during the High Middle Ages. The adulterous liaisons of Lancelot and Guinevere and of Tristan and Isolde may have provided an emotional outlet for readers during an age in which relationships between men and women were largely determined by dynastic politics.

Whereas works such as the *Nibelungenlied* (Song of the Nibelungs, circa 1200) can be traced back to the heroic deeds of Germanic warriors and peoples, the tales of Arthur have their historical origin in the Celtic resistance in Britain to the advance of Saxons, Angles, and Jutes in the fifth and sixth centuries, after the Roman government in provincial Britannia had begun to break down. The exact nature of that resistance is unclear, but it is possible that Saxons and Angles were invited into Britain to help Celtic peoples ward off invasions by perennial enemies such as the Picts. Pressure from the Germanic peoples seems to have driven the Brythonic peoples westward, and large numbers migrated across the English Channel to settle in the Armorican peninsula (today Brittany). There are diverse theories about the historical Arthur, all based on the same scant and fragmentary evidence. If a historical Arthur existed at all,[6] he may have been the leader of Welsh resistance to the advance of Germanic peoples around 500. Knowledge of a historical Arthur mainly comes from the *Historia Britonum* (History of the Britons), composed around 829 and attributed to a priest of southern Wales, Nennius. The *Historia Britonum* says that Arthur, who is designated not as king but as *dux bellorum* (commander in chief), fought against Octa, son of the Jute Hengist, and won twelve great victories. There is no scholarly consensus on when and where these battles were fought. Notable in the list of battles is the eighth victory, at Castellum Guinnion. There Arthur bore the image of the Virgin Mary on his

Perceval on his first visit to the Grail castle, an illustration in a North French manuscript, dated 1274, for Chrétien de Troyes's Perceval *(Paris, Bibliothèque Nationale, MS Fr. 342, f. 84ᵛ)*

shoulders (it has been suggested that that depiction has resulted from a mistranslation into Latin of the Welsh word for shield[7]), and, with the help of Jesus Christ and the Virgin Mary, the pagans were put to flight and slaughtered in great numbers, suggesting that Arthur's struggle had become a Crusade-like campaign against the heathen enemy. The final battle, that of Badon Hill, is the only one of the twelve battles that is mentioned in an earlier source. In approximately the fourth decade of the sixth century another priest of southern Wales, Gildas, in his *De excidio Britanniae* (On the Destruction of Britain), mentions the siege of Badon Hill as occurring forty-four years before he wrote, which would mean around 489, but does not mention Arthur.

Scholars have voiced skepticism about the accuracy of the account of Arthur's military career in the *Historia Britonum*. It has been conjectured that its ninth-century author was in need of a hero who seemed to hold forth the promise of future glory for the Welsh, that a certain Arthur celebrated in popular poetry seemed to fill this role perfectly, and that events were manipulated and battles attributed to that Arthur that may have been fought by others.[8] The Nennian Arthur may be based on orally transmitted poetry about Arthur that is now inaccessible. Thus, it is difficult to determine whether the *Historia Britonum* is an accurate depiction of history or a propagandistic employment of popular legend that tells little or nothing about Arthur's historical existence.[9] The *Annales Cambriae* (Annals of Wales, circa 950), an anonymous list of important dates in Welsh history, is another source with historical pre-

tensions. Two brief entries deal with Arthur. The first, which may be based on the *Historia Britonum*, lists the battle of Badon Hill as occurring around 516 and says that "Arthur carried the cross of our Lord Jesus Christ on his shoulders three nights and days, and the Britons were victorious." The second lists the battle of Camlann, around 537, "in which Arthur and Medraut fell, and many died in Britain and Ireland." This entry, which anticipates the great literary depictions of Arthur's tragic end by poets such as Sir Thomas Malory, is based on an unknown source.

With respect to the explosion of Arthurian literature in the High Middle Ages, the most significant document with historical pretensions is the *Historia regum Britanniae*. Geoffrey, who was probably born in the Welsh town of Monmouth, was connected from 1129 to 1151 with events in Oxford, where he was a priest and possibly a teacher (he possessed the title of *magister,* meaning master or teacher), although the university did not yet exist in his day. Geoffrey's signature appears on lists of witnesses with that of Walter, archdeacon of Oxford, from whom Geoffrey says he obtained a "Britannici sermonis librum vetustissimum" (very old book in the British language)[10] with a request to translate it into Latin. The existence of such a book has been a matter of much scholarly debate, with many positing that it is merely an invention of Geoffrey, who in fact based the *Historia regum Britanniae* on the *Historia Britonum*, the *Annales Cambriae*, and medieval Welsh regnal lists and genealogies. It is also fairly certain that Geoffrey employed orally

The procession of the Grail, an illustration in an early-fourteenth-century Parisian manuscript for Chrétien de Troyes's Perceval (Paris, Bibliothèque Nationale, MS Fr. 12557, f. 84ᵛ)

transmitted, popular tales about Arthur and that he mixed diverse historic events and poetic elements in his own design. Whatever Geoffrey's sources may have been, it is difficult to consider his work, which Roger Sherman Loomis has called "one of the world's most brazen and successful frauds,"[11] a historical one. Nevertheless, although its claim to historical accuracy was criticized even in Geoffrey's day, the *Historia regum Britanniae* was for the most part taken as such, thus contributing to the amalgamation of the historic and the fantastic that was typical of Arthur's reception in the twelfth century.

It is in Geoffrey's history that Arthur first appears as the great king of Britain that he is in the French and German romances that began to be written in the latter half of the twelfth century. Describing Britain as "insularum optima" (the best of all islands), Geoffrey relates that British civilization was founded by Brutus, great-grandson of the Trojan Aeneas. Britain, according to Geoffrey, traces its name back to Brutus, who arrived there after many years of wandering and reigned over the island when Eli ruled in Judea and the ark of the covenant was captured by the Philistines (circa 1115–1075 B.C.). The history of Britain subsequent to Brutus is one of warfare, treachery, and degradation interspersed with occasional moments of greatness. The third part of the history contains a description of the arrival of the Romans under Julius Caesar and their victory over the Britons with the assistance of a disaffected British duke. The rise of Christianity

among the Britons coincides with a series of rebellions against Roman overlordship, to which the Romans eventually respond with the construction of Hadrian's Wall from 122 to 128. After the Romans withdraw from Britain, a British king named Maximianus settles with one hundred thousand Britons in Armorica, a conquered section of Gaul, in the fourth century. This event, which seems to record the historic settlement of Brittany by Celtic peoples, brings about a crucial moment in British history. Britain is deprived of its best men and is seemingly defenseless before the onslaught of Picts, Angles, and Saxons.

Britain is ruled at this time by King Constantine, whose three sons, Constans, Aurelius, and Utherpendragon, are too young to succeed him when he dies. A usurper, Vortigern, takes control and forms alliances with the Saxons under Hengist and Horsa. The Saxons, who are invited by Vortigern into England, eventually become too numerous, and Vortigern is forced to take up arms against them and subsequently to flee to Wales. There, on the advice of his magicians, he begins to build a tower that is to be the last bastion against the Saxons. But whenever an attempt is made to lay the foundation, it is swallowed up by the earth. For an explanation of this strange event Vortigern's magicians advise him to seek out a boy without a father, to kill him, and to sprinkle the mortar and stone with his blood. The boy turns out to be Merlin, who in Geoffrey's history is linked for the first

A fourteenth-century ivory casket from Paris, decorated with scenes from two romances by Chrétien de Troyes; from Perceval: *Gawain at the Castle of Marvels overcoming the lion that guards the entrance (first panel) and surviving the test of the perilous bed (third panel) while three girls wait to congratulate him (fourth panel); from* Lancelot: *Lancelot crossing the sword bridge (second panel; New York, Metropolitan Museum)*

time, albeit indirectly, to Arthur.[12] Merlin's magical skills enable him to avoid the bloody end recommended by the magicians, and he explains that in a pool beneath the earth where Vortigern wishes to build his fortress there are two dragons, one red and one white, which engage in a life-or-death battle symbolic of the struggle between Britons and Saxons. When asked for the significance of this battle, Merlin falls into a trance and utters many prophesies concerning the future of Britain, particularly regarding the *aper Cornubiae* (Boar of Cornwall), Arthur, who has yet to be born. The prophesies, the *Prophetia Merlini,* were originally an independent work by Geoffrey that was later incorporated into his history as book 7. One of them indicates Arthur's future popularity, with which the twelfth-century Geoffrey was, of course, familiar: "In ore populorum celebrabitur et actus eius cibus erit narrantibus" (The Boar shall be extolled in the mouths of its peoples, and its deeds will be as meat and drink to those who tell tales).[13]

After deposing the usurper Vortigern, Aurelius becomes king and engages in battles with the ever-present Saxon enemy. He wins victories over Hengist and his son Octa, and after the Saxons beg for mercy and convert to Christianity, he grants them land and allows them to settle in Britain. During the reign of Aurelius, Merlin reappears: with his assistance great stones with a variety of medicinal virtues are taken by force from the Irish and assembled on Salisbury plain as a monument to British

leaders and princes who had been betrayed by the Saxons. (Although Stonehenge was more than a millennium older, Geoffrey seems to have believed, or wished his readers to believe, that it was constructed in the fifth century.) After Aurelius is poisoned by the Saxon Eopa, Utherpendragon becomes king. Utherpendragon also has to fight against the newly rebellious Saxons led by Octa, but he is better known for falling passionately in love with the beautiful Ygerna, the wife of Gorlois, Duke of Cornwall. With Merlin's aid Utherpendragon is made to resemble Gorlois, and in this form he lies with the unsuspecting Ygerna at the castle of Tintagel, where he begets the future King Arthur. At this point Merlin disappears from Geoffrey's history; he does not come into direct contact with Arthur as he does in later versions of Arthur's life.

On the death of Utherpendragon by poisoning, rule over the Britons is assumed by the fifteen-year-old Arthur, whose deeds are clearly the focal point of Geoffrey's history. Arthur's courage, generosity, and goodness are praised in a manner that sets him apart from all previous British kings. Although Arthur is obliged to fight, as his predecessors had, against the Saxons, this perennial struggle assumes under Arthur the unprecedented status of a Crusade: Arthur encourages his followers, who include familiar figures such as Kay, Bedivere, and Gawain, with assurances that those who die fighting for the fatherland will be absolved from their sins; those who died fighting against the infidels in the

Crusades were promised the same reward. After Arthur establishes order by defeating all the traditional enemies of the Britons, a moment of political and social harmony occurs that is like no other in Geoffrey's history: Arthur marries Guinevere, a descendant of a noble Roman family, and adopts a way of life that is quite different from that of his royal predecessors:

> Tunc invitatis quibusque probissimis ex longe positis regnis, coepit (Arturus) familiam suam augmentare tantamque facetiam in domo sua habere, ita ut aemulationem longe manentibus populis ingereret. Unde nobilissimus quisque incitatus nihili pendebat se, nisi sese sive in induendo sive in arma ferendo, ad modum militum Arturi haberet.

> (Arthur then began to increase his personal entourage by inviting very distinguished men from far-distant kingdoms to join it. In this way he developed such a code of courtliness in his household that he inspired peoples living far away to imitate him. The result was that even the man of noblest birth, once he was roused to rivalry, thought nothing at all of himself unless he wore his arms and dressed in the same way as Arthur's knights.)[14]

It is difficult to say whether Geoffrey is describing an Arthurian fashion that had already taken hold of parts of twelfth-century Europe or whether the fashion developed later as a result of Geoffrey's work and its vernacular reworkings, such as the French verse *Roman de Brut* (1155), by Wace. The ideal harmony under Arthur in Britain's otherwise turbulent history seems to be expanded and made the basis of the great romances in French and German that were written later in the twelfth and early thirteenth centuries. The Arthur of Chrétien de Troyes, Hartmann, and Wolfram presides over a similar exemplary courtly order. Omitted from their Arthurian romances is the warfare waged by Arthur – in one battle in Geoffrey's history he single-handedly slays 470 Saxons – which brings about a brief moment of peaceful courtly harmony, as well as the chaos and betrayal that ends it. While authors of verse romances based their works on Geoffrey or his translators, they passed over these negative elements in Arthur's history, which returned in the French *Prose-Lancelot* (circa 1215–1235) and in Malory's *Morte D'Arthur* (1485), and lingered on in passages such as the following, which anticipates the ideal of *Minnedienst* (love service):

> Ad tantum etenim statum dignitatis Brittania tunc reducta erat, quod copia divitiarum, luxu ornamentorum, facetia incolarum, cetera regna excellebat.

> Quicumque enim famosus probitate miles in eadem erat, unius coloris armis atque vestibus utebatur. Facetae etiam mulieres, consimilia vestimenta habentes, nullius amorem habere dignabantur, nisi tertio in militia probatus esset. Efficiebantur ergo castae et meliores et milites pro amore illarum probiores.

> Britain had reached such a standard of sophistication that it excelled all other kingdoms in its general affluence, the richness of its decorations, and the courteous behavior of its inhabitants. Every knight in the country who was in any way famed for his bravery wore livery and arms showing his own distinctive colour; and women of fashion often displayed the same colours. They scorned to give their love to any man who had not proved himself three times in battle. In this way the womenfolk became chaste and more virtuous and for their love the knights were ever more daring.)[15]

The period of harmony comes to an end when Rome demands tribute from Britain, basing its claim on the rule it once held over the island. Arthur sets out to submit Rome to his authority, leaving his land in the hands of Guinevere and his nephew Mordred. He defeats the Roman forces but is prevented from taking Rome by the news that Mordred has placed the crown on his own head and is living adulterously with Guinevere. A series of battles between Arthur and his traitorous nephew culminates in the terrible slaughter at Camblam, in which Mordred is killed and Arthur meets a somewhat ambiguous end after going to Avalon and relinquishing his crown to his cousin Constantine.

Predictably, Arthur's successors are not up to the task of recapturing the greatness of Arthur. As a result of their sinfulness and arrogance, Britain lapses into civil war, and the last of the British kings, Cadwaller, leaves for Armorica with a handful of followers in the latter seventh century, leaving the island to Scots, Picts, and Saxons. It is made clear by the departing monarch that the British have not been defeated by their enemies but by the hand of God, who is punishing the Britons for their evil and folly. The Saxons assume control over Britain, and it is said that they ruled more wisely and kept peace among themselves.

Geoffrey's history and its translations, which were being disseminated throughout twelfth-century Europe, played a role in the rise of Arthurian romance, but it is difficult to posit any direct influences. Geoffrey's history includes elements from popular poetic traditions with which the romance authors may also have been familiar. These poetic traditions may have played their own role, independently of possible influences from Geoffrey and his translators, in the composi-

The Round Table at the feast of Pentecost, an illustration in a late-fourteenth-century North Italian manuscript for Chrétien de Troyes's
Perceval *(Paris, Bibliothèque Nationale, MS Fr. 343, f. 3)*

tion of these romances. The earliest poetic work mentioning Arthur is the *Gododdin,* a Welsh poem that was written in northern Britain around 600. It laments British warriors who fell in battle against the Angles and says that a British warrior named Gwawrddur glutted the black ravens (with the bodies of his enemies), "ceni bei ef arthur" (although he was no Arthur).[16] This indirect reference indicates that Arthur, whatever his historical origins, was early becoming a legendary figure renowned for his fighting prowess. In an appendix to the *Historia Britonum,* the *Mirabilia* (Wonders), there are two references to Arthur. The first refers to a stone that bears the footprint of Arthur's hound Cabal, made while hunting the boar Troit. This hunt is clearly part of the legendary lore about Arthur, for it recurs in "Culhwch and Olwen" in the *Mabinogion,* a collection of Welsh tales compiled by Charlotte Guest in 1849. The second refers to the grave of Arthur's son, Amr, the dimensions of which change each time it is measured. Curiously, Amr was slain by his father. The broader context for this bloody deed, which is difficult to reconcile with Arthur's later de-

velopment, is not mentioned. *The Black Book of Carmarthen,* which was probably composed around 1250 but contains much older material, portrays Arthur as the leader of a group of warriors that include Kay, Bedivere, and other figures who may originally have been Celtic deities, some imported from Ireland: Mabon; Manawidan, son of Llyr; and Luch Llaugnnauc.[17] Similarly, *The Book of Taliesin,* composed in the fourteenth century, includes older material, such as "Spoils of Annwn," an obscure poem that depicts Arthur as the leader of an expedition to Annwn, a kind of Celtic Elysium inhabited by gods and fairies that seems alternatively to be an island in the sea and a subterranean region. A magic cauldron, which may be the predecessor of later testing vessels such as the Holy Grail, is stolen by Arthur at the cost of all but seven of his men. Preserved also are the triads, mnemonic texts probably used by Welsh bards to organize their tales. The triads, in which Arthur is the most prominent figure, mention briefly many familiar figures and events without providing precise information about their relationships. One triad says that Mordred raided

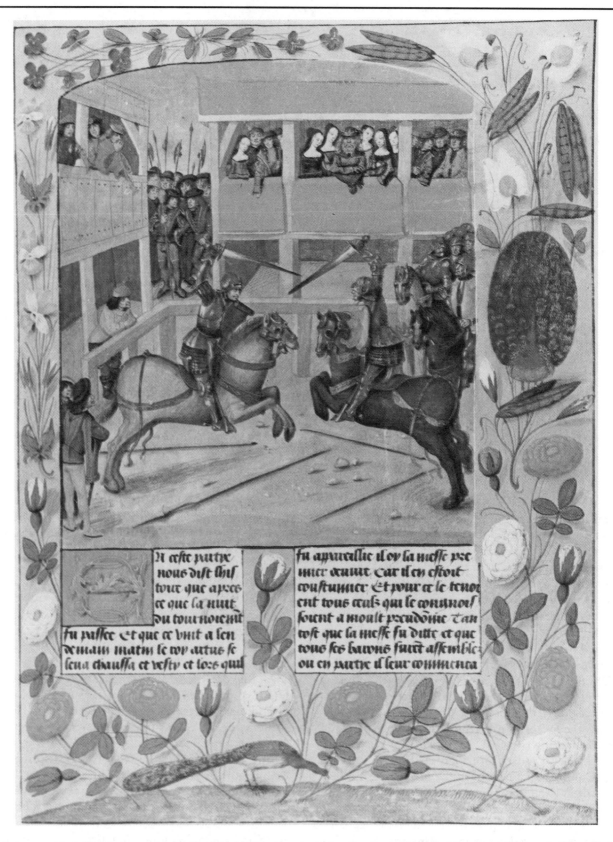

A tournament in Arthur's presence and a damsel arriving in Arthur's court, miniatures in a manuscript for the late romance of Guiron le Courtois, *by Hélie de Barron, written circa 1475–1500 and illuminated by a Flemish artist (Oxford, Bodleian Library, MS Douce 383, f. 16)*

Arthur's court in Cornwall, dragged Guinevere from her chair, and struck her. In another, Drustan (Tristan), son of Tallwch; Essyllt (Isolde); and Merchyon (Marke) are mentioned, although their relationships to one another are unclear. Also mentioned in the triads is Owein (Iwein), son of Urien, who may have been a historical prince in the sixth century who was later absorbed, in a manner similar to Arthur, into Celtic legend. Especially significant are the tales in the *Mabinogion.* Some – "Gereint and Enid"; "Owein, or, The Countess of the Fountain"; and "Peredur" – were written down around the same time as the courtly romances, and it is possible that they were based on the works of Chrétien or on common sources. Others, most notably "Culwch and Olwen," represent an older layer of the Arthurian tradition. In that tale Arthur and his men come to the assistance of the young man Culhwch in his attempt to win the beautiful Olwen, daughter of the giant Ysbaddaden. Motifs observed elsewhere recur in this story, including the hunt for the boar Troit and a magic cauldron that is used to boil the meat for Culhwch's wedding feast. Furthermore, the arrival and reception of Culhwch at the court of Arthur, as Loomis has pointed out, seems to anticipate a similar episode in Chrétien's *Perceval.*[18]

The Arthur of these early poetic documents, and of the vast oral traditions on which they seem to be based, is above all a courageous and mighty warrior, but his morality is questionable: he is by no means the ideal king he is in later romances. Authors of twelfth-century Welsh saints' lives exploit both his greatness and his perceived moral shortcomings by employing him negatively as a foil to the holy figures they portray. In *The Life of Saint Cadoc* (circa 1075) Arthur plays dice on a hilltop with Kay and Bedivere, then attempts to rape a girl who is eloping before he is persuaded to defend the couple from their pursuers. In a quarrel over blood money Arthur insists on cattle of a certain color as payment until he is cured from that obsession by a miracle brought about by Saint Cadoc. In *The Life of Saint Gildas* (circa 1130), by the monk Caradoc, appears an early version of the abduction of Guinevere, a recurring episode in the later romances. The guilty party in this case is Melwas, who violates Arthur's queen and brings her to his castle. After Arthur raises armies and besieges Melwas's castle, the holy Gildas counsels Melwas to return the lady to Arthur and thus brings about a harmonious conclusion. A similar episode is portrayed in a sculpture, likely made before 1120, on the Porta della Pescheria of the Modena cathedral. The sculpture is a striking testimony to Arthur's fame throughout Europe in the early twelfth century.

The development of Arthurian romance by Chrétien, the next major breakthrough in the Arthurian tradition, was not an isolated occurrence but stands in relationship to the broader European fascination with Arthur in the twelfth century. Little is known about the life of Chrétien besides his association with the courts of Champagne and Flanders. The dedication of his *Lancelot* (circa 1172) indicates that this poem was written for Countess Marie de Champagne, the daughter of Louis VII of France and Eleanor of Aquitaine, and *Perceval* was commissioned by Philippe of Alsace, who became count of Flanders in 1190. Chrétien's works, which include a translation of Ovid, indicate that he was well educated, possibly a cleric, with a knowledge of Latin and of rhetoric. Although the chronology is uncertain, his first works probably include *Erec et Enide* and have been dated in the 1160s, while his last work, the unfinished *Perceval,* may have been written around 1190.

One of the great mysteries in the Arthurian tradition is the relationship of Chrétien to his sources. Many other French works dealing with Arthur in the latter twelfth century, such as some of the lays (circa 1160–1170) of Marie de France and the *Merlin* (circa 1200) of Robert de Boron, provide indirect clues. In the composition of her lays Marie apparently employed a procedure similar to that of Chrétien: putting into verse brief stories that had been in prose. Robert's *Merlin* employs elements that were not in Geoffrey's history and did not find their way into the romances of Chrétien or of the German authors but that later appeared with Malory, such as the story of Arthur's revealing himself as king by drawing the sword from the stone and the association of the Holy Grail with the vessel used by Christ at the Last Supper and with the legend of Joseph of Arimathea. Another significant work of Arthurian lore, in which Arthur does not appear, is the *Tristram* (circa 1170) of Thomas of Brittany, which was based on a now-lost Tristan romance in French, the *estoire* (Story, circa 1150), and which in turn was the source for Gottfried's version of the Tristan legend. Other works also testify to the existence of a great variety of stories dealing with Arthur and his knights that were probably disseminated throughout Europe by wandering bards and *conteurs* (storytellers) from Brittany after the Norman invasion of England in 1066. Because of the invasion the Bretons, who were allied with the Normans, would have been in a position to reestablish links to the literary traditions of their Welsh ancestors and to infuse these traditions with a new energy.[19] Thus, Chrétien was apparently able to choose his materials from an Arthurian tradition that included Geoffrey's Latin history, its vernacular translations (the "Bruts," the most important of which was Wace's, in which the Round Table appears for the first time), and a great corpus of tales told by wandering Breton *conteurs*. Where the German authors diverge from Chrétien's version – one thinks particularly of Wolfram's *Parzival* – they are possibly selecting different elements from this tradition, with which they would have been familiar.

It is impossible to determine whether Chrétien based his work closely on longer tales about Arthur that were already in existence and are now lost, or whether he invented Arthurian romance by creating narratives of relatively great length and complexity out of the simpler tales that were available. Whatever the intermediary steps may have been, the Arthurian tradition greatly evolves in Chrétien's works. An integral aspect of Chrétien's elaborate narrative structure is the alternation of perspectives. One perspective is that of the Arthurian court, which is presented for the most part in a condition of ideal social harmony.[20] The other significant perspective is that of a single knight (or, in the case of *Erec et Enide,* a knight and his wife) who rides into unknown regions to undertake a series of adventures or military encounters. The adventures of these individual knights – in fantastic landscapes populated by renegades, giants, dwarfs, dragons, and other adventuring knights – occupy, by virtue of the amount of attention given them, the central position in Chrétien's Arthurian romances.

The interlacing of narrative perspectives is tightly organized in a bipartite structure that is also visible in the "classical" Arthurian romances in Germany by Hartmann and Wolfram. An essay by Hugo Kuhn on *Erec*[21] first drew attention to that narrative structure, which organizes the series of adventures constituting the plot of the Arthurian works into two structural segments, each of which involves the hero's departure from court (generally the court of Arthur), a series of adventures, and finally his return to court. As important as the content of these segments is their relationship to one another. Although in the first segment the hero wins a wife and land along with *êre* (honor) and *prîs* (fame), his achievements are not real and lasting until the second segment has occurred. Kuhn perceives a religious form of thinking[22] in this structure. Despite the hero's best intentions, in the first segment he is involved in *Schuld* (guilt), which is analogous to original sin. The guilt is presumably

not of an individual nature, as it might be understood today, but one that derives from the constitution of human flesh and the unredeemed world. The second segment does not so much respond to the first as transcend it (the analogy being the action of God's grace). The illusory harmony that the hero achieved at the end of the first segment by corresponding to external or formal codes of behavior is made substantial during the second segment. The presence of such a religious form of thinking in Arthurian works is not surprising in a religious age, and it would be inappropriate to mistake the structural analogy for a religious intention on the part of the authors. Instead, the structure is employed as a framework within which social values of various kinds can be presented and discussed. In the case of Erec, for example, the failure in the first segment is generally identified as his intense devotion to a life of love with his wife and the neglect of his other social responsibilities in which this single-minded devotion results. The second segment restores him to court society with a more balanced set of priorities. The invention of this structure may be Chrétien's greatest contribution to the Arthurian tradition: with it he transforms the tradition into a framework in which many of the social values and concerns of his age – those of chivalry and courtliness – could be articulated. The emphasis placed on the adventures of the individual knights – even if always linked to the concerns of court society as a whole – can also be seen in terms of the increasing emphasis on the individual that is visible in other cultural spheres in the High Middle Ages.

The Arthurian works of Hartmann and Wolfram, the most celebrated romance authors in German court literature, are indebted to romances by Chrétien (*Erec et Enide, Ivain,* and *Perceval*), particularly to their structural and thematic innovations. Those German authors, in turn, serve as models for the subsequent development of the romance in Germany. Although it is generally considered the most aesthetically productive development of Arthurian romance, their narrative structures are by no means exclusive. Romances composed around the same time as those of Hartmann (for example, Ulrich von Zatzikhoven's *Lanzelet,* circa 1194–1203) and many of the romances of the thirteenth century (perhaps most notably Heinrich von dem Türlîn's *Diu Crône* [The Crown], circa 1230) manifest other structural characteristics. Those romances have been appraised negatively by scholars who see them as diverging from the superior model set by Chrétien, although increasingly there is an attempt to evaluate them on their own literary merits.

Tristan fighting Palamedes in a tournament and Tristan and Iseult embarking for England, illuminations by Everard d'Espingues in a 1479–1480 manuscript for Tristan *(Chantilly, Musée Condé, MS 315–317, f. 59 and f. 234)*

The static ideality of King Arthur, and the generally harmonious balance of his court's concerns and interests with those of the individual knights as achieved in the Arthurian romances of Chrétien, Hartmann, and Wolfram, may have corresponded to a political and social situation that was of short duration. Whatever its connections to extraliterary reality, the harmonious stasis of the classical model was only temporarily satisfactory, judging by subsequent literary developments. It seems that authors and audiences in the thirteenth century once again began to view Arthur not just as the ideal embodiment of chivalry and courtliness but as a historical figure of dubious origins, wed to an unfaithful queen and destined to die in a tragic battle against his own nephew while the peaceful order over which he once presided lies in shambles. The poetry of the verse romances gradually gave way to prose. The French *Prose-Lancelot,* or Vulgate cycle, a vast work by unknown authors, portrays the entire career of Arthur, focusing on episodes – such as Guinevere's adulterous relationship with Lancelot,

and Mordred's betrayal – that shed a different light on King Arthur and his knights and provide them with shades and nuances they had not previously possessed. The *Prose-Lancelot* brings together for the first time what became, with inevitable changes in the individual elements, the authoritative version of the story of King Arthur that eventually was a major source for Malory's *Le Morte D'Arthur.*

The legend of Arthur has continued through the centuries to be employed by diverse peoples and groups to express their values and aspirations. The Arthurian legend has fared best among the English poets, such as Ben Jonson, Edmund Spenser, and Alfred Tennyson, although it has also provided material for writers such as the German Dorothea Schlegel in her "Geschichte des Zauberers Merlin" (Story of the Magician Merlin, in *Sammlung romantischer Dichtungen des Mittelalters* [Collection of Romantic Writings of the Middle Ages], 1804).[23] The *Tristan und Isolde* (1859) and *Parsifal* (1877) of Richard Wagner suggest that the Arthurian tradition played a role – albeit a limited one in comparison to the more purely Germanic *Der Ring des Nibelungen* (Ring of the Nibelungs, 1863) – in nineteenth-century Germany's cultural quest for a national identity. Wagner's *Parsifal,* in particular, marked the beginning of the prevalence of this knight's spiritual-mystical quest in later German reworkings of the Arthurian tradition, such as Tankred Dorst's drama *Merlin oder Das wüste Land* (Merlin; or, the Wasted Land, 1981). The dominance of Parsifal in Germany subsequent to Wagner has been such that one observes an "Artus-Rezeption ohne Artus" (a reception of Arthur without Arthur).[24] These and myriad other examples suggest that the Arthurian legend has continued through the centuries to provide an archetypal model for the expression of the best and worst aspects of Western culture.

NOTES

1. Hartmann von Aue, *Iwein,* edited by G. F. Benecke and Karl Lachmann; seventh edition, revised by Ludwig Wolff (Berlin: De Gruyter, 1968).

2. In his *Historia Anglorum* Matthew Paris states that the times of Arthur seem to have come again in the greatness of the English king's court. Cf. Robert Huntington Fletcher, *Arthurian Material in Chronicles* (New York: Haskell, 1965), p. 186.

3. After Henry's death in the early 1190s, the claim was made that the bodies of Arthur and Guinevere had been found at Glastonbury with a cross inscribed: "Here lies the famous king Arthur, buried in the isle of Avalon."

4. The *ministeriales* were an unfree class of servants fulfilling a variety of different functions, some important, at the larger courts. That class was in the process of solidifying a position in the lower echelons of the feudal nobility.

5. Cf. Gert Kaiser, *Textauslegung und gesellschaftliche Selbstdeutung: Aspekte einer sozialgeschichtlichen Interpretation von Hartmanns Artusepen* (Frankfurt am Main: Athenaeum, 1973).

6. Earlier in this century many scholars felt that Arthur was probably a mythical being with little or no basis in historical fact. Cf. Roger Sherman Loomis, *The Development of Arthurian Romance* (London: Hutchinson, 1963), p. 16.

7. Cf. Loomis, p. 17.

8. Richard Barber, *King Arthur: Hero and Legend* (New York: St. Martin's Press, 1986), p. 8.

9. Cf. the recent essay by Thomas Charles-Edwards, "The Arthur of History," in *The Arthur of the Welsh,* edited by Rachel Bromwich (Cardiff: University of Wales Press, 1991), p. 28: "One cannot help suspecting that the account of Arthur's battles has in part been moulded by the concerns of the seventh and eighth centuries, in England as well as in Wales."

10. *History,* p. 22. Subsequent Latin citations are from this text.

11. Loomis, p. 35.

12. The legend of Merlin, or Myrddin, had once been an independent tradition. Cf. A. O. H. Jarman, "The Merlin Legend and the Welsh Tradition of Prophecy," in *The Arthur of the Welsh,* pp. 117–145.

13. Geoffrey's text is cited from *Historia regum Britanniae,* edited by Jacob Hammer (Cambridge, Mass.: Medieval Academy of America, 1951), p. 124. The English translation is taken from *The History of the Kings of Britain,* translated by Lewis Thorpe (Baltimore: Penguin, 1966), p. 172.

14. Hammer, p. 158; Thorpe, p. 222.

15. Hammer, p. 164; Thorpe, p. 229.

16. The Welsh is cited from Charles-Edwards's article, p. 15.

17. Cf. Loomis, pp. 19–20.

18. Loomis, p. 27.

19. Cf. Loomis, pp. 32–43. Cf. also the more recent essay by Rachel Bromwich, "First Transmission to England and France," in her *The Arthur of the Welsh,* pp. 273–298.

20. This is a moot point among scholars, some of whom feel that the ideality is supposed to be recognized as suspect or fake, while others posit that it is to be taken seriously, even if it is dependent on the adventures of the individual knights.

21. Hugo Kuhn, "Erec," in *Dichtung und Welt im Mittelalter* (Stuttgart: Metzler, 1959).

22. Kuhn calls it a "Denkstruktur."

23. See Barber (pp. 140–200) for a discussion of modern reworkings of the Arthurian tradition.

24. U. Müller, "Artus-Rezeption ohne König Artus: Zur deutschen Artus-Rezeption unter dem Einfluß von Richard Wagner," in *Moderne Artus-Rezeption: 18.–20. Jahrhundert,* edited by Kurt Gamerschlag (Göppingen: Kümmerle, 1991), p. 160.

Wolfram von Eschenbach's *Parzival,* Prologue
Manuscript Facsimiles

No presentation of the literature of the high medieval period would be complete without providing a sampling of that literature in its original form. Unlike the literature that arose after the invention of movable type, the epics, poems, and romances of the early and high medieval periods were preserved in manuscripts, first predominantly of parchment, then increasingly of paper from the fourteenth century on. The manuscripts were copied by professional scribes with varying degrees of ornamentation, and, over time, variations, sometimes significant ones, arose in the texts. It has been the difficult task of philologists of the nineteenth and twentieth centuries to determine which versions are most likely to be authentic – that is, to represent most accurately the wording of the original version of the work. This task involves tracing the family tree of a manuscript, trying to determine "family relationships" between them, and determining in which tradition a particular manuscript stands.

The following pages provide (in chronological order, to the extent this can be determined) sample leaves from the sixteen extant manuscripts that provide Wolfram von Eschenbach's *Parzival* in its entirety. All other *Parzival* manuscripts are fragments. The sample text is that of the prologue. Of interest in the illustrations are several points: the different levels of care (and skill) with which they were transcribed, the varying states of preservation of the leaves, and the gradual changes occurring over time in the scribal hand. The last sample, though it will not be obvious, is not a manuscript but an early printed version with an initial executed by hand.

At the end of this section is an English translation, from standard Middle High German editions, by Helen M. Mustard and Charles E. Passage (*Parzival* [New York: Vintage, 1961]).

The manuscripts are reproduced from Uta Ulzen, ed., *Wolfram von Eschenbach "Parzival": Abbildungen und Transkriptionen zur gesamten handschriftlichen Überlieferung des Prologs* (Göppingen: Kümmerle, 1974).

Parzival, *Prologue Ms. D (Saint Gall, Stiftsbibliothek, Nr. 857, f.5ᵃ–6ᵇ)*

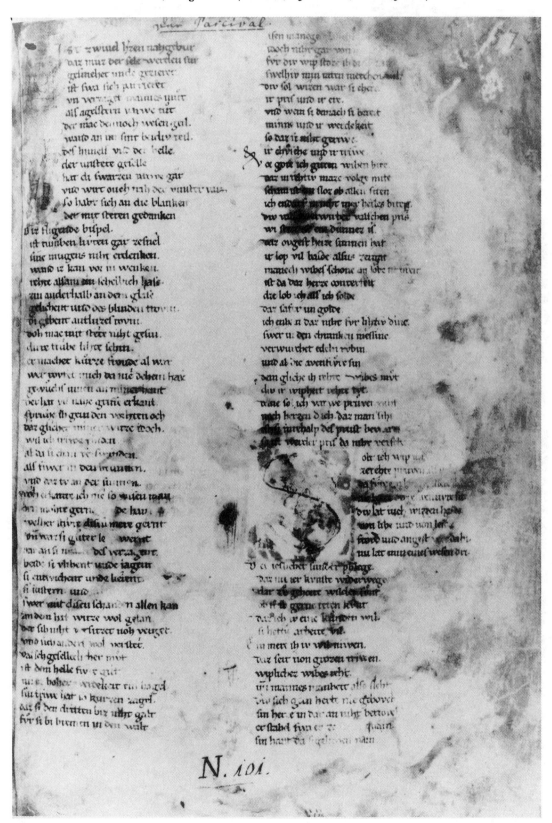

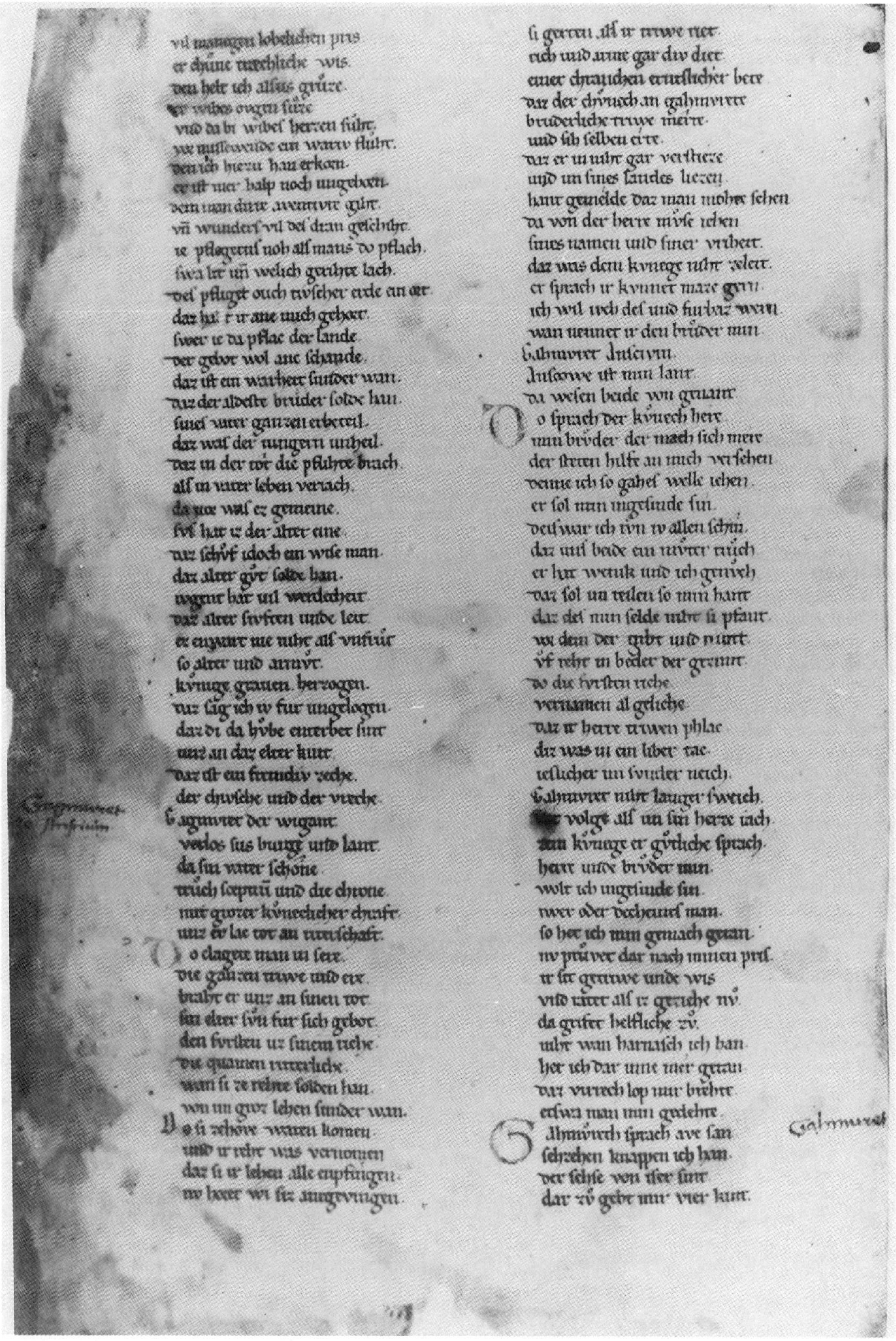

Parzival, Prologue Ms. G (Munich, Bayerische Staatsbibliothek, cgm 19, f.1r)

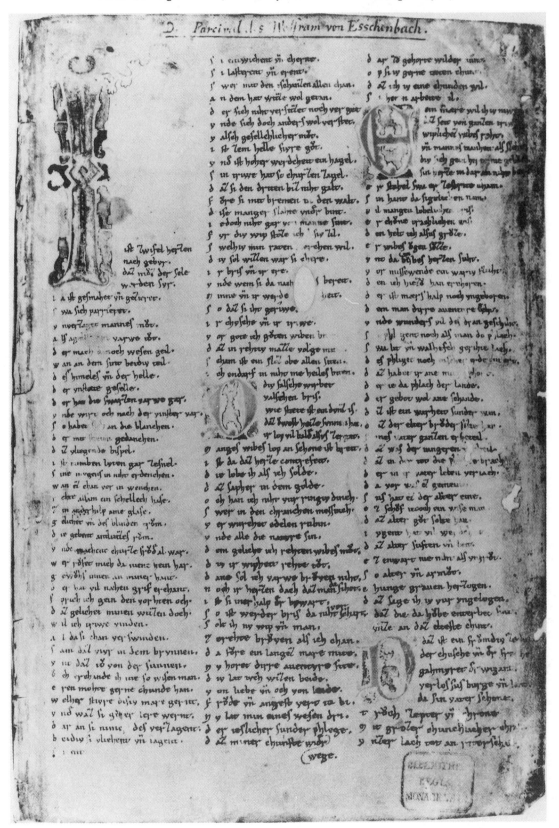

Ms. G^k (Munich, Bayerische Staatsbibliothek, cgm 18, f.1r–1v)

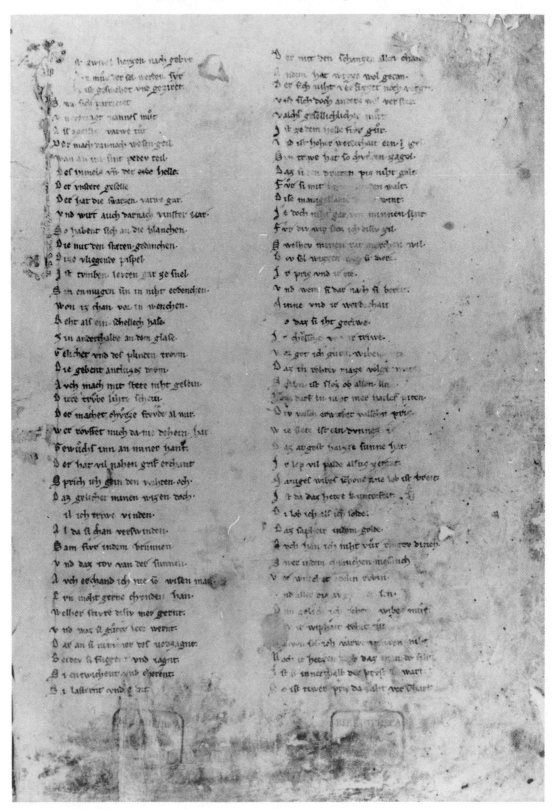

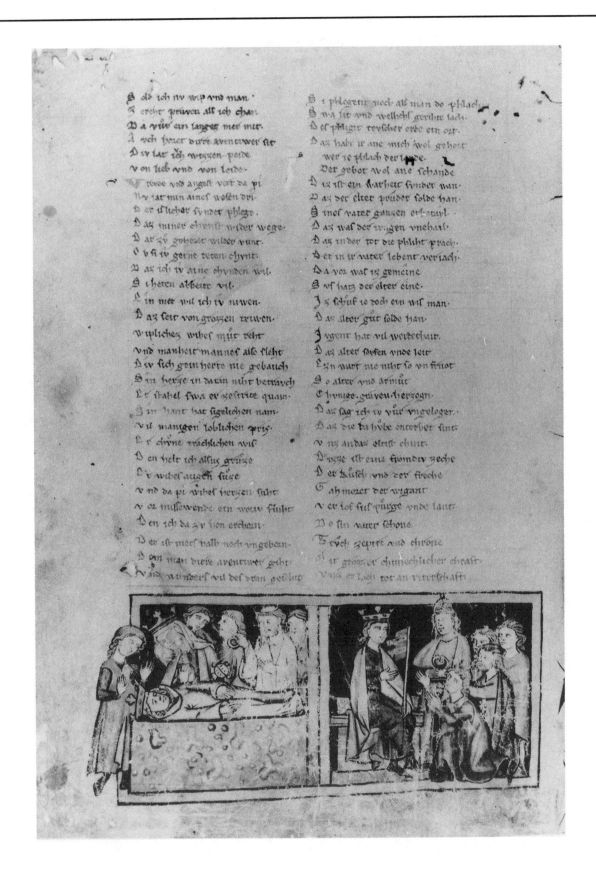

G^{r} (Zurich, Zentralbibliothek, Ms. Car C 182, Fragment f. 1r)

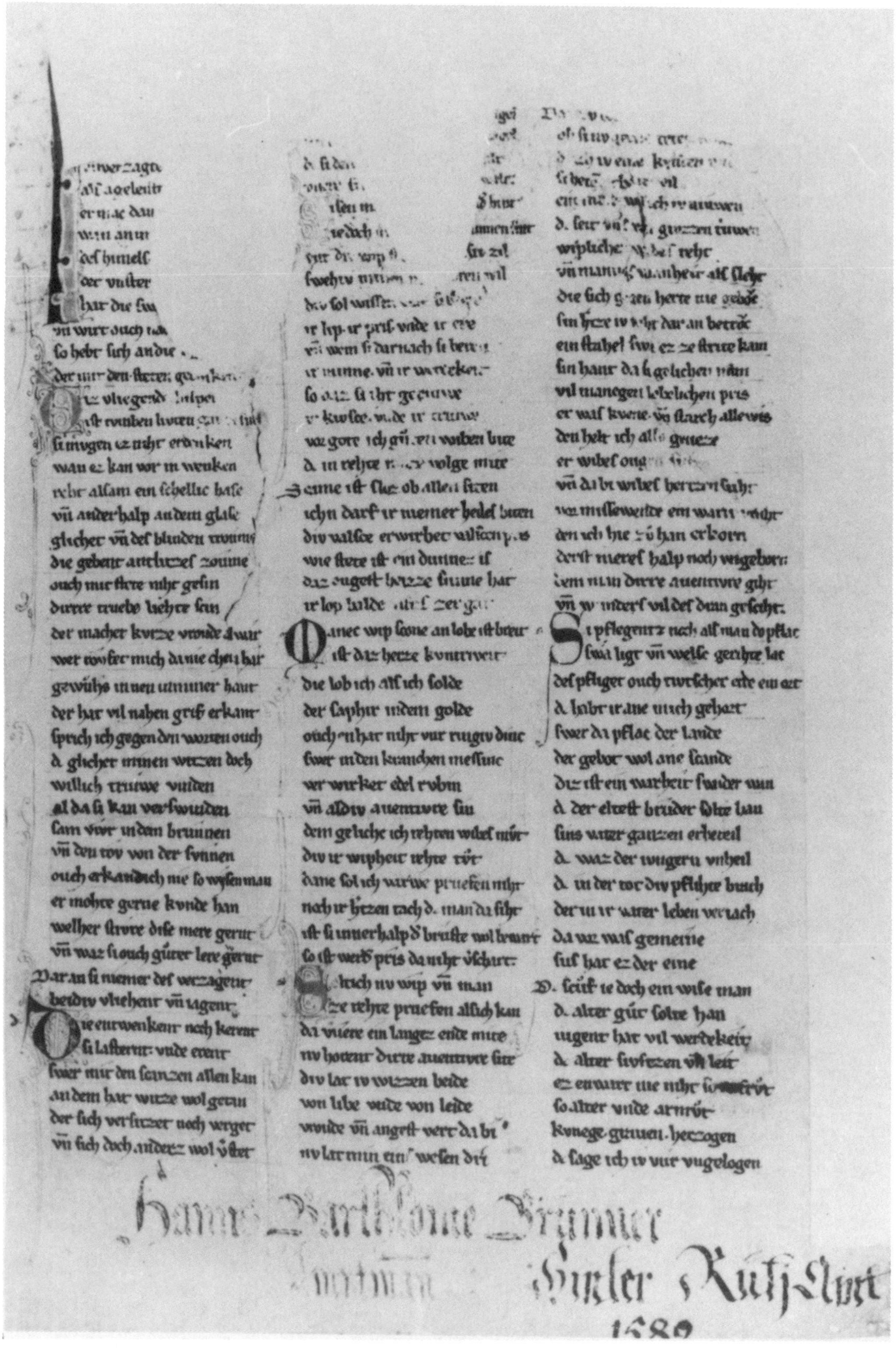

Gⁿ (Vienna, Österreichische Nationalbibliothek, Cod. 2708, f.1r–1v)

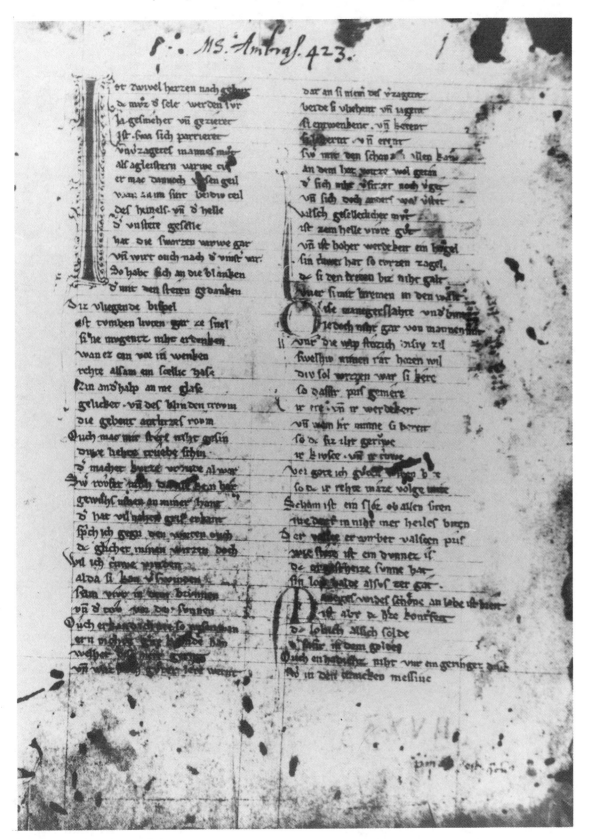

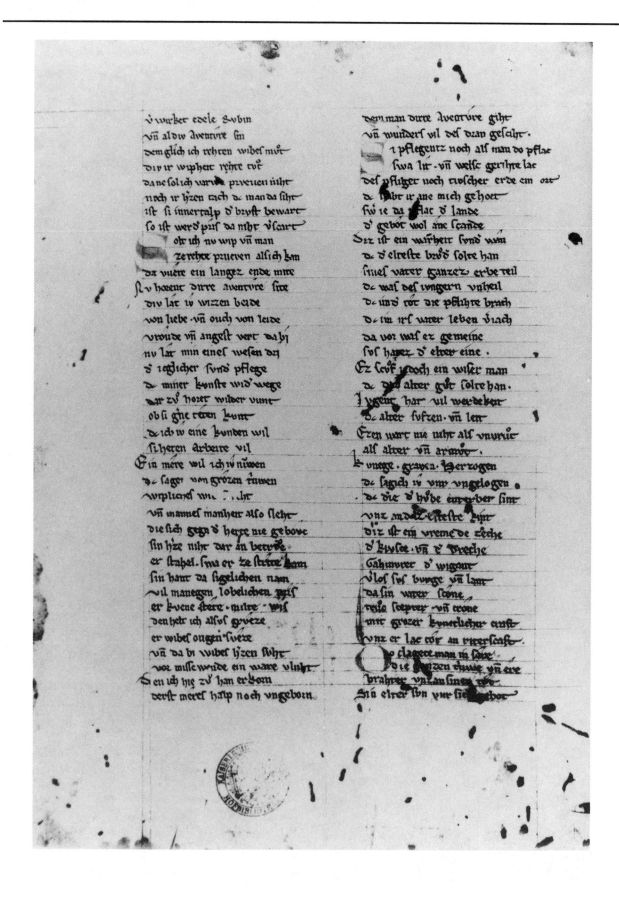

G^μ (Vienna, Österreichische Nationalbibliothek, Cod. 2775, f.1r–1v)

den ich hie zu han erkorn
der ist meres halp noch vngelost
den man dirre auenture git
vn vunders vil des dan geschit
Sie plegedes noch als ma
do plac . wa hie vnd
welihs gerihte lac .
des plegere noch dutscher
erde ein cu .

Daz hat ane mich gehort
wer ie do plac der lande
Da gelwt wol ane schande
vn ist ein warher kunt wa
daz der edeliste bud soler han
sines vater ganz erbeteil
Daz was der iungern vnheil
Daz in der tot plihte brach
Der in ir vater leben vsach
Da vor was ez gemeine
sus here der alter eine .
Er schuf iedoch ein wiser ma
Daz dn alter gut solte han .
Jugent hat vil wirdekeit .
Daz alter suften vnd leit
En wart nie nie als vnwut .
Als alter vnd armut .
kunegx grauen herzogen
Daz sag ich iu vor vngelogn
Daz die der hulen enterbet sint
vns an der eldeste kint
Daz ist ein vreinede zeche
Der 　　　 vnd der vreche
Gahmureth der wigant
verlos sus burge vn lant
Da sin vater schone .
Drug scepter vn crone
mit grozer kuncheit euah
vns er lac tot an ritterschaft

Do clagete man in sere .
Die ganze truwe vn ere
Smachter vns an sinen tot
din eler sin vur sich gebot .
Den wursten vz sime riche
Die komen ritterlichen
wan sie zu rehte solden han
ven im grove lehen sunt wa
Do sie zu hove waren kome
vn ir reht was vernome
vn do sie irlehin enpfhinge
hoer wie sie ez ane vinge
sie geben als ir truwe riet
Riche vnd arme gar die diet
Einer ersunken ernstlichen rede
Daz des kunig an gahmurete
Bruderliche truwe merte
vn sich selber ere .
Daz er in nit gar versherze
vn in sines landes liere schi
han gemahel daz maumohe
Da von d hie mochte lehen
sines name vn siner vriheit
Daz was d kiunige nit zu leit
Er sprach ir kunnet maze gern
Jch wil in des vn vurlaz wern
Man nenne dem bruder min
Gahmurt anscheutin
An schowin ist min lant
Da wesen beide von genant
Do sprach d kiunig here
Jch sol min bruder mere
Der stete helfe an mir vselhin
Dannoch so gehens wille uehi
Er sol min ingesinde sin .
Des was ich dun in alle schi
Daz vns leide ein mutter drug
Er har wene vn ich gnune

Daz sol im deilen so mi han
daz deo min selde ir si pane
vor dem der gir vn nimer
vf reht in beiden d gezimen
Do die vursten riche
vernanie alle geliche
Daz ir hie truwen plac
Daz was in ein vil beß bac
iegelich in lesunder nac
Gahmurte nit langer swete
Der volge als im sin hie rach
Zu ein kiunge er guclichie sprach
herre vn bruder min .
wolde ich ingesinde sin .
wer oder deheines ma
So hoe ich min gemach gedan
Dar nach puiver min pris
Jr sit getruwe vn wis .
Nu ratet als ez geriche nu
Da grisento helfichin zu
Siv wan hernach ich han
Hoe ich dar inne mer getan
Dar verlo lob mir vrethe
ethyo man min gedehte
Gahmurt sprach ab san
Sie nehin knappen ich
han selle die von ysern siue .
Dar zu gelo mir viere kint
An guder zuch vo hoh art
vor den wir nimer nie gespart
Des ir leidhin mac min hant
Jch wil heirn in din lant
Jch han ein dal auch e geварn
Ob mich geluke wil lewarn
So erwerbe ich gut wip grot
ob ich in dar nach diene mir
vn ob ich des wirdic bin
So radet mir min best sin .

G^δ (Donaueschingen, Fürstl. Fürstenberg. Hofbibliothek, Ms. Nr. 97, f.1r–1v)

Ist zwuuel herzen nachgebur
daz mus der selen werden sur
ja gesmehet vñ gezieret
Ist swa sich parrieret
Vnverzaget mannes mut
als agelaster varwe tut
Der mag dannoch wesen geil
wand an ime sint beide teil
Des himels vñ der helle
Der vnstere geselle
hat die swarze varwe gar
vñ wurt och nach der vinstere var
So habet sich an die blanken
Die mit den steten gedanken
Dů fliegende bispel
Ist dumben litten gar ze snel
Sü enmugent es niut erdenken
wan es kan wor in wenken
Echt alsam ein schellig hase
Zim anderthalben am glase
Flichet vñ des blinden tröm
Die gebent antlitzes röm
Och mag niut stete niht gesin
Durre trube liehte schyn
Der machet kurze fröude al war
Swer rofet mich do nie kein har
Gewuhs mman an miner hant
Der het vil nohen grif erkant
Spich ich gege den forhten noch
Daz glichet mmer wiezen iedoch
Wi bich wil truwe vinden
Ida sü kan verswinden
Sam fiur in dem brunnen
vñ der tô vð der sunnen
Och erkant ich nie so wisen man
er enmöhte gne kunde han
welicher stiure dise mere gerint
vñ war sü och giter lere wunt
Dar an sü niemer des vragent
beide sü fluchent vñ iagent
Sü ent wenkent vñ kerent
Sü lesterent vñ erent
Swr mit den schanczen allen kan
An deme hat wize wol geran
Der sich niut vsiget noch vset
Vñ sich doch anders wol vster
Falsch geselleclicher mut
Ist zer hellefiure gut
Vñ ist hoher wirdikeyt ein hagel
Sin truwe het so kurzen zagel

Daz sü den dritten biez niut galt
Fuir sü mit bremen in den walt
Dise maniger slahte vnderbint
Jedoch niut gar von mannen sint
Fur die wip stoize ich dise zil
wele minen rat hoizen wil
Die sol wissen war sü kere
Iren pris vñ ire ere
Vñ weine sü do nach si bereit
Ire minne·irre werdikeit
So daz sü iht geruwe
Ir kusche vñ ir truwe
Vor gotte ich gůten wiben bitte
Daz in rehte moize volge mitte
Schame ist ein schlos ob allen sitten
Sen darf in niut me heiles bitten
Dů falsche·erwirbet falschen pris
Wie stete ist ein dvinn es is
Daz in öisteste heisse sunne hat
Ir lop vil balde also zergat
Si amiges wibes schöne an lobe ist breit
Ist do daz herze guntrafeit
Die lobe ich als ich solde
Das saphir in deme golde
Ich enhan daz niut für lihte ding
Swer in den kranken messing
Vir wurket edelen rubin
Vñ alle die auentiure sin
Dem gliche ich rehte wibes mut
Die ir wipheit rehte tut
Do hnsol ich varwe priuuen niht
Noch irs hzie rach·daz man siht
Ist sü innerhalb der brust bewart
So ist ir wider pris do niht vschart
Solte ich wip·vñ man
Prüfen·als ich zerehte kan
Do fürte ich ein langes mere mitte
Nv horzent dirre auentiur sitte
Die lat uch wissen beide
Vo liebe·vñ och von leide
Fröude vñ angest fert do bi
Nv lant min eines wesen dri
Der ieglicher sunder pflege
Daz immer kunste wider wege
Dar zů hoizte wilder funt
Ob sü uch gerne tetent kunt
Daz ich uch eine kunden wil
Sü hettent alle erbette vil
Eine mere wil ich iuch nuwen
Daz seit von grossen truwen

w ibes wipliches reht
v n manes manheit alse sleht
D ie sich gegen herte me gebog
S in lize in dar an nie betrog
E r was stahel swo er ze strite kam
S in hant vil sigelichen nam
V il manigen lobelichen pris
E r kvne stere milte wis
D en helt ich alsus gruoze
E r was wibes ogen suoze
V n do bi wibes herzen suht
V or missewende eine ware fruht
D en ich darzuo han erkorn
D er ist merels halb noch vngeborn
D em man dirre auentiure giht
V n wunders vil des dran geschiht

S v pflegent es noch als mans do pflag
S wo lit vn welsch gerihte lag
D es pfliget tiutsch erde noch ein ort
D az hant ir one mich gehort
S w ie do pflag der lande
D er gebot wol one schande
D az ist ein worheit sunder won
D az der elter bruoder solte hon
S ines vater ganzes erbeteil
D az was der iungen vnheil
D az inder tot die pflihte brach
D es in ir vater lebende iach
D o vor was es gemeine
S us hat es der elte eine
E s geschuf iedoch ein wiser man
D az daz alter guot solte han
I vgent hat vil werdekeit
A lter sufzen vnde leit
E s enwart nie nvt so vnfruit
S o alter ist vn armuot
K vnige · frauen herzogen
D az sage ich iuch vur vngelogen
D az die der huoben enterber sint
V nz an daz elteste kint
D az ist eine fromede zeche
D er kiusche vn der freche
G amuret der wigant
V erlos sus burge vn lant
D o sin vater schone
T ruog zepter vn crone
M it grozer kvniclicher craft
V nz er tot lag an ritterschaft
D o clagete man in sere
D ie ganzen truwe vn ere

B raht er vnze an sinen tot
S in elter svn fur sich gebot
D en fursten in sime riche
D ie koment ritterliche
W ande sy zerehte solten han
V on im gros lehen svnd wan
D o sv zehove woren komen
V n ir reht was svnomen
D az sy alle ire lehen enpfiengen
N v horent wie svs ane viengen
S v gerten alse ir trve riet
R ich vn arm gar div diet
E iner crauclicher steter bette
D az der kvnig an Gamurette
B ruderliche truwe merte
V n sich selben erte
D az er in niht gar vsliesse
V n ine sines landes liesse
H ant gemahel daz man mohte sehen
D o w der lsre mohtæchen
S ines namen vn siner friheit
D az was deme kunige niht zeleit
E r sprach ir kvnnet ze moze gern
I ch wil iuch des vn furbas wern
W an nemet ir den bruoder min
G amuret anschefin
A nschowe ist min lant
D o sint wir beide von genant
S us sprach der kvnig herre
S im bruoder sol sich mere
D er steten helfe an mir vsehen
D an ich so guhes welle iehen
E r sol min ingesinde sin
D es swar ich tun iuch allen schin
D az vns beide ein muot truog
E r hat wenig · vn ich gnuog
D az sol ine teilen so min hant
D az des min selde iht si pfant
V orde der sit vn nimet
V f reht in beider daz gezimmer
D o die fursten riche
V ernomet al geliche
D az ir herre truwen pflag
D az was in ein vil lieber tag
I eglicher ime bisvnd neig
G amuret niht lang hveig
D er volge als im sin herze iach
Z v deme kunige er gutliche sprach
B re vn bruder min
w olte ich ingesinde sin

G^{x} (Heidelberg, Universitätsbibliothek, cpg 364, f.1r–1v)

Parcifall vnd Lanngen

st zwifel hertzen nach gebvr
Daz muz der sele werden svr
Gesmelzet vnd geʒieret
Swo sich parrieret
Vnverzagtes mannes mvt
Als agelaster varwe tvt
Der mac dannoch wesen geil
Wan an im sint beide teil
Des himels vnd der helle
Der vnstete geselle
Der hat die swartzen varwe gar
Vnd wirt ovch nach der vinster var
So habt sich an die blanken
Swit steten gedanken
Daz fligenden bispel
Ist tvmmen levten gar zv snel
Sie enmugent ins niht erdenken
Wan ez kan vor in wenken
Reht alsam ein schellich hase
Zin anderhalp Anime glase
Gelich vnd des blinden trovm
Die gebent antslutzes rovm
Doch mac mit stete niht gesin
Dirre trvbe liehter schin
Der machet kurtze frevde al war
Wer rovft mich da nie kein har
Gewuhs innen an miner hant
Der hat vil nahen griffe erkant
Sprich ich gein den vorhten och
Daz gelichet minen witzen doch
Wil ich treive vinden
Alda sie kan verswinden
Sam fevr in dem brunnen
Vnd daz towe vor der sunnen
Ovch erkant ich nie so wisen man
Er mohte gern kunde han
Welher stevr dise mere gernt
Vnd waz sie gvter lere wernt
Dar an sie nimmer des verzagent
Beide sie fliehent vnd sie iagent
Sie entwichent vnd kerent
Sie lasternt vnd erent
Der mit den schantzen allen kan
An dem hat witze wol getan
Der sich niht ver sitzet noch verget
Vnd sich anders wol ver stet
Valsch gesellichier mvt
Ist zv dem helle fevr gvt
Vnd ist hoher werdikeit ein hagel
Sin treive hat so kurtzen zagel
Daz sie den dritten biz niht kalt
Fvr sie mit prennen inden walt
Dise maniger slaht vnder bint
Iedoch niht gar von mannen sint
Fvr die wip stozz ich dise zil
Swelhe minen rat merken wil

Die sol wizzen war sie kere
Ir pris vnd ir ere
Vnd wem sie dar nach si bereit
Anne vnd ir werdikeit
So daz sie iht gerewe
Ir kevsche vnd ir treve
Vor got ich gvten wiben bit
Daz in rehte mazze volge mit
Scham ist ein sloz ob allen siten
Ich endarf in niht mer heils biten
Die valschen werbent valschen pris
Wie stete vnd wie trvwez is
Der owest hertze sumen hat
Ir lop vil balde alsus zvr gar
Aniges wibes schone an lobe ist breit
Ist daz des hertzen gunderfeit
Die loben ich solte
Daz saphir in golte
Ich han daz niht fur wehe dinc
Swer in den cranken messinc
Fvr wurket den edlen rubin
Vnd al die aventevr sin
Dem glich ich rehten wibes mut
Die ir wipheit reht tvt
Da sol ich farwe prvfen niht
Sch ir hertzen dach daz man da siht
Ist sie innerhalp der brvst bewart
So ist werder pris da niht verschart
Wold ich nu wip vnd man
Zv rehte prvfen als ich kan
Da fvr ein langez mere mvt
Sv hort dirre aventevre sit
Die let vch wizzen beide
Von liebe vnd von leide
Frevde vnd angest vert da bi
Sv lat min eins wesen dri
Der ieglicher sunter pflege
Daz miner kunste wider wege
Daz zv gehort wilder kunt
Ob ev gerne teten kunt
Daz ich ein kunden wil
Sie heten arbeite vil
Ein mere wil ich ev newen
Daz sagt von grozzen trewen
Wipliches wibes reht
Vnd mannes manheit also sleht
Die sich gein herte nie gebove
Sin hertze in dar an niht betrove
Er stahel swar er zv strite qvam
Sin hant dar sigeliehen nam
Vil manigen lobelichen pris
Er kvne tregeliehen wis
Den helt ich alsus grvzze
Er wibes ovgen svzze
Vnd da bi wibes hertzen svht
Vor missewende ein ware flvht

q, fragment Ir (Freiburg, Universitäts-Bibliothek, Fragm.-Hs. Nr. 530)

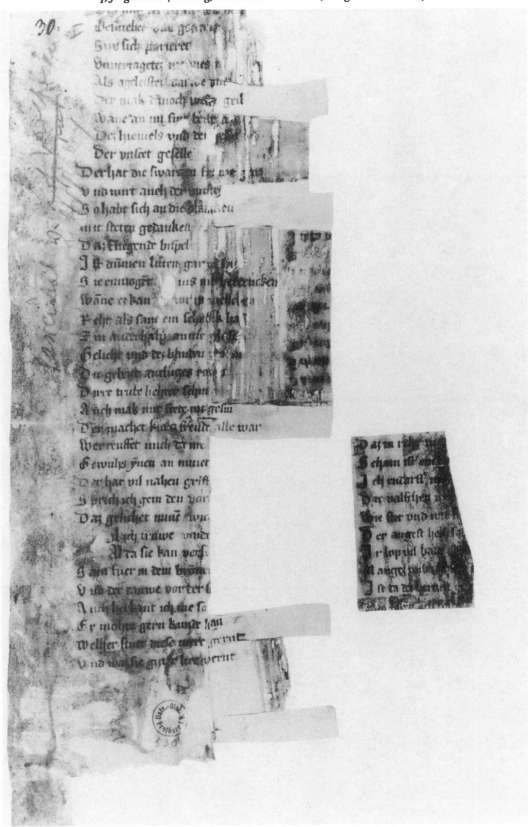

q, fragment IIv (Freiburg, Universitäts-Bibliothek, Fragm.-Hs. Nr. 530)

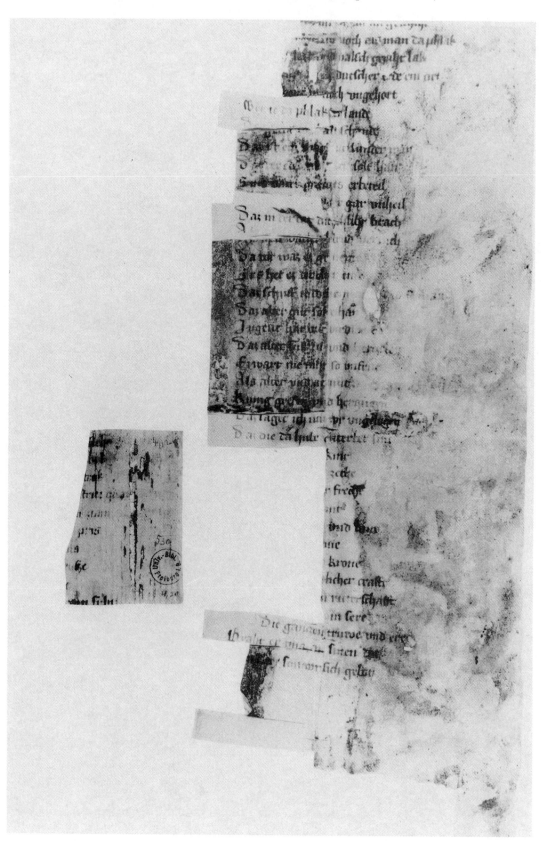

G° (Hamburg, Staats- und Universitätsbibliothek, Cod. germ. 6, f.8ᵃ–9ᵇ)

8.

hie hebet an das buch von Gahmuret der was parzi[...]

Ist zwivel hertzen nachgebur
Das muß der sele werden swer
Ja ist gesmahet vnd gezieret
Swa sich parrieret
Man saget mannes mut verzagten
Als agelster varwe tut
Der mag dannoch wesen geil
Wan an im sint beide teil
Des himels vnd der helle
Der vnstate geselle
Der hat die swartzen varwe gar
Vnd wirt och nach der vinster var
So hat sich an die blanchen
Der mit steten gedanchen
Dis vliegende byspel
Ist tumben luten gar zu snel
Sie mugen es niht erdenchen
Wan ez kan vor in wenchen
Rechte als schellich hase
Schin anderhalp an dem glase
Gelichet sich des blinden troum
Die gebent antlutzes roum
Doch mag nut stæte niht gesin
Dvrre trübe lychte schin
Er machet kurtze freude alwar
Wer ruffet mich da niemen sehen kan
Geswulst ynnerhalp an mannes lip
Der vil valschen grieff erkant
Sprich ich gegen den worte och
Das gelichet mynen witze och
Wil ich truwe vinden
Da sie kan verswinden
Dan fiur in dem brunnen

Vnd der tov von der sunnen
Ouch erkunde ich me so wise man
Er mohte gerne kunde han
Welicher stiure dise mere gerut
Vnd was sie guter mere weren
Dar an sie niemer des verzagen
Beide sie vliehent vnd iagent
Sie entwichent vnde kerent
Sie lesterent vnde erent
Der mit allen schantzen kan
An dem hat wunde wol getan
Der sich versitzet noch verget
Vnd sich anders des wol verstet
Valsch gesellecliche mut
Ist zu dem helle fure gut
Vnd ist hoher werdicheit ein hagel
Sin truwe hat so kurtzen zagel
Das sie den dritten biz niht galt
Fure sie mit roemen in den walt
Dise manger slahte vnderbint
Iedoch niht gar von warte sint
Fur die wip stosse ich dise zil
Welche minen rede merken wil
Die wisse war sie kere
Ir pris vnd ir ere
Vnd wem sie sy dar nach bereit
Minne vnd ir wirdikeit
So das sie ist gerüwe
Gekusche vnd in truwe
Vor got ich gutte wiben bitte
Das in rehte maße volget mitte
Scham ist ein sloß ob allen sitte
Ich darff in niht mere heiles bitte
Die valsche winbet valschen pris
Wie stette ist ein dunnes ys

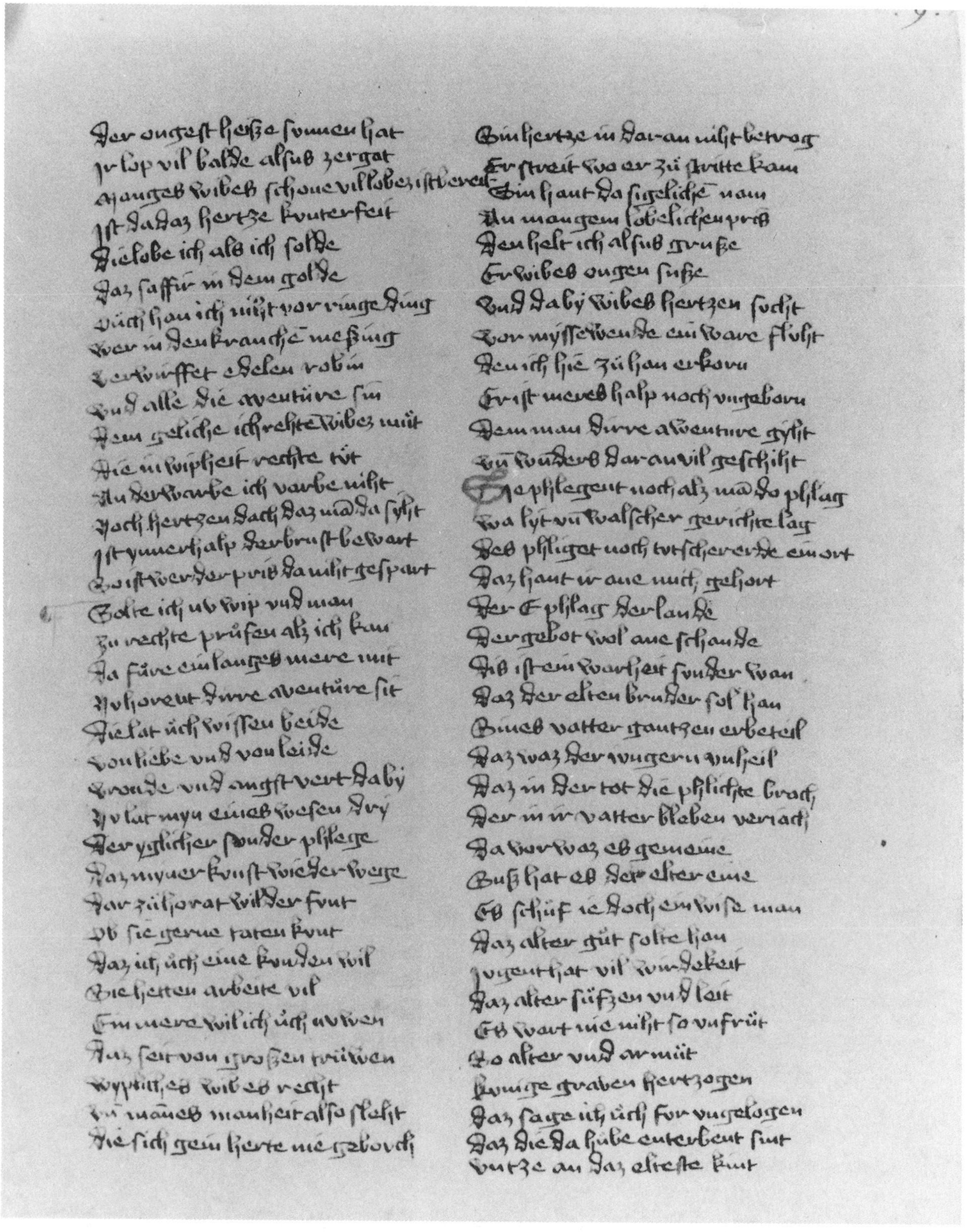

*G*ᵗ *(Donaueschingen, Fürstl. Fürstenberg. Hofbibliothek, Ms. Nr. 70, f.1ᵃ–2ᵇ)*

Ist da das hertze kunterfeyt
Die lobe als ich solde
Den affter in dem golde / durch
Ich en han das nicht verlichte
Wer in den krancken mässneck
fur wircker edeln tuben
Vnd alle die abentewre sein
Tem gleich ich rechte weibes müt
Die ir weypheit recht thut
Da en sol ich sarben preise nicht
Noch ich hertzen trag das ma do sicht
Ist sie inwendig der prust bewart
So ist werd preyss do nicht österhart
Solt ich und weyp vnd ma
Tzu rechte preisen als ich kan
Do fure ein langes mere mite
Nu horet diese abentewre sitte
Die lat euch wissen perde
Von lieb vnd von leyde
Not vnd angst sere do bey
Nu lot in eines wesen drey
Der pglicher sind pflege
Das nimmer kunste wid wege
Dor tzu gehorte wilder funt
ob sie euch gerne tett kunt
Das ich euch eine kunde wol
Ire keten erbeyte wol
Ein mer wil ich euch newe
Das sagt vo grossen treuen
Weypliches weybes recht
Vnd manes maheit also schlegt
Die sie geherte nye gebore
Sein hertze der an nicht trach
Er schel sich er tzu in quam
Sein haut da sich elwachd nam
Vil manchen loblichd preyss
Er kune treglichen weyss

Den kelt ich alsus grusse
Er weybes augen süsse
Vnd do bey weibes hertzen sucht
Vor mistrende ein ware feucht
Den ich sie han tzu erkoren
Der ist meres halb noch ungeboren
Dem ma diese abentewre gicht
Vnd wunders vil das dan geschicht

Nu sin gamuret vater me
Ire pflege noch als ma pflag
So ligt vnd welches ge
rechte lag
Das pflegt auch der erde ein ort
Das ir habt one nich gehort
Wer do pflagt der lande
Der gehort wol ane schande
Diss ist ein warheit sund wan
Das der elste bruder solde han
Seines vater gantzen erb teyl
Das was der iungern unheyl
Das in der tod die pflichte brach
Der in irs vater lebn verrach
Do vor was es gemeine
Sunst hies der elterin eine
Das schuff doch ey weyset ma
Das alter gute solte han
Iugent hot vil vonrikeit
Das alter sufftzen vnd leys
Des tzu wart me nicht so vnfeut
Als alter vnd armut
Konige grossen vnd hertzogen
Das sag ich euch fur ungelogen
Das die da ande enterbent seind
Vnd an das elteste kint
Das ist ein fremde zecke
Der kreusch vnd der frecke
Gamuret der weygant

G^v (Schwerin, Wissenschaftliche Allgemeinbibliothek des Bezirkes Schwerin, ohne Signatur, f.69r–69v)

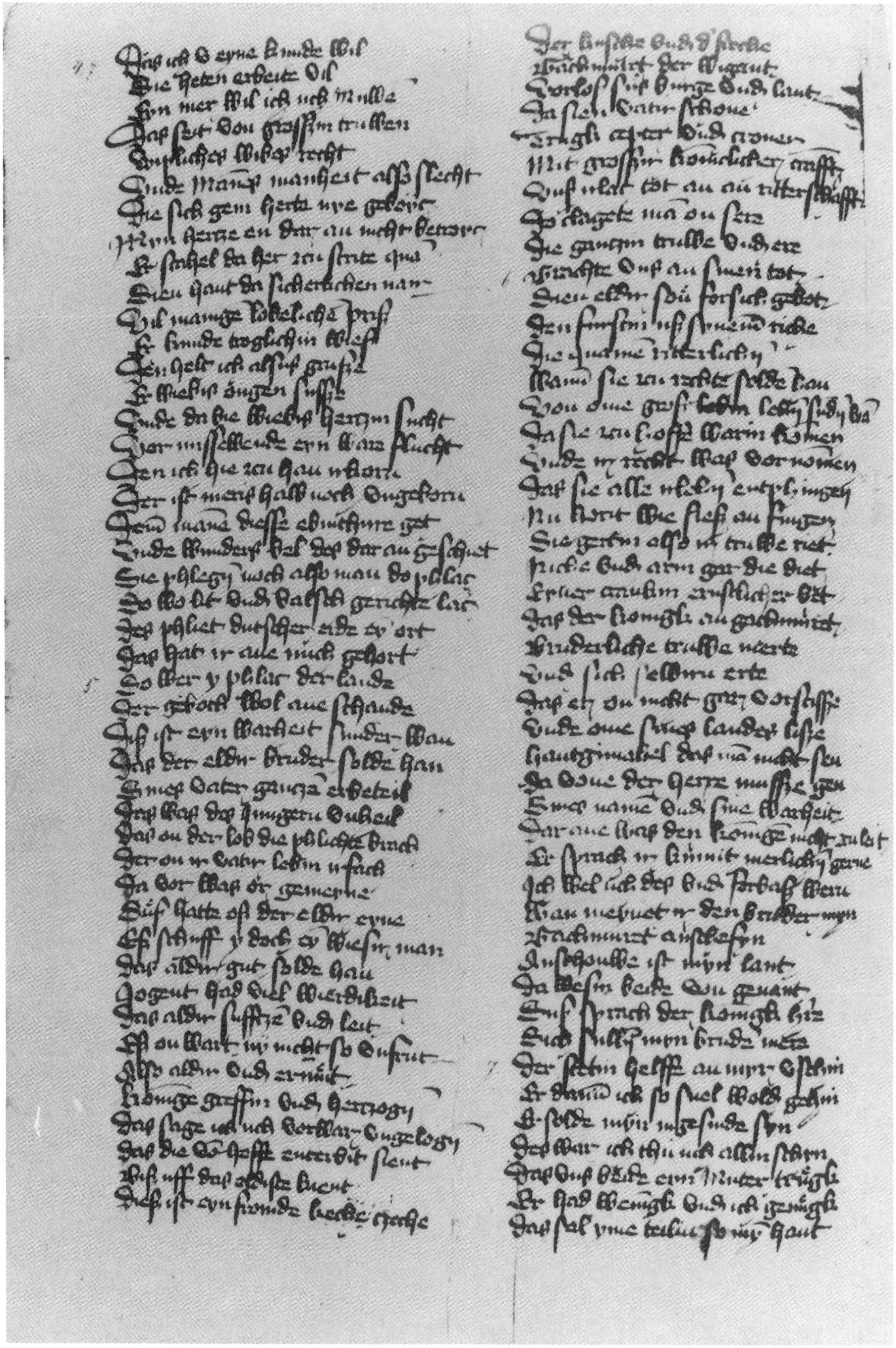

m (Vienna, Österreichische Nationalbibliothek, Cod. 2914, f.1r–3r)

Also fure in der burmen
vnd der ton von der siunen
Doch erkant ich nie so wysen man
Er mochte gerne kunde han
welcher tōre die freuden gerent
vnd was sye guter lere werent
Dar an sy myoner vzageit
seide sye fliechend vnd jagend
Sye verwichnt vnd karent
Sye lasterent vond erent
wer mit disen schantzen allen kan
An dem hat witze wol getan
Der sich mit dirre vnd verstatt
vnd sich anders wol vergat
valsch gesellecklicher mut
Ist zu der helle fure gut
vnd ist hoher wirdikeit ein hagel
vntruwe hett so kurtzen zagel
Das sye den druten biß mit galt
sure sye mit brenen in den walt
Dye mannicher slachte conderbint
Doch mit gar von manen sind
sur die wis stosse ich dise zil
walse hye myn ratten mercken wil

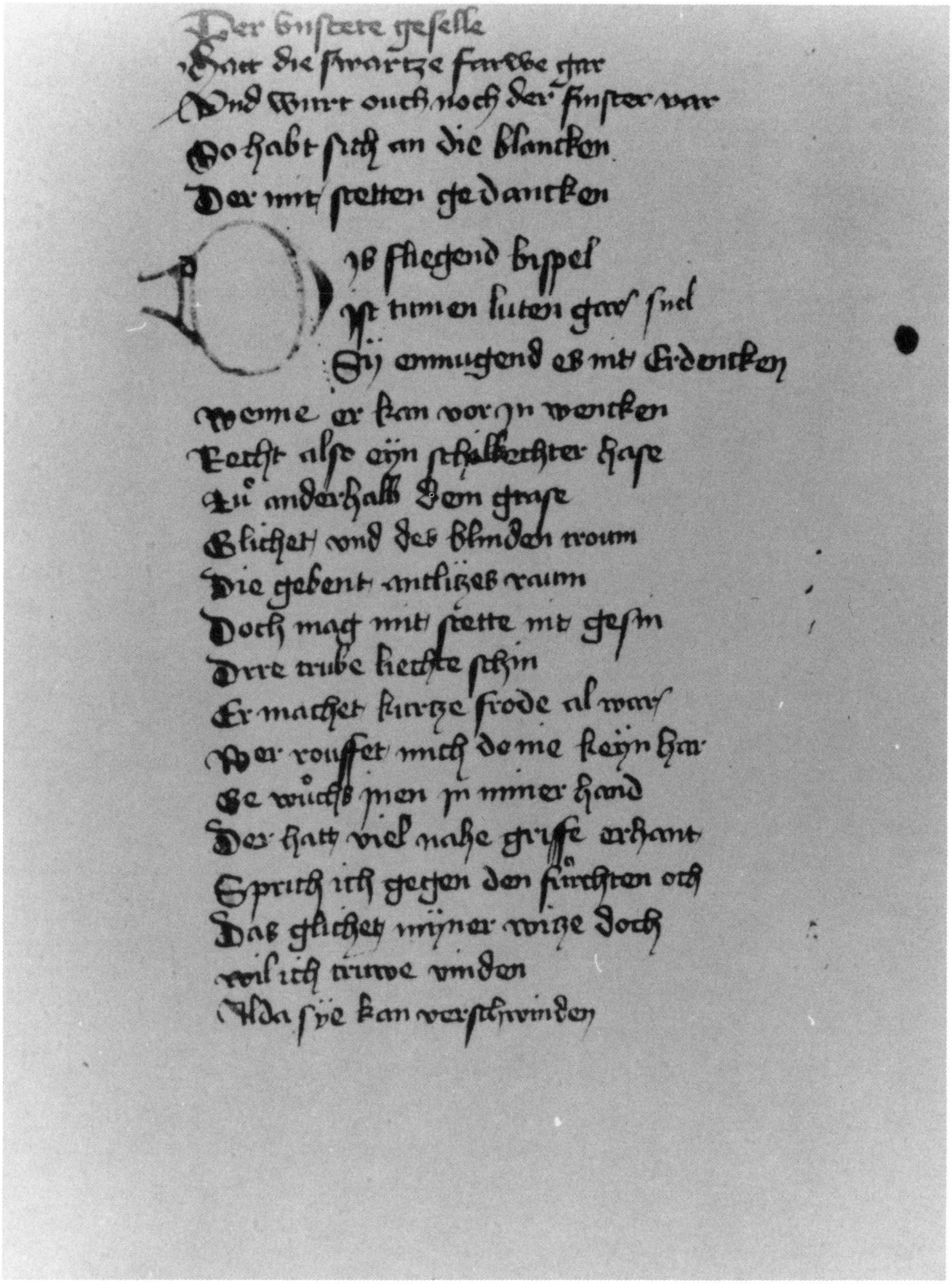

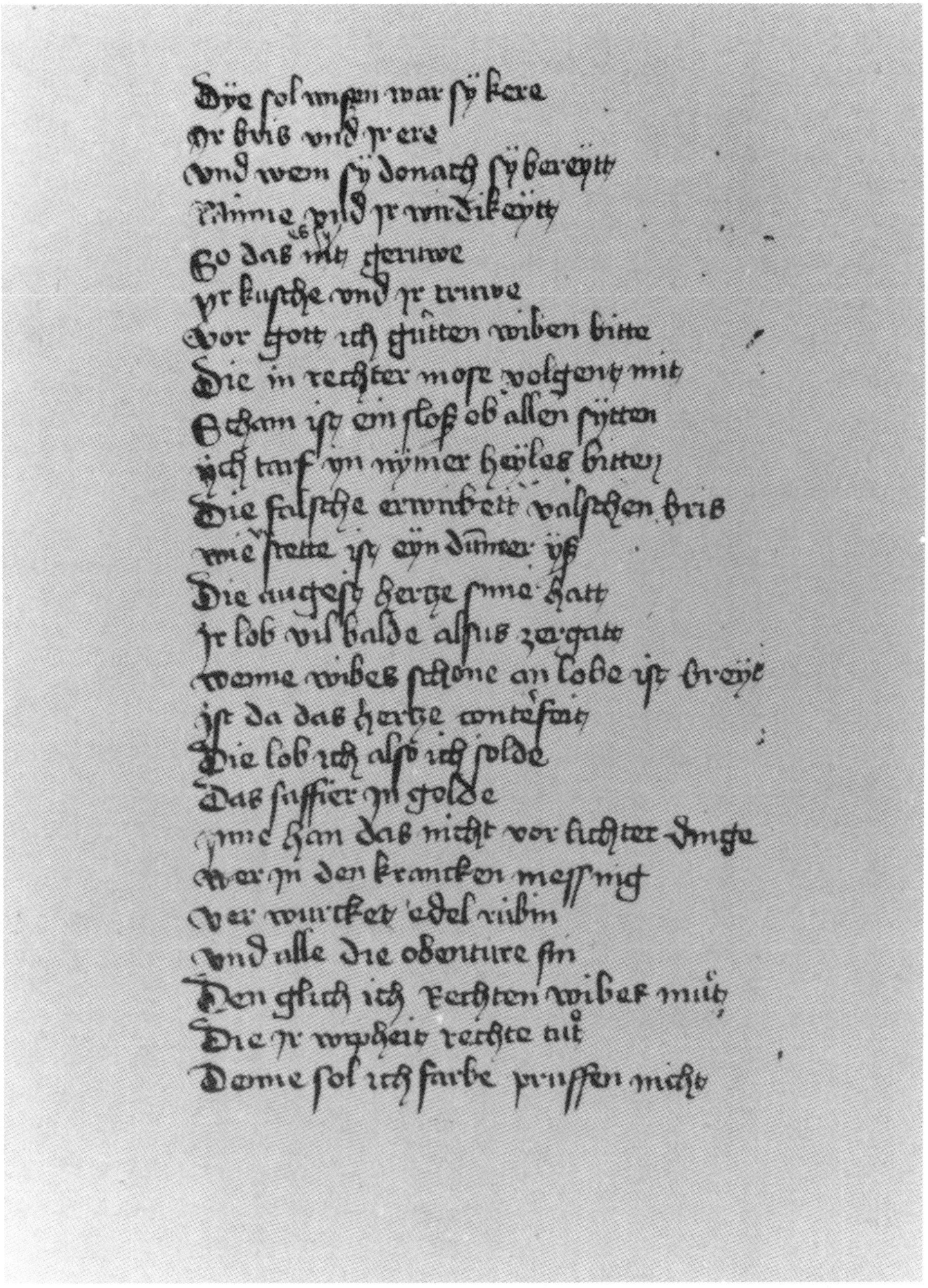

Dye sol man war sy kere
yr bris vnd yr ere
vnd wen sy donach sy bereytt
Rimme vnd yr vindikeytt
So das mit geruwe
yr kusche vnd yr truwe
vor gott ich gutten wiben bitte
Die in rechter mose volgent mit
Ocham iff ein floß ob allen yitten
ich tarf yn nymer heyles bitten
Die falsche erwirbett valschen bris
wie stette yst ein dunnen yß
Die auch sy hertze ynne hatt
yr lob vil balde alsus zergatt
wanne wibes schone an lobe yst breyt
yst da das hertze contrefait
Die lob ich also ich solde
Das saffier yn golde
yne han das nicht vor lichter smige
wer yn den krancken mess nit
ver wurcket edel rubin
vnd alle die oventure syn
Den glich ich rechten wibes muht
Die yr wipheit rechte tut
Dome sol ich farbe prissen nicht

Noch ires hertzen rach do man da sicht
ist sinnenthalb der bruste bewart
So ist worden pris do mit verswart
Jn mere ich hye wil hurwen
Das seyt von grossen truwen
wiplicher wibes recht · schlecht
vnd mannes manheit also slepht
Die sy gegen hertz nie gebock
Ein hertz jn dar an nie betrog
Er stahel wo er zu strite kam
Eine hand do gehelichen nam
eyn rechten loblichen pris
Der küne trachslicher wis
Den helt ich alsus grüsse
Der wibes ougen süsse
vnd do by wibes hertzen sucht
vor missewende ay varibe flucht
Den ich hare han zu erkenen
Er ist meiner half noch vngeborn
Den man dare auenture gicht
vnd wonders viel das dar angesicht

Je pflegend es noch es als man
do pflag
wo luthend welych gerichte lagt
Das pflegend ouch nützher er de eyn ort

n (Heidelberg, Universitätsbibliothek, cpg 339, f.6r–8v)

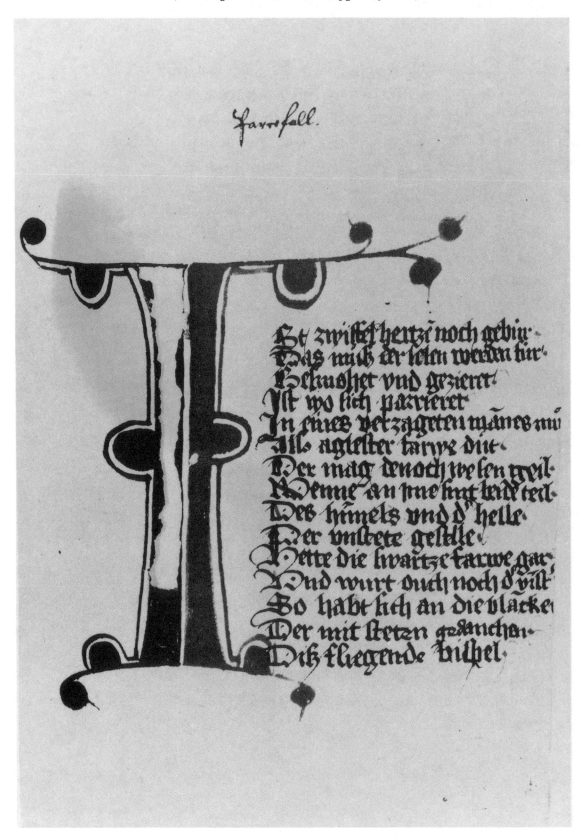

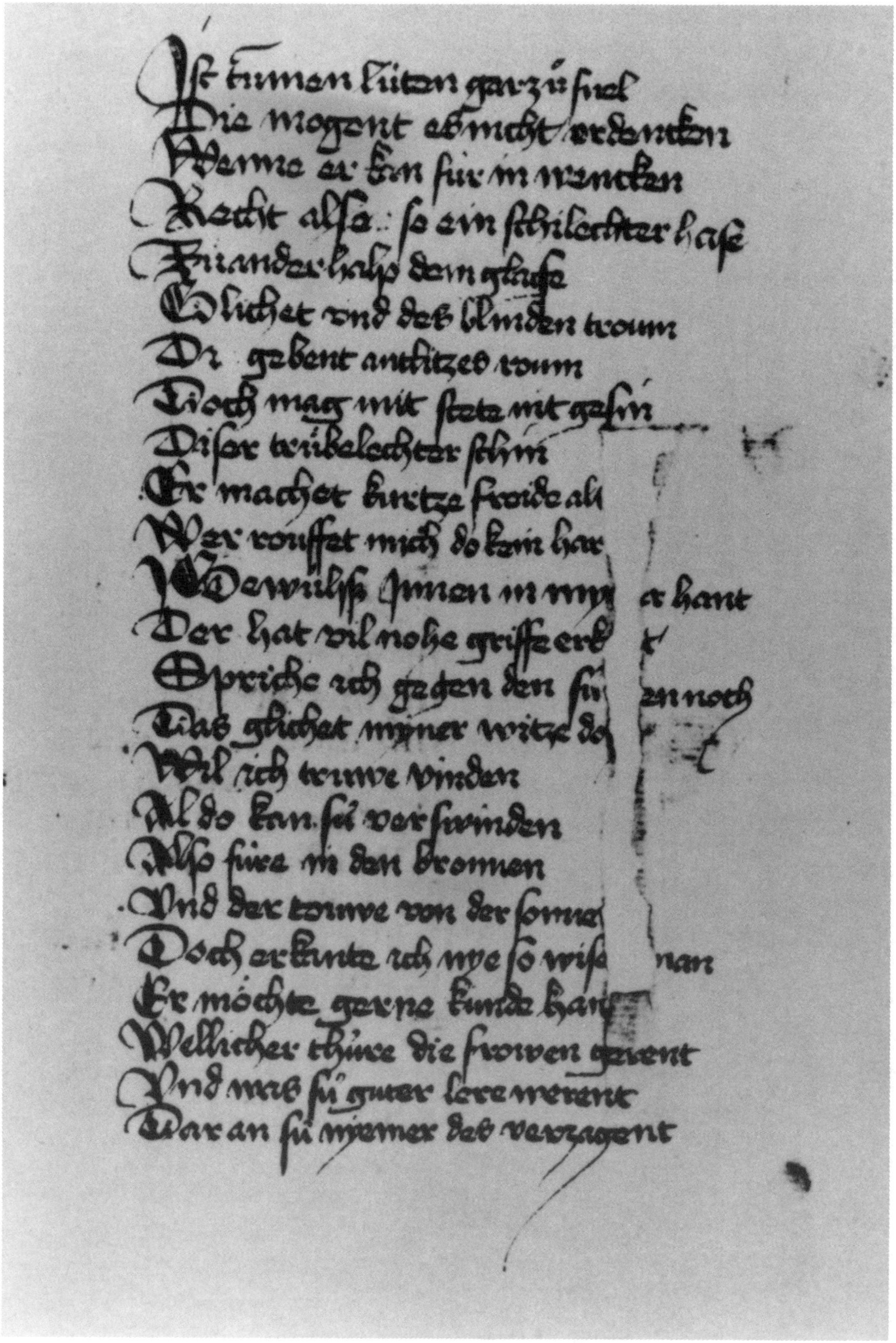
Ist tumen lüten gar zü snel
Die mogent es nicht erdenken
Wenne er kan für in wencken
Rehte alse so ein schilechter hase
Zin anderhalp dem glase
Glichet und des blinden troum
Die gebent antlitzes roum
Doch mag mit stete nit gesin
Diser trübelechter schim
Er machet kurtze froide al
Wer rouffet mich do kein har
Gewuchs innen in myn er hant
Der hat vil nohe griffe erk t
Spriche ich gegen den s en noch
Das glichet myner witze do
Wil ich truwe vinden
Al do kan sei verswinden
Also füre in den bronnen
Und der touwe von der sonne
Doch erkante ich nye so wise man
Er möchte gerne künde han
Wellicher stiure die frowen gerent
Und was si guter lere werent
War an si niemer des verzagent

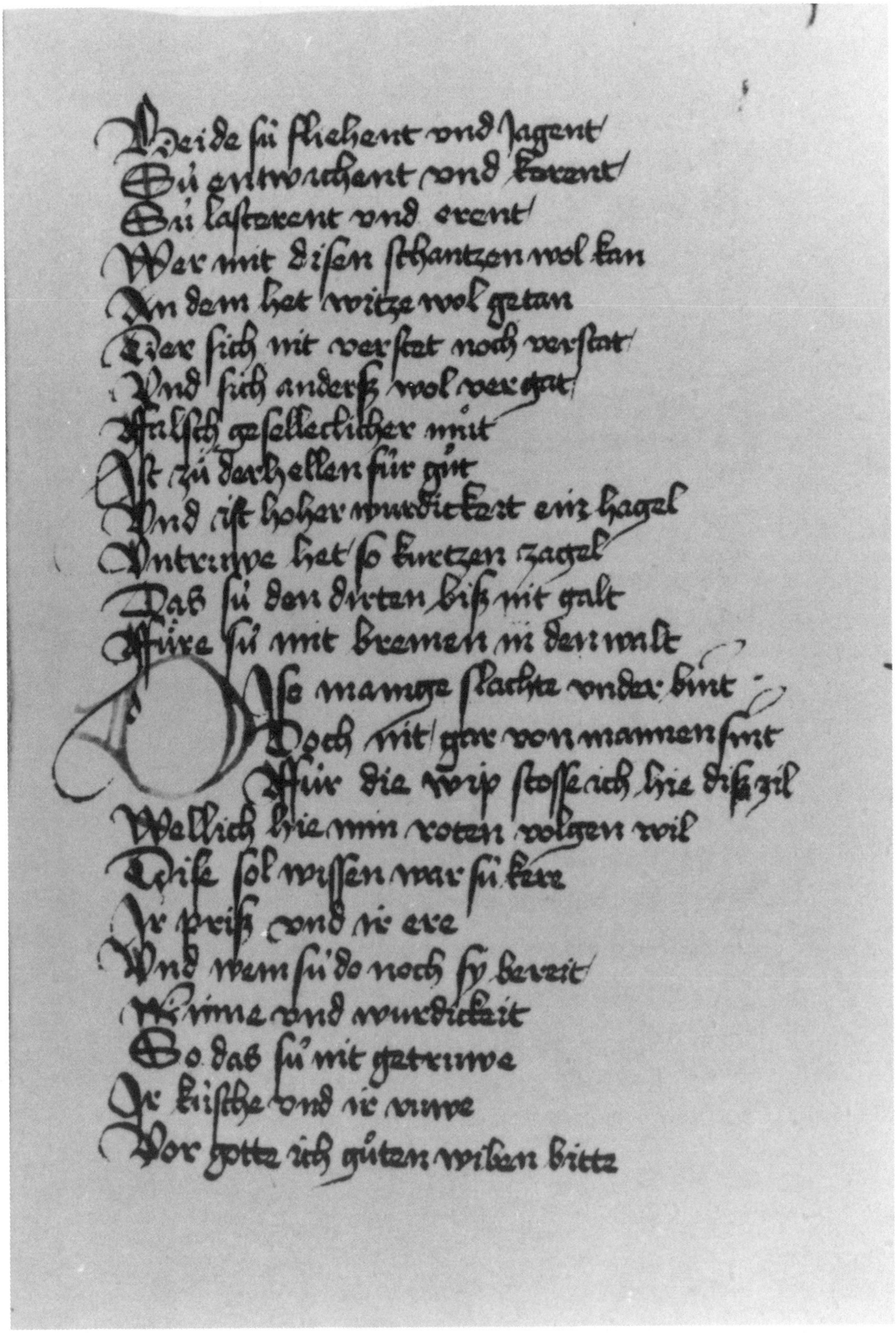

Beide su fliehent vnd Jagent
Su entwichent vnd kerent
Su lasterent vnd erent
Wer mit disen schantzen wol kan
An dem het witze wol getan
Der sich mit verstat noch verstat
Vnd sich anders wol verstat
Falsch geselleclicher mut
Ist zu der hellen fur gut
Vnd ist hoher wurdickeit ein hagel
Vntruwe het so kurtzen zagel
Das su den dritten biss nit galt
Fure su mit bremen in den walt
So manige slachte vnder bint
Doch sit gar von mannen sint
Fur die wip stosse ich hie dis zil
Wellich hie min roten volgen wil
Die sol wissen war su kere
Ir pris vnd ir ere
Vnd wem su do noch sy bereit
Minne vnd wurdickeit
So das su mit getruwe
Ir kusche vnd ir ruwe
Vor hotte ich guten wisen bitte

Dis in rechter mosse volge mitte
Betham ist ein floss ob allem sitten
Ich darff in nymer heiles bitten
Di die falsch er wirbet / falschen preiß
Wie stete ist ein dünner iß
Div angest hertze sinne bît /
Sin lop wil balde alsus verzert
Wenne wibes schöne an lobe ist bereit
Ist do das hertze hunterfert
Die lobe ich also ich solde
Das saffier in golde
Ich han das nicht für lichter ding
Wer in den brancken messing
Der wircket / edel rubin
Und alle die offenture sin
Die glich ich rechter wibes mut
Die ir wipheit recht dut
Den sol ich farwe prüfen nicht
Noch ires hertzen tach do man sicht
Ist innerhalp der brust bewart
So ist worden preiß do mit / verstat
Swie mere ich hie wil muwen
Das sait von grossen truwen
Wiplicher wibes recht.

Vnd mannes manheit also slecht
Die su sich gegen hertze nye gebog
Sin hertze in der an nye betrog
Gestahel wo der zü strite kam
Sin hant do sigelichen name
Manigen löbelichen priß
Der kúne trachelichen wiß
Den helt ich alsus gruisse
Der wibes ougen suisse
Vnd do sy wibes hertzen sucht
Vor misservende ein sarme flucht
Den ich hie han erkorn
Er ist morgens halp noch vnzeborn
Dem man diser offentine sicht
Vnd wunders vil dar an geschicht
Sú pflegen es noch also man pflag
Alo lúte vnd welsche gerichte lag
Das pfliget ouch ~~bos~~ tútscher eran act
Das habent ir an mir gehart
Wer Je do pflag der lande
Silber gebot wol one schande
Das ist an worheit sunder wan
Das der altest bruder solte han
Sines vatter gantzen erbe teil

o (Dresden, Sächsische Landesbibliothek, M 66, f.1r–3v)

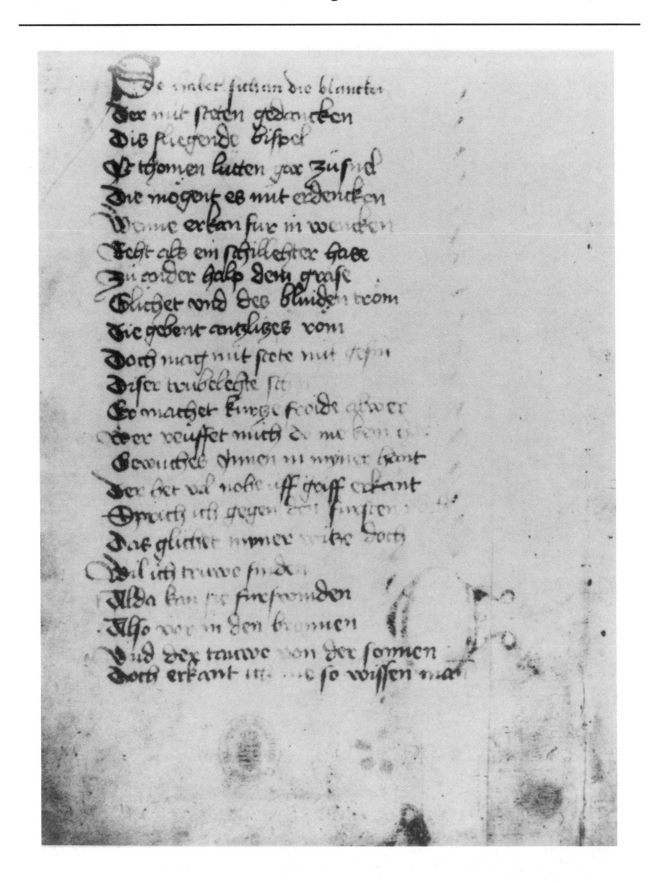

Er möhte gerne kunde tün
Velscher müre die frowen ye erent
Vnd was sie guter lere werent
Dar an sie niemer des fürzagent
Bede sie fliessent vnd zagent
Sie entwichent vnd kerent
Sie lasterent vnd lerent
Wer mit disen stangen alle kan
An dem ist witze wol getan
Der sich nut ustert noch verstat
Vnd sich anders wol verstat
Valsch geselliche nut
Ist zu der hellen für gut
Vnd ist töifer wridikeit ein hagel
Vntruwe hette so kurzen zagel
Das sie den biten biz nit galt
Fure sie nit breenen in den walt
Ist manicher slahte vnder int
Doch nit gar von mannen sint
Vor dise wip hosse uti dise zil
Velich sie min taten merken wil

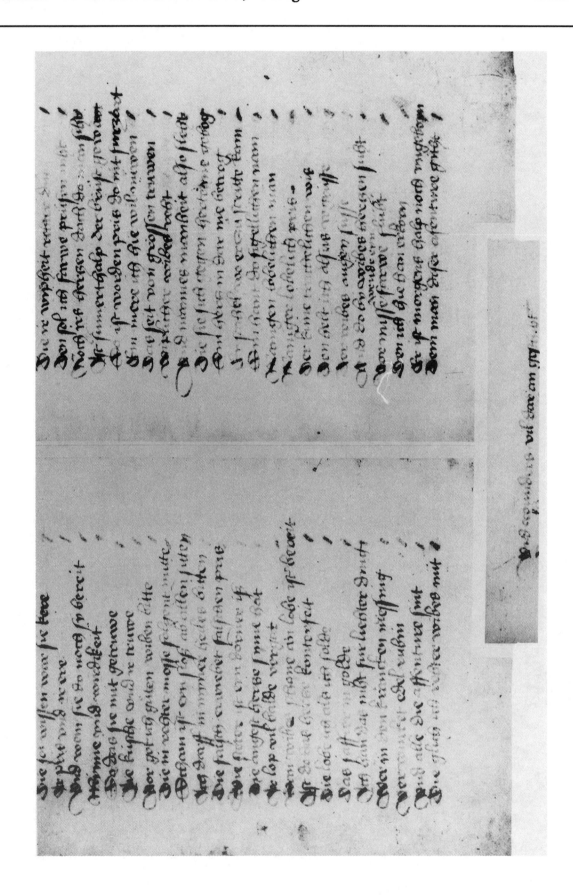

G✠ (Strasbourg: Printed by Johann Mentelin, 1477, f.1r–1v)

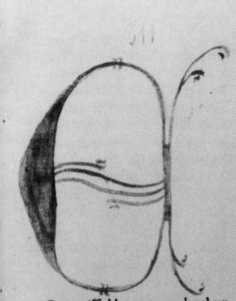

St zweiffel hertzen nachgebur
Das muß der selen werden sur
Geschmehet vnd gezieret
Ist wo sy parieret
In eines verzagten mannes müt
Also agelaster varbe thüt
Der mag darnach wesen gail
Wan an im sein baide tail
Des himels vnd der hellen
Der vnstendige gesellen
Het die schwartze varbe gar
Vnd ist nach der vinsteruar
So hebent sich an die blancken
Der mit steten gedancken
Diß fliegende beispel
Ist tummen leuten gar schnel
Die mügen es nit erdencken
Wann es kan vor in wencken
Recht als ein erschelter hase
Zü anderthalb dem glase
Gleichet vnd des blinden trom
Die gebent alle antlütz rom
Doch mag mit stete nit gesein
Diser trübelechte schein

Er machet kurtze fröde alwar
Wer ropffet mich do nie kein har
Gewüchß innen in meiner hand
Der het so nahe griff erkand
Sprich ich gegen den fürsten hoch
Das gleichet meiner witze doch
Wil ich trü we vmden
Also kan sy verschwmden
Als faur m dem brunnen
Vnd der tauwe von der sunnen
Doch erkant ich nie so weisen man
Er möchte gerne kinde ban
Welcher rüre die frauwen gerent
Vnd was sy güter lere werent
Dar an sy nimer des verczagent
Beide sy fliehen vnd iagent
Sy entweichent vnd kerent
Sy lasterent vnd erent
Wer mit disen schantzen allen kan
An dem hat witz wol getan
Der sich nit versinnet vnd verstat
Vnd sich anders nit vergat
Valsch gesellicher müt
Ist zü der hellen güt
Vnd ist höher würdikait ein hagel
Vntreüw hat so kurtzen zagel
Das sy den dritten biß nit galt
Eür sy mit bremen in den walt
Alse manigschlachte vnderbinde
Doch nit gar von mannen sint
Vor die weib stoß ich dise zil
Wellich bie mein raten merckë wil
Die sol wissen war sy kere
Ir preiß vnd ir ere
Vnd wem sy noch do sy berait
Mynne vnd würdikait
So das sy nit gereüwe
Ir keüsch vnd ir treüwe
Vor got ich güten weiben bitte
Die in rechter masse volgent mitte

Scham ist ein schloß ob allen sitten
Ich darff in minner heils bitten
Die valscher wirbet valschen preiß
Wie stete ist ein dünnes eiß
Die angst hertzen sinne hat
Ir lob vil balde suß zergat
Wan weibes schöne ist ein lob brait
Ist do das hertze kunterfait
Die lobe ich als ich solde
Das saffir in dem golde
Ich han das nit für leichter ding
Wer in den krancken messing
Verwürcket edel rubin
Vnd alle auentüre drin
Die gleich ich rechter weibes gut
Die ir weibhait nit rechte thut
Den sol ich varbe preisen nicht
Noch irs hertzen doch do man sicht
Ist sunderhalb der prüfe bewart
So ist worden preiß nit verstart
OVn mere ich hie wil neuwen
Das seit von grossen trüwen
Weiblicher weibes recht
Vnd mannes manhait also schlecht
Die sich gegen herte nie geboug
Sein hertze in dar an nie betroug
Er stahel wo er zu streite kan
Sein hand do sigelichen nam
Mangen löbelichen preiß
Der küne trachenliche weiß
Den helt ich alsuß grüsse
Der weibes augen süsse
Vnd do bey weibes hertzen sicht
Vor miswende ein varbe schlicht
Den ich hie han erkorn
Er ist morgens halb noch vngeborn
Dem man diser auentüre gicht
Vn wunders vil dar an beschicht
Sy pfleget es noch als man es pflag
Wo leute vnd wellich gericht lag

Das pfliget teütscher erde art
Das habent ir an mir gehart
Wie er do pflag der lande
Der gebot wol on schande
Das ist ein warhait sunderwan
Das der eltest bruoder sol han
Seins vatter gantzen erbtail
Das was der iungen michel hail
Das in der tot die pflicht brach
Als in ir vatter leben veriach
Dan do vor was es gemain
Suß het es der elter ain
Das schuff iedoch ein weiser man
Das alter gut sol han
Iuget het vil wirdikait
Do alter seufftzen vnd lait
Es wart nieman so frut
So alter vnd armut
In her iaget zu seinem zil
So ist seiner witze nit zu vil
Künig grefen vnd hertzogen
Das sag ich euch für vngelogen
Das die iungen enterbet sint
Vntz an das eltest kint
Das was ein fremde zeche
Der küsche vnd der freche
Gamuret der wigand
Verloß suß bürge vnd land
Do sein vatter schone
Trüg zepter vnd krone
Mit grosser küniglicher krafft
Vntz er lag tot an ritterschafft
Do clagte man in sere
Die gantze treuw vnd ere
Bracht vntz an seinen tot
Sein alter sun für sich gebot
Die fürsten auß seinem reiche
Sy koment ritterleiche
Wan sy recht solten han
Von im groß lehen sunderwan

Parzival, Prologue
Translation*

If inconstancy is the heart's neighbor, the soul will not fail to find it bitter. Blame and praise alike befall when a dauntless man's spirit is black-and-white-mixed like the magpie's plumage. Yet he may see blessedness after all, for both colors have a share in him, the color of heaven and the color of hell. Inconstancy's companion is all black and takes on the hue of darkness, while he of steadfast thoughts clings to white.

This flying metaphor will be much too swift for dullards. They will not be able to think it through because it will run from them like a startled rabbit. Mirrors coated on the back with tin, and blind men's dreams, these catch only the surface of the face, and that dim light cannot steadfastly endure even though it may make fleeting joy real. Anyone who grabs the hair in the palm of my hand, where there isn't any, has indeed learned how to grab close. And if I cry Ouch!, it will only show what kind of a mind *I* have. Shall I look for loyalty precisely where it vanishes'[2]
as fire in running water, dew in the sun?

Never have I met a man so wise but that he would have liked to find out what authority this story claims and what good lessons it provides. On that score it never wants for courage, now to flee, now to charge, dodge and return, condemn and praise. Whoever can make sense out of all these turns of chance has been well treated by Wisdom, or whoever does not *sit* too tight, or *walk* astray, but in general under*stands*. The thoughts of a false man lead to hellfire, but they beat upon high dignity like hail; his loyalty has a tail so short that it couldn't slap back at the third bite if it were flicking flies in a forest.

These various definitions are by no means directed at men solely: for women I will set up these same goals. Any woman willing to mark my advice shall know where to bestow her praise and honors,

and, accordingly, on whom to bestow her love and respect, so that she will not rue[3]
the giving of her purity and devotion. I pray to God that good women may follow the proper mean. Modesty is a capstone over all virtues; I need not wish them anything better than that. She who is false shall win false praise. How durable is thin ice that gets the hot August sun? Just so quickly will her renown decay. Many a woman's beauty is praised afar, but if the heart within is counterfeit, I would praise her as I would praise a jewel of blue paste set in gold. I count it no trifling thing if someone mounts a noble ruby, with all its magic virtue, in paltry brass. To such a jewel I liken a faithful woman's way. Any one true to her womanhood I will not examine as to her complexion or the heart's external roof, for if she is well protected *within* her heart, her praise will not be paid amiss.

If I were to tell of men and women aright, as I understand them, it would be a long tale. But now listen to the manner of this story. It will bring you word of both joy and sorrow, and delight and distress accompany it as well. Assuming there were three men instead of me[4]
alone, each possessed of ability equal to mine, it would still be fantastic skill if they set forth to you what I, singlehanded, mean to set forth. They would find it a task indeed. I mean to tell you once again a story that speaks of great faithfulness, of the ways of womenly women and of a man's manhood so forthright that never against hardness was it broken. Never did his heart betray him, he all steel, when he came to combat, for there his victorious hand took many a prize of praise. *A brave man slowly wise* – thus I hail my hero – sweetness to women's eyes and yet to women's hearts a sorrow, from wrongdoing a man in flight! The one whom I have thus chosen is, story-wise, as yet unborn, he of whom this adventure tells and to whom many marvels there befall.

*Superscript numbers in the text refer to Lachmann strophe numbers.

341

Wolfram von Eschenbach's *Parzival,* Book 3
Manuscript Facsimiles

The manuscripts D and G of *Parzival,* reproduced here, are especially important because, in the view of philologists such as Karl Lachmann, one of the pioneers of the study of Middle High German literature in the early nineteenth century, those manuscripts best represent two divergent manuscript traditions of Wolfram von Eschenbach's *Parzival.*

The leaves for book 3 in versions D and G are reproduced below, one following the other. At the end of this section is an English translation of book 3 by Helen M. Mustard and Charles E. Passage (*Parzival* [New York: Vintage, 1961]). This translation is chiefly based on the Middle High German edition compiled from several manuscripts by Lachmann (Berlin: Reimer, 1833).

The first manuscript reproduced, D, is preserved in the Monastery Library in Saint Gall, Switzerland, Cod. Sangall. 857. It dates from the thirteenth century and is part of a collection of manuscripts that altogether consists of 318 parchment leaves. The G manuscript, Cod. germ. 19, is found in the Staatsbibliothek Munich. It is a work of the thirteenth century and of unknown provenance. It consists of 75 parchment leaves.

Each manuscript page reproduced here has a tag at the bottom that correlates the manuscript with the standard High Middle German edition by Lachmann. On the tags, the designations D and G, respectively, identify the manuscript; S. refers to the manuscript page; Sp. refers to columns (with columns on a page referred to by superscript letters), and L followed by a series of numbers refers to the Lachmann edition by strophe and line number. Thus, "D S. 36 Sp.36^a = L 112,30–114,25" states that this is manuscript D, p. 36 (S. 36) in which column a (Sp.36^a) corresponds to text in strophe 112, line 30, to strophe 114, line 25, of the Lachmann edition.

At the end of this section is an English translation, from standard Middle High German editions, by Helen M. Mustard and Charles E. Passage (*Parzival* [New York: Vintage, 1961]).

The manuscripts are reproduced from Jürgen Kühnel, ed., *Wolfram von Eschenbach "Parzival" : Lachmanns Buch III. Abbildung und Transkription der Leithandschriften D und G* (Göppingen: Kümmerle, 1971).

Parzival, *MS. D*

D   S. 36   Sp. 36[a] = L 112,30–114,25

Sp. 36[b] = L 114,26–116,19

* Apology begins; **Book 3 begins

des wart ir gabe niwe.
zehmel mit eideloser gebe.
ich ir nv vil wenich lebe.
die iunch der erden rihtvm.
liezen dvrch des himeles rvm.
ich ercheine ir nehein.
man vn wip mir sint al ein.
die mident if al geliche.
fro Herzeloyde div riche.
ir drier lande wart ein gast.
si trveh der freuden mangels last.
der valsch an ir so gar verswant.
oge noch ore in nie da vant.
an nebel was ir div synne.
si vloch der werelde winne.   *Werelde wale*
ir was geliche naht vnt der tach.
ir herze niht tamers phlach.
ich zoch div frowe tamers balt.
vz ir lande in einen walt.
zer waste in soltane.
nihe dvrch blvmen vf die plane.
ir herzen tamer was so ganz.
sine cherte sich an cheinen chranz.
er ware rot odr val.
si brahte dar dvrch flvhsal.
des werdn Gahmvretes kint.
livte die bi ir da sint.
mvzen buwen vn riuten.
si chvnde wol getriuten.
ir svn e daz sich der versan.
ir volch si gar fvr sich gewan.
ez ware man odr wip.
den gebot si allen an den lip.
daz si nimmer ritters wrden lut.
wan friesche daz mins herzen trvt.
welch ritters leben ware.
daz wrde mir vil sware.
nv habt iwch an der witze chraft.
vnd helt in alle ritterschaft.
der site fvr angestliche vart.
der knappe alsvs geborgen wart.
zer waste in soltane erzogn.
an chvneclicher fvre betrogn.
ez enmohte an eime site sin.
bogen vn bolzelin.
die snet er mir sin selbes hant.
vn schoz vil vogele die er vant.
swenne abr er den vogel erschoz.
des schal von sange e was so groz.
so weinde er vnd rofte sich.
an sin har chert er gerich.
sin lip was clar vn fier.
vf dem plan ame rivier.
twgut sich alle morgen.

erne chvnde niht gesorgen.
ez enware ob im der vogel sanch.
div svze in sin herze dranch.
daz erstrachte im siniv prvstelin.
al weinende er lief zer kvnegin.
So sprch si wer hat dir getan.
dv ware hin vz vf den plan.
ern chvnde ir gesagen niht.
als chinden lihte noch geschiht.
Dem mare giench si lange nach.
eins tages si in chapfen sach.
vf die bome nach der vogele schal.
si wart wol innen daz ir swal.
von der stimme ir chindes brvst.
des twanch ir art vn sin gelvst.
fro Herzeloyde chert ir haz.
an die vogele sine weste vmb waz.
si wolt ir schal verchenchen.
ir bvlivte vn ir enchen.
die hiez si vaste gahen.
vogele wrgen vnd vahen.
vogele waren dar geriten.
etsliches sterben wart vermiten.
der beleip da lebendich ein teil.
die sit mit sange wrden geil.
er knappe sprch zer kvnegin.
waz wizet man den vogelin.
er gert in frides sa zest vnt.
sin mvter chvst in an den mvnt.
Div sprch wes wende ich sin gebot.
der doch ist der hohste got.
svlen vogele dvrch mich freude lan.
der knappe sprch zer mvter san.
owe mvter was ist got.
svn ich sage dirz ane spot.
er ist noch liehter denne der tach.
der antlvzes sich bewach.
nach mennischen antlvzze.
sv merche eine witze.
vn flehe in vmb dine not.
sin triwe der werlde ie helfe bot.
So heizet ener der helle wirt.
der ist swarz vntriwe in niht verbirt.
von dem chere dine gedanche.
vn och von zwivels wanche.
Sin mvter vndersciet im gar.
daz vinstr vnt daz lieht gewar.
dar nach sin snelheit verre spranch.
er lernte den Babylots swanch.
da mit er manegn hirz erschoz.
des sin mvter vn ir volch genoz.
ez ware aber odr snie.
dem wilde ter sin schiezen we.
nv horet frombdiv mare.

D   S. 37   Sp. 37a = L 116,2o–118,13
            Sp. 37b = L 118,14–12o,7

swenne er schoz daz swære.
des wære ein mul geladen gnuoch.
als vnverworht hin heim erz truoch.
ines tages gie er den weide ganch.
an einer halden div was lanch.
er brach durch blates stimme ein zwich.
da nahen bi im gie ein stich.
da hôret schal von huffslegen.
sin gabylot begvndr wegen.
do speh er waz han ich vernomn.
wan wolt er nv der tivuel chomn.
mit grimme zornecliche.
den bestunde ich sicherliche.
min muoter freisen von in saget.
ich wæne ir ellen si verzagt.
Alsus stvont er unstrites get.
nv seht dort chom geschruft her.
rittr nach wnsche var.
von fvz vf gewapent gar.
der kaape wande svndr spot.
daz ieslicher wære ein got.
Do stvnt och er niht langer hie.
in daz phat viel er vf sinv chnie.
lute rief der knappe san.
hilf got dv maht wol helfe han.
der vodr zortus sich bewach.
do der knappe ime phade lach.
dirre tôrsche waleise.
vnsich wender gaher reise.
ein pris den wir beier tragn.
muz ich von waleisen sagn.
die sint tôrscher denne beiersche her.
vn doch bi manlicher wer.
swer in den zwein landen wirt.
gefvge ein wilde an im birt.
o chom geleischieret.
vn wol gezimieret.
an rittr dem was harte gach.
er reit in stritecliche nach.
di verre waren von im chomn.
zwene ritter hetten in genomn.
eine iuncfrowen in sime lande.
den helt er dulte schande.
in mvte der iuncfrowen leit.
div iæmerliche vor in reit.
dise dri waren sine man.
er reit ein schône kastelan.
sines schildes was vil wenich ganz.
er hiez karnahkarnanz.
Laheons vtrerlech.
er spoh wer irret vns den wech.
svs fvr er zime knappen san.
den duht er als ein got getan.
eren here so sines niht erchant.

vfem tôwe der wapenroch erwant.
mit gvldinen schellen ebleine.
vor iewederm beine.
waren die stegreif erchlenger.
vn zerehter maze erlenger.
sin zeswer arm von schellen ehlanch.
swar er den bot odr swanch.
der was durch swertslege so hel.
der helt was gein prise snel.
svs fvr der fvrste riche.
gezimieret wunnecliche.
Aller manne schône ein blumen chranz.
den wagete karnahkarnanz.
Juncherre sahet ir fvr iuch varn.
zwene ritter die sih niht bewarn.
chvnnen an ritlicher zunft.
si ringet mit der not nunft.
vn sint an werdecheit verzagt.
si fvrent robel eine magt.
Der knappe wande swaz er spoh.
ez wære got als im veriach.
frô Herzeloyde div kvnegin.
do si im vndirschiet den lihten schin.
do rief er lute svndr spot.
nv hilf mir hilfe richer got.
vil diche viel an sin gebet.
fulu roy Bahmvret.
der fvrste spoh ich pin niht got.
ich leiste abr gerne sin gebot.
dv maht hie vier ritter sehn.
ob dv zerehte chvndest spehn.
Der knappe vragete furbaz.
dv nennest rittr waz ist daz.
hastv niht gotlicher chraft.
so sage mir wer git rittrschaft.
daz tvt der kvnec Artvs.
iuncherre chomt ir in des hvs.
der bringet iuch an rittrs namn.
daz irs iuch nimmer durfet schamn.
ir mvgt wol sin von rittrs art.
von den helden er geschôwet wart.
o lach div gotes gunst an im.
von der aventivre ich daz nim.
div mich mit warheit des beschiet.
nie mannes varwe baz geriet.
vor im sit Adames zit.
des wart sin lop von wiben wit.
Aber spoh der knappe san.
da von ein lachen wart getan.
ay ritter got waz mahtv sin.
dv hast svst manech vingerlin.
an dinen lip gebunden.
dort oben vnt hie vnden.
alda begreif des knappen hant.

swaz er yser ame fvrsten wut.
der hurnasch begvnde er schowen.
miner mvtr ivnchfröwen.
ir vingerlin an snvren tragt.
die niht sos an ein andr ragit.
der knappe spch dvrch sinen mvt.
zen fvrstn. war zv ist diz gvt.
daz dich so wol chan sluchen.
ine mages niht ab gezwichen.
der fvrste im zaigete sa sin swert.
nv sich swer an mich strites gert.
des selbn wer ich mich mit flegn.
fvr die sine mvz ich an mich legn.
vn fvr den schvz vn fvf den stich.
mvz ich alsvs wapen mich.
aber spch der knappe snel.
ob die hurze trvgen svs ir vel.
sone wvnt ir niht min gabylot.
der veller manget von mir tot.
ue ritter zv reron daz er hielt.
bi dem knappen der vil tvmpheite wielt.
der fvrste spch got hvte din.
owi wan wære din schöne min.
dir hete got den wnsch gegebn.
ob dv mit witzen soldest lebn.
div gotes chraft dir virre leit.
die sine vn och er selbe reit.
vn gahten harte balde.
zeinem velde in dem walde.
da vant der gefvge.
frö Herzeloyden phvge.
ir volche leidr nie geschach.
die er balde eren sach.
si begvnden sæn dar nach egen.
ob starchen ohsen wegn.
der fvrste in gvten morgen bot.
vn vraget ob si sæhen not.
eine ivnchfröwen liden.
sine chvnden niht vermiden.
swes er vragete daz wart gesagt.
zwene ritter vn ein magt.
da riten hivte morgn.
div fröwe fvr mit sorgn.
mit sporn si vaste rvrten.
di die ivnchfröwen fvrten.
Ez was Melukanz.
den erjaht karnach karnanz.
mit stritte er　　im die fröwen nam.
div was da　　　vor an freden lam.
si hiez Jmane.
von der Beafontane.
ue bvlrute verzageten.
do die helde fvr sie iageten.
si spchen. wie ist vns svs geschehen.

han vnser ivncherre ersehen.
an disen ritern helme schart.
sone han wir vns niht wol bewart.
wir svlen der kvneginne haz.
von schvlden hören vmb daz.
wand er mit vns da her lief.
hivte morgen do si dannoch slief.
Der knappe enrvelrte och wer do schoz.
die hurze cleine vnd groz.
er hvp sich gein der mvtr widr.
vn sagt ir mære do viel si nidr.
siner worte si so sere erschrac.
daz si vnversvnnen vor im lach.
Do div kvneginne.
widr chom zir sinne.
swie si da vor wære verzagt.
do spch si svn wer hat gesagt.
dir von ritters orden.
wa bist dvs innen worden.
herre ich sach vier man.
noch liehter danne got getan.
die sagetn mir von ritterschaft.
Artvs kvnechlichiv chraft.
sol mich nach ritters eren.
an schildes ambt cheren.
Sich hvp ein niwer iamer hie.
div fröwe enwesse rehte wie.
daz si ir den list erdæhte.
vn in von dem willen bræhte.
Der knappe tvmp vn wert.
iesch von der mvtr diche ein pfert.
daz begvnde si in ir herzen chlagn.
si dahte. ine wil im niht versagn.
ez mvz abr vil böse sin.
do gedahte mer div kvnegin.
der livte vil bi spotte sint.
toren cleidr sol min kint.
ob sine liben libe tragn.
wirt er geröfet vnt geslagn.
so chvmt er mir her widr wol.
owe der iamerlichen dol.
Div fröwe nam ein sach tvch.
si sneit im hemde vn brvch.
daz doch an eine stvche erschein.
vnz enmitten an sin blanches bein.
daz wart fvr toren cleit erhant.
ein gvgelen man obene drvfe vant.
al frisch rvch chelberin.
von einer hvte zwei rbbalin.
nach sinen beinen wart gesnitn.
da wart groz iamer niht vermitn.
Div kvnegin was also bedaht.
si bat beliben in die naht.
dune solt niht hinnen cheren.

ich wil dich liste leren.
an vngebawten straxen.
soltu tunchel furte lixen.
die sihte vnd luter sin.
da solt du al balde riten in.
du solt dich site nieten.
der werelde gruxen bieten.
Ob dich ein gra wise man.
xuht wil leren alser wol chan.
dem soltu gerne volgen.
vn wis im niht erbolgen.
Sun la dir bevolhen sin.
swa du gvtes wibes vingerlin.
mugest erwerben vnt ir grvz.
dax nim. ex tvt dir chumbers bvz.
du solt zvr chusse gahen.
vn ir lip vaste vmbe vahen.
dax git gelvche vnd hohen mvt.
ob si chvsche ist vn gvt.
Du solt och wizzen svn min.
der stolze chvne Lehelin.
dinen fvrsten ab ervaht xwei lant.
die solten dienen diner hant.
Wales vnd Norgals.
ein din fvrste Tvrkentals.
den tot von siner herde enphiench.
din volch er slvch vn viench.
Dix rich ich mveter rchtes got.
in verwndet noch min gabylot.
Des morgens do der tag erschein.
der knappe balde wart ein.
im was gegen Artvse gach.
frö Herxeloyde in chusse vn lief im nach.
der werelde riwe al geschach.
do si ir svn niht langer sach.
der reit enwech wem ist deste lax.
da viel div fröwe valsches lax.
vf die erde al da si xamer sneit.
so dax si ein sterben niht vermeit.
ir vil getriwlicher tot.
der fröwen wert die helle not.
O wol si dax si mveter wart.
svs fvr div lones vernde vart.
ein wrcel der gvte.
vn ein stam der diemvte.
owe dax wir nv niht enhan.
ir sippe vnx an den elften span.
des wirt gevelschet manech lip.
doch solten nv getriwiv wip.
heiles wunschen disem knabn.
der sich hie von ir hat erhabn.

...eir der knabe wolgetan.
...gin dem forest in Prizlian.
...er chom an einen bach gerin.
...un here ein han wol vberschriten
...vre da stvnden blvmn vn gras
durch dax stvflvx so tunchel was.
der knappe len fvrt dar an vermeit.
den tag er gar dernebn reit.
als er sinen witzen tohte.
er beleip die naht swi er mohte.
vnx im der liehte tag erschein
der knappe sich dan al ein.
hvp xeime fvrte luter wolgetan.
da was andrhalp der plan.
mit eime gexelt geheret.
grox richeit dran gecheret.
von drier slahte samit.
ex was hoh vnd wit.
vf den neten lagen porten gvt.
da hiench ein liderin hvt.
den man drvber xiehen solte.
immer swenne ex regenen wolte.
Der herxoge Orilvs de Lalander.
des wip doit vnde vander.
ligende minnecliche.
div herxoginne riche.
geliche eime ritters trvte.
Si hiez Jeschvte.
Div fröwe was entslafen.
si trvch der minne wafen.
einen mvnt dvrch liehtich rot.
vn gerndes ritters herxen not.
innen des div fröwe slief.
der mvnt ir von ein andr lief.
der trvch der minne hitze fiwer.
svs lach des wunsches aventiwer.
von sne wixen beine.
nahe bi ein andr cleine.
svs stvnden ir die liehten xene.
ich wæne mich innen chvssens wene.
an einen svss gelobten mvnt.
dax ist mir selten worden chvnt.
ir dechelachen xobelin.
erwant an ir hvffelin.
dax si dvrch hitze von ir stiez.
da si der al eine liez.
si was geschichet vnt geslihten.
an ir was chvnt   niht verniht.
got selbe worht ir   svzen lip.
och here dax mine   ehliche wip.
langen arm vnd blanche hant.
der knappe ein vingerlin da vant.
dax in gein dem bette twanch.
do er mit der herxoginne ranch.

do dahr er an die mvtr fin.
div riet an wibes vingerlin.
ich fpch der knappe wolgetan.
von dem teppiche an daz bette fan.
iv fvze chvfche vnfamfte erferfach.
do der knappe an ir arme lach.
fi mvft idoch erwachen.
mit feltame alfvndr lachen.
div frowe xvht geleret.
fpch wer hat mich enteret.
ivncherre ez ift iv gar zevil.
ir mohtet iv nennen andr zil.
div frowe lvte chlagete.
ern rvchte waz fi fagete.
ir mvnt er an den finen twanch.
da nach waf do niht zelanch.
eer drvhte an fich die herzogin.
vn nam ir ôch ein vingerlin.
an ir hemde ein fvrfpan er da fach.
vngefvge erz dannen brach.
div frowe waf mit wibes wer:
ir waf fin chraft ein ganzes her:
doch wart da ringens vil getan.
Der chnappe chlagete den hvnger fan.
div frowe waf ir liebes liht.
fi fpch ir fvlt min ezzen niht.
wært ir zefrvmen wife.
ir nemet iv andr fpife.
dort ftet brot vnd win.
vn ôch zwei pardrifekin.
alf ein ivnchfrowe brahte.
divf wenech iv gedahte.
zn rvchte wa div wirtin faz.
einen gvten chropf er az.
dar nach er fwære trvnche tranch.
die frowen dvhte gar zelanch.
fines wefens in dem Polvn.
fi wande er wære ein garzvn.
gefcheiden von den wizzen.
ir fcham begvnde fwizzen.
idoch fpch div herzogin.
ivncherre ir fvlt min vingerlin.
hie lazen vnt min fvrfpan.
hebt ivch enwech wan chvmt min man.
ir mvzet zvrnen liden.
daz ir gerner mohzet miden.
Do fpch der knappe wol geborn.
owe waz fvrht ich iwer mannes zorn.
van fchadet ez iv an eren.
fo wil ich hinnen cheren.
do giengez zv dem bette fan.
ein ander chvff da wart getan.
daz waf der herzoginne leit.
der knappe an vrlop dannen reit.

idoch fpch er got hvte din.
alfvf riet mir div mvtr min.
Der knappe des rôbes waf gemeit.
do er eine wile von dan gereit.
wol nach grin der mile zil.
do chom von dem ich fprechen wil.
der fpvrte an dem rôwe.
daz gefchefer waf fin frowe.
der fnvre ein teil waf vz gezert.
da hete ein knappe daz griz gewert.
ez fvrfte wert vnt erchant.
fin wip dort vn al trvrich vant.
do fpch der ftolze Orilvs.
owe frowe wie han ich fvs.
min dienest grin iv gewendet.
mir ift nach laster gendet.
manech riterliche priz.
ir habt ein andr amis.
Ott warzer richen ôgen.
div frowe bot ir lôgen.
so daz fi vnfchvldich wære:
ern gelôbte niht ir mære.
idoch fpch fi mit forte fiten.
da chom ein tore her zv geriten.
fwaz ich livte erchennet han.
me gefach me lip fo wolgetan.
min fvrfpan vn ein vingerlin.
daz nam er ane den willen min.
Hey fin lip iv wol gevellet.
ir habt iv ziun gefellet.
do fpch fi nv ne welle got.
finv ribbalin fin gabilot.
waren mir doch zenahen.
div rede iv folte fmahen.
fvrftinne ez vbelz zæme:
ob fi da minne næme.
Aber fpch der fvrfte fan.
frowe ine han iv niht getan.
iren welt iveh einer ftrv fchamn.
ir liezet kvnnegvnde iuwern.
vn hiezet dvrh mich ein herzogin.
der chôf git mir vngewin.
in manheit ift doch fo qwech.
daz iwer brvder frech.
min fwager fillu roylach.
ich wol dar vmbe hazzen mach.
mich erchennet idoch der wife:
an fo bewartem prife:
der nidr mach enteret fin.
wan daz er ivch vor Prvrin.
mit finer tiost valte:
an im ich fie bezalte:
hohen priz vor karnant.
zerehter tiost ftach in min hant.

D S. 41 Sp. 41^a = L 130,29–132,22
          Sp. 41^b = L 132,23–134,16

~42

hinderz ors durch harxe:
dvrch sin schilt mit lanxe.
twer chleinode brahte.
vil wenich ich do gedahte.
twerr myine einem anderm trvte:
min frowe jesevte.
frowe ir svlt geloben des.
dar der stolze baloes.
fillu roy Gandin.
tot lach von der tioste min.
Jr hielt och da nahen bi.
da Lihoplihen.
gein mir dvrch tivstiren reit.
vn mich sin striten niht vermeit.
min tioste in hinderz ors verswanch.
dar mder satel nmder dranch.
ich han dicke pris bexalt.
vn manegen ritt ab gewalt.
des enmoht ich nv gemexen niht.
ein hoher laster mir des giht.
Si harxent mich besvndr:
die von der tavelrvndr.
der ich ahte nider stach.
da ez manech wert ivnchfrowe sach.
vmbe den sperware ze kanedich.
ich behielt iv pris vn mir den sich.
dar sahet ir vnt Artvs.
der mine swestr hat ze hvs.
die frxen svnnewaren.
ir mynt chan niht gebaren.
mit lachen e si den gesiht.
dem man des hohsten prises giht.
wan chome mir doch der selbe man.
so wrde ein striten hie getan.
als hivte morgen do ich streit.
vn eime fvrsten frvnte leit.
der mir sin tivstiren bot.
von miner tioste lager tot.
Jch enwil iv niht von xorne sagen.
dar manger hat sin wip geslagen.
vmb ir ehrencher schvlde.
het ich dienest odr hvlde.
dar ich iv solte bieten.
ir mvst iwch mangell nieten.
ich ensol niht me erwarmen.
an iweren blanchen armen.
da ich etswenne dvrch minne lach.
manegen winneclichen tach.
ich sol velwen iweren roten mvnt.
vn iwern ogen machen rote chvnt.
ich sol iv frode enteren.
vn iwer herxe sivften leren.
iv fvrstin an den fvrsten sach.
ir mvnt do iamerlichen sprch.

nv eret an mir ritters pris.
ir sit getriwe vn wis.
vn och wol so gewaldich min.
ir mvget mir gebn hohen pin.
ir svlt e min gerihte nemn.
dvrch elliv wip lat iwch xemn.
ir mvgt mir dannoch fvgen not.
lage ich von andern handen tot.
dar iv niht pris geneichte.
swie schiere ich denne veichte.
dar ware mir ein svriv rit.
sit iwer harxen an mir lit.
Aber sprch der fvrste mere.
frowe ir waret mir gar xe here.
des sol ich an iv marxen.
gesellesehaft wirt laxen.
mir trinchen vn mir erxen.
bi ligens wirt vergexxen.
ir enphahet mer dehein gewant.
wan alsich iwch sxrrent vant.
iwer rom mvx sin ein paltin sel.
iwer phert belagt wol hvngers teil.
iwer satel wol gexieret.
der wirt enschvmphieret.
Vil balde er xarte vn brach.
den samit drab do dar geschach.
er xerslvch den satel da si nne reit.
ir chivsche vn ir wiphert.
im harxen liden mvsten.
mit bestinen bvsten.
pant er aber widr xv.
ir chon sin harxen al xefrv.
So sprch er an den xiten.
frowe nv svlen wir riten.
chome ich an des wrde ich geil.
der hie nam iwerr minne teil.
ich belvnde in doch dvrch aventivr.
ob sin atem gæbe fivr.
als eines wilden trachen.
Al weinende svndr lachen.
div frowe vns iamers riche.
schiet dannen trvrechliche.
si nemvte niht swax ir geschach.
wan ir mannes vngemach.
des trvren gap ir grоe not.
dar si noch iampfter ware tot.
Hv svlt ir si dvrch triwe chlagn.
si beginnet nv hoher chvinbr tragn.
ware mir aller wibe hax bereit.
mich mvte doch frоn Ieschvten leit.
Svs riten si vه der fla hin nach.
dem knappen vor im och was vil gach.
doch weste der vnvrxagter.
niht dar man in iagete.

D   S. 42   Sp. 42^a = L 134,17-136,1o
            Sp. 42^b = L 136.11-138.4

wan swenne sin ogen sahen.
so er dem begvnde nahen.
den givrte der knappe gvter.
vn nach sys riet mir min mvter.
s chom vnser torscher chnabe.
geriten eine halden abe.
wibes stimme er horte.
vor eines velses orte.
n frowe vz rehtem iam schrei.
vn div wurt frede enzwei.
der knappe reit ir balde zv.
nv horet waz div frowe tv.
da brach frv Sigvne.
ir langen zopfe brvne.
vor iamer vz ir swarten.
der knappe begvnde warten.
Seunatvlandr.
den fvrsten tot da vandr.
der ivnchfrowen tot in ir schoz.
aller schimphe si verdroz.
Er si trvrich odr freuden var.
die lat min mvter grvzen gar.
gor halde rvch sich des knappen mvnt.
ich han hie iemerlichen fvnt.
in iwerm schoze fvnden.
wer gap iv den rittr wnden.
geschah ez mir eine gabylot.
mich dvnchet frowe er lige tot.
welt ir mir da von iht sagn.
wer iv den man habe erslagn.
ob ich in mag erriten.
ich wil gerne mit im striten.
do greif der knappe mære.
ez sine chochære.
vil scharphiv gabylot er vant.
er fvrt och dannoch beidiv phant.
div er von Jeschvten brach.
vn in tvmpheit da geschach.
het er gelernet sines vatr site.
die werdechliche un wolten mite.
div bvkel wære gehvrt lax.
da div herzoginne al eine saz.
div sit vil chvmbers dvrch in leit.
mer danne ein ganzez iar si meit.
grvz von ir mannes libe.
vnrehte geschach dem wibe.
Hort och von Sigvnen sagn.
div chvnde ir leit mit iamer chlagn.
si sprich zem knappen dv hast tvgnt.
geret si din svziv ivgent.
vn din antlvzze minneclich.
deiswar dv wirst noch sælden rich.
disen rittr meit daz gabylot.
er lach zetvstieren tot.

si den knappen riten hiez.
si vragete in wie er hiez.
vn iach er trvge den gotes vliz.
von fiz iein fiz beafix.
alsvs hat mich genennet.
der mich da heime erchennet.
So div rede was getan.
si erchant in bi den namn san.
nv hort in rehter nennen.
daz in wol mvget erchennen.
wer dirre aventivre herre si.
der hielt der ivnchfrowen bi.
ir roter mvnt sprch svndr twal.
deiswar dv heizest Parzival.
der nam ir rehte mitten dvrch.
groz liebe ir solhe herzen fvrch.
mit diner mvtr triwe.
din vatr liez ir riwe.
ich engihe dirs niht zervme.
din mvtr ist min mvme.
vn sag dir svndr valschen list.
die rehten warheit wer dv bist.
Din vatr was ein Ansevin.
ein waleis von der mvtr din.
bistv geborn von kanvolerz.
die rehten warheit ich des werz.
dv bist och chvnech ze norgals.
in der hovpt stat ze kingrivals.
sol din hovbet chrone tragen.
dirre fvrste wart dvch dich erslagen.
wand er din lant ie werte.
sine triwe er nie verscherte.
ivch vlætich svzer man.
die gebrvder hant dir vil getan.
zwei lant nam dir Læhelin.
disen rittr vn den vatr din.
ze rivsieren slvch orilvs.
der liez och mich in iamer fvs.
ia diende an alle schande.
dirre fvrste von dime lande.
do zoch min din mvtr.
lieber neve gvter.
nv war disiv mære sin.
ein brachen seil gap im dem pin.
in vnser zweier dienste den tot.
hat er beiagt vn iamers not.
mir nach siner minne.
ich hete chranche sinne.
daz ich im niht minne gap.
des hat der sorgen vrhap.
mir frede verschroten.
nv minne ich in also roten.
Do sprch er nistel mir ist leit.
din chvmber vn min laster breit.

D   S. 43   Sp. 43^a = L 138,5 −139,30
             Sp. 43^b = L 140,3 −141,26

44

swenne ich daz mac gerechen.
daz wil ich gerne zechen.
Do was im gein dem strite gach.
si wiste in unrehte nach.
si vorhte daz er den lip verlur.
vn daz si grozen schaden chur.
eine straze er do gevinch.
div gein den verteoysen giench.
div was gestrichet vn breit.
swer im widr giench odr widr reit.
ez ware ritr odr chofman.
die selben grvzter alle san.
vn nach daz wart siner mvtr rat.
div gaben och ane missetat.
der abent begvnde nahen.
groz mvde gein im gahen.
do ersach der tvmpheit groz.
ein hvs regvter maze groz.
da was inne ein arger wirt.
als noch vf vngelahte birt.
daz was ein vischare.
vn aller gvte lare.
den chnappen hvnger leite.
daz er dergein cheite.
vn chlagete dem wirte hvngers not.
der spch ine gabe iv ein halbez brot.
niht zedrizech iaren.
swer miner mitte varen.
vergebn wil der synet sich.
ine sorge vmb niemn danne vmb mich.
dar nach vmb minv kindelin.
ir enchomt zalaneh da her in.
het ir phenninge odr phant.
ich beheit iveh al zehant.
Do bot im der knappe san.
frön iesevten fvrspan.
do ez der vilan ersach.
sin mvnt do lachete vn spch.
wiltv beliben liebez kint.
dich erent alle die hinne sint.
wiltv mich hivte wol spisen.
vn morgen rehte wisen.
gein artvse dem bin ich holt.
so mach beliben dir diz golt.
Diz tvn ich sprach der vilan.
ine gesich nie lip so wolgetan.
ich pringe dich dvrch wnder.
fvr des kvneges tavelrvnder.
Die naht beleip der knappe da.
man sah in sinorgens uidrswan.
des tages er chivnie erbeite.
der wirt och sich bereite.
vn liefim vor der knappe nach.
reit. do was in beiden gach.

Vnn her Hartman von Owe.
vn frö Ginover iwer fröwe.
vn iwer herre der kvneg Artvs.
den chvmt ein min gut ze hvs.
bitt hvten sin vor spotte.
ern ist gige noch div rotte.
si svlen ein ardor gampel nemn.
des lazen sich dvrch zvht gezemn.
Andrs iwer frö snide.
vnt ir mvter karsnafide.
werdent dvrch die mvl gerochet.
vn ir lop gebvchet.
sol ich den mvnt mitt spotte zern.
ich wil minen frivnt mitt spotte vern.
Do chom der vischere.
vn och der knappe mare.
einer höptstat so nahen.
al da si Nantes sahen.
do spch er. kint got hvte din.
nv sich. dort soltv riten in.
Do spch der knappe an wizzen laz.
dv solt mich wisen furbax.
wie wol min lip daz bewart.
div massenie ist al sölher art.
genahete ir immer vilan.
daz ware vil sere misseran.
ez knappe aleine furbax reit.
vf einen plan niht zebreit.
der stvnt von blvmen liht gemal.
in zoch dehein Cvrvenal.
er chvnde kvrtosie niht.
als vngevarnen man gesicht.
sin zöm der was paltin.
vn lvrte chranch sin phardelin.
daz tet von strvchen manegen val.
och was sin sattel vberal.
vnbeslagen mit niwen ledern.
samit herminer vedern.
man da vil lvzzel an im silt.
ern bedorfte der mantel snvre niht.
fvr svkenie vnd fvr svrkot.
da fvr nam er sin gabylot.
des site man gein prise maz.
sin vatr was gvcleidet baz.
vfem teppiche vol kanvoleiz.
der geliez nie vorthlichen sweiz.
jm chom ein ritr widr riten.
den gervter nach sinen siten.
got halb ivch riet min mvtr mir.
ivncherre got lone iv vn ir.
spch Artvs basin svn.
den zoch Grepandragvn.
och spch der selbe wigant.
erbeschaft ce Bertane vn daz lant.

D   S. 44   Sp. 44ᵃ = L 141,27–143,20
              Sp. 44ᵇ = L 143,21–145,14

er was vrier von kukeviez.
den roten riter man in hiez.
sin harnas was gar so rot.
daz ez den ogen rote bot.
sin ors was rot vn snel.
al rot was sin gugrel.
rot samit was sin covertivre.
sin schilt noch roter danne ein fivr.
al rot was sin kursit.
vn wol an in gesimten wit.
rot was sin schaft. rot was sin sper.
al rot nach des heldes ger. was im sin swert
gerotet. nach der scerpfe idoch gelotet.
Der kvnec von chuchumerlant.
al rot von golde vf siner hant.
stvnt ein kopf vil wol ergrabn.
ob tavelrvnde vf erhabn.
blanch was sin vel rot was sin har.
der sprch zem knappen svndr var.
geert si din svzer lip.
dich braht zer werelde ein reine wip.
owol der mvtr div dich gebar.
me gesach nie lip so wol gevar.
dv bist der waren minne blich.
ir sevmpheit riwet vn ir sich.
vil wibes frede an dir gesigt.
dar nach dir zimt swærer wigt.
Lieber frivnt wil dv da hin in.
so sage mir dvrch den diezest min.
dem kvnege vn al den sinen.
me syle niht flvhtich schinen.
ich wil hie gerne beiten.
swer zer tiost sich sol bereiten.
z neheiner hubz fvr wider.
ich reit fvr tavelrvnder.
mins landes ich mich vnderwant.
disen koph min vngefvgiv hant.
vf zehte daz der win vergoz.
frôn ginovern in ir schoz.
vnderwinden mich daz lerte.
ob ich schobe vmbe cherte.
so wide rvzech mir min vel.
daz meit ich sprch der degen snel.
jne hanz ôch niht dvrch rôp getan.
des hat min chrone mich erlan.
frivnt nv sager der kvnegin.
ich begvzzet an den willen min.
alda die werden saxen.
die reht zuer vergaxen.
ez sin kvnege odr fvrsten.
wes laxerez si ir wirt erdvrsten.
wan holet si un hie sin golt vaz.
ir sneller pris wirt anders laz.
Der knappe sprch ich wirbe dir.

swaz dv gesprochen hast ze mir.
er reit von un ze llantes in.
da volgeten un div kindelin.
vf den hoff fvr den palas.
da maneger slahte fvre was.
schiere wart vmb in gedranch.
swanet dar naher spranch.
ein knappe valches yrie.
der bot un kvmpanie.
Der knappe sprch got halde dich.
vur reden min nivtr mich.
ê daz ich schiede von ir lws.
ich sihe hie manegen dirvs.
wer sol mich riter machen.
swanet begvnde lachen.
er sprch. dvne silzt des rehten niht.
daz aber schiere nv geschiht.
er fvrten in zem palas.
da div werde massenide was.
svs vil chvndr in schalle.
er sprch got halde weh herren alle.
benamn den kvnec vn des wip.
mir gebot min mvtr an den lip.
daz ich die gvrte svndr.
die ob der tavelrvnde.
von rehtem prise heten stat.
die selbn si mich grvzen bat.
Dar an ein chvnst mich verbirt.
ine weiz niht welher hiune ut wirt.
dem hat ein ritter her enborn.
den sah ich allenthalben rôrn.
er welle sin da vze biten.
mich dvnchet er welle striten.
jm ist ôch leit daz er den win.
vergoz vf die kvnegin.
owi wan het ich sin gewant.
enphangen von des kvneges hant.
so were ich freden riche.
wan ez stet so riterliche.
Der knappe vnbetwngen.
wart harte vil gedrvngen.
gehvrt her. vnt dar.
si namen siner varwe war.
diz was selpscowet.
gelert noch gerowet.
wart me minnechlicher frvht.
got was in einer svzen zvht.
do er parzivalen worhte.
der vreise wenitch vorhte.
svs wart er fvr drvsen braht.
an dem got wisshel het erdaht.
un chvnde niemn viertv sin.
do besah in ôch div kvnegin.
ê si schiede von dem palas.

da si da vor begozzen was.
Artvs an dem knappen sach.
zv den zwinben er do spch.
wnherre. got vergelde iv grvz.
den ich gerne dienen mvz.
mit dem libe vñ mit dem gvte.
des ist mir wol zemvte.
wolt er got wan wære daz war:
der wile dvnchet mich ein iar.
daz ich niht ritter wesen sol.
daz tvt mir wirs denne wol.
nyne svmet mich niht mere.
phlegt man nach ritters ere.
daz tvn ich gerne spch der wirt.
ob werdecheit mich niht verbirt.
v bist wol so gehvre.
rich an edile stivre.
wirt dir min gabe vndertan.
desvar ich solz vngerne lan.
dv solt vnze morgen beiten.
ich wil dich wol bereiten.
der wol geborne knappe:
hielt gagernde als ein trappe:
er spch ine wil hie nihtes biten.
mir chom ein ritter wider riten.
mach mir des harnasche werden niht:
ine rvche wer kvneges gabe gilt.
so git aber mir div mvter min.
ich wæne doch div ist ein kvnegin.
Artvs spch zem knappen san.
daz harnasch fvrt an im ein man.
daz ich dirz niht getorste gebn.
ich mvz doch svs mit chvmber lebn.
an alle mine schvlde.
sit ich darbe siner hvlde.
ez ist ither von Gaheviez.
der trvren mir dvrch frede stiez.
Jr wæret ein kvnec milte.
ob ivch solher gabe bevilte:
gebtz im dar: sprach keye san.
vñ lat in zv zim vf den plan.
sol znnen bringen vns den kopf:
ir heit div geisel dort der topf.
lat kint in vmbe triben.
so lobt manz vor den wiben.
ez mvz noch diehe hagen.
vñ solhe scanze wagen.
One sorge vmb ir dewedrs lebn.
man sol hvnde nach ebers höpte gebn.
vngerne wolt ich in versagn.
wan daz ich fvrhte er werde erslagn.
den ich heizen sol der riterschaft.
spch Artvs vz trvwen ernaft.
Der knappe idoch die gabe emphiench.

da von ein iamer sit ergiench.
do was im von dem kvnege gach.
ivnge vñ alte im drvngen nach.
Jwanet in an der hende zoch.
fvr eine löben niht zegroz.
do sah er fvr vnd widr:
och was div löbe so nidr:
daz er drvffe horte vñ och ersach.
da von ein trvren im geschach.
Da wolt och div kvnegin.
selbe an dem venstr sin.
mit rittern vñ mit fröwen.
die begvnden in alle schöwen.
da saz frö Cvnneware.
div fiere vñ div clare.
div enlachete decheinen gwis.
sine sæhe in div den hohsten pris.
here or solte erwerben.
si wolt e svs ersterben.
aller lachen si vermeit.
vnz daz der knappe fvr si reit.
do erlachete ir minnechlicher mvnt.
des wart ir rvkke vngesvnt.
O nam keye senescalt.
frön Cvnnewaren de lalant:
mit ir reiden hare:
ir lange zöpfe clare.
die want er vmbe sine hant.
er spanetese ane tvrbant.
ir rvke wart dechein eit gestabt.
doch wart ein stab so dran gehabt.
vnze daz sin sivsen gar verswanch.
dvrch die wat. vnt dvrch ir vel ez dranch.
Do spch der vnwise.
iwerin werdem prise:
ist gegebn ein smahlv lere:
ich pin sin wangech nezze.
ich solen widr in ivch sniden.
daz irz empfindet vf den liden.
ez ist dem kvnege Artvs.
vf sinen hoff vnt in sin hvs.
so manech werdr man geriten.
dvrch den ir lachen hat vermiten.
vñ lachet ir dvrch einen man.
der niht mit ritters fvre chan.
Jn zorne widers vil gestalt.
svs slages wart im erteilet niht:
vorim riche vf dise magt.
div vil von frivnden wart geschlagt.
ob si halt seit solde tragn.
div vnfvge ist da geslagn.
wan si was von arde ein fvrstin.
Orilvs vnd Lähelin.
ir brvdr heten die geschehen

der slege muñte ware geschehen.
Der verswigene Anthanor·
der durch swigen dohte an tor·
sin rede vñ ir lachen.
was gezilt mit einen sachen.
ern wolde nimmer wort gesagn.
sine lachете div da wart geslagn.
do ir lachen wart getan.
sin munt sprch ze keyen san.
got weiz her Seneschalt.
daz Cunnewаre de Lalant.
durch den knappen ist zerbert.
weit frede es wirt verzert·
noch von siner hende.
ern si nie so ellende.
Sit iwer erste rede mir drot.
ich wæne ir wenich rich gerrot.
sin brat wart galvnet.
mit slegen vil gervnet.
dem wirzehaftem toren.
mit fivsten in sin oren.
daz ret kaye svndr twal.
So muse der ivnge Parzival.
disen chvmber scowen.
Anthanors vñ der frowen.
im was von herzen leit ir not.
vil dicher greif zem gabilot.
vor der kynegin was solh gedranch.
daz er durch daz vermeit den swanch.
vrlop nam do Jwanet.
zem fillv roy bahmvret.
ez reise aleine wart getan.
hin vz gein Jther vf den plan.
dem saget er solhiv mare.
daz niemn dinne wære.
Ich sagte als dv mir verzihe.
wi ez ane danch geschæhe.
daz dv den win vergvze.
vnfvge dich verdrvze.
ir decheinen wider strites.
gip mir da dv offe rites.
vñ dar zu al din harnasch.
daz enpfieng ich vf den pelas.
dar inne ich ritter werden mvz.
wider sagt si dir min grvz.
ob dv mirz vngerne gist.
war mich ob dv bi wirzen sist·
Der kynec von kvchvmerlant.
sich hat artvs hant.
dir min harnasch gegebn.
daz tætr öch min lebn.
mohtestv mirz an gewinnen.
svs chan er friwende minnen.
was er dir abr e iht holt. *1 holt*

din dienst gedient so schiere den solt.
Ich getar wol dienen swaz ich sol.
öch hat er mich gewert vil wol.
gip her vñ laz din lantreht.
ine wil niht langer sin ein kneht.
ich sol schildes ambet han.
er greif vm nach dem zome san.
dv maht wol wesen zehelin.
von dem mir chlaget div mvttr min.
Der ritter vmbe chert den schaft.
vñ stach den knappen so mit chraft.
daz er vñ sin pfæredlin.
mvsen vallende vf die blvmen sin.
Der helt was zornes dræte·
er slvg in daz vm wæte.
wome schafte zter swarte blvt·
Parzival der knappe gvt.
stvnt al zornich vf dem plan.
sin gabylot begreif er san.
da der helm vñ div barbier·
sich locheten ob dem harsnier·
durchz öge in sneit daz gabylot.
vñ durch den nach so daz er tot.
viel der valscheite widrsatz·
wibe svfzen herzen iamers chratz.
gap Jthers tot von baheviez·
der wiben nazziv ögen liez.
swelhiv siner minne enphant.
durch die frede ir was gezant.
vñ ir scimpf entschvmpfieret·
gein der rivhe getondwieret·
Parzival der tvmbe.
cherten diche al vmbe·
er chvnde im ab geziehen niht·
daz was ein widerlich geseiht.
helmes snvre noch siniv scinnelier·
mit sinen blanchen handen fier·
chvnd ers niht vf gestriehen.
noch svs her ab gezwiehen.
vil dicherz doch versvchte.
wisheit der vmbervchte.
Daz ors vñ daz pfæredlin.
erhvben einen so hohen grin.
daz ez Jwanet erhorte.
vor der stat ans graben orte.
frön ginovern knappe vñ ir mach.
der von dem orse erhorte den bach.
vñ do er niemn drvffe sach.
von sinen triwen daz geschach.
di er nach Parzivale trvch.
do dahte daz der knappe chlvch.
Er vant Jthern tot.
vñ Parzivalen in vmber not.
snellich er zin beiden spranch.

D   S. 47   Sp. 47^a = L 152,22–154,17
Sp. 47^b = L 154,18–156,11

48

do sageter Parzivale danch.
priss des erwarp sin hant.
an dem Chvchvmerlant.
got lone dir: nu rate was ich tv.
ich chan hie harte wenich tv.
wie brinege ich ab vn an mich.
daz chan ich wol gelern dich.
sus sprch der stolze Jwaner.
zein sun roy Gahmuret.
entwapent wart der tote man.
al da vor Hattes vf dem plan.
vn an den lebenden geleit.
den dannoch groziv tvmpeit reit.
Jwaner sprch div ribbalin.
svlen niht vnderein isern sin.
dv solt niv tragen rittrs chleit.
div rede was Parzivale leit.

Do sprch der knappe gvter:
swaz mir gap min mvter.
des sol vil wenich von mir chomn.
ez ge zescaden odr ze frvmn.
daz dvhte wnderlich genvch.
Jwaner der was chlvch.
idoch mvser im volgen.
ern was im niht erbolgen.
zwo liehte hosen iserin.
schvht erem vber div ribbalin.
svber leder mit zwein porten.
zwene sporen dar zv gehorten.
er spien im an daz goldes werch.
e er im brite dar den halperch.
er strichte im vmbe div seinnelier:
svndr twale vil harte sein:
von fvz vf gewapent wol.
wart Parzival mit gerendr bol.
Do iesch der knappe mare.
sinen chochare:
ich enreiche dir dechein gabylot.
div ritterscaft dir daz verbot.
sprch Jwaner der knappe wert.
der gvrte im vmbe ein scarpfez swert.
daz lert ern vz ziehen.
vn widr riet im fliehen.
do zoh er im dar naher sin.
des roten mannes kastelan.
daz trvch pein hoh vn lanch.
der gewapent in den satel spranch.
ern gerte stegreifes niht:
dem man noch svelheit gyht:
Jwaneren niht bevilte.
ern lerten vnderm scilte.
chvnstechlich gebarn.
vn der viende scaden warn.
er bot im in die hant ein sper:

daz was gar ane sine ger:
doch vragt ern. war zv ist diz frvm.
swer gein dir zer tiost chvm.
da soltvz balde brechen.
dvrch sinen scilt verstechen.
wiltv des vil getriben.
man lobt dich vor den wiben.
Als vns div aventvre gieht:
von Chölne noch von Mastriht:
dechein sciltare entwrfen hiez.
denn alser vsem orse saz.
Do sprch er zywaneren san.
lieber frivnt min kvmpan.
ich han hie erworben des ich pat.
dv solt min dienst in die stat.
dem kvnege dreuse sagen.
vn öch min hohez laster chlagen.
bring im widr sin golt vax.
ein ritter sich an mir vergax.
daz er die ivnchfröwen kiiscch.
dvrch daz si lachens mvn gewch.
mich mvrit ir iamerlichen wort.
dine rvrent mir dechein hercen ort.
ia mvz ein mitten drinne sin.
der fröwen vngedienter pin.
nv trev dvrch dine geselleckeit.
vn lax dir sin min laster leit.
got hvte din ich wil von dir warn.
der mag vns bede wol bewarn.
Ithern vn Gahoviez.
er iamerliche lügen hiez.
der was doch rot so minnechlich.
lebende was er selden rich.
ware ritrschaft sin endes wer:
zer tiost dvrch schilt mit eime sper:
wer chlagetv denne die widers not:
er starp von eime gabylot.
Jwaner vs im do brach.
der liehten blvmen reinis dach.
er stiez den gabylotes stil.
zv im nach der martr zil.
der knappe chvsche vn stolz.
drvchte euchtvziefwis ein holz.
dvrch des gabylotes snident.
done wolder niht vermiden.
hin in die stat er sagete.
des manech wip verzagete.
vnt des manech ritter weinde.
der chlagende triwe erdeinde.
Da wart iamers vil gedolt.
der tote scone wart geholt.
div kvneginne reit vz der stat.
daz heuichevin si fvren bat.
ob dem kvnege von Chvchvmerlant.

den tote parzivales hant.
zo ginover div kvnegin.
sprach iamerlicher worte sin.
owe vnd heia hei.
...vil werdecheit erwer.
...l brechen noch dir wudt.
...der ob der tavelrvndr.
den hohsten pris solde tragn.
...ar der von hantes lit erslagn.
sins erbteils er gerte.
da man in sterbens werte.
...r was doch massenide alhie.
also dax dechein ore rue.
...cheine sin vntat vernam.
...r was vor wildem valsce zam.
der was vil gar von im geschabn.
...nv mvz ich alxefrv begrabn.
ein floz ob dem prise.
sin herze an zvhten wise.
ob ensloze ein hant veste.
...ner im benamn dax beste.
...wa man nach wibes minne.
mit ellenthaftem sinne.
...lt er zeigen mannes triwe.
...n bereidiv frvhe al niwe.
...st tvreis vf div wip gesaz.
...v diner wriden iamer wirt.
...r was doch wol so rot din har.
...az din blv die blvmen clar.
...niht roter dorfte machen.
...w swendest wiplich lachen.
...zez der lobt riche.
...wart bestatet kvnecliche.
...zror schop svfzen in div wip.
...in harnasc im verlos den lip.
...ar vmbe was sin eidel wer.
...es tvmben parzivales ger.
...ir do er sich dax verstan.
...ngern her erz do getan.
...dax ors einer site pflach.
...zvz arbeit er ringe wach.
...zz ware chalt oder heiz.
...r enliez dvrch reise cheinen swerz.
...mvte stein oder ronen.
...r dorft im cheines gvrtens wonen.
...doch eines loches naher baz.
...so er zwene tage drvfte saz.
...gwapent reit er der tvmbe man.
...den tach so verre erz bete lan.
...an blox wiser solt erz han geritten.
...zwene tage erz warte vermitten.
...e liez er sevften selten drabn.
...r chvnde in lvzzel vf gehabn.
...inn gein abende er resach.

eines tvrnes gvpfen vnt des dach.
den tvmben dvhte sere.
wie der tvrne whse mere.
der stvnt da vil vf eime hvs.
do wunde si sere drvs.
des uher im fvr heilicheit.
Vnt dax sin selde ware breit.
Also sprach der tvmbe man.
Ammer mvrt volch niht pruven chan.
iane wehset niht so lanch ir sat.
swaz si ir vnden walde hat.
grox regen si setzen da verbirt.
Gvrnemanz de grahart hiez der wirt.
vf dirre bvrch. dar zv er reit.
da vor stvnt ein linde breit.
vf einen grvnen anger.
der was breiter noch langer.
niht wan ze rehter maxe.
dax ors vn ôch div strâxe.
in trvgen da er sizzen vant.
des was div bvrch vn ôch dax lant.
sin groxiv mvde in des betwanch.
dax er den schilt vnrehte swanch.
ze verte hindr odr fvr.
er nndit nach der site chvr.
die man da gein prise max.
Gvrnemanz der vvrste al eine saz.
ôch gap der luiden tolde.
ir saxen alf si solde.
dem hoptman der waren zvht.
des site was vor valsce ein flvht.
der enpfiench den gast dax was sin reht.
bi im was ritter noch chneht.
Svss antwrte im do parzival.
vz tvmben wizzen svndr twal.
mich pat min mvter nemn rat.
ze dem der grawe lohe hat.
da wil ich iv dienen nach.
sir mir min mvter des veriach.
Ist iv dvrch ratef schvlde.
her chomn iwer hvlde.
mvzzet ir mir dvrch raten lan.
vn wolt ir ratef volge han.
Do wrf der vvrste mare.
einen mvter sparwarre.
von der herde. in die bvrch er swanch.
ein gvldin scelle dran erchlanch.
dax was ein bote do quam in sin.
vil inncherren wolgetan.
er bat den gast den er da sach.
in fvren vn scaffen sin gemach.
der sprch. min mvter sagt alwar.
alte mannes rede stet niht ze var.
Hin in fvren si in al zehant.

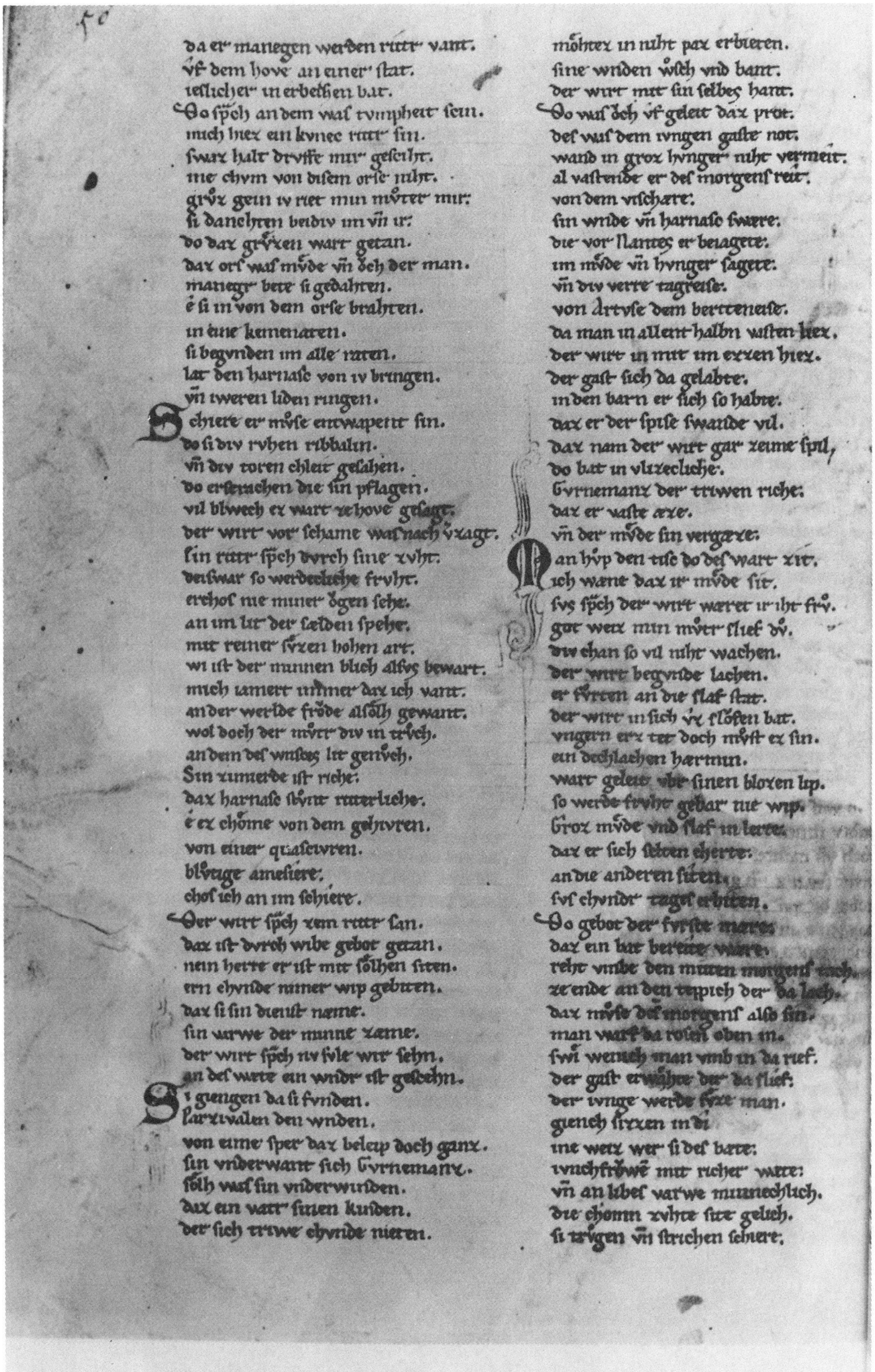

da er manegen werden ritter vant.
vf dem hove an einer stat.
iesliche in erbeizen bat.
Do sprach an dem was tumpheit schin.
mich hiez ein kunec ritter sin.
swaz halt drvffe mir geschiht.
ine chvm von disem orse niht.
grvz gein iv riet min mvter mir.
si danchten beidiv im vñ ir.
do daz grvzen wart getan.
daz ors was mvde vñ doch der man.
manegr bete si gedahten.
ê si in von dem orse brahten.
in eine kemenaten.
si begvnden im alle raten.
lat den harnasch von iv bringen.
vñ twerern liden ringen.
Schiere er mvse entwapent sin.
do si div rvhen ribbalin.
vñ div toren chleit gesahen.
do erschrachen die sin pflagen.
vil blvwech ez wart ze hove gesagt.
der wirt vor schame was nach verzagt.
sin ritter sprach durch sine zvht.
deiswar so werdechliche frvht.
erchos nie miner ogen sehe.
an im lit der saelden spehe.
mit reiner svzen hohen art.
wi ist der minnen bluch alsus bewart.
mich iamert immer daz ich vant.
an der werlde frode alsolh gewant.
wol doch der mvter div in trvch.
an dem des wunsches lit genvch.
Sin zimierde ist riche.
daz harnasch stvnt ritterliche.
ê ez chôme von dem gehvren.
von einer quaschvren.
blvtige amesiere.
chos ich an im schiere.
Der wirt sprach zem ritter san.
daz ist durch wibe gebot getan.
nein herre er ist mit solhen siten.
ern chvnde nimer wip gebiten.
daz si sin dienst naeme.
sin varwe der minne zaeme.
der wirt sprach nv sule wir sehn.
an des wate ein wnder ist geschehn.
Si giengen da si fvnden.
parzivalen den wnden.
von eime sper daz beleip doch ganz.
sin vnderwant sich Gvrnemanz.
solh was sin vnderwinden.
daz ein vatter sinen kinden.
der sich triwe chvnde nieten.

mohter in niht baz erbieten.
sine wnden wsch vnd bant.
der wirt mit sin selbes hant.
Do was doch vf geleit daz prot.
des was dem ivngen gaste not.
wand in groz hvnger niht vermeit.
al vastende er des morgens reit.
von dem vischaere.
sin wnde vñ harnasch swaere.
die vor Nantes er beiagete.
im mvde vñ hvnger sagete.
vñ div verre tagreise.
von artvse dem bertenoise.
da man in allenthalbn vasten liez.
der wirt in mit im ezzen hiez.
der gast sich da gelabte.
in den barn er sich so habte.
daz er der spise swande vil.
daz nam der wirt gar zeime spil.
do bat in vlizecliche.
Gvrnemanz der triwen riche.
daz er vaste aeze.
vñ der mvde sin vergaeze.
Man hvp den tisc do des wart zit.
ich waene daz ir mvde sit.
sus sprach der wirt waeret ir iht frv.
got weiz min mvter slief dv.
div chan so vil niht wachen.
der wirt begvnde lachen.
er fvrten an die slaf stat.
der wirt in sich vz sloufen bat.
vngern erz tet doch mvst ez sin.
ein dechlachen hermin.
wart geleit vber sinen bloxen lip.
so werde frvht gebar nie wip.
Groz mvde vnd slaf in lerte.
daz er sich selten cherte.
an die anderen siten.
sus chvnde er tages erbiten.
Do gebot der fvrste maere.
daz ein bat bereite waere.
reht vmbe den mitten morgens zich.
ze ende an den teppich der da lach.
daz mvse des morgens also sin.
man warf da rosen oben in.
swi weinech man vmb in da rief.
der gast erwahte der da slief.
der ivnge werde svze man.
giench sitzen in di
nie weiz wer si des bate.
ivnchfrowen mit richer wate.
vñ an libes varwe minnechlich.
die chomn zvhte site gelich.
si twvgen vñ strichen schiere.

D S. 5o Sp. $5o^{a}$ = L 163,18-165,11
Sp. $5o^{b}$ = L 165,12-167,5

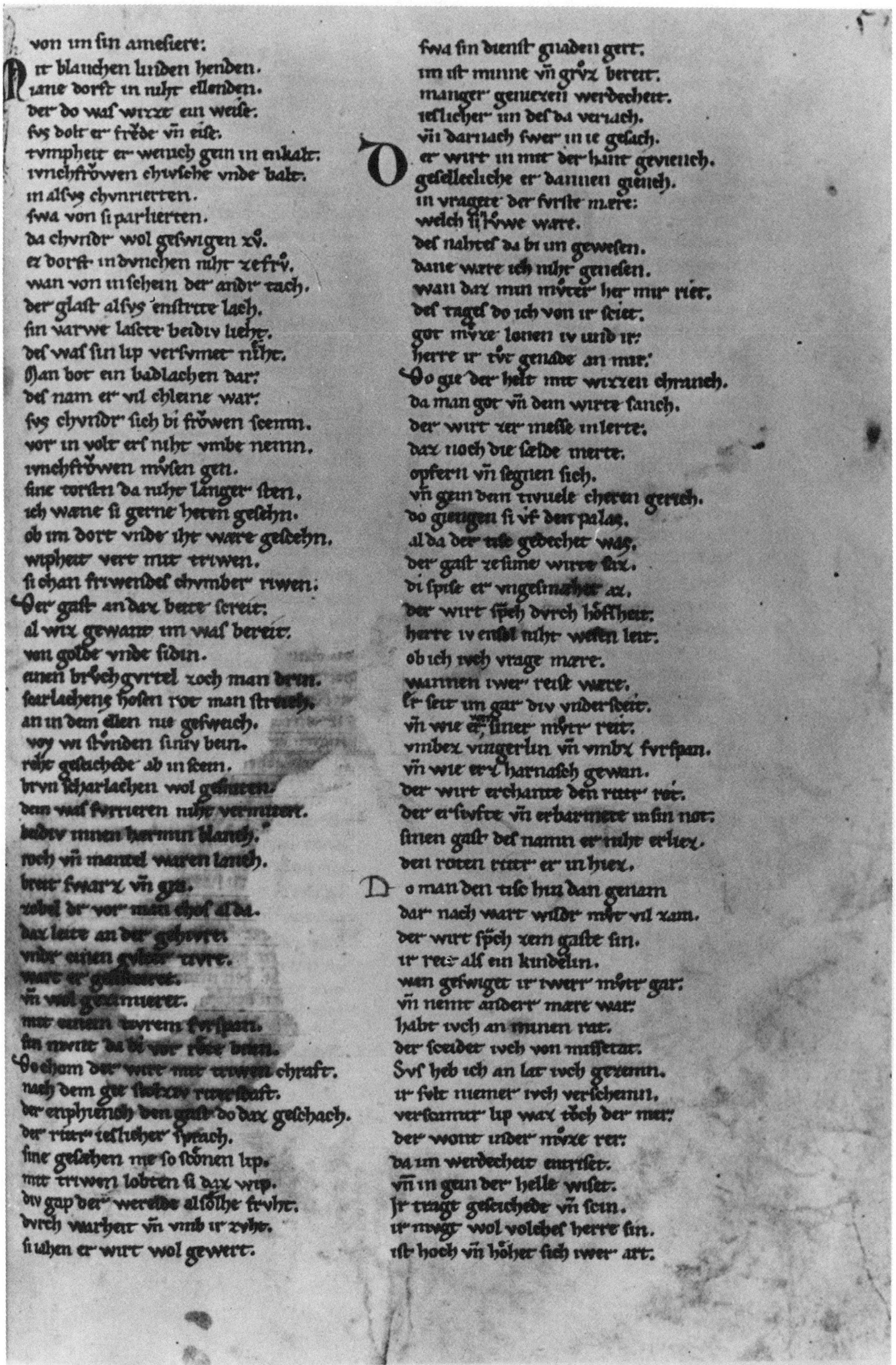

von im sin amesiere:
Nv blanchen linden henden.
wane dorst in niht ellenden.
der do was wizze ein weise.
sus dolt er frĕde vn̄ eise.
tumpheit er weinch gein in enkalt.
ivnchfrŏwen chiwsche vnde balt.
in alsus chvnrierten.
swa von si parlierten.
da chvndr wol geswigen zv̊.
ez dorst in dvnchen niht zefrv̊.
wan von in schein der andr tach.
der glast alsus enstritte lach.
sin varwe laschte beidiv lieht.
des was sin lip versvmet niht.
Man bot ein badlachen dar:
des nam er vil chleine war:
sus chvndr sich bi frŏwen schemn.
vor in wolt ers niht vmbe nemn.
ivnchfrŏwen mv̊sen gen.
sine torstn da niht langer sten.
ich wæne si gerne heten gesehn.
ob im dort vnde iht wære geschehn.
wipheit vert mit triwen.
si chan friwendes chumber riwen.
Der gast an daz bette screit:
al wiz gewant im was bereit:
von golde vnde sidin.
einen brŭchgurtel zoch man [illegible].
scarlachens hosen rot man [illegible].
an in dem ellen nie gesweich.
wy wi stv̊nden siniv bein.
rehte gesachede ab in schein.
brvn scharlachen wol [illegible].
dem was furrieren niht [illegible].
beidiv innen hermin blanch.
roch vn̄ mantel waren lanch.
[illegible] swarz vn̄ [illegible].
zobel [illegible] vor man chos al da.
daz leite an der [illegible].
vnde einen [illegible] tivre.
[illegible]
vn̄ wol [illegible].
mit [illegible] fvrspan.
sin munt [illegible].
Dochom der wirt mit triwen chraft.
nach dem gie [illegible] riterschaft.
der enphiench den gast do daz geschach.
der riter iesliher sprach.
sine gesæhen nie so schonen lip.
mit triwen lobten si daz wip.
div gap der werelde also[l]he fruht.
durch warheit vn̄ vmb ir zuht.
si iahen er wirt wol gewert.
swa sin dienst gnaden gert.
im ist minne vn̄ grv̊z bereit.
manger geniezen werdecheit.
iesliher im des da veriach.
vn̄ darnach swer in ie gesach.
Der wirt in mit der hant gevienech.
gesellecliche er dannen gienech.
in vrageter der furste mere:
welch si frŏwe wære.
des nahtes da bi im gewesen.
dane wære ich niht genesen.
wan daz min mv̊ter her mir riet.
des tages do ich von ir schiet.
got mvze lonen iv vnd ir:
herre ir tvt genade an mir:
Do gie der helt mit wizzen chranch.
da man got vn̄ dem wirte sanch.
der wirt zer messe in lerte:
daz noch die selde merte.
opfern vn̄ segnen sich.
vn̄ gein dem tivuele cheren gerich.
do giengen si vf den palas.
al da der tisch gedechet was.
der gast ze sime wirte saz.
di spise er vngesmacher az.
der wirt sprach durch hofsheit:
herre iv ensol niht wesen leit:
ob ich iwch vrage mære.
wannen iwer reise wære.
Er seit im gar div vndersceit.
vn̄ wie er [...] siner mv̊ter reit:
vmbez vingerlin vn̄ vmbz furspan.
vn̄ wie erz harnasch gewan.
der wirt erchante den riter rot.
der ersiufte vn̄ erbarmete in sin not:
sinen gast des namn er niht erliez.
den roten riter er in hiez.
Do man den tisch hin dan genam
dar nach wart wilder mvt vil zam.
der wirt sprch zem gaste sin.
ir ret als ein kindelin.
wen geswiget ir iwer mv̊ter gar:
vn̄ nemt ander mære war:
habt iwch an minen rat.
der scheidet iwch von missetat.
Sus heb ich an lat iwch gezemn.
ir solt niemer iwch verschemn.
verschamter lip waz tŏch der mer:
der wont in der mv̊ze rer:
da im werdecheit entriset.
vn̄ in gein der helle wiset.
Ir tragt gesichede vn̄ schin.
ir mugt wol volches herre sin.
ist hoch vn̄ hoher sich iwer art.

D S. 51 Sp. 51[a] = L 167,6 -168,29
Sp. 51[b] = L 168,3o-17o,23

lat iweren willen des bewart.
ich sol erbarmen noteeh her.
gein des chumbr sit ze wer.
mit milte vn mit gvte.
vlrzet iweh dieenvte.
der chvmberhafte werde man.
wol mit staete ringen chan.
dax ist ein vnsvr arbeit.
dem svlt ir helfe sin bereit.
swenne ir dem toe chvmbers bvr.
so nahet iv der gotes grvr.
irn ist noch wirs denne den di gent.
nach porte al da div venster stent.
Ir svlt bescheidenliche.
sin aren vn riche.
wan swa der herre gar vertvt.
dax ist niht herrenlicher mvt.
samnet er aber scax ze sere.
dax sint doch vnere.
gebt rehter maxe ir orden.
ich pin wol innen worden.
dax ir rates dvrftich sit.
nv lat der vnfvge ir strit.
Iren svlt niht vil gevragen.
doch ensol iveh niht betragen.
bedahter gegen rede div ge.
reht als iener vragen ste.
der iveh wil mit worten spehen.
ir chvnthet horen vn sehen.
entseben vn braehen.
dax solt iveh wixxen naehen.
lat die erbarme bi der vravel sin.
svs tvt mir rates volge schin.
An swem ir strites sicherheit.
bezalt. ern hab iv solhiv leit.
getan. div herxe chvmbr wesn.
div nemt vnd laxet in genesn.
ir mvxer diche wapen tragn.
sox von iv chom dax ir getwagn.
vndr ogen vn an handen sit.
des ist nach isters rame xit.
sit manlich vn wol gemvt.
dax ist ze werdem priset iv gvt.
Vnd lat iv liep sin div wip.
dax tiwert ivnges mannes lip.
gewenchet nimer tag an in.
dax ist rehte manlicher sin.
welt ir in gerne liegen.
ir mvget ir vil betriegen.
gein werdr minne valscer list.
hat gein prise cbvrxe vrist.
da wirt der slichaere ehlage.
dax dvrre holx ime hage.
dax prister vn ehrachet.

der wahtaere erwachet.
vngeverte vnd hamit.
dar gedihet manech strit.
Dix relt gein der minne.
div werde hat sinne.
gein valsce listeclich ehvnst.
swenn ir belaget ir vngvnst.
so nixxet ir gvneret sin.
vn imer dvlten scamenden pin.
dise lere svlt ir nahe tragn.
ich wil iv mer von wibes orden sagn.
Man vn wip die sint al ein.
als div svnne div hivte scein.
vn doch der name der heixet tach.
der enwederx sich gescheiden mach.
si blvnt vx ame cheyne gar.
des nemt chvnstechiche war.
Der gast dem wirte dvrch raten nach.
siner mvter ergesweich.
mit rede vn in dem herxen niht.
als noch getriwem man gesihet.
Der wirt spch sin ere.
noch svlt ir lernen mere.
chvnst an riterliche siten.
wie quamet ir xv mir geriten.
ich han bescowet manege want.
da ich den scilt bax hangen vant.
denn er iv ze halse taete.
ex ist vns niht ze spaete.
wir svlen xe velde gahen.
da svlt ir chvnste nahen.
Bringet um sin ors vn mir x min.
vn ietlichem ritter sin.
ivncherren svlen doch dar chomn.
der ietlicher habe genomn.
einen starchen schaft vn bringen dar.
der nach der niwe si gevar.
Svs chom der fvrste vf den plan.
da wart mit riten chvnst getan.
sime gaste er raten gap.
wi erx ors vxem walap.
mit sporn grvier pine.
mit scenesleien fliegen seine.
vf den poridr solde wenchen.
vn den scaft xerehte senchen.
vn den scilt gein rioste fvr sich nnnen.
er speh des laxer iveh gexennen.
Vnfvge er im svs werte.
dax denne an swanchel gerte.
div argen ehunden brichet vel.
do inez er chomn ritter snel.
gein im dvrch rivstieren.
er begvrste in condwieren.
einem xeggen an den rinch.

D   S. 52   Sp. 52^a = L 17o,24–172,19
                Sp. 52^b = L 172,2o–174,13

do brahte der ivngelinch.
sin ersten riost dvrch einen schilt.
des von in allen wart bevilt.
vn dar er hinders ors verswanch.
einen starchen riter niht ze chranch.
sin tiostiure was chomn.
do het och Parcival genomn.
einen starchen niwen schaft.
sin ivgent het ellen vn chraft.
der ivnge svze arte hart.
den twanch div bahmvrets art.
vn an geborniv manheit.
uax ors von Rabbine er reit.
mit volleclicher hvrte dar.
er nam der vier nagele war.
des wirtes riter niht gesax.
al vallende er den aecher max.
do mvsen chleiniv stvchelin.
al da von trvnxvnen sin.
svs stach er ir fvnve nidr.
der wirt in nam vn fvrten widr.
al da behielt er seumpfes pris.
er wart och sit an strite wis.
ir sin riten gesahen.
al die wisen im des iahen.
da fvre chvnst vn ellen bi.
nv wirt man herte iamers vri.
ich mach nv ivngen wol sin lebn.
er sol im zewibe gebn.
sine tohter vnser frowen.
ob wir in bi wixxen schowen.
so lider im sin iamers not.
fvr siner drier svne tot.
ist in ein gelt ze hvs geriten.
nv hat in helde nihte vermiten.
svs chom der fvrste sabenes in.
der tisc gedechet mvse sin.
sine tohter bat er chomn.
ze tisce alsvs han iche vernomn.
do er die magt chomn sach.
nv hoeret wie der wirt sprach.
vn der schonen Liaxen.
dv solt in chvssen laxen.
disen riter bive un ere.
er vert mit saelden lere.
och solt an iwch gedinget sin.
dax ir der meide ir vingerlin.
bieter ob siz mohte han.
nvne hat siz niht noch forspan.
wer gaebe ir solhen volleist.
so der frowen in dem foreist.
div het erlwen von dem si enpfiech.
dax iz zenpfahene sir ergiench.
ir mvget Liaxen niht genemn.

der gast begvnde sich des scemn.
doch chviterse an den mvnt.
den was wol siwers varwe chvnt.
Liaxen lip was minneclich.
dar xv der waren chivsce rich.
der tise was nidr vnd lanch.
der wirt mit niemn sich da dranch.
er sax al eine an den ort.
sinen gast hiex er sixxen dort.
xwisen im vnt sine kinde.
ir blanchen hende linde.
mvsen sniden so der wirt gebot.
den man da hiex der ritter rot.
swax der exxen wolde.
niemen sie weiden solde.
sine gebarten heimliche.
div mage mit xvhten riche.
leiste ir vater willen gar.
si vnt der gast waren wol gevar.
Dar nach sciere gie div mage widr.
svs pflach man des heldes sidr.
vnx an den vierxehenden tach.
bi sime herxen chvmbr lach.
anders niht wan vmbe dax.
er wolde gestriten dax.
e dax er dar an wider waren.
dax man da heizet frowen aren.
in dvhte wert gedinget.
dax waere ein hohiv linge.
zednsem libe lie vnt dort.
dax sir noch vngelogeniv wort.
ines morgens vrlobes er bat.
do rvmter Graharx die stat.
der wirt mit im zevelde reit.
do hvp sich niwex herxenleit.
do spch der fvrste vz triwe erchorn.
ir sit min vierdr svn verlorn.
ia wand ich ergexxet waere.
drier iaemerlichen maere.
der waren dennoch niht wan driv.
der nv min herxe envieriv.
mit siner hende slvge.
vn ieslicher stvche trvge.
dax divhte mich ein grox gewin.
einex fvr iwch ir riter hin.
div driv fvr minv werden kunt.
div ellenthaft erstorbn sint.
svs loner doch div riterschaft.
ir xagel ist iamer striche haft.
ein tot mich lerit an freden gar.
mius svns wol gevar.
der was geherxen Scentreflvrs.
da svndwir amvrs.
lib vn ir lant niht wolde gebn

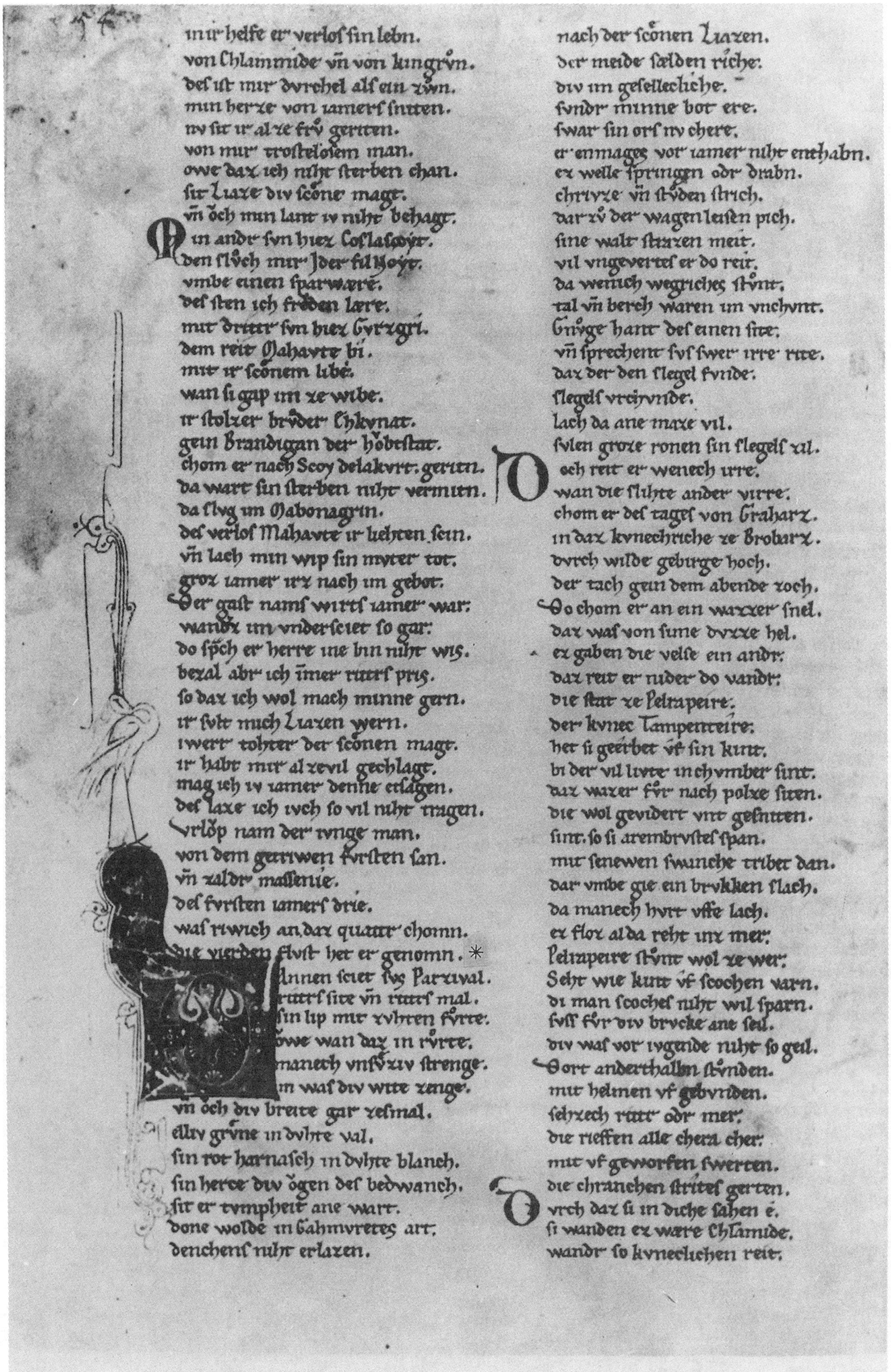
in ir helfe er verlos sin lebn.
von Chlamide vñ von kingrvn.
des ist mir dvrchel als ein zvn.
min herze von iamers snitten.
nv sit ir al ze frv geritten.
von mir trostelosem man.
owe daz ich niht sterben chan.
sit Liaze div scone magt.
vñ och min lant iv niht behagt.
Min ander svn hiez Cos lasoyr.
den slvch mir Jder fil Noyt.
vmbe einen sparware.
des sten ich freden lare.
min dritter svn hiez Gvrzgri.
dem reit Mahavte bi.
mit ir sconem libe.
wan si gap in ze wibe.
ir stolzer brvder Chkvnat.
gein Brandigan der hobestat.
chom er nach Scoy delakvrt geritn.
da wart sin sterben niht vermitn.
da slvg in Mabonagrin.
des verlos Mahavte ir liehten schin.
vñ lach min wip sin mvter tot.
groz iamer irz nach in gebot.
Der gast nams witts iamer war.
wandz im vnderseiet so gar.
do sprach er herre ine bin niht wis.
bezal abr ich imer ritters pris.
so daz ich wol mach minne gern.
ir svlt mich Liazen wern.
iwer tohter der sconen magt.
ir habt mir al ze vil gechlagt.
mag ich iv iamer denne erlagen.
des laze ich ivch so vil niht tragen.
Vrlop nam der ivnge man.
von dem getriwen fvrsten san.
vñ zaldr massenie.
des fvrsten iamers drie.
was riwich an daz quatr chomn.
die vierden flvst het er genomn. *
...nnen seiet svs Parzival.
...tters site vñ ritters mal.
...sin lip mit zvhten fvrte.
...we wan daz in rvrte.
...manech vnsvziv strenge.
...m was div wite zenge.
vñ och div breite gar ze smal.
elliv grvne in dvhte val.
sin rot harnasch in dvhte blanch.
sin herze div ogen des bedwanch.
sit er tvmpheit ane wart.
done wolde in Gahmuretes art.
denchens niht erlazen.
nach der sconen Liazen.
der meide sælden riche.
div im gesellecliche.
svndr minne bot ere.
swar sin ors nv chere.
er enmages vor iamer niht enthabn.
ez welle springen odr drabn.
chrivze vñ stvden strich.
dar zv der wagen leisen pich.
sine walt strazen meit.
vil vngevertes er do reit.
da wenich wegriches stvnt.
tal vñ berch waren im vnchvnt.
Gnvge hant des einen site.
vñ sprechent svs swer irre rite.
daz der den slegel fvnde.
slegels vrchvnde.
lach da ane maze vil.
svlen groze ronen sin slegels zil.
Doch reit er wenech irre.
wan die slihte ander virre.
chom er des tages von Graharz.
in daz kvnechriche ze Brobarz.
dvrch wilde gebirge hoch.
der tach gein dem abende zoch.
Do chom er an ein wazzer snel.
daz was von sime dvzze hel.
ez gaben die velse ein andr.
daz reit er nider do vandr.
die stat ze Pelrapeire.
der kvnec Tampenteire.
het si geerbet vf sin kint.
bi der vil livte in chvmber sint.
daz wazer fvr nach polze siten.
die wol gevidert vnt gesnitten.
sint so si arembrvstes span.
mit senewen swanche triben dan.
dar vmbe gie ein brvkken slach.
da manech hvrt vffe lach.
ez floz al da reht in z mer.
Pelrapeire stvnt wol ze wer.
Seht wie kint vf scochen varn.
di man scoches niht wil sparn.
svs fvr div brvcke ane seil.
div was vor ivgende niht so geil.
Dort anderthalbn stvnden.
mit helmen vf gebvnden.
sehzech ritter odr mer.
die riefen alle chera cher.
mit vf geworfen swerten.
die chranchen strites gerten.
Dvrch daz si in diche sahen e.
si wanden ez wære Chlamide.
wandr so kvnechlichen reit.

D S. 54 Sp. 54[a] = L 178,2 -179,25
Sp. 54[b] = L 179,26-181,19

* *Book 3 ends*

Parzival, *MS. G*

G　Bl. 1o^v　　Sp. 1o^{va} = L 1o7,3o–11o,2

　　　　　　　　Sp. 1o^{vb} = L 11o,3 –112,7

　　　　　　　　Sp. 1o^{vc} = L 112,8 –114,14

* *Apology begins*

G　　Bl. 11^r　　Sp. 11ra = L 114,15–116,16
　　　　　　　　　Sp. 11rb = L 116,19–118,18
　　　　　　　　　Sp. 11^{rc} = L 118,19–12o,22

* Book 3 begins

```
G   Bl. 11ᵛ      Sp. 11ᵛᵃ = L 120,23–122,18
                 Sp. 11ᵛᵇ = L 122,19–124,26
                 Sp. 11ᵛᶜ = L 124,27–127,7
```

G　Bl. 12^r　　Sp. 12ra = L 127,8 –129,17
　　　　　　　　Sp. 12rb = L 129,18–131,24
　　　　　　　　Sp. 12^{rc} = L 131,25–133,30

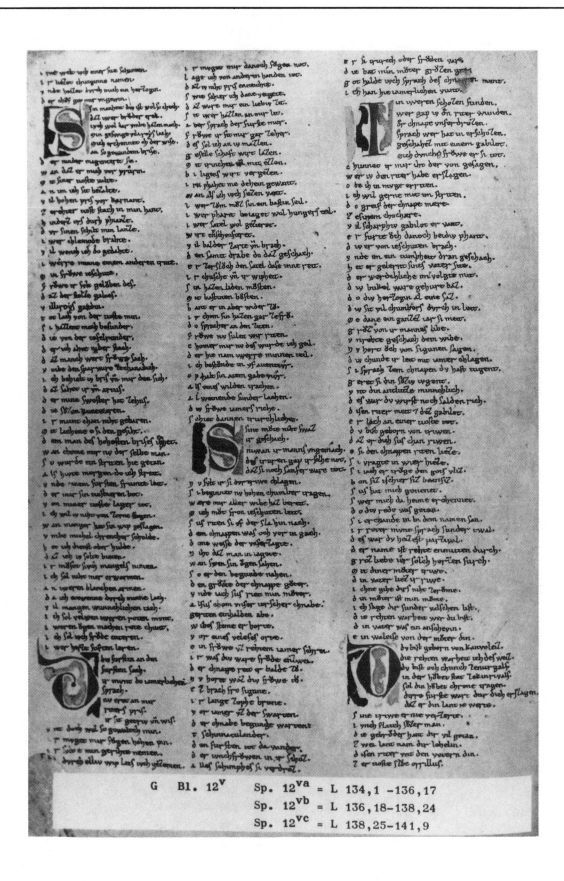

G Bl. 12ᵛ   Sp. 12ᵛᵃ = L 134,1 –136,17
            Sp. 12ᵛᵇ = L 136,18–138,24
            Sp. 12ᵛᶜ = L 138,25–141,9

13

G   Bl. 13^r   Sp. 13ra = L 141,10–143,18
                Sp. 13rb = L 143,19–145,26
                Sp. 13^rc = L 145,27–148,10

G　　Bl. 13^v　　Sp. 13va = L 148,11–150,13

Sp. 13vb = L 150,14–152,23

Sp. 13^{vc} = L 152,24–155,2

G   Bl. 14^r Sp. 14ra = L 155,3 –157,10

Sp. 14rb = L 157,11–159,22

Sp. 14^{rc} = L 159,23–162,4

G　Bl. 14ᵛ　　Sp. 14ᵛᵃ = L 162,5 −164,14

Sp. 14ᵛᵇ = L 164,15−167,26

Sp. 14ᵛᶜ = L 167,27−169,4

G   Bl. 15^r Sp. 15ra = L 169,5 –171,12
Sp. 15rb = L 171,13–173,19
Sp. 15^{rc} = L 173,20–175,30

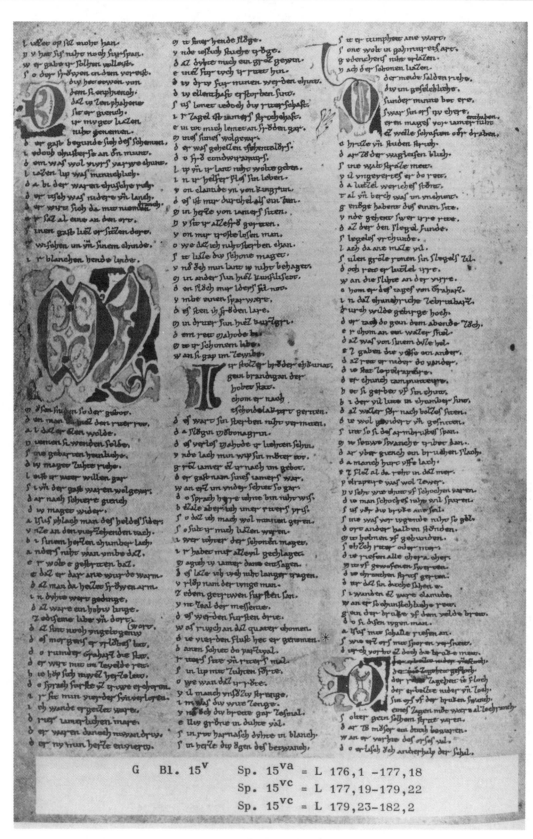

G   Bl. 15ᵛ   Sp. 15ᵛᵃ = L 176,1 –177,18
            Sp. 15ᵛᶜ = L 177,19–179,22
            Sp. 15ᵛᶜ = L 179,23–182,2

Book 3 ends

Parzival, Book 3
Translation*

Apology

If there is anyone who praises women better than I, I will surely not be the one to hold it against him. I would be glad to hear their joys extended far and wide. For only one of them am I unwilling to do loyal service, and against her my anger is still fresh – ever since I found her in disloyalty. I am Wolfram von Eschenbach, and I know a thing or two about poetry, and I am a tongs at holding my anger against a woman. This one has offered me such an offense that I cannot do other than hate her. On the account of this the others hate *me*. Why, alas! do they do so? Though their hatred troubles me, it is their womanhood that is to blame, since I did go too far and I have done myself harm. This will probably never happen again, but they should not be overhasty to storm my bastion, or else they are likely to run into defensive combat. I have not forgotten how to judge both their manners and their lives. To any woman ¹¹⁵ following propriety I shall be a defending champion of her reputation: her distress troubles me to the depths of my heart.

A man's praise limps like a spavined horse when he declares all women are off the board just to show his own lady to advantage. Any lady that wants to inspect my rights, both see them and hear them, I will not deceive her. My birth was to the knightly trade, and if my bravery is underrated by one who loves me for my poetry, I consider that she is weak in her wits. If I seek a good woman's love, and if I am not to win her love's reward by my shield and my spear, then let her bestow her favor accordingly. A man aiming at love through knightly deeds is, after all, playing for very high stakes.

If the woman would not take it for flattery, I would add further unknown words to this story for you, I would continue the adventure for you. But if anyone requests me to do so, let him not consider it a book. I don't know a single letter of the alphabet.

Plenty of people get their material that way, but this adventure steers without books. Rather than have anybody think it is a book, I would sit ¹¹⁶ naked without a towel, the way I would sit in a bath–if I didn't forget the bouquet of twigs.

♦

It grieves me that so many share the name of woman. They all have the same clear voices, but plenty of them are quick to falsity, while others are free from falsity, and thus things vary. But that they should bear the same name, shames my heart. Womanhood, with your true nature goes fidelity, and always has gone. A good many people say that poverty serves no good, but anyone enduring it for fidelity's sake, his soul will escape hellfire. There was a woman who endured it for fidelity's sake, and thereby her gift was compensated in heaven with eternal giving. I fancy there are few such now alive who would renounce the world's riches while still young for the glory of heaven. *I* know of none such. Man or woman, they are all the same, all alike shirk it.

Lady Herzeloyde, the mighty, became a stranger to her three kingdoms, bearing with her the burden of joylessness. Falsity had so utterly vanished from her heart that neither eye nor ear could detect it. ¹¹⁷ For her the sun was a mist. She fled the world's delight. To her night and day were the same; her heart dwelt on sorrow alone.

This lady full of sorrow withdrew from her kingdom to a forest, to the clearing in Soltane, and not for the sake of flowers on the meadow. Her heart's grief was so complete that she cared for no garland, neither red nor faded. And there, for refuge, she brought noble Gahmuret's child. The people who are with her have to clear and till. *She* well knew how to care for her son. Before he came of years she summoned her people before her and

* Superscript numbers in the text refer to Lachmann strophe numbers.

charged them on their lives, men and women alike, never to utter a word about knights. "For if my heart's darling should find out what knights' life is, it would pain me deeply. Now use your wits and keep all knighthood from him."

The custom traveled an anxious road. The boy thus hidden away was brought up in the forest clearing of Soltane, cheated of his royal heritage except on one count: [118] with his own hands he whittled himself a bow and little arrows and shot many birds that he came upon. But whenever he shot the bird whose song was so loud before, he would weep and tear his hair – and his hair came in for grief. His body was fair and proud. Every morning he washed in the stream by the meadow. Of sorrow he knew nothing, unless it was the birdsong above him, for the sweetness of it pierced his heart and made his little bosom swell. Weeping he ran to the queen, and she said, "Who has hurt you? You were out on the meadow." He could tell her nothing, as is still the way with children.

For a long time she kept pursuing the matter. One day she saw him gaping up at the trees toward the song of the birds, and then she realized it was their voices that made her child's bosom swell. His heritage and his desire thus compelled him. Without quite knowing why, Lady Herzeloyde turned her anger against the birds and wanted to destroy their song. She bade her plowmen and her [119] field hands make haste to snare the birds and twist their necks. The birds were better mounted. Quite a number of deaths were avoided and a share of them remained alive, which afterwards were merry with singing.

The boy said to the queen, "What do they have against the birds?" and asked peace for them at once.

His mother kissed him on the mouth and said, "Why should I alter His commandment Who is, after all, Supreme God? Should birds lose their delight because of me?"

Then the boy said to his mother, "O, what is God, Mother?"

"Son, I will tell you in all earnest. He is brighter than the daylight, yet He took upon Himself the features of man. Son, mark this wisdom and pray to Him when in trouble, for His fidelity has ever offered help to the world. But there is one called the Master of Hell, and he is black and faithlessness is his mark. From him turn your thought away, and also away from inconstant wavering!" His mother fully explained for him the dark and the light. And then his alacrity was off and away. [120]

He learned the swing of the javelot and with it brought down many a stag, which his mother and her people put to good use. Thaw or snow, his shooting brought the wild animals grief. Now hear a strange thing: when he shot a weight that would have been load enough for a mule, he would carry it home carcass-whole.

One day he went out hunting along a mountain slope. He broke off a branch from a tree for the whistle the leaf would make. Right near him ran a path, and there he heard the sound of horses' hooves. He began to brandish his javelot and said, "What is this I hear? O, if only the Devil would just come along now in his furious rage! I would stand up to him for sure. My mother says he is a terror, but I think her bravery is a little daunted." And thus he stood eager for battle, when look! there came three knights galloping along, as fair as anyone could wish and armed from the feet upward. The lad thought for sure that each one was a god, and so he stood there no longer but fell to his knees on the path. Loud cried the lad then, "Help, God! You surely have help to give!" [121] The rider in front flew into a rage to see the lad lying there in the path: "This stupid Waleis is holding up our swift journey." – A thing we Bavarians get praise for I have to say about Waleis people too: they are stupider than Bavarian folks, and yet, like them, of manly stout-heartedness. Anyone born in these two countries grows up a marvel of cleverness.

Just then there came along at a gallop a splendidly adorned knight who was in a great hurry. He was riding in pursuit of those who had got a head start on him, two knights, namely, who had abducted a lady in his land. He considered this a disgrace and grieved at the plight of the maiden, who had ridden on before him in a deplorable state. These three knights here were his own vassals. He was riding a fine Castilian horse; there was very little of his shield that was whole; and his name was Karnahkarnanz, *le comte* Ulterlec. "Who is blocking our way?" said he, and rode over to the lad, to whom he seemed to have the form of a god, for never had he seen anything so bright. His surcoat swept the dew, his stirrups, [122] adjusted to either foot to just the right length, rang with little golden bells, and his right arm chimed with bells whenever he raised it in greeting or to strike. It was meant to ring loud at his sword strokes, for this hero was eager for renown. Thus rode the rich prince, wondrously adorned.

Then of him who was a garland of all the flowers of manly beauty Karnahkarnanz asked, "Young

Sir, have you seen two knights ride past who could not keep the knightly code? They are perpetrating rape and are lacking in honor. They are abducting a maiden."

But say what he might, the lad still thought he was God, just as Lady Herzeloyde the Queen had told him when she explained His bright shining. And so he cried out in all seriousness, "Help me now, God of help!" And *le fils du roi* Gahmuret fell down in an attitude of prayer.

The prince said, "I am not God, though I gladly do His commandment. What you see here are four knights, if you would only look aright." [123] The lad asked further, "You speak of *knights:* what is that? If you do not have God's kind of power, then tell me: who bestows knighthood?"

"That King Arthur does. Young Sir, if you come to his house, he will give you the name of knight so that you will never need to be ashamed of it. You may well be of knightly race." – And by the warriors he was scrutinized, and God's handiwork was manifest in him. – I have this from the adventure, which with truth was told me so. Never had man's beauty been more nobly realized since Adam's time, and hence his praise was wide among women.

But then the lad spoke again, and laughter arose at it, "Ay, Knight God, what may you be? You have so many rings tied around your body, up there, and down here." And therewith the lad's hand laid hold of iron wherever he could find it on the prince, and he began to inspect the armor. "My mother's ladies wear their rings on strands and they don't fit so close together as these." The lad spoke further to the prince, just as the thoughts came [124] to him, "What is this good for, that fits you so well? I can't pick it off."

Then the prince showed him his sword. "You see, anyone seeking battle with me I ward off with blows, and to protect myself against his, I have to put this on, and both for shot and for stab I have to wear armor like this."

But the lad quickly replied, "If stags wore pelts like that, my javelot would not wound a single one. And a good many fall dead before me."

The knights were chafing at his delay with the lad who was so simple. "God shield you," said the prince. "Would that your beauty were mine! God would have conferred upon you the uttermost that could be wished for, if only you had intelligence. May God's power keep you from harm."

He and his men rode on at rapid gait and soon came to a field in the forest where the courteous man found Lady Herzeloyde's plows at work.

Never did greater distress befall her people. Those whom he saw plowing now, began to sow and then to harrow, wielding their goads upon stout oxen. The prince bade them good morning and [125] asked whether they had seen a maiden in distress.

There was no way out of it: what he asked, that they answered: "Two knights and a maiden rode past this morning, the lady lamenting and those that had the maiden using their spurs liberally." It was Meljacanz, whom Karnahkarnanz now outrode, taking the lady from him by force. Joyless enough had she been until then. Her name was Imane of the Beafontane.

The farm hands were dismayed as the heroes spurred past them. "How did this happen?" they said. "If our young master has glimpsed the dinted helmets on those knights, we have not kept a good lookout. We will hear the queen's hatred for this, and rightly so, for he came along here with us this morning while she was still asleep."

As a matter of fact the lad no longer cared who shot the stags small and large. He went straight to his mother and told her the story. At which she collapsed. So greatly was she terrified by his words that she lay unconscious [126] before him.

When the queen came to her senses again – whereas before she had not been equal to it – she spoke: "Son, who told you about the order of knighthood? How did you come to know of it?"

"Mother, I saw four men more shining than God, and they told me about knighthood. The royal power of Arthur shall in knightly honor turn me to chivalric service."

Here was a fresh sorrow. The lady did not rightly know what stratagem to invent to keep him from his purpose.

The simple yet noble lad kept begging his mother for a horse, so that she grieved in her heart. "I will not deny him," she thought, "but it must be a thoroughly bad one." And the queen thought further, "People are much given to mockery. Fool's clothing shall my child wear on his fair body. If he is pommeled and beaten, perhaps he will come back to me again." – Alas for her grievous sorrow! – The lady took sack cloth and cut for him shirt and [127] breeches which, all of a piece, came halfway down his white leg. Such was the regular garb of fools. On top was a hood, while from a hide of untanned calfskin boots were cut for his feet. But all this did not keep sorrow away. The queen, having pondered the matter, begged him to stay yet that night. "You shall not leave here until I teach you cunning:

On untrodden ways you must beware of dark fords;
where they are shallow and clear, there ride boldly in.

You must be polite and give people your greeting.

If a man grey with age is willing to teach you behavior,
as he well knows how to do, you must follow him willingly and not show him temper.

Son, bear this in mind: wherever you can win a good
woman's ring and greeting, take them; it will set you
free from care. You must make haste to kiss her and
clasp her tight in your embrace. That brings happiness
and a stout spirit, if she is chaste and [128]
good.

"You must know further, my son, that the proud,
bold Lehelin wrested two countries away from your
nobles, which were to have served your hand,
Waleis and Norgals. One of your vassal princes,
Turkentals, met death at his hand. Your people he
slew or took captive."

"This I will avenge, Mother. God willing, my
javelot will wound him yet."

Next morning when daylight came the lad
quickly made up his mind that he would go straight
to Arthur. Lady Herzeloyde kissed him and ran
after him. Then the sorrow of the world befell.
When she no longer saw her son – he rode away:
who could be glad of that? – then that lady without
falsity fell upon the ground, where grief stabbed her
until she died. – Her death from sheer loyalty saved
her from the pains of hell. Well for her that she became a mother! Thus she traveled the journey that
brings reward, a root of goodness she, and a branch
of humility. Alas that we do not now have her like
even to the eleventh generation! Lacking such,
many are turned to falseness. Yet [129]
all loyal women should wish this lad well, who has
ridden away and left her.

Then this handsome lad turned toward the
forest in Brizljan, where he came upon a brook as
he rode. A rooster could probably have crossed it,
but there were flowers and grass there which made
its stream so dark that the lad avoided fording it.
All day he rode alongside, as befitted his wits. He
spent the night as best he could until the bright day
shone upon him.

Then the lad went on all by himself to a fine
clear ford. On the other side was a meadow
adorned with a tent upon which great luxury had
been expended. It was of samite in three colors,
high and wide, and with fine ribbons attached to the
seams. Above it hung a leathern screen that could
always be pulled over it when the rain came on.

Inside he found the wife of Duke Orilus de
Lalander, the noble duchess, Jeschute by name,
winsomely reclining like a knight's beloved. The
lady had fallen asleep. [130]
She bore Love's weapon, a mouth gleaming red, the
heart's sorrow of a yearning knight, and as she slept
her lips parted, warm with the fire of Love's ardor.
So lay this marvel of uttermost desire. Of snow-
white ivory, and small and close-set, were her teeth.
– I guess no one will ever get me accustomed to
kissing such high-praised lips. *I* have seldom
known anything of the sort. – Her sable coverlet
reached only to her hips, for because of the heat she
had pushed it down when her lord had left her by
herself. She was beautifully shaped and molded; no
art had been spared on her, for God Himself had
fashioned her sweet body. This lovely lady had also
a slender arm and a white hand, and there the lad
discovered a ring which drew him toward the bed
for a struggle with the duchess. He was thinking of
his mother who had counseled him about women's
rings. And so the handsome lad leaped from the carpet onto [131] the bed.

The sweet, chaste lady was rudely startled to
find the lad lying in her arms. Naturally she could
not help waking. With shame in which there was no
laughter the gently bred lady said, "Who has dishonored me? Young Sir, you presume too far. You
might choose a different goal!"

Loudly the lady protested, but he paid no
heed to what she said and he forced her mouth to
his. Then it was not long before he hugged the
duchess to him and took her ring besides. On her
smock he caught sight of a brooch, and he roughly
snatched that. The lady had only a woman's weapons; *his* strength was to her a whole army. All the
same, there was a great struggle there.

Then the lad complained of hunger. The
lady's body was radiantly lovely.

"You shan't eat *me!* " she said. "If you were
sensible, you would take some other food. There
stand bread and wine, and two partridges too,
though when the young lady brought them she by
no means had you in mind."

He paid no heed to where his hostess sat, but
[132] ate a good bellyful and then drank lusty drafts.

To the lady his stay in the pavilion seemed all
too long. She thought he was a boy who had lost his
wits. Her shame began to sweat; yet the duchess
said, "Young Sir, you must leave my brooch and
my ring here. And now begone. If my husband
comes, you will endure some anger that you had
better avoid."

To which the well-born lad replied, "What do I care of your husband's anger? But if it does any harm to your honor, I will be off." And with that he went up to the bed and there, to the dismay of the duchess, another kiss was taken. Without saying farewell the lad rode off, and yet he did say, "God shield you. That's what my mother told me to say."

The lad was delighted with his spoils. When he had ridden on for a time, perhaps a mile, there arrived he of whom I am about to tell. By the dew he perceived that his lady had had a visitor. Some of the tent ropes had been ridden down, and around them some lad had trodden [133]down the grass. Inside, this noble and renowned prince found his wife all woebegone.

"Aha! my lady!" said the haughty Orilus. "For what have I devoted my service to you? A shameful end to many a knightly prize: you have another *ami*."

With tear-filled eyes the lady protested that she was innocent, but he did not believe her story. Timidly, however, she went on to say, "A fool came riding along here. Of all the people I have ever known, I never saw anybody so comely. And against my will he took my brooch and my ring."

"Oh, so he pleases you, and you gave him your company!"

"God forbid!" she said. "But his boots and javelot were all too close to me just the same. You should be ashamed to talk that way. It does not beseem a noblewoman to accept love from the likes of that."

But the prince said, "Lady, I have done you no harm, unless you are ashamed of one thing, that you [134] gave up the title of Queen to receive the title of Duchess by marrying me. I have the worst of the bargain. But my manhood is so mettlesome that your brother Erec, my brother-in-law, *le fils du roi* Lac, may well hate you on account of it. All the same, that clever man knows that I am of such renown as can nowhere be gainsaid, except that he unhorsed me in the lists at Prurin. But afterwards, at Karnant, I paid him back richly. In the single combat with lance my hand knocked him backwards off his horse to get his oath of surrender. My lance carried your token right through his shield. Little then did I intend your love would go to some other lover, my Lady Jeschute. Lady, I want you to realize that the proud Galoes, *fils du roi* Gandin, fell in death before my jousting. And you were right there when Plihopliheri rode against me in a tourney and did not spare me his battleskill. But my thrust toppled him from his horse so his saddle didn't pinch him any more. I [135]have often won re-

nown and I have brought down many a knight. But now I can no longer profit from that: a great disgrace tells me so. They hate me, every one of them at the Round Table, eight of whom I unhorsed where many a noble maiden could see it at the joust for the sparrow hawk at Kanedic. For you I won the prize, and victory for myself. You saw that, and so did Arthur, in whose house lives my sister, the sweet Cunneware. Her mouth cannot produce laughter until she beholds him to whom the highest praise is given. If only that man would come! Then there would be a battle like the one this morning when I fought and did some harm to a prince who had challenged me with his jousting. *He* fell dead from *my* joust. I will forbear to mention that many a man has beaten his wife in anger for a lesser fault. If I owed you service or homage, you would have to do with the lack of it. No longer will I bask in those white arms of yours where, for [136]love's sake, I used to lie many a blissful day. I'll turn your red mouth pale and put redness in your eyes. I'll undo your joy and teach your heart to sigh."

The princess looked at the prince and her lips said piteously, "Honor in me your knightly fame. You are faithful and wise, but you also have such power over me that you can inflict great pain on me. You should first hear my defense. In the name of all women, deign to do so – you can still make me wretched enough after that. If I lay dead at another's hands, so long as it did not impair *your* honor, that hour would be sweet to me, even if I died at once, since your hatred is turned against me."

But the prince went right on: "Lady, you're getting just too proud for me, and I'm going to curb that in you. Our companionship is over, so is our common eating and drinking, and our common bed shall be forgotten. You'll receive no clothing from me except what I find you sitting in now. Your bridle shall be a cord of bast, your horse [137] shall go hungry, your saddle with all its adornment shall be despoiled!" And all of a sudden he ripped and tore the samite covering from it, and when that was done he smashed the saddle in which she rode – her chasteness and her womanhood had to endure his hatred – and with bast cords he tied it together again. His hatred had come all too soon upon her. And then he said, "Lady, now we shall ride. I would be happy to come upon him who shared your love here. I would face him in battle even if his breath blew fire like a wild dragon."

Unsmiling, full of tears, this lady rich in sorrow departed wretchedly. What had happened to *her* did not distress her: what distressed her was her husband's chagrin. His sorrow grieved her greatly;

she would rather have been dead. Now you shall lament for her faithfulness' sake, for now she begins to endure high affliction. – Even if all women hated me, the Lady Jeschute's sorrow would still grieve *me.* – and so they rode following the trail. The lad ahead of [138]

them was also very swift. Nor did that dauntless youth know that he was being pursued. Whenever his eyes caught sight of someone, he would approach him and the good lad would greet him and say: "That's what my mother told me to do."

Thus our simple boy came riding down a slope. He heard a woman's voice. There, beside a cliff, a lady was wailing in real anguish. Her true joy had been torn in twain. The lad quickly rode over to her. Now hear what the lady was doing. There was Sigune tearing her long brown braids out of her head for grief. The lad looked, and there was Schianatulander the Prince, dead in the maiden's lap. She was aweary of all mirth.

"Sad or of joy's color, my mother bade me greet everybody. God help you!" said the lad. "I find a piteous object here in your lap. Who gave you the wounded knight?" And eagerly the lad went on, "Who shot him? Was it [139]

done with a javelot? I think he is dead, Lady. Won't you tell me something about who killed the man? If I can overtake him I will gladly fight him."

The good lad reached into his quiver and found sharp javelots aplenty there. He was also still carrying both the tokens which he had wrested from Jeschute when he committed his stupidity there. If he had learned his father's habitual ways, he would have hit the target better, since the duchess was alone. But she was yet to suffer much grief because of him: more than one whole year she missed the welcome of her husband's body. Injustice was done that woman.

But now let me tell you about Sigune, who might well bemoan her sorrow. She said to the lad, "You have virtue in you. Honor be to your sweet youth and to your lovely face. In truth you will be rich in blessings. This knight did not die by the javelot, he perished in a joust. Fidelity was born in you, that you can feel pity this way for [140]

him." Before she allowed the lad to ride on she asked him his name, remarking that he showed the evidence of God's handiwork.

"'*Bon fils, cher fils, beau fils,*' that is what I was called by those who knew me at home."

As soon as he said this she recognized him by those names. Now hear him more correctly named so that you will know who is the lord of this adventure.

As he stood there with the maiden her red mouth made haste to speak: "In truth, your name is Parzival, which signifies *'right through the middle.'* Such a furrow did great love plow in your mother's heart with the plow of her faithfulness. Your father bequeathed her sorrow. I tell you, and not to boast: your mother is my aunt. And without any base deception I tell you the sure truth of who you are: your father was an Angevin, and you were born a man of Waleis on your mother's side, at Kanvoleis. I know this for a certainty. You are also the King of Norgals, and in your capital city of Kingrivals your head shall some day bear the crown. *This* prince was slain for your [141]

sake because he defended your lands steadfastly. Never did his fidelity slacken. O fair, sweet young man, those two brothers have done you much harm: Lehelin seized two kingdoms of yours, and this knight, as well as your father's brother, was slain by Orilus. And he it was who left me in the grief you here behold. This prince of your kingdom served me in unstained honor. I was then your mother's ward. Dear, good cousin, hear how this came about. It was a hound's leash that brought him mortal pain. In the service of us two he gained death for himself and for me the grievous yearning for his love. What a fool I was not to grant him my love! Utter sorrow has cut my joy to pieces. Now that he is dead, I love him."

Then he said, "Cousin, I grieve for your sorrow and for my own disgrace. If I can avenge these things I will surely do so."

He was eager for battle then and there, but she showed him the wrong direction, fearing that he would lose his life and that she would thereby only sustain [142]

greater harm than before. Then he took a road, smoothtrodden and wide, that led to the Britons. And to whomever he met, afoot or on horseback, knight or merchant, he gave his greeting and said that that was what his mother had told him to do. And she had given him that advice with no thought of ill.

Evening was coming on and suddenly great weariness came over him. Then Simplicity's companion caught sight of a house of fair size. There dwelt a greedy owner of the sort that still spring from base birth, a fisherman who lacked all kindliness. Hunger instructed the lad to turn in there and tell the owner of hunger's pangs.

· But he said, "I wouldn't give you half a loaf of bread, not in thirty years. Anybody that looks for my generosity for nothing is wasting his time. I don't care about anybody but myself, and after that, about my children. You won't get in here today. If you had money or valuables, I would keep you, sure enough."

Whereat the lad offered him Lady Jeschute's [143] brooch.

As soon as the churl saw that, his mouth became a smile and said, "If you would like to stay, dear child, all who live here will show you honor."

"If you will feed me tonight and in the morning show me the way to Arthur – I am in his service – the gold can stay with you."

"That I will," said the churl. "I never did see such a handsome fellow. And just for a change I'll take you up to the King's Table Round."

And so the lad passed the night there, but the morrow saw him elsewhere.

He could hardly wait for daylight. His host also made ready and ran on in front while the lad rode after, and both were in a hurry.

Sir Hartmann von Ouwe! To the house of your Lady Ginover and your lord, King Arthur, a guest of mine is coming. Please to protect him from mockery there! He is neither a fiddle nor a rote: let them get some other plaything and out of courtesy amuse themselves with that. Or else your Lady Enite and her mother Karsnafite will be put through the mill and have their fame bent down. [144] If I am forced to misuse my mouth for mockery, then with mockery I will defend my friend.

Then the fisherman and the brave lad came to where they could see a capital city close by, and that was Nantes.

Then the fisherman said, "Child, God shield you! Look now, there is where you ride in."

The lad, scant of wit, said, "You must lead me further than this."

"I should say not! Those courtiers are all so high bred that if ever a peasant came near them it would be a serious offense."

So the lad rode on by himself across a meadow not too broad that was bright with the color of flowers. No Curvenal had brought him up. He knew nothing of *courtoisie*, as is the way with those who have not traveled. His bridle was made of bast, and his pony was mighty weak so that it stumbled to many a fall, and his saddle was nowhere covered with new leather. Of samite or downy ermine there was very little to be seen on him, he had no use for tie cords to a cloak, and instead of fur-lined jacket and surcoat he carried his javelot. His father, who was adjudged [145]

a model knight, was better attired on that carpet before Kanvoleis.

He who never knew the sweat of fear now saw a knight riding toward him. He greeted him in his usual fashion: "God help you! That's how my mother taught me."

"Young Sir, may God reward you and her," said the son of Arthur's aunt.

This warrior had been brought up by Utepandragun and claimed hereditary rights to the land of Britain. Ither von Gaheviez was his name, though people called him the Red Knight. His armor was so red that it made your eyes red to look at it. His swift horse was red, all red was his horse's hood piece, red samite were its trappings, his shield was redder than a flame, all red was his gambeson and tailored full, red was his spear shaft, red was his spear point, and at the hero's own desire his sword had been dyed red, though tempered for sharpness all the same. This King of Kukumerlant had in his hand a goblet of red gold and finely engraved, snatched away from the Round Table. [146] White was his skin, red was his hair.

Straightforwardly he said to the lad, "Blessed be your sweet body: a pure woman brought you into the world. Well for the mother that bore you! I have never seen anyone so fair. You are the very luster of love, her defeat and her victory. Much joy in woman will triumph in you, but afterwards grief will weigh you down. Dear friend, if you intend to ride in here, then tell the King for me, and all his men, that I have not taken flight and that I will gladly wait here for anyone who may be preparing to joust. Let none of them think it strange. I rode up to the Round Table to claim possession of my kingdom. In token of my claim my hand picked up this goblet, but the wine spilled in Lady Ginover's lap. If I had overturned the torches I would have got my skin all sooty, so I chose not to do that." The bold warrior went on: "Not that I did this as a theft. Being a king, I have no need for that. Now tell the Queen, friend, that I spilled the wine on her unintention- [147] ally. And those worthy gentleman sat there and offered no defense. Kings or princes they may be, but why do they let their host die of thirst? Why don't they come out here and get his golden goblet for him? Otherwise their reputations will be lost."

"I will do as you have told me," the lad said, and rode away from him into Nantes. There the children followed him to the courtyard in front of the palace where all sorts of things were going on. A crowd gathered dense around him. Up ran Iwanet, a lad free of falseness, and offered to bear him company.

The lad said, "God keep you! as my mother told me to say before I left her house. I see many Arthurs here: which one will make me a knight?"

Iwanet burst out laughing and said, "The right one you do not see, but it won't be long before you do." He led him inside the great hall where the worthy company was.

In spite of the din he was able to say, "God keep you gentlemen all, and especially the King and his wife. My mother charged me on my life to greet[148]

them in particular. And those that have a place at the Round Table because of their deserved renown, she bade me greet them too. But one piece of knowledge I lack: I don't know which one of you is the host. To *him* a knight has sent a message – I saw him and he was red all over – and he says he will wait for him outside there. I think he wants to fight. Also, he is sorry that he spilled wine on the Queen. O, if only I had received those clothes of his from the King's hand! I would be very pleased: they look so knightly!"

The free-spoken lad was much elbowed about, hustled this way and that. They noticed his beauty. Their own eyes saw that never was more lovely form lorded or ladied, for god was in a good humor when He created Parzival. And thus he who feared terror but little was brought before Arthur. No one could be hostile to him in whom[149] God invented perfection. The Queen too gazed at him before she left the great hall where she had had the wine spilled on her.

Then Arthur looked at the lad, and to the simple youth he said, "Young Sir, may God repay your greeting. I will gladly serve you with my life and my possessions. I am indeed of a mind to do so."

"God grant that that is really so! The time seems to me a year since I was supposed to become a knight, and that is more bad than good. Now do not make me wait any longer, grant me the honor of knighthood!"

"That I will, and gladly," said his host, "if my dignity suffices. You are so pleasing that my gift to you shall be of precious worth. Indeed I will not fail to do it, but you must wait until tomorrow morning and I will fit you out properly."

The high-born lad halted there awkward as a crane, and said, "I will not beg for anything here. A knight came riding toward me. If I can't get his armor I don't care who talks about kingly gifts. Those my

mother can give me, for after all she is a queen."[150]

Then Arthur said to the lad, "That armor is worn by such a man that I would not dare give it to you. I have had to live with worry as it is, and through no fault of mine, ever since I lost his homage. He is Ither of Gaheviez, who rammed sorrow through my joy."

"A generous king *you* would be, if a gift like that were too great for you!" said Keie then. "Let him have it, and let him go out there and face him on the meadow! As long as someone has to bring us the goblet, here is the string and there is the top: let the boy do the spinning. He will be praised for it among the women. He will often have to risk quarrels and take such chances, and I don't care about either of their lives. You have to lose a dog or two to get a boar's head."

"I hate to deny him," said Arthur in good faith, "only I fear he may be killed just when I am about to help him to knighthood."

But the lad obtained the gift, from which subsequently was to come grief. Now he was in a hurry to leave the King. Young and old crowded after him. Iwanet took him by the hand and led him past a roofed balcony not[151] too high up but that he could see the length and breadth of it. In fact, the balcony was so low that he saw and heard something there that grieved him greatly. The Queen herself chose to be at the window with knights and ladies around her, and they were all looking at him. There too sat Lady Cunneware, the proud and fair, she who was never to laugh until she beheld him who had won, or was to win, supreme honor, otherwise she would die never having laughed. She *had* never laughed – until the lad came riding past, and then her lovely mouth burst forth laughing. Her back paid for that later in soreness, for Keie the senseschal took Lady Cunneware de Lalant by her wavy hair and wound her long fair braids around his hand and fastened them without a bolt. Her back had taken no oath on a judge's staff, and yet on her back a staff was used until, by the time the whirr had gone out of it, it had cut right through her clothes and through her skin.

Then the unwise fellow said, "Your noble reputation[152] is brought to a disgraceful end, but I am the net that catches it, and I'm going to pound it back into you till you feel it in every limb. To King Arthur's court and household has come riding so many a worthy man for whom you failed to laugh, and now you laugh for a man who has no knightly breeding at all."

Many odd things happen in anger. No royal
decree would have awarded him the right to flog
that maiden, who was much pitied by her friends.
Even if she had been a knight, it was a disgraceful
way to beat her, and she was a princess by birth. If
her brothers, Orilus and Lehelin, had seen it, there
would have been fewer blows.

Her laughter and the speech of silent Antanor,
who because of his silence was considered a fool,
were dependent on the same event: he was never to
speak a word unless she laughed, she who was
flogged. But when she did laugh, his mouth said to
Keie, "God knows, Sir Seneschal, [153]
that Cunneware de Lalant is being thrashed because
of that lad, but by his hand your own joy will yet be
destroyed, however far away he may go."

"Since your first words are a threat to me, I
think they will bring you little joy yourself!" Then
his hide got tanned, and fists whispered a lot of
things into that clever fool's ears: that is what Keie
did with no delay.

Young Parzival could not help seeing this misery of Antanor's and of the lady's, and his heart was
sick beholding their distress. More than once he
seized his javelot, but there was such a press around
the Queen that he refrained from the throw.

Then Iwanet took leave of *le fils du roi*
Gahmuret, whose trip was made alone out to Ither
on the meadow. To him he reported that there was
no one inside who wanted to joust. "The King bestowed a gift on me. I told him, just as you had told
me, how it happened unintentionally that you
spilled the wine, and how you were sorry for your [154]
clumsiness. None of them wants to fight. Now give
me what you're riding on there, and all your armor
too, because that is what I was given at the great
hall, and I have to be made a knight in it. I'll deny
you my greeting if you refuse it to me. So give it to
me, if you're in your right mind."

The King of Kukumerlant said, "If Arthur's
hand has made you a gift of my armor, he would do
as much with my life – if you could win it from me.
That's the way he loves his kinsmen. Tell me
though, was he ever so well disposed toward you
before? Your service has won its reward so fast."

"I dare to earn whatever I deserve, and he did
give it to me. Hand it over, and stop this foolish
talk. I'm not going to be a squire any longer. I'm
going to carry the shield of a knight." He reached
over and grabbed his bridle. "Maybe you are
Lehelin about whom my mother complains."

The knight reversed his spear shaft and struck
the lad with such force that both he and his pony

were tumbled onto the flowers. That hero was
quick to anger [155]
and he struck him with his shaft so the blood
spurted from his scalp. The good lad Parzival stood
there furious on the meadow. Then he seized his
javelot. Just where the helmet and the vizor had
holes over the cap beneath, there the javelot went
through his eye and right on through his head, so
that he fell dead, that foe of falsity. Women's sighs
and the rending of hearts were the result of the
death of Ither of Gaheviez, and all women who
loved him found their eyes wet with tears. Their joy
was ridden down, their delight was defeated and led
onto rough roads.

The simple Parzival rolled him over and over
but did not know how to get the armor off him.
Here was something odd: neither helmet laces nor
kneepieces could his strong white hands untie or
pull off, though he tried again and again in his simplicity. Now both steed and pony set up such a
whinnying that Iwanet heard it, Lady Gin- [156]
over's page and kinsman, where he was standing at
the end of the moat by the city wall. When he heard
the outcry from the horse, and when he saw no one
on it, the nimble-witted lad hurried out – he did so
from the loyalty he bore Parzival – and found Ither
dead and Parzival in childish distress. He ran over
to both of them. Then he praised Parzival for the
fame his hand had won over the King of Kukumerlant.

"God reward you for that! Now tell me what
to do. I don't know how to go about this. How do I
get it off from him and onto me?"

"I can soon show you that," said the proud
Iwanet to *le fils du roi* Gahmuret.

And the armor was stripped from the dead
man right there on the meadow before Nantes and
put onto the living one, whom great simplicity still
ruled.

"Those boots won't go with iron hose," said
Iwanet. "You have to wear knightly attire now."

These words vexed the good lad Parzival, and
he said, "Anything my mother gave me is not going
to be cast off, whether for the better or for the
worse." [157]

To Iwanet that seemed odd enough – *he* was
courtly-bred – but he had to comply all the same.
He was not angry with him at all. So he shod him
with two shiny iron hose over the boots. With them
went two golden spurs, and these he fastened on,
not with leather straps, but with two bands of rib-
bon. Before offering him the gorget he tied on the

kneepieces, and in short order there was the impatient Parzival in armor from the foot upward.

Then the lad asked for his quiver too.

"I won't let you have a javelot," said Iwanet, the worthy lad. "Knighthood has forbidden you that."

And he girded a sharp sword around him, and taught him how to draw it, and told him he must never flee. Then he brought over the dead man's Castilian, with its long slim legs. The youth leaped in full armor into the saddle without asking for stirrups. People still talk about his swiftness. Iwanet did not think it too much trouble to teach [158] him how to use his shield properly and how to aim for an opponent's harm. Then he put a spear into his hand, but he would have none of that.

"What's the good of that?" he asked.

"If someone comes riding against you in a joust, you're supposed to break it on him boldly and run it through his shield. The more you do that, the more you will be praised before the women."

As the adventure tells us, he sat better upon his horse than any painter from Maestricht or Cologne could have painted him.

Then to Iwanet he said, "Dear friend and comrade, I have won here what I asked for. Commend my service to King Arthur in the city. Take his golden goblet back to him and tell him also about the great insult to me. A knight forgot himself with me and beat a maiden because she was moved to laughter at me. Her cries of pain trouble me yet. The lady's undeserved suffering does not touch just the edge of my heart but lies at its very center. Now do this, by our friendship, and feel for me in my grief. God [159] keep you. I leave you now. May He preserve us both."

Ither of Gaheviez he left lying pitiably on the meadow, who was so fair in death and who had, in life, known the fullness of joy. If knightly action had been the cause of his death in a joust, with a spear through his shield, who then would mourn the great calamity? But he died by a javelot. Then Iwanet brought him bright flowers for a covering. The javelot shaft he set in the ground at his side, and in the manner of Christ's Passion this lad pure and proud pressed a piece of wood through the javelot blade to make a cross. Nor did he fail to go back to the city and tell the news, at which many a woman was dismayed and many a knight wept as they gave vent to their faithful grief. Great was the lamentation. The dead man was brought in in state. The Queen rode forth from the city and bade them lift up the Monstrance over the King of Kukumerlant whom Parzival's hand had slain.

Lady Ginover the Queen spoke words of sorrow: [160] "Alas and alas, the renown of Arthur may break in twain at this strange event, that he who had been destined to win the highest fame of those about the Round Table lies here slain before Nantes. He claimed his heritage and they gave him death. He was of our company here, and no ear ever heard of any misdeed on his part. In wildness of treachery he was tame, for that had been stripped from him. Now I must bury all too soon this treasure-lock of fame. His heart wise in courtesy, a seal upon that lock, taught him the noblest conduct wherever a man should with bravery show a man's fidelity for a woman's love. A seed bearing ever new fruit of sorrow is sown among women. Grief wafts from your wounds. So red was your hair that your blood could not make these bright flowers any redder. You have banished laughter from women."

Ither the rich in renown was buried as a king, [161] and his death taught sighing to women. His armor had cost him his life; the simple Parzival's desire for it was the cause of his death. Later, when he learned better, he would not have done it.

There were certain qualities in his horse: it took great exertion as nothing; cold weather or hot, over rocks or tree trunks, it never sweated from travel; there was no need to tighten its girth by a single notch even if he rode for two days. In his armor that simple man rode further that day than a sensible man without armor would have ridden in two. He rode at a gallop, rarely at a trot, because he did not know how to check the speed.

Toward evening the pinnacle and roof of a tower came into view. The simple man actually thought that more and more towers were growing up out of the ground, for there were a great many of them on a house. He imagined that Arthur had planted them, and therefore thought of him as a saint whose blessings reached far and wide.

"Well," said the simple man, "my mother's peo- [162] ple don't know how to farm. Their crops don't grow this tall, any that she has them sow there in the forest. She always gets too much rain."

Gurnemanz de Graharz was the name of the lord of this castle toward which he was riding. In front of it there stood a broad linden tree on a green meadow that was neither broader nor longer than the proper size. The horse, and the road too, led him to where he found sitting him to whom the castle and the land belonged. A great weariness made him carry his shield improperly, swinging it too far back or too far forward but not at all in the manner that was deemed praiseworthy there. Gurnemanz the Prince was sitting alone. The linden's mass cast its shade — as it should — upon that captain of true courtesy. Then he, whose ways were a refuge from falsity, received the guest, as was his duty. He had neither knights nor squires with him.

Then from his simple wits and without delay Parzival answered him thus: "My mother told me to accept advice from any man having grey hair. I will serve you for it, since that is what my mother said." [163]

"If you have come here for advice, you will have to guarantee me your friendliness before I assent to give you such advice."

Then the famed prince cast from his hand a yearling sparrow hawk that swooped off into the castle. It wore a little golden bell that tinkled. That was a messenger, and immediately there appeared a number of handsomely attired pages whom he bade escort the stranger in and attend his needs.

"My mother was right," said he. "There is no danger from an old man's talk."

They took him in at once to where he found many noble knights. At one spot in the courtyard they all begged him to dismount.

But he in whom simplicity was evident said, "A king bade me be a knight, and I don't care what happens, I'm not going to get off this horse. My mother told me to greet all of you."

They thanked both him and her, and then when the greetings were over, though the horse was tired and so was the man, they thought up many a plea before they got him off the horse and into a warm room. Then they [164] all began to urge him: "Let them take your armor off and lighten your limbs."

Directly his armor was removed, but when the attendants saw the rough boots and the fool's garment they were startled. With much embarrassment this was reported at court, and the host was all but overcome with shame.

But one knight, of fine manners, said, "Truly, my eye has never beheld one so noble. In him there is surpassing beauty, as well as a lofty nature pure and sweet. How is it that the glory of love should be dressed like this? I am grieved to find the World's Joy in such attire. And yet, well for the mother that bore him, for in him there is all that can be desired. His knightly gear is rich and his armor was

gallantly worn before it was removed from the handsome fellow. But I noticed the bloodstains of a great bruise on his body."

"This," said the host to the knight, "has been done for some woman's sake."

"No, Sir, his manners are such that he would not know how to ask a woman to accept his service, al- [165] though his looks are of Love's color."

"Well," said the host, "let us go and have a look at this fellow whose clothes are so very strange."

They went to Parzival and found him wounded with a spear — an unbroken spear. Then Gurnemanz took him under his special care, care such that no father who strove for loyalty to his children could treat them any better. With his own hand the host washed and bandaged the wound. Then supper was laid, of which the youthful guest was in need, for great hunger had not passed him by. He had ridden away from the fisherman that morning without breakfast. His wound and the heavy armor that he won before Nantes had brought him weariness and hunger, as well as the long day's travels from Arthur of Britain. Everywhere they had let him fast. The host bade him eat with him, and the guest fell to with a will. He tackled the manger with such eagerness that he put away a quantity of food. That amused the host, and Gurnemanz, the rich in loyalty, earnestly bade him go right on eating and forget his fatigue. [166]

When the time came and the table was removed, the host said, "I guess you are tired. Were you up early?"

"God knows my mother was still asleep. She can't stay awake so much."

The host could not help laughing. Then he took him to the sleeping quarters and told him to slip out of his clothes. He did so unwillingly, but it had to be. An ermine coverlet was laid over his naked body: never did woman bear fairer fruit. Great weariness and sleep kept him from turning on one side and the other. Thus he waited for day to come.

Then the famed prince ordered a bath to be prepared for mid-morning at the foot of the couch where he lay – this was regularly done in the morning – and roses were strewn in the water. As little noise as they made around him, the sleeping guest still awoke and went, that sweet and worthy young man, directly to the bath.

I don't know who told them to, but maidens in [167]

rich apparel and lovely to see came in with all propriety, and with their soft white hands washed and rubbed away his bruises. He had no cause to be surprised, that orphan of wisdom, and he just enjoyed the pleasure and _aise,_ nor did they mind his simplicity. Thus maidens modest yet bold tended him, but chatter as they might, he merely remained silent. He could not imagine it was too early, for a second daylight shone from them. Thus radiance clashed with radiance, until _his_ brightness outshone them both — he did not lack in that. They offered him a bath sheet but he would have none of it: he was so ashamed before ladies that he would not put it around him. The maidens had to leave, they dared not stay any longer. — I think they would have liked to see if anything had happened to him down below.

Womanhood is loyal ever;
Friend's woe is their endeavor.

The guest walked over to the bed, where a garment[168] all of white was ready for him. Through it they passed a gold and silken belt, and hose of scarlet wool they drew up smooth on the legs of him whom bravery never failed. Ah! How fine his legs looked in them, and how his fine form was revealed! Of gleaming scarlet wool and well cut, both lined with ermine white, were his long coat and mantle, and trimmed in front with wide sable fur both black and grey. These the fine young man put on. Girt with a costly belt, the coast was fastened and beautifully adorned with a precious brooch. His lips burned red as well.

Then came the loyal host followed by proud knights, and greeted his guest. When this was over, the knights all said they had never seen anyone so handsome, and in all sincerity they praised the woman who had given the world such progeny. From their courtly breeding and in honesty too they said, "He will be well rewarded wherever he seeks for favor. Love and greeting await him. May he profit[169]

by his worth." All said the same, and so did all who saw him thereafter.

The host took him by the hand and they walked off together. The famed prince inquired how his rest had been that night under his roof.

"Well, I would not be alive now if my mother had not advised me to come here that day when I left her. May God reward you and her, Sir! You do me great kindness."

Then our simple-witted hero went where Mass was being sung for God and for his host. During Mass the host taught him the things that increased blessedness: how to make his offering, how to make the sign of the Cross, and how to foil the Devil thereby. Then they went to the palace hall where the table was laid, and there the guest sat down with his host and ate with gusto.

Courteously the host said, "Sir, you must not mind my asking where you come from."

He explained to him how he had ridden away and left his mother, and about the ring and the brooch,[170]

and how he had won the armor. The host had known the Red Knight and now sighed in pity at his fate. His name he now transferred to his guest and called _him_ "the Red Knight."

When the table was removed, then a wild will received its taming. The host said to his guest, "You talk like a little child. Why not stop talking about your mother and think of other things? Follow _my_ advice: it will keep you from wrongdoing. I will begin thus:

See that you never lose your sense of shame. A man without a sense of shame, what good is he? He lives in a molting state, shedding his honor, and with steps directed toward hell.

You have beauty and bearing, you may well be the lord of some people. If you are of high origin and rising still higher, bear in mind that you must have compassion on the host of the needy. Shield them from distress with generosity and with kindness, and strive for humility. The poor man of good birth may well wrestle with shame — it is a sour business — and you should be ready with[171]

help. When you lighten his load God's blessing is near you. He has it worse than those who come to the window for bread.

Be both poor and rich appropriately: if a lord squanders, that is not lord-like; if he hoards treasure too much, that is dishonor also. Make your rule the true mean.

I have observed that you are in need of advice.

Leave bad manners to their own quarrel.

Do not ask too many questions.

Do not disdain thoughtful answers that go straight to the question of one who is sounding you out with words. You can hear and see, taste and smell: these should bring you wisdom.

Let mercy go along with daring. *There* will be the test of my counsels. Once a man gives you his oath of surrender in battle, take his word of honor and let him live, unless he has done you such wrong as would burden your heart with grief.

You will frequently have to wear armor. As 172
soon as it is removed, see that you wash your hands and around your eyes to get the iron rust off. That way you will be of love's color, and women's eyes will note that.

Be manly and cheerful of spirit: that is good for winning honor and praise.

Let women be dear to you, for that enhances a young man's worth. Do not waver a single day toward them: that is true manly conduct. If you choose to tell them lies you may deceive many of them, but in true love base deception does not enjoy honor long. It is the prowler's complaint that the dry branches in the park snap and crack and rouse the watch. Pathless places and felled-tree barriers, there is where many a battle thrives. Measure this against love. Noble love has judgment with which to outwit sly deceptive trickery. If you incur her disfavor you will be dishonored and suffer painful shame forever. Take this lesson to heart.

I will tell you more about womankind. Husband and wife are one, as are the sun that shone to- 173
day and the thing called day itself; neither can be separated from the other; they blossom from a single seed. Strive to understand this."

The guest bowed thanks to his host for his counsel. He gave up talking about his mother — in his speech, but not in his heart, as is still a true man's way.

The host spoke what redounded to his honor. "Also, you must learn more skill in knightly arts. They way you came riding here to me! I have seen many a wall where I found the shield more properly hung than yours was around your neck. It is not too late: let us go out on the field and learn some skills. Bring him his horse and me mine, and every knight his. Have squires come too, and have each one take a stout spear and bring it along, and see that they are new ones."

Then the prince came out on the meadow, and there some practice was had at riding. He showed his guest how to bring the horse out of a gallop with a sharp dig of the spurs, how to urge it to the charge by a pressure 174
of the thighs, how to lower the spear properly, and how to bring up the shield in front against a spear thrust. Then he said, "Be so good as to do the same."

Thus he saved him from mishap better than the lithe switch that tears the skin of wayward children. Then he called for hardy knights to come out against him in joust and himself led him to the lists against one of them. There the youth made his first spear thrust through a shield, so that all were astonished, and there he knocked a stout rider, who was no slight fellow, back off his horse. A second jouster had come up, and Parzival had taken a fresh strong spear. His youth and strength and spirit, this sweet young man without a beard, and his heritage from Gahmuret, together with innate manhood, drove him on. He rode at full career head on and aimed at the four rivets. His host's knight did not keep his seat but measured the field in a fall. Little bits of splintered lance were 175
all around. In this manner he struck down five of them. Then the host took him and led him home. He had won the prize in the games: later he was to prove adept at real combat. All who saw him ride and who understood these matters said that he had skill and courage.

"Now my lord will see the end of his cares and he can become young again. Let him bestow his daughter, our lady, on him for a wife. If he is sensible his sorrows will be at an end. Here is someone that has ridden into his house to make up for the deaths of his three sons. Fortune has not passed him by."

And so the prince came in at evening, the table was set, and he bade his daughter come to table with them — that is how I heard the story.

Now hear what the host said to the lovely Liaze when he saw the maiden coming: "Allow this knight to kiss you, and do him honor. He travels with Fortune's instruction. — And you, Sir, are supposed to leave my daughter her ring — assuming she has one. But she hasn't. Nor any 176
brooch either. Who would give her such expensive things as were given to the lady in the forest? *She* had someone from whom she received those things that you managed to take, but from Liaze there is nothing to be taken."

The guest felt shy, but all the same he kissed her on the lips, and they were the color of fire. Liaze was lovely to look at and rich in true purity besides. The table was long and low, and the host was crowded by no one but sat alone at one end. His guest he bade sit between him and his daughter, and at his command her soft white hands had to cut up whatever was to be eaten by this man whom they called "the Red Knight." No one was to disturb them if they exchanged little intimacies. The maiden with all propriety was doing her father's will. She and the guest made a comely pair. Directly thereafter the maiden withdrew.

In this way our hero was entertained until the fourteenth day. His heart was troubled by just one thing: he [177] wanted to have fought better before enjoying the warmth of what they term "a lady's arms." He felt that noble striving was a lofty goal both in this life and yonder. And that is still no lie.

One morning he asked permission to depart, and thus he left Graharz the town. His host rode out with him, but then a new heart's sorrow came to pass.

"You are the fourth son that I have lost," said the prince, truest of the true. "I thought that I had recompense for those three sorrows. There were, after all, only three of them. But now if someone were to take his hand and strike my heart into four pieces and carry each piece away, I would be glad of it, one for you – you are riding away – and the other three for my noble sons who died bravely. But such is knighthood's reward; it has a knotted whip of sorrows for a tail.

"One death lamed all my joy, that of my fair son whose name was Schentaflurs. Since Condwiramurs was not willing to bestow herself and her kingdom, helping [178] her, he lost his life at the hands of Clamidê and Kingrun. From that, my heart is slashed by sorrow so that it has holes like a fence. You have ridden away from me all to soon, disconsolate as I am. O, to think I cannot die, since Liaze the lovely maid and my country do not satisfy you!

"My second son was Count Lascoyt, who was killed by Ider, *fils de* Noyt, in a contest for a sparrow hawk. Because of that I am empty of joy.

"My third son's name was Gurzgri. With him rode Mahaute in her beauty, whom her haughty brother Ehkunat had given him for a wife. To the capital city of Brandigan he rode to Schoydelakurt, where death did not fail to find him. Mabonagrin slew him. Wherefrom Mahaute lost her beauty, and my wife, his mother, died. Great grief drew her after him."

The guest perceived his host's sorrow, for he had recounted it so clearly, and he said, "Sir, I am not wise, but if I ever win knightly fame so that I am fit to ask for love, you shall give me Liaze your daughter, the [179] lovely maid. You have told me too much sorrow. If I can relieve it then, I will not let you bear so great a burden of it."

Then the young man took his leave of that loyal prince and of all his retinue. With that, the prince's trey of sorrows was sadly raised to a four. He had just suffered his fourth bereavement.

Translators' note: In general we have followed the Lachmann text (*Wolfram von Eschenbach,* edited by Karl Lachmann, revised by Eduard Hartl, Berlin, 1952), but we have felt free to use the Leitzmann text whenever it seemed to give a preferable reading (*Wolfram von Eschenbach,* edited by Albert Leitzmann, vol. I, 5th edition, Halle, 1948; vol. II, 3rd edition, Halle, 1947; vol. III, 2nd edition, Halle, 1933) – Helen M. Mustard and Charles E. Passage.

Books for Further Reading

Barber, Richard. *The Reign of Chivalry*. Newton Abbot, U.K.: David & Charles, 1980; New York: St. Martin's Press, 1980.

Bertau, Karl. *Deutsche Literatur im europäischen Mittelalter*. Munich: Beck, 1972.

Bevington, David. *Medieval Drama*. Boston: Houghton Mifflin, 1975.

Bloch, Marc. *Societé Féodale*, 2 volumes. Paris: A. Michel, 1939, 1940. Translated by L. A. Manyon as *Feudal Society*, London: Routledge & Kegan Paul, 1961; republished, with a new foreword by T. S. Brown. London & New York: Routledge, 1989.

Bumke, Joachim. *Geschichte der deutschen Literatur im hohen Mittelalter*, volume 2 of *Geschichte der deutschen Literatur im Mittelalter*. Edited by Bumke, Thomas Cramer, and Dieter Kartschoke. Munich: Deutscher Taschenbuch Verlag, 1990.

Bumke. *Höfische Kultur: Literatur und Gesellschaft im hohen Mittelalter*. Munich: Deutscher Taschenbuch Verlag, 1986. Translated by Thomas Dunlap as *Courtly Culture: Literature and Society in the High Middle Ages*. Berkeley: University of California Press, 1991.

Curtius, Ernst Robert. *Europäische Literatur und Lateinisches Mittelalter*. Bern: A. Francke, 1948. Translated by Willard R. Trask as *European Literature and the Latin Middle Ages*. New York: Pantheon, 1953.

De Boor, Helmut. *Die höfische Literatur: Vorbereitung, Blüte, Ausklang 1170–1250*, volume 2 of *Geschichte der deutschen Literatur*. Edited by de Boor and Newald, fourth edition. Munich: Beck, 1969.

De Boor. *Das späte Mittelalter: Zerfall und Neubeginn, Erster Teil 1250–1350*, volume 3 of *Geschichte der deutschen Literatur*. Edited by de Boor and Richard Newald, fourth edition. Munich: Beck, 1973.

Duby, Georges. *Les trois ordres: ou, L'imaginaire du feodalisme*. Paris: Gallimard, 1978. Translated by Arthur Goldhammer as *The Three Orders: Feudal Society Imagined*. Chicago: University of Chicago Press, 1980.

Eggers, Hans. *Deutsche Sprachgeschichte*, volume 1 of his *Das Althochdeutsche und das Mittelhochdeutsche*. Reinbek bei Hamburg: Rowohlt, 1986.

Ehrismann, Gustav. *Geschichte der deutschen Literatur bis zum Ausgang des Mittelalters*, 2 volumes in 4. Munich: Beck, 1918–1935.

Elias, Norbert. *Über den Prozeß der Zivilisation: soziogenetische und psychogenetische Untersuchungen*, 2 volumes, second edition. Bern: Francke, 1969. Translated by Edmund Jephcott, with notes and revisions by Elias, as *The Civilizing Process*, 2 volumes. New York: Pantheon, 1982.

Haug, Walter. *Literaturtheorie im deutschen Mittelalter. Von den Anfängen bis zum Ende des 13. Jahrhunderts: Eine Einführung*. Darmstadt: Wissenschaftliche Buchgesellschaft, 1985.

Haymes, Edward. *Mündliches Epos in mittelhochdeutscher Zeit*. Göppingen: Kümmerle, 1975.

Kuhn, Hugo. *Dichtung und Welt im Mittelalter*. Stuttgart: Metzler, 1959.

Loomis, Roger Sherman. *Celtic Myth and Arthurian Romance*. New York: Columbia University Press, 1927.

McMahon, James V. *The Music of Early Minnesang*. Columbia, S.C.: Camden House, 1990.

Ruh, Kurt. *Höfische Epik des deutschen Mittelalters,* 2 volumes. Berlin: Schmidt, 1967, 1980.

Ruh, ed. *Die deutsche Literatur des Mittelalters: Verfasserlexikon,* second edition, revised, 7 volumes to date. Berlin: De Gruyter, 1978–

Sayce, Olive. *The Medieval German Lyric 1150–1300*. Oxford: Clarendon Press / New York: Oxford University Press, 1982.

Simon, Eckehard, ed. *The Theatre of Medieval Europe*. Cambridge & New York: Cambridge University Press, 1991.

Vivian, Kim, ed. *A Concise History of German Literature to 1900*. Columbia, S.C.: Camden House, 1992.

Waterman, John. *A History of the German Language: With Special Reference to the Social and Cultural Forces that Shaped the Standard Literary Language,* revised edition. Seattle: University of Washington Press, 1976.

Contributors

Michael S. Batts ....*University of British Columbia*
Ralph J. Blasting ....*Towson State University*
Alexander Mark Buckholtz ....*Yale University*
Albrecht Classen..*University of Arizona*
Ernst S. Dick ....*University of Kansas*
Danielle Egan ....*University of Southern California*
Will Hasty ....*University of Florida*
Hubert Heinen ....*University of Texas at Austin*
Timothy R. Jackson ....*Trinity College, Dublin*
William E. Jackson...*University of Virginia*
Dennis M. Kratz ....*University of Texas at Dallas*
Henry Kratz..*University of Tennessee*
R. William Leckie, Jr...*University of Toronto*
Winder McConnell ....*University of California, Davis*
James V. McMahon ....*Emory University*
Kathleen J. Meyer...*Bemidji State University*
Linda B. Parshall ....*Portland State University*
Michael Resler ....*Boston College*
Klaus M. Schmidt...*Bowling Green State University*
Margit M. Sinka..*Clemson University*
Adrian Stevens ....*University College, London*
J. Wesley Thomas ....*University of Kentucky*
Marianne Wynn ....*University of London*

Cumulative Index

Dictionary of Literary Biography, Volumes 1-138
Dictionary of Literary Biography Yearbook, 1980-1992
Dictionary of Literary Biography Documentary Series, Volumes 1-11

Cumulative Index

DLB before number: *Dictionary of Literary Biography,* Volumes 1-138
Y before number: *Dictionary of Literary Biography Yearbook,* 1980-1992
DS before number: *Dictionary of Literary Biography Documentary Series,* Volumes 1-11

B

H

N

P

Q

ISBN 0-8103-5397-0

90000

9 780810 353978

Documentary Series

Yearbooks